Communications in Computer and Information Science   **1028**

Commenced Publication in 2007
Founding and Former Series Editors:
Phoebe Chen, Alfredo Cuzzocrea, Xiaoyong Du, Orhun Kara, Ting Liu,
Krishna M. Sivalingam, Dominik Ślęzak, Takashi Washio, and Xiaokang Yang

More information about this series at http://www.springer.com/series/7899

Ji-Hyun Lee (Ed.)

Computer-Aided Architectural Design

"Hello, Culture"

18th International Conference, CAAD Futures 2019
Daejeon, Republic of Korea, June 26–28, 2019
Selected Papers

 Springer

Editor
Ji-Hyun Lee
Korea Advanced Institute of Science
and Technology
Daejeon, Korea (Republic of)

ISSN 1865-0929 ISSN 1865-0937 (electronic)
Communications in Computer and Information Science
ISBN 978-981-13-8409-7 ISBN 978-981-13-8410-3 (eBook)
https://doi.org/10.1007/978-981-13-8410-3

This Springer imprint is published by the registered company Springer Nature Singapore Pte Ltd.
The registered company address is: 152 Beach Road, #21-01/04 Gateway East, Singapore 189721, Singapore

Preface

In 1985, the Computer-Aided Architectural Design Foundation was established with the goal of providing a strong base for the stimulation of rigorous research and lively academic discussions on the analysis and the synthesis of architectural designs through computers, and it persists to promote groundbreaking research through conferences and publications to this day.

The 18th CAAD Futures Conference in 2019 was hosted in Daejeon, the fifth largest metropolis of South Korea. Daejeon is considered to be one of the South Korean administration hubs with a Daejeon Government Complex and has earned its name as a "Silicon Valley of Asia" with 18 universities including KAIST, 28 government-funded research institutions, and 79 private research institutions. Moreover, Gongju, a nearby city of Daejeon, was the Capital of the Baekje Dynasty from AD 475 to 538 and an important center of cultural heritage. To connect culture and science as well as old and new, the theme of the conference was "Hello, Culture." Since things are nothing without being defined by someone, everything including the created artifacts and social phenomena has been given meaning through being understood. Just like saying hello to a new world, we looked forward to welcoming a new cultural era. In this CAAD Futures Conference, new and diverse cultural areas were analyzed and defined through contemporary architectural designers, engineers, and other researchers.

In the first stage of the paper evaluation, from the initial 194 abstracts received from 33 different countries, only 34 papers were selected for the Springer proceedings based on the reviewers' comments. Each paper was double-blind reviewed by at least three experts from an international committee of 66 experienced researchers. In the same process, 40 other papers were selected for publication in the conference proceedings and in Cumincad (cumincad.scix.net).

The papers in this book have been categorized under six headings: (1) Theory, Methodology, and Practice of Architectural and Interior Design, (2) Support Systems for Design Decisions, (3) Tools, Methods, and Implementation of Urban Design, (4) Rethinking Space and Spatial Behavior, (5) Fabrication and Materialization, (6) Shape Studies. The first group is about research in architectural and interior design. The second offers a broad range of studies in optimizing the creation and sustaining of the built environment. The third provides examples of various tools, methods, and applications of computation in the urban environment. The fourth group presents studies of the analysis of space or human behaviors. The fifth group includes research into new ways of making, which incorporate materials and computational thinking. The sixth group comprises research on mathematics of shapes in design. The contributors of this book are researchers from the fields of architecture, design, urban design, computer science, engineering, and other disciplines that address issues of computational design.

The editors are very grateful to Professors Bauke de Vries and Tom Kvan, CAAD Futures presidents, for their support for this book and preparing the conference. We also thank all the scientific committee members for their competent reviews and comments to authors, which resulted in the highest academic standard for the papers selected. Thank you to Taeha Yi, Mi Chang, and Meereh Kim for managing the overall conference and submission and the Graduate School of Culture Technology, KAIST, for supporting the conference. Finally, the conference would not have been possible without the sponsorship of Daejeon International Marketing Enterprise and Bentley Institute.

June 2019   Ji-Hyun Lee

Organization

CAAD Futures Board

Bauke de Vries	Eindhoven University of Technology, The Netherlands
Tom Kvan	University of Melbourne, Australia
Mark Gross	Carnegie Mellon University, USA

Organizing Committee

Ji-Hyun Lee (Chair)	Korea Advanced Institute of Science and Technology, South Korea
Taeha Yi	Korea Advanced Institute of Science and Technology, South Korea
Mi Chang	Korea Advanced Institute of Science and Technology, South Korea
Meereh Kim	Korea Advanced Institute of Science and Technology, South Korea
Minkyu Choi	Korea Advanced Institute of Science and Technology, South Korea
Po Yan Lai	Korea Advanced Institute of Science and Technology, South Korea
Gyueun Lee	Korea Advanced Institute of Science and Technology, South Korea
Sukjoo Hong	Korea Advanced Institute of Science and Technology, South Korea

Scientific Program Committee

Ahu Sökmenoğlu Sohtorik	Istanbul Technical University, Turkey
Andrew Li	Kyoto Institute of Technology, Japan
Andrzej Zarzycki	New Jersey Institute of Technology, USA
Arzu Gönenç Sorguç	Middle East Technical University, Turkey
Athanassios Economou	Georgia Institute of Technology, USA
Axel Kilian	Princeton University, USA
Başak Uçar	TED University, Turkey
Benay Gürsoy	Penn State University, USA
Bige Tuncer	SUTD, Singapore
Birgül Çolakoğlu	Istanbul Technical University, Turkey
Bob Martens	Vienna University of Technology, Austria
Brady Peters	University of Toronto, Canada

Surapong Lertsithichai	Mahidol University
Sule Tasli Pektas	Baskent University, Turkey
Terry Knight	MIT, USA
Tomohiro Fukuda	Osaka University, Japan
Tuba Kocatürk	University of Liverpool, UK
Tuğrul Yazar	Bilgi University, Turkey
Weixin Huang	Tsinghua University, China
Werner Lonsing	Independent Researcher, Germany
Yüksel Demir	Istanbul Technical University, Turkey

Sponsors

Daejeon International Marketing Enterprise

Bentley Institute

Contents

Fabrication and Materialization

Shape Studies

Theory, Methodology and Practice of Architectural and Interior Design

A Graph Theoretical Approach
for Creating Building Floor Plans

Krishnendra Shekhawat[1(✉)] 🆔, Pinki[1] 🆔, and José P. Duarte[2] 🆔

[1] Department of Mathematics, BITS Pilani, Pilani Campus, Pilani, India
krishnendra.iitd@gmail.com
[2] SCDC, School of Architecture and Landscape Architecture,
The Pennsylvania State University, University Park, PA 16802, USA

Abstract. Existing floor planning algorithms are mostly limited to rectangular room geometries. This restriction is a significant reason why they are not used much in design practice. To address this issue, we propose an algorithm (based on graph theoretic tools) that generates rectangular and, if required, orthogonal floor plans while satisfying the given adjacency requirements. If a floor plan does not exist for the given adjacency requirements, we introduce circulations within a floor plan to have a required floor plan.

Keywords: Adjacency · Algorithm · Graph theory ·
Rectangular floor plan · Orthogonal floor plan

1 Introduction

A *floor plan* (FP) is a polygon, the plan boundary, divided by straight lines into component polygons called *rooms*. The edges forming the perimeter of each room are termed *walls*. Two rooms in a floor plan are *adjacent* if they share a wall or a section of wall; it is not sufficient for them to touch at a point only.

A *rectangular floor plan* (RFP) is a FP in which plan's boundary and each room are rectangles. Any RFP with n rooms is represented by RFP(n). An *orthogonal floor plan* (OFP) has a rectangular plan boundary with the walls of each room parallel to the sides of the plan boundary, i.e., an OFP may have some non-rectangular rooms, such as L-shaped, T-shaped, etc. A FP with non-rectangular and rectilinear plan boundary is called *non-rectangular floor plan* (NRFP). For an illustration, refer to Figs. 1A, B and C demonstrating a RFP, an OFP and a NRFP respectively.

An essential task in the initial stages of most architectural design processes is the construction of planar floor plans, that are composed of non-overlapping rooms divided from each other by walls while satisfying given constraints. In this paper, we aim to construct a floor plan for any given adjacency graph, where an *adjacency graph* provides specific neighborhood between the given rooms. Constructing a floor plan involves the following sub-problems:

© Springer Nature Singapore Pte Ltd. 2019
J.-H. Lee (Ed.): CAAD Futures 2019, CCIS 1028, pp. 3–14, 2019.
https://doi.org/10.1007/978-981-13-8410-3_1

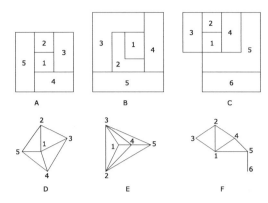

Fig. 1. Illustrating different concepts used in the paper

1. Checking the existence of a floor plan
   There may or may not exist a floor plan for the given adjacency graph. If it exists, then there may or may not exists a RFP. If it does not exist, then there may or may not exists an OFP. Hence, for constructing a floor plan, we first need to derive some conditions for checking the existence of a floor plan for the given adjacency graph.
2. Identifying the position of rooms
   Rooms need to be positioned in a way that each room should only be surrounded by its neighbors. Also, we need to consider their adjacencies with the exterior, if asked by the user.
3. Identifying the shape of rooms
   We need to look for the shape of a room that would make it adjacent to its neighbors. Initially, we prefer a room to be rectangular, otherwise we look for a shape that is made up of more than one rectangles, for example, L-shape is made up of 2 rectangles while U-shape is made up of 3 rectangles.
4. Identifying the shape of the layout
   We need to place all rooms inside a polygon while satisfying the above-discussed constraints. Here, we prefer to have a rectangular boundary, if possible.
5. The size of rooms and the layout
   At this stage, we are not considering the dimensional constraints, i.e., we will construct a floor plan corresponding to a given adjacency graph only.

1.1   Comparison with Existing Work

In the past, many researchers have presented graph theoretical techniques for the generation of a FP while satisfying given adjacency requirements. A brief literature review is as follows:

This approach was first presented by Levin [1] where a method was proposed for converting an adjacency graph into a FP. Then in 1970, Cousin [2] talked about the construction of a RFP for a given adjacency graph. In both the approaches, the problem of realizing the adjacency structure as a FP was not presented very clearly. In the same year, Grason [3] proposed a dual graph representation of a planar graph for generating a RFP. In this direction, Steadman [4] exhaustively generates all topologically distinct RFP (illustrating all possibilities up to six component rooms). These packings were produced by hand. In 1975, Sauda [5] designed a computer algorithm for generating all topologically distinct RFP having 8 rooms. In 1977, Lynes [6] showed that "all rooms of a FP may have windows if and only if the adjacency graph is outer-planar[1]." In 1980, Baybars and Eastman [7] demonstrated a systematic procedure for obtaining NRFP from a given underlying maximal planar graph (MPG)[2]. In 1982, Roth et al. [8] presented the construction of a dimensioned RFP from a given adjacency graph. In this method, the given graph is first split into two sub-graphs by a colouring technique; each of these graphs is then converted into a dimensioned graph; at the end, a set of alternative plans were derived where the size of FP is determined using the PERT algorithm [9]. In 1985, Robinson and Janjic [10] showed that, for a given maximal outer-planar graph, if areas are specified for rooms, then any convex polygon with the correct area can be divided into convex rooms to satisfy both area and adjacency requirements. In 1987, Bhasker and Sahni [11] gave a linear time algorithm for the existence of a RFP corresponding to a properly triangulated planar graph (PTPG)[3]. In 1988, Rinsma [12] provided conditions for the existence of a RFP and an OFP for a given tree[4]. In 1990, Rinsma et al. [13] demonstrated the automated generation of an OFP corresponding to a given MPG. In 1993, Yeap and Sarrafzadeh [14] showed that every planar triangulated graph (PTG) has a floor-plan using 1-, 2-, and 3-rectangle modules. In 1995, Giffin et al. [15] gave a linear time algorithm for constructing an OFP where rooms are at worst topologically equivalent T-shapes. In 1999, He [16] presented a linear time algorithm that constructs a floor-plan for PTG using only 1- and 2-rectangle modules. In 2000, Recuero et al. [17] presented a heuristic method for checking the existence of a RFP for a given graph. In 2003, Liao et al. [18] gave a linear time algorithm for constructing an OFP for any n-vertex PTG, which is based upon the concept of orderly spanning trees.

As a recent work, in 2011, Jokar and Sangchooli [19] introduced face area concept for constructing an OFP corresponding to a particular class of MPG. In the

---

[1] An undirected graph is an *outer-planar graph* if it can be drawn in the plane without crossings in such a way that all of the vertices belong to the unbounded face of the drawing.

[2] A planar graph G is *maximal* if no edges can be added to G without losing planarity.

[3] A *properly triangulated planar graph* (PTPG), G, is a connected planar graph that satisfies the following properties:

   i. Every face (except the exterior) is a triangle (i.e., bounded by three edges),
   ii. All internal vertices have degree ≥ 4,
   iii. All cycles that are not faces have length ≥ 4.

[4] Any connected graph without cycles is a tree.

same year, Zhang and Sadasivam [20] studied adjacency-preserving transformations from MPG to PTPG. In 2012, Regateiro et al. [21] proposed an approach for architectural layout design problems, which is based on topological algebras and constraint satisfaction techniques. In 2014, Shekhawat [22] proposed the enumeration of a particular class of RFP, i.e., the RFP having $3n - 7$ edges in their dual graphs. In 2017, Shekhawat et al. [23] gave an algorithm to generate a NRFP corresponding to the given weighted adjacency matrix. In 2018, Slusarczyk [24] introduced the notion of hierarchical layout graph (HL-graph) and present a theoretical framework for extending local graph requirements to global requirements on HL-graphs. Recently, Shekhawat [25] presented an algorithm for enumerating all distinct maximal RFP.

It can be seen that most of the work done related to the existence and construction of a FP falls into any one of these categories:

i. Construction of a RFP corresponding to PTPG [8,11,22,26,27],
ii. Construction of an OFP corresponding to maximal outer planar (MOP) graphs [6,10,12] and MPG [13–16,18,19],
iii. Construction of a NRFP corresponding to MPG [7] or corresponding to weighted adjacency matrix [23].

Hence, most of the work related to the generation of a FP is restricted to a particular class of adjacency graphs. And to the best of our knowledge, there does not exist an algorithm for constructing a FP corresponding to adjacency graphs, other than PTG and MPG. In this work, we aim to provide a FP for any given adjacency graph, i.e., this work is not restricted to any particular class of adjacency graphs.

In 2006, Steadman [28] showed that rectangular packings offer the best flexibility of dimensioning and this is why most of the buildings are rectangular. Hence, in this paper, we first aim to have a RFP for a given adjacency graph. If RFP does not exist, then we look for an OFP. If both of them do not exist, then we insert some circulations within the floor plan.

Notations:
FP: floor plan/s,
FP_G: floor plan graph,
RFP: rectangular FP,
RFP(n): RFP with n rooms,
MFP and MFP_G: maximal FP and maximal FP_G respectively,
OFP: orthogonal FP,
G_n: $n-$vertex simple connected adjacency graph,
n: the number of rooms in a RFP or the number of vertices in an adjacency graph,
v_i: i^{th} vertex of an adjacency graph,
R_i: i^{th} room of a FP.

2 An Algorithm for Constructing Floor Plans

In this section, our aim is to construct a FP for a given adjacency graph G_n. We prefer to derive a RFP for G_n, otherwise we proceed for an OFP. If a floor plan does not exists, then we introduce some circulations within a FP. To proceed further, we introduce the following new terminologies.

Definition 1. An adjacency graph for which a FP exists is called *floor plan graph*, abbreviated as FP$_G$.

For example, the adjacency graph in Fig. 1D is a FP$_G$. In particular, it is a RFP$_G$ because of the presence of a RFP in Fig. 1A while it is interesting to verify that the adjacency graph in Fig. 1E is an OFP$_G$ but not a RFP$_G$ (it is not possible to construct a RFP for the adjacency graph in Fig. 1E).

Definition 2. A FP$_G$ is called *maximal* FP$_G$, abbreviated as MFP$_G$, if adding any new edge to it results in a graph that is not a FP$_G$. A FP corresponding to a MFP$_G$ is called *maximal floor plan*, abbreviated as MFP.

Similarly, maximal rectangular floor plan and maximal orthogonal floor plan are abbreviated as MRFP and MOFP respectively.

It is easy to verify that the FP in Fig. 1A is a MRFP (it is not possible to make two non-adjacent rooms adjacent in Fig. 1A while maintaining other adjacencies and rectangularity). Similarly, the FP in Fig. 1B is a MOFP (we cannot make two non-adjacent rooms adjacent while maintaining other adjacencies).

In 2018, Shekhawat [25] presented the enumeration of all distinct MRFP. Furthermore, it has been proved that if an adjacency graph G_n is not a sub-graph of any of the MRFP$_G(n)$, then there does not exist a RFP(n) for G_n. It leads us to the following cases:

1. G_n is not a sub-graph of a MRFP$_G(n)$
   In this case, there does not exist a RFP for G_n but there may or may not exist an OFP for G_n. If it exists, we construct an OFP for G_n. If it does not exist, we construct a FP with circulations.
2. G_n is a sub-graph of a MRFP$_G(n)$
   In this case, there may or may not exist a RFP for G_n. If it exists, we construct a RFP otherwise we construct an OFP.

The steps for the construction of a FP are as follows (for a better understanding of all the steps involved, refer to the flow chart in Fig. 2):

1. Check if G_n is a sub-graph of any one of the MRFP$_G(n)$
2. If G_n is a sub-graph of any one of the MRFP$_G(n)$
   For example, G_6 in Fig. 3A is a sub-graph of MRFP$_G(6)$ in Fig. 3B. The red edges in Fig. 3B are the extra connections, which are not a part of adjacency constraints. Similarly, G_6 in Fig. 4A is also a sub-graph of the MRFP$_G(6)$.
   (a) Consider a MRFP(n) corresponding to the MRFP$_G(n)$.
      For example, corresponding to the adjacency graphs G_6 in Figs. 3A and 4A, the required MRFP(6) are illustrated in Figs. 3C and 4B respectively.

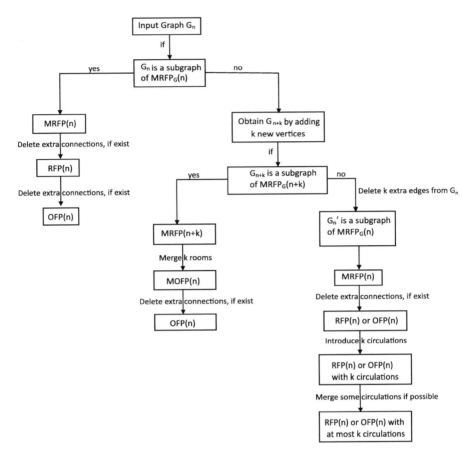

Fig. 2. Flow chart illustrating the different cases for constructing a floor plan corresponding to a given adjacency graph

(b) Reduce the obtained MRFP(n) into a required FP(n) by eliminating the extra connections.

One of the most common ways which has been used by many researchers to eliminate the extra connections is to introduce doors between adjacent rooms such that there are no doors between non-adjacent rooms. For example, refer to Fig. 3E with a RFP(6) from the given G_6, where the extra connections with no doors are shown in red. But, in this approach, we are compromising with the position of the rooms. As an example, G_6 in Fig. 3A clearly indicates that all rooms must be adjacent to exterior but RFP(6) in Fig. 3E have two rooms which are not adjacent to the exterior. Hence, the best possible approach is to adjust the shape and size of some rooms to have a required FP. For example, the reduction of MRFP(6) in Fig. 3C into a RFP(6) in Fig. 3F is shown in Figs. 3G to K. Further, the MRFP(6) in Figure cannot be reduced in a RFP, hence an OFP for G_6 in Fig. 4A has been shown in Fig. 4D.

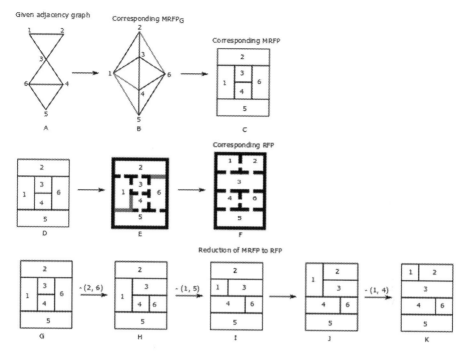

Fig. 3. Deriving a RFP from MRFP corresponding to a given adjacency graph (Color figure online)

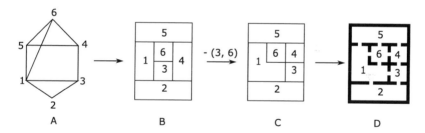

Fig. 4. Deriving an OFP from MRFP corresponding to a given adjacency graph

3. If G_n is not a sub-graph of any of the MRFP$_G(n)$

   For example, G_8 in Fig. 5A is not a sub-graph of any of the MRFP$_G(8)$ (for all MRFP$_G(8)$, refer to [25]).

   (a) In this case, there does not exist a RFP corresponding to G_n. Hence, we need to construct an OFP for G_n.

   For example, G_8 in Fig. 5A is not a RFP$_G(8)$.

   (b) Let k be the minimum number of edges of G_n whose deletion results in a graph G'_n such that G'_n is a sub-graph of at least one of the MRFP$_G(n)$ (an algorithm for computing k is given in Sect. 3.1).

For example, for G_8 in Fig. 5A, we have $k = 2$, corresponding to the edges joining vertices (v_1, v_7) and (v_3, v_5).

(c) Subdivide each of the k edges, obtained in above step, into two edges, by adding a vertex to each of them, to have a new graph, say G_r with $r = n + k$.

For example, two vertices, v_9 and v_{10}, have been added to G_8 in Fig. 5A to derive graph G_{10}, illustrated in Fig. 5B.

(d) If G_r is a sub-graph of any one of the $\mathrm{MRFP_G}(r)$

   i. Consider a $\mathrm{MRFP}(r)$ corresponding to the $\mathrm{MRFP_G}(r)$.

      For example, G_{10} in Fig. 5B is a sub-graph of $\mathrm{MRFP_G}(10)$ in Fig. 5C and corresponding $\mathrm{MRFP}(10)$ is shown in Fig. 5D.

   ii. Let e_{ij} denotes an edge with endpoints v_i and v_j and v_p is the added vertex on e_{ij}.

      Corresponding to each new vertex v_p, $n < p \leq n + k$, either merge rooms R_i and R_p, or merge rooms R_p and R_j, to have a MOFP with k orthogonal rooms.

      For example, corresponding to G_8 in Fig. 5A, a $\mathrm{MOFP}(8)$ is shown in Fig. 5E, that is obtained from $\mathrm{MRFP}(10)$ by merging (R_3, R_9) and (R_7, R_{10}).

   iii. Reduce the obtained $\mathrm{MOFP}(n)$ into a required $\mathrm{OFP}(n)$ by eliminating the extra connections.

      For example, an $\mathrm{OFP}(8)$ for G_8 in Fig. 5A is shown in Fig. 5H. The steps for deriving the $\mathrm{OFP}(8)$ in Fig. 5H from $\mathrm{MOFP}(8)$ in Fig. 5F are shown in Fig. 5I to L.

(e) If G_r is not a sub-graph of any one of the $\mathrm{MRFP_G}(r)$

   For example, G_7 in Fig. 6B is not a subgraph of any of the $\mathrm{MRFP_G}(7)$.

   i. Consider the graph G'_n (obtained by deleting k edges in Step 3b).

      For example, G'_5 for G_5 in Fig. 6A is shown in Fig. 6C.

   ii. Obtain a $\mathrm{MRFP}(n)$ for G'_n.

      For example, a MRFP for G'_5 in Fig. 6C is illustrated in Fig. 6D.

   iii. Eliminate extra connections, if exist in the obtained MRFP.

      For example, there does not exist extra connections in the MRFP corresponding to G'_5 in Fig. 6C.

   iv. Introduce k circulations corresponding to the deleted edges. If possible, insert circulations such that they are adjacent to exterior.

      For example, two circulations have been introduced in Fig. 6E corresponding to the edges deleted from G_5 in Fig. 6A.

   v. Merge circulations with the rooms, if possible.

      For example, a circulation has been merged to room R_3 to have a required floor plan for G_5 in Fig. 6A, as shown in Fig. 6G.

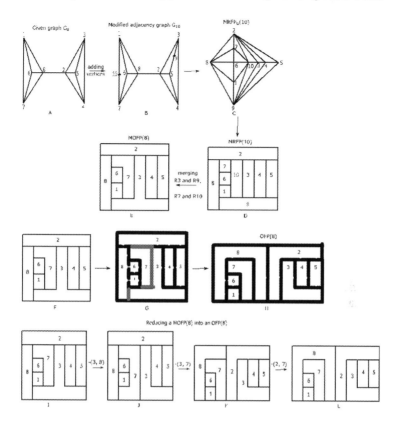

Fig. 5. Deriving an OFP from MOFP corresponding to a given adjacency graph

2.1 Computing Extra Edges

If a given adjacency graph G_n is not a $RFP_G(n)$, we need to construct an OFP corresponding to it. To have an OFP, we require k, where k is the minimum number of edges of G_n whose deletion results in a graph G'_n such that G'_n is a sub-graph of at least one of the $MRFP_G(n)$. The steps for computing k are as follows:

1. Compute power set of edge set of G_n and denote it as $P(E(G_n))$, where $E(G_n)$ is the edge set of G_n.
   Let the members of $P(E(G_n))$ are denoted as $S_1, S_2, \ldots, S_{2^m}$.
2. Order $S_1, S_2, \ldots, S_{2^m}$ in decreasing order on the basis of size of each set S_i.
   Let the members of $P(E(G_n))$ in the descending order be $S'_1, S'_2, \ldots, S'_{2^m}$.
3. Let $i = 2$.
4. Choose S'_i.
5. If $S'_i \subseteq E(MRFP_G(n))$, then $k = m - n(S'_i)$ and edges corresponding to k are $E(G_n) - S'_i$.
6. If condition in Step 5 holds, stop the algorithm otherwise increase i by 1.
7. If $i \leq (2^m)$ go to Step 4 otherwise stop.

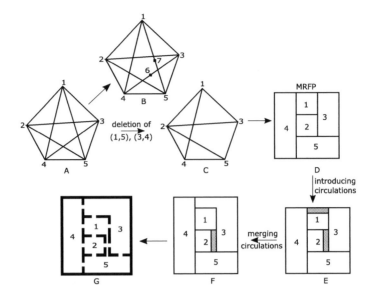

Fig. 6. Deriving a FP with circulations corresponding to a given adjacency graph

3   Conclusion and Future Work

In this paper, we first aim to check the existence of a floor plan corresponding to a given adjacency graph, and if it exists, we aim to construct it.

To the best of our knowledge, there does not exist a mathematical theory for checking the existence of a FP for a given adjacency graph, other than PTPG and MPG. In this paper, we are the first one to categorize the adjacency graphs on the basis of existence of a RFP, or OFP, or none of them. In addition, we propose a method to construct a FP for any given adjacency graph, where we prefer to have a RFP first, then an OFP. If both of them do not exist, then we go for a floor plan with circulations.

We know that in architectural design, a multitude of aspects with different nature need to be considered. In this paper, we are dealing with adjacency requirements in the strict sense only. In the future, we first aim to introduce dimensional constraints for constructing a floor plan. Then, we will cover other aspects, like (aesthetic) composition, style, functionality, access to light, etc.

Acknowledgement. The research described in this paper evolved as part of the research project Mathematics-aided Architectural Design Layouts (File Number: ECR/2017/000356) funded by the Science and Engineering Research Board, India.

References

1. Levin, P.H.: Use of graphs to decide the optimum layout of buildings. Archit. J. **7**, 809–817 (1964)
2. Cousin, J.: Topological organization of architectural spaces. Architectural Des. **40**, 491–493 (1970)
3. Grason, J.: A dual linear representation for space filling location problems of the floorplan type. In: Moore, G.T. (ed.) Emerg. Methods Environ. Des. Plann., pp. 170–178. MIT Press, Cambridge (1970)
4. Steadman, J.P.: Graph theoretic representation of architectural arrangement. Architect. Res. Teach. **2**(3), 161–172 (1973)
5. Sauda, E.J.: Computer program for the generation of dwelling unit floor plans. March thesis, University of California, Los Angeles-Architecture (1975)
6. Lynes, J.A.: Windows and floor plans. Environ. Plan. B. **4**, 51–55 (1977)
7. Baybars, I., Eastman, C.M.: Enumerating architectural arrangements by generating their underlying graphs. Environ. Plan. B. **7**, 289–310 (1980)
8. Roth, J., Hashimshony, R., Wachman, A.: Turning a graph into a rectangular floor plan. Build. Environ. **17**(3), 163–173 (1982)
9. Radcliffe, P.E., Kawal, D.E., Stephenson, R.J.: Critical Path Method, vol. III. Cahner, Chicago (1967)
10. Robinson, D.F., Janjic, I.: The constructability of floorplans with certain given outerplanar adjacency graph and room areas. In: Proceedings Xth British Combinatorics Conference, Ars Combinatoria, vol. 20B, pp. 133–142 (1985)
11. Bhasker, J., Sahni, S.: A linear time algorithm to check for the existence of a rectangular dual of a planar triangulated graph. Networks **17**(3), 307–317 (1987)
12. Rinsma, I.: Rectangular and orthogonal floorplans with required room areas and tree adjacency. Environ. Plan. B: Plan. Des. **15**, 111–118 (1988)
13. Rinsma, I., Giffin, J.W., Robinson, D.F.: Orthogonal floorplans from maximal planar graphs. Environ. Plan. B: Plan. Des. **174**, 67–71 (1990)
14. Yeap, K.-H., Sarrafzadeh, M.: Floor-planning by graph dualization: 2-concave rectilinear modules. SIAM J. Comput. **22**(3), 500–526 (1993)
15. Giffin, J.W., Watson, K., Foulds, L.R.: Orthogonal layouts using the deltahedron heuristic. Australas. J. Comb. **12**, 127–144 (1995)
16. He, X.: On floor-plan of plane graphs. SIAM J. Comput. **28**(6), 2150–2167 (1999)
17. Recuero, A., Río, O., Alvarez, M.: Heuristic method to check the realisability of a graph into a rectangular plan. Adv. Eng. Soft. **31**, 223–231 (2000)
18. Liao, C.-C., Lu, H.-I., Yen, H.-C.: Compact floor-planning via orderly spanning trees. J. Algorithm **48**, 441–451 (2003)
19. Jokar, M.R.A., Sangchooli, A.S.: Constructing a block layout by face area. Int. J. Manuf. Technol. **54**, 801–809 (2011)
20. Zhang, H., Sadasivam, S.: Improved floor-planning of graphs via adjacency-preserving transformations. J. Comb. Optim. **22**, 726–746 (2011)
21. Regateiro, F., Bento, J., Dias, J.: Floor plan design using block algebra and constraint satisfaction. Adv. Eng. Inf. **26**, 361–382 (2012)
22. Shekhawat, K.: Algorithm for constructing an optimally connected rectangular floor plan. Front. Archit. Res. **3**(3), 324–330 (2014)
23. Shekhawat, K., Duarte, J.P.: Rectilinear floor plans. Commun. Comput. Inf. Sci. **724**, 395–411 (2017)
24. Slusarczyk, G.: Graph-based representation of design properties in creating building floorplans. Comput. Aid. Des. **95**, 24–39 (2018)

25. Shekhawat, K.: Enumerating generic rectangular floor plans. Autom. Constr. **92**, 151–165 (2018)
26. He, X.: On finding the rectangular duals of planar triangular graphs. SIAM J. Comput. **22**, 1218–1226 (1993)
27. Shekhawat, K., Duarte, J.P.: Automated best connected rectangular floorplans. In: Gero, J.S. (ed.) Design Computing and Cognition '16, pp. 495–511. Springer, Cham (2017). https://doi.org/10.1007/978-3-319-44989-0_27
28. Steadman, P.: Why are most buildings rectangular? ARQ Mag. **10**(2), 119–130 (2006)

Environmental Performance-Driven Urban Design: Parametric Design Method for the Integration of Daylight and Urban Comfort Analysis in Cold Climates

Francesco De Luca[(✉)] (iD)

Tallinn University of Technology, Tallinn, Estonia
francesco.deluca@taltech.ee

Abstract. Shape of built environment and image of cities are significantly influenced by environmental factors such as access to natural light, air temperature and wind. Adequate quantity of daylight in building interiors is important for occupant wellbeing and energy saving. In Estonia minimum quantity of daylight is required by building standards. Wind speed increased by urban environment at northern latitudes can significantly reduce pedestrian perceived temperature during winter inducing strong cold stress. This paper presents a method for the integration of parametric modeling and environmental simulations to analyze interiors and exteriors comfort of tower building cluster variations in different urban areas in Tallinn. Optimal pattern characteristics such as buildings distance and alignment favoring improvement of interiors daylight and decrease of pedestrian cold stress are presented and discussed.

Keywords: Daylight · Urban comfort · Environmental analysis ·
Performance-driven urban design · Parametric design

1 Introduction

Environmental factors such as access to daylight and protection from direct sun light, exploitment of summer cooling breezes and protection from winter cold winds, have largely contributed to shape urban environments and to outline the image of cities through history.

Already in Ancient Greece the distance between buildings, their orientation and height were taken into account to provide the appropriate quantity of solar access for dwellings and were considered important urban planning factors. The plan of Priene, an ancient Greek city in Asia Minor, was characterized by an east-west alignment of the main streets to maximize southerly exposure of dwelling main facades hence to exploit solar radiation in winter time [1].

Vitruvius, in his treatise The Ten Books on Architecture, recommends to take into account climatic conditions of the site to plan streets and alleys to limit the flow of local winds that are unpleasant in the cold season, debilitating in the hot season and unhealthy during days characterized by moist weather [2].

© Springer Nature Singapore Pte Ltd. 2019
J.-H. Lee (Ed.): CAAD Futures 2019, CCIS 1028, pp. 15–31, 2019.
https://doi.org/10.1007/978-981-13-8410-3_2

Adaptation to wind conditions has been the driving factor of the urban layout development of Korčula historic center in Croatia. The street pattern minimizes air flows of northerly cold winds during winter and maximizes the easterly and westerly flow of summer breezes which help to cool the buildings [3].

In more recent times daylight regulations had a significant influence on the urban structure and image of cities. The New York Zoning Resolution of 1916 allowing to use the whole footprint of a building as floor size for a limited height and requiring a gradual recession for higher floors, influenced architects and developers to use the terraced building massing characteristic of New York skyscrapers of first half of past century [4].

In UK the Doctrine of Ancient Lights included in the Rights to Light Act of 1959 states that a window that is receiving a specific amount of natural light for 20 years has the right to continue to receive it and new buildings on neighboring lands cannot reduce it. Though not suggesting a specific building shape this daylight regulation favors urban fragmentation [5].

1.1 Daylight Requirements

During last few decades daylight importance has steadily gained consensus. Nowadays it is considered one of the main factors to improve buildings energy efficiency, occupant comfort and workers productivity [6]. Daylight is the most appreciated source of interiors illumination and its variability has proven to be beneficial for the occupant physiological and psychological well-being entraining humans' circadian rhythm [7].

Building natural illumination requirements exist in most countries. They require either minimum quantity of hours of direct sun light or minimum level of interiors daylight. The first type is more difficult to accomplish. Nevertheless, recently calculation methods have been developed which can be efficiently used to include direct solar access in the design process [8]. The second type is easier to accomplish because it considers also the diffused and reflected light components, and is more reliable in predicting occupant comfort because it takes into account interiors layout.

Different procedures and metrics exist to quantitatively estimate daylight performance of building interiors through computer simulations. Daylight Factor (DF) is an efficient metric which predicts interiors natural light levels as a percentage of external illuminance levels. DF takes into account room size and proportions, windows size and glazing visible transmittance, interior surfaces reflectance and external obstructions, though does not take into account building orientation and location climate.

In Estonia access to natural light is regulated by the building standard "Daylight in Dwellings and Offices" [9]. The standard, soon to become compulsory regulation, sets the minimum mean Daylight Factor (mDF) for a number of interior spaces such as residential, educational and commercial. For office buildings the standard requires a minimum mDF of 2% to be calculated on a grid located at desktop height (0.75 m). Estonian DF requirement has been used to assess relation of daylight with energy efficiency of buildings [10]. Studies used successfully DF requirement to investigate planning principles for occupant comfort and energy conservation in Estonia [11].

1.2 Urban Comfort

Contemporary cities alter local climate conditions influencing significantly pedestrian comfort during winter time at northern latitudes. Hence specific urban design strategies need to be adopted [12]. Pedestrian comfort along with building interiors comfort and energy use are closely related to urban form. Environmental factors such as solar radiation, air temperature and wind velocity, which influence the comfort of pedestrian, can be significantly altered by the urban environment to generate discomfort or even danger [13]. Taking their variation into account during the design process can help architects to improve comfort of building interiors and open urban areas.

The modification of air flow in urban environments can generate consistent wind acceleration due to aerodynamic affects around buildings and structures [14]. At northern latitudes increased wind velocities can significantly decrease the perceived temperature by pedestrian during cold season due to wind chill effect [15].

Wind Chill Equivalent Temperature (WCT) metric has been developed to determine for which combination of air temperature and wind velocity the exposed skin of a person is at risk of frostbite [16]. It is possible to calculate WCT through the specific equation for all the possible combinations of air temperature and wind speed or using a chart based on discreet increments.

Universal Thermal Climate Index (UTCI) is a metric particularly efficient in determining both increased and decreased perceived temperature which become the standard in urban comfort studies [17]. Taking into account solar radiation, radiant temperature, air temperature, humidity and wind speed it is mostly used in urban heat island analysis. The large spectrum of environmental factors and the use of different levels of thermal stress for the human body, makes UTCI an efficient metric also in assessing cold stress in urban environments. UTCI accounts as well for clothing on the basis of people behavior and uses average values for age and body mass.

The present research investigates daylight performance of office premises and urban comfort for cold stress in proximity of tower buildings during winter in the city of Tallinn, Estonia (Lat. 59°26'N Lon. 24°45'E). The scope is to analyze optimal or conflicting characteristics of building cluster patterns such as distance and alignment through integration of parametric design methods, simulations and environmental performance analysis tools. The study can help to improve local building culture providing methods and solutions to be used by architects and planners to improve interior occupant and exterior pedestrian comfort for future developments.

2 Method

A parametric design workflow is developed to integrate different urban environments, building cluster variations, daylight analysis, Tallinn weather data, Computational Fluid Dynamics (CFD) wind simulations and urban thermal comfort assessments of cold stress.

Daylight analysis is performed in the interiors of office tower buildings to assess compliance with the mean Daylight Factor requirement of the Estonian standard "Daylight in Dwellings and Offices". Urban thermal comfort analysis is performed to assess cold stress due to decreased perceived temperatures in winter time, as a consequence of wind acceleration, simulated by CFD, through and around tall buildings in urban areas. The main metric used for cold stress assessment is UTCI. In the study WCT is used as well to assess possible health dangers for pedestrian due to frostbite.

The study arises from the necessity to assess interiors and exteriors comfort of tower building clusters in the city of Tallinn. In recent years similar office and residential developments have been realized and more are planned in different parts of the city, from center to areas by the sea, characterized by buildings located close to each other, modifying consistently local microclimate (Fig. 1).

The climate type of Tallinn is cold with warm summer. The analysis periods used in the study are the months from December to March. During winter pedestrian comfort is particularly at risk because wind velocities are the highest of the year increasing significantly the discomfort due to seasonal low temperatures. Thus the urban form has an important role in improving comfort and attenuating possible health risks.

Fig. 1. View of Tallinn financial and commercial city center (Source of image: author).

2.1   Urban Areas

The research is conducted on building clusters located in 3 different urban areas. The scope is to analyze possible daylight and urban comfort performance variations due to different surrounding buildings density and urban morphology (Fig. 2).

The case study area of Liivalaia Street is located in the city center. The analysis plot is surrounded on three sides by medium and high density areas with buildings up to 10 floors. The financial and commercial district on the north side is densely populated by medium height and tower buildings up to 30 floors. The plot used for the study is located in a residual urban area used for parking and paths with trees.

Mustamäe Street case study area is located in a mixed use and medium density area of the city populated by housing buildings up to 10 floors, smaller residential buildings of average 5 floors, single family houses, large and low commercial buildings. The plot used for the study is located in an area used as car depot.

The case study area of Logi Street is situated in the Tallinn port area between the sea toward north and city center toward south. The close urban area is populated by dispersed low and medium height large buildings such as the port terminal and the landmark Linnahall of about 15 m and 18 m in height respectively. The plot used for the study is located in an unused land.

Fig. 2. The three case study areas of Liivalaia Street (left), Mustamäe Street (center) and Logi Street (right) (Source of images: Estonian Geoportal).

2.2 Building Cluster

The building cluster used in the study presents 3 office towers characterized by a footprint of 30 m by 30 m, a height of 100 m for 25 floors of 4 m height each. The size of the plot is 138 m by 114 m. Due to the different morphology of the three urban areas the study plots have different orientations (Fig. 2)

For each study area are tested 9 building cluster variations, different for pattern layout and buildings distance (Fig. 3). Variation 1 presents the 3 buildings located at the same reciprocal distance of 12 m between each other. Two buildings occupy symmetrically one half of the plot and the third building occupies the other half of the plot in a position symmetrical in regard to the other two buildings.

The most recent developments of this type in Tallinn present 2 or 3 tower buildings, thus the layout has been chosen to investigate different wind patterns, and consequently pedestrian cold stress on the area surrounding the buildings. The variations from 2 to 8 present different incremental distances between buildings of 18 m, 24 m and 30 m using the asymmetrical pattern. Variation 9 presents the same pattern of Variation 1 with a reciprocal distance of 30 m between the three buildings.

Fig. 3. Building cluster patterns for Variation 1 (left), 4 (center) and 7 (right).

2.3   Algorithm Design

The workflow developed for the study is composed of 4 main integrated algorithms: parametric design of building cluster; daylight analysis; wind simulations; urban comfort analysis calculations (Fig. 4). An additional algorithm automates pattern variation and the processes of simulation and analysis.

The algorithms are realized using visual scripting in Grasshopper for Rhinoceros [18] through specific tools realized by the author, the daylight design and urban thermal comfort analysis plug-ins DIVA [19] and Ladybug Tools [20], and the wind simulation plug-in Swift [21].

The first algorithm, for each study area, generates the rectangular building cluster plot and locates it in the urban environment previously modeled up to a distance of 500 m and imported in the parametric design software. The plot is subdivided in cells 3 m by 3 m. The cell centers are used in the third and fourth main algorithm to probe wind velocities and for urban comfort mapping.

Consequently the 3 tower buildings are created with footprints in correspondence with 100 cells each. The algorithm generates 9 cluster pattern variations selecting automatically pre-defined non-uniform distances between the three buildings with increments of 3 m.

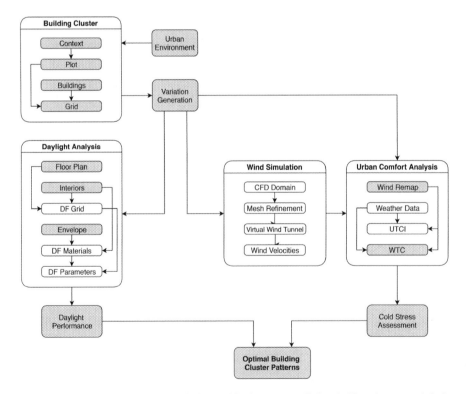

Fig. 4. Flowchart for the algorithm design. White boxes are off-the-shelf environmental design plug-in components. Grey boxes are algorithm functions and tools developed by the author.

The second, third and fourth algorithms of the workflow concern specific analysis, simulation and calculation workflows and are discussed in the following relative sections. Environmental simulations and analysis, and comfort performance calculations are preformed automatically through a recursive tool and results are collected at every building cluster variation generation.

2.4   Daylight Analysis

The first section of the second algorithm creates schematic floor plans and building envelopes (Fig. 5). Floors 4 m high are generated, divided in a core zone of 10 m by 10 m and a daylight zone 10 m deep subdivided in 8 open plan offices of 100 m² each with ceilings at 2.8 m. The algorithm subdivides the outer floor envelope in a glazed portion of height 2.8 m and in an opaque portion of 1.2 m on top of it.

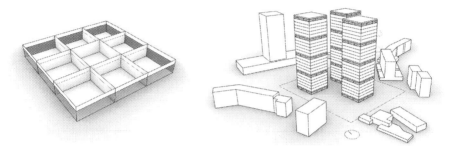

Fig. 5.   Floor layout (left). The 5 floors used for DF analysis for the tower buildings of Liivalaia Street study area (right).

The metric used for daylight performance analysis is the mean Daylight Factor (mDF) and the minimum 2% benchmark is used as required by the Estonian daylight standard to assess the comfort of the building interiors. Minimum mDF is calculated for the 8 open plan offices, 5 floors every building, 3 towers, 9 cluster variations, and 3 urban environments for a total of 3240 simulations (Fig. 6).

The floors used are the 1st (ground floor), the 25th (last floor) and 3 intermediate floors i.e. the 7th, 13th and 19th (Fig. 5). The use of 5 floors is due to limit the computationally intensive simulations. Nevertheless, the floors used represent with sufficient accuracy daylight variations due to different heights for the entire buildings.

Daylight Factor analysis is performed using the validated simulation software Radiance through DIVA. The grid used has cell size of 2 m and is placed at a height of 0.75 m. The main Radiance parameters used (−aa .1 −ab 5 −ad 1500 −ar 300 -as 20) guarantee results accuracy. Material properties are presented in Table 1.

Table 1.   Values of Reflectance (R) and Visible Transmittance (VT) used in Radiance.

	Floor	Walls	Ceilings	Ground	Exterior	Glazing
R	20%	50%	70%	20%	30%	–
VT	–	–	–	–	–	56%

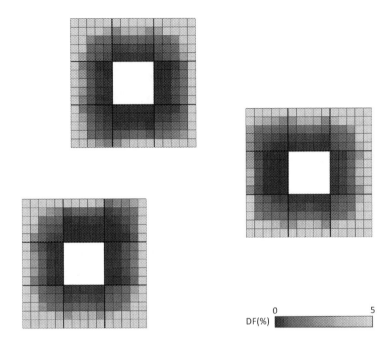

Fig. 6. Daylight Factor analysis grids of the open plan offices of cluster building 7th floor, variation 3 for the Liivalaia case study area.

2.5   Wind Simulation

Wind is a critical factor, together with air temperature, for the assessment of urban thermal comfort and cold stress in areas around and between buildings since in winter time and at high latitudes solar radiation, humidity and radiant temperature have a small or negligible effect.

The third algorithm is built using specific components to realize the wind analysis model, run CFD simulations using the validated software OpenFOAM through the plug-in Swift for each building cluster variation in every urban environment and probe wind velocities on the grid cells of the study area. In order to guarantee a proper level of results accuracy the methods of the Grasshopper CFD plug-in Swift are integrated with simulation recommendations [22].

A first component generates the computational domain realized almost entirely of hexahedral cells (Fig. 7). Surrounding buildings are modeled for a distance of 500 m from the study area and imported in the component. The square CFD domain is built with the same length and width, as required by Swift plug-in. In the flow direction the downstream length of 15 h (where h is the height of the highest modeled building) permits redevelopment of flows in the wake region. The same considerable upstream length permits flow establishment. The domain height is 10 h in order to not create wind flow alteration between the highest buildings and the domain upper side (Fig. 7). The size of the hexahedral cells of the domain before refinement is 16 m.

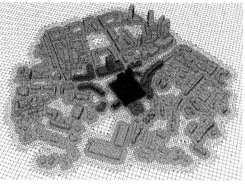

Fig. 7. CFD domain of Liivalaia Street study area with the urban environment modeled for a distance of 500 m (left). The different refinement regions of the domain: urban environment; buildings surrounding the plot; cluster buildings; ground (right).

Consequently a component of the algorithm refines the mesh domain, using the smallest possible number of non- hexahedral cells, in regions where more accuracy is needed in order to guarantee quality of simulation results. The following refinement levels are used: 2 for the urban environment which generates 4 m cells; 3 for buildings surrounding the study area which generates cells of 2 m; 4 for the cluster buildings of the study area which generates cells of 1 m; 5 for the cluster plot ground which generates cells of 0.5 m (Fig. 7).

After the domain mesh is built, for every building cluster variation and urban environment, 16 CFD simulations are run through the Virtual Wind Tunnel (VWT) component, one every 22.5° starting from 0° (north) clockwise, using a fixed wind velocity of 5 m/s. The VWT component is a circular extension of the computational domain which permits to run automatically multiple wind direction simulations without repeating the CFD domain meshing procedure for each of them, thus allowing considerable computation time saving. The 16 wind direction simulations guarantee accuracy of calculations for long analysis periods such as months as used in this study.

The VWT furthermore permits to change Boundary Conditions (BC) for different wind directions. This allows for more accurate simulation results in case of different urban areas and different surrounding morphologies. The values of terrain roughness length (Z_0) used in the CFD simulations are presented in Table 2.

For every cluster variation and urban area a last component of the CFD simulation algorithm probes the wind velocities of the domain cells on a grid of 1448 points corresponding to the center of the plot cells 3 m by 3 m located at 1.5 m height for WCT analysis and at 10 m height for UTCI analysis (Fig. 8).

Table 2. Values of terrain roughness length used in the CFD simulations.

Z_0	Liivalaia Street	Mustamäe Street	Logi Street
0.0002 - Sea	–	–	0°–90°, 292.5°–337.5°
1 - Urban areas	45°–247.5°	0°–337.5°	112.5°–270°
2 - City center	0°–22.5°, 270°–337.5°	–	–

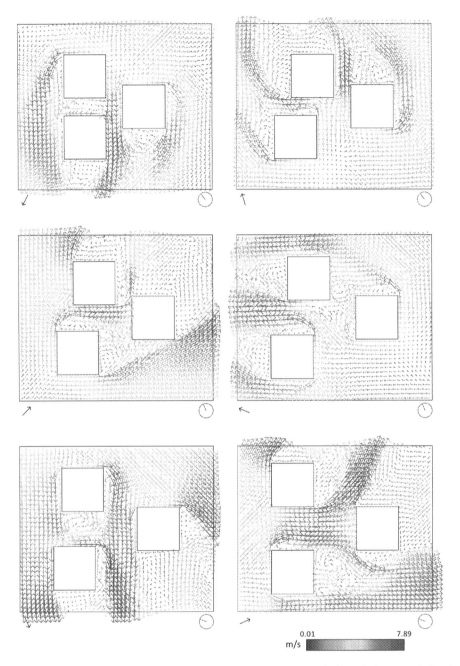

Fig. 8. Wind velocities and patterns (10 m). Top to bottom: area of Liivalaia Street variation 1 direction 67.5° (E-NE) (left) and variation 3 direction 202.5° (S-SW) (right), area of Mustamäe Street variation 4 direction 247.5° (W-SW) (left) and variation 6 direction 135° (SE), area of Logi Street variation 7 direction 45° (NE) (left) and variation 9 direction 315° (NW) (right).

2.6 Urban Comfort Analysis

For cold stress analysis the metrics UTCI and WCT are used on the basis of data from Tallinn weather file and simulated wind velocities. Four different analysis periods during winter season are used corresponding to the months of December, January, February and March. Due to consistent differences of air temperature and wind velocities between the 4 months, using different analysis periods allows for differentiation and greater significance of results which would be otherwise averaged.

The fourth algorithm is build using Grasshopper parametric design components and off-the-shelf tools of the environmental design plug-in Ladybug Tools.

A tool developed by the author remaps wind velocities according to weather data. The wind velocity of every hour during the analyzed month obtained from the weather file is associated to one of the 16 CFD simulation directions on the basis of its measured direction. Each of the 1448 wind probed velocities of every CFD direction are normalized (divided by the simulation fixed wind velocity value of 5 m/s) and multiplied for every weather data wind velocity of the same CFD direction.

In this way it is possible to obtain remapped wind velocities for every hour of the analysis period for every grid point. Additionally wind velocities of the plots without buildings are remapped on full plot grids for comparison of cold stress results.

The variables accounted for UTCI calculations of perceived temperature are radiant temperature, air temperature, humidity and wind speed. An off-the-shelf component of the algorithm calculates solar adjusted Mean Radiant Temperature for every point of a grid at 1.5 m from the ground (human body location) for every hour of each analysis period taking into account direct normal and diffuse horizontal solar radiation, dry bulb temperature and context shading. Surface temperature of cluster buildings is not taken into account due to its negligible effect during cold season. Hourly data of air temperature and humidity are obtained from the weather file.

An environmental design component finally calculates the percentage of time during the analysis period of different comfort levels of a person located in correspondence of each grid point. For the present study the UTCI Equivalent Temperature −13 °C or lower is used to assess the percentage of time each grid point of every cluster variation in each study area is in the condition of "strong cold stress" [17] (Fig. 9).

A section of the algorithm developed by the author performs cold stress analysis using WCT. According to this metric frostbite risk occurs at WCT −27 °C. The variables accounted for WCT are air temperature and wind velocity. Hourly air temperatures of winter months used as analysis periods are retrieved from the weather data file and wind velocities are obtained remapping CFD simulation wind velocities probed at 1.5 m height. WCT is computed using Formula 1 [16].

$$\text{WCT}\,(^\circ\text{C}) = 13.12 + 0.6215 \cdot T - 11.37 \cdot V^{0.16} + 0.3965 \cdot T \cdot V^{0.16} \qquad (1)$$

Here, T is the air temperature (°C) and V is the wind velocity (km·h^{-1}).

Through an automation component of the algorithm the process of calculation of UTCI and WCT is iterated for the 9 building cluster variations in each one of the 3 study areas.

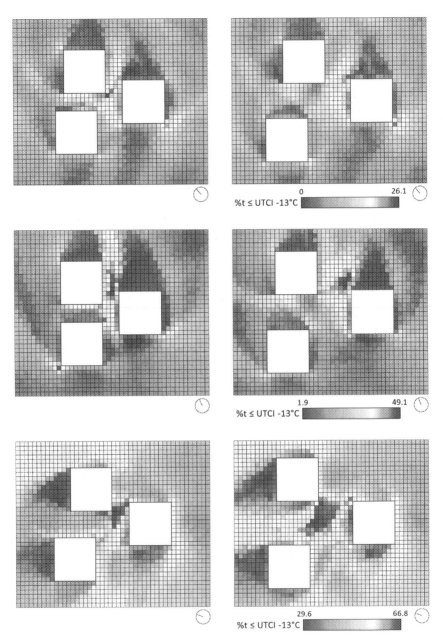

Fig. 9. Urban comfort maps for cold stress of percentage of time during analysis period body locations (grid points) experience a temperature ≤ UTCI −13°C. Top to bottom: area of Liivalaia St. period March variation 2 (left) and 6 (right), area of Mustamäe St. period December variation 1 (left) and 7 (right), area of Logi St. period January variation 4 (left) and 8 (right).

3 Results

The present section presents and discusses results of daylight analysis and urban comfort assessment for cold stress. The scope is to investigate optimal cluster patterns in terms of building distances and mutual position which improve both environmental performances together or possible conflicts between them.

Daylight performance of building cluster variations are evaluated against the Daylight Factor requirement of minimum 2% mDF of the Estonian daylight standard thus using a fixed threshold. Additionally average DF is analyzed. In Estonia urban comfort is not regulated by building codes hence cold stress analysis using UTCI and WCT are evaluated in terms of differences of performance between pattern variations.

3.1 Daylight Analysis Results

Minimum and average mDF is calculated for 8 offices of 5 floors each tower building, for 9 building cluster variations and 3 urban environments (Fig. 10). Daylight performance are very similar in the different urban areas with slightly larger DF values for less dense environments. This outcome shows that the urban environment has negligible impact on daylight performance of tower building clusters.

Results of average mDF among open plan offices show that the majority receive the minimum 2% as required by the Estonian standard "Daylight in Dwellings and Offices". Due to most of the views to the outside not obstructed by the other two tower buildings the average mDF per cluster ranges from 4.77% of variation 1 for Liivalaia Street case study to 5.49% of variation 9 for Logi Street case study.

Results of minimum mDF show that not all the open plan offices of all the building cluster variations and urban areas receive the required daylight. When tower buildings are very close (12 m) as in variation 1 minimum mDF for the 3 urban areas ranges from 0.61% to 0.63%. As expected daylight performance increases with increasing of distance between cluster buildings. All the open plan offices receive the required daylight for variation 7 of Logi Street case study with minimum mDF 2% and for variations 8 and 9 for all the 3 urban areas. Results show that for this type of building cluster interiors receive adequate daylight when opposite building distance is equal their width or slightly less in case buildings are not aligned.

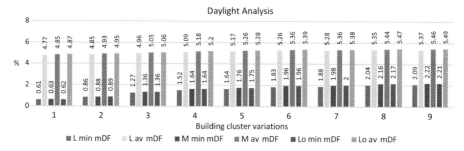

Fig. 10. Values of minimum (min) and average (av) Daylight Factor for 9 cluster variations in the 3 urban environments of Liivalaia Street (L), Mustamäe Street (M) and Logi Street (Lo).

28   F. De Luca

3.2   Urban Comfort Results

Cold stress results are presented for the 4 analyzed months, the 9 building cluster variations (V1-9) in the 3 urban areas. Frostbite risk is presented only for January because not present in other periods. Existing situation (no building cluster) is also presented for analysis and comparison (V0). Values are the maximum percentage of time a body located in the study area is below thresholds during the analyzed period.

In the area of Liivalaia Street cold stress duration due to the presence of cluster buildings increase from a minimum of 38% for V1 during January up to 12.9 times for V1 during February comparing empty plot (Fig. 11). During the months of December and February increased distance of buildings of V9 decreases cold stress 20.9% and 27.7% of time comparing V1 respectively. During months of January and March no significant difference of maximum cold stress is due to cluster variations. Percentage of time with frostbite risk is very small and similar for different clusters.

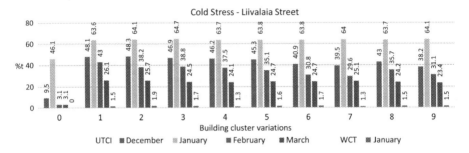

Fig. 11. Percentage of time (%t) perceived temperature is $\leq$ UTCI $-13°C$ and $\leq$ WCT $-27°C$ for existing situation and cluster variations during analysis months for Liivalaia Street area.

Increased cold stress time between existing situation and building cluster for the area of Mustamäe Street range from 30.3% for V1 during January to 5.4 times for V2 during February (Fig. 12). During January and March no significant difference of cold stress is shown between clusters. During December increasing building distances do not decrease cold stress linearly being V5 the cluster with least cold stress 13.2% time less than V1. During February increased distances of V8 decreases cold stress time of 22.9% comparing V2. Frostbite risk is small and uniform among clusters.

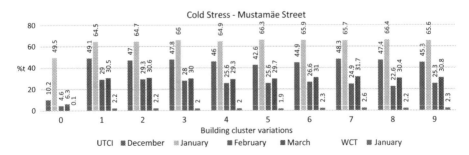

Fig. 12. Percentage of time (%t) perceived temperature is $\leq$ UTCI $-13°C$ and $\leq$ WCT $-27°C$ for existing situation and cluster variations during analysis months for Mustamäe Street area.

The area of Logi Street presents the highest maximum percentages of cold stress time and increases between existing situation and building clusters for almost all the cluster variations and analyzed months (Fig. 13). Frostbite risk percentage of time is also higher than the other two areas though still not significant.

As for the other two analyzed areas variations of building cluster pattern do not influence significantly cold stress maximum percentage of time during January and March. Building clusters V6-9 present smaller cold stress percentage of time comparing clusters V1-5 during December for an average of 17.4% and a maximum of 27.6% between V6-7 and V1. During February decrease of maximum percentage of cold stress time due to cluster pattern is 38.5% between V5 and V1. Minimum cold stress increase comparing existing situation is 37% for V2 and V5 during January, whereas maximum cold stress increase is 6.45 times for V1 during February.

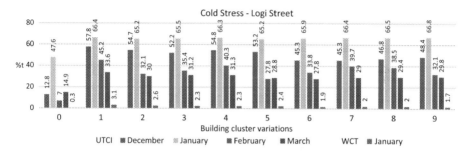

Fig. 13. Percentage of time (%t) perceived temperature is $\leq$ UTCI $-13°C$ and $\leq$ WCT $-27°C$ for existing situation and cluster variations during analysis months for Logi Street area.

4   Discussion

Results show that maximum percentage of times a body is exposed to "strong cold stress" is higher for Logi Street study area than the other two due its location by the sea, though not in the same way for the different months and cluster variations. Maximum cold stress percentage of time difference is 57.4% between Logi Street V4 (higher) and Mustamäe Street V4 in February and average difference between all cluster variations of the same two study areas in the month of February is 37.3%.

The 3 analyzed study areas present different variations of cold stress between building clusters during different months. During December and February variations are consistent whereas during January and March are small. After an analysis of wind data the author argue that the reason is the different impact that monthly dominant wind directions have on building cluster patterns.

Evidence show that smallest distance patterns are those mostly associated with highest cold stress, though in a number of cases least cold stress is not associated with largest distance patterns but with an intermediate one favored by building disalignment. Larger distance between buildings is an advantage also for interiors daylight, thus the two environmental performance are synergetic. The study underlines the importance of performing simulations and analysis to determine optimal building cluster patterns for specific environmental and urban conditions.

5   Conclusions

The presented study develops a parametric design workflow for integrated environmental analysis of interiors daylight and exteriors urban comfort of building cluster variations in different urban areas during winter in the city of Tallinn, Estonia. The scope is to investigate optimal cluster pattern characteristics such as distance and alignment in order to provide required quantity of natural light in the interiors and decrease cold stress in public areas around buildings in winter. The building cluster is formed by 3 close office towers. The type of cluster has been selected on the basis of the current construction culture in Tallinn, where several such developments are being built. For the study 9 cluster variations in 3 different urban areas are investigated.

Daylight performance is assessed on the basis of the Estonian standard "Daylight in Dwellings and Offices". Since in the country are not in force planning requirements for urban comfort, the present study uses Universal Thermal Climate Index and Wind Chill Equivalent Temperature metrics to assess "strong cold stress" and frostbite risk due mostly to the combined action of low air temperature and wind.

The parametric design workflow is composed of different integrated algorithms to generate building cluster variations and perform Daylight Factor analysis, CFD wind simulations and urban comfort assessment through UTCI and WCT.

Daylight analysis outcome show that for this type of building cluster a distance equal the two opposite buildings width is recommended to provide adequate quantity of natural light for all of the office interiors. For patterns with shifted buildings the distance can be reduced. Daylight results show as well the negligible effect of the surroundings for the analyzed building cluster type and urban areas.

Cold stress analysis results underline the dramatic impact of built environment on local micro climate during winter time. The maximum percentage of time a body located in proximity of cluster buildings experiences "strong cold stress" is up to 12.9 times higher comparing being located in the same area without buildings. Development by the sea can increase percentage of time of cold stress up to 57.4% comparing other areas of the city.

Findings show that increasing buildings distance and shifting the cluster buildings location increases interiors daylight and reduces percentage of time of experienced pedestrian cold stress. Nevertheless, it is important to notice that the first performance varies linearly whereas smaller cold stress can be obtained in some cases by closer building patterns for the influence of urban surroundings and buildings orientation. This underline the importance of performing analysis and simulations to determine optimal building clusters for the specific location and urban area. The author recommends that the presented method is used in the everyday work of architect and planner offices through the creation of interdisciplinary teams. After acquiring specific scientific knowledge and practical skills on computational and simulation software, every designer can contribute significantly to improve the environmental performance of projects and consequently the quality of future built environment.

Acknowledgements. The research has been supported by the European Regional Development Fund grant ZEBE 2014-2020.4.01.15-0016.

References

1. Butti, K., Perlin, J.: A Golden Thread: 2500 Years of Solar Architecture and Technology. Cheshire Books, Palo Alto (1980)
2. Morgan, M.H.: Vitruvius. The Ten Books on Architecture. Translation of Marcus Vitruvius Pollio: De Architectura (15 BC). Harvard University Press, Cambridge (1914)
3. Krautheim, M., Pasel, R., Pfeiffer, S., Schultz-Granberg, J.: City and Wind: Climate as an Architectural Instrument. DOM Publishers, Berlin (2014)
4. Willis, C.: Form Follows Finance: Skyscrapers and Skylines in New York and Chicago. Princeton Architectural Press, New York (1995)
5. Howard, D.: The future of ancient light. J. Arch. Plan. Res. **6**(2), 132–153 (1989)
6. Andersen, M., Mardaljevic, J., Lockley, S.M.: A framework for predicting the non-visual effects of daylight – Part I. Light. Res. Technol. **44**(1), 37–53 (2012)
7. Reinhart, C.F.: Daylighting Handbook I: Fundamentals Designing with the Sun. Building Technology Press, Cambridge (2014)
8. De Luca, F.: Solar form finding: subtractive solar envelope and integrated solar collection computational method for high-rise buildings in urban environments. In: Disciplines and Disruption - Proceedings Catalog of the 37th Annual Conference of the Association for Computer Aided Design in Architecture, ACADIA 2017, pp. 212–221, Cambridge (2017)
9. Estonian Centre for Standardization: Standard 894:2008/A2:2015. EVS, Tallinn (2015)
10. Voll, H., De Luca, F., Pavlovas, V.: Analysis of the insolation criteria for nearly-zero energy buildings in Estonia. Sci. Technol. Built Environ. **22**(7), 939–950 (2016)
11. Voll, H., Thalfeldt, M., De Luca, F., Kurnitski, J., Olesk, T.: Urban planning principles of nearly-zero energy residential buildings in Estonia. Manag. Environ. Qual.: Int. J. **27**(6), 634–648 (2016)
12. Ebrahimabadi, S., Nilsson, K.L., Johansson, C.: The problems of addressing microclimate factors in urban planning of the subarctic regions. Environ. Plan. B: Plan. Des. **42**, 415–430 (2015)
13. Shishegar, N.: Street design and urban microclimate: analyzing the effects of street geometry and orientation on airflow and solar access in urban canyons. J. Clean Energy Technol. **1**(1), 52–56 (2013)
14. Gendemer, J.: Discomfort Due to Wind Near Buildings: Aerodynamic Concepts. U.S. Department of Commerce/National Bureau of Standards, Washington (1978)
15. Hyungkeun, K., Kyungsoo, L., Taeyeon, K.: Investigation of pedestrian comfort with wind chill during winter. Sustainability **10**(1), 274–286 (2018)
16. Osczevski, R., Bluestein, M.: The new wind chill equivalent temperature chart. Bull. Am. Meteorol. Soc. **86**(10), 1453–1458 (2005)
17. Bröde, P., Jendritzky, G., Fiala, D., Havenith, G.: The universal thermal climate index UTCI in operational use. In: Proceedings of Adapting to Change: New Thinking on Comfort, Windsor (2010)
18. Grasshopper. http://www.grasshopper3d.com. Accessed 28 Mar 2019
19. DIVA. http://solemma.net. Accessed 28 Mar 2019
20. Sadeghipour, M., Pak, M.: Ladybug: a parametric environmental plugin for grasshopper to help designers create an environmentally-conscious design. In: Proceedings of IBPSA 2013, pp. 3128–3135, Chambéry (2013)
21. Swift. https://www.ods-engineering.com/Accessed 28 Mar 2019
22. Franke, J., Hellsten, A., Schlünzen, H., Carissimo, B.: Best Practice Guideline for the CFD Simulation of Flows in the Urban Environment. COST Office, Brussels (2007)

Fresh Eyes

A Framework for the Application of Machine Learning to Generative Architectural Design, and a Report of Activities at Smartgeometry 2018

Kyle Steinfeld[1]([⊠]), Kat Park[2], Adam Menges[3],
and Samantha Walker[2]

[1] University of California, Berkeley,
230 Wurster Hall, MC 1800, Berkeley, CA 94720, USA
ksteinfe@berkeley.edu
[2] Skidmore, Owings & Merrill LLP,
1 Front St #2400, San Francisco, CA 94111, USA
{kat.park, samantha.walker}@som.com
[3] Lobe Artificial Intelligence, Inc., 3507 Palmilla Drive,
San Francisco, CA 95134, USA
adam@adammenges.com

Abstract. This paper presents a framework for the application of Machine Learning (ML) to Generative Architectural Design (GAD), and illustrates this framework through a description of a series of projects completed at the Smart Geometry conference in May of 2018 (SG 2018) in Toronto. Proposed here is a modest modification of a 3-step process that is well-known in generative architectural design, and that proceeds as: generate, evaluate, iterate. In place of the typical approaches to the evaluation step, we propose to employ a machine learning process: a neural net trained to perform image classification. This modified process is different enough from traditional methods as to warrant an adjustment of the terms of GAD. Through the development of this framework, we seek to demonstrate that generative evaluation may be seen as a new locus of subjectivity in design.

Keywords: Machine learning · Generative design · Design methods

1 Introduction

This paper proposes a framework for the synthesis of Machine Learning (ML) and Generative Architectural Design (GAD), and reports on an initial set of probes, undertaken at the Smart Geometry conference in May of 2018 (SG 2018), into the practical and conceptual ramifications.

1.1 Context

Machine learning has made rapid gains in recent years in a broad range of application domains. One class of ML models – generative models broadly, and generative

© Springer Nature Singapore Pte Ltd. 2019
J.-H. Lee (Ed.): CAAD Futures 2019, CCIS 1028, pp. 32–46, 2019.
https://doi.org/10.1007/978-981-13-8410-3_3

adversarial networks (GANs) in particular - have demonstrated remarkable capacity for tasks previously out of reach for AI (such as image synthesis), and have suggested relevance to creative architectural design. Here, before discussing the position of this work, we take a moment to reflect on the ramifications of an algorithmic process that is capable of synthesizing images, of "drawing" pictures, with convincing fidelity in the specific context of the discipline of architectural design, which is rooted in a long history of geometric description and modes of representation (Fig. 1).

Fig. 1. The reflective loop of design activity.

The mode of authorship enabled by traditional architectural drawing tools is a well-studied (Evans 1997) and, while not a straightforward affair, is one in which the complexities have been long articulated and are well-understood. It is a mode that, in the opinion of the authors, remains well-described by an account first articulated almost fifty years ago by Donald Schon. Following in the tradition first established by Schon, we may trace a lineage that leads to what is now termed by cognitive scientists (Visser 2006) as the 'reflective loop' of design activity. Despite the changes brought about by the digital transformation of architecture in the early 2000's, this understanding of design as an iterative cycle of making and seeing basically held true. Even as computers offered new forms of acting - forms that included, for example the indirect defining of the shape of curves and surfaces via NURBS control points, and the assembling of ornate chains of logic via scripting and visual programming - these advances were primarily concentrated as **design actions**, offering little in support of aesthetic **design evaluations**. Broadly speaking, and with only a handful of notable exceptions, since their introduction into the design studio computers in architecture have left the seeing to us humans. In the late 2000s, the advent of parametric modelling changed things slightly, in that at this time, a new mode of design action found its way into practical application. This was a mode that formalized not only computational modes of acting, as had long been practiced, but also sought to formalize modes of evaluation, and also structured the mechanisms of iteration. This design method, novel in the early 2000s, has come to be known as **generative design** (Fig. 2).

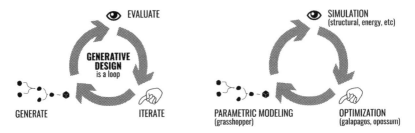

Fig. 2. The cycles of generative design (left). The means by which GAD proceeds (right).

Generative design in architecture has been described as a three-stage cycle[1], which may be summarized as: Generate, Evaluate, Iterate. In the generation step, new potential forms are proposed using a computational process. In the evaluation step, the performance of these forms are quantified, again relying on computational analysis rather than the subjective eye of the designer. Finally, in the iteration step, the parameters of design generation are manipulated to find better results.

In contemporary architectural design practice, this approach typically employs a combination of parametric, simulation, and optimization tools. Design generation is the domain of parametric modeling, such as Grasshopper or Dynamo; Design evaluation is typically handled by numerical simulation models, such as structural analysis software, thermodynamic simulation, or a heuristic stand-in thereof; Walking a design space (as required by the iteration step) is a significant topic of study in engineering, and various optimization approaches have been encapsulated by a number of software plug-ins, such as Galapagos (Rutten 2018) and Opossum (Wortmann 2017) for Rhino.

1.2   Summary of the Approach

Seen as an intervention into this well-known workflow, the contribution of this work in synthesizing ML and GAD comes into focus. Proposed here is a modest modification of the GAD process. We proceed by swapping the traditional approaches to the evaluation step of the cycle for a machine learning process, specifically a neural net trained to perform image classification (Fig. 3).

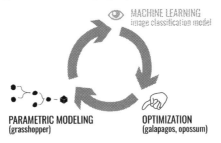

Fig. 3. The cluster proposes the replacement of the traditional means by which the evaluative step is performed.

---

[1] We find echos of these three steps as far back as (Simon 1973), who included among the qualities of well-structured problems generative mechanisms, clear means of analysis, and a definable solution space.

This modified process is different enough from traditional methods as to warrant an adjustment of the terms of GAD. And so, with the personification implicit in the dialog surrounding machine learning in mind, we propose to re-define the generative design cycle from imperative verb forms to pronoun forms, such that:

Generate, Evaluate, Iterate
becomes:
Actor, Critic, Stage

As in the generative step of traditional GAD, the role of an actor is to generate new forms, and describe them in a format preferred by ML. As discussed below, the issue of format is a crucial one. Since for a variety of reasons, the most developed ML models relevant to architectural design operate on images, in the examples presented below actors re-present architectural form as image. As such, one important contribution of work preparing for the SG 2018 workshop involved the developing and testing of methods for describing architectural forms and spaces as images (Fig. 4).

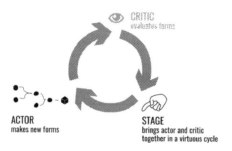

Fig. 4. Modified as proposed in this text, the terms employed to describe each step of the generative design workflow also require modification.

Next, we define a critic as an ML process that evaluates candidate architectural forms based on patterns and types learned from experience. In this regard, the importance of training a critic should not be underestimated. Rather, it should be regarded as an important new locus of creative action in design, and a rich new form of subjectivity. The authors contend that to cede this space to existing processes and models would be a significant loss for the discipline. Finally, we define a stage as the system which brings together actor and critic, allowing an actor to progressively improve his performance. Here, traditional optimization techniques are employed, as with the actor and critic in place as described above, no modification is required.

2 Background and Relevance

In a 2002 essay, Manuel DeLanda offered both a criticism of and a guidebook for the more creative application of an emerging technology of his time: the genetic algorithm (GA). Writing in the context of an expanded field of architectural practice that had recently been brought about by the advent of parametric modeling, DeLanda highlighted the important role that genetic algorithms could potentially play in generative design. As described above, if we understand this process as 'generate, evaluate, iterate', we find a tidy account of a whole range of recent innovations in design methods. Parametric modeling is a clearly generative tool, one that radically expands the space of possible designs available to the design imagination, and that arguably has done more for the creative application of computation in design than any other recent innovation. Genetic algorithms, along with similar optimization processes, are iterative tools, as they offer methods for exploring spaces of design for well-performing or surprising solutions. As an advocate for the GA, Delanda also presented a convincing case for the creative potential of the iterative step in general. This call was clearly heard by design researchers at the time, given the level of interest in optimization from 2000–2010. In contrast with the two steps, few have presented a compelling case for the creative potential of the second step of the generative design process: evaluation. Often regarded as the domain of architectural simulation - be it thermodynamic, structural, or lighting - the evaluation of candidate solutions has remained almost entirely in the domain of readily quantifiable metrics, and has historically been seen as the least fertile ground for creative use. Recent experience tells us that it need not be so.

Updating his work ten years later, at a keynote for the ACADIA conference in 2012 (DeLanda 2012), DeLanda expanded his position on the GA, and offered a succinct but noteworthy addition in his related article. Writing prophetically on the integration of neural nets into the generative design process, Delanda briefly speculates on the encapsulation of the *"taste or stylistic preferences of the designer so that they can be applied automatically"*. Implicit in his argument is that an application of neural nets to replace the *"eye of the beholder"* would hold profound ramifications for the creative potential of design evaluation. It was a radical proposal in 2012, and for all practical purposes at the time, it was impossible. While such an application remains radical, thanks to developments in ML in the intervening years this approach has not only become possible, but precisely the approach adopted in the examples described below.

Just as DeLanda advocated for the creative use of genetic algorithms - and through this advocacy, drew needed attention to the iterative step in generative design more broadly - so we advocate for the creative use of machine learning, and for the cultural practice of automated design evaluation.

3   Methods

In this section, we describe the technical methods employed to develop and test the proposed framework, including the requisite workflows and software produced in this scope of research. Following this technical account, to illustrate latent potentials and limitations, we offer an overview of projects completed at SG 2018 that probe, extend, elaborate, and (at times) present challenges to the framework as proposed. This latter discussion is organized around the three stages of the modified GAD workflow, as projects are selected to reveal the salient issues surrounding design through the metaphor of actor-critic-stage. As a provocation for future work, we conclude with a discussion of those projects completed at SG 2018 that adopted techniques that move outside of or present challenges to the proposed framework.

To illustrate how the three pieces of the proposed design framework relate, we begin by describing through a simple example how an actor and a critic come together on a stage. In this illustrative example, a portion of which is described in more detail below, an actor is constructed that proposes new architectural forms (houses), a critic is trained to discern and select among potential forms (based on a pre-defined ontology of house forms) and to assign a value to candidates with an objective of finding those that best adhere to a given typology, and a stage brings these two entities together in a virtuous cycle of optimization.

To begin, a critic is trained on 3d models, such as the ones seen in Fig. 5 that describes typologies of detached single-family homes. This dataset was constructed by hand based on real-world examples by students at UC Berkeley, and includes well-known types such as Cape Cod, Shotgun, Dogtrot, and the Toronto Bay and Gable.

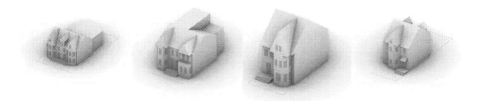

Fig. 5. Selected 3d models, each of which describes a Bay and Gable style house. The dataset contains 576 3d models that describe 16 house types.

To train the ML model, each 3d model must be described as a raster image, such as the tiled image shown on the right of the nearby figure. A number of approaches to extracting images from architectural forms are possible, and a range of these are supported in the current toolset as described in the section on software method, below. In this case, a single tiled image synthesizes multiple projective views such that the critic may be trained on one image per training sample. The multi-view tiled image on the right of the nearby diagram shows that each row of the tiled image represents a different slice direction: the top row, shows a series of cuts parallel with the world x–y plane, the next two rows show front and side cuts, and the final two rows are cut at oblique angles in plan (Fig. 6).

Fig. 6. A 3d model of a Bay and Gable style house (left), a multi-view tiled projection image that represents this house to a ML model (middle), candidate architectural forms generated by the actor (right).

The job of the critic is to evaluate the performance of an actor. In the case of this simple example, the actor is a parametric model that is capable of generating a range of candidate house-like forms, and to represent each these forms as a raster image, as described above. The forms produced by this sample actor are similar in character to the ones used to train the critic. The limited nature of such an actor is discussed in a section below, as are the potential repercussions of an **amicable** (as opposed to **adversarial**) actor-critic relationship that may be seen in this example. The two processes are brought together in an optimization, wherein the actor generates new potential house forms, and these forms are scored by the critic in terms of how much they resemble a known type of house, and then the process iterates. This relationship follows the pattern of a classic optimization.

3.1   Software Developed and Required by the Proposed Framework

Here we describe in summary the technical methods required for adopting the proposed design framework. While some of these steps require off the shelf software or tools developed outside of the current scope of work, others were developed with the proposed framework in mind, and specifically to address the needs of the SG workshop.

Technical Overview
At a minimum, the following steps are required for constructing an actor, training a critic, and staging an optimization.

To Train a Critic
First, training sets of 3d models are constructed or collected via a variety of informal methods. Some of the participants at SG 2018 employed custom Python scripts to assist in these tasks. In order to serve as training sets for an ML image classification model, collected 3d models must be re-presented as raster images. For this purpose, a number of methods for extracting raster data from 3d models were developed, and expressed as components or chains of related components for the Grasshopper visual scripting environment for Rhino. These are described in the section on Fresh Eyes for Grasshopper, below. Once a set of training images has been produced, an image classification model is trained using Tensorflow, and with the assistance of a web-based graphical interface for creating, manipulating, and serving ML models called Lobe, described in detail below. Once trained, the critic must be made available to the stage. For this, the ML model is hosted (either using a Lobe server API or on a server running locally) and accessed via API requests. A number of the components developed for the Grasshopper plugin address issues in translating and formatting geometric information in JSON format in the construction of requests, and in parsing JSON responses from the server such that the information may be used in the construction of the fitness function of an optimization.

To Construct an Actor
Actors produce new potential forms using any traditional parametric modeling processes, so long as the candidate form may be appropriately represented as a raster image using one of the methods supported by the Fresh Eyes plugin and articulated below. To best interface with the specific optimization processes employed by the SG 2018 workshop, participants were encouraged to package their actors as a single

Grasshopper clustered object that accepts some number of normalized inputs. Constructed in this way, actors are somewhat interchangeable, and may be set in partnership with different critics.

To Stage an Optimization

An optimization is staged within a Grasshopper model, which brings together an actor (in the form of a packaged component with normalized parameters), a critic (in the form of a trained ML model from which predictions may be requested via API calls), and an iteration routine. For this iterative step, a number of off-the-shelf optimization packages were tested. Ultimately, the Opossum plugin for Grasshopper was established as the preferred method.

Lobe.ai

As argued above, the authors assert that if architects are to remain relevant in the age of ML, designers must take ownership of the training of critics. To ensure that those that adopt the proposed framework are not disenfranchised by an inability to train models relevant to them, architects must find practical means for training their own ML models, and do not passively or uncritically accept existing ones. For this reason, in the context of the SG 2018 workshop, we partnered with a company called Lobe, which provided a platform that became an essential means for training ML models relevant to architectural evaluation.

Lobe is a browser-based graphical programming environment for creating neural nets. It was developed by one of the cluster campions, Adam Menges, outside of the scope of work described here. We might describe it with the analogy: as Grasshopper is to Rhino, so Lobe is to Tensorflow.

Participants in the SG 2018 workshop used Lobe to establish training datasets, train image-based models using Tensorflow, host these models on cloud servers dedicated to this purpose, and establish structures to call upon them using an application program interface (API). Using the Grasshopper-like graphical programming environment provided by Lobe, workshop participants were able to design a model, train it (or use a pre-trained one), and receive predictions from the cloud (Fig. 7).

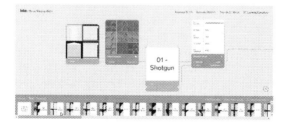

Fig. 7. A screenshot of the Lobe.ai user interface, which provides a visual programming interface (similar to Grasshopper) for creating neural networks. Node runs Tensorflow, an open-source library for machine intelligence.

Fresh Eyes for Grasshopper

The framework described in this paper requires a number of operations that are not commonly included in the software toolkit employed by architects. To support these operations, a number of procedures were developed and package into components for the Grasshopper visual programming environment.

Broadly speaking, these operations may be divided into six categories: 1. Components for constructing API requests and receiving responses (see the "API" tab in the image below). 2. Components for interacting with the 3d environment of Rhino, such as painting geometry to the screen in controllable ways and taking screenshots (see the "Doc Util" tab in the image below). 3. Components for programmatically manipulating images (see the Image tab in the image below). 4. Components for constructing and parsing JSON strings (see the "JSON" tab in the image below). 5. Finally, two categories of components for rasterizing architectural forms, as described below.

One crucial function of the Fresh Eyes for Grasshopper plugin is support for the rasterization of architectural form. This proceeds through two basic methods: parallel projection and isovist raycasting. The former strategy, based on parallel projection, is employed for extracting raster images of forms as they appear from the exterior. A range of options for defining cutting planes in various patterns is provided. This often results in an image comprised of smaller tiled view, wherein a single tiled image may be used to describe a single sample from the dataset of 3d models. The latter strategy, based on a isovist raycasting strategy and inspired by established work in this area (Peng 2017), is employed for extracting raster images of forms as they appear from arbitrary positions in space. Using this strategy, each 3d model in the dataset may be sample any number of times to produce multiple images in the training set.

With the technical methods outlined above, the following sections are free to further articulate issues in each of three stages of the proposed framework, and to illustrate issues using examples drawn from participant work at SG 2018.

3.2 Actors

While the technologies involved in the construction of actors is unmodified relative to the traditional GAN workflow, and is in some ways no different from those employed in typical parametric design processes, new problems arise in this step unique to the modified design framework proposed here. For example, certain limitations naturally arise from the constraint that the actor must present a description of a candidate design in a format comprehensible to the critic: images. This limitation, combined with certain practical constraints on image resolution and computing time, presents a barrier to certain categories of study. Consider the challenges faced by the example described below, in which a number of actors are set in relation to a critic trained to predict structural performance under wind load.

An Actor for Tall Buildings Under Wind Load

A number of parametric models were authored by participants at the SG 2018 workshop that described a range of approaches to the massing design of tall towers. These actors were set in relationship to a single critic, pre-trained and provided by the cluster organizers, intended to predict the performance of tower forms under wind load. Here, issues were raised surrounding the resolution of the raster images employed, and if the pixel density required to capture formal details that drive wind performance could be practically employed.

3.3   Critics

Machine learning requires large datasets, often carefully crafted for the purpose they serve. Since architectural design does not typically require the sorts of vast datasets called for by other fields, few sources of data useful for the training of critics have been established. For this reason, the identification or construction of datasets appropriate to ML and relevant to architectural design is likely to remain a topic of concern for years to come. With this larger problem in mind, some participants in the workshop chose to focus on the crafting of datasets and the training of critics. For these participants, a useful deliverable was a well-trained critic that is relevant to architectural design.

A Critic of Architectural Volumes

Here, building on an existing thread of research (Peng 2017), participants defined a new dataset of 3d models that describes a variety of architectural ceiling forms. These forms were organized according to two levels of hierarchy, resulting in four distinct critics. The first "major" critic is charged with distinguishing between three volumetric spatial types: box, vault, and dome. After this critic has made his distinction, one of three "minor" critics is activated, further refining the prediction of the first, and sub-categorizing forms according to their perceived experiential qualities (Fig. 8).

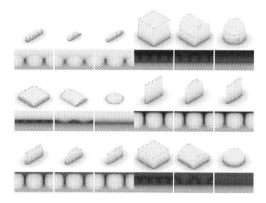

Fig. 8. Depictions of a dataset used to train an ML model to discern three categories of volumetric spatial type (box, vault and dome) from an interior isovist perspective.

A Critic of Floor Plans

Armed with a large dataset of residential floor plans that display a consistent graphic character, this group of participants trained a critic to recognize certain features, such as doors, windows, and other graphic notes common to architectural plans. The participants produced network graphs of features extracted by a ML model trained to detect elements of a floor plan of a small apartment. The model identifies windows and doors of a floor plan, which are then used to construct a network graph standard parametric tools.

3.4   Stages

A stage is an iterative system which brings together actor and critic, and proceeds through traditional optimization techniques. The interaction of actor and critic introduce new complexities, and suggest that different relationships (such as "agreeable" performances as opposed to "adversarial" ones) may bring about different affordances.

A Stage for Single-Family Homes

Building on the illustrative example at the start of this section, here we further examine the coming together of a simple actor and critic on a stage. In this case, the actor and critic may be seen as "agreeable", in that the characteristics of the forms produced by the actor are roughly similar to those used to train the critic. This relationship stands in contrast to the "adversarial" relationship described in the section below.

As shown in the nearby figure, the critic is a ML model trained to discern among typologies of detached single-family homes, and receives descriptions of candidate designs as multi-view tiled projection images (top). The actor is a parametric model capable of generating new candidate forms as a simple combination of solid forms (bottom). These two come together in an optimization that seeks to maximize the critics prediction that the candidate form matches its expectation for a Bay and Gable type. The image shown displays the last step of the optimization cycle. The lower left form shows the last candidate design to be evaluated. The middle form shows the best of the most recent 20 iterations. The form on the right shows the global best (Fig. 9).

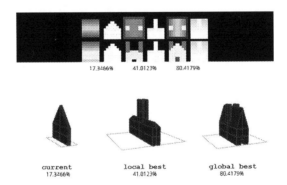

Fig. 9. A diagram showing how actor and critic come together on a stage.

A Stage for Forest-Like Forms

This project compares different formal and spatial ideas about trees and how a ML model can be used to mimic the visual image of a "forest." A set of ideal forest types, alder, elm, tall conifer - are used to train a critic. The critic, in turn, discerns from a series of proposals for potential "forests" produced by an actor to identify those which best satisfy the criteria of elm, tall coniferous, etc. The process uses an isovist critic and actor, evaluating the forests perspectivally (Fig. 10).

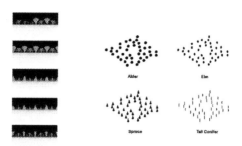

Fig. 10. A series of isovist images that were used to train a critic to discern the spatial characteristics of a number of forest types, including Alder, Elm, Spruce, and Tall Conifer.

3.5   Non-conforming Related Explorations

The actor-critic-stage framework presented in this paper is but one of many potential workflows in which machine learning processes are applied to creative design. In this section we present a number of successful explorations were undertaken at SG 2018 which did not rigidly conform to this framework, and yet produced compelling results nonetheless. We present these non-conforming examples in the interest of demonstrating the limits of the framework as proposed, and to suggest directions for future research.

House GAN

In AI, a Generative adversarial network (GAN) is a special class of unsupervised machine learning model (Goodfellow 2014) that shares many characteristics with the framework outlined in this paper. Like the actor and critic of the modified GAD method outlined here, in a GAN, two entities, one generative and one evaluative, are set in relation to one another in an iterative process. However, where the actor is expressed as a traditional parametric model and set in relation to an ML evaluator, both the generator and the evaluator are ML models in a GAN. As its name would imply, a GAN is an adversarial process, in which two models are trained at the same time: a generative ML model (called a generator) that learns to produce new forms that are intended to "fool" a second ML model (called a discriminator) that estimates the probability that a given sample came from training data rather than from the generator (Fig. 11).

Fig. 11. A diagram that expresses the difference between a three-dimensional model generated by the an actor (top), a multi-view image that allows this actor to communicate a form to a critic (middle), and a reconstructed three-dimensional model based on this tiled image (bottom). We may understand this last row as illustrative of how the critic "sees" in three-dimensions.

In the context of SG 2018, what started as an interest in better understanding the nature of the difference between what the actor and critic "see" when looking at a given design, evolved into an implementation of a GAN that was trained on the house typology training set described above. The results of this HouseGAN are shown in a nearby image. This particular thread of research, still nascent at the time of writing, is the first example known to the authors of a generative adverserial network applied to a three-dimensional architectural massing. This work continues to bear fruit and will be presented in detail in a future paper (Fig. 12).

Fig. 12. New house forms generated by a generative adversarial network (GAN). The top row shows images directly produced by the GAN, and are equivalent to the multi-view tiled projection images shown in the middle row of the previous figure, but are synthetic images and not extracted from any training set. The bottom row shows reconstructed three-dimensional models based on this tiled image, and are equivalent to the bottom row of the previous figure).

4   Results and Reflections

The creative use of machine learning in architectural design offers a wealth of new opportunities, new affordances, and new subjectivities. The framework presented here, in which ML is employed as the evaluation step of a traditional generative design process, is but one of many potential workflows in which machine learning processes are applied to creative design. This paper has demonstrated that, even within the scope of this limited subset of applications, entirely new modes of authorship are evident and wholly new issues must be addressed. First, the construction of an actor, while expressed through the medium of parametric modeling, must address new concerns in terms of the actor-critic relationship. Next, the training of a critic is an entirely new form of authorship for architectural designers, proceeding as all ML processes in a "design by example" mode. Finally, the combination and interaction of actor and critic introduce new complexities and opportunities for creative expression, such as setting up "amicable" performances as opposed to "adversarial" ones.

The work presented here offers a framework for future investigations of an emerging mode of creative expression. It is our aim that the re-imagining of generative design through the lens of ML, and the specific set of terms and metaphors of action offered here, provides a useful guide for future research. In particular, we envision that entirely new territories of opportunities will emerge if ML models are developed that, in contrast with those that deal in raster images, are able to be trained on formats more appropriate to architectural design, such as point clouds, graphs, polygon meshes, or other descriptions of three-dimensional form.

5   Conclusion and Reflection

The authors argue that this novel design framework, by modestly adjusting the nature of the evaluation step of the GAD process, offers a potential way to move beyond optimization for quantifiable objectives, as is typical in GAD, to more qualitative, tacit, and intangible objectives, such as architectural typology or spatial experience. The ramifications of such a shift are profound.

The authors would like to express appreciation to the SmartGeometry organization for its support of this research, and of the participants of the SG 2018 cluster: Ben Coorey, Marantha Dawkins, James Forren, Timothy Logan, Antoine Maes, Jenessa Man, Sebastian Misiurek, Gabriel Payant, Aseel Sadat, Nonna Shabanova, and Jenny Zhu.

References

DeLanda, M.: Deleuze and the use of the genetic algorithm in architecture. Archit. Des. **71**(7), 9–12 (2002)

DeLanda, M.: The use of genetic algorithms in art. In: Proceedings of the 32nd Annual Conference of the Association for Computer Aided Design in Architecture (ACADIA), pp. 25–31. San Francisco (2012). http://cumincad.scix.net/cgi-bin/works/Show?acadia12_25

Evans, R.: Translations from Drawing to Building. MIT Press, Cambridge (1997)

Goodfellow, I.J., et al.: Generative Adversarial Networks. arXiv:1406.2661 [Cs, Stat], 10 June 2014. http://arxiv.org/abs/1406.2661

Isola, P., Zhu, J.-Y., Zhou, T., Efros, A.A.: Image-to-Image Translation with Conditional Adversarial Networks. arXiv:1611.07004 [Cs], 21 November 2016. http://arxiv.org/abs/1611.07004

Peng, W., Zhang, F., Nagakura, T.: Machines' perception of space. In: Proceedings of the 37th Annual Conference of the Association for Computer Aided Design in Architecture (ACADIA), Cambridge, MA. Association for Computer Aided Design in Architecture (2017)

Rutten, D.: Galapagos Evolutionary Solver. http://www.grasshopper3d.com/groups/group/show?groupUrl=galapagos. Accessed 16 May 2018

Simon, H.: The structure of Ill structured problems. Artif. Intell. **4**(3–4), 181–201 (1973)

Visser, W.: Designing as construction of representations: a dynamic viewpoint in cognitive design research. Hum. Comput. Interact. **21**(1), 103–152 (2006)

Wortmann, T.: Opossum - introducing and evaluating a model-based optimization tool for grasshopper. In: Janssen, P., Loh, P., Raonic, A., Schnabel, M.A. (Eds.) Protocols, Flows, and Glitches - Proceedings of the 22nd CAADRIA Conference, Xi'an Jiaotong-Liverpool University, Suzhou, China, 5–8 April 2017, pp. 283–292. CUMINCAD (2017)

Recognizing and Classifying Unknown Object in BIM Using 2D CNN

Jinsung Kim, Jaeyeol Song, and Jin-Kook Lee[✉]

Department of Interior Architecture and Built Environment,
Yonsei University, Seoul, Republic of Korea
wlstjdl320@gmail.com, songjy92@gmail.com,
leejinkook@yonsei.ac.kr

Abstract. This paper aims to propose an approach to automated classifying building element instance in BIM using deep learning-based 3D object classification algorithm. Recently, studies related to checking or validating engine of BIM object for ensuring data integrity of BIM instances are getting attention. As a part of this research, this paper train recognition models that are targeted at basic building element and interior element using 3D object recognition technique that uses images of objects as inputs. Object recognition is executed in two stages; (1) class of object (e.g. wall, window, seating furniture, toilet fixture and etc.), (2) sub-type of specific classes (e.g. Toilet or Urinal). Using the trained models, BIM plug-in prototype is developed and the performance of this AI-based approach with test BIM model is checked. We expect this recognition approach to help ensure the integrity of BIM data and contribute to the practical use of BIM.

Keywords: 3D object classification · Building element ·
Building information modeling · Data integrity · Interior element

1 Introduction

1.1 Research Objective

This paper aims to automatically recognize the information of an unknown object in building information model (BIM) instances using a deep learning-based technique. BIM and its applications have shown the various benefits in the architecture, engineering, construction, and facility management (AEC/FM) industry. Practically execution of such BIM applications presupposes that the BIM model has the appropriate data for each of specific domains [1]. However, it is difficult to ensure the BIM data integrity due to error, mistake or omission of object information for various reasons including; (1) technical problems resulting from the process of data conversion between BIM tools, (2) Human error such as input from the writing process, and (3) Utilization of dummy geometry objects created from non-BIM design tools or obtained from the cloud points. Although a neutral format, the industry foundation class (IFC), and various translation frameworks, the model view definition (MVD), have been proposed to ensure interoperability of BIM data, tasks to input and validate

© Springer Nature Singapore Pte Ltd. 2019
J.-H. Lee (Ed.): CAAD Futures 2019, CCIS 1028, pp. 47–57, 2019.
https://doi.org/10.1007/978-981-13-8410-3_4

the data should have been done by workers. For solving this problem, researches about automatically recognizing and validation BIM data have been introduced. Bloch and Sacks (2018) showed that a machine learning-based approach is more successful in automatically classifying the name of spaces then rule-based approaches. Koo et al. (2019) proposed automated recognizing category of basic building objects such as a wall, column, slab, door and etc. using a machine learning-based classification technique. These researches utilize geometry data such as (width, height, volume and etc.) and relationships between the object to the training machine learning model. However, it is difficult to recognize the category of detailed and complex objects (e.g. Interior elements and complex building fixtures) and various types of each category with only low-level geometry data. This research aims to look for ways to recognize category and detailed sub-types of various building objects using 2D-CNN-based approaches that have demonstrated excellence in complex and diverse 3D object classification. The visual information including a visual image (shape) and geometry data such as mass, area, height, and width is less likely to be missing or an error and the domain experts also rely on such information in validation task. The proposed mechanism includes the deep learning-based CNN model and machine learning-based classification algorithm using multi-view rendering image and geometry data of building object (Fig. 1).

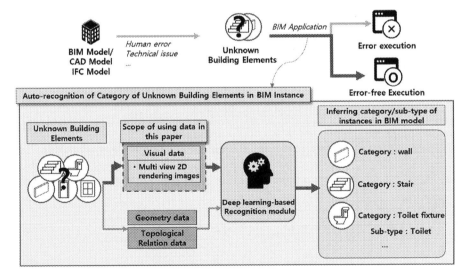

Fig. 1. The objective of this research

1.2   Research Scope and Method

2D CNN model is the proven approach to effectively making computer train and classify 3D CAD object using 2D captured images at various viewpoints. The target classes of the object include not only general building objects such as walls, columns, and stairs, but also interior object that may have more variations such as furniture, and toilet fixture. There are two different scopes of classification. The first is a high-level classification of the category. The second is a low-level classification of sub-type on specific categories. The level of detail of the object covered in this paper is LOD 200 that basically could be visually classified. The flow of research is as follows: (1) Preparing object data and multi-view images using image generator API we developed, (2) Training the CNN models according to classification scopes, (3) Demonstrating the prototyping plug-in of auto-classification on the BIM tool. Through the application, the user could check undetermined objects in IFC instances and override the class data automatically. It is expected to help practical operations for further BIM applications.

2 Background

2.1 Researches on Ensuring Data Integrity of BIM Object

Researches on improving the accuracy of building information models and ensuring the interoperability of BIM data has been studied. Eastman (2009) described that syntactic pre-checking is required to determine that the BIM instance has the objects and their properties required to execute a function in the application. It has been explained that the inaccuracy in the information model derives from various reason causes. The most critical cause is occurred in exchanging the BIM data between different BIM applications. The Industry Foundation Class (IFC) is the standard data format for BIM data exchange. Most BIM software generally implements heterogeneous translators that bind their native data format to the IFC format. This results in the syntactic errors of BIM data exchanged [2]. The other cause is related to a human error in the BIM authoring and exchanging process. The probability of human mistakes and omissions become stronger according to increasing the size and complexity of the BIM models [3].

Researches on the mapping framework for BIM and IFC have been conducted. Model view definition (MVD) is the most popular approach and the generic definition of MVD is "the standard methodology and format documenting the software implementation requirements for standard IFC based data exchange" [4]. MVD is IFC sub-schemas that represents interoperable requirements data for applications of specific domains, so helps software vendors develop translator of IFC import and export [5]. Solibri Model Checker (SMC) [6] which is known as the most popular rule-checking software has pre-checking module such as name and properties conventions, object existence and others.

However, these tools and approaches can't validate directly the correctness of properties in building information models such as name, class or type of object. Recently, studies on validating BIM data and inferring missing information using a third "engine" have been introduced. The logic rule-based approach is common and well known. Sacks, et al. (2017) described a logic rule-based approach to object classification using single-object features and topological relationships between pairs of objects [7]. However, the logic rule-based approach has a limitation on generalization because every building object has different features and different rules are needed to set respectively. Unlike this deductive approach, Machine learning-based approach to classification of building element was presented as an alternative method that can effectively classify complex object with no specific rules [8]. Koo, et al. (2019) proposed the machine learning-based approach to classifying 8 different IFC class of object (wall, slab, door, window, railing, covering, column and beam) in building information model instance [9]. Geometry information (e.g. width, height, length, volume and etc.) and some representative relationship information (e.g. relation with the wall, door and window) is used as an input value, and support vector machine algorithm was utilized to train "ifc class classifier". The approach showed 94.39% accuracy of classifying the basic building element in the test phase. These results show that the machine learning approach can successfully inductively infer the class information without specific logic rule. Thus, it is shown that there are differences between geometric information and relationship information for each BIM object, and it is possible to create a model that can learn the differences and recognize them. However, this approach can be applied to common building objects, but different approaches may be needed for interior objects that may be similar in size and relationship. For example, how can you distinguish between a sofa and a toilet using the geometry data? People classify these by visual differences rather than geometric information. As a part of these inductive approaches to recognizing building element, this paper explores a different approach using the deep learning based image recognition techniques, which has shown human-level performance.

2.2   3D Object Classification Approaches

Classification of a 3D object is one of the main researches subject in the computer vision field. The Princeton ModelNet [10] is the representative project with well-structured collections of generic 3D CAD files labeled with 10–40 different classes. This dataset is commonly used for developing a 3D object classification model and validating the accuracy of the model. The study of 3D object recognition can be broadly divided into what features to target and what algorithm or methods to target to create a classification model. Recently, machine learning or deep learning approaches have shown more successful performance in terms of accuracy and efficiency than rule-based approaches. Especially, Deep Learning-based approaches that utilize voxel data or object images data are drawing attention.

The voxel-based approach generally utilizes the $n \times n \times n$ grid of voxels that is usually given by the intersection of 3D CAD models as input. On the other hand, the image-based approach utilizes the rendering images of 3D CAD models as input. Like human generally recognizes a 3D object with the composition of 2D images, the image-based approach models have shown as better performance then models trained with the voxel data [11]. It may result from the relative efficiency of 2D and 3D representations [12]. Convolutional neural network (CNN) has been known as the most powerful deep learning algorithm to train the computer model to recognize and classify 2D image [13]. A CNN model [12] with single view images showed higher accuracy (85.1%) than one (77.3%) of a model that trained voxel data [14]. Su, et al. (2015) compared the single-view and multi-view models and showed that the multi-view models are averagely more accurate by 5%. In this paper, Multi-view based CNN approach is applied to a training model to classify building object.

We do not train the model from scratch, but fine-tuning Inception-v3 [15] that trained ImageNet [16] data on TensorFlow framework [17]. The main feature of the Inception-v3 model is the inception modules that includes multiple convolution layers and pooling layer. It is confirmed that the inception-v3 shown a better performance than the VGG model. It is beyond the scope of this study to describe the structure and detailed operating principles of the inception-v3 model, so this paper only explains how the model is utilized (Fig. 2). Generally, the architecture of the CNN model can be divided into two parts: the image feature extraction part and classifier part. We reuse the image feature extraction part of the inception-v3 and then retrain the 4 different classifiers regarding tasks. As a result, 4 different models that recognize building element categories, sub-type of the door, seating and toilet are trained.

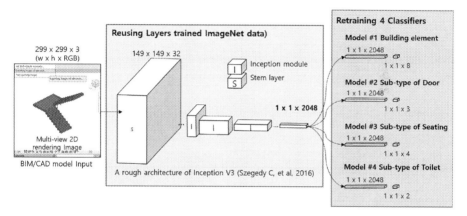

Fig. 2. The pipeline of utilization of pre-trained Inception-v3 model [15] to retrain the building elements and sub-types

3   Auto-Recognition of Category of Building Element Using 2D-CNN

3.1   Preparation of Data of Building Element

The objects covered in this study include the basic building elements and specific interior elements that make up the building. Information about architectural objects is basic and essential, and information about more specific objects, such as interior furnishing, is increasingly required. For example, information of more detailed building element is required for a detailed code compliance checking (such as the Installation Standards for Public Toilets, etc.) Specific information such as sub-type of the door (e.g. single swing, double swings, rotation and etc.) is required. Therefore, this paper aims to recognize the categories as well as sub-types of some building elements. Building object data for training consist of the BIM files as well as the simple CAD files such as .dwg, .skp and .3 dm files. The object data being studied in the paper were collected from a variety of BIM libraries [18, 19] as well as from a simple CAD library [20] without object information. 80% of the data collected is used for training and 20% for validation.

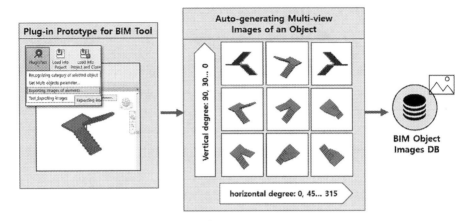

Fig. 3. A module to generate multi-view images of BIM object on BIM tool

Data of the building objects used in this paper consists of 2D rendering bitmap image data and geometric text data (width, depth, height, and volume). First of all, the rendering image of an architectural object means the multi-view images that are generated from various angles of each object. For automatically creating the rendering images of selected objects, the multi-view images generator module was developed as a plug-in tool for using the API [21] of BIM authoring software. To obtain images of different angles, the sets of horizontal angle are preset in 45° from 0 to 315°, the sets of vertical angle in 30° from 0 to 90°, and 32 images can be created per object (Fig. 3). This is used to build an image DB for learning and to create an object cache image to be used in the inference process. Collecting the geometry data of building objects is also conducted by using API of BIM tool. The volume and minimum bounding box of the object are calculated. The bounding box is utilized to calculate the width, depth, and height.

3.2 2D-CNN-Based Training a Model of 3D Object Recognition

In this paper, two types of recognition models are addressed. The first model aims to recognize the category of building element, while the second model aims to recognize the sub-type of some building elements. For example, if an element is recognized as a door, it can be re-recognized whether the door is a single wing, a double swing, or a revolving type. This approach can give the possibility to validate the more detail information of BIM data. The target building objects and sub-types to be covered are shown in Fig. 4. The configuration and name of categories are referred to IFC entity and Omniclas [22]. As the target of first-stage, the category of building element includes slab, wall, ceiling, columns, a staircase that can be described basic building elements and only toilet fixtures that are considered as the interior element. As the target of second-stage, sub-types of door and toilet fixture are covered. The training of these recognition models is processed by fine-tuning the Inception-v3model that train the ImageNet dataset and show the successful performance. The training process is conducted in the TensorFlow environment.

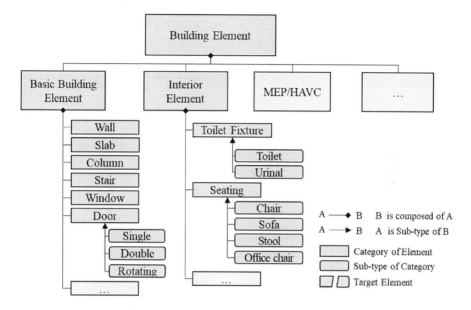

Fig. 4. An abstraction of the building element

4 Evaluation of Recognition Module and Prototype Application for Classification

4.1 Evaluation of Recognition Module with Test BIM Model

The training result can be examined with quantitative values such as accuracy of classification and cross entropy value. Accuracy shows the ratio of the overall classification data to the label information that matches the classification results, i.e. to the correct classification. Cross-entropy, on the other hand, shows the value of the lost function in the classifier learning of this model, the closer the function is to zero, the total number of objects for which the function is intended, the result is for training and validation, respectively. Tensorboard which is the visualization tool of training on TensorFlow allows drawing a graph about changing the value of accuracy and cross entropy of training and validating session respectively. In training the deep learning model, it is important to avoid seeing models over-fitting and under-fitting. In the case of under-fitting, it means that the model is more possible to train. The under-fitting situation can be confirmed by a graph that the price of cross entropy continues to fall. This means that the more training steps are needed. This can be checked with the value of Cross entropy is continuously falling. On the other hand, overfitting refers to cases in which training is classified accurately, but it is classified incorrectly in validating. This situation can be also confirmed by a graph that the cross-entropy value of training is falling, but the cross-entropy value of validation appears to be stagnant or even rising.

In this paper, two stages of training model are executed. The first stage is related to classification of category types of building element (e.g. wall, column, slab, window and etc.). The other stage is related to classification of sub-type of a specific element (e.g. double, single or revolving door). The first stage training set and the result are shown in Table 1. The training was executed with a different number of data by categories, considering the visual variance and redundancy of objects. The accuracy of training is 96.0%. The second stage training set and results are shown in Table 2.

Table 1. Building element categories training and validating set and the training accuracy

Categories	Training set	Validation set	Total	Accuracy of training
Column	48	12	60	96.0%
Wall	200	48	248	
Slab	32	8	40	
Stair	32	8	40	
Door	84	21	105	
Window	90	25	115	
Seating	160	40	200	
Toilet fixture	64	16	80	

Table 2. Sub-type training and validating set and the training accuracy

Categories	Sub-type	Training set	Validation set	Total	Accuracy of training
Door	Single	32	8	105	97.4%
	Double	32	8		
	Revolving	20	5		
Seating	Chair	48	12	200	94.8%
	Office chair	48	12		
	Sofa	32	8		
	Stool	32	8		
Toilet fixture	Toilet	32	8	80	97.9%
	Urinal	32	8		

4.2   Demonstration of Prototype Plug-in Application for Auto-Classification of Unknown Object in BIM

We developed a prototype plug-in on the Revit tool that automatically recognizes and input the result values of category or sub-type information of unknown objects using the trained models. The recognizing engine was developed in Python language, and is called on Revit interface that was developed using Revit's C # API. Through this plug-in, it can be conducted to infer category of unknown dummy geometry objects. These kinds of objects are generally recognized as generic models in Revit. It is possible to change the entity of BIM object (e.g. stairs, lighting fixture, walls and etc.) additionally Therefore, this plug-in inputs the result value of recognition into the general field such as comments. The results of recognition are expressed in the general name of each category and sub-type, but lately, it can be replaced with the IFC entity or Omniclass title or number.

Figure 5 shows examples of application execution for stair and toilet objects modeled in the 3D CAD tool. They are the dummy geometry object so there are not category data. The recognition engine recognized these objects. The object looking like a stair was recognized as a stair with 99.3% of the probability and the result value was input into the comment field of the object. Another object looking like a toilet was recognized as a toilet with 97.8% of probability and the result value was input into the comment field.

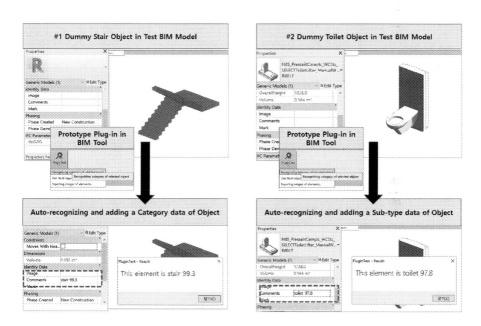

Fig. 5. Demonstration of Prototype Plug-in application with test dummy geometry objects

5   Conclusion

This paper proposed an approach to automated classifying building element instance according to category and sub-type using 2D CNN-based 3D object classification technique Training of object recognition was executed in two stages; The first stage training results showed the 96.0% accuracy of classification of building elements (column, stair, slab, wall, door and window) and interior elements categories (seating furniture and toilet fixture). The second stage training result showed the average 96.7% accuracy of classification of sub-type of door, seating and toilet fixture. Unlike previous literature, this paper showed the possibility of recognizing interior element that has more complex geometry then the basic building element with 2D convolutional neural networks model. The number of target elements and volume of data is very limited, but this approach shows the possibility of generalization and extension to other building element that is needed to be recognized. The prototyping plug-in of auto-classification on the BIM tool using independent python-based recognition engine is demonstrated. Through the application, the user could quickly check undetermined objects in BIM instances and override the category and sub-type data automatically. Since the recognition engine is independent of the BIM tool, it has the advantage that it can be easily attached to a variety of tools that have a 3D object rendering engine. In future research, this approach and result will be used to pre-check IFC object data for IFC-based design review application such as a code compliance.

Acknowledgement. This research was supported by a grant (19AUDP-B127891-03) from the Architecture & Urban Development Research Program funded by the Ministry of Land, Infrastructure and Transport of the Korean government.

References

1. Eastman, C., et al.: Automatic rule-based checking of building designs. Autom. Constr. **18** (8), 1011–1033 (2009)
2. Lee, Y.-C., et al.: Validations for ensuring the interoperability of data exchange of a building information model. Autom. Constr. **58**, 176–195 (2015)
3. Koo, B., Shin, B.: Applying novelty detection to identify model element to IFC class misclassifications on architectural and infrastructure building information models. J. Comput. Design Eng. **5**(4), 391–400 (2018)
4. IFC Solutions Factory: Model View Definitions Site. http://www.blis-project.org/IAI-MVD. Accessed 29 Mar 2019
5. Weise, M., et al.: Integrating use case definitions for IFC developments, eWork and eBusiness in architecture and construction, pp. 637–645 (2009)
6. SMC: Solibri Model Checker. http://www.solibri.com. Accessed 29 Mar 2019
7. Sacks, R., et al.: Semantic enrichment for building information modeling: procedure for compiling inference rules and operators for complex geometry. J. Comput. Civ. Eng. **31**(6), 256–272 (2017)
8. Bloch, T., Sacks, R.: Comparing machine learning and rule-based inferencing for semantic enrichment of BIM models. Autom. Constr. **91**, 256–272 (2018)
9. Koo, B., et al.: Using support vector machines to classify building elements for checking the semantic integrity of building information models. Autom. Constr. **98**, 183–194 (2019)
10. The Princeton ModelNet. http://modelnet.cs.princeton.edu/. Accessed 29 Mar 2019
11. Maturana, D., Scherer, S.: VoxNet: a 3D convolutional neural network for real-time object recognition. In: 2015 IEEE/RSJ International Conference Proceedings of Intelligent Robots and Systems (IROS), pp. 922–928 (2015)
12. Su, H., et al.: Multi-view convolutional neural networks for 3D shape recognition. In: Proceedings of the IEEE International Conference on Computer Vision, pp. 945–953 (2015)

13. Krizhevsky A., et al.: ImageNet classification with deep convolutional neural networks. In: Proceedings of Advances in Neural Information Processing Systems, pp. 1097–1105 (2012)
14. Wu, Z., et al.: 3D ShapeNets: a deep representation for volumetric shapes. In: Proceedings of the IEEE Conference on Computer Vision and Pattern Recognition, pp. 1912–1920 (2015)
15. Szegedy, C., et al.: Rethinking the inception architecture for computer vision. In: Proceedings of the IEEE Conference on Computer Vision and Pattern Recognition, pp. 2818–2826 (2016)
16. Deng, J., et al.: Imagenet: a large-scale hierarchical image database. In: Proceedings of Computer Vision and Pattern Recognition, pp. 248–255 (2009)
17. Abadi, M., et al.: Tensorflow: large-scale machine learning on heterogeneous distributed systems, arXiv preprint arXiv:1603.04467 (2016)
18. KBIMS Library. http://www.kbims.or.kr/lms. Accessed 29 Mar 2019
19. BIMObject: BIM Libarary. https://www.bimobject.com/. Accessed 29 Mar 2019
20. 3Dwarehouse. https://3dwarehouse.sketchup.com/. Accessed 29 Mar 2019
21. Revit and Revit API. https://www.autodesk.co.kr/products/revit/overview. Accessed 29 Mar 2019
22. Omniclass: a classification system for the construction industry. http://www.omniclass.org Accessed 29 Mar 2019

Supporting Architectural Design Process with FLEA
A Distributed AI Methodology for Retrieval, Suggestion, Adaptation, and Explanation of Room Configurations

Viktor Eisenstadt[1]([✉]), Christoph Lanhgenhan[2], and Klaus-Dieter Althoff[1,3]

[1] Institute of Computer Science, University of Hildesheim,
Samelsonplatz 1, 31141 Hildesheim, Germany
{ayzensht,althoff}@uni-hildesheim.de
[2] Chair of Architectural Informatics, Technical University of Munich,
Arcisstrasse 21, 80333 Munich, Germany
langenhan@tum.de
[3] German Research Center for Artificial Intelligence (DFKI),
Trippstadter Strasse 122, 67663 Kaiserslautern, Germany

Abstract. The artificial intelligence methods, such as case-based reasoning and artificial neural networks were already applied to the task of architectural design support in a multitude of specific approaches and tools. However, modern AI trends, such as Explainable AI (XAI), and additional features, such as providing contextual suggestions for the next step of the design process, were rarely considered an integral part of these approaches or simply not available. In this paper, we present an application of a distributed AI-based methodology FLEA (Find, Learn, Explain, Adapt) to the task of room configuration during the early conceptual phases of architectural design. The implementation of the methodology in the framework MetisCBR applies CBR-based methods for retrieval of similar floor plans to suggest possibly inspirational designs and to explain the returned results with specific explanation patterns. Furthermore, it makes use of a farm of recurrent neural networks to suggest contextually suitable next configuration steps and to present design variations that show how the designs may evolve in the future. The flexibility of FLEA allows for variational use of its components in order to activate the currently required modules only. The methodology was initialized during the basic research project Metis (funded by German Research Foundation) during which the architectural semantic search patterns and a family of corresponding floor plan representations were developed. FLEA uses these patterns and representations as the base for its semantic search, explanation, next step suggestion, and adaptation components. The methodology implementation was iteratively tested during quantitative evaluations and user studies with multiple floor plan datasets.

Keywords: Room configuration · Distributed AI ·
Case-based reasoning · Neural networks · Explainable AI

J.-H. Lee (Ed.): CAAD Futures 2019, CCIS 1028, pp. 58–73, 2019.
https://doi.org/10.1007/978-981-13-8410-3_5

1   Introduction

Current trends of information technology established artificial intelligence (AI) as one of the most ubiquitous techniques for decision and creativity support in different business and research areas. Architecture, being an interdisciplinary domain, i.e., active in both business and research, is not an exception: continuously increasing complexity and the industrial digitization of the architectural design process require consistent modernization and consolidation of methods that support creativity in form of digital assistance during the inspiration and exploration phases. Still, many approaches that implement the recent AI trends, such as convolutional and recurrent neural networks (CNN, RNN), are in the process of research and not yet ready to be used in the daily design process. However, many of them showed potential for standalone application or integration in the existing computer-aided architectural design (CAAD) software.

This paper presents a novel AI-based methodology *FLEA* (named after its four main steps/components: *Find, Learn, Explain, Adapt*) and its implementation for the phase of creating a room configuration: an essential process of the initial design phase that is responsible for the basic setup of the building design as it influences the later utilization and interior of the currently designed architectural unit. The goal of FLEA is to inspire and guide the designer during the early conceptual phase by providing her with a collaborative assistance system in order to create a proper room layout for the design task at hand.

The key advantage of FLEA is its high flexibility: each main component can be decoupled and used separately, without being dependent on other modules, provided that the data required for the component to work is available. A combination that consists of a subset of the main components is possible as well. Each main component itself possesses a certain grade of flexibility too, e.g., a conditional choice of the most suitable neural network to suggest the next step. The methodology was implemented as the underlying structure for the mode of operation of *MetisCBR* [7], a framework for support of the early design phases in architecture. MetisCBR uses methods of case-based reasoning (CBR), multi-agent systems (MAS), and artificial neural networks (ANN). The architectural design case in the framework is represented as a *graph-based room configuration* that uses *semantic fingerprints of architecture* [21] for description with well-known architectural concepts (see Fig. 1 and also Fig. 3). This paper describes the current status of FLEA's integration in the framework (see Fig. 2).

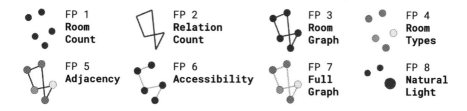

Fig. 1. Semantic fingerprints of architecture currently implemented in MetisCBR.

2   Related Work

In the last decades, many research initiatives from the AI-related domains developed approaches to support the early phases of the architectural design process. During the early years of CBR, a multitude of design-related case-based systems established case-based design (CBD) as an essential part of the entire CBR domain. The approaches, such as ARCHIE [30], FABEL [29], or, later, DIM [19] and CBArch [9], provided different variations of case-based techniques to examine how CBR can improve the design process by recommending, modifying, or explaining the floor plans and their corresponding (semantic) representations. Richter's work [23] summarizes the activity of CBR in the CAAD domain and provides an overview of problems that the case-based approaches need to solve or keep in mind if the acceptance of CBR among the representatives of the architecture domain should be increased. Among these problems are the optimization of retrieval strategies and the lack of variability and flexibility in the systems.

From the distributed AI perspective, the MAS-related research provided the most influential approaches for development and enhancement of the FLEA methodology. The work of Anumba et al. [3] examines research and technical foundations of use of multi-agent systems in construction and architecture domains. Gerber et al. [16] developed a research framework for prototyping of agents for support of generative parametric design process for the tasks of, e.g., façade generation or shell form finding. Simeone et al. [26] present an agent-based simulation and modeling approach for building design construction that enhances the Building Information Modeling (BIM) structure by extending it with agents that take into account the building's future users and use. Chu et al. [11] use agents to create a system for collaborative distributed 3D design: agents run on the server as well as on the user side, negotiate the design parameters, and generate the geometric model based on these parameters.

The research domain of deep learning in form of ANNs extended its activities for the CAAD domain as well and provided a number of related approaches during the last years. One of these approaches, DANIEL (Deep Architecture for fiNdIng alikE Layouts), uses deep learning for extraction of semantic features from floor plan images and applies convolutional neural networks for retrieval of similar building layouts [25]. An approach that combines case-based reasoning strategies with multi-agent systems and artificial networks was developed by González-Briones et al. for optimization of energy management in office buildings [17]. These two approaches are structurally the closest ones to FLEA and its implementation in MetisCBR, however, they are either conceptualized for one phase only, e.g., retrieval, or do not deal with the room configuration phase.

3   FLEA Methodology

Case-based reasoning, being a versatile knowledge-based technique, can be used to cover a number of phases of the design process and many tasks during these phases. For example, CBR can be used in early conceptual phases as well as in the cost calculation phase. For the former, CBR can offer the designer a collection of structurally similar past designs, pick the features that should be adapted in the current design, or create a variety of design recommendations based on the current design and the similar designs. For the latter, CBR-based approaches can search for past designs with similar features, present the cost for each of these designs, and estimate the budget for development of the current design. The accomplishment of such tasks is possible thanks to the human-alike reasoning structure of CBR's 4R-cycle [1] that includes the phases *Retrieve*, *Reuse*, *Revise*, and *Retain*. By combining CBR with distributed AI, it is also possible to distribute the R-steps among autonomous agents that assume responsibility for one or more tasks and collaborate to solve the given common problem.

However, a completely collaborative process with voluntary participation of autonomous agents is not possible with 4R, as the current step always depends on the results of the previous step. This also means that combinations of some of the steps can't be made flexible: e.g., retrieval is always required. Furthermore, for the design domain, the problem of CBR-specific separation of case in *problem and solution* exists as well: usually, the problem is described as a failure or a (feature-based) search request for which the most similar case from the case base should be retrieved, its solution adapted and implemented, and, if positively revised, saved in the case base. Designs, however, usually do not contain explicitly described failures, and reduction to a set of abstract features does not represent its complex structure and so is not suitable for use as a query for structurally similar designs and the adaptation. The approaches that used the structure of an architectural design as query [2], mostly contain the retrieval step only.

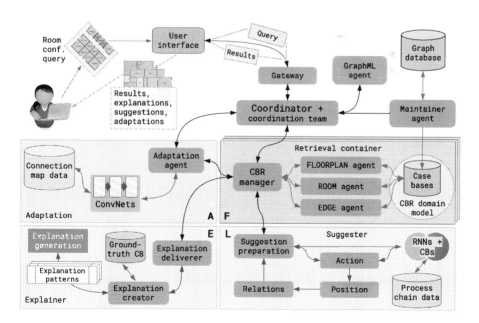

Fig. 2. The current implementation of FLEA in MetisCBR.

To overcome these shortcomings, we developed FLEA, a more flexible alternative to the classic CBR cycle. FLEA was created specifically for the architectural design domain, however, it can also be applied to other domains that provide a similar case structure. FLEA's main task is to provide a flexible assistance methodology to support the early phase of the design process by recommending inspirational similar designs (*Find*, see Sect. 3.1) and contextually suitable next steps of the process (*Learn*, see Sect. 3.2), explaining why and how a design can be helpful (*Explain*, see Sect. 3.3), and adapting the design by generating varieties of alternatives (*Adapt*, see Sect. 3.4). The FLEA methodology deliberately does not provide a strict execution sequence of its steps: unlike the 4R cycle, steps of FLEA can be almost arbitrary combined or used separately, provided that the correct data for the step could be inferred from the previous steps and/or the current state of the design process. Examples of such combinations in the context of the architectural design process are provided in Sect. 4.

3.1   Find

Find is historically the first phase that was developed for FLEA and MetisCBR in order to find similar architectural designs with methods of CBR. *Find's distributed domain model* [6] (see Fig. 3) defines the underlying structure for all room configuration cases of the system. It is based on semantic fingerprints and AGraphML [20], the architectural implementation of the graph description language GraphML. Three main concepts are available to describe the case: *ROOM*, *EDGE* (room connection, relation), and *FLOORPLAN* (metadata). ROOM and EDGE can have multiple instances per case and describe the atomic parts of the floor plans with the corresponding AGraphML attributes and a number of specific additional attributes (such as `source` and `target` for EDGE). FLOOR-PLAN contains the meta information about the case and is enriched with specific attributes too (e.g., `roomTypes` for the list of room functionalities of the room graph). The main concepts are connected with the `is-part-of` connection. For retrieval, MetisCBR uses the so-called *Basic* strategy (see also Fig. 3 and [6]), which is based on the main premise of CBR: similar problems have similar solutions. *Find's case base of floor plans* contains the cases for the case-based comparison with the query. Each case is constructed with respect to the domain model, incomplete cases (e.g., those without metadata) are not permitted.

Based on the results of the most notable experiments, e.g. [24], performed to evaluate MetisCBR's retrieval coordination component and the retrieval strategy in the context of other methods, the retrieval component of MetisCBR was extended with improvement of the search functionality, making it more flexible and responsive [5]. During a specific study, the representatives of the architecture domain were asked to play the role of the framework with the goal to examine their working and thinking processes during the early conceptualization process, with emphasis on the search for similar references during the room configuration process, in order to transfer a meta model of these processes to the framework.

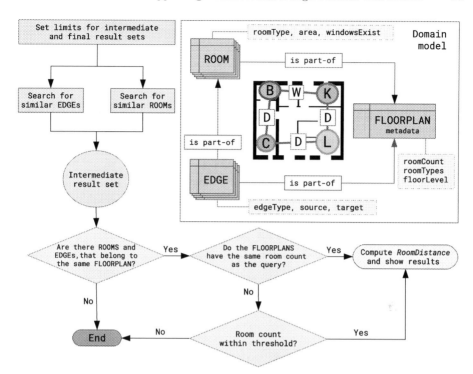

Fig. 3. The current state of the Basic retrieval strategy, together with the distributed domain model. The main concepts of the model, *ROOM, EDGE*, and *FLOORPLAN* are accompanied by a selection of their corresponding attributes (yellow rectangles). An example of a room configuration case is placed in the middle of the model. **L** stands for the *Living* room, **K** – *Kitchen*, **C** – *Corridor*, **B** – *Bath*, **D** – *Door*, **W** – *Wall*. (Color figure online)

One of the results of this study is the generic definition for retrieval strategy that became a base for creation of new and modification of already available strategies. The most recent research work [28] presents a new strategy, the *Room Type Dominance* (RTD) strategy, as well as the extension of the Basic strategy according to the definition. The RTD strategy is based on the new criterion for floor plan comparison, the *room type dominance*: a measure of dominance of a room type within the room configuration (e.g., in a room configuration {Living, Living, Living, Sleeping, Kitchen, Bath} the room type Living is highly dominant). The RTD strategy uses it as the main comparison criterion along with the semantic fingerprint-based criteria and the abstraction levels [5] of the floor plans. The extension of the Basic strategy adds a special similarity value, *Neighborhood Similarity Coefficient* to the last step of the strategy. The evaluations of both new strategies have proven their suitability for use in MetisCBR under different scenarios: the RTD strategy for scenarios where specific functionalities of rooms or the floor plan should be detected, the modified Basic strategy for situations where a set of inspirational designs is required, however, with a very high structural similarity to the query [28].

3.2   Learn

The phase *Learn* of the implementation of FLEA represents a collection of machine learning methods to learn the context or purpose of the current room configuration process and to suggest a set of possible next actions for this process. In particular, the system module the *Suggester* (that implements and executes the *Learn* phase, see Fig. 4) analyzes the previous steps of the process recorded by the system, tries to determine which context the process most likely belongs to, and produces a number of possible continuations of the configuration based on the previous processes from this context. The key components of the Suggester module of MetisCBR are the process chain, the contextual clusters, the contextual recurrent neural networks, and the context footprint case bases [12].

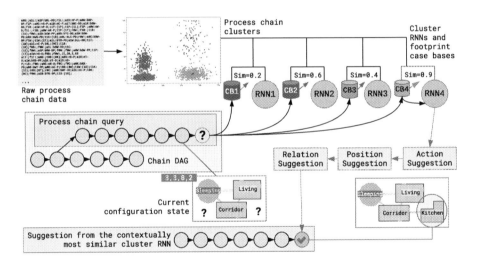

Fig. 4. The mode of operation of the Suggester in MetisCBR. An example of a visualized query with possible similarity values for each context and an example of a visualized suggestion are added for demonstration purposes. Figure adapted from [12].

The *process chain* represents an ordered record of the particular steps of the room configuration process. It is an emblematization of user's actions and is represented by a directed acyclic graph (DAG). For each step of the process, a notation of its action is mandatory. The Suggester can differentiate between room-related actions, such as *Addition, Removal, Reshaping,* or *Type modification*. Each action also contains specific information about the level of abstraction of the room, and the room type. For the Addition action, a set of additional information can be appended: a position within the configuration and the connections that should be used to connect the new room with rooms from the position suggestion. Each step in the process chain is accompanied by a metadata label (see Fig. 4) that consits of the current room and edge counts, the current amount of actions, and the amount of semantic fingerprints used in the latest search. The latter is the only attribute that connects *Find* and *Learn* in MetisCBR.

The *contextual clusters* represent the process chain dataset divided into a number of clusters based on the metadata described above. That is, each process chain is assigned to a cluster with contextually similar chains. The contexts are determined automatically with the *K-Means* clustering method that takes the metadata of the last step in the chain as the input vector. This contextual separation is a direct connection to our research [13] where the specific contextual classes define relations between the configurations in the retrieval result set.

After the cluster creation has been performed, a *contextual RNN* is created for each cluster as basis for training and the actual suggestion of the most suitable configuration step. In the past, RNNs have provided the best performance for sequential data (e.g., time series) as the mode of operation of their network cells allows for remembering the states of previous time steps in order to predict the next step. That is, RNNs are able to remember dependencies between the past steps over time. The Suggester uses *GRU* (Gated Recurrent Unit) [10] for the cells of cluster RNNs. To determine which cluster RNN is the most suitable one for suggestion of the next step for the current configuration, a special case base is created for each context cluster. This case base represents the cluster with a *footprint* – a selection of cases that provide the most typical metadata values for this cluster. This method is inspired by the footprint similarity-based retrieval [27]. The initial set of footprint cases is a product of random selection. Every new process chain query that is processed by the Suggester gets compared with all footprint cases of all cluster case bases, the RNN of the cluster case base that provides the highest similarity value is then queried and returns a set of possible next actions. The case that provided the highest similarity value remains in the case base, all others are removed and the case base gets filled up with new random cases from the cluster data. This repeats for every new query.

If the context RNN suggests to add a new room to the configuration, then the Suggester needs to find the proper position within the configuration and to determine which connections can be used to connect this new room to the adjacent rooms. The position suggestion uses a histogram of position entries of the corresponding action (for each of the possible addition actions such a histogram exists that was created from the initial process chain dataset) and suggests the positions consecutively starting with the position with the highest number of occurrence. The suggestion of connections is performed in a similar way: an instant histogram of all connections of each room type available in the current configuration is used. The Suggester then tries to find the best connection guess for the given number of the adjacent rooms, starting with the connections set with the highest number of occurrence.

For implementation of *Learn* in MetisCBR, an initial quantitative evaluation was conducted to examine the general suitability of the module [12]. A generated dataset with an amount of 1000000 process chains was used. 100 clusters/RNNs were created from this data with 50 chains per cluster footprint case base. 1000 generated queries were used to perform two suggestion phases. In the first phase 86% of suggestions were valid, i.e., accepted as suitable for the current configuration. In the second phase this value increased to $\approx 97\%$.

3.3   Explain

The current directions of the AI-related research domains emphasize the importance of human-understandable explanations of the internal processes of the AI systems. The research domain of Explainable AI (XAI) gained much attention within the last decade, resulting, for example, in multiple XAI-related workshops at the major AI conferences. The phase *Explain* of FLEA follows the current XAI development and requires an explanation feature for the systems that implement the methodology. To provide MetisCBR with explanation abilities, the *Explainer* module (see Fig. 2) was created as part of the system according to this methodology requirement. The main task of the Explainer is to support the retrieval process by providing explanations for the search results in form of textual expressions that contain information about system's decisions and reasons to include these results in the final result set. The mode of operation of the Explainer is based on the *Explanation Patterns* for CBR-based approaches [8]:

- *Justification* – Answers the question of why a particular result was returned.
- *Relevance* – Provides the context of the question that the system has asked.
- *Transparency* – Explains how exactly the system was able to find results.

Over time, a number of different Explainers have been conceptualized and implemented in MetisCBR. All of them have in common that they implement the explanation patterns and the validation of the produced explanations, i.e., they check the explanation for correlation between its expression or value and the requirements for understandable domain-specific explanations.

The *CBR-Explainer-1* [4] was the first one to implement the concept of explanation patterns and validation. Its task was to detect the patterns within the retrieval results by means of applying a specific ruleset that was conceptualized to cover all possible combinations of semantic fingerprints. After the pattern recognition phase, the corresponding explanation expression was generated, based on detected patterns (see Fig. 5), and evaluated with the case-based validation process based on comparison with ground-truth explanation cases from a case base of 'golden-standard' explanations that were checked for validity by a CAAD expert. During an evaluation with a case base of 225 room configurations, the CBR-Explainer-1 achieved 84.825% of validation processes with a positive outcome and so proved the suitability of its mode of operation.

The *CBR-Explainer-2* [13], an enhanced, however, more restrictive version of the CBR-Explainer-1, provides more deeply in detail going explanations that do not consider the semantic fingerprints only for patterns detection, but also take particular attributes of the domain model's main concepts into account. The detection process of each pattern was reworked, extensively enhanced and assigned a particular agent responsible for this pattern only. The Relevance detection is based on analysis of attributes of all ROOMs and EDGEs available in case and query, where each of them is checked for predefined requirements that determine if this instance is suitable for similarity assessment. If no Relevance was detected in either query or case, then the pattern detection process proceeds with recognition of the Justification pattern. Here, a Justification score that is based on similarity values of the particular rooms, edges, and the result as a whole, serves as a classification means to categorize the result into a justification class. The detection of the Transparency pattern then depends on similarity assessment history of the attributes of the main concepts. The Transparency agent collects all available data on this history and constructs the assessment summary report. The explanation validation process of the CBR-Explainer-2 is an enhancement of the CBR-Explainer-1's validation, the most notabe modification is the inclusion of *undetected* patterns which provides a more exact detection picture. Besides pattern detection, the CBR-Explainer-2 is also able to detect contextual relations between the results by assigning different context classes to them. These classes represent specific features such as *RoomTypeDominance* (see Sect. 3.1) or *SparseConnections* [13]. The evaluation of the CBR-Explainer-2 with a dataset of 119 room configurations resulted in ≈ 80.4% of validations with a positive outcome. The subsequent user study, during which the understandability of explanations was rated, resulted in satisfactory feedback with comments on visualization of explanations and improvement suggestions from the participants.

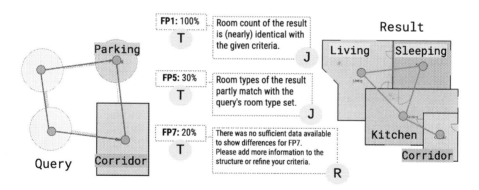

Fig. 5. An example of explanations produced with CBR-Explainer-1. T, J, and R stand for Transparency, Justification, and Relevance respectively. Figure adapted from [4].

The *DA-Explainer* [14] is based on the classification method *discriminant analysis*. This Explainer was conceptualized and implemented to predict the explanation and validation classes of the result. The explanation classes, denoted by the letters A-D and assigned by means of applying the discriminant function and decision trees, represent the detection grade of the corresponding pattern and so can describe how likely a sufficient amount of explanation-related information will be available in both query and result to produce an understandable explanation. The validation classes, denoted by V1–V4, estimate the likelihood of validity of the explanations. The DA-Explainer was compared in a joint evaluation [15] with the CBR-based Explainers. This experiment used a dataset of 120 room configurations and showed that the CBR-Explainer-1 produces the most constant validation values, whereas the DA-Explainer delivered the most inconsistent performance.

The last of the currently existing Explainers is the *BDI-Explainer* [22] that is based on the *Belief-Desire-Intention* architecture well-known from the MAS domain. This Explainer was influenced by the explainable BDI agent concept [18]. The BDI-Explainer provides a high-level structure for construction of other Explainers where each concept of the BDI architecture is connected to a specific task and/or the corresponding knowledge basis. Beliefs describe the domain-specific technical knowledge, i.e., the technical terms and relations of the CAAD domain. Desires represent the goals of the Explainer: detection of explanation patterns and validation of the generated explanation. Intentions stand for the most suitable next steps to achieve the desired goal by means of applying the beliefs knowledge, e.g., to contextually activate one of the available Explainers. The concept of the BDI-Explainer was examined by a group of 4 architects [22]. The results showed a general acceptance rate of 75% for the concept of knowledge- and pattern-based explanation generation. Additionally, it was also determined that the enrichment of results with explanations helps to avoid mistakes during the conceptualization process, but does not stimulate creativity.

3.4   Adapt

Modification of solutions of retrieved cases, emblemaized by the phase Reuse of the 4R CBR cycle, by adapting them (or just the parts of them) to the current situation, is an essential phase that influences the success of the reasoning process as it provides the user with a possible solution to her problem. For design cases, this means that a selection of generated variations of the current design at hand can be presented. FLEA's *Adapt* provides the implementation of the methodology with such functionality to give the designer another source of inspiration that shows how the current design can evolve over time.

The implementation of *Adapt* in MetisCBR is based on *Generative Adversarial Nets* (GAN), an approach for ANN-based generation of data objects. GAN makes use of two neural networks, where the Generator generates objects and the Discriminator decides if this object would appear real to a human. Our approach (see Fig. 6) takes the GAN methodology as a basis and extends it with a pre-generation step, the *adaptation complexity classification* phase implemented in the specific Classificator network that defines how strong the current design should be adapted. The outcome of this classification is the grade on the specific *complexity scale* **1**(slight)–**3**(heaviest) that is then used to select a proper mode of adaptation for the Generator that modifies the current room configuration according to the requirements of this grade. After that, all of the generated room configuration variants are forwarded to the Discriminator whose task is to determine if this configuration can be considered a descendant of the original configuration. The chosen variations are then saved in the case base and marked as descendants of the query design producing its particular case tree. All three steps of our adaptation approach use a convolutional neural network (CNN, ConvNet) as its corresponding underlying technique and work with a connection map as the floor plan representation (see Fig. 6).

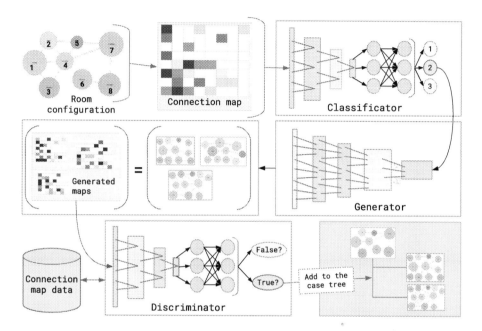

Fig. 6. The main structure of the GAN-based adaptation module of MetisCBR.

A connection map is a *modified adjacency matrix* of the floor plan's graph, however, instead of weights, a special *connection code* is used to mark the connection between two rooms. This code represents a numerical signature of the connection, where the first two numbers represent the connected rooms and the last number stands for the type of connection. For example, the connection code 241 stands for *Living and Kitchen connected by a Door*. Both directions, e.g., Living→Kitchen and Kitchen→Living are allowed, e.g., if they are connected with two different connection types. For use in ConvNets, these numbers are then converted into the grayscale values, e.g., 241 to 0.241. In Fig. 7, an example visualization of the original and the corresponding adapted connection maps is shown. The outcomes from the Generator's network are decoded afterwards, if they have been accepted by the Discriminator. The dataset of connection maps is a reflection of the case base for retrieval, with adaptation complexity classes derived from different steps of the process chains described in Sect. 3.3.

Currently the adaptation component is under active development, especially the configurations of different adaptations modes of the Generator are being tested. However, in an initial evaluation of the Classificator, classification accuracy of $\approx 93\%$ could be achieved, based on 30000 generated connection maps.

4   Example Usages of FLEA Components

The following examples demonstrate how FLEA's components can be combined together or used separately in order to accomplish different tasks that can occur during the room configuration process (see Fig. 7).

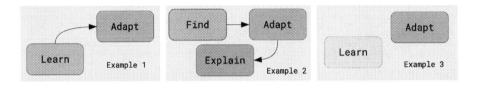

Fig. 7. Examples of FLEA component combinations.

4.1   Example 1: *Learn* and *Adapt*

If the architect does not wish to take a look on floor plans similar to the currently developed one, but instead only to know how this current design can or could evolve, then the system can combine *Learn* and *Adapt* components in order to present variations of the design by using the past design process steps history saved in the process chain (see Sect. 3.2). In this case, the *Adapt* component takes the different, in the most simple case manually or randomly selected, configuration states from the history (including the current state) and produces a number of adaptations that can show how the current state can evolve as well as what would happen if at some other point in the current room configuration history another configuration decision could have been made. This combination can help the designer reconsider her decisions and try to correct them if required.

4.2   Example 2: *Find - Adapt - Explain*

The most classic case, where the designer looks for the most similar cases in the dataset of past cases in order to find inspiration or take a look how the current configuration is embedded in a similar context can be extended with explanations of why these designs are useful for further design development process and also how they are related to each other (which is already implemented in MetisCBR). Additionally, this combination can be enhanced with an intermediate adaptation functionality that can adapt the current design state as well as a number of the most similar designs found in the case base. Furthermore, these selected most similar designs can themselves be used as the adaptation basis. Subsequently, the Explain component can be used to make retrieval as well as adaptation results more reasonable by showing the similarity-based relationship between them.

4.3 Example 3: *Learn* or *Explain* Separately

If computational resources are to be considered then only the modules can be active that are currently required most, while other modules can be disabled. For example, *Explain* can be used separately to find out how two designs can be helpful for each other, which is the easiest possible use of *Explain*. In this case, the explanation component does not need much resources, as pattern detection and validation will only be performed for the evaluation of one design. Other example is the usage of *Learn* as the only active component that concentrates the system performance on suggestions for the next step only. As *Learn* generally requires more computational resources than other modules, it is recommended to periodically (re)consider how many clusters and RNNs should be created.

5 Future Work and Conclusion

In this paper, we presented FLEA, a methodology for support of the early conceptual design phase in architecture. FLEA is implemented in a framework for room configuration support, where all steps, namely *Find*, *Learn*, *Explain*, and *Adapt*, are implemented in particular system components for retrieval of similar floor plans, explanation of the returned results, suggestions of the next configuration steps, and generation of adapted variations of the current configuration. Future work will be conducted mostly for *Learn* and *Adapt* to improve these components and perform a number of quantitative and qualitative experiments.

References

1. Aamodt, A., Plaza, E.: Case-based reasoning: foundational issues, methodological variations, and system approaches. AI Commun. **7**(1), 39–59 (1994)
2. Ahmed, S., Weber, M., Liwicki, M., Langenhan, C., Dengel, A., Petzold, F.: Automatic analysis and sketch-based retrieval of architectural floor plans. Pattern Recogn. Lett. **35**, 91–100 (2014)
3. Anumba, C., Ren, Z., Ugwu, O.: Agents and Multi-agent Systems in Construction. Routledge, Abingdon (2007)
4. Ayzenshtadt, V., Espinoza-Stapelfeld, C.A., Langenhahn, C., Althoff, K.D.: Multi-agent-based generation of explanations for retrieval results within a case-based support framework for architectural design. In: ICAART 2018. Scitepress (2018)
5. Ayzenshtadt, V., Langenhan, C., Bukhari, S., Althoff, K.-D., Petzold, F., Dengel, A.: Extending the flexibility of case-based design support tools: a use case in the architectural domain. In: Aha, D.W., Lieber, J. (eds.) ICCBR 2017. LNCS (LNAI), vol. 10339, pp. 46–60. Springer, Cham (2017). https://doi.org/10.1007/978-3-319-61030-6_4
6. Ayzenshtadt, V., Langenhan, C., Bukhari, S.S., Althoff, K.D., Petzold, F., Dengel, A.: Distributed domain model for the case-based retrieval of architectural building designs. In: Petridis, M., Roth-Berghofer, T., Wiratunga, N. (eds.) UKCBR-2015, Cambridge, United Kingdom, 15–17 December (2015)

7. Ayzenshtadt, V., Langenhan, C., Bukhari, S.S., Althoff, K.D., Petzold, F., Dengel, A.: Thinking with containers: a multi-agent retrieval approach for the case-based semantic search of architectural designs. In: Filipe, J., van den Herik, J. (eds.) ICAART-2016, Rome, Italy, 24–26 February. SCITEPRESS (2016)

8. Cassens, J., Kofod-Petersen, A.: Designing explanation aware systems: the quest for explanation patterns. In: ExaCt, pp. 20–27 (2007)

9. Cavieres, A., Bhatia, U., Joshi, P., Zhao, F., Ram, A.: CBArch: a case-based reasoning framework for conceptual design of commercial buildings. In: Artificial Intelligence and Sustainable Design - Papers from the AAAI 2011 Spring Symposium (SS-11-02), pp. 19–25 (2011)

10. Cho, K., et al.: Learning phrase representations using RNN encoder-decoder for statistical machine translation. In: EMNLP-2014. Association for Computational Linguistics (2014)

11. Chu, C.H., Wu, P.H., Hsu, Y.C.: Multi-agent collaborative 3D design with geometric model at different levels of detail. Robot. Comput. Integr. Manuf. **25**(2), 334–347 (2009)

12. Eisenstadt, V., Althoff, K.D.: 'what is the next step?' Supporting architectural room configuration process with case-based reasoning and recurrent neural networks. In: FLAIRS 2019 (2019)

13. Eisenstadt, V., Espinoza-Stapelfeld, C., Mikyas, A., Althoff, K.-D.: Explainable distributed case-based support systems: patterns for enhancement and validation of design recommendations. In: Cox, M.T., Funk, P., Begum, S. (eds.) ICCBR 2018. LNCS (LNAI), vol. 11156, pp. 78–94. Springer, Cham (2018). https://doi.org/10.1007/978-3-030-01081-2_6

14. Espinoza-Stapelfeld, C.: Case-based classification of explanation expressions in search results of a retrieval system for support of conceptual phase in architecture (2018)

15. Espinoza-Stapelfeld, C., Eisenstadt, V., Althoff, K.-D.: Comparative quantitative evaluation of distributed methods for explanation generation and validation of floor plan recommendations. In: van den Herik, J., Rocha, A.P. (eds.) ICAART 2018. LNCS (LNAI), vol. 11352, pp. 46–63. Springer, Cham (2019). https://doi.org/10.1007/978-3-030-05453-3_3

16. Gerber, D.J., Pantazis, E., Marcolino, L.S.: Design agency. In: Celani, G., Sperling, D.M., Franco, J.M.S. (eds.) CAAD Futures 2015. CCIS, vol. 527, pp. 213–235. Springer, Heidelberg (2015). https://doi.org/10.1007/978-3-662-47386-3_12

17. González-Briones, A., Prieto, J., De La Prieta, F., Herrera-Viedma, E., Corchado, J.: Energy optimization using a case-based reasoning strategy. Sensors **18**(3), 865 (2018)

18. Harbers, M., van den Bosch, K., Meyer, J.J.C.: Design and evaluation of explainable BDI agents. In: 2010 IEEE/WIC/ACM International Conference on Web Intelligence and Intelligent Agent Technology, vol. 2, pp. 125–132 (2010)

19. Lai, I.C.: Dynamic idea maps: a framework for linking ideas with cases during brainstorming. Int. J. Architectural Comput. **3**(4), 429–447 (2005)

20. Langenhan, C.: A federated information system for the support of topological BIM-based approaches. Forum Bauinformatik, Aachen (2015)

21. Langenhan, C., Petzold, F.: The fingerprint of architecture-sketch-based design methods for researching building layouts through the semantic fingerprinting of floor plans. Int. Electron. Sci. Educ. J.: Architect. Mod. Inf. Technol. **4**, 13 (2010)

22. Mikyas, A.: Concept for development of an explanation component for BDI agents to support the design phase in architecture (2018)

23. Richter, K.: What a shame-why good ideas can't make it in architecture: a contemporary approach towards the case-based reasoning paradigm in architecture. In: FLAIRS Conference (2013)
24. Sabri, Q.U., Bayer, J., Ayzenshtadt, V., Bukhari, S.S., Althoff, K.D., Dengel, A.: Semantic pattern-based retrieval of architectural floor plans with case-based and graph-based searching techniques and their evaluation and visualization. In: ICPRAM 2017, Porto, Portugal, 24–26 February (2017)
25. Sharma, D., Gupta, N., Chattopadhyay, C., Mehta, S.: DANIEL: A deep architecture for automatic analysis and retrieval of building floor plans. In: 2017 14th IAPR International Conference on Document Analysis and Recognition (ICDAR), vol. 1, pp. 420–425. IEEE (2017)
26. Simeone, D., Cursi, S., Coraglia, U.M.: Modelling buildings and their use as systems of agents. In: eCAADe-2017 (2017)
27. Smyt, B., McKenna, E.: Footprint-based retrieval. In: Althoff, K.-D., Bergmann, R., Branting, L.K. (eds.) ICCBR 1999. LNCS, vol. 1650, pp. 343–357. Springer, Heidelberg (1999). https://doi.org/10.1007/3-540-48508-2_25
28. Standke, S.: Strategical extension of similarity assessment of the retrieval module in a system for support of conceptual design phase in architecture (2018)
29. Voss, A.: Case design specialists in FABEL. In: Issues and Applications of Case-based Reasoning in Design, pp. 301–335 (1997)
30. Zimring, C.M., Pearce, M., Goel, A.K., Kolodner, J.L., Sentosa, L.S., Billington, R.: Case-based decision support: a case study in architectural design (1992)

Visualizing Mackintosh's Alternative Design Proposal for Scotland Street School

Danilo Di Mascio[⊠]

Department of Architecture and 3D Design,
School of Art, Design and Architecture,
The University of Huddersfield, Huddersfield, UK
D.DiMascio@hud.ac.uk

Abstract. This paper describes the process of creation of a set of visualizations (elevations, perspective views and a short animation) of C.R. Mackintosh's original but unrealized first design proposal for Scotland Street School (dated January 1904). Moreover, the piece of writing reflects upon some key aspects of the project such as how architectural historians were involved and how ambiguities due to the discrepancies between the drawings and missing details were resolved by studying multiple drawings and transferring clues from other Mackintosh's built works. The contributions of this research are important for several reasons: it proposes a methodology that can be applied to similar research projects; it explains the educational value of the development work, which can be defined as digitally handcrafted, behind the visualizations; it contributes to studies of buildings designed by C.R. Mackintosh by using digital technologies that open up new insights to aspects still overlooked of his architectural production.

Keywords: Digital handcrafted · Digital heritage ·
3D digital reconstruction · Visualization · Charles Rennie Mackintosh

1 Introduction

This paper describes the process of creation of a set of visualizations of C.R. Mackintosh's original but unrealized first design proposal for Scotland Street School (dated January 1904), and identifies and reflects upon some key aspects of the project such as how the architectural historians were involved in the process and how ambiguities due to the discrepancies between the drawings and missing details were resolved. Hence, the work goes beyond the sole creation of the visualizations of the building and considers aspects related to the interpretation of archival information and collaboration. Furthermore, the whole development process of the visualizations can be defined as digitally handcrafted because the CAD drawings, the investigation of the 3D shape and architectural details of the building, the making of the 3D model and the creation of the textures/materials have been time-consuming works that presented a level of care similar to a handcrafted work, with solutions personalised to this specific project.

Charles Rennie Mackintosh is one of the most important names in the history of architecture and a pioneer of modern movement [1]. However, despite another

© Springer Nature Singapore Pte Ltd. 2019
J.-H. Lee (Ed.): CAAD Futures 2019, CCIS 1028, pp. 74–87, 2019.
https://doi.org/10.1007/978-981-13-8410-3_6

publication where digital technologies were used to investigate the narrative features of the Glasgow School of Art [2], there are no other known research publications that have explored other buildings designed by him through the use of digital tools and related methods.

Digital technologies have already been used in several projects that focused on architectural analysis and critique of existing, lost or unbuilt works. In each of these projects, digital tools supported by specific theoretical and methodological approaches allowed the development of a better understanding of several aspects of those projects and the discovery and dissemination of relevant information [3–5].

In all the previous projects, one of the constant elements that the scholars had to deal with was the scarcity of information available that, in most cases, also presented many inaccuracies and discrepancies. Considering the subcategory of unbuilt projects designed by famous architects, this lack of information was often overcome by interpreting the archival material and by studying the architect's life and the historical, cultural, social and economic context when he or she operated [4]. Also in this project, one of the main challenges was to manage missing, incomplete and inaccurate information presented in the original drawings by C.R. Mackintosh. This situation was handled by studying multiple drawings and transferring clues from other Mackintosh's built works, and by the support of architectural historians.

The lessons from this case study are multiple, starting with the proposal of a methodology that can be applied to similar research projects.

1.1 Main Aims of the Paper

The main objective of this paper is to describe the process of creation of a set of visualizations of C.R. Mackintosh's original but unrealized first design proposal for Scotland Street School and identify and reflect upon key aspects including:

- The educational values of the whole project;
- How and when the architectural historians were involved in the process;
- How ambiguities due to the discrepancies between the drawings and missing details were resolved;
- The methodology and the tools that were used.

The main aim of the set of rendered images (the four elevations and a few perspective views) and the animation was to communicate the different materials and the main architectural elements of Mackintosh's first design proposal which differs from the final design. The visualizations deepen the knowledge of the design of this remarkable building and allow further comparisons and reflections between Mackintosh's works.

2 Scotland Street School: Design Proposal and Built Version

Scotland Street School is one of the most relevant buildings designed and built by Charles Rennie Mackintosh in Glasgow [6–8], and today, after the tragic fire that recently destroyed the Glasgow School of Art [9], it can be considered as the main existing educational building designed by him in the Scottish city. Nowadays it is used as a museum of education.

One of the most remarkable features of the building is constituted by the two glazed towers located on the North façade which is the main elevation of the building. These towers accommodated the two separated main entrances and staircases: one for girls and one for boys. The two towers represent a modern reinterpretation of traditional Scottish architecture, and it is evident the influence of Scottish castles, especially for the shape and the conical roofs, that Mackintosh studied and recorded in his notebooks when he travelled around Scotland [10]. Hence, these two towers have a strong link with the architectural heritage of his home country. As for other details of Mackintosh's architectural production, the big glazed surfaces and the interior staircase of the tower anticipated similar solutions adopted during the modern movement by Walter Gropius [11].

The first design is different from the built version for several small details, but mainly for the proposal of a different material. The existing building is made in red limestone (red Locharbriggs sandstone ashlar) while the proposed building was meant to be made with white Dullatur stone (Fig. 1). Hence, the color and the stonework were very different. Other differences encompassed architectural elements and decorations.

Fig. 1. (Left) Original drawing showing of the North Elevation (Source: © CSGCIC Glasgow Libraries Collection. All rights reserved); (Right) Photo of the actual building in Glasgow (Source: Personal archive of the author).

3 Methodology: How to Visualize Mackintosh's Alternative Design Proposal

The methodology was based on approaches developed during, and applied on, other digital heritage projects, such as [2] and [12].

The main aim of this research was to contribute to a significant project, titled "Mackintosh Architecture: Context, Making and Meaning" [13], by developing a set of elevations, a 3D model of Scotland Street Public School (1904–1906) and a short animation, for inclusion on the website of the project.[1] Hence, the work was also a contribution to a significant research project. The 3D digital reconstruction phase and the creation of the visualizations were supported by conversations with two architectural historians, including the principal investigator of the research project, Professor Pamela Robertson.

The following diagram (Fig. 2) shows the main steps that characterised the process by readapting the visual framework developed for 3D digital reconstructions of lost buildings and described in [14]. This visual framework supports the reading and classification of existing projects, the development of new works and foster sharing of information. To some extent, each step of the 'How' phase has aspects linked to content and interpretation on one side, and digital technologies and their applications on the other side.

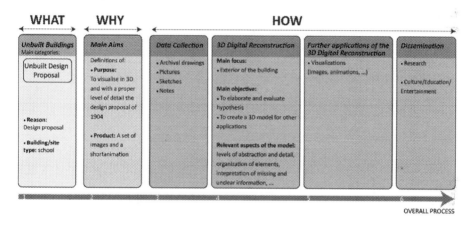

Fig. 2. Visual framework of the overall process and its main steps (Source: Personal archive of the author).

3.1 Collection, Analysis and Interpretation of the Available Information

The first step of the project was the collection of all the available archival information. The Hunterian Art Gallery provided a set of high-resolution scans of 9 original drawings that show the design proposal of January 1904. The drawings' set included: a

---

[1] "Mackintosh Architecture: Context, Making and Meaning" was funded by the Arts and Humanities Research Board of the U.K. and was based at the University of Glasgow. It aimed to provide the first authoritative catalogue raisonne of the architecture of Charles Rennie Mackintosh (1868–1928). Its major output was the website www.mackintosh-architecture.gla.ac.uk, which contains 350 projects, over 870,000 works, over 3,000 images, 380 biographies, contextual and analytical essays, and supporting features. More information can be found on the website: https://www.mackintosh-architecture.gla.ac.uk/.

block plan, the three plan views (ground-floor plan, first-floor plan and second-floor plan, the four elevations, two cross sections and one longitudinal section) (Fig. 3).

The analysis and interpretation of the drawings constituted an essential step. A first careful observation of the drawings showed several discrepancies that were confirmed and increased in number after the drawings were imported into AutoCAD.

Once the drawings were imported in the CAD environment, and placed in correspondence to each other based on the main vertical and horizontal axes and alignments, it was possible to compare them and identify other discrepancies accurately. Furthermore, the original drawings, being at a design stage, lacked information about various elements and decorations.

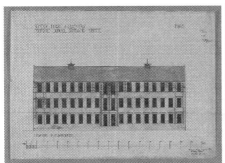 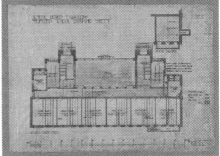

Fig. 3. Two of the original drawings of the first design proposal of January 1904 (Source: © CSGCIC Glasgow Libraries Collection. All rights reserved).

The following list summarises some of the main issues identified during a first analysis of the collected graphical documentation:

- The same elements (e.g. walls and windows) present slightly different dimensions on different drawings;
- Details or technical elements, such as chimneys, shown in one elevation are missing in another one;
- The W. and E. elevations do not present any details about the two towers; this makes complicated any interpretation of the carved mouldings and decorations;
- On the top of the long central windows of the north facade, Mackintosh did not indicate lintels; considering the presence of cast-iron internal columns noticeable on one of the two transverse sections, it has been assumed that the lintels appearance might look like those on the N. facade of the GSA building;
- In general, information about the dimensions of the reliefs of cornices, edges and other carved decorations, are missing because, as with other technical elements, they seem unresolved in the original drawings of this first design proposal.

3.2   Redrawing Process

The imported drawings in AutoCAD were carefully arranged, scaled, and aligned with each other. Then, each vector drawing was traced over the related original drawing and compared to the other orthographic projections in order to create an accurate and consistent set of CAD drawings (Fig. 4). Even if the final aim of the project was to produce visualizations of the exterior of the building, the redrawing process also involved the main interior elements which were used as further visual references. Once the basic 2D representations were completed, they were coloured in order to understand the different materials, edges and the projections of different volumes and elements (Fig. 10 - right).

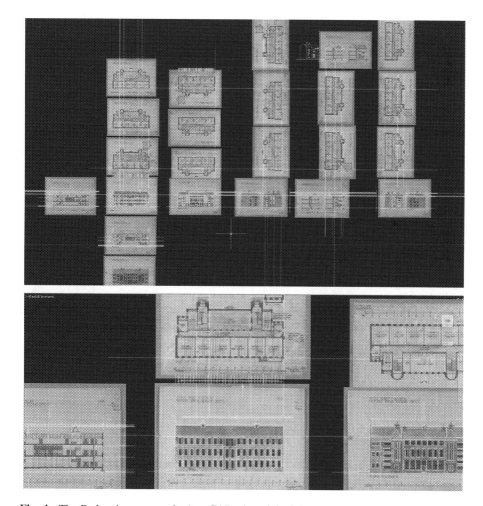

Fig. 4. The Redrawing process in AutoCAD: the original drawings were arranged and aligned in order to create a consistent set of vector drawings (Source: Personal archive of the author).

The 2D and 3D modelling processes were supported by hand sketches and notes which allowed to investigate and clarify details at several levels: from the shape, ridges and slopes of the pitched roof to the shape and measures of the windows' frames (Fig. 5)

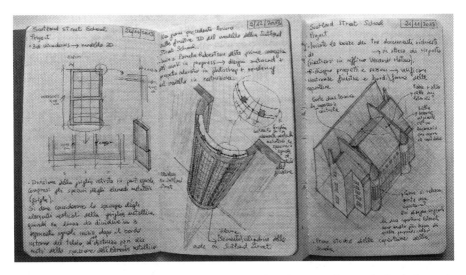

Fig. 5. Sketches and notes from a personal notebook to interpret the standard windows, the glazed surfaces of the towers, and the shape, ridges and slopes of the pitched roof (Source: Personal archive of the author).

3.3   3D Digital Reconstruction

The main challenge of the 3D digital reconstruction was to translate into 3D architectural and technical elements that were implied and unresolved in the original drawings of January 1904. This difficulty was tackled by looking at other projects designed by Mackintosh (and in particular the Glasgow School of Art) and by sharing hypothesis with the architectural historians and receiving their points of view.

At the beginning of the 3D Digital Reconstruction process, the CAD drawings produced in AutoCAD were imported into Rhinoceros v5.0 and used as a metrically accurate base to create the 3D model of the building. Hence, they were aligned in a way that supported the 3D modelling process (Fig. 6). However, other discrepancies were discovered during the translation of the 2D drawings into a 3D model, and this required a continuous check and update of the 2D drawings in AutoCAD and reimported them into Rhinoceros. This process was time-consuming. For this reason, and considering the improvement of Rhinoceros v5.0's 2D drafting tools, it was decided to undertake the whole work directly within this software package. This decision brought several benefits. One of the main ones was to have flexible and precision tools while exploring the possible geometry of architectural elements in 2D and 3D. Like in a handcrafted work, the geometry of each architectural element was carefully evaluated, and each 3D object modelled.

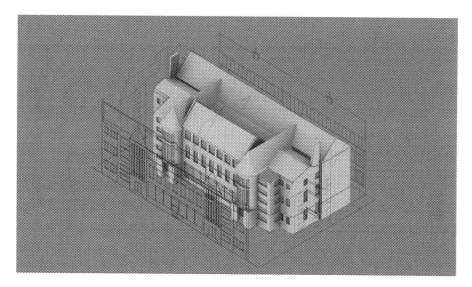

Fig. 6. During the 3D digital reconstruction phase, the vector drawings were arranged and aligned in order to support the 3D modelling process (Source: Personal archive of the author).

3.4   Study and Representation of the Materials

An essential step in the project was represented by the definition of the pattern and the color of the primary material, the snecked[2] pale yellow Dullatur sandstone selected by Mackintosh. The original drawings were the starting point to create a texture to convey the stonework. However, Mackintosh suggested the stonework in selected areas only. Hence, the plan was to try a schematic approach to convey the stonework following Mackintosh's draughtsmanship. The observation of the stonework of the Glasgow School of Art provided other vital information to define a stonework pattern for a wider wall surface (Fig. 7). Moreover, from an analysis of the selected windows of the Glasgow School of Art, it was noticed that the snecked sandstone was used for the overall stonework with the only exception of the areas around the windows (including lintels and sills) that were made with ashlar[3].

---

[2] Snecked describes small pieces of stone used to fill the gaps between larger stones in a wall. 'Snecked rubble' describes masonry that has a mixture of squared stones of different sizes.

[3] Ashlar: masonry in regular blocks with a smooth surface (These two definitions were provided by Professor Pamela Robertson).

Fig. 7. Photos of two windows of the East Façade of the Glasgow School of Art. Around the windows, it is possible to recognize the ashlar. The photos also show the variation of the stone color (Source: Personal archive of the author).

In order to avoid the annoying tiling effect caused by the repetition of the same texture, a basic set of textures was created (by tracing over Mackintosh's original drawings in AutoCAD and coloring them in Photoshop), and then they were stitched together and customized for each façade. In this way, the stonework of each façade looks different and more consistent.

For the colours different references were used, starting from the Orrock Johnston tombstone (the Dullatur stone there is now aged, however, as a reference it was selected an area where the stone looked fresh and relatively clean), also designed by Mackintosh, plus other buildings that used the same kind of stone, in this case one of the primary references was the Pearce Institute in Govan (Glasgow).

Observations of the facades of the Glasgow School of Art showed that the stonework presented some variations in the stone color (Fig. 7) which was replicated on the textures/materials of the digital model. The final images communicate the snecked sandstone, the ashlar and the masonry's joints.

The color of the slates of the roof matched the colour as built.

3.5   Lighting, Mood and Presentation of the Final Images and Animation

The four elevations were lit respecting the actual orientation of the building and a specific time to create a more dramatic visual effect. The images were rendered in 3ds Max using sunlight and a skylight for indirect illumination (scanline renderer).

The short animation used a path target and a camera target and focused on the North elevation. The main value of the animation is to provide better communication of the tridimensional qualities of the building (Fig. 8).

Fig. 8. N. elevation, rendering based on Mackintosh's earliest surviving drawings of January 1904 and showing his specification for pale yellow Dullatur sandstone © Mackintosh Architecture, University of Glasgow; CAD by Danilo Di Mascio (Source: www.mackintosh-architecture.gla.ac.uk).

4   Reflections on the Key Aspects of the Project and Their Values

4.1   The Visualization Process and the Communication with the Architectural Historians

One of the most relevant aspects of the project was related to the communication with the architectural historians who provided essential support along the whole process.

The whole work was carried out by a scholar with a background in architecture and research experiences in digital heritage. A background in architecture is useful in order to evaluate architectural and technical elements also during the analysis of the original drawings, and it is even more helpful during the 3D digital reconstruction. In fact, it is beneficial to understand shape, function, meaning and technological/material aspects of each architectural element while creating its 3D digital representation. Moreover, the knowledge of the scholar covered also aspects related to other buildings designed by Mackintosh in Glasgow.

The two architectural historians provided expert knowledge related to the whole of Mackintosh's architectural production, and the architecture of Glasgow during Mackintosh's period.

The communication with the architectural historians was undertaken on a quite regular basis. Updates were shared every time there was a doubt about missing information on the drawings or when the available data led to an uncertain result, such as the shape of a decoration.

The below diagram (Fig. 9) shows the main steps of the process and when updates were sent to the architectural historians in order to let them provide their comments and pieces of advice. In total, there had been 18 updates, with the last one about the delivery of the final visualizations. Each update or set of updates covered one or more aspects of the work in progress. For example, 4 updates covered the creation and application of the primary material/texture of the stonework. Some updates also covered more than one single aspect. As shown in the diagram, once the first draft of the 3D digital model was completed, the work was carried out on multiple levels simultaneously. Considering the visual nature of the project, the updates were constituted by drawings or rendered views of the work in progress or by images where some important element where highlighted (Fig. 10). All the visual information were accompanied by descriptive text, such as personal reflections and interpretations, and questions. The extensive use of visual material proved to be very effective and made the communication process straightforward and the comments always precise and useful.

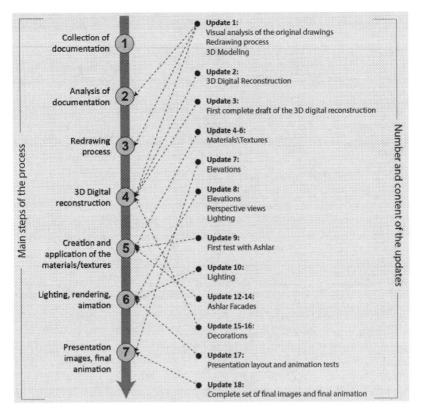

Fig. 9. Diagram that shows the main steps of the process and the number and content of the updates sent to the architectural historians (Source: Personal archive of the author).

Fig. 10. Examples of two drawings shared during one of the updates to the architectural historians (Source: Personal archive of the author).

4.2 Educational Aspects of the Development Process

Like in design works, both in practice and in an educational environment, the development process (in this case the set of visualizations, in a design work a final design proposal) has strong educational value. Firstly, the methodological process can be applied, adapted and expanded by other scholars in order to study other unbuilt works in any cultural context.

Secondly, all the information produced and recorded along the process can be useful to let other scholars, students and laypeople understand the amount and variety of work and tools involved in this kind of research projects. Usually, people that are not familiar with this kind of research projects may find it difficult to imagine how those visualizations were made.

Part of the information produced and recorded along the process is constituted by ca. 500 rendered images that document the 3D digital reconstruction process, including tests related to materials and lighting. A selection of these images can be disseminated in several ways, including during public exhibitions.

The process has been defined 'digitally handcrafted' because of, as mentioned in the introduction, the similarities with a handcrafted work. Studies of architectural heritage always require personalized approached and a modelling care similar to the creation of physical models and objects. The variety of architectural elements and shapes about different historical and cultural contexts do not allow using automated and standard approaches that are becoming more and more common in the design and construction of new building.

4.3 Digital Tools

The 2D redrawing and 3D digital reconstruction processes let also reflect upon the digital tools. Producing 2D drawings and 3D models within the same digital environment gives many benefits. Rhinoceros provides a wide range of precision and 2D drafting tools that are usually missing in pure 3D modelling software such as 3DS Max or Cinema 4D. At the same time, a powerful 2D drafting tools as AutoCAD does not offer the same range of 3D modelling tools and the flexibility provided by Rhinoceros.

Also, a BIM tool does not provide the same flexibility required in these kinds of research projects. In a BIM environment, the architectural elements are represented as 3D components. However, as in this case, there are situations when it is not necessary to create walls as 3D objects because it is not required by the project to represent the interior spaces. Hence, in this work, a 3D surface is the preferable solution.

In this kind of project, it is important to have a high level of control of the geometry of the architectural objects, in both 2D and 3D. In this regard, a software package as Rhinoceros may be more and more useful in architectural/digital heritage projects.

Texturing, rendering and animation were done in 3DS Max which offered powerful tools for UVW Unwrap. Improved and new tools within Rhino 6.0 will be explored in further projects.

5   Conclusions

This paper presented the process of creation of a set of visualizations and a short animation of Mackintosh's first design proposal for Scotland Street School.

Moreover, this piece of writing allowed to reflect on the work done and on key aspects that are usually overlooked such as the communication with the architectural historians and the educational aspects of the development process.

The digitally handcrafted quality of the work, which involves all the main phases of the process from the 2D drawings through the 3D digital modelling until the creation of the materials/textures, and its educational values have never been properly critically analyzed in other pieces of writing. A future paper will further explore this topic (together with the material produced during the development work) and its value, especially for architecture students.

This is the second piece of writing that investigates aspects of a building designed by Charles Rennie Mackintosh by using digital technologies. The research about the Glasgow School of Art presented in the previous paper [2] is still in progress, and new findings will be presented in future publications.

The application of this methodology to other historic buildings is also under consideration. Other case studies will allow exploring further and new functionalities of the used software packages and alternative digital tools.

Acknowledgements. The work was commissioned as part of the research project Mackintosh Architecture (Principal Investigator Professor Pamela Robertson, The Hunterian, The University of Glasgow). This major project was funded by the Arts and Humanities Research Board of the U.K. and was based at the University of Glasgow. The author also wants to thank Professor Pamela Robertson and Dr Robert Proctor, the two architectural historians who followed and supported the project with precious pieces of advice, and Professor Tom Maver for an informative visit of the building.

References

1. Pevsner, N.: Pioneers of Modern Design Penguin Books. Middlesex, Harmondsworth (1970)
2. Di Mascio, D., Maver, T.: Investigating a narrative architecture, Mackintosh's Glasgow School of Art. In: Proceedings of the 32nd eCAADe Conference, Newcastle upon Tyne, United Kingdom (2014)
3. Webb, N., Brown, A.: Augmenting critique of lost or unbuilt works of architecture using digitally mediated techniques. In: Proceedings of the 29th eCAADe Conference, Ljubljana, Slovenia (2011)
4. Webb, N., Brown, A.: Digital forensics as a tool for augmenting historical architectural analysis. case study: the student work of James stirling. In: Proceedings of the 16th CAADRIA Conference, Newcastle, Australia (2011)
5. Novitski, B.J.: Rendering Real and Imagined Buildings. Rockport Publisher, Gloucester (1998)
6. Cooper, J.: Mackintosh Architecture: The Complete Buildings and Selected Projects. Academy Editions/St. Martins Press, London (1978)
7. Billcliffe, R.: Visiting Charles Rennie Mackintosh. Frances Lincoln Limited Publishers, London (2012)
8. Crawford, A.: Charles Rennie Mackintosh. Thames and Hudson, London (2002)
9. Carrell, S., Brooks, L., Rawlinson, K.: Heartbreaking: fire guts Glasgow School of Art for second time. Mackintosh building restoration was nearly finished after smaller 2014 blaze (2018). https://www.theguardian.com/uk-news/2018/jun/16/firefighters-tackle-blaze-at-glasgow-school-of-art. Accessed 24 December 2018
10. Billcliffe, R.: Architectural Sketches & Flower Drawings by Charles Rennie Mackintosh. Academy Editions, London (1977)
11. Kliczkowski, S.: Charles Rennie Mackintosh, teNeues Publishing Group, Düsseldorf (1998)
12. Di Mascio, D.: Digital reconstruction and analysis of turchinio's trabocco: a method of digital reconstruction of a complex structure as a way to improve our knowledge of a cultural heritage artifact. In: Proceedings of the 4th ASCAAD Conference, Manama, Kingdom of Bahrain (2009)
13. Robertson, P., Sharples, J., Imrie, N.: Mackintosh Architecture: Context, Making and Meaning (2014). www.mackintosh-architecture.gla.ac.uk
14. Di Mascio, D., Chiuini, M., Fillwalk, J., Pauwels, P.: 3D digital reconstructions of lost buildings a first critical framing. In: Proceedings of the 34th eCAADe Conference, Oulu, Finland (2016)

Support Systems for Design Decisions

A Multi-resolution Design Methodology Based on Discrete Models

Manuel Ladron de Guevara[1]($\boxtimes$) (ID), Luis Borunda[2] (ID),
and Ramesh Krishnamurti[1] (ID)

[1] Carnegie Mellon University, Pittsburgh, PA 15213, USA
{manuelr, ramesh}@andrew.cmu.edu
[2] Universidad Politecnica de Madrid, 28040 Madrid, Spain
lborunda.eco@etsav.cat

Abstract. The use of programming languages in design opens up unexplored and previously unworkable territories, mainly, in conventional architectural practice. In the 1990s, languages of continuity, smoothness and seamlessness dominated the architectural inquiry with the CNC milling machine as its manufacturing tool. Today's computational design and fabrication technology look at languages of synthesis of fragments or particles, with the 3D printer as its fabrication archetype. Fundamental to this idea is the concept of resolution–the amount of information stored at any localized region. Construction of a shape is then based on multiple regions of resolution. This paper explores a novel design methodology that takes this concept of resolutions on discrete elements as a design driver for architectural practice. This research has been tested primarily through additive manufacturing techniques.

Keywords: Multi-resolution design methodology ·
Discrete-based computational design · Resolutions · Additive manufacturing

1 Introduction

Resolution is defined as the amount of data in a given region. Its application in architecture is relatively new, since conventional design processes do not operate on such raw data. Instead, architects manipulate geometries. In other fields, for example, imaging, the term resolution reflects the detail an image holds. Digital images measure resolution by its number of pixels each containing a masked color or grayscale value as data. Historically, resolution has been an issue in communication systems, as the transmission of images entails data conversion from the transmitting station to the receiving station; inventors Sharp and Thompson designed methods for augmenting resolution [1].

In architecture, resolution has been explored by architects Dillenburger and Hansmeyer [2] who define it as the number of voxels per volume, looking at the maximum resolution at which an additive manufacturing (AM) method can fabricate. In this research, however, resolution is the quantity of information at a localized region of a discretized 3-dimensional shape. It is important to note that a shape designed by a conventional design model cannot be measured by its resolution, for instance, when

© Springer Nature Singapore Pte Ltd. 2019
J.-H. Lee (Ed.): CAAD Futures 2019, CCIS 1028, pp. 91–104, 2019.
https://doi.org/10.1007/978-981-13-8410-3_7

geometry is manipulated using a modeling software. A resolution-based methodology is necessarily driven by manipulation of data through the use of programming tools.

Today's computational technologies offer the possibility to directly design in 3-dimensions without recourse to encoding and decoding shapes via 2-dimensional drawings. Furthermore, programming languages provide a means of constructing shapes through raw data without geometrical manipulation. Prior to the use of algorithms, the design process was purely intuitive, and designers normally made decisions based on what they perceived from visual feedback [3].

Technological advancement often comes with a period of exploration in which architects learn how to implement them [4]. In the late 1980s, with the introduction of CAD software, manual drafting was substituted by digital drafting; during the 1990s, software developed for industries such as film–Autodesk's 3D Studio, or aeronautics–Dassault Systemès' CATIA, were appropriated. Nonetheless, the essential paradigm remained the same: manipulation of geometry and modification based on visual feedback. On the fabrication side, the combination of CAD/CAM technologies created a seamless connection between design and manufacturing, which gave architects the possibility to re-gain their lost status as master builders [5].

Parametric tools, such as Grasshopper and Dynamo, have generalized visual scripting, augmenting the design process by the insertion of procedural logic and data management, facilitating contemporary avant-garde architectural styles such as, parametricism [6]. However, such tools neither, necessarily, address design in terms of discreteness nor resolution.

Discrete methods are normally used by analytical frameworks, for instance, finite element method (FEM), a numerical technique for solving problems such as structural analysis, heat transfer or fluid flow. An object is discretized into smaller units that are studied separately, yet as part of an integrative process. Karamba 3D by Clemens Preisinger or STAAD.Pro by Bentley, are examples of force distribution solvers. While these analyses can be integrated in the design process, there is no such generalized discrete design methodology.

This paper provides a step towards a new methodology of design, based on multi-resolution adjustments, using a discretization technique, which crafts raw data, without manipulating geometry. Resolution measured by the quantity of data in a given region is natural to this method. A localized region comprises a cluster of neighboring fragments, with information stored in a set of dictionary data structures, containing numerical and textual values, such as coordinates, material information, location, context awareness and Boolean values. Shape is understood as multiple dictionaries of information, which define its resolutions levels. In essence, this data construes discrete geometrical units informed by the fabrication process.

Additive fabrication technology needs a certain amount of data and machine time, does not involve reusable cast, mold or stamp, and does not require any voxel-generated volume to be identical to any other, regardless of scale or size. The marginal cost of a voxel is always the same, no matter how many we print. In this way, 3D printing brings the logic of customization from the macro to the micro scale of production of physical matter, and at previously unimagined levels of complexity and granularity [7]. Utilization of additive manufacturing methods is clearly ideal when designing with different resolutions.

2 State of the Art

2.1 Resolution

The notion of resolution as a driver in design fields is relatively new–it is linked to a recent computational revolution in which brand new science begets a new way of thinking, and to the advent of additive fabrication such as 3D printing [4]. The following designers include the word "resolution" in their descriptions. Voxel Chair and Curvoxels by Garcia and Retsin [8, 9], use a discrete approach specifically to directly design for a 3D Spatial printing fabrication. However, their design approach is not driven by concepts of resolution and is rather a medium for a specific fabrication method. The Computational Chair Design Studies by Phillipe Morel of EZCT Architecture & Design were among the earliest demonstrations of discrete approaches. Interestingly, a Finite Element Analysis (FEA) framework is used as a design tool. Digital Grotesque, by Dillenburger and Hansmeyer [2], is the first work to tackle resolution as a driver in design and fabrication. Their work is a manifestation of exuberance and a celebration of computational power. While resolution is their main motive, their project looks at the highest resolution possible, rather than taking resolution as a platform for multiple inquiry.

Recently, Andrasek [10] showcased the Croatian National Pavilion, Cloud Pergola, at the Venice Biennale. A large-scale robotic spatial printing workpiece is designed using algorithms for multi-agent systems (MAS). Her algorithm computes active discrete elements whose behavior is determined by a collection of rules. Although the resolution is the same across the piece, we can see the potential in designing through discrete approaches: this strategy yields a high performance at structural, material wastage and aesthetic capacities.

In other fields, common use of discrete methods includes volumetric imaging in medicine, representation of terrain in games and simulations, and granular flows and rock mechanics in engineering. A crucial stage in volume graphics is the synthesis of voxel-represented objects. This stage, called voxelization, is concerned with converting geometric objects from their continuous geometric representation into a set of voxels that approximates the object [11].

2.2 Fabrication

Additive manufacturing enables the fabrication of complex physical designs. One substantial research development specific to AM is the use of spatial deposition techniques [12, 13] capable of continuously extruding cellular lattice members in a spatial organization with minimal waste [14, 15]. Foams and spatial lattices provide multifunctional lightweight structures, high strength and relatively low mass [16, 17] and robotic AM [18] the precision required to manufacture. In order to manufacture complex geometries through a continuous deposition method, fabrication and computational methods that serialize the deposition process into a concatenation of units have been developed [9].

Research efforts focus on adapting resolution in the discretization process while maintaining the index concatenation required for the geometrically correct continuous deposition (Fig. 1). We can build upon advances in AM application to other disciplines such as bone reconstruction of graded porosity [19–21], in particular, to study bones at an architectural level in order to establish hierarchically and topologically different design principles [22, 23]. This research provides a spatial organization system of indexable units with differentiated performance, boundary and neighboring conditions of manufacture through continuous deposition maintaining geometrical continuity.

With resolution based design, such strategies may be translated into functional large-scale architectural components with potential for complex design of engineered anisotropy [24, 25] feasible through spatial AM.

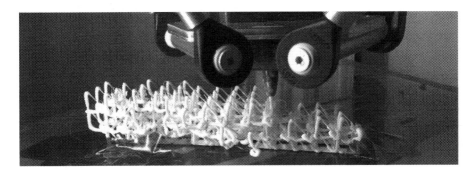

Fig. 1. 3D Spatial printing technique with a commercial delta 3D printer.

3 Method

3.1 Overview

The method proposed here examines the potential of designing an object using a discrete elements approach in order to configure its morphology to specific conditions through multi-resolution adjustments. This approach differs from resolution operations in other fields in that, here, resolution levels are seen as design opportunities, rather than understanding resolution as a measure of quality, particularly, as an operation for optimization. That is a characteristic from other areas such as imagery or medicine. Since we find potential niches in intertwining different resolution levels, this design technique is planned anew. The balance between higher and lower resolutions across the object corresponds to different design criteria such as aesthetic values, structural behavior, density, and material properties. Higher resolutions correspond to *interesting* regions, and lower resolutions target less *interesting* regions. That is, the algorithm behaves differently according to the degree of resolution, where the subdivision level quantifies the interesting regions and the type of information that qualifies them.

The number of regions of interest follow a design criterion, which depends on user demand, thus, the algorithm solution can be expanded, more or less, upon this. For this particular research, the algorithm considers variable density, opacity levels, and printable in-budget implementations. The algorithm is divided into three main parts:

shape analysis, grid structure, and discrete elements design. Understanding the fabrication end is imperative in this approach, since the affordances and limitations of material and tool define the design possibilities.

This research provides a step towards a design methodology based on multi-resolution adjustments. For simplicity, we show the potential of the method through the study of an ulna bone (Fig. 2) both as a design example, and as a potential application of this design and fabrication approach to other fields. Current research focuses on expanding the algorithm to a larger scale for architectural practice.

The algorithms are written in Python, and for visualization purposes, Grasshopper is used to transform numerical data into geometrical values, using the Rhino Common library.

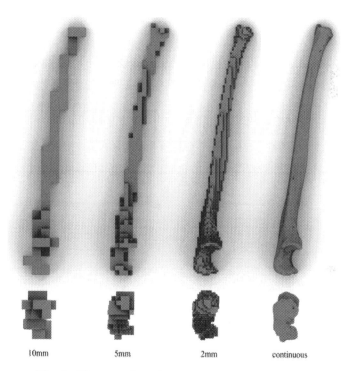

10mm   5mm   2mm   continuous

Fig. 2. Discrete and continuous models of the ulna bone.

3.2 Shape Analysis and Discretization Structure

The design process begins by taking the main geometry to be discretized as a closed mesh, surface or poly-surface. Its boundaries are calculated, and the mesh repositioned at the origin. A 3-dimensional multi-sized grid is constructed and automatically adjusted to the size of the initial volume, based on the number of rows, columns and floors, with values corresponding to the respective boundary dimensions divided by a default resolution size. This resolution value, R, specifies the size of a voxel $R \times R \times R$ (Fig. 3). The grid structure is used to specify the voxels that lie inside or outside the initial volume through an octree data structure [26] of true/false values. Computationally, the grid defines an object class, containing dictionaries of data of the interesting region, subdivision levels, and geometry and material properties.

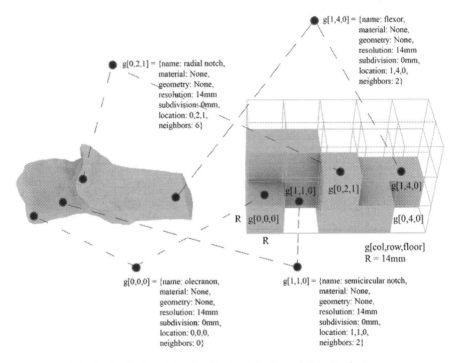

Fig. 3. Studied model and grid at a default resolution R of 14 mm.

3.3   Arxel

An *Arxel* is an informed digital architectural unit. It is a voxel with an overlapping agenda of material properties, economy, geometry and performative data such as structural behavior, opacity and density variations. Arxels are understood in dependency with their surrounding arxels. As a data unit an arxel is an information container, rather than a geometrical element, and it is structured as a set of dictionaries. Its boundary is defined by eight coordinates corresponding to its vertices. The boundary, however, is only for visualization purposes; it does not possess any geometrical value.

3.4   Multi-resolution

The resolutions of the main volume are constructed by the scrutiny of interesting regions. A volume can have one or more different resolutions. A default resolution is defined at the beginning of the process, normally informed by the fabrication tool, and new resolutions are given by the said interesting regions. In our implementation these are selected directly in the Rhino view-space and linked to Grasshopper. The subdivision level corresponding to these regions responds to a design criterion and limitations on the fabrication, where the algorithm is able to compute different degrees of resolution altogether (Fig. 4). Ray casting is used to retrieve the Boolean value at each arxel, yielding true, if its centroid falls inside the interesting regions, and false, otherwise. This information is passed in the form of a dictionary, which is then read by a function that subdivides the arxels based on the subdivision level. Level = 1 subdivides the arxel into 8 smaller units, level 2 subdivides it into 64 units, and so on. An algorithm similar to an octree approach is developed to form a multi-resolution grid. The algorithm restricts each arxel with a false value to level 0, the default level of resolution. In order to bridge between a conventional IDE and the Rhino-3D environment and geometry created in GH-Python, the grid information is exported as a Javascript json file.

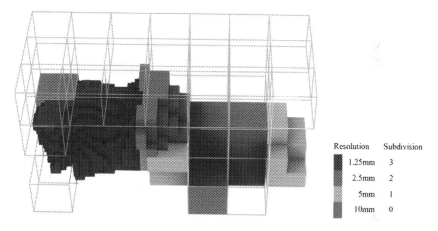

Fig. 4. Resolutions levels

3.5 Design Discreteness

This section has two parts. The first describes a general approach to design discreteness without considering limitations of fabrication; the second implements specific features such as material budget responsiveness and consideration of constraints on the 3D spatial printing technique for manufacturing purposes, such as printing order and collision checks.

3.6 Basic Configuration

This process takes, as input, information relating to the resolutions of the object from the previously exported data file, to start the design. This is informed by the fabrication side, and natural to the process is the creation of a linear language where the geometry is directly used as toolpath [9, 27]. However, we insert different XYZ-coordinates that are connected with lines only for purposes of visualization. The creation and manipulation of geometry is restricted to the management of numerical values (1). For instance, a rotation of an arxel through angle α is given by:

$$x' = x \cos \alpha - y \sin \alpha \qquad (1)$$

$$y' = x \cos \alpha + y \cos \alpha$$

No direct manipulation of geometrical models is made. A set of six numerical matrix configurations is designed, increasing in shape complexity to ensure disparity between the options at shown in Fig. 5. For instance, an region within the given volume that may require a higher structural reinforcement could be achieved by placing denser geometries to the detriment of simpler ones. Similarly, regions with higher degrees of opacity might be better determined by denser geometries. Each geometrical configuration is placed within the boundary of an arxel, selected upon design specifications. In order to increase options for design and fabrication, four 90° rotations along the Z axis are also added to the set, augmenting each initial grammar by four, having a set of 24 shapes.

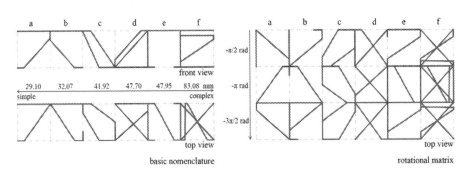

Fig. 5. Matrix configurations

3.7 Design for Manufacturing

Fabrication is based on 3D spatial printing techniques: we create a design language based on linear segments, constrained by material and tool properties. For instance, a delta type 3D printer, which extrudes 1.75 mm filaments of polylactic acid (PLA) or acrylonitrile butadiene styrene (ABS), will constrain certain design decisions. The nozzle of the printer defines the angle between the linear segments of a polyline and the height of an arxel.

The printing order informs the position of the numerical configurations at each arxel to avoid collisions with already printed geometries. The printing order follows the logical positioning of the arxels within the grid, in the order of columns (Y axis), rows (X axis) and floors (Z axis). That is the algorithm starts positioning the first numerical matrix at the 0th column, 0th row and 0th floor indices, the next matrix is placed at the 1st column, 0th row, and 0th floor. At this point it is necessary to check whether the chosen matrix may collide with an already printed neighboring arxels. For instance, at the position col = 1, row = 0, floor = 0, only the arxel at position (col-1, row) needs to be checked. At the position, say, col = 3, row = 5, floor = 0, the list of arxels [(col − 1, row − 1), (col − 1, row), (col + 1, row), (col, row − 1)] should be checked. A backtracking algorithm is implemented to find a valid solution following the pseudo-code below:

```
def solvePrintable(i, printedD):
if isCompleted:
return geometries
  for matrix in matrixSet:
    if grid[col,row,floor] == subdivided:
      k = [col+i, row, floor]
      printedD[col,row,floor] = matrix
      if isValidMatrixForSubdivision:
        sol=solvePrintable(i+1, printedD)
        if sol != None:
          return geometries
    else:
      k = [col+i, row, floor]
      printedD[col,row,floor] = matrix
      if isValidMatrixNonSubdivided:
        sol=solvePrintable(i+1, printedD)
        if sol != None:
          return geometries
    printed[col,row,floor] = -10
  return None
```

To check whether an arxel might collide with previously printed arxels, a comparison is made between each of its coordinates and the already printed coordinates, such that $zP > z$, $-xP < x < xP$ and $-yP < y < yP$, being xP, yP, zP already printed coordinates. The domains {−xP, +xP} and {−yP, +yP} correspond to the nozzle dimensions. The complexity of the algorithm increases at the subdivided voxels, since these arxels are formed by matrixes of matrixes equivalent to the level of resolution.

Similar to the backtracking strategy explained above, an algorithm that finds a valid solution responding to material length limit is computed. To adjust the overall piece within a material constraint, calculation of the distance of the coordinates at each voxel is required in order to know the total printed length of the piece. If the total length is more than the given material budget value, the algorithm selects pseudo-randomly non-subdivided arxels, since these correspond to less interesting regions. Their matrix is changed and tested procedurally, passing tests if the overall length is less than the previous state and still above the material budget. If so, another arxel is selected, changed and tested until finding a solution that fits in the budget. If no solution is found, earlier design decisions such as the size or quantity of interesting regions, or the base resolution should be modified.

4   Case Study

An ulna bone is used as the case study since its complex morphology requires different levels of resolutions. Furthermore, applying our design approach at a human scale first will inform bigger and more complex architectures. Our approach is tested through a bone structure as it does not demand those real-world requirements that a building component would, thereby, avoiding factors such as load forces or environmental considerations. Furthermore, we acknowledge that the spatial printing technique is still under research, making it difficult to apply directly to a larger scale such as a building component. Rather, we focus the research on the natural alignment that a cancellous bone tissue provides with a cellular 3d spatial printable structure. We apply a higher degree of resolution to the ulna's radial and semicircular notch through the definition of a localized sphere, and also, we reinforce the ulna's coronoid process via definition of a spline (Fig. 6). We maintain lower resolutions in the rest of the bone.

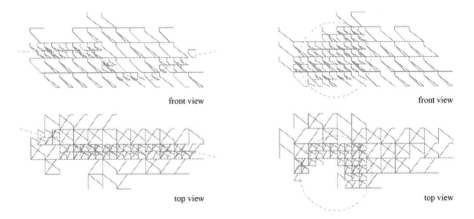

Fig. 6. Selection by spline (left) and by volume (right)

The case study begins with an analysis of the ulna, extracting its dimensions and decreasing the scale by two thirds for fabrication in a conventional 3D delta printer. Initial tests with different defaulted resolution are made to assess the degree of information that satisfies the purposes of this research. For the initial analysis, we use the arxels' boundary representation, that is, equilateral cuboids, for visualization purposes. Upon determining the interesting regions of the ulna, we compute the levels of subdivision based on the amount of information at the notch and at the internal stress line as shown in Fig. 6. The design process continues by automated selection of the type of geometry that best suits the specific location at the bone. That is, since the grid stores information on the piece such as the number of components or parts, regions of interest or structural analysis, we define denser regions where a higher structural capacity is required, and the algorithm selects those grammars within the set that fit the needs.

Once the selection of the resolutions and type of geometry of the discrete elements that form the bone satisfies the design conditions, the backtracking algorithm for fabrication is enacted, where a fabrication solution is found without altering the situated conditions across the piece. For simplicity, no multi-material is implemented since we use a conventional nozzle in the 3D printer. Instead, PLA is used for early prototyping (Fig. 7).

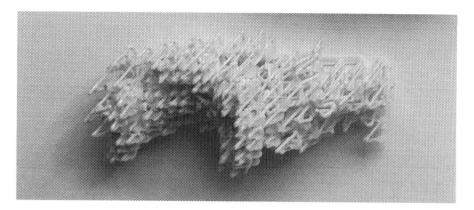

Fig. 7. 3D printed ulna bone applying multi-resolution algorithm

5   Results and Discussions

This paper contributes to a design methodology based on multi-resolution adjustments as avenues of opportunity. This is only now feasible as the design methodology represents a change in design thinking spurred by a computational revolution and the advent of 3D printers. It is now when we can start talking about resolution in architecture.

The design method presents numerous limitations that should be overcome with more research in both the computational part and physical tool development. This research uses recursion as a main strategy for subdivision; this is computationally expensive and relatively complex. On the other hand, subdivision follows a recursive logic that might be quicker to apply than other alternatives. Data structures such as dictionaries or sets are used, as their hashable nature optimizes the operation time. Also, designing within a frame of spatial printing presents even more constraints. The fidelity between the digital model and the physical model fabricated in a 3D delta printer differs around a 17%. The segment-like nature of the geometry also limits the design scope. Combined strategies between spatial printing and conventional 3D printing is under research by the authors.

The ulna bone was chosen as the design study, since the degree of complexity of a bone is convenient to assess the potential benefits and limitations of this design approach. Moreover, understanding it at a human scale informs possible design considerations at an architectural scale. The authors of this paper acknowledge that this is only a small step towards a larger design process. However, this design approach can be understood at a higher level, by considering new computational and fabrication tools available to explore alternative design methods. We have used a multi-resolution approach that is limited to different geometrical and scale outputs that define structural behavior and different density levels. However, this approach can be expanded in multi-materiality and multi-fabrication techniques, and also the exploration of novel aesthetic meanings. Similar to the shift of the meaning of the value of the ornament in architecture [7], new aesthetic values might arise as the result of design alternatives.

Although this paper attempts to generalize a discrete approach, we understand that a relatively high level of computation is needed in order to follow this design process. Also, a sophisticated understanding of the material and the machine is required if the design seeks to leave the digital environment. The physical pieces presented in this paper (Fig. 8) require some level of knowledge about hacking commercial 3D printers. The design space is conducive to creative exploration, and the understanding of resolution through other fabrication techniques remains open.

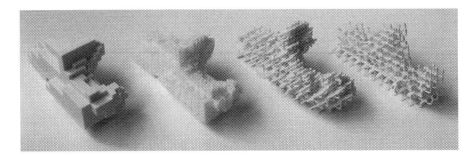

Fig. 8. Studied ulna 3D printed pieces

Acknowledgements. The authors would like to thank the following organizations that funded this research; The Frank Ratchye Fund for Art @ the Frontier (FRFAF), Consejo Social de la Universidad Politécnica de Madrid and the National Council of Science and Technology of Mexico.

References

1. Sharp, J.V., Thompson, D.R.: Method and apparatus for increasing image resolution (1971)
2. Dillenburger, B., Hansmeyer, M.: The resolution of architecture in the digital age. Commun. Comput. Inf. Sci. **369**, 347–357 (2013). https://doi.org/10.1007/978-3-642-38974-0_33
3. Oxman, R.: Educating the designerly thinker. Des. Stud. **20**, 105–122 (1999). https://doi.org/10.1016/S0142-694X(98)00029-5
4. Carpo, M.: The Second Digital Turn: Design Beyond Intelligence. MIT Press, Cambridge (2017)
5. Cardoso, D.: Builders of the Vision, p. 208 (2012)
6. Schumacher, P.: Parametricism: a new global style for architecture and urban design. Archit. Des. **79**, 14–23 (2009). https://doi.org/10.1002/ad.912

7. Carpo, M.: Excessive resolution: from digital streamlining to computational complexity. Archit. Des. **86**, 78–83 (2016). https://doi.org/10.1002/ad.2114

8. Garcia, M.J.: A generalized approach to non-layered fused filament fabrication. In: ACADIA 2017 Disciplines & Disruption, pp. 562–571 (2017)

9. Retsin, G., Jiménez García, M.: Discrete computational methods for robotic additive manufacturing. In: Fabricate 2017, pp. 178–184 (2017). https://doi.org/10.14324/111.9781787350014

10. Sanchez, J., Andrasek, A.: Bloom. In: Fabricate 2014, DGO-Digi, pp. 98–103. UCL Press (2017)

11. Yagel, R., Cohen, D., Kaufman, A., et al.: Volume graphics. Computer (Long Beach Calif) **26**, 51–64 (1993). https://doi.org/10.1109/MC.1993.274942

12. Wu, R., Peng, H., Guimbretière, F., Marschner, S.: Printing arbitrary meshes with a 5DOF wireframe printer. ACM Trans. Graph. **35**, 1–9 (2016). https://doi.org/10.1145/2897824.2925966

13. Mueller, S., Im, S., Gurevich, S., et al.: WirePrint. In: Proceedings of the 27th Annual ACM Symposium on User Interface Software and Technology - UIST 2014, pp. 273–280. ACM Press, New York (2014)

14. Reynolds, D., Tam, K.-M.M., Otani, R., Poulsen, E.: Equivalent material modelling of complex additive manufactured conformal lattices. In: Proceedings of the IASS Annual Symposium 2017. International Association for Shell and Spatial Structures (IASS), Hamburg, pp. 1–10 (2017)

15. Pasquarelli, G., Sharples, W., Sharples, C., et al.: Additive manufacturing revolutionizes lightweight gridshells. In: Proceedings of the IASS Annual Symposium 2017. International Association for Shell and Spatial Structures (IASS), Hamburg (2017)

16. Cheung, K.C.: Digital Cellular Solids: Reconfigurable composite materials. Massachusetts Institute of Technology (2012)

17. Gibson, L., Ashby, M.: Cellular Solids: Structure and Properties. Cambridge University Press, Cambridge (1999)

18. Willmann, J., Gramazio, F., Kohler, M., Langenberg, S.: Digital by material. In: Brell-Çokcan, S., Braumann, J. (eds.) Rob | Arch 2012, pp. 12–27. Springer, Vienna (2013). https://doi.org/10.1007/978-3-7091-1465-0_2

19. Feng, J., Fu, J., Shang, C., et al.: Porous scaffold design by solid T-splines and triply periodic minimal surfaces. Comput. Methods Appl. Mech. Eng. **336**, 333–352 (2018). https://doi.org/10.1016/j.cma.2018.03.007

20. Wang, S., Zhou, L., Luo, Z., et al.: Lightweight of artificial bone models utilizing porous structures and 3D printing. Int. J. Perform. Eng. **13**, 633–642 (2017). https://doi.org/10.23940/ijpe.17.05.p8.633642

21. Yoo, D.J.: Porous scaffold design using the distance field and triply periodic minimal surface models. Biomaterials **32**, 7741–7754 (2011). https://doi.org/10.1016/j.biomaterials.2011.07.019

22. Gibson, L.J.: The mechanical behaviour of cancellous bone. J. Biomech. **18**, 317–328 (1985). https://doi.org/10.1016/0021-9290(85)90287-8

23. Liebschner, M., Wettergreen, M.: Optimization of bone scaffold engineering for load bearing applications. In: Topics in Tissue Engineering Bone II, Part II, vol. 1, chap. 6, pp. 1–39 (2003)

24. Oxman, N.: Virtual and physical prototyping variable property rapid prototyping. **6**, 3–31 (2011). https://doi.org/10.1080/17452759.2011.558588

25. Fleck, N.A., Deshpande, V.S., Ashby, M.F.: Micro-architectured materials: past, present and future. Proc. R. Soc. A Math. Phys. Eng. Sci. **466**, 2495–2516 (2010). https://doi.org/10.1098/rspa.2010.0215

26. Meagher, D.: Geometric modeling using octree encoding. Comput. Graph. Image Process. **19**, 129–147 (1982). https://doi.org/10.1016/0146-664X(82)90104-6
27. Liu, S., Li, Y., Li, N.: A novel free-hanging 3D printing method for continuous carbon fiber reinforced thermoplastic lattice truss core structures. Mater. Des. **137**, 235–244 (2018). https://doi.org/10.1016/j.matdes.2017.10.007

An Experimental Archaeology of CAD

Using Software Reconstruction to Explore the Past and Future of Computer-Aided Design

Daniel Cardoso Llach[(⊠)] and Scott Donaldson

Computational Design Laboratory, School of Architecture,
Carnegie Mellon University, Pittsburgh, USA
dcardoso@cmu.edu

Abstract. This paper proposes software reconstruction as a method to shed new light into the material, gestural, and sensual dimensions of computer-aided design technologies. Specifically, it shows how by combining historical research and creative prototyping this method can bring us closer to distant ways of seeing, touching, drawing, and designing—while raising new questions about the impact of CAD technologies on present-day architectural practices. It documents the development of two software reconstructions—of Ivan Sutherland's "Sketchpad" and of Steven A. Coons's "Coons Patch"—and reflects on the responses they elicited in the context of two exhibitions. The paper shows how software reconstruction can offer access to overlooked aspects of computer-aided design systems, specially their material and sensual dimensions, and how we may explore its broader potential for research, preservation, pedagogy, and speculative design of design technologies.

Keywords: Software reconstruction · Media archaeology · CAD · Sketchpad · Steven A. Coons · Ivan Sutherland · Computational design history

1 Introduction

Computer-aided design (CAD) systems are artifacts of cultural and technical significance which shape the intellectual labor and professional identities of many architects, engineers, and other designers. Recent scholarship on these technologies, and their impact on architecture, has examined their intellectual and institutional origins [1, 2], studied the dynamics of their adoption by practitioners and educators [3–6], examined their implications in professional cultures [7, 8], and explored their effects on architectural organizations and labor [9–11]. However, the usual vehicles of scholarly research—text and, at best, illustrations—fail to account for their material, sensual, and gestural dimensions, which are central to the new experiences, and the new types of practice, that they elicited. This paper reports on Archaeology of CAD, a research project initiated by the first author combining historical research and creative technology design in order to enrich our understanding of these systems by experimentally reconstructing some of its pioneering technologies. Accordingly, the paper introduces software reconstruction as a method of inquiry into computer-aided design and—more

© Springer Nature Singapore Pte Ltd. 2019
J.-H. Lee (Ed.): CAAD Futures 2019, CCIS 1028, pp. 105–119, 2019.
https://doi.org/10.1007/978-981-13-8410-3_8

generally—software artifacts, with ties to media archaeological and historical recon-struction practices. It then documents our reconstruction of two foundational CAD technologies: Steven A. Coons's "Coons Patch", and Ivan Sutherland's "Sketchpad". It offers details about their development, which involved the analysis of both original archival and oral sources, as well as a creative process involving technological re-interpretations, translations, and adaptations.

The paper further documents the public installation of the two reconstructions in exhibitions at the Miller Gallery at Carnegie Mellon University, Pittsburgh, and in the SIGGRAPH 2018 Art Gallery, Vancouver. It shows how by approximating the logical, gestural, and ergonomic signature of these systems, the reconstructions helped make visible (and tangible) the new forms of design, drawing, and human-machine inter-action that emerged with the rise of interactive computing. Finally, the paper discusses some avenues for future work, as well as implications of software reconstruction for scholarly research, pedagogy, preservation, and speculative technology design.

2   Software Reconstruction as Method

Software reconstruction draws inspiration from well-established practices of experi-mental reworking in archaeology and the historiography of science and technology. Archaeologists studying material culture have long used the term "experimental archaeology" to describe a host of research methods aiming at reproducing the material conditions of specific practices and processes [12]. More recently, historians of science and technology have used experimental reworkings as a complement to textual anal-ysis, and as a method to shed light on gaps in archival documentation—which typically overlooks "sensual" aspects of scientific practices such as smell or touch [13: 91]. In this way reworkings of historical experiments can offer richer portraits of the material and social conditions surrounding scientific and technological production.

Software reconstruction also derives insight from the "undisciplined discipline" of media archaeology [14: 323], which has sought to enrich the analytical repertoire of media scholars by re-covering and re-contextualizing media artifacts, and by reflecting upon the "regimes of memory" they elicit [15: 2]. In a similar vein, recent work in human-computer interaction (HCI) has sought, for example, to enliven material prac-tices of early computing incorporating them into renewed, feminist accounts of the history of technology [16], or to revisit, through playful prototyping, salient artifacts in the history of cybernetics [17]. These practices strand the scholarly and the artistic, and involve the "creative remediation" [15: 142] of technological artifacts as a path towards scholarly and/or creative inquiry. As proposed here, software reconstruction shares with these works a desire to "thinker" with the past [18], and to performatively "re-presence" it [14] in ways that foreground the materialities and dispositions of tech-nological objects, rather than focusing on their narrative disclosures. Unique to soft-ware reconstruction as proposed here is its concern with recuperating and reflecting upon the gestural, ergonomic, and visual repertoires enabled by past design tools.

It is important to note that the goal of software reconstruction is not to replicate or restore the original hardware and software systems as an antiquarian would do—this would result on a cybernetic version of Madame Tussaud's museum—filled with uncanny, glass-eyed look-alikes of technical artifacts. Accordingly, software reconstruction does not require, for example, old mainframe computers or CRT monitors, nor re-writing programs in assembly language. As the examples documented below show, they can be constructed with modern languages (Java and JavaScript), digital fabrication devices (laser cutters and CNC routers), and hardware components (low-cost screens and controllers). However productive exact replicas might be, the more humble—and more agile—technical repertoire of software reconstruction suits best its goal of approximating the experience of using these technologies by enacting their fundamental logic and their key visual, gestural, and ergonomic signatures.

3   Two Reconstructions

3.1   Reconstructing the "Coons Patch"

The "Coons Patch" is a mathematical technique to calculate curved surfaces, developed in the early 1960s by MIT professor of mechanical engineering, computer graphics pioneer, and early CAD theorist and promoter Steven A. Coons [19]. A direct ancestor of non-uniform rational B-splines (NURBS), Coons's technique was, in essence, a clever interpolation algorithm. It allowed early computer graphics researchers to create smooth surfaces between any four parametrically defined curves (Fig. 1). Displayed in the phosphorescent light of CRT monitors, these "patches" were photographed, animated, and then circulated in both research and industry circles through books, films, and research reports. Robin Forrest, one of Coons's students, offers a succinct overview of Coons's technique: "the algorithm provides a means of generating a free-form curved surface from any four arbitrary, boundary-defining curves, parameterized such that for any t between 0 and 1, one can find the point on the curve at parameter t, and with the curves joined at the endpoints" [20]. These patches were key in demonstrating the computer's potential as a modeling and visualization tool with applications in a variety of fields including aeronautic, automotive, and architectural design. Further, they helped trigger a fledgling computer graphics community as it formed across dispersed university and industry laboratories on both sides of the Atlantic—many of whose members came to see Coons as an inspiring, founding figure [1: 49–72]. The "Coons Patch" thus foreshadowed present-day methods for parametric surface representation and manipulation, which are ubiquitous in architectural, engineering, and product design today.

As an algorithm, the "Coons Patch" does not have an associated hardware interface —it is "platform independent". Its earliest implementations involved direct manipulation of numerical values in matrices, and working with memory registers in mainframe computers such as the TX-2 at Lincoln Labs [21]. Given that a curve in its cubic form can be represented mathematically by two end points and two control points, a "Coons Patch" may be represented by 36 floating point numbers: four three-dimensional endpoints, and eight three-dimensional control points. Individually adjusting 36 numbers in order to transform a design would surely exceed the patience of the average present-day designer, but this is how a computational designer of this era operated. For example, a 1967 Ford Motors product research film produced at the MIT

Lincoln Labs shows the construction of patches and their placement as car parts [22]. The process of preparing this two-and-a-half minute animation "hardcoding" the numerical values describing the shape of the patch at each frame—as well as the coordinates of the camera's position—must have been painstaking.

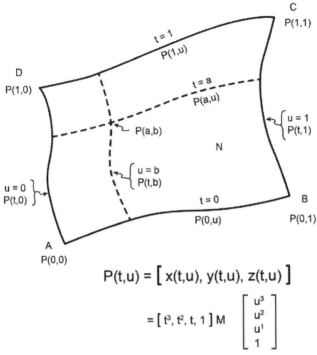

$$P(t,u) = \left[\, x(t,u),\, y(t,u),\, z(t,u) \,\right]$$

$$= \left[\, t^3, t^2, t, 1 \,\right] M \begin{bmatrix} u^3 \\ u^2 \\ u^1 \\ 1 \end{bmatrix}$$

where M is a 4 x 4 matrix of 3-component vectors
defining points, slopes and twists.

Fig. 1. The "Coons patch" foreshadowed modern methods of surface representation, such as NURBS, which have since become commonplace in architectural and engineering design. Image based on a drawing by Robin Forrest (c. 1970).

Our reconstruction streamlines this process in order to emphasize the geometric plasticity of Coons's technique, and make visible its mathematical structure. A small keypad interface and a knob placed on a 10″ × 10″ podium in front of a projection wall allow users to toggle the point controls on and off, and manually move them along the X, Y, and Z axes. When points are active, their changing numerical coordinates are displayed, making visible the mathematical structure of the patch as the user transforms it (Fig. 2). Aside from manipulating individual points in sequence, a user may choose to randomly transform the entire surface.

Our reconstruction does this by translating each end and control point by a random amount within a bounded range for each dimension, and animating the transformation between the current and target states. Users may then rotate or zoom the camera to view the surface from another perspective, manipulate individual points, or restore the surface to its initial form—a unit square on the XY plane, centered at the origin. When left unattended, the patch randomly transforms itself every 20 s.

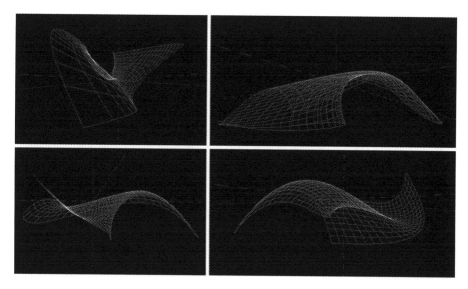

Fig. 2. Examples of patches generated using the software reconstruction of the "Coons Patch". The images illustrate the geometric plasticity of shapes generated using Coons's technique.

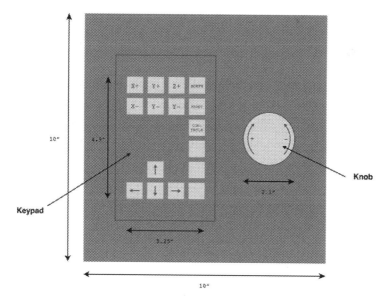

Fig. 3. A simple hardware interface allows users of the reconstruction to visualize and manipulate "Coons Patches".

Our reconstruction is a web-based app implemented using Three.js, a 3d graphics and rendering library for the web and React, a user interface development framework streamlined to work with present-day browsers. An advantage of Three.js is its harnessing of WebGL, a powerful low-level language for web graphics that is hardware-accelerated to optimize computational geometry and rendering. React is a popular component-based framework that streamlines the process of making HTML elements interactive, and centralizes the state of an app. In this reconstruction the state may change depending on whether a user is manipulating the geometric surface, rotating the camera, or viewing the tutorial. The app's visual display updates based on this state (for example, to zoom in or out, or show the tutorial overlay).

On the hardware side, a keypad and control knob integrate with the "Coons Patch" software via user events native to the web (Fig. 3). The app 'listens' for keypress and scroll events and, depending on the React state, performs computations and updates the visual display, a wall projection, accordingly.

3.2   Reconstructing "Sketchpad"

"Sketchpad" is a computer program developed in 1963 by Ivan Sutherland, which famously pioneered graphic user interfaces and laid out the foundations of present-day CAD systems. "Sketchpad" was the centerpiece of Sutherland's PhD thesis at MIT, for which Steven A. Coons was an advisor [23]. In contrast with Coons's "patch", Sutherland's "Sketchpad" was platform specific. It was in fact made possible by the TX-2 computer at Lincoln Labs, which allowed Sutherland to develop "Sketchpad" as an interactive, rather as a batch processing, system. Using a "light pen", a keypad, and control knobs "Sketchpad" users could conduct a variety of drawing operations on $7'' \times 7''$ CRT monitor. Aside from functions for drawing lines, circles, polygons, and other shapes, Sutherland also implemented functions that extended beyond the capabilities of traditional drafting media. For example, he included "save" and "transform" functions, as well as "rubber-banding" and "linkages"—known today in parametric modeling lingo as "constraints". Notably, many of the innovative features that Sutherland included in "Sketchpad" remain central to modern 3-D modeling and computer-aided design systems today, more than 60 years after its development. "Sketchpad" thus remains a milestone in the history of computing, and an essential point of reference for computer-aided design.

Sutherland programmed "Sketchpad" directly in assembly language on the TX-2 computer—its entities were written, retrieved, and manipulated directly in the computer's memory at the hardware level. In order to store these entities, Sutherland used an innovative data structure he calls "n-component elements". The "n" refers to the variable size of geometric entities—for example, a line segment may require less storage space than a more complex shape. Objects occupying variable amounts of space in memory could be stored as "n consecutive registers in storage", all locatable in TX-2's core memory [23: 35]. Thanks to the higher-level abstractions made available by present-day programming languages, this way of working—addressing memory locations directly in the hardware—is mostly a relic of the past. In our reconstruction geometric entities are simply instances of custom objects implemented in the object-oriented programming language Java. A line segment in our reconstruction, for example, contains references to two points, which we call *p1* and *p2*. This is nearly identical to the way "Sketchpad" stored line segments by referring to its points externally. However, instead of relying on machine-specific registers and memory addresses, we use object named classes and instance data. This abstraction, as well as the support of drawing APIs and the Android software development kit (SDK), allow our code to run, with small concessions, on any Android device. Approximating the original "Sketchpad" interface, a user may use a combination of "light pen" and knobs gestures to draw geometric elements on the screen and to move, manipulate, copy, or delete them (Fig. 4). It is also possible to create compound objects such as, for example, a triangle inscribed in a circle, and for the individual entities to then act as one —moving, scaling, rotating, copying, and deleting in tandem.

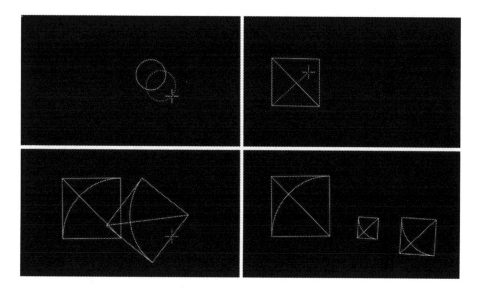

Fig. 4. Examples of drawings made using the "Sketchpad" reconstruction. Top left illustrates the "copy" function. Top right illustrates "rubberbanding". Bottom left illustrates the "rotate function". Bottom right illustrates the instantiation of compound objects.

Our reconstruction relies on modern devices to approximate many of "Sketchpad's" functions, as well as its key visual, gestural, and ergonomic traits. It evokes the TX-2's original user interface of flywheels, switches, and keypad with low-cost hardware including an Android tablet, a series of control knobs, a keypad, and a stylus (Fig. 5). These hardware elements are organized in a custom work station designed to approximate the ergonomics of the TX-2 desk. Instead of reconstructing or restoring an actual mainframe computer, we use a small Android touch-screen tablet. Instead of using a "photodiode and transistor preamplifier" [23: 55] as a light-pen, we use the tablet's stylus, which requires no additional hardware or software integration.

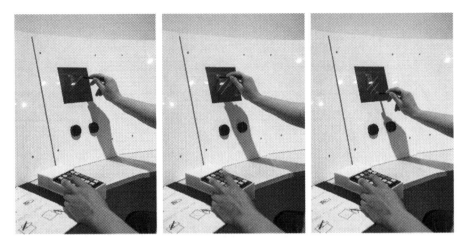

Fig. 5. Demonstration of a drawing procedure using the "Sketchpad" reconstruction. Photo credit: Tom Little (2017).

4   Results

This section documents the software reconstructions in the context of two different exhibitions, and our observations of their engagements with the public.

4.1   Engaging an Architectural and Academic Audience

The reconstructions were first included as elements of the design of the exhibition *Designing the Computational Image, Imagining Computational Design*, curated by the first author. The exhibition, which was on display between September 22 and November 12 of 2017, showcased "rare photographs, film, high-quality reproductions, and interactive software reconstructions examining the formative period of numerical control and Computer-Aided Design technologies, along with a selection of experimental work by computational designers working today" [24]. The exhibition, which was free and open to the public, was visited by an estimate of 1,600 people, in addition to the 200 who visited the exhibition during the opening. In this context, the software reconstructions complemented the exhibition's curated artworks, which comprised mostly visual materials.

The "Coons Patch" reconstruction was placed in a section entitled "Structured Images" among a selection of historical materials describing the origins of computer graphics and computational geometry. Directly behind the reconstruction was a series of handwritten notes by Steven A. Coons describing the technique, and its potential for design (Fig. 6). Nearby video screens displayed works from Lincoln Labs [22] along with contemporary pieces. The "Sketchpad" reconstruction was placed in a separate section of the exhibition entitled "Interaction and Intelligence" among a selection of materials and artworks describing the influence of early artificial intelligence ideas in design (Fig. 7). "Sketchpad" was placed besides a 1963 procedurally-generated painting by design theorist George Stiny. Juxtaposing two radically different paradigms of computational design—one visual, and another numerical—were thus juxtaposed.

Aside from offering additional context to the historical and contemporary pieces, the reconstructions helped enliven the space and became points of attraction. Additionally, as weeks passed bugs and areas of improvement were identified, some of which were addressed for the reconstructions' second show.

Fig. 6. At the Miller Gallery, the "Coons Patch" software reconstruction was installed among a curated selection of materials from the history of computer graphics. Image Credits: Tom Little (top and bottom right) and Joshua Brown (bottom left).

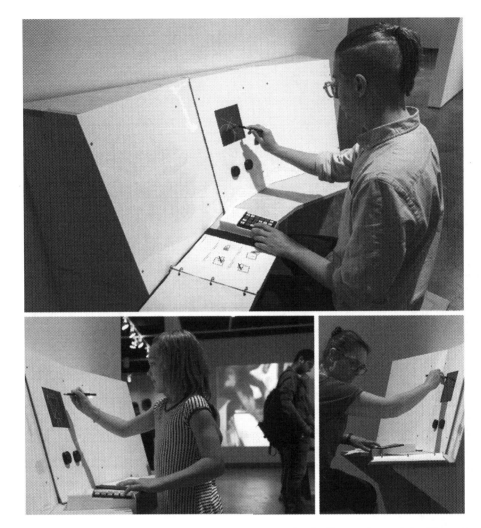

Fig. 7. The reconstruction of "Sketchpad" was placed in the "Interaction and Intelligence" section of the exhibition, among artworks that described the postwar intersection of ideas about artificial intelligence, cognition, and design. Photo credits: Tom Little (2017).

4.2   Engaging a Diverse, Computer-Focused Audience

The second exhibition took place in the SIGGRAPH 2018 Art Gallery in Vancouver. The show was "conceived as a dialogical space that enables the viewer to reflect on man's diverse cultural values and rituals through contemporary creative practices" and explored the concept of "origins"—broadly understood to encompass not only the technological but also the cultural and ethnic dimensions of the term.

Accordingly, in contrast to the previous exhibition, which had a clear focus on the history and contemporary practice of computer-aided design, this exhibition encompassed a more diverse selection of artworks and themes, including new media artworks by native American artists, interactive films, and historical pieces by computational art pioneers, curated by Andres Burbano. Featured artists included Ruth Wilson, Skawenatti, Nicole L'Huillier, and John Edmonds, among others. During this relatively short period the reconstructions were used by hundreds of people.

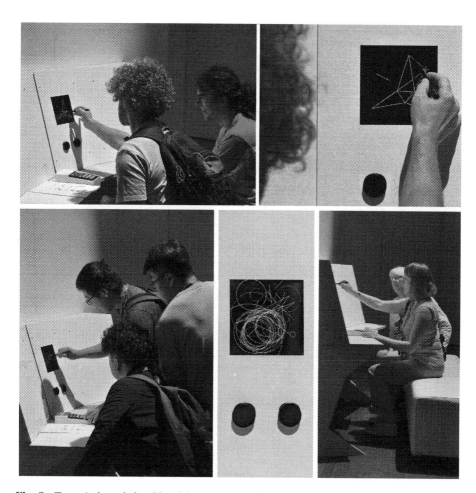

Fig. 8. Top: A knowledgeable visitor uses the "Sketchpad" reconstruction to explain the concept of parametric linkages. Bottom: The reconstruction encouraged different kinds of social interaction—from the playful to the rigorous. Photos by the authors.

In this context, the reconstructions addressed the exhibition's concept of "origin" by invoking the earliest computer graphics and computer-aided design techniques, which were central to the origin of the conference itself. Given the different context, both pieces were concentrated in a single space—on opposite sides of a "fat wall". Which also and incorporating a tablet for the interactive display of contextual information about the pieces. The whole installation occupied an area of 120″ × 190″ with the "fat wall" dividing it through the short side at 60″. Instead of additional pieces from the history of CAD, on the "Sketchpad" side a wall mounted iPad was installed offering additional context through a selection of historical materials and films.

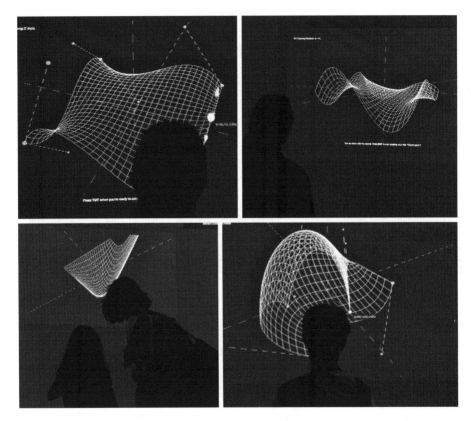

Fig. 9. The "Coons Patch" reconstruction attracted different kinds of users: the geometry savvy, and the curious. Photos by the authors.

Located among a diverse collection of artworks—many of which employing more sophisticated technologies—the reconstructions were a constant point of attraction for visitors and groups in the gallery, many of whom recognized the historical context and welcomed the opportunity to engage with it visually and tangibly. At times, the reconstructions became pedagogical tools visitors used to explain the core concepts of the technologies (Figs. 8 and 9).

5   Discussion

Two key insights can be drawn from the above experiences concerning the potentialities of software reconstruction as a method in the study of computer-aided design and—more generally—interactive technologies.

Defamiliarizing Technologies to See Them Anew
The software reconstructions forced experienced users of CAD systems to temporarily "unlearn" the logic of present-day CAD software in order to adopt an unfamiliar repertoire of postures and gestures. It was common during the two exhibitions to see such users spending a significant amount of time—between 5 and 10 min—in a mixture of amusement and bewilderment, trying to figure out how to use the pen, knobs, and keypad, to draw. A tutorial left on the "Sketchpad's" desk helped guided them on this. "Sketchpad" thus had the effect of de-familarizing conventional CAD tools, and—by invoking an alien paradigm of interaction—prompting a reflection on the embodied experience of designing computationally both *then*, and *now*.

De-mystifying Technological Novelty to Explore the Poetics of Computation in Design
Beyond the functional advantages they offered, architects adopted computer-aided design software because of the novel visual languages that they made possible [25]. However, close to sixty years after their inception and widely adopted by the profession, these languages are far from novel. As a result, computationally-generated imagery has become a new vernacular language of architectural representation, prompting a "post-digital" reaction in many present-day architects and designers. This attitude is often expressed through a nostalgic attachment to analog drawing media and (somewhat ironically) through the simulation of these analog media through software remediations. While architects in the "post-digital" space reserve the romanticism to hand drawing, the software reconstructions described here recuperate the undeniable sense of wonder that arises when one draws a line on a screen and stretches it, twists it around, and entangles it with others to form more intricate shapes.

6   Conclusion

This paper has outlined software reconstruction as a method combining historical research and creative technology prototyping, and documented its potential to shed new light into the material, gestural, and sensual dimensions of computer-aided design technologies. Specifically, it shows how software reconstruction can bring us closer to distant ways of seeing, touching, drawing, and designing while raising new questions about the impact of these historical practices on our present. As playful artifacts of scholarly and design inquiry, software reconstructions can operate at multiple registers, and for multiple publics.

From an architectural and design perspective, software reconstruction confront us with the origins of a visual, gestural, and ergonomic repertoire that has shaped the ideas, practices, and professional identities of those in these fields over the last 30 years. By creating a situation in which present-day CAD systems are *defamiliarized*, software reconstructions create the opportunity for the tacit knowledge [26] involved in their operation to be recuperated and made subject to historical analysis. In other words, software reconstruction makes computer-aided design technologies visible (and tangible) again as devices that fundamentally re-structure architectural labors, bodies, and the intellectual life of practitioners. While focusing on CAD, software reconstruction is naturally transferable to other systems.

From a media and science and technology studies perspective, we acquire a deeper understanding of the decision-making process behind the systems we study, and of the logical and material constraints confronted by their authors. Experimentally reconstructing "Sketchpad", for example, highlighted for us the limitations of early data structures for geometric representation and hardware, and the critical interplay between these constraints and the image of design that emerged in conjunction with it. This insight was organic to the messy processes of adapting, translating, and re-interpreting the system's functionality in a modern programming language, and would be difficult to acquire (let alone convey) through documentary accounts. Therefore, software reconstruction complements and adds nuance to our reading of the historical texts and interpretation of oral accounts.

Finally, from a pedagogical perspective, the process of making experimental reconstructions is useful to introduce students to concepts of interaction, programming, digital fabrication, and hardware design. Software reconstruction then not only enriches our understanding of technological and design histories, outlining the origins of contemporary architectural languages and subjects, but also engages with present-day technological frameworks, thus opening avenues for speculative tool-making and design.

Acknowledgments. The first author wishes to thank CAD pioneers Timothy E. Johnson, Robin Forrest, and Malcolm Sabin for valuable contributions to this project through interviews, documents, and informal conversations—any inaccuracies and undue liberties in this paper are not their fault; Francois Penz, The Martin Centre of Architectural and Urban Studies at the University of Cambridge, UK, and Allan Blackwell, who helped make some of these conversations possible; and The Graham Foundation for Advanced Study in the Fine Arts and the Berkman Fund for Faculty Development at Carnegie Mellon, for granting essential material support. Thanks also to Margaret Cox and Kara Skylling at the Miller Institute of Contemporary Art for valuable assistance as coordinators of the 2017 exhibition *Designing the Computational Image, Imagining Computational Design*. Thanks to the SIGGRAPH 2018 Art Gallery team, specially to curator Andres Burbano for selecting the two installations for the *Original Narratives* exhibition in Vancouver, and to Elizia Artis for expert management and coordination.

References

1. Cardoso Llach, D.: Builders of the Vision: Software and the Imagination of Design. Routledge, London; New York (2015)
2. Steenson, M.W.: Architectural Intelligence: How Designers and Architects Created the Digital Landscape. The MIT Press, Cambridge (2017)
3. Fallon, K.K.: The AEC Technology Survival Guide: Managing Today's Information Practice, 1st edn. Wiley, Hoboken (1997)
4. Andia, A.: Reconstructing the effects of computers on practice and education during the past three decades. J. Archit. Educ. **56**(2), 7–13 (2002). https://doi.org/10.1162/1046488026 0472512
5. Coyne, R.: The impact of computer use on design practice. In: Computer Aided Architectural Design Futures: Education, Research, Applications [CAAD Futures 1991 Conference Proceedings/ISBN 3-528-08821-4] Zürich (Switzerland), pp. 413–424 (CUMINCAD 1991), July 1991. http://papers.cumincad.org/cgi-bin/works/paper/403c

6. Akin, Ö.: Computational design instruction: toward a pedagogy. In: The Electronic Design Studio: Architectural Knowledge and Media in the Computer Era [CAAD Futures 1989 Conference Proceedings/ISBN 0-262-13254-0] Cambridge (Massachusetts/USA), pp. 302–316 (CUMINCAD 1990) (1989). http://papers.cumincad.org/cgi-bin/works/paper/450c

7. Downey, G.L.: The Machine in Me: An Anthropologist Sits Among Computer Engineers. Routledge, Abingdon (1998)

8. Loukissas, Y.A.: Co-Designers: Cultures of Computer Simulation in Architecture. Routledge, New York (2012)

9. Gutman, R.: Architectural Practice: A Critical View, 5th edn. Princeton Architectural Press, New York (1997)

10. Yaneva, A.: Mapping Controversies in Architecture, 1 edn. Routledge, London; New York (2016)

11. Cardoso Llach, D.: Architecture and the structured image: software simulations as infrastructures for building production. In: Ammon, S., Capdevila-Werning, R. (eds.) The Active Image. PET, vol. 28, pp. 23–52. Springer, Cham (2017). https://doi.org/10.1007/978-3-319-56466-1_2

12. Ingersoll, D., Yellen, J.E., Macdonald, W. (eds.): Experimental Archeology. Columbia University Press, New York (1977)

13. Fors, H., Principe, L.M., Sibum, H.O.: From the library to the laboratory and back again: experiment as a tool for historians of science. Ambix **63**(2), 85–97 (2016). https://doi.org/10.1080/00026980.2016.1213009

14. Sobchak, V.: Afterword: media archaeology and re-presencing the past. In: Huhtamo, E., Parikka, J. (eds.) Media Archaeology: Approaches, Applications, and Implications, pp. 323–333. University of California Press (2011)

15. Parikka, J.: What Is Media Archaeology? 1 edn. Polity, Cambridge (2012)

16. Rosner, D.K., et al.: Making core memory: design inquiry into gendered legacies of engineering and craftwork. In: Proceedings of the 2018 CHI Conference on Human Factors in Computing Systems, CHI 2018, pp. 531:1–531:13. ACM, New York (2018). https://doi.org/10.1145/3173574.3174105

17. Pangaro, P., et al.: "Colloquyofmobiles," Colloquy 2018 (2018). https://www.colloquyofmobiles.com

18. Huhtamo, E.: Thinkering with media: on the art of paul DeMarinis. In: Beirer, I., Himmelsbach, S., Seiffarth, C. (eds.) Paul DeMarinis: Buried in Noise, pp. 33–46. Kehrer Verlag, Heidelberg and Berlin (2010)

19. Coons, S.A.: Surfaces for Computer-Aided Design of Space Forms, MAC-TR, 41. M.I.T. Project MAC, Cambridge (1967)

20. Forrest, R.: Interview with the first author (2016)

21. Johnson, T.E.: Personal communication with the first author (2016)

22. Surface Generation by Computer: Ford Motors Product Research at MIT Lincoln Labs, 16 mm (1967). Courtesy of Timothy E. Johnson

23. Sutherland, I.E.: Sketchpad, a Man-Machine Graphical Communication System. Massachusetts Institute of Technology (1963)

24. Cardoso Llach, D.: Designing the Computational Image, Imagining Computational Design (Exhibition Catalogue). Carnegie Mellon University School of Architecture, Pittsburgh (2017)

25. Bruegmann, R.: The pencil and the electronic sketchpad: architectural representation and the computer. In: Blau, E., Kaufman, N. (eds.) Architecture and Its Image. Montreal (1989)

26. Collins, H.: Tacit and Explicit Knowledge. Reprint edition. University of Chicago Press, Chicago (2012)

Digital Design Ecology to Generate a Speculative Virtual Environment Reimagining New Relativity Laws

Jessie Rogers$^{(\boxtimes)}$ ⓘ, Marc Aurel Schnabel ⓘ, and Tane Moleta ⓘ

Victoria University of Wellington, Wellington, New Zealand
{Jessie.Rogers,MarcAurel.Schnabel,
Tane.Moleta}@vuw.ac.nz

Abstract. This paper presents the trilogy of virtual classifications, the speculative environment, the virtual inhabitant and the virtual built-form. These combine, generating a new realm of design within immersive architectural space, all to be designed relative to each other, this paper focuses on the speculative environment portion. This challenged computational design and representation through atmospheric filters, visible environment boundaries, materiality and audio experience. The speculative environment was generated manipulating the physical laws of the physical world, applied within the virtual space. The outcome provided a new spatial experience of architectural dynamics enhanced by detailed spatial qualities. Design concepts within this paper suggest at what immersive virtual reality can evolve into. Following an interconnective design methodology framework allowed a high level of complexity and richness to shine through the research case study throughout the process and final dissemination stages.

Keywords: Virtual reality · Relativity · Methodology · Immersive · Speculative

1 Introduction

Wiggins suggests, from a period where computer-aided architectural design software capabilities were very limited on the early desktop and portable computers, that many designers believe that their ability to design will be impaired by the study of the design process [1]. Large quantities of research conducted to investigate design processes, give designers a vast range of knowledge, inspiration and techniques to exercise or avoid making their own processes more informative and efficient while harnessing their boundless creativity. Beginning to slowly phase out, while still extremely important to exercise, are the traditional methods of design such as paper sketching ideation and two-dimensional vector techniques, these fail to provide such complex representation elements to acquire such richness of design work within the concept, development and presentation phases [2]. Many new evolving tools of architectural design are becoming more common to use, which provide wide ranges of digital and immersive features, used to aid architectural design processes within an early concept, development, and presentation phases. However, these are typically limited to just a few applications

© Springer Nature Singapore Pte Ltd. 2019
J.-H. Lee (Ed.): CAAD Futures 2019, CCIS 1028, pp. 120–133, 2019.
https://doi.org/10.1007/978-981-13-8410-3_9

throughout the duration of design projects. Within those projects, the methodologies and procedures currently established are usually adequate for the profession to be time and cost effective, and for studio design projects to be built or as a design exercise within education.

Spatial environments are dynamic, relative to acoustics, form, materiality, light and place, details unless experienced first-hand, cannot be completely conveyed using digital media [3]. Conventional tools of design representation do not give the user the replicated ability of reality to move freely within a temporal and three-dimensional environment, leaving the architecture's dynamic nature and detailed spatial qualities unable to completely comprehended [4]. The construction of architecture within immersive virtual reality environments differs greatly from real-world environments. While being purely digital, its deep structure is pure code, generated through various forms of software, defined as virtually built. Beginning as a blank canvas, every single element must be generated, ranging anywhere from the environment to inhabitation. Dissemination is the concluding factor in the majority of design projects, when it comes to residing within spaces, architectural design gives much significance to the inhabitants' perception and experience of this activity [5], virtual reality provides a high-quality option for the first-hand experience of such spaces [6].

This paper is part of a result from a case study following the design methodology Digital Culture: An Interconnective Design Methodology Ecosystem [7], which proposed a new architectural design framework, urging professional designers and andragogy to increase their design potential with richness and complexity (Fig. 1). Commonly, many designs remain within one or two computer-aided design programs from initiation to completion, typically resulting with the lack of richness and complexity [2]. Whereas the paper provides details of a successful case study with the outcome being highly resolved and intricate, exercising a range of evolving design tools. It follows the process of dynamically implementing evolving design tools in an interconnective manner (Fig. 1).

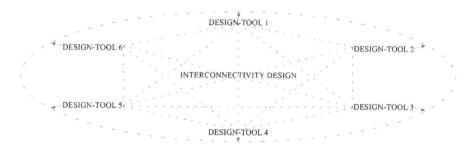

Fig. 1. Interconnective design methodology ecosystem [7].

Enhancing the immersive virtual environment design process intensifies architectural design in virtual reality culture, introducing new innovative opportunities within the vast architectural realm. One of three parts of a case study here is investigated, extremely abstract from current styles of built architecture, as it is entirely virtual with its own generated relativity laws. To design the relativity laws, a trilogy of virtual classifications has been established, defined as vital ingredients which combine to form the virtual new-relativity environment, these are the speculative environment, the virtual inhabitant and the virtual built-form, this paper focuses on the speculative environment component, currently limited to atmospheric filters, visible environment boundaries, materiality and audio experience.

2 Methodology

Influencing this research is the design cycle as shown in Fig. 2, encompassing the translation, exploration and manipulation of conceptual ideas alternating between physical and virtual tools, in this case study, physical modelling tools are obsolete as the result and process were kept entirely virtual. This continuous testing of ideas was carried out through each technical design alteration, developing the design outcome, engaging deeper to create intense complexity and richness. As Wiggins also suggests, the study of the design process allows the exercised design tools to be analyzed, based on performance and ease of use, in relation to the design process and outcome [1]. As such, for these successful design frameworks to be generated, the art of study and practice results in legitimate reasoning, contributing to their intellectual structure [2].

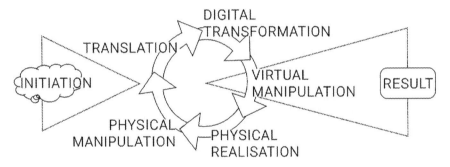

Fig. 2. Design cycle [2].

Following the framework from Digital Culture: An interconnective design methodology ecosystem in Fig. 1 [7], tools were chosen for this case study, the speculative environment component of the trilogy of virtual classifications, based on efficiency, access and existing knowledge. Atmospheric filters were created in *Unity3D* and *MonoDevelop*. Visible environment boundaries were created in *Adobe Photoshop,* Unity3D and MonoDevelop C# Scripting. Materiality was created in Unity3D and MonoDevelop C# Scripting. Lastly, the audio experience was created in *Audacity,* Unity3D and MonoDevelop C# Scripting. These combined with the other trilogy of virtual classifications inhabitant components create a wide range of evolving tools exercised within the framework. All of these components were designed relative together in an interconnective, and dynamic way, always changing, developing and enhancing. Continuous testing of the design environment was carried out through the use of the *HTC Vive* in conjunction with *SteamVR* by the designer.

3   Trilogy of Virtual Classifications

To generate a new-relativity law governed virtual environment, a trilogy of virtual classifications was established. The trilogy is formed by the virtual inhabitant, the virtual built-form and the speculative environment, all three consist of crucial components within. These components were determined before and during the entire research case study as new findings and necessities became apparent.

3.1   Virtual Inhabitant

One of the three virtual classifications, the virtual inhabitant focuses on the user and every aspect of their representation within the immersive virtual space, crucial components determined within the research were the virtual body (Fig. 3), spatial loco-motion, spatial orientation [8], local scale and user population. These were all set up as a rig within the virtual space which could be duplicated to represent multiple inhabitants.

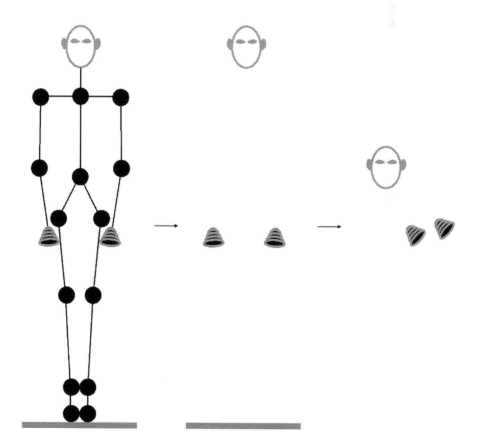

Fig. 3. Transitioning the physical body into the virtual body.

3.2   Virtual Built-Form

Considered as all geometry existing within the virtual space. Defined as virtually built, the virtual built-form portion within this research was designed to test the effects of the designed virtual inhabitant and speculative environment components. Various separate styles of geometry were selected and generated focusing on the main aspects of orthogonal, polygonal, curved rotational fractals and minimal surfaces (Fig. 4). These were designed within *Rhinoceros 3D* and imported into Unity3D as '.OBJ' mesh files.

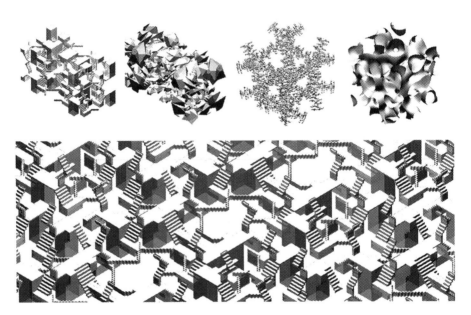

Fig. 4. Virtual built-form geometry, orthogonal, polygonal, curved rotational fractals and minimal surfaces, also showing the orthogonal tessellation.

3.3   Speculative Environment

The speculative environment trilogy portion focused on the all aspects within the virtual space which were neither geometry or the virtual inhabitants rig. Crucial components determined within research were atmospheric filters, environment boundaries, materiality and audio experience all designed relative to each other. Following this guideline, all future modifications and additions to the components of this segment will greatly enhance the user's experience, reimagining inhabitation within the space in any way desired.

4   Speculative Environment Components

The following outlines the speculative environment components applied within this case study.

4.1 Atmospheric Filters

Unlike reality, virtual environments begin as a blank canvas, therefore all components desired within the space need to be designed. Such as light, material, sound and time. These effects could either be implemented as a source or material within the spatial environment, global, or applied to the camera as a scripted filter, local.

In this research, the atmospheric filters were applied specifically to the stereoscopic camera, considered as a local filter, giving the illusion of a global effect, such as antialiasing bloom and fog. While none of these qualities were necessary within the virtual space, these as such, did not directly affect the user physically, but they altered their perception of the space. Spatial perception illusions consisted of form visibility, depth of environment and geometry appearance within the space.

This limited range of filters applied within this research was determined to generate an alien-like atmosphere to reimagine inhabitation of reality. Antialiasing reduce while flicker and smoothed the edges of geometry, giving a realistic appearance.

A subtle bloom generated a sufficient amount of halo around bright spots within the geometry and materials within the space (Fig. 5). These examples of intensities in Fig. 5 give the illusion of crisp geometry ranging to fluid but messy geometry, by using light effects to hide great amounts of detail, blending the foreground and background together. While choosing to use no fog within the space maximized the visual range and allowed accurate and high-quality reflections on the various geometric built-form surfaces comparing the left image in Fig. 5 to all images in Fig. 6. The ability to change how a user perceives a space through these few camera filters gave illusions.

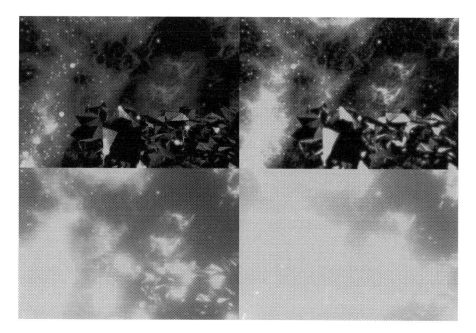

Fig. 5. 'Bloom' post-processing camera filter at low and high intensities.

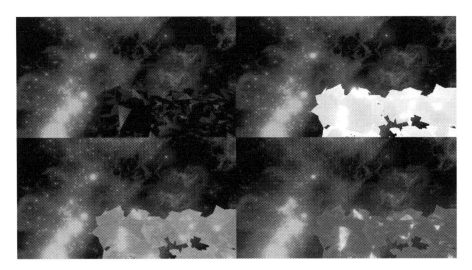

Fig. 6. 'Fog' post-processing camera filter using various coloration.

4.2   Environment Boundaries

Natural environment visible boundaries in reality typically consist of varied landscapes, ground planes and skies, whereas a virtual environment can have almost anything desired as the visible environment boundary, only represented as an image or video. Designing the visible environment boundary, technically identified as the skybox or sky-dome, are either represented as a six-sided cube, panoramic image or panoramic video, scripted to remain the furthest visible element within the inhabitable scene [9].

Within this research, a galaxy-like visual environment boundary was adopted, developing on from the alien-like atmosphere to reimagine inhabitation of reality.

Typically, on earth, the ground plane and sky suggest a singular source of orientation, the galaxy notions the absence of this singular orientation within the space. Eliminating preconceived notions, the user might have had regarding gravity and orientation when they enter the speculative virtual environment.

Constructed as a six-sided cube, the detailing within the high-definition seamless galaxy imagery provided intriguing textures, to be reflected by the geometry within the scene. Additionally, a C Sharp script, as presented below, allowed smooth transitioning between various color tints based on timed values, mimicking the geometric events unfolding within the scene.

```
using System.Collections;
using System.Collections.Generic;
using UnityEngine;

public class SkyboxSTARTfade : MonoBehaviour {

  public Material skyOne;
  public float sec1 = 15f;
  public float sec2 = 15f;
  public float sec3 = 15f;
  public float sec4 = 15f;
  public float rbou = 15f;
  float duration = 5f;
  float smoothness = 0.02f;

  void Start () {
    RenderSettings.skybox = skyOne;
    RenderSettings.skybox.SetColor("_Tint", Color.grey);
    RenderSettings.reflectionBounces = 2;
    DynamicGI.UpdateEnvironment();
    StartCoroutine ("change");
    StartCoroutine ("rb");
    StartCoroutine ("change2");
    StartCoroutine ("change3");
    StartCoroutine ("change4");  }

  IEnumerator change() {
    yield return new WaitForSeconds (sec1);
    RenderSettings.reflectionBounces = 2;
    DynamicGI.UpdateEnvironment();
    float progress = 0f;
    float increment = smoothness/duration;
    while (progress < 1f) {
      RenderSettings.skybox.SetColor ("_Tint", Color.Lerp
(Color.grey, new Color(0f, 0.5f, 1f, 0.5f), progress));
      progress += increment;
      yield return new WaitForSeconds (smoothness);
      DynamicGI.UpdateEnvironment ();    } }

  IEnumerator rb() {
    yield return new WaitForSeconds (rbou);
    RenderSettings.reflectionBounces = 1;
    DynamicGI.UpdateEnvironment(); }

  IEnumerator change2()  {
    yield return new WaitForSeconds (sec2);
```

```
RenderSettings.reflectionBounces = 1;
DynamicGI.UpdateEnvironment();
float progress = 0f;
float increment = smoothness/duration;
while (progress < 1f) {
   RenderSettings.skybox.SetColor ("_Tint", Color.Lerp
(new Color(0f, 0.5f, 1f, 0.5f), new Color(0.75f, 0f,
0.75f, 1f), progress));
      progress += increment;
      yield return new WaitForSeconds (smoothness);
      DynamicGI.UpdateEnvironment ();    } }

 IEnumerator change3()  {
   yield return new WaitForSeconds (sec3);
   RenderSettings.reflectionBounces = 1;
   DynamicGI.UpdateEnvironment();
   float progress = 0f;
   float increment = smoothness/duration;
   while (progress < 1f) {
     RenderSettings.skybox.SetColor ("_Tint", Color.Lerp
(new Color(0.75f, 0f, 0.75f, 1f), new Color(1f, 0f, 1f,
1f), progress));
      progress += increment;
      yield return new WaitForSeconds (smoothness);
      DynamicGI.UpdateEnvironment (); } }

 IEnumerator change4()  {
   yield return new WaitForSeconds (sec4);
   RenderSettings.reflectionBounces = 1;
   DynamicGI.UpdateEnvironment();
   float progress = 0f;
   float increment = smoothness/duration;
   while (progress < 1f) {
     RenderSettings.skybox.SetColor ("_Tint", Color.Lerp
(new Color(1f, 0f, 1f, 1f), new Color(1f, 0f, 0.3f, 1f),
progress));
      progress += increment;
      yield return new WaitForSeconds (smoothness);
      DynamicGI.UpdateEnvironment ();    } } }
```

[Script that allows smooth transitioning between various color tints based on timed values, mimicking the geometric events unfolding within the scene]

This altering coloration of the skybox texture through scripting deemed the most efficient way to have a completely time-dynamic environment with the least lag possible. Seamless transitions from gentle tones of green and blue to more intense tones of purple and pink mimicked the intensity and complexity of the virtual built-form geometric styles in Fig. 7, which were animated in a hide and reveal sequence with similar time values. This acted as a visual aid for the inhabitant to understand the environment's evolving nature, reimagining their speculative environment spatial inhabitation.

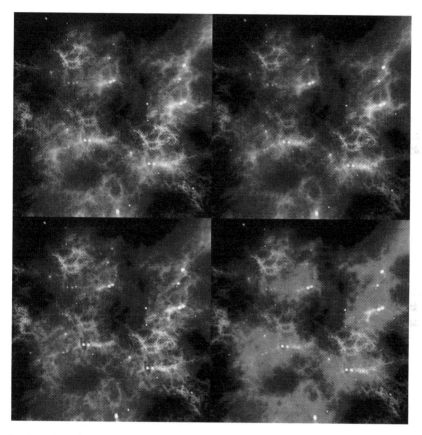

Fig. 7. One side of a six-sided cube shown in different tints, green, light blue, dark blue, and purple/pink. (Color figure online)

4.3   Materiality

Materials applied within virtual spaces typically attempt to represent those within reality. Physical texture, physical properties and aesthetics are technical elements which each have their own challenge to accurately represent the materiality of a geometrical built-form within a virtual environment.

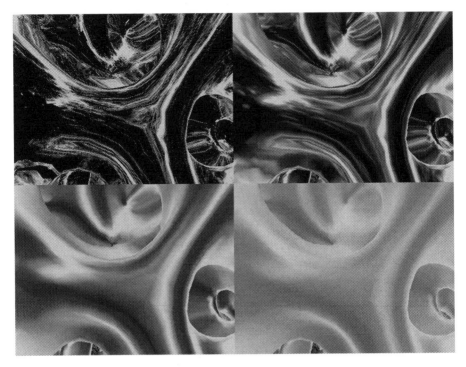

Fig. 8. Metallic lerp ping-pong effect on material reflections.

Physical textures in reality, require nerves within the skin to sense the texture and temperature of an object, this is difficult to convey within virtual environments. In this research, as a user felt the HTC Vive hand-controller, its temperature and texture mostly remained constant, except for the hands of the user slowly heating up the plastic material. Based on this technology used, gaining a felt physical texture response within the virtual environment could only be conveyed to the user through haptic feedback within the hand-controllers to represent a bumpy surface. This, however, was unrealistic due to the smooth material chosen for the built-form geometry with the space.

Physical properties of materials were limited within the virtual environment based on the few available pre-made choices and limited experience in this scripting area. Smooth materials used within the virtual environment was scripted such that the camera rig would glide along surfaces smoothly.

Aesthetic materiality of the virtual built-form within the virtual space consisted of many options for the material properties within Unity3D. Greatly used was a reflective material, applied to the virtual built-form within the space, with a light-bounce factor of two, giving the illusion of geometry within geometry, suggesting an infinite environment. A script was then generated to allow a seamless fade between material property values like a ping-pong effect. The metallic property as the reflectivity of the material transitioned between values 1.0, pure mirror, and 0.8 which appeared as frosted.

These transitions were on a time-loop within the virtual scene, enhancing the dynamic nature of the environment (Fig. 8). In everyday environments, it is not often an inhabitant sees their environment material fade between appearances, unless it is the sky or a digital screen. This dynamically designed material creates the illusion of an infinite environment and living structure while dynamically changing aesthetic material (Fig. 9), reimaging the way in which one inhabits space.

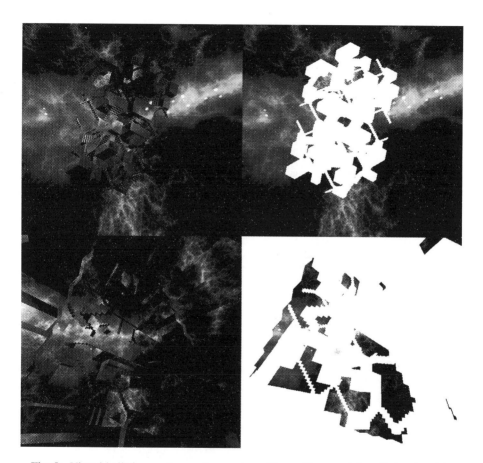

Fig. 9. Virtual built-form orthogonal geometry with metallic material applied, value 1.0.

4.4   Sonification

While some architects aim to manipulate sound through their designs, there is always noise to begin with within the real environment, such as a hum in the distance, wildlife, or traffic. External sound within the virtual space does not initially exist, except for the odd technology static in an earpiece. This required the audio experience to be designed and implemented within the virtual environment.

Throughout this research, three types of sound were designed and implemented within the immersive space, heartbeat as the local source, screeching metal as a distant source, and an ambient pulse as a global source as in Fig. 10. These manipulated the inhabitant's experience by contradicting their visual perception within the environment. These audio techniques with different intensities were timed specifically to the events unfolding within the space, reimagining their inhabitation, as their spatial perceptions were otherwise completely different. Such as fluid forms paired with the rough metal screech and dynamic material aesthetics of the virtual built-form paired with faint pulses, suggesting the form is alive.

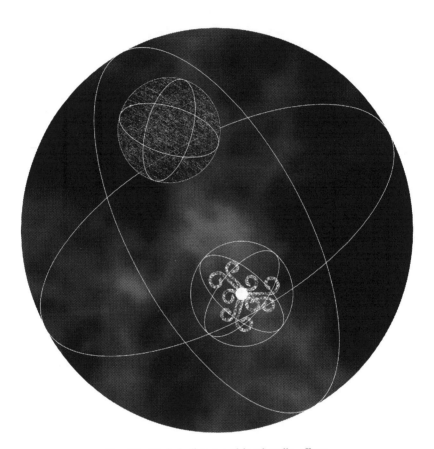

Fig. 10. Global, distant and local audio effects.

5   Conclusion

The interconnective methodology framework allowed a high level of complexity and richness to shine through the research case study throughout the process and final dissemination stages [10]. This case study established the trilogy of virtual classifications, the speculative environment, virtual inhabitant and the virtual built form. These combine, generating a new realm of design within immersive architectural space, all designed relative to each other, this paper focused on the speculative environment portion. This leveraged computational design through atmospheric filters, visible environment boundaries, materiality and audio experience. As a result, a new-relativity law governed virtual environment was generated manipulating the physical laws of the physical world and applied within the virtual space [11]. The outcome provided a new spatial experience of architectural dynamics enhancing detailed spatial qualities, encouraging architects to break out of the norm and dive into the realm of designing inhabitable virtual environments. The design concepts within this paper suggest at what immersive virtual reality can evolve into to reimagine the way in which users inhabit virtual space.

References

1. Wiggins, G.E.: Methodology in architectural design, Ph.D. Thesis, Massachusetts Institute of Technology (1989)
2. Schnabel, M.A., Kvan, T., Kuan, S.K.S., Li, W.: 3D crossover: exploring objects digitalis'e. Int. J. Archit. Comput. 2(4), 476–490 (2004)
3. Senagala, M.: Architecture, speed, and relativity: on the ethics of eternity, infinity, and virtuality, eternity, infinity and virtuality in architecture. In: Proceedings of the 22nd Annual Conference of the Association for Computer-Aided Design in Architecture, Washington, pp. 29–37 (2000)
4. Mitchell, W.J.: City of Bits: Space, Place, and the Infobahn. MIT Press, Cambridge, Mass (1995)
5. Szenasy, S.: Designing the Metaverse: The Role of Architecture in Virtual Environments (2017). https://www.metropolismag.com/architecture/architecture-virtual-environments/
6. Pandit, A.S.: How Virtual Environments Could Help Architects? (2016). https://www.arch2o.com/how-virtual-environments-could-help-architects/
7. Rogers, J., Schnabel, M.A., Lo, T.T.: Digital culture - an interconnective design methodology ecosystem, learning, adapting and prototyping. In: Proceedings of the 23rd International Conference of the Association for Computer-Aided Architectural Design Research in Asia (CAADRIA), Beijing, China, pp. 493–502 (2018)
8. Escher, M.C.: 1953, Relativity (2016). https://www.moma.org/collection/works/61398
9. Rogers, J., Moleta, T.J., Schnabel, M.A.: Future virtual heritage – techniques. In: 3rd Digital Heritage International Congress (Digital Heritage) and 24th International Conference on Virtual Systems & Multimedia (VSMM 2018), San Francisco, CA, USA, 4 p. (2018)
10. Rogers, J., Schnabel, M.A.: Digital design ecology: an analysis for an intricate framework of architectural design. In: Proceedings of the 36th eCAADe Conference Computing for a better tomorrow, Lodz, Poland, pp. 459–468 (2018)
11. Rogers, J., Schnabel, M.A., Moleta, T.J., Reimagining relativity: transitioning the physical body into a virtual inhabitant. In: Intelligent & Informed, Proceedings of the 24th International Conference of the Association for Computer-Aided Architectural Design Research in Asia (CAADRIA), Wellington, New Zealand, vol. 2, pp. 727–736 (2019)

Optimizing Spatial Adjacency in Hospital Master Planning

ZhouZhou Su[✉]

EYP, Houston, TX 77002, USA
zhouzhousu@gmail.com

Abstract. Hospitals are one of the most complex building types. Each is comprised of a wide range of service areas and functional spaces. Spatial relationships comprise one of the most critical design criteria, to be considered early-on in the master planning stage. Proper adjacency contributes to shorter travel distances, better wayfinding, improved patient care, higher satisfaction, and reduced overall cost. However, there is a lack of research on the automatic generation of design solutions that can be applied to real-world hospital master planning projects. Moreover, given the complexity of hospital design, an optimization tool is needed that is capable of evaluating both machine- and human-generated solutions. This study proposes a rating system for evaluating existing plans and proposed designs in hospital master planning, and explores optimal design solutions through rapid computational simulations. The first stage of this work presents interviews with senior professionals in the industry to explore best practices regarding spatial relationships in hospital planning. The second stage describes an automatic analysis tool for ranking the design options generated by healthcare planners and examining optimal design solutions that feature the best spatial adjacencies. This tool was employed in a recent master planning project with over fifty programming spaces, in order to test its validity.

Keywords: Optimization · Spatial adjacency · Hospital master planning

1 Introduction

1.1 Interdepartmental Relationships

Among the various types of architectural design, healthcare facilities are one of the most complex. The reasons for this are threefold. First, there are a vast number of possible solutions to any given design problem. Second, healthcare facilities involve a significant number of design objectives. Third, hospitals not only impact the wellbeing of patients [1, 2], but also affect physicians, staff members, caregivers [3], and patients' families [4]. Given the complexity of healthcare design, an important concept used in prioritizing emerging needs that should be incorporated early on in the planning stage is the spatial adjacency of functional areas. The movements of patients, staff, materials, and information from one place to another can significantly affect both time and cost. Consequently, departments should be arranged in a manner that shortens travel distances and improves efficiency [5, 6].

© Springer Nature Singapore Pte Ltd. 2019
J.-H. Lee (Ed.): CAAD Futures 2019, CCIS 1028, pp. 134–144, 2019.
https://doi.org/10.1007/978-981-13-8410-3_10

Poor adjacency can dramatically increase travel distances. Walking has been identified as one of the most significantly time-consuming activity for nurses; the time saved by reducing travel routes can be better spent on patient care activities [7]. Individual nurses can travel between 1.0 and 5.0 miles in a 10-hour daytime shift. Average travel distances range from 2.4 to 3.4 miles, with a median of 3.0 miles per every 10 h worked [8]. This unnecessary walking leads to wasted time and increased fatigue and stress. Proper adjacency not only reduces travel distances, it assists in the improvement of health, wayfinding, patient care and satisfaction, resource sharing, and the mitigation of overall cost [9]. Consequently, it is recommended that departmental relationships be evaluated during the early planning stage [6]. Space planning matrices have frequently been used by architects and healthcare planners to visualize departmental adjacency in two-dimensional diagrams. Various studies have employed a variety of weighting systems to rank the relative desirability of physical connections among departments. Such weighting systems have included the following factors: criticality, volume, importance, and frequency among departments.

Such interdepartmental closeness matrices can be of substantial value to younger planners, serving as visual guides and planning references [5]. Several employ the same three-scale rating system, the categories of which are: essential, important, and desirable [5, 6]. Color is used [10] to indicate the three different levels of importance. Some matrices, however, are more complicated. Hardy and Lammers [5] offered one example with 10 scales, addressing numerous topics such as whether the two departments are on the same or different floors. However, most of these matrices are outdated and do not reflect the ever-changing nature of the healthcare industry. For instance, while the matrix in [10] is recent, it does not systematically group and color-code departments; thus, it is difficult to locate particular branches, especially when a large project is being depicted. Moreover, senior health care planners have recommended the use of a five-point scale (instead of three) to represent complicated adjacency requirements (see Sect. 2).

1.2   Adjacency Optimization Methods in Hospital Planning

Currently, in architectural design, spatial relationship studies tend to focus on simple forms such as bubble diagrams and preliminary sketches. However, since the 1960s, researchers have explored the possibility of using automated solutions to solve spatial layout problems [11, 12]. While Moseley [11] was the first study to introduce a layout optimization program for a hospital operating unit, many of these early studies used physical space-planning methods to automate the conceptual design process, applying the physics of motion such as Newtonian laws of gravitation [13] and spring forces to boundary edges [14].

Since architectural design problems often have discrete, nonlinear, and stochastic decision variables with multiple objectives, more recent studies have used genetic algorithms (GA) as their optimization tool. GA mimics natural selection and the process of evolution [15], providing a robust search process that has been used in optimizing complex and poorly-understood scientific and engineering problems [16]. Among the tools with a built-in GA function, the integrated Rhino/Grasshopper program provides the most efficient ready-to-use GA plugins for optimization. Galapagos is a single-objective GA optimization tool; Octopus is used for multi-objective optimization. A recent study [10] highlighted the usefulness of both Grasshopper and Galapagos as analytical tools for optimizing adjacency criteria.

Although design computation and optimization are becoming increasingly popular in architecture, they have yet to become an integral part of the hospital design process. First, they are considered to be tools that deprive architects of the opportunity to use their creativity. Second, most of the current research is theory-based and requires knowledge outside of architects' general fields of expertise, such as that of coding and physics. Third, it's challenging to incorporate this type of research into the traditional design process. Due to these issues, the intent of the present study is not to suggest a comprehensive process of computational design automation that would replace architects' creativity, but rather to use design automation as a means of assisting architects in better understanding the nature of this type of problem, as well as locating and comparing useful design options.

To achieve this, the current study was designed to create a rating system for evaluating existing plans and proposed designs in hospital master planning and look for optimal design solutions through rapid computational simulations. The first stage presents interviews with senior professionals in the industry, in order to explore best practices regarding spatial relationships in hospital planning. The second stage describes an automatic analytical tool for ranking the design options generated by healthcare planners and looking for optimal design solutions that feature the best spatial adjacency. This tool was used in a recent master planning project to test its validity.

2   Part 1 – Interdepartmental Matrix

Every hospital is comprised of a wide range of functional units and departments. These include diagnostics and treatment areas, inpatient and outpatient spaces, support locations, and administration and public centers. The physical relationships among these divisions define the composition of the hospital. Besides the wide range of functions that must be accommodated, hospitals need to serve and support a variety of users such as patients, families, visitors, physicians, nurses, etc.

In the first part of this study, in-depth interviews were conducted with senior planners at WHR Architects (now EYP), as a means of facilitating a thorough understanding of the spatial relationships in hospital master planning, and creating an interdepartmental matrix that would best depict the complexity of hospital master planning and serve as a template for future projects. A detailed description of the interview process will be provided in a separate publication.

In creating the proposed matrix, departments were grouped into six categories (see Fig. 1). A color-coding system (the standard color palette used by WHR Architects across projects for various drawings, including floor plans, sections, site plans, etc.) was implemented for differentiation, as follows: Diagnostics and Treatment – Red, Inpatient – Blue, Outpatient – Green, Support – Orange, Administration and Public Areas – Yellow, and Access – Gray. The names of the departments were placed in alphabetical order under each category title. For simplification, some departments (e.g., LDR and LDRP) were grouped on the premise that their connection would not affect the adjacencies and ranks of the matrix. In other words, these departments had an interdepartmental relationship similar to that of other departments in the matrix.

A ranking system with five hierarchies was proposed and agreed upon by all interviewees, as a means of representing the priorities and rankings of each design element in relation to all of the others. The five departmental adjacency scales were as follows:

Scale 1: Critical; should be physically connected
Scale 2: Important; although physical connection is preferred, the two departments could be separated with a minimum of travel distance
Scale 3: Preferred; within reasonable travel distance
Scale 4: Low frequency; periodic contact
Scale 5: No relationship needed

It was not the purpose of the study to create a universal matrix that would work for all hospital types in all locations. Hospitals are becoming more and more sophisticated, and require different sizes, functions, locations, strategic goals, specialty focuses, and configurations, all of which translate to different interdepartmental relationships. In hospital master planning projects, planners should first identify the number of departments on the matrix and prioritize them to reflect the scale and purpose of the endeavor. Then, the adjacency relationships should be carefully evaluated. Finally, the needs and associations should be confirmed with the users. Figure 1 shows an example of a typical interdepartmental matrix. This matrix was extracted from the space program of a community hospital in New Jersey.

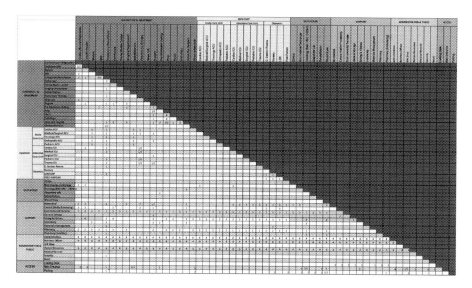

Fig. 1. Example of an interdepartmental matrix (Color figure online)

3   Part 2 – Design Optimization

The second part of this study used Rhino and Grasshopper as analytical tools to: (1) evaluate an existing hospital campus, (2) compare the proposed master plan design options, and (3) identify optimal design solutions with regards to spatial adjacency requirements and travel distances. This tool will help planners to better understand the nature of this unique problem and explore design alternatives across important departmental adjacency criteria.

This study used a master planning project for a community hospital in New Jersey as a case study to demonstrate and validate the proposed method. In early 2016, the hospital collaborated with WHR Architects to update and reevaluate the existing master plan. The core group, along with WHR, prioritized users' immediate needs, a choice that yielded several major drivers, including enlarging several key programs. Most of the key program drivers were located on the first two floors of the campus, so in order to simplify the computer model, only those programs located on the first two floors were included. Figure 2 shows the simplified version of the interdepartmental matrix that corresponds to these programs.

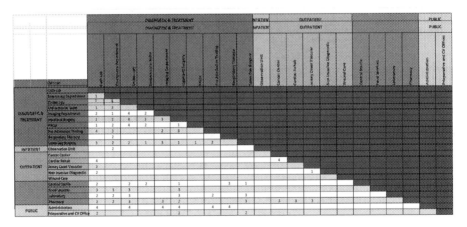

Fig. 2. Simplified interdepartmental matrix.

3.1   Fitness Function

In this optimization study, the fitness function (i.e., the design objective) was defined as the numerical value derived from the sum of the product of the adjacency levels of two departments (measured from 1 to 5) and the distance between those two departments (considering all interconnected program elements). A lower fitness score meant that the given design solution provided better departmental relationships and shorter walking distances between highly related departments.

Fitness Score

$$= \textbf{Sum Department 1} - \textbf{2}_{\text{Adjacency Level}} (\text{from 1 to 5}) \times \textbf{Department 1} - \textbf{2}_{\text{Travel Distance}} (\text{in feet})$$

$$= \sum_{i=1}^{n} (\textbf{Department } i - (i+1)_{\text{Adjacency Level}} \times \textbf{Department } i - (i+1)_{\text{Travel Distance}})$$

The adjacency values for this case study are shown in Fig. 2. For travel distances, measurements were taken from the center point of the first department to the entrance/exit, along the center line of the corridor(s), to the entrance/exit of the second department, and finally to the center point of the second department.

3.2 Vertical Transportation

There were multiple elevators in this facility. It was essential to quantify the vertical travel distances because patients, staff, and physicians at the hospital frequently traveled between the first two levels. However, there were only a few existing methodologies available to systematically convert vertical travel distances to be comparable with horizontal distances. Based on the Vertical Transportation Handbook [17], in hospital-type buildings, the handling capacity is generally approximately 12%, the interval time ranges from 30 to 50 s, and the average wait time is between 15 and 25 s. We assumed that the average wait time at the hospital was 20 s for all elevators, and the average walking speed was approximately 3.1 miles per hour (1.47 fps) [18]. Hypothetically, if someone needed to use the elevator to go up or down one level, he or she could walk horizontally about 30 feet (20 s × 1.47 feet per second = 29.4 feet) in the same amount of time. Thus, to account for someone traveling from a department on Level 1 to a department on Level 2 (or vice versa), 30 feet was added to the horizontal travel distance. It is worth noting that 30 feet was somewhat arbitrary, and could change from one project to another depending on many factors such as elevator type, number of elevators, number of floors traveled, handling capacity, traffic, patient volume, etc.

3.3 Geometry

We customized the first steps in creating the geometry in Grasshopper/Rhino for this project. Each floor was translated into a user-defined boundary as a potential floor space. The floor-to-floor height was adjustable. A reasonable number of points (the amount defined by the user) was generated inside the grid; these points were used as the department centers. Generally, the number of control points correlates to the time consumed in the optimization process. The more points given, the longer the computer requires for calculation, but the more realistic the final layout will be.

Both the total number of points and the site boundary were adjustable. In this case study, a total of 305 points were generated on the grid; Pt0 was located at the lower left, and Pt304 was situated in the upper right (see Fig. 3). All departments were simplified as squares with circles inside, and constructed around a center point. Once the first department was allocated on the grid, all of the points inside were removed from the list used in the generation of the next department; this prevented overlapping among various programs. Figure 3 illustrates two of the department locations generated by the computer. The Emergency department appears in Fig. 3 as a blue square around a red circle; Pt152 is at the center. The circle indicates a space with a radius of 118 feet (see Fig. 4). Figure 4 shows the square footage and radii of all key departments addressed in this study.

In the next step, the computer located the second department. The computer repeated this process until all departments were mapped. Users were able to search, locate, and change the departments' locations, based on the fitness scores and by using the sliders to change the origin points.

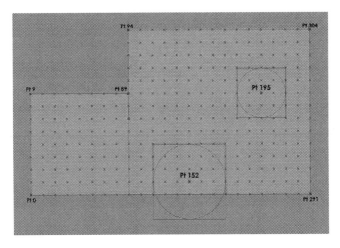

Fig. 3. Design boundary and control points. (Color figure online)

		Current Level	Proposed Level_Option 1	Proposed Level_Option 2	Current Square Footage	Propsed Square Footage	Current Radius	Proposed Radius
	CV Institute		2	2		14,750		69
	Emergency Department	1	1	1	44,000	44,000	118	118
	Endoscopy	2	2	2	6,800	6,800	67	47
DIAGNOSTIC & TREATMENT	Endovascular Suite	2	2	2	2,670	2,670	29	29
	Imaging Department	1	1	1	19,170	19,170	78	78
	Inpatient Surgery	2	2	2	12,900	12,900	64	64
	Pre Admission Testing	1	1	1	576	576	14	14
	Respiratory Therapy	2	2	2	1,400	1,400	21	21
	Same Day Surgery	2	2	2	11,025	11,025	59	59
INPATIENT	Observation Unit	2	2	2	6,500	6,500	45	45
	Cancer Center	1	1	1	18,000	18,000	76	76
	Cardiac Rehab	1	1	1	2,743	2,743	30	30
OUTPATIENT	Jersey Coast Vascular	2	2	2	3,575	3,575	34	34
	Non Invasive Diagnostic		2	2		3,500		33
	HBO Wound Care	1	1	1	1,000	1,000	18	18
	Central Sterile	2	4	2	6,500	6,500	31	45
	Food Services	2	2	2	9,825	9,825	56	56
	Laboratory	2	2	4	6,000	6,000	44	44
	Pharmacy	1	1	1	3,352	3,352	33	33
PUBLIC	Administration	1	1	1	6,266	6,266	45	45
	Prioperative and CV Offices	2	2	2	2,700	2,700	29	29

Fig. 4. Square footage and radii of key departments.

3.4   Divide and Conquer

Only 20 programmatic elements were involved in this simplified case study. In Galapagos, each department was identified as a variable/genome with approximately 150 to 305 solutions. The first department on the grid had 305 possible solutions. The number of candidate solutions for the next department was 305, less the number of points inside the previous iteration. For simplicity, it was assumed that each program had an equal option of 150; thus, for 20 programs, the total possible number of solutions was 10520 = 3.3 × 1043. In design optimization, the computing time needed to solve a problem increases as the population of the candidate solution grows. For 1043 possibilities, even today's fastest computers would require an extremely long computing time.

Unfortunately, architects and planners usually work with short design schedules. Thus, Divide and Conquer (D&C) was introduced to lighten the load on computer processing systems [19, 20]. D&C divides a large problem with a sizeable population into manageable sub-problems with smaller populations. The solution to the original problem can be obtained by combining the resolutions of the smaller sub-problems. In this study, the 20 programmatic elements were broken down into six groups (see Fig. 5). Each member needed to be adjacent to the others within the same group. Galapagos found the best locations for each group, a process that involved significantly fewer possibilities than locating all 20 programmatic elements at the same time.

Application of the D&C method minimizes the search space. The algorithm can run with less computing time, or the search space within the same timeframe can be enlarged. However, it is important for planners to identify which programs are highly related to one another.

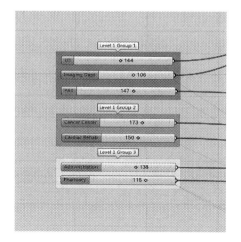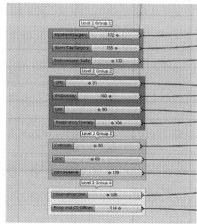

Fig. 5. The "Divide and Conquer" program groupings.

4 Results

To better evaluate the existing campus and proposed options, the best-fit layout with the most desirable adjacency and shortest travel distances between departments (i.e., the lowest fitness score) was assigned an arbitrary score of 100; the worst-fit layout with the least desirable adjacency and longest travel distance between departments (i.e., the highest fitness score) was given a score of 0 (see Table 1). With the highest and lowest numbers assigned, it was possible to convert the fitness score of the existing campus and both proposed options to scores between 0 and 100. The reason behind this conversion was to provide a rating system to help hospital owners and architects better evaluate the various possible layouts. It should be noted that the score given to the existing campus, 74.6, was an arbitrary number; it was not the purpose of this study to inform the hospital's owners of how good or bad their current facility layout was. On the contrary, this project was designed as a way of comparing existing layouts with the best possible solutions, assuming the facility could be built anew. This process will help hospital owners and designers find the bottlenecks in their existing facilities.

Surprisingly, after comparing selected programs in both proposed options to the existing campus, it was found that Option 1 had a lower score than the existing layout; Option 2 had a better score. Option 1 expanded most of the key departments on their existing Levels 1 and 2. Some departments were expanded in their current locations, while others were expanded and relocated to different locations on the same floor. Since the first two floors are considered "prime real estate," the floor plates quickly reached maximum capacity, leaving little space for expansion. A department cannot be expanded in its current location without moving another nearby department to a new location, sacrificing the connectivity between them. Thus, some departments were relocated far from their current locations, which also contributed to the score being lower than the existing layout.

Option 2 tested a different strategy. It expanded and relocated several key departments to underutilized spaces on different floors. Although going vertical might not be ideal, this approach maintained critical connectivity among departments that were not growing, and the travel distance between key departments on different floors (considering vertical travel distance) was less than the horizontal travel distance when one department moved far away but remained on the same floor.

Table 1. Scores assigned to the existing campus and proposed options, based on the best and worst fit results.

Example	Existing Campus	Proposed Option 1	Proposed Option 2	Worst Fit Result	Best Fit Result
Fitness Score	13,617	14,219	13,115	22,000	8,664
Score	62.9	58.3	66.6	0	100

5   Discussion and Conclusion

This study provided data- and performance-driven methods designed to assist with traditional architectural design and planning. This work was performed in two stages. The first included interviews with senior professional medical planners. These discussions explored the industry's best practices in terms of spatial relationships in hospital planning. An interrelationship matrix was created from the data gathered, using a 1-to-5 scale in which 1 indicated that a physical connection was preferred, and 5 meant that no direct relationship was needed. The second stage involved using Rhino and Grasshopper in the creation of a framework to: (1) rank an existing hospital campus, (2) hierarchize the proposed master plan design options generated by the interviewed medical planners, and (3) develop an automated computational tool to identify optimal design solutions that consider spatial adjacency requirements and travel distances between key departments and areas.

The major benefit to using this tool in healthcare planning is that it can manage a large number of program spaces and adjacency requirements. Additionally, it is capable of searching for and locating a vast number of design possibilities. Given the complexity inherent in healthcare design, it is often challenging to consider all adjacency requirements. Thus, this tool can be used in a variety of ways and along numerous design scales to find the best-fit layouts for everything from a large hospital facility master plan like the one in our case study, to much smaller projects such as an inpatient wing layout. It should be noted that the present work did not intend to replace architects' work with artificial intelligence; on the contrary, it was developed to assist designers with their process and provide them with evidence-based data to support their decisions. It can also offer useful information to hospital owners, helping them to better understand their facilities and locate adjacency and travel-distance bottlenecks.

This study has several limitations. It considered two important design goals in the realm of healthcare design: adjacency and travel distance. However, many other equally important design goals were not addressed, such as building shape, daylighting, sustainability, net-to-gross ratio, etc. The best-fit layout only presented the most favorable relationships and shortest travel distances among departments; it did not take into account any of the other above-mentioned design objectives. Designers should manually evaluate best-fit layouts and verify if they also facilitate other design objectives and work within essential architectural constraints. Additionally, the programmatic elements in this research were simplified as squares. Further development of this tool would be necessary to provide free forms for each program element. Some key spaces that might significantly affect the layout were not included, such as entrances and loading docks, because both remained untouched in our case study. Additionally, to a certain extent this tool was customized, and therefore will not be useful to a non-user of Grasshopper. Future work should develop a control panel for non-Grasshopper users. We would also like to study the possibility of using building information modeling (BIM) tools such as Revit and Dynamo as design media. Finally, the proposed methods and prototype tools should be presented to management-oriented audiences in order to promote optimization and improve industry methods.

References

1. Dettenkofer, M., Seegers, S., Antes, G., Motschall, E., Schumacher, M., Daschner, F.D.: Does the architecture of hospital facilities influence nosocomial infection rates? A systematic review. Infect. Control Hosp. Epidemiol. **25**(1), 21–25 (2004)
2. Ulrich, R.: View through a window may influence recovery. Science **224**(4647), 224–225 (1984)
3. Harris, D.D., Shepley, M.M., White, R.D., Kolberg, K.J.S., Harrell, J.W.: The impact of single family room design on patients and caregivers: executive summary. J. Perinatol. **26**, S38–S48 (2006)
4. Conner, J.M., Nelson, E.C.: Neonatal intensive care: Satisfaction measured from a parent's perspective. Pediatrics **103**(1 Suppl. E), 336–349 (1999)
5. Hardy, O.B., Lammers, L.P.: Hospitals, the Planning and Design Process. Aspen Publishers, New York (1977)
6. Kobus, R.L.: Building Type Basics for Healthcare Facilities, vol. 13. Wiley, Hoboken (2008)
7. Zimring, C., Joseph, A., Choudhary, R.: The Role of the Physical Environment in the Hospital of the 21st Century: A Once-in-a-Lifetime Opportunity. The Center for Health Design, Concord (2004)
8. Hendrich, A., Chow, M., Skierczynski, B., Lu, Z.: A 36-hospital time and motion study: how do medical-surgical nurses spend their time? Permanente J. **12**(3), 25–34 (2008)
9. Vangelatos, G.: Health Care Design Needs To Take Adjacency Into Consideration (2012). http://www.facilitiesnet.com/green/article/Health-Care-Design-Needs-ToTake-Adjacency-Into-Consideration-Facilities-Management-Green-Feature–13601. Accessed 25 Aug 2016
10. Boon, C., Griffin, C., Papaefthimious, N., Ross, J., Storey, K.: Optimizing spatial adjacencies using evolutionary parametric tools: using grasshopper and galapagos to analyze, visualize, and improve complex architectural programming. Perkins Res. J. **07.02** (Special), 25–37 (2015)
11. Moseley, L.: A rational design theory for planning buildings based on the analysis and solution of circulation problems. Architects' J. **138**, 525–537 (1963)
12. Gross, M.D., Ervin, S.M.: Designing with constraints (1987)
13. Lorenz, W.E., Bicher, M., Wurzer, G.X.: Adjacency in hospital planning. IFAC-PapersOnLine **48**(1), 862–867 (2015)
14. Arvin, S.A., House, D.H.: Modeling architectural design objectives in physically based space planning. Autom. Constr. **11**(2), 213–225 (2002)
15. Holland, J.H.: Adaptation in Natural and Artificial Systems: An Introductory Analysis with Applications to Biology, Control, and Artificial Intelligence. U Michigan Press, Ann Arbor (1975)
16. Gero, J.S., Louis, S.J.: Improving Pareto optimal designs using genetic algorithms. Comput. Aided Civ. Infrastruct. Eng. **10**(4), 239–247 (1995)
17. Strakosch, G.R., Caporale, R.S.: The Vertical Transportation Handbook, vol. 4. Wiley, Hoboken (2010)
18. Aspelin, K. Establishing pedestrian walking speeds, pp. 5–25. Portland State University (2005)
19. Su, Z., Yan, W.: A fast genetic algorithm for solving architectural design optimization problems. Artif. Intell. Eng. Des. Anal. Manuf. **29**(4), 457–469 (2015)
20. Su, Z., Yan, W.: Creating and improving a closed loop: design optimization and knowledge discovery in architecture. Int. J. Architectural Comput. **13**(2), 123–142 (2015)

Oriole

A Parametric Solution for Animation-Based Robotic Motion Design

Ebrahim Poustinchi[(✉)] [iD]

Architecture, Kent State University, Kent, OH 44240, USA
mpoustin@kent.edu

Abstract. This paper presents a project-based research study using Oriole—a custom-made plug-in for robotic motion control solutions in grasshopper 3D visual programming environment. Oriole is a parametric tool that enables users/designers to design robotic motion-paths, based on the notion of keyframing and animation. Using Oriole, designers are able to simulate—and ultimately develop robotic movements in more intuitive free-form ways.

Using Rhino 3D as a digital modeling platform and Grasshopper 3D and its robotic simulation platforms for different industrial robots such as KUKA, ABB, and Universal, Oriole enables designers to create a precise interaction between the robot, its spatial "performance" and the physical environment through animation.

Keywords: Robotics · Parametric design · Human-computer interaction

1 Introduction

1.1 Robotic Design

In the past few years and after the introduction of robotics to design disciplines, many designers and architects started to use robots to translate/convert the outcome of their digital design process into the physical manner, similar to the use of CNC (Computer Numerical Control) machines in the design discipline. Given the five to eight-axis freedom of robots, multiple designers, architects, and academic set-ups started to rethink the potential of this freedom in identifying creative fabrication/production processes. Projects such as "Robotic Softness" [1], Bartlett RC4 and multiple "chair" projects [2], and ICD/ITKE Research Pavilions—2013–14 research pavilion for instance [3] just to name a few, are challenging the conventional ways of thinking about robots in the realm of fabrication through new means of communication or fabrication.

Although creative fabrication/production is an invaluable reason to use robots in an architectural/design set-up, there is a missed opportunity to use the performative aspects of robots as performers and possibly architectural components. In another word, in some of the mentioned projects and similar ones, although the process is tremendously innovative, the performance of the robot follows conventional thinking

© Springer Nature Singapore Pte Ltd. 2019
J.-H. Lee (Ed.): CAAD Futures 2019, CCIS 1028, pp. 145–154, 2019.
https://doi.org/10.1007/978-981-13-8410-3_11

methods of "engineered" efficiency in finding the optimized "path" to perform a task or avoid any unexpected collisions. These limitations mostly come from the design of the robotic motion through data/path based code-generating methods.

Later, some professions, academic set-ups, and creative platforms, started to create new methods for developing custom motion design platforms for robots, with a focus on designing the "performance" of the robot in conjunction to its operation. Esperant.O platform at Sci-Arc by Kruysman-Proto [4], BDMove at UCLA and Bot and Dolly by Bot and Dolly, and RobotAnimator [5] are some examples of these intuitive controlling platforms. The "Impossible Objects" design series by Kruysman-Proto and Curime Batliner [6] and the "Aether Project" by Guvenc Ozel studio at University of California Los Angeles [7] are some examples of using these robot-controlling methods to design the robotic motion in a performative way. Another familiar example of the use of robotic motion design to curate a performative spatial effect—as a direct result of new means of robotic controlling, is the work of Bot and Dolly—creative robotic studio, in designing and shooting special effects of the movie Gravity [8].

Although these robotic motion design platforms and projects had a priceless impact on "creative" robotics, all of them are restricted to highly customized software platforms that are limited to the developer's design studio. In another word, despite the universal impact of these tools on the contemporary discourse of creative robotics, none of these "animation-based" robotic controlling platforms were/are open to the public. Oriole research, as a parametric robotic controlling platform, seeks the potential of similar methodologies in controlling robots, in a more conventional/open source yet creative design platforms such as Rhino and Grasshopper 3D. Using familiar design software platforms, and in the context of an advanced graduate research studio, Oriole investigates the potentials of animation-based robotic motion control as a possible medium to study and design dynamic architectural spaces.

1.2   Animation in Design

In the past three decades and after the introduction of digital design, architecture and other design disciplines started to adopt changes and shifts—triggered by the digital wave, as design opportunities. Following this digital movement, and as a cultural shift in design, in his book Animate From, Greg Lynn calls for attention to the possibilities of animation as a design-tool in architecture [9]. Immediately after, animation became an accepted important experimental architectural design, simulation, and representation tool through which, animation concepts—such as deformation, blend-shapes, constraining, keyframing, graph-editing and gradual transformations, and physic simulations—to name a few, grown into architectural, formal and spatial strategies and language. As a result of this growth and in today's conversation about design and architecture, animation and its frame of mind play a serious role when it comes to design thinking.

1.3   Oriole

Many software developers—when it comes to their designer/architect users tend to build on the culture of design as a mean of communication and expanding their users.

Introduction of node-based visual programming platforms such as Grasshopper 3D, Touch-Designer or SOFT-MODELLING [10] for instance or developing hardware controllers such as a 3D mouse, Palette interface and NKNM platforms [11], are a few examples of acknowledging design-culture from software/hardware developing point of view.

As mentioned above, robotics is not far from the conversation of animation when it comes to its controlling process (discussed in further detail below). Given the established position of animation as a thinking medium for designers and architects in today's world, on one hand and the rapidly growing desire and culture of robotics as design and fabrication tool on the other hand, it seems to be essential to have controlling methods for design software platforms, to use animation strategies to "animate"/move robots.

By investigating design students' and designers' experiences in using Oriole platform, this study demonstrates the potential of a keyframe-based parametric animation controlling platform for robots. This method enhances the design experience with robots not only as fabrication/production tools, but also as a new outlook to interactively design and evaluate the physical performance of the robot as potentially a solution for animated architecture and space. Building on previous experiences with animation—in design disciplines as well as robotic controlling solutions, Oriole research proposes a new way of controlling robots through a familiar design software (Rhino 3D) and with a familiar thinking/design process (animation keyframing).

2   Research Questions and Methods

Developed based upon earlier studies in robot controlling and animation-based software development, Oriole is part of ongoing research that questions two potentials of animation-based robot controlling in design:

1. How an animation-based parametric controlling platform for robots, can change/expand the use of robots in design-oriented disciplines, from fabrication tool to design tool?
2. How moving from code-based/path-based robotic programming to animation based motion design—as a more intuitive way of designing robotic motion, diversifies the possible robotic motion designers with a minor technical background?

To study these questions, and to maximize the diversity of potential users, Oriole has been developed as a plug-in independent from the robotic/controlling software/plug-ins and act as an addition to the digital simulation. In another word, independent from the robotic software/plug-in that generates the move-commands, Oriole can serve as a bridge, which converts key-framed positions into understandable data for the robot post-processor (discussed in further detail below). This independence/flexibility enables the end-user to use Oriole to design motion for any brand of robots—KUKA, ABB and Universal to name a few, as long as there is a post-processor for them in Grasshopper 3D environment.

Developed for the use in the context of a research studio at the College of Architecture and Environmental Design, at Kent State University, Oriole has four main components: (a) Inverse Kinematic (IK) Direct Frame, (b) Key Frame Solver, (c) Wait Solver, and (d) Robot Lab (Fig. 1). In addition to the components mentioned above, and to complete an Oriole-based project, there is a need for a robot arm and a robotic post-processor software/plug-in (Fig. 2).

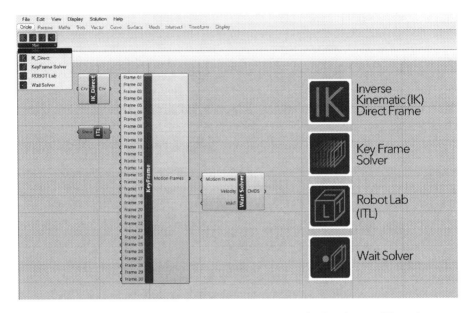

Fig. 1. An overview of Oriole—custom plug-in/components in Grasshopper 3D environment.

Fig. 2. Oriole can provide 3D information for most of the available robotic post-processors in Grasshopper 3D to generate readable commands for KUKA, ABB, and Universal Robots.

As an additional feature, Oriole can directly generate controlling codes for KUKA industrial robots or can use any other parametric robot controlling platforms (post-processors) in Grasshopper 3D such as KUKA|prc, HAL, and Taco—to name a few, to drive industrial robots. This adaptability is one of the distinctive features of Oriole.

For the current research, we produced a platform to use Oriole as a part of a graduate studio, using KUKA KR6 R900 Sixx robot arm and with a focus robotic motion as a medium to study the potential of three-dimensional architectural re-configurability. Besides, some students used Oriole as a method to study formal, spatial, and compositional qualities of the design through the physical model and as a feedback system to inform the digital design.

3 Oriole: A Parametric Solution for Animation-Based Robotic Motion Design

As part of the promises of Oriole research, Oriole serves as a plug-in for the node-based visual programming environment of Grasshopper 3D in Rhino 3D software. Early studies with Oriole—presented in this paper as Oriole Alpha, demonstrates the potential of the first version of the plug-in, as a tool to animate robots in the context of a design studio, looking into possibilities of architecture as a moveable three-dimensional puzzle. Oriole Alpha contains four main components of Oriole, as well as KUKA|prc [12] as the robotic post-processor plug-in and KUKA KR6 R900 Sixx as the robot arm.

3.1 Oriole Component: Inverse Kinematic (IK) Direct Frame

As the first component, Oriole Alpha uses a costume mechanism to develop robotic motion, based on keyframing logic. Using the notion of inverse kinematics (IK), Oriole Alpha enables users to interactively design the movement of the robot, "Frame by frame." In both robotics and animation, inverse kinematics (IK) uses kinematics equations to move joints and axis of an "arm"—or any joint-based model, to provide a desired position for the end-effector (a tool attached to the last axis—in six-axis robot arms, the 6th axis of the arm). The significant difference in this method is the possibility of controlling the robot arm spatially. Using IK frame component of Oriole, user can design and save different positions and orientations for the robot end-effector in the format of an adjustable frame without moving each axis of the robot individually—known as forward kinematics (FK) (Fig. 3).

3.2 Oriole Component: Key Frame Solver

Developing IK frames using the first Oriole component, users can use the Key Frame Solver component to generate a robotic animation—up to 30 frames in Oriole Alpha. Key Frame Solver uses animation logic to calculate the transitional frames between the "keyed" frames. Similar to most of the digital animation platforms, Key Frame Solver uses mathematical equations to parametrically divide the "transformation" between frames (Fig. 4). Through this method, Oriole Alpha users can assign 30 different keyframes to the solver, and make a robotic animation between those frames using KUKA|prc post-processor (discussed in further detail below).

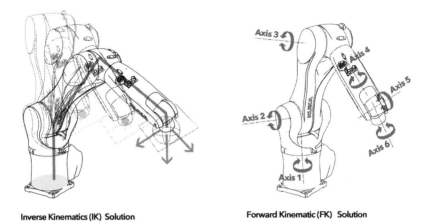

Inverse Kinematics (IK) Solution   **Forward Kinematic (FK) Solution**

Fig. 3. Difference between IK and FK solutions for robotic motion. IK interactively moves all the joints/axis of the robot to "solve" the position/orientation of the end-effector, however in FK solution; users can control the robot through the rotation of each axis.

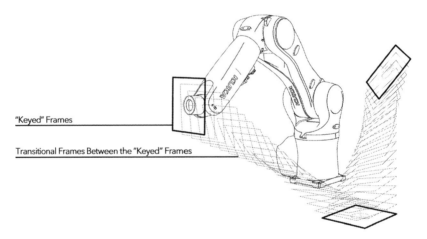

Fig. 4. Key Frame Solver calculates the transitional frames between the keyed frames as a way to define the "resolution"/smoothness of the robotic motion.

3.3   Oriole Component: Wait Solver

As the next component, Oriole Alpha offers a Wait Solver to define the numbers of seconds for each of the frames. The robot arm will stop for the specified duration of time at each keyframe, and continues through the transitional frames with a regular (defined on the robot) speed. For KUKA robots, Wait Solver embeds a KRL wait commend into the final KRL code generated for the robot.

3.4   Oriole Component: Robot Lab

To avoid any damages or unexpected collisions, Oriole Alpha provides a possibility to import the digital model of the robotic set-up into the Grasshopper 3D environment as a way to secure the physical simulation afterward.

3.5   Robotic Post-processor: KUKA|Prc

Although the data produced through Oriole is usable by different post-processors, in Oriole Alpha research, we used KUKA|prc to generate KRL code for KUKA robots. In the first iteration—Oriole Alpha, and as a way to make the platform more usable for users with no programming/coding background—students at the College of Architecture and Environmental Design, at Kent State University, we embedded some of KUKA|prc components into Oriole Alpha components (IK Frame, Key Frame Solver, and Wait Solver). Students later used the "updated"/"upgraded" Oriole components in connection to KUKA|prc Core component to generate KRL codes to be then uploaded to the robot arm.

3.6   Robot Arm: KUKA KR6 R900 Sixx

As the last module of the Oriole Alpha, we used KUKA KR6 R900 Sixx for all of the digital simulations as well as physical tests. Capable of moving up to six kilograms, with six axes of freedom, KR6 R900 Sixx robot was an ideal choice to test Oriole robotic animation in a context of a design studio and as part of the research on animated/moving architecture.

4   Operation and Testing

To test Oriole system as part of an architectural project, we used Oriole Alpha in a design-research studio at the College of Architecture and Environmental Design, at Kent State University. Applying Oriole Alpha, students looked into possibilities of literal motion [1]—through robotics as a design tool to study inside-outside relationships through moving architectural components.

To simulate the physical architectural motions at the desktop scale, students developed architectural massing models digitally. Each of these compositional studies had a super-component [13] which could serve as part of the primary composition or detach from the whole and live as an individual object (Fig. 5).

Later in the process and using digital simulation power of Oriole Alpha, each student studied the potential of super-component as a moving chunk of the architectural composition using the key-framing solutions. Through this method, students were able to animate the super-component using IK frame component of Oriole. This feature enabled a precise animation Key Framing as a way to define the right position for the robot to control the position of the moving component both in relation to the architectural composition and as an independent object on the base (Fig. 6).

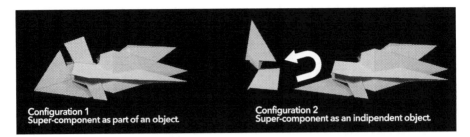

Fig. 5. As part of the studio scenario and in response to Wiscombe's idea of super-component, studio revisited part of an architectural composition that can be a part of the whole (object), –and through some re-configurations, an individual whole (object).

Fig. 6. The precision of Oriole enabled students to design the robotic animation/motion digitally, with almost no issues when it translated to physical robotic motion.

Through a back and forth digital-study of the model using Oriole Alpha and developing multiple iterations based on the robotic digital simulation, students started the production of the final physical models using additive fabrication methods (3D printing and composite fabrication techniques) to initiate the physical simulation set-up. By having the Robot-Lab component of the Oriole Alpha, students precisely measured the position of the physical model in relation to the actual robot—based on the digital simulation. Placing the model in its designed position/set-up, as the last step of the process before running the physical test, each student used their Oriole animation to activate the KUKA|prc plug-in in Grasshopper 3D to generate the KRL code.

Exporting the KRL code via KUKA|prc plug-in, and uploading it to the KUKA robot, students were able to animate the robot—and ultimately the super-component of the physical model, as designed in the digital keyframed animation (Fig. 7).

Fig. 7. An example of robot moving the super-component precisely as digitally animated.

5   Conclusion

Oriole as a parametric animation-based robotic controlling plug-in for Grasshopper 3D enables designers to design the motion path for industrial robot arms interactively using IK frame solutions and Key Frame Solver. The initial studies with Oriole Alpha showed that students with a minor programming background could immediately learn how to design a robotic motion using notions of animation.

In the context of creative robotics, one of the significant features of Oriole is to assist users in designing the motion of the robot independent from the robot path. Focused on the concept of inverse kinematics, using Oriole, designers can "design" the position of the end-effector step-by-step. This possibility is critical when it comes to non-fabrication-based use of robots. In custom pick-and-place set-ups, experimental fabrication, 3D puzzle scenarios, and robotic videography to name a few, it is critical to have control over the precise position of the end-effector and Oriole opens up possibilities to design those correct positions through keyframing.

6   Limitations and Suggestions for Future Research

Two main limitations of this research are the small group of users for the first experiment and limited type of robot to test Oriole—only KR6 R900 Sixx robot. Another limitation of Oriole Alpha research is that the plug-in has been used just for one specific task of custom pick-and-place, to move a component of a physical model and place it in a new position. Given the possibilities of the plug-in, there is a lot more possible in the light of parametric animation-based key-framing.

We are currently working on developing a videography project, using Oriole as a way to animate physical camera utilizing a robot. Different from previous experiences with animation software platforms—such as MAYA to animate robots, the advantage of this future research is the opportunity of controlling the robotic camera through Grasshopper 3D as a native node-based visual programming platform for designers/architects. Another component of future research is to use different types and scales of robot arms to calibrate Oriole as a possible platform. Diversifying users/audiences of the plug-in is a crucial next step, as one of the promises of Oriole is to be adaptable with different design/programming backgrounds.

References

1. Brugnaro, G., Baharlou, E., Vasey, L., Menges, A.: Robotic softness: an adaptive robotic fabrication process for woven structures. In: Proceedings of the 36th Annual Conference of the Association for Computer Aided Design in Architecture (ACADIA), Ann Arbor, MI, USA, pp. 154–163 (2016)
2. Soler, V., Retsin, G., Jimenez, G.M.: A generalized approach to non-layered fused filament fabrication. In: Proceedings of the 37th Annual Conference of the Association for Computer Aided Design in Architecture (ACADIA), Cambridge, MA, USA, pp. 562–571 (2017)

3. Yunis, L., Kyjánek, O., Dörstelmann, M., Prado, M., Schwinn, T., Menges, A.: Bio-inspired and fabrication-informed design strategies for modular fibrous structures in architecture, Fusion. In: Proceedings of the 32nd eCAADe Conference, pp. 423–432. Publisher, Newcastle upon Tyne (2014)
4. Testa, P.: Robot House. Thames & Hudson Inc., New York (2017)
5. Ibrahim, K.: AndyRobot—Robot Animator® for Programming KUKA Robots. www. andyrobot.com/. Accessed 15 Dec 2018
6. Brandon, K., Johnathan, P.: Impossible objects. In: Sheil, B. (ed.) Architectural Design, no 227, pp. 106–111 (2014)
7. Ozel, G.: Case for an architectural singularity: synchronization of robotically actuated motion, sense-based interaction and computational interface. In: Gerber, D., Huang, A., Sanchez, J. (eds.) Proceedings of the 34th Annual Conference of the Association for Computer Aided Design in Architecture (ACADIA), ACADIA/Riverside Architectural, Los Angeles, CA, USA, pp. 399–408 (2015)
8. Bot & Dolly Fuses 3D Animation and Industrial Automation. https://www.robotics-businessreview.com/consumer/bot_dolly_fuses_3d_animation_and_industrial_automation/. Accessed 25 Nov 2013
9. Lynn, G.: Animate FORM. Princeton Architectural Press, New York (1999)
10. Garcia, M.J.: Soft modelling: open source Java application for flexible structural systems. In: Aulikki, H., Österlund, T., Markkanen, P. (eds.) Complexity & Simplicity - Proceedings of the 34th eCAADe Conference, Oulu, Finland, vol. 2, pp. 265–274 (2016)
11. Poustinchi, E., Wang, S., Luhan, G.: NO KEYBOARD, NO MOUSE-hybrid digital-analog hardware design for enhancing design UI and UX. In: Fukuda, T., Huang, W., Janssen, P., Crolla, K., Alhadidi, S. (eds.) Learning, Adapting and Prototyping - Proceedings of the 23rd CAADRIA Conference, Beijing, China, vol. 1, pp. 535–544 (2018)
12. Braumann, J., Brell-Cokcan, S.: Adaptive robot control: new parametric workflows directly from design to KUKArobots. In: Proceedings of the 33rd International Conference on Education and Research in Computer Aided Architectural Design in Europe (eCAADe) 2016, Vienna, Austria, vol. 2, pp. 243–250 (2015)
13. Wiscombe, T.: Discreteness or towards a flat ontology of architecture. Project (Issue 3), 34–43 (2014)

Tools, Methods and Implementation of
Urban Design

A Method of Mesh Simplification for Drone 3D Modeling with Architectural Feature Extraction

Chi-Li Cheng$^{(\boxtimes)}$ and June-Hao Hou

National Chiao Tung University, Hsinchu, Taiwan
{micky, jhou}@arch.nctu.edu.tw

Abstract. This paper proposes a method of mesh simplification for 3D terrain or city models generated photogrammetrically from drone captured images, enabled by the ability of extracting the architectural features. Compare to traditional geometric computational method, the proposed method recognizes and processes the features from the architectural perspectives. In addition, the workflow also allows exporting the simplified models and geometric features to open platforms, e.g. OpenStreetMap, for practical usages in site analysis, city generation, and contributing to the open data communities.

Keywords: Mesh reconstruction · Photogrammetry · Mesh simplification · Procedural mode · Machine learning

1 Introduction

Designer and Researcher have been exploring approaches that convert photos into 3D models effectively for a long time, such as the reconstruction algorithm proposed by Qing et al. back in 1994 [1]. Such development brings about a great convenience to generate 3D models and capture the physical reality for wide range of applications.

Recently, tools utilizing photogrammetric modeling technology, such as VisualSFM, Recap Pro, Altizure...etc., have becoming more and more mature and popular in many industries, especially in content production, asset management and land survey. Moreover, there are artists and architects use photogrammetry to create fascinating works, such as oddviz [2].

Nonetheless, the 3D mesh model with a huge number of faces usually causes issues when it is utilized. First, when architects want to employ photogrammetry to survey the city, the majority of their computers are inadequate to process it for modify or display. Second, in the scenario that users attempt to 3D print it, the unclosed, the self-intersecting, and rugged mesh might make it impossible. Therefore, it is necessary to reduce the faces of the mesh model while retaining the critical geometric features, making the model feasible to be used in common applications. Although there are certain methods to reduce the mesh, they are not mainly meet the need of architects. In architectural design process, the requires are distinct building volumes and terrain with less faces.

© Springer Nature Singapore Pte Ltd. 2019
J.-H. Lee (Ed.): CAAD Futures 2019, CCIS 1028, pp. 157–167, 2019.
https://doi.org/10.1007/978-981-13-8410-3_12

However, the simplification or retopology processes in most of the mesh-editing tools are unable to recognize architecture features; besides, the achieving models still contain too many meshes and lose architectural details. In order to deal with them, we speculate what the method should be, developing it.

What if we can employ certain architectural knowledge and use Artificial Intelligence (AI) to assist and recognize architectural features to further simplified a wall into only few meshes rather than few hundreds? What if the simplified model (Fig. 1) can be directly shared on the open platform such as OpenStreetMap (OSM) through this process?

Fig. 1. Reconstructing the photogrammetric model

2   Method

The function of this reconstruction process uses the mesh generated by photogrammetry software (VisualSFM) as input. Then, it outputs the reduced model which contains ground and buildings. To achieve the effect, the strategy that we use is slicing the model into contour polylines (Fig. 2) for feature attraction. The approach has several advantages. For instance, to analysis 2D polylines is more efficient than to analysis the 3D mesh. Based on our preliminary test, we realize that those center points of contours can be grouped by certain distance appropriately majority of the time; therefore, we use it as the means to derive individual buildings roughly.

Additionally, polylines are more practical than 3D model to show the relationships between buildings and spaces because of the fact that the majority of architectural design process based on plan view; therefore, the process in this research is similar to the scenario that architects view architectural plan, comparing and analyzing the relationships between different elevations.

Fig. 2. Contours of terrain and buildings for analysis.

Moreover, it references colors from the texture of the photogrammetric model and implements unsupervised machine learning to discriminate and group these polylines. After grouping these contours to represent each of buildings, the process removes inappropriate parts and reconstruct the building volumes, retaining the details of buildings.

In previous steps, it derives certain preliminary information, such as contours, ground model, and colors from the texture, thereby, it enables this reconstruction process to analyze the contours of the model based on geometric features and colors. It is useful to deal with the difficulties when the tree canopy and building are stuck together; thereby, the process can evaluate the quality of the building's contours, extracting proper contours that are without non-building parts to represent the building. Following is the process diagram of the method (Fig. 3).

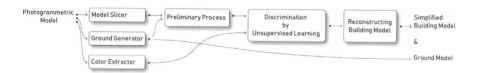

Fig. 3. The overall process of this method

In this research, we take the model of NCTU (National Chiao Tung University, Taiwan) (Fig. 4) campus as an example to demonstrate the reconstruction process. The campus model is generated through the cloud service Altizure from a series of drone-captured photographs. In the model there are enormous elements such as buildings, sport field, trees, cars, street furniture, etc. We use this complex composition to test this method.

Fig. 4. The original Altizure model

2.1   The Preliminary Process

The process starts with generating ground model. The ground model can be output as terrain for further usage. Besides, the ground model will be used in the subsequent process to distinguish parts of buildings from the entire model. Following are two steps to process it.

Step 1. Generating Underneath Surface (terrain). First of all, this reconstruction process calculates the best fit plane (Fig. 5a) from the point group in the model, using this plane to generate the bounding box of this model. The underneath plane (Fig. 5b) of the bounding box will be use as the preliminary ground model.

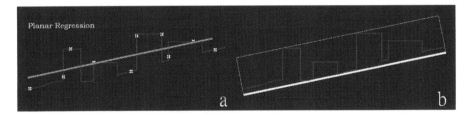

Fig. 5. The way to generate appropriate bounding box (section perspective).

Step 2. Fitting the Terrain. In this section, the mechanism is like taking a pattern by rubbing upside down. It finds the closest points from the preliminary ground model to the original model, then fitting them (Fig. 6a). It will neglect buildings parts because the buildings parts on the model are viewed as holes when the program viewing it upside down; while finding the closest points on the original model, those points in these holes (building parts) will not be picked (Fig. 6b).

In detail, after gaining these closest points on original model, it only modifies the control points in the z-axis in order to keep the surface tidy and even; otherwise, the terrain will be uneven.

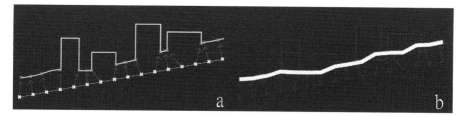

Fig. 6. Reconstructing the ground (section perspective)

The result shows that it removes most of convex parts on the ground, such as buildings, trees, etc. Consequently, the result will be the pure and empty ground (Fig. 7). Besides, the terrain model will be appropriate to generate contour line.

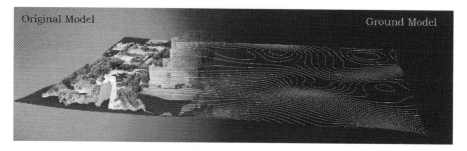

Fig. 7. The result of the terrain

2.2 Building Model Reconstruction

The procedure of the reconstructing process includes four steps. Step 1 is filtering the models that are separated from the ground. The preliminary process is grouping these contours to represent buildings. However, it contains certain elements are useless. Majority of the time, the mesh near ground are distorted because of the dead angles while taking these aerial pictures, as a result, these contour of the parts near the ground can be viewed as improper elements. Besides, somehow, some convex parts are very subtle, and the contour might be extremely short. It is necessary to remove these improper elements before group them to speed up the process and to avoid null result. The below image shows the result after filtering (Fig. 8).

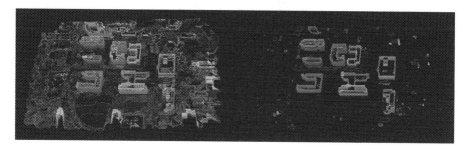

Fig. 8. The result of the filter

Step 2 is grouping these elements; after filtering them, it begins group them. In detail, we utilize the polygon center component to derive the center of polylines. The component contains three kinds of output from different kinds of average, such as vertices, edges, and area. In order to group them appropriately, the approach that we opt is area centroid because other options are too sensitive to the distribution of control points and make these center points scattered. Those scattered points cause excessive grouping, making the model complex. Following figure is the test of these three conditions. The performance of using area center is better than others (Fig. 9).

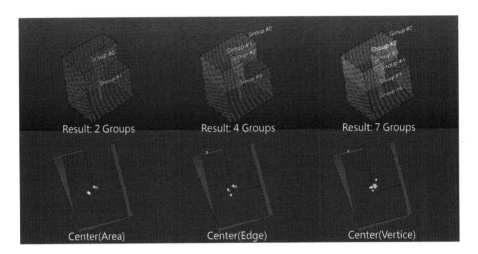

Fig. 9. The example shows results of three approaches

Step 3 is picking the most typical contour in each group. Each group of contours will be converted to a building volume. To keep the fidelity of the shape, we use the number of corners, the length of polyline and area of the region as features to estimate them. Then, the most typical contour will be picked up to represent the outline of the building volume (Fig. 10). The method that we gain the number of corners is referred to the Corner Finder for Polylines proposed by Wolin et al. [3].

Furthermore, the number of each group manifests its continuity in z-axis. The continuity can be a feature that assists the discrimination process to classify contours. In general, the groups of building contour contain larger number; in contrast, the groups of trees and articles of street furniture contain smaller number because they are irregular relatively.

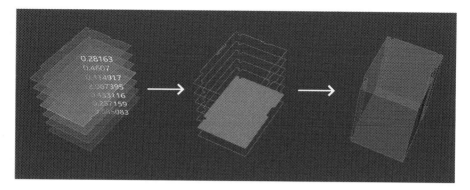

Fig. 10. Picking proper contour to represent a building volume

Step 4 is the discrimination process. Although these qualities of building volumes are not bad, they still have some defects on certain contours. For example, when the trees attach the face of the building. continuously, these contours might be viewed as building part.

In this situation, those outlines that mix tree and building bring about deficiency of the reconstructing result. To deal with it, we employ unsupervised machine learning as means to filter the model with texture information.

Unsupervised machine learning has been utilized to segment 3D mesh. It is similar to the methods proposed by Lavoue et al. [4]. However, in this section, the aim is to remove improper building volumes. There is a research that demonstrates using GMMs (Gaussian mixture models) to classify the texture data efficiently [5]. The condition more suitable for ours because we attempt to develop the process that performs the perception of the texture (materials).

The unsupervised machine learning tool that we used is the Gaussian mixture model component of the Lunchbox plugin in Grasshopper (Fig. 11).

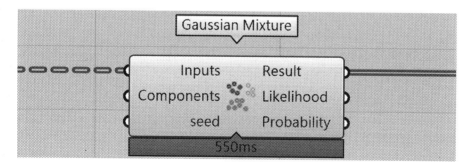

Fig. 11. The Gaussian mixture that we utilize in the section (Color figure online)

This method is useful to classify the condition with complex features. In this research, we use GMMs to separate select these improper contours and to remove them. We make the dataset includes RGB information and the continuity of each building volume (number). RGB information is from the texture image. In order to gain RGB information, we decode the OBJ format to get the texture coordinates of each face's vertices. Then, we pair each control points of contours and the closest vertices' colors from the texture. Therefore, the discrimination process acquires the perception of materials and shapes' continuity. Those red parts in Fig. 11 are determined as non-building or inappropriate contours by this approach (Fig. 12).

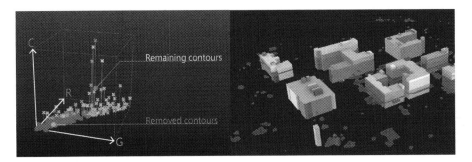

Fig. 12. Using GMMs to discriminate those building volumes (Color figure online)

3   Result

Our method has the ability to refine building volumes and simplify the extremely complex photogrammetric model by about 99% (In this case, the original mesh contains 142,900 faces while the result contains 918 faces). Furthermore, certain details can remain, such as the skylight, the roof of elevator shaft, etc. (Figure 13) Besides, each building volume is placed in a neat stack. It makes these models accessed and utilized easily. The below render image demonstrates the effect of the building volumes that this method produces (Fig. 14). Running this method in Grasshopper on a laptop equipped with Core i7 8 Gen CPU takes about 20 s.

Fig. 13. The result retains certain details

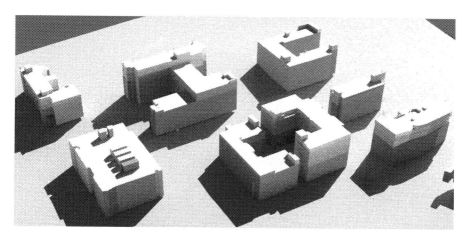

Fig. 14. The rendering of the output model with shadow

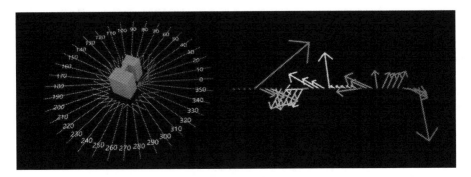

Fig. 15. The directions of a building's contour segments

4   Conclusion

The approach is inspired by tomography technique because the algorithm mainly deals with the contours (polylines) of the subject, focusing on the geometric features of horizontal contours. This perspective of view is similar to figure-ground perception that the majority of architects rely on. It gives substantial information of space even though it is so simple.

This reconstruction process has the ability of simplifying complex mesh models, simplifying them appropriately by referring architectural knowledge through machine learning, generating building outlines and elevations, and exporting the geometric features for further usage. Eventually, this process will be suitable for rapid modeling of an urban region, the analysis of up-to-date building outlines, and data collection of buildings as buildings not meshes.

It can be applied at several purposes, such as environmental analysis [6], urban research [7], Building Information Model [8], reconstruction of simulation environment, etc. Therefore, this approach is multifunctional and is able to make design process and investigation efficiently. Besides, we develop the reconstruction process as toolkit in grasshopper as a means to enable the majority of architects and designer to utilize the design tool efficiently.

5   Future Work

After developing this method, the next work is to convert the result model with the height value to the format that can be upload onto OpenStreetMap. Besides, we will develop several analysis tools with the converter, making the entire toolkit completed.

By now, this method can be used for exporting building volumes. However, when the contours of buildings in the photogrammetric model are not closed, the building will be neglected. The next work that we attempt to do is enhancing the guessing ability of the buildings' appearances. In addition, the reconstruction of trees and articles of street furniture are not developed yet. These elements are also crucial when investigating the urban during the architectural design; therefore, the developments of these functions are in the list of future work.

Moreover, we assume that it might have further usages by using more features of contours when this research demonstrates the performance of construction based on contour analysis. The direction is crucial in architectural design because sunlight influences whether the architect are comfortable to live. The direction of each segments in contours might be vital features. The hypothesis in the further research is that whether the continuity and direction of segments of contours can let the method based on deep learning has the strong perception to recognize types of architecture; additionally, artificial intelligent might have the ability to design based on this approach. As a result, regarding to the orientation through retrieving and analysis the normal vectors from the contour segments will be the approach in our future studies (Fig. 15).

Acknowledgment. The research is partially supported by the Ministry of Science and Technology under Grant Number MOST 108-2634-F-009-013 through Pervasive Artificial Intelligence Research (PAIR) Labs, Taiwan

References

1. Qing, W.Y., Philip, C.L., Chen, Z.T.: Efficient algorithm for the reconstruction of 3D objects from orthographic projections. Comput.-Aided Des. **26**(9), 700–717 (1994)
2. Oddiviz: a collective that uses photogrammetry to document in three dimensions. https://www.oddviz.com/. Accessed 1 Dec 2018
3. Wolin, A., Eoff, B., Hammound, T.: ShortStraw: a simple and effective corner finder for polylines. In: EUROGRAPHICS Workshop on Sketch-Based Interfaces and Modeling (2008)
4. Lavoue, G., Wolf, C.: Markov random fields for improving 3D mesh analysis and segmentation (2008)
5. Permuter, H., Francos, J., Jermyn, L.: A study of Gaussian mixture models of color and texture features for image classification and segmentation. Pattern Recognit. **39**, 695–706 (2005)
6. Roberts, A., Marsh, A.: ECOTECT: environmental prediction in architectural education. In: 19th eCAADe Conference Proceedings of Architectural Information Management, Helsinki (Finland) 29–31 August 2001, pp. 342–347 (2010). ISBN 0-9523687-8-1
7. Akdag, S.G., Cagdas, G., Guney, C.: Analyzing the changes of Bosphorus Silhouette, FUTURE CITIES [28th eCAADe Conference Proceedings/ ISBN 978-0-9541183-9-6] ETH Zurich (Switzerland) 15–18 September 2010, pp. 815–823 (2010)
8. You, C.F., Yang, S.S.: Reconstruction of architectural model from orthographic drawings reconstruction of curvilinear manifold objects from orthographic views. Comput. Graph. **20**(2), 275–280 (1996)

Citizen Visual Search Engine:
Detection and Curation of Urban Objects

Immanuel Koh$^{(\boxtimes)}$ ⓘ and Jeffrey Huang

École polytechnique fédérale de Lausanne (EPFL), 1015 Lausanne, Switzerland
{Immanuel.koh, jeffrey.huang}@epfl.ch

Abstract. Increasingly, the ubiquity of satellite imagery has made the data analysis and machine learning of large geographical datasets one of the building blocks of visuospatial intelligence. It is the key to discover current (and predict future) cultural, social, financial and political realities. How can we, as designers and researchers, empower citizens to understand and participate in the design of our cities amid this technological shift? As an initial step towards this broader ambition, a series of creative web applications, in the form of visual search engines, has been developed and implemented to data mine large datasets. Using open sourced deep learning and computer vision libraries, these applications facilitate the searching, detecting and curating of urban objects. In turn, the paper proposes and formulates a framework to design truly citizen-centric creative visual search engines – a contribution to citizen science and citizen journalism in spatial terms.

Keywords: Deep learning · Computer vision · Satellite imagery ·
Citizen science · Artificial intelligence

1 Introduction

The collection and analysis of satellite imageries have been increasingly used by organizations or companies as a means to infer new spatial and temporal insights at the local and global scales. What was once only accessible to the military intelligence is now made almost ubiquitous. On the one hand, there are the new satellite players who send private micro-satellites into space to capture the Earth's images; on the other hand, there are the new startups using machine learning to gather actionable intelligence from these images to predict market movements. In near real-time, cultural, social, financial and political insights can be gained by simply harnessing the visual data of the Earth's conditions from above. In addition, we are also witnessing a surge in the resolution of satellite imagery – from the 60 m/pixel in the 1970s, to 30 m/pixel in the 1980s, to 20 m/pixel in the 1990s, to 2.5 m/pixel in 2000s and now as much as 0.5 m/pixel [1]. Yet, the public is denied access to very high-quality satellite imagery often controlled by commercial entities and political organizations. We argue that this denial is not only technological and monetary, but fundamentally political. It is a loss of the citizen's power to detect, search and make sense (curate) of the world. It is what Eyal Weizman refers to as *the threshold of detectability*, a condition between what is and is not detectable [2]. In the past, this detectability is dependent on the grain size of a single

J.-H. Lee (Ed.): CAAD Futures 2019, CCIS 1028, pp. 168–182, 2019.
https://doi.org/10.1007/978-981-13-8410-3_13

silver salt particle on analogue film and now, in our case, the pixel size of today's digital satellite imagery.

How can we, as designers and researchers, empower citizens to understand and participate in the design of our cities amid this new technological shift? As an initial step towards this broader ambition, a series of creative web applications, in the form of visual search engines, has been developed and implemented to data mine large datasets using open sourced deep learning libraries to facilitate in the detection, recognition, tracking and classification of a selection of visible urban artifacts. These applications are in fact the computational apparatus for our envisioned citizen science and citizen journalism. By gathering insights from the curated urban data and presenting them as playful interactions, citizens will be empowered to explore and reflect on their current territorial conditions and implications. A total of 6 different projects will be discussed in varying detail to highlight the opportunities found and strategies used. All projects used Switzerland as their site, with the exception of one in Africa and one in Colombia. All projects are also full stack web developments, implementing different deep neural network architectures and image processing algorithms, on both raster and vector tiles as their raw datasets. The collective contribution of this design research is the prototyping of creative visual applications to search for a specific territorial reality and framing its potential urban meaning and values, while democratizing GIS for all.

2   Definitions

Urban Objects. What are urban objects? In the Sydney Urban Objects Dataset, there are altogether 26 classes of objects 3D scanned (LIDAR), ranging from umbrella, bench, tree to bus and buildings [3]. In the SpaceNet dataset on Amazon Web Services (AWS) [4], probably the largest dataset of this sort, a corpus of prelabelled satellite imagery of up to 0.3 m/pixel resolution featuring selected cities, such as Paris, Shanghai and Rio de Janeiro, has recently been made publicly available for the machine learning research community. In our paper, we define an urban object as any entity that is visible on a satellite image. Our concept of urban objects is closely related to Google's Data Center Mural project by artist Odell [5]. This 2016 project featured the ways in which Odell manually cropped objects found on Google Maps and organized them in an artistic fashion according to their types, shapes, colors and other visual criteria. Her artworks from this series are predominantly an aesthetical endeavor and suggest to us that when urban objects are removed from their contexts, a comparative analysis and an alternative reading of their meanings could emerge in surprising ways. Another strand of our motivation comes from the work of Forensic Architecture [2] whose use of satellite maps and crowdsourced datasets provide the basis to critically interrogate society's political, economic and social issues in visual and temporal terms.

3 Detection with Deep Learning

There are 4 different projects in this section that have used deep neural network architecture to implement their creative visual search engine. Each project discussion is organized in the following order – objective, data, model and engine, to better facilitate a common reading structure. Inspired by Google Map route planning capabilities, the first project ('Roads') uses a publicly available dataset of Africa that contains a higher resolution of satellite imagery to develop an app that will plot the list of safest routes from one location to the other, according to the prediction of a deep neural network trained with pre-labelled data of 'non-road', 'paved-road' and 'dirt-road'. The second project ('Photovoltaics') trained a neural network to recognize and detect every solar panel found on any building in the entirety of Switzerland. As a timely example of citizen science and journalism, it then uses this as a proxy to measure and visualize the solar energy production in each municipality and canton during the May 2017 Swiss Energy Voting. The third project ('Roofs') uses deep learning for ethnographic purposes, as well as to experiment with the process of human-machine collaboration, specifically in the task of data labelling and object classification. This application detects the indigenous Colombian houses in the tropical forest of La Sierra Nevada, and in the process provides users the opportunity to both visually discover and understand its specific spatial and social configurations, while verifying the accuracy of the machine's own predictions. The last project ('Trees'), concerned with the effects of deforestation, trained a convolutional neural network to classify and calculate tree coverage from satellite imagery, according to their pixel spatial density and sparsity. This interactive app not only allows users to pick, compare and visualize any city or canton, but also see their ecological ranking in Switzerland.

3.1 Urban Object: *Roads*

Objective. The urban object of concern in this project is the *road*, more specifically the quality of roads in the African city of Ouagadougou in Burkina Faso – paved road versus dirt road. According to the World Economic Forum and World Health Organization [6], 40 of the 50 countries with the highest road traffic deaths are all African. Compared to Europe, Africa has 10 times fewer cars and yet 3 times higher road traffic deaths. The prototype is akin to a Google Map interface, except that the recommended routes are ranked based on inferred safety, rather than duration of travel. In addition, the generated data from our deep learning model could serve as a proxy to measure economic development of African city neighborhoods, thus creating awareness to both citizens and other stakeholders.

Data. The pre-labelled dataset is available at Kaggle [7] consisting of 1 km × 1 km satellite images in 3-band and 16-band formats. For our purposes, we only utilize the 3-band format and the 2 class types – *poor_dirt_cart_track* and *good_roads*. To ensure a balanced training set of our 3 classes ('non-road', 'good road', 'bad road'), tiles without roads are removed from our training set. To improve the training process, we have also applied normalization to the images by removing the mean and dividing them by the standard deviation. For our supervised learning process, each RGB satellite image tile is labelled according to the 3 masks of each class. The class labels are originally in the vector format of the given GeoJSON file but are converted as raster format corresponding to the image pixels distribution. Each mask is a black and white image with the same number of pixels as the tile. Each pixel is white when it is associated with the given category.

Model. After several trials, the U-Net with two phases of upscaling and downscaling is chosen as the most appropriate convolutional neural network architecture. Our U-Net consists of 4 blocks in each phase. Each block in turn consists of 2 convolutions (kernel 3×3) with a RELU activation function and a bias. For the downscaling (1st phase), each block ends with a max pooling layer; while for the upscaling (2nd phase), each block begins with a upsampling layer. Finally, the model ends with a 2-dimensional convolutional layer using a sigmoid activation function, the binary cross entropy as loss function and Adam as the optimizer. This last layer is to predict the final classification of each pixel according to the combined 3 classes of binary masks ('non-road', 'good road', 'bad road') given a RGB satellite imagery input. Thus, it is similar to an image segmentation classification problem. We then generate an infinite stream of training data for our neural network model with the following data augmentation procedure:

- Picking a random 4-uples (satellite image and the 3 masks)
- Select a random rotational angle and position displacement
- Crop the 4-uples as 160×160 images according to the new rotation and displacement
- Check if at least 1 pixel corresponds to a road label and return the 4 crops. Otherwise, restart the procedure with a new randomly selected 4-uples.

The training lasted 10 days on a NVIDIA GTX Titan (GK110) with 3000 epochs of 212 batches (24 tiles measuring 160×160 pixels each). The inference process proceeds by first reading a given satellite image, cutting it into 160×160 pixels tiles (with overlaps and normalization), reconstructing as 512×512 pixel tile, merging all three classes with 'non-road' pixel as transparent channel, 'good road' pixel as green channel and 'bad road' pixel as red channel.

Engine. (Figure 1) The user interface (React application) consists of a simple web map visualization and a sidebar allowing the user to type in the desired origin and destination with the additional autocomplete functionality from Google Maps Places API. Multiple itineraries are then generated with the same API and serialized to JSON and sent to the 1st server (Node.js). Upon receiving the routes, the server determines the tiles traversed by these routes and trigger a 2nd server to classify the pixels in the tiles. The 1st server then receives the inferred tiles for reading and extracting all the pixels along the itineraries before computing a score that represents the safety measure (blue for good and red for bad parts of the trajectories). The inferred tiles are also displayed as an overlay on the web map and red-blue trajectories.

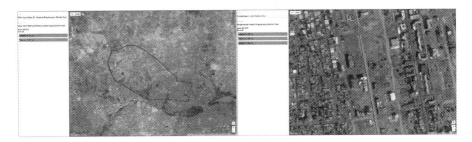

Fig. 1. (LEFT) Screenshot of the 'ROADS' project interface. The side menu lists the user's origin and destination in Ouagadougou, followed by the sorted generated itineraries according to the computed safety measures in percentages. The web map visualizes the generated itineraries (red = unsafe route, blue = safe route). (RIGHT) Another screenshot with zoom-in details. The web map shows the satellite image tiles being overlaid with pixels mask (red = bad road, green = good road) inferred by our deep learning model. (Color figure online)

3.2   Urban Object: *Photovoltaics*

Objective. The urban object to be searched in this project is the *photovoltaic panels* installed on the roofs of buildings in the entirety of Switzerland. Related works, such as the recent Google's Project Sunroof [8] and the Swiss Sonnen Dach [9] projects, have demonstrated the use of satellite imagery in predicting the amount of sunlight a given building receives on its roof and facade per year, in order to then calculate the optimal solar plan for economical energy production and savings. However, our project is closer to the 2013 Big Atlas of Los Angeles Pools [10], where the focus is about the searching and classifying of urban objects. Instead of mapping LA pools with crowdsourcing mechanism (e.g. Amazon Mechanical Turk services) and traditional computer vision algorithms, our project maps and classifies all the buildings in Switzerland based on the presence or absence of solar panels using deep neural networks and web scraped datasets. Apart from the non-existent tag category of 'solar panels' on OpenStreetMap, the varying shapes and colors of solar panels makes using a standard image processing algorithm ineffective for our project. More philosophically speaking, the project is concerned with a citizen science approach of mapping and measuring urban objects, thus making visible their correlations with the invisible forces of economy, politics and ecology. For instance, in the case of the 2016 Swiss vote for/against "Exiting Nuclear Energy", our project could be used to predict the result based on the distribution of solar panels in each Swiss canton.

Data. There exists no pre-labelled training dataset for our classification problem, thus necessitating both the collection of our own datasets and the creation of their corresponding labels. Using the Overpass Turbo API, we extract the WGS84 coordinates of every building footprint polygon in the city of Lausanne from OpenStreetMap formatted as GeoJSON. We then download every satellite tile at zoom level 20 (the maximum allowable resolution via the Google Maps Static API), with its center according to our computed barycenter of each building polygon. The square bounding box of the intersection between the building polygon and the satellite tile (640 × 640) is used to crop and resize the final image to 224×224 pixels, which is the default input size of our chosen deep learning model. Since this dataset is still unlabeled, we created a minimalist web interface showing a pre-labelled satellite image and 3 different buttons ('yes', 'no', 'redo') for the user to verify if a solar panel is visible. With our manual labelling interface, we manage to label 15000 satellite images by simply clicking the corresponding buttons at a rate of 5000 images per hour. However, only 1000 out of these 15000 images actually contain solar panels and we end up using a balanced training set of 900 positive and 900 negative images, and another 100 positive and 100 negative images for the validation set of our neural network. In addition to the training set, we need to download the remaining satellite tiles for the rest of Switzerland to be used for our prediction. The same workflow is used, except with 4 API keys to overcome the API daily limits and with 50 downloads in parallel, thus achieving a rate of downloading 100,000 images per day in approximately 1 h. The cropping process takes 2 h while the classification rate is 12000 images per hour. Due to Overpass Turbo API's internal memory limit of 2 GB when processing queries, the queries are done canton by canton and even split into successive queries for big cantons.

Model. We use a transfer learning approach with an existing pre-trained convolutional neural network called ResNet50 for our classification problem. The advantage of using such an approach is the capability to train a model with little data, in our case, a labelled dataset of 2000 images. Although more complex than the VGG-16 architecture due to its residual architecture and 50 layers of convolutions, the ResNet50 is much lighter and faster to train. We first remove the last fully connected layer (FC) and do a forward pass through this network to obtain the output features and save them as.npy files. We then train our own 1-layer fully connected neural network with a binary output by loading the previously saved.npy files and achieve an accuracy of 85%. For the final prediction model, we replace the last fully connected layer (FC) of the original ResNet50 model with our newly trained small neural network.

Engine. (Figure 2) In total, 1.5 million buildings have been classified with the initial 500 GB of downloaded satellite images. Each canton is represented with a single JSON file containing the number of buildings with and without solar panels, as well as all the building coordinates. An interactive map (rendered as SVG) is made with D3js for the data visualization. This interactive exploration can be experienced at the level of country, canton, municipality and individual building. All the regions are shaded and mapped on a color scale, representing their respective percentages of buildings with solar panels, such that users could compare their statistical differences at any zoom level. Additionally, the interface provides the mechanism for users to verify the presence or absence of the solar panels when viewing the satellite imagery, thus crowdsourcing from the users to improve the accuracy and revealing the potential biasness of our trained model during their online interactions. Due to the huge number of SVG objects, to facilitate a smooth and fluid interaction, the web client only loads on-demand. In other words, without loading all the files in the browser, the SVG elements from previous canton are removed when clicking on another canton during the interactive session.

Fig. 2. Screenshot of the 'PHOTOVOLTAICS' project interface. A web map application showing the distribution of buildings with solar panels (in yellow) and those without (in black), based on the prediction of a trained deep learning neural network. The different Swiss municipalities are shaded based on a color scale (from light red to dark red) that maps the percentages of buildings with solar panels within their respective regions. (Color figure online)

3.3   Urban Object: *Roofs*

Objective. The urban object to be searched in this project is the *roof* itself, more specifically the roofs of the Colombian indigenous house distributed among the tropical forests of La Sierra Nevada that are visible from satellite imagery. Recent online projects like GlobalXplorer [11], which allow citizen explorers to identify culturally important ruins with high-resolution satellite images, serves as our initial inspiration. The additional features of our project are that the user will have the choice to do some guided exploration, as well as verify data labeled by our algorithm. More precisely, the focus is on images containing (or not) Colombian indigenous houses. This way, the user will participate in improving an algorithm that could potentially detect global settlements from different tropical forests.

Data. We use the Google Map API to fetch 1700 satellite tiles as the training set (1500 as positive and 200 as negative labels), and another 360 tiles as the validation set (100 as positive and 260 as negative labels). Each of the satellite tiles is 224×224 in size and is cropped to remove any unnecessary overlaid annotations by Google Maps. The tile colors are also normalized before feeding them to our deep learning model – using transfer learning with a pre-trained convolutional neural network (CNN).

Model. The VGG-16 that we are using for our transfer learning has already been pre-trained with the ImageNet dataset, containing millions of images, to classify 1000 classes of objects. The VGG-16 model consists of 5 blocks of convolutional layers and 1 block of fully-connected layers. We have removed this top block of 3 fully-connected layers, as well as, the last layer (max-pooling layer) of the last convolutional block. Such that we could use their output features as inputs for our smaller fully convolutional network (FCN) of 4 layers to predict if an image contains (or not) any indigenous settlement. Our trained model has an accuracy of close to 98% (validation set). The advantage of using FCN is the ability to visualize the regions of the image that have activated the last convolutional layer in the form of a heatmap, thus serving our purpose in visually understanding how the neural network has perceived the given satellite imagery.

Engine. (Figures 3 and 4) In addition to crowdsourcing the locations of potential indigenous settlements, this project also provides a means for users to confront the predictive accuracy of our deep learning model. Here, users are able to see what our 'black box' machine is 'seeing' (activations) and are empowered to make their own data verification as a community. Technically, it also helps to improve our deep learning model with human curated data.

Fig. 3. Screenshot of the 'ROOFS' project interface. A web map application guiding the user in exploring and detecting the presence of Colombian indigenous house settlements distributed among the tropical forests of La Sierra Nevada.

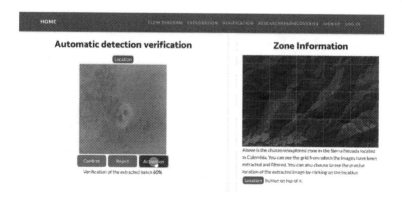

Fig. 4. Another screenshot of the 'ROOFS' project interface. On the left panel, users are empowered to verify the accuracy of our deep learning model and at the same time understand how the model sees via the visualization of its neural networks' activations. The panel on the right displays the unexplored areas, while providing users with the geographical context in which the satellite image is taken from.

3.4   Urban Object: *Trees*

Objective. The urban object to be computed in this project is the *tree* itself. By conceptualizing trees as pixels found on satellite imagery, a measure of their spatial density and sparsity per satellite tile (fixed at a specified zoom level) can be framed as a measure of deforestation. The curation is comparatively visualized: displaying 2 regions, side-by-side, at a selected hierarchical level of the canton and the municipality in Switzerland.

Data. In order to have a realistic representation of trees as pixels, we have opted for a zoom level of 16, which gives a resolution of 2.387 m/pixel with a tile size of 256×256, or 512×512 if we upscale it with MapBox's added functionality. For a supervised learning approach like ours, the only available source of training labels is OpenStreetMap (OSM) via the Overpass Turbo API, such as querying for the tag *"natural = tree"* which is an OSM node that represents a single tree or *"landuse = forest"* which represents wooded plantations. The tree density could then be calculated and each tile labelled. However, it soon became clear that the labels are very incomplete and thus no longer an option for our purposes.

Model. 3 different Deep Neural Networks architectures were initially considered – the Convolutional Neural Networks (CNN) where the input is an image tile and the output is a number representing tree density; the Fully Convolutional Networks (FCN); and the U-Nets where the input is also an image tile and the output is a categorically segmented version of the same image. However, none of these architectures which each requires a huge number of pre-labelled training dataset was eventually found appropriate and a novel approach of Per-Pixel classification was adopted instead. Our approach only requires 15 manually labelled satellite tiles which translates to almost 4 million inputs ($15 \times 512 \times 512$). After balancing the ratio of tree/non-tree pixels in this dataset, 768622 inputs were used for the training model. Two different machine learning models were tested and both yield good results with around 92% accuracies. The first model is an AdaBoost with 512 decision trees as base classifiers, while the other is a simple fully connected Neural Network with 3 hidden layers of 256 nodes each. The input feature vectors of length 10 is used which consists of the pixel colors in CIELAB color space, entropy values and illumination invariant values.

Engine. (Figure 5) After the tile classification, both the density and sparsity of the trees are calculated. Several other measures based on the statistics fetched from the Federal Statistical Office of Switzerland are used as well, namely cars per inhabitant, relative area and relative population. Together, these 5 features with their corresponding weights of 160, 240, 30, 2, 1 form the basis for the curatorial ranking of the most/least air polluted cities and cantons in Switzerland. Since this is a prototype, only all the tiles from the cantons of Vaud and Geneva are classified, which already amounts to 20 GB of 5 million records. The size could have been in the billions if each pixel and its coordinate is saved. Instead, what we have done here is to save them as tile of 32×32 pixels each. We are aware that our Per-Pixel approach is probably contrary to the region-based visual perception of objects by humans. Thus, 2 image processing filters (erosion and dilation) are used on the predicted outputs to take into consideration the neighboring pixels while removing any potential noise. The final interface allows a side-by-side visualization, measurement and comparison of different spaces in Switzerland at any scale, from individual cities to cantons and even arbitrarily user drawn areas. Their respective rankings and scores are also indicated according to our custom-made scale index of the 5 weighted features.

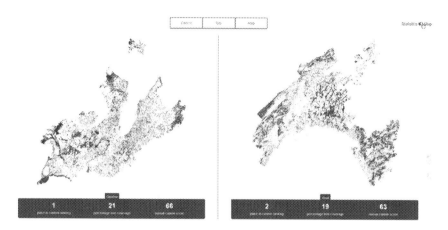

Fig. 5. Screenshot of the 'TREES' project interface. A web application showing side-by-side 2 different cantons (Geneva vs Vaud) in Switzerland with their respective statistics and predicted tree coverage.

4   Curation with Computer Vision

Even though the use of deep neural networks has proved to be highly effective in the previously discussed projects, the following projects take on a non-deep learning approach in the implementation of their curatorial applications. Instead, computer vision and image processing algorithms are used which allow more explicit feature selection and finer-tuned differentiation beyond a binary one. Here, there is also a greater emphasis on alternative user interaction in curating the visual data. One project ('Pitches') visually ranks artifacts from satellite imagery by looking at ways to grade the quality of football pitches and tennis courts found in Switzerland. Instead of using deep learning, OpenCV (an open source computer vision library) is used for template matching, to detect and score key parts of the pitches, such as the end lines, sidelines and goal lines. This application thus not only provides a means for the respective city council to ensure the maintenance and quality of their sport infrastructure, but also to potentially notify OpenStreetMap (OSM) of any missing or mislabeled vector tiles in their databases. For the pleasure in playful curation, one project ('Lakes') rethinks the process of visual search as one of simply sketching a line on screen. With this simple gestural input, the application will search for lakes in Switzerland with the best matching geographical boundaries and rank them accordingly. Again, each project discussion is organized in the following order – objective, data, algorithm and engine, to better facilitate a common reading structure.

4.1   Urban Object: *Pitches*

Objective. The urban object to be curated in this project is the *pitch*, more specifically the quality of football pitches and tennis courts found in the entire Switzerland. It is a curatorial engine where users can search and explore pitches according to their qualitative score – in our case, the measured clarity of the field line markings as seen on the satellite imagery. In doing so, the application also indirectly illustrates the economic well-being and social infrastructural investment of different neighborhoods, cities and cantons in Switzerland.

Data. During the initial dataset investigation, we found that the existing OSM vector dataset shows a considerable amount of discrepancies, namely inaccurate outlining and incorrect tagging of fields. Further data irregularity is also found in the Google Map raster dataset, mainly occlusions of the fields by other urban objects, such as humans, shadows from nearby buildings and trees, as well as other conjoining sport fields. Fortunately, unlike other urban objects discussed thus far, the dimensions of these sport field urban objects are generally standardized – football (1110 by 970, ratio of 0.87) and tennis (530 by 280, ratio of 0.53). The data preprocessing consists of the extraction of field location coordinates, extraction of images and their analysis with computer vision algorithms. First, we use the simple OSM query by specifying the relation type as "facility" and the subtypes as "tennis", "football" or "soccer", to obtain the necessary GeoJSON files describing the corner coordinates of all the fields. Next, for each field polygon, we fetch the raster satellite image with Google Maps API and fit their corresponding corners. A duplicate of this image is made but overlaid with a fill color, thus acting like a mask, such that a bitwise operation could be applied on both images to crop the field. Since all the fields have different orientations, we extract their median axis to reorient them vertically for our subsequent image analysis.

Algorithm. Various computer vision algorithms have been tested to extract the field line markings in order to measure their quality. These include applying Canny edge detector with Hough transform on either grayscale or HSV images and Viola-Jones algorithm with Adaboost. The former's result is not satisfying, while the latter requires more and cleaner data. The final solution is to use a template-matching approach by searching and scoring the field according to a set of key patterns representing various field line markings. More concretely, there are 5 different templates ('full', 'frame', 'center,' 'top' and 'bottom'), each varyingly scaled and consists of thick white outlines. The higher the confidence score implies the more vivid the line markings are and therefore the higher the quality of the field is. Lastly, for each field, a vector is computed that represents all the 5 confidence scores, as well as, another hue color distance score. Using L1 distance function between each pair of fields, we can compute their similarity score and save them in a database for our curatorial engine.

Engine. (Figure 6) The interactive web app is made with the React framework which provides easy implementation of interactivity, as well as, easy communication among the client, the server and the mongo database. The various components of the user interaction include the map navigation, search curation, field inspection, similar fields display and scoring weights adjustment. The user could begin by choosing the type of pitch (either tennis or football), setting the score interval (desired quality of the pitch) and the range of distances to search other similar pitches. Once a pitch (polygon) is clicked on the web map, its corresponding satellite image is displayed on the right panel, alongside its matched templates as overlays. These scoring templates are displayed as color-coded frames with different thicknesses according to their respective numerical scores along the indicative sliders. At the same time, the 6 most similar pitches are also displayed at the bottom panel, allowing the user to seamlessly zoom in and out between different pitches as they explore them on the web map. Lastly, the user could use the bottom right panel to reset the template weights that are used to compute the similarity score. By laying out the logic of our algorithmic curation on the interface, we are opening up creative ways of visually searching and curating urban objects.

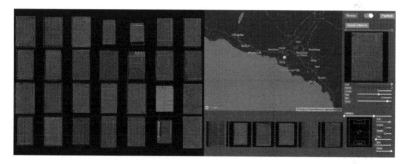

Fig. 6. (LEFT) Screenshot showing the OpenCV algorithm at work to compute the quality of football pitches from the web-crawled satellite imageries. (RIGHT) Screenshot of the 'PITCHES' project interface.

4.2   Urban Object: *Lakes*

Objective. The urban object to be curated in this project is the *lake*, more specifically the shapes and colors of lakes found in the entire Switzerland. The early inspiration for the project is Google Chrome Experiment's Land Lines [12] which is a web app running on the smartphone that allows users to explore Google Earth satellite imagery simply through the gesture of the fingers - searching by drawing lines. In our case, we sketch a shape and our engine will present us with the most similar Swiss lakes. It is a simple search and curation engine that uses visual inputs instead of words. Admittedly, this project seems to lack the degree of clarity with regard to its targeted audience and stated value, as compared to most of the other projects discussed in the paper. However, in the spirit of Land Lines [12], we foresee the advantages of such an open-ended application, in terms of their potential for aspiring future appropriation by other citizen-developers or even experts in lake morphology. For example, by knowing the lake's length-to-width ratio and its shoreline profile, one could already infer the nature of the local weather, as well as the biological diversity of the lake and its surrounding areas.

Data. Using the tags *"natural = water"* and *"water = lake"* in our OpenStreetMap query, we downloaded all the lakes' vector shapes in GeoJSON format with their names included. We then crop the corresponding raster satellite images fetched from Google Maps API within the vector shape boundary and store them in Google Cloud Storage.

Algorithm. Given all the extracted data, the task is to have an algorithm to calculate their similarity in shape and color. An image processing pipeline is adopted as follows:

- Convert each vector shape to a 50 × 50 pixels binary image
- Perform medial axis skeletonisation on the binary image
- Find principal axis of the medial axis
- Rotate the shape such that the principal axis is aligned to the x-axis
- Calculate a distance function between the pixels of every pair of lakes using L1-norm, while satisfying non-negativity, identity of indiscernible, symmetry and triangle inequality.

Once the above image processing is done, we implement a Vantage-point tree structure to organize all the lakes according to their similarity as neighbors using the value computed with the distance function. The color similarity function is eventually not implemented due to the visible color discrepancy and glitch when lakes are composed of satellite images aggregated from varying temporal and cloud coverage conditions.

Engine. (Figure 7) Implemented in the Flask framework, the application interface is done with a mix of D3js and plain javascript. The user is first presented with an empty canvas to sketch in the browser. Instead of a single line, the user draws a self-closing polygon to query lakes with a similar polygonal shape, regardless of orientation and size. The user is then presented a sorted list of 5 most similar lakes on the right panel. By hovering over any one of these lakes, an expanded view of the satellite image is displayed. By clicking on the name of the lakes shown, the application will open up a new browser window with an OSM view showing the lake's location in context.

Fig. 7. (LEFT) Poster showing the curatorial organization of different lakes in Switzerland based on their computed visual features. (RIGHT) Screenshot of the 'LAKES' project interface. The user draws a shape on the left panel, while the engine computes and presents the sorted 5 most similar lakes on the right panel, regardless of their actual geographical orientations and sizes.

5   Discussion

All the design research projects discussed thus far, have directly or indirectly, contributed to a broader understanding of what might constitute a citizen visual search engine. In formulating such a conceptual framework for creating meaningful urban values, we have identified the following key characteristics:

- The visual satellite imagery data is often publicly available for download or for querying via free APIs. For example, the use of Kaggle competition dataset and Google Maps API.
- The inaccuracy and inconsistency of open source dataset, as a result of human error, needs to be recognized and considered in the design of the creative visual search engine. For example, the polygon and tag errors in OpenStreetMap and the color glitch in Google's satellite imagery.
- The common nonexistence of specific labelled dataset often necessitates the design of interfaces to rapidly crowdsource their corresponding labels. For example, the creation of minimalistic web interface to manually label satellite images by simply clicking a set of 'yes' and 'no' buttons.
- The desire of citizens to see, understand and interact with algorithmic 'black boxes' is a form of empowerment. For example, the visualization of deep learning model's neural activation layers allows user to intuitively discover and critique their potential data biasness.
- The nature of the urban object to be searched can have a direct impact on the type of computer vision algorithms and learning models used. For example, urban objects with invariant sizes or shapes or colors could use less data-intensive approaches by designing explicit high-level feature extraction mechanisms, instead of deep learning models.
- The selection and modification of deep neural network architecture is often dependent on the type of classification problem and the size of dataset available. For example, the use of transfer learning is extremely effective when only higher-level features classification is needed, thus opportunistically reusing weights already trained with lower-level visual features.
- The frontend design of the user interaction is of paramount importance and is a determining factor in the creative experience of search and curation. For example, even without having a clearly defined practical use for the project, through the process of gestural play and visual exploration, users are given the space for imagination.
- The framing of a citizen visual search engine often begins with a simple or native pairing of an urban object and a societal issue. Yet, the result often suggests multiple and unforeseen potential appropriation or extension of existing applications. For example, the simple classification of safe/unsafe satellite image pixels eventually becomes the basis to extend Google Map's itinerary generation logic.

6   Future Work

The lack of pre-labelled datasets encountered by many of the deep learning projects discussed here poses a glaring concern. Data annotations, either manually labelled by us or made available occasionally at Kaggle, is essential for any supervised learning models like ours. Our future research in creative visual search engine needs to move beyond the paradigm of supervised learning and incorporate both unsupervised deep learning models and self-supervised machine learning algorithms. In addition, instead of the single urban object type, we plan to implement applications that provide the capabilities to detect, search and curate multiple urban objects at different scales. We hope this paper will provide the first step towards the formulation and design of a truly citizen-centric creative search engine, one that is liberated from the current epistemology that is often motived politically and commercially.

References

1. Kurgan, L.: Close up at a Distance: Mapping, Technology and Politics. Zone Books, New York (2013)
2. Weizman, E.: Forensic Architecture: Violence at the Threshold of Detectability. Zone Books, New York (2017)
3. Quadros, A., Underwood, J., Douillard, B.: Sydney Urban Objects Dataset, Australian Centre for Field Robotics (2013). http://www.acfr.usyd.edu.au/papers/SydneyUrbanObjects-Dataset.shtml
4. SpaceNet on Amazon Web Services (AWS). "Datasets." The SpaceNet Catalog. https://spacenetchallenge.github.io/datasets/datasetHomePage.html. Accessed 30 Apr 2018
5. Odell, J.: Mayes County. Google (2016). https://datacentermurals.withgoogle.com/mayes-county
6. Worse than Malaria. The Economist. https://www.economist.com/middle-east-and-africa/2015/10/24/worse-than-malaria. Accessed 24 Oct 2015
7. Dstl Satellite Imagery Feature Detection: Can you train an eye in the sky? Kaggle (2016). https://www.kaggle.com/c/dstl-satellite-imagery-feature-detection/data
8. Project Sunroof - Solar Calculator. Google. https://www.google.com/get/sunroof. Accessed 29 Dec 2018
9. Wie Viel Strom Und Wärme Kann Mein Dach Produzieren? Bundesamt für Energie BFE, Sonnendach.ch. http://www.sonnendach.ch. Accessed 29 Dec 2018
10. Groß, B.: The Big Atlas of LA Pools, June 2013. https://benedikt-gross.de/projects/the-big-atlas-of-la-pools
11. GlobalXplorer° (2016). https://www.globalxplorer.org/
12. Lieberman, Z., Felsen, M., and Google Data Arts Team: Land Lines (2016). https://lines.chromeexperiments.com/

Computing and Visualizing Taxi Cab Dynamics as Proxies for Autonomous Mobility on Demand Systems

The Case of the Chicago Taxi Cab System

Dimitris Papanikolaou$^{(\boxtimes)}$

University of North Carolina at Charlotte, Charlotte, NC 28223, USA
dpapanik@uncc.edu

Abstract. Despite the expansion of shared mobility-on-demand (MoD) systems as sustainable modes of urban transport, a growing debate among planners and urban scientists regarding what constitutes cost and how to compute it, divides opinions on the benefits that autonomous MoD systems may bring. We present a comprehensive definition of cost of traveling by MoD systems as the cost of the vehicle hours (VH), the vehicle-hours-traveled (VHT), the vehicle-hours-dispatched (VHD), and the vehicle-hours-parked (VHP) required to serve a pattern of trips. Next, we discuss an approach to estimate empty (dispatch) trips and idle periods from a user trip dataset. Finally, we model, compute, and visualize the relationship between the dynamics of VHP, VHT, and VHD using Chicago's taxi cab system as a case. Our results show that the total fleet of taxis in Chicago can decrease by 51% if all trips, currently served by conventional taxis, were served by autonomous ones.

Keywords: Mobility on Demand systems · Taxi cab systems ·
Data-driven dynamic modeling · Autonomous Vehicles · System dynamics

1 Introduction

Widely considered as emerging modes of sustainable transport, mobility on demand (MoD) systems utilize shared vehicles, parking spaces, and advanced information technology, allowing citizens to move from point to point on demand while minimizing resource utilization and carbon footprint [1]. With an industry doubling biannually, and pilot autonomous vehicles (AV) already cruising in streets of cities, MoD systems are one of the most rapidly growing sectors of urban transport. Yet, a growing debate among scholars and practitioners on what constitutes cost and how to compute it, has divided opinions on the benefits that autonomous MoD systems may bring. Some studies claim that sharing reduces congestion, improves air quality, and enhances accessibility while reducing dependence on private ownership [2–4]. Others, however, show that vehicle-miles traveled (VMT) and traffic congestion will increase up to 8% and 14.0% respectively due to increased empty trips for charging and pickup [5–7]. Understanding what aspects, and how, affect performance is important, not only for

© Springer Nature Singapore Pte Ltd. 2019
J.-H. Lee (Ed.): CAAD Futures 2019, CCIS 1028, pp. 183–197, 2019.
https://doi.org/10.1007/978-981-13-8410-3_14

assessing the potential of on-demand mobility, but also for designing, planning, and operating future MoD systems that perform better than today's ones.

For planners and urban scientists, estimating the quantities of vehicles, parking land, and dispatch flows (movements of empty vehicles from one drop-off to the next pickup), required to mobilize a demand for trips, is essential because they determine the cost, the infrastructure size and planning requirements, and the environmental impact of a MoD system. While recent studies have used microsimulation techniques to address such questions for AV MoD systems [4–6, 8], their modeling assumptions of how vehicles move in space and time are often too idealized. It is therefore important to complement results from such theoretical models with similar results from data-driven evidence-based simulation models that describe real systems in high detail.

In this paper, we analyze a dataset of user trips from taxi cabs, asking the question: How many vehicles, parking land, and dispatch work are required to serve the same trips with AVs, and how would these quantities change as technology improves? We consider a taxi system as the closest contemporary analogy to an AV MoD system. Since an AV is a taxi with a restless computerized driver, studying taxi systems can reveal important information about a lower bound in performance of AV MoD systems. At each moment, a taxi cab can be in one of three possible states: *active* (carrying a passenger), *dispatched* (driving empty in search of a new passenger), or *parked* (either temporarily or overnight). In particular, we focus on three questions in estimating the minimum capacity of a MoD system: *how many taxis are required to serve a given demand for trips? How much parking land do these taxis occupy when not in use? How much traffic do these taxis create when in use or being dispatched?*

In previous work [9] we developed a novel method to reconstruct and visualize accumulation dynamics of MoD systems by numerically integrating trip data over time, and we used this method to model the dynamic relationship between the active, dispatched, and parked portions of the fleet in Boston's bike sharing system. In this paper, we expand this method to compute and visualize the dynamics of the actual and minimum quantities of vehicles, parking land, and dispatch work, required to mobilize a pattern of trips in a taxi cab system. We analyze a trip dataset from Chicago's taxi system with over 100 million rides dating back to 2013, and focus on July 13, 2017 as a case.

Our paper makes three contributions in the fields of Smart Cities, Data Analytics, and Urban Modeling and Simulation. (1) We present a holistic definition of cost of traveling by taxi. (2) We discuss a novel method to estimate dispatch trips and idle periods from user trips in taxi systems and we apply this method to estimate the number of dispatch taxi trips and idle periods in Chicago. (3) We model, compute, and visualize the relationship between the dynamics of the vehicle-hours-traveled (VHT), the vehicle-hours-dispatched (VHD) and the vehicle-hours-parked (VHP) for serving users with taxi MoD systems in Chicago.

The rest of the paper is organized as follows. Section 2 discusses related works. Section 3 defines the cost of shared mobility from a dynamics' perspective. Section 4 describes the Chicago taxi trip dataset. Section 5 describes the method to estimate the empty (dispatch) trips and idle periods from the user trip dataset. Section 6 describes the method to reconstruct dynamics of vehicle accumulations and a validation method. Section 7 presents a scenario analysis in Chicago visualizing both the existing and the hypothetical accumulation dynamics if all current trips were served by autonomous taxi cabs that minimize empty trip and idle durations. Finally, Sect. 8 discusses significance and future steps of our work, specifically in relation to MoD systems.

2 Background

Sizing and rebalancing, is the fundamental planning and operations problem of deciding the optimal combination of infrastructure size (number of vehicles, parking spaces, road capacity) and rebalancing work (dispatches of empty vehicles from full to empty locations) for serving a pattern of trips. The two quantities are in a tradeoff relationship. Increasing one, decreases the need for the other. Sizing-rebalancing problems in MoD systems summarize into three directions: sizing optimization [10]; routing optimization [11–13]; and joint sizing-rebalancing optimization which are significantly more complex [4, 14]. State-of-the-art approaches use stochastic microsimulations [4–6, 8, 14], however, developing such models is laborious, data intensive, and computationally expensive, without guaranteeing results [15]. Estimating rebalancing work requires solving routing but routing depends on assumptions about network structure and trip demand, which in MoD systems are often random. This makes micromodeling approaches speculative and, for the scope of our research, unnecessarily complex.

Recent studies on various data sources show that even though individual trip patterns are random, human mobility patterns are macroscopically consistent and predictable [16–21]. In particular, intra-city commuting patterns are found to be periodic [22–24] and universal across cities [25, 26] with a trip duration consistent at 25–35 min [25]. This relationship has been observed in multiple data sources from taxi [16, 23, 27] and bike sharing [28, 29] trips. Finally, other studies on bike sharing [11, 29, 30] and car sharing [8] data found that trip patterns are not only periodic but also cumulatively imbalanced, creating increasingly uneven distributions of vehicles. These studies suggest that accurate dynamic macromodeling is scientifically possible [18].

There are two cultures in building dynamic models from time series data. The first, coming from data science, views time series data as samples from an unknown stochastic process and uses machine learning techniques to invent a mechanism that can emulate them without explicitly knowing the physical system that may have generated them. Despite their usefulness in modeling data patterns when the system that created them is unknown, these techniques work as black boxes without explaining why data have been clustered one way or another [31], or what the resulting model and its parameters mean. As such, they cannot substitute valid theoretical models for planners. The second approach is hypothesis-based and comes from areas of physics, complex systems, and dynamics. It views time series data as measurements of a dynamic physical system which aims to reconstruct by postulating its structure and behavior based on first principles, empirical evidence, or established theories [32]. System dynamic (SD) models, lump accumulations of quantities into compartments representing different states (called stocks), and compute accumulation levels by numerically integrating inflows and outflows to and from each compartment over time.

By describing mathematically flow rates with equations, SD models can simulate a variety of what-if scenarios, with applications in urban studies [33–35].

Our work extends the aforementioned works in three ways. First, we introduce a novel general method to derive empty trips and idle periods from a user trip dataset. Second, we show the relationship between cost and accumulation dynamics, and we introduce a novel method to reconstruct accumulation dynamics and to find the minimum fleet for serving demand, as a time-series dynamic problem. Third, we introduce a novel way to visualize accumulation dynamics and, to our knowledge, for the first time, we visualize the dynamic relationship between accumulation dynamics of all areas in the city for taxicab systems.

3   Cost as Rent and Work

Every shared mobility system requires four fundamental types of resources to mobilize a pattern of trips: vehicles, parking land, work to mobilize user trips, and work to dispatch empty trips (also known as rebalancing). We quantify these quantities as vehicle-hours (VH), vehicle-hours-parked (VHP), vehicle-hours-travelled (VHT), and vehicle-hours-dispatched (VHD), and we define as cost, the cost of these quantities over time, measured as vehicle rent, parking rent, useful work, and rebalancing (empty) work.

From a dynamics' perspective, trip paths are unimportant. If two trips between a pair of locations have the same duration, their effect on accumulations at locations is the same even if their paths are different. What matters instead is where and when departures (outflows) and arrivals (inflows) occur and, consequently, which locations, at what rate, and to what extent, fill with or empty from vehicles. These fluctuations determine minimum fleet size, parking size, and traffic requirements.

If a dataset of user and dispatch trips is available, then VH, VHP, VHT, and VHD can be directly computed by numerically integrating the difference of departures and arrivals over time. The vehicle and land rent of each location during a period, is the cost of the net number of vehicle-hours or parking-hours required to serve a pattern of outgoing and incoming trips during that period. If 10 vehicles depart from a location and arrive after 8 h, the location will require 80 vehicle-hours of vehicle rent for the temporary absence of vehicles. If the 10 vehicles arrive and then depart after 8 h, the location will require 80 parking-hours of land rent to accommodate the temporary presence of vehicles. If each of the 10 vehicles traveled 30 min for each one-way trip, then a total of 10 vehicle-hours-traveled of work was done (5 VHT in each direction) to move them. The vehicle and land rent of a system during a period is the sum of the individual vehicle and land rents of its locations during that period. Since the system is closed and mass is conserved, VHT and VHD can be calculated from the VHP: if a portion of vehicle mass is absent from parking areas then it must be traveling in streets. VHP can be directly computed from locations from their occupancy. We define as occupancy of a location, the aggregate presence or absence of vehicle mass during a period of time. Positive occupancy indicates net presence while negative occupancy indicates net absence of vehicles. In this paper, we show that minimum VH, VHP, VHT, and VHD can be estimated from a user trip dataset, even if no information about dispatch trips is available, using the average dispatch duration as a parameter. The next sections describe a method to derive empty trips from a user trip dataset and a method to compute the dynamics of VHT, VHD, and VHP over time.

4 Chicago Taxi Trip Data

The study is based on a dataset that the City of Chicago started publishing on November 16, 2016. Today, the dataset includes over 100 million taxi ride entries, dating back to 2013. The data can be accessed through the Chicago Socrata API in JSON, XML and CSV formats. Our study focuses on three weekdays of July 12–15, 2017 using the 13th as a reference day. Each entry in the dataset describes a trip and contains 23 attributes:

Trip ID, Taxi ID, Trip Start Timestamp, Trip End Timestamp, Trip Seconds, Trip Miles, Pickup Census Tract, Dropoff Census Tract, Pickup Community Area, Dropoff Community Area, Fare, Tips, Tolls, Extras, Trip Total, Payment Type, Company, Pickup Centroid Latitude, Pickup Centroid Longitude, Pickup Centroid Location, Dropoff Centroid Latitude, Dropoff Centroid Longitude, Dropoff Centroid Location.

All start and end times were rounded to the nearest 15 min. In order to preserve costumer and driver's privacy, location is provided only at Census Tract and Community Area level ("*pickup_community_area*", "*dropoff_community_area*"). Census Tract data is not available for some trips for privacy purposes. The data attributes "*fare*", "*tips*", "*tolls*", "*extras*", "*trip_total*" and "*payement_type*" are all cost related and provide details about the cost of each trip and how costumers paid the cost. The pickup and dropoff centroid latitudes and longitudes, as well as the pickup and dropoff centroid location attributes, provide geographic coordinates for the pick-ups and drop offs. These coordinates are either the center of the census tract in which the trip began and ended or the community area if the census tract has been removed for privacy.

Initial exploration of the data revealed that certain entries seem either implausible or have specific meanings that are not described in the dataset. For example, several trip entries appeared to have either zero-second duration or zero-mile distance. Other entries appeared to have non-zero durations but zero-miles distance or non-zero-miles distance but zero-seconds durations. To avoid unsupported interpretations, we contacted the Chicago Data Portal and inquired about these specific cases. According to Chicago data portal, due to the unavoidable circumstances in data collection having 0 values for trip_seconds and trip_miles may occur and these values are wrong. Therefore, we decided to remove all entries with 0 durations. Another problem with data is that several trips had as start or end locations, areas with no name and 0 latitude and longitude. To address these inconsistencies, we filtered out these data trip entries. In total, from the 105,037 entries of the 3-day focus period, we filtered-out 8,941 such entries.

5 Identification of Empty Trips and Idle Periods

We consider as *empty trip*, the movement that a taxi makes from the dropoff location of a client to the pickup location of the next client. We consider as *idle period*, the duration that a taxi remains parked at a rest area. Therefore, we consider three possible states for each taxi: "full", when the taxi is occupied by a passenger; "empty", when the taxi driver is driving to find the next passenger; and "idle", when the taxi is parked without looking for passengers (sleeping, having lunch, waiting, etc.). Since the dataset contains only user trips, we developed a method to identify empty trips and idle periods from the periods between consecutive rides from the same taxi ID. We labeled each such period as a *combined duration* because it combines both the duration of an empty trip and the duration of a potential idle period. The distribution of full trip durations has one sharp peak that centers at about 900 s and is skewed to the left. This means that while most user trips are short and similar (about 15 min), there are several user trips that are longer and have durations that vary. The histogram in Fig. 1 shows the distribution of combined durations (empty and idle). The distribution has a sharp peak that centers at about 1,000 s and is skewed to the left. A closer look reveals a second peak, shorter and fatter, that centers at about 8,000 s. This means that while many durations between consecutive drop-offs and pickups are similar to the duration of a typical ride, there is a smaller cluster of such durations that are much longer, with a range of 1 to 8 h, and an average of 2.2 h.

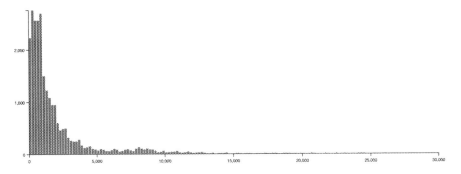

Fig. 1. Histogram of the durations of empty trips.

We interpreted the first peak of short durations as empty trips (trips from a dropoff to a pickup similar in duration to user trips) and we interpreted the second peak of long durations as idle periods. The interpretation is based both on empirical evidence and on common sense: idle periods include overnight rests during sleep hours and can therefore be several hours long. On the other hand, empty trips cannot be overly long: if they were, on average, longer than idle periods, then empty taxis in streets would outnumber occupied ones. This, however, cannot be the case: first, because demand during peak hours is higher than supply, and second, because during off-peak hours, spending more time empty than occupied would be financially unsustainable for taxi operators.

To distinguish between empty trips and idle periods, we analyzed the duration between a user drop-off and the next user pickup for each pair of consecutive trips with the same taxi ID. Some of these durations signify an empty trip while others include idle periods (driver rests temporarily or overnight). We consider three possible cases (Fig. 2).

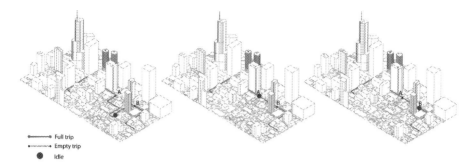

Fig. 2. Three cases for an empty trip. Left: a taxi drives empty from dropoff area A to a rest area (blue dot), remains idle, and then drives empty to pickup area B. Middle: a taxi remains idle after dropping off a client and then drives empty to a pickup area. Right: a taxi drives empty after dropping off a client to a rest area, remains idle, and then picks up the next client. (Color figure online)

In the first case, the taxi is assumed to do an empty trip from the drop-off location of the last client to a parking location (presumably the house of the taxi driver or the central taxi facility) and an empty trip from the parking location to the pickup location of the next client. In the second and third cases, the taxi is assumed to stay idle immediately after dropping-off a client and then perform an empty trip to pick up the next new client (second case) or perform an empty trip to the location of the next client pickup and sojourn at that location until the next pickup (third case). While the first case is more plausible than the second and third cases, we have no data that suggest whether rest areas are different than last dropoff or first pickup areas. On the other hand, while second and third cases are less plausible today, they imply a future scenario in which an AV, if not in use, parks anywhere and stays idle until someone calls it. We therefore decided to choose either the second or third cases. Since these cases make no practical difference for the dynamics of the system, we chose the third case.

To identify empty trips, we developed an algorithm that takes as input a user trip dataset and a duration threshold, and it outputs a dataset of full and empty trips. The duration threshold is used as a classifier. If the duration between a consecutive dropoff and pickup is below the threshold, we assume the duration to signify an empty trip from the dropoff location to the pickup location. If the duration is above the threshold, we assumed that at least one empty trip and an idle duration exist.

To define the threshold duration that is used as a classifier to distinguish empty trips from idle periods, we used a duration of 1,800 s (30 min) which is close to twice the mean trip duration. By filtering the duration values, we labeled trips longer than 5,455.60 s as "idle" and the rest as "empty". While this method is crude, it provides an empirical separation between empty trips and idle periods and can therefore be used in combination with a sensitivity analysis, in which, a range of datasets are computed and tested for a range of possible thresholds. A future improvement of this method will use the application of a mixture bivariant model and use of Machine Learning (Expectation Maximization) to find the mean times of the two peaks.

6   Reconstruction of Accumulation Dynamics

After calculating the empty and full trips, we used them to reconstruct the accumulation dynamics of the system. A central concept in dynamic analysis and modeling is the reconstruction of the *trajectory* of the system, which is the collection of all the states that the system takes over a time period [19–21]. The state of a taxi system at each moment, is defined by the accumulation levels of stationary, in-use, and in-dispatch taxi vehicles. A dynamic system is defined by its inflow/outflow time series, the difference equations (conservation laws), and the state of the system at a reference time, known as the initial state. Any state can be derived by the initial state by numerical integrating inflows and outflows. In this section, we show that, by combining data (uncontrollable input) with mathematical functions (controllable input), we can build interactive data driven dynamic models that can be used for scenario analysis.

To reconstruct dynamics of VHP, VHT, and VHD, first, we obtain the set of community areas from the origins and destinations of trip data. Next, we create inflow and outflow time series data from user and empty (dispatch) trip data, by computing departures and arrivals per location per unit of time. Next, we compute accumulation level time series data per community area, by integrating numerically inflow and outflow time series over timeline. Finally, we compute the accumulation time series data for the stocks in transit and in dispatch. The total stock of the system is the sum of the stock in locations, in dispatch, and in transit, and remains constant over time. Initial values for accumulation levels may be obtained from any known state of the system with backward numerical integration.

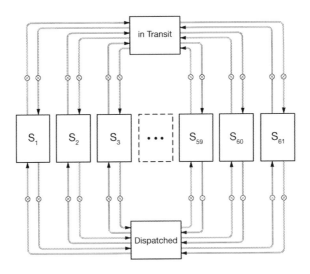

Fig. 3. Stock-flow diagram of a taxi system consisting of all community areas (represented by different stocks) and two stocks representing vehicles in transit (full and empty).

Create Closed System of Locations. To construct a trajectory that conserves mass, it is important that the number of locations derive from trip data. To create locations: (1) Create empty array for locations. (2) For each trip in trips array, for each location in locations array: if location is the same as origin or destination location of trip, go to next trip; else, add origin or destination location of trip in locations array, and go to next trip. (3) End. Figure 3 shows the resulting stock-flow model from this process consisting of stocks for each community area containing parked vehicles (s_1, s_2,..., s_n) and of two additional stocks containing vehicles in transit and dispatched vehicles.

Create User Inflow and Outflow Time Series. To create user inflow and outflow time series per location: (1) Divide timeline into timesteps. (2) For each location in the locations array, create four empty arrays: departures, arrivals, outflows, and inflows. (3) For each trip in trips array, get origin and destination locations of trip; add one departure event in the departures array of the origin location; add one arrival event in the arrivals array of the destination location. (4) For each time-step, for each location in the locations array: add the sum of all departures that occurred within the time-step in the outflows array; add the sum of all arrivals that occurred within time-step in the inflows array. (5) End. The resulting system contains the set S of $|S|$ locations (where $|S|$ is the size of S). Each location s_i contains 4 time-series with $|T|$ data points each (where $|T|$ is number of time-steps within timeline T): user outflows X_i, user inflows Y_i, dispatch outflows $\hat{X}_i$, and dispatch inflows $\hat{Y}_i$:

$$S = \left\{ s_1, s_2, \ldots, s_{|S|} \right\} : s_i = \left\{ \begin{array}{l} X_i = \left\{ x_1, x_2, \ldots x_{|T|} \right\} \\ Y_i = \left\{ y_1, y_2, \ldots y_{|T|} \right\} \\ \hat{X}_i = \left\{ \hat{x}_1, \hat{x}_2, \ldots \hat{x}_{|T|} \right\} \\ \hat{Y}_i = \left\{ \hat{y}_1, \hat{y}_2, \ldots \hat{y}_{|T|} \right\} \end{array} \right\} \tag{1}$$

Compute Accumulation Dynamics at Locations. The user accumulation level L_i of location s_i, at time-step j, is computed by adding and subtracting inflows and outflows from $t = 1$ to $t = j$, where $\overline{\overline{L}}_i$ is the initial level $(t = 0)$:

$$L_i(j) = \overline{\overline{L}}_i + \sum_{t=1}^{j} x_i(t) - y_i(t) \tag{2}$$

Likewise, the corrected accumulation level $\hat{L}_i$ of location s_i at time-step j is:

$$\hat{L}_i(j) = \overline{\overline{L}}_i + \sum_{t=1}^{j} x_i(t) - y_i(t) + \hat{x}_i(t) - \hat{y}_i(t) \tag{3}$$

Compute Accumulation Dynamics of Stocks in Transit. The stock of vehicles in transit (stock-in-transit) contains vehicles in use by users. Since the system is closed, inflows to stock-in-transit equal outflows from locations, and outflows from stock-in-transit equal inflows to locations. In the model diagram, stock-in-transit's compartment connects to each location's compartment through the departure and arrival flow rates (pipelines). The level of stock-in-transit L_T at time-step j, is computed by adding and subtracting user outflows and inflows from $t = 1$ to $t = j$ for each of the $|S|$ locations, where $\overline{\overline{L}}_T$ is the initial level:

$$L_T(j) = \overline{\overline{L}}_T + \sum_{i=1}^{|S|} \sum_{t=1}^{j} y_i(t) - x_i(t) \tag{4}$$

Add Dispatch Flows and Reconstruct System Trajectory. To reconstruct the trajectory of the system with dispatching, we add dispatch inflows and outflows and recompute accumulation levels. The dispatch stock contains empty vehicles. In the model diagram, the dispatched compartment connects to each location's compartment through the dispatch departures and dispatch arrivals flow rates (pipelines). The level of the dispatch stock L_D at time-step j, is computed by adding and subtracting dispatch outflows and dispatch inflows from $t = 1$ to $t = j$ for each of the $|S|$ locations where $\overline{\overline{L}}_D$ is the initial level:

$$L_D(j) = \overline{\overline{L}}_D + \sum_{i=1}^{|S|} \sum_{t=1}^{j} \hat{y}_i(t) - \hat{x}_i(t) \tag{5}$$

Set Minimum Initial Values of Accumulation Levels. Initial values for accumulation levels may be obtained from any known state of the system with backward numerical integration. If no such state is known, then the minimum initial level $\overline{\overline{L}}_i$ of any location s_i, is the opposite of the minimum value $L_{i_{min}}$ that L_i had over timeline T:

$$\overline{\overline{L}}_i = -L_{i_{min}}, L_{i_{min}} = min_{t \in T} \sum_{z=1}^{t} x_i(z) - y_i(z) \tag{6}$$

The minimum parking capacity P_i of location s_i is the range (max-min) of its accumulation level values over timeline:

$$P_i = L_{i_{max}} - L_{i_{min}}, L_{i_{max}} = max_{t \in T} \sum_{z=1}^{t} x_i(z) - y_i(z) \tag{7}$$

Set Actual Initial Values of Accumulation Levels. Finding the initial values for the actual accumulation levels was a two-step process. First, we found initial levels of all trips that were considered in the time window. Second, we found initial levels at locations at the beginning of the time window. To find initial levels for each location, for each vehicle ID, we filtered all trips from the same vehicle ID, and we obtained the first trip. Then, we got the start location of the first trip and we incremented unitarily the initial level of that location. This process provided the initial levels of the first trips that either ended or started from the time window. To get the initial levels at time zero, we constructed accumulation dynamics from the start time of the first trip till the end time of the desired range, and we then trimmed the timeseries to the desired length.

6.1 Validation

In reconstructing an empty trip dataset from a given user trip dataset, two possible types of inconsistencies may occur: inconsistencies in time and inconsistencies in space. Inconsistencies in time occur if (1) an estimated empty trip appears to start before the previous full trip of the same vehicle ends, (2) an estimated empty trip appears to end after the next full trip of the same vehicle starts, or (3) an empty trip appears to end before it has started. Inconsistencies in space occur if an estimated empty trip appears to start from, or end to, different locations than its previous and next full trips. Results of such inconsistencies create accumulation dynamics that violate the law of mass preservation. For example, if a vehicle departs from a location before its previous trip arrives at that location, or if a vehicle arrives at a location after its next trip departs from that location, then the quantity of the vehicle at the location appears negative while the quantity of the vehicle in the streets (travelling) appears double. Likewise, if a vehicle arrives at a location but then departs from another location, then there must two vehicles in the system with the same ID. The resulting dataset of both empty and full trips can be validated for topological connectivity as follows. For each chain of trips of the same vehicle, the origin location of each trip is the same as the destination location of the previous trip, and the departure time of each trip is after the arrival time of the previous trip and before the departure time of the next trip. Likewise, the destination location of each trip is the same as the origin location of the next trip, and the arrival time of each trip is after the departure time of the trip and before the departure of the next trip. To validate the reconstructed accumulation dynamics, we analyzed the resulting empty and full trips dataset for mass preservation. If reconstructed empty trips were valid, then the mass of each individual vehicle in the system should remain constant over time. If a vehicle is removed from an area, it must be added to the transitionary stock and if it added in another area, it must be first removed from the transitionary stock. For each vehicle, we traced the chains of empty, idle, and full durations, and we analyzed whether there was any timestep during which the vehicle mass in the system increased or decreased. Moreover, for each location, we found the initial values for each vehicle. In total, the sum of the initial values for all locations for a vehicle were found to be 1, and the sum of all departures and arrivals in the system for that vehicle were found to be zero.

7 Scenario Analysis

An extensive scenario analysis is beyond the scope of this paper. Here, we present two scenario cases: The actual-fleet accumulation dynamics (Fig. 4), and the minimum-fleet accumulation dynamics (Fig. 5). For each case, we used a threshold duration of 1,800 s which classifies every combined duration below 30 min as an empty trip, and every combined duration above 30 min, as a 30-min empty trip and the remainder as idle period. The actual fleet was found to be 2,398 which matches the number of distinct vehicle IDs in the trip dataset. The minimum fleet was found to be 1,220 vehicles or 50.9% smaller than the actual fleet size. In total, for the selected day, taxis in Chicago spent 57,552 VH, 43,550 VHP, 8,071 VHT, and 5,931 VHD.

8 Discussion

We presented a definition of cost for shared mobility and a novel method to compute and visualize dynamics of VHP, VHT and VHD for a taxi cab system. Moreover, we presented a method for exploring how this cost changes in two scenario cases: actual and minimum fleet accumulation dynamics. In this section, we discuss insights from the results, and limitations of the presented method. First of all, the cost of traveling by taxi is substantially dominated by the size of the inactive stationary stock compared to the active transitionary stock. While this hidden stock is a consequence of the current business model for most taxi cab systems around the world, it also constitutes an inefficiency that can be greatly reduced in a future scenario of autonomous vehicles (AVs).

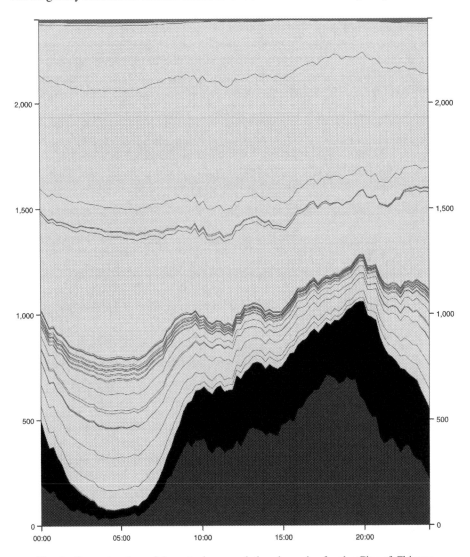

Fig. 4. Reconstruction of the actual accumulation dynamics for the City of Chicago.

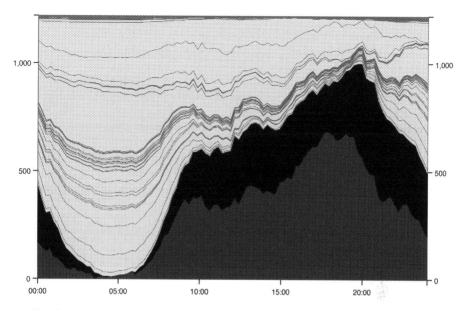

Fig. 5. Reconstruction of the actual accumulation dynamics for the City of Chicago.

In such scenario, an autonomous cab can immediately drive to pick up the next client, reducing the total VHP for the system. In particular, we showed that if each empty vehicle arrival to an idle area coincided with an empty vehicle departure from the same area, the total fleet could reduce by 50% assuming that empty trip duration is not increasing. While our results show that the fleet can reduce by roughly 50%, this reduction reflects only the reduction in vehicle rent. The total cost change i Atefeh Mahdavi Goloujeh <amahdavi@uncc.edu>s different. In particular, the total work that must be done to mobilize full and empty trips (VHT and VHD) either does not change or it increases, assuming that AVs must travel longer distances for empty trips. What decreases instead is the rent that must be paid for locations and parked vehicles (measured as VHP). Second, a strength of the presented method is that, in contrast to existing approaches that rely on solving routing for calculating cost, we showed that by using a very simple assumption, we can show that using MoD, we can significantly reduce the cost of travel in our system by enabling cars to stay idle and wait for other passengers rather than searching for passengers. Constructing empty trips data from full trips allow us to understand approximately how efficient and cost effective the mobility system in Chicago is. First, it shows the true cost of traveling by taxi as the distribution in time of VHP, VHT, and VHD. The main current limitation of the method is that the classification of combined durations into empty trips and idle periods uses an average empty trip duration which is obtained empirically, by observing the shape of the bimodal distribution of combined durations. A future improvement of this approach involves using Machine Learning (ML) techniques to distinguish between empty trips and idle periods.

Acknowledgments. The research presented in this paper has been partially funded by UNCC's Faculty Research Grant (funding cycle 2018-2019). The Chicago taxi trip dataset is publicly available and can be downloaded via the Socrata Open Data API through the following link: https://dev.socrata.com/foundry/data.cityofchicago.org/wrvz-psew. Figure 2 credits: Atefeh Mahdavi Goloujeh.

References

1. Shaheen, S., Cohen, A.: Innovative Mobility Carsharing Outlook. Transportation Sustainability Research Center, University of California, Berkeley (2016)
2. Steininger, K., Vogl, C., Zettl, R.: Car-sharing organizations: the size of the market segment and revealed change in mobility behavior. Transp. Policy **3**, 177–185 (1996)
3. Shaheen, S., Rodier, C.: Travel effects of a suburban commuter carsharing service: CarLink case study. Transp. Res. Rec. J. Transp. Res. Board. **1927**, 182–188 (2005)
4. Spieser, K., Treleaven, K., Zhang, R., Frazzoli, E., Morton, D., Pavone, M.: Toward a Systematic Approach to the Design and Evaluation of Automated Mobility-on-Demand Systems: A Case Study in Singapore. Frazzoli (2014)
5. Fagnant, D.J., Kockelman, K.M.: The travel and environmental implications of shared autonomous vehicles, using agent- based model scenarios. Transp. Res. Part C **40**, 1–13 (2014)
6. Chen, T.D., Kockelman, K.M., Hanna, J.P.: Operations of a shared, autonomous, electric vehicle fleet: implications of vehicle & charging infrastructure decisions. Transp. Res. Part A **94**, 243–254 (2016). https://doi.org/10.1016/j.tra.2016.08.020
7. Papanikolaou, D.: The Potential of On-demand Urban Mobility: Lessons from System Analysis and Data Visualization (2016)
8. Fagnant, D.J., Kockelman, K.M., Bansal, P.: Operations of shared autonomous vehicle fleet for Austin, Texas. Market. Transp. Res. Rec. J. Transp. Res. Board. **2536**, 98–106 (2015). https://doi.org/10.3141/2536-12
9. Papanikolaou, D.: Data-driven state space reconstruction of mobility on demand systems for sizing-rebalancing analysis. In: Proceedings of the 2018 Symposium on Simulation for Architecture and Urban Design (SimAUD 2018). Technical University of Delft, Netherlands (2018)
10. George, D., Xia, C.: Fleet-sizing and service availability for a vehicle rental system via closed queueing networks. Eur. J. Oper. Res. **211**, 198–207 (2011). https://doi.org/10.1016/j.ejor.2010.12.015
11. Dell'Amico, M., Hadjicostantinou, E., Iori, M., Novellani, S.: The bike sharing rebalancing problem: mathematical formulations and benchmark instances. Omega **45**, 7 (2014)
12. Chemla, D., Meunier, F., Wolfler Calvo, R.: Bike sharing systems: solving the static rebalancing problem. Discrete Optim. **10**, 120–146 (2013). https://doi.org/10.1016/j.disopt.2012.11.005
13. Kloimüllner, C., Papazek, P., Hu, B., Raidl, G.R.: Balancing bicycle sharing systems: an approach for the dynamic case. In: Blum, C., Ochoa, G. (eds.) EvoCOP 2014. LNCS, vol. 8600, pp. 73–84. Springer, Heidelberg (2014). https://doi.org/10.1007/978-3-662-44320-0_7
14. Pavone, M., Treleaven, K., Frazzoli, E.: Fundamental performance limits and efficient polices for transportation-on-demand systems. In: 49th IEEE Conference on Decision and Control, CDC 2010, pp. 5622–5629 (2010). https://doi.org/10.1109/cdc.2010.5717552
15. McNally, M.G., Rindt, C.: The Activity-Based Approach (2008)

16. Liu, Y., Wang, F., Xiao, Y., Gao, S.: Urban land uses and traffic 'source-sink areas': evidence from GPS- enabled taxi data in Shanghai. Landsc. Urban Plan. **106**, 73–87 (2012)
17. González, M.C., Hidalgo, C.A., Barabási, A.-L.: Understanding individual human mobility patterns. Nature **453**, 779 (2008)
18. Song, C., Koren, T., Wang, P., Barabási, A.-L.: Modelling the scaling properties of human mobility. Nat. Phys. **6**, 818 (2010). https://doi.org/10.1038/nphys1760
19. Chowell, G., Hyman, J.M., Eubank, S., Castillo-Chavez, C.: Scaling laws for the movement of people between locations in a large city. Phys. Rev. Stat. Nonlinear Soft Matter Phys. **68**, 066102 (2003)
20. Liang, X., Zheng, X., Lv, W., Zhu, T., Xu, K.: The scaling of human mobility by taxis is exponential. Phys. Stat. Mech. Appl. **391**, 2135–2144 (2012)
21. Phithakkitnukoon, S., Veloso, M., Bento, C., Biderman, A., Ratti, C.: Taxi-aware map: identifying and predicting vacant taxis in the city. In: de Ruyter, B., et al. (eds.) AmI 2010. LNCS, vol. 6439, pp. 86–95. Springer, Heidelberg (2010). https://doi.org/10.1007/978-3-642-16917-5_9
22. Kang, C., Ma, X., Tong, D., Liu, Y.: Intra-urban human mobility patterns: an urban morphology perspective. Phys. Stat. Mech. Appl. **391**, 1702–1717 (2012)
23. Scholz, R.W., Lu, Y.: Detection of dynamic activity patterns at a collective level from large-volume trajectory data. Int. J. Geogr. Inf. Sci. **28**, 1–18 (2014)
24. Sun, J.B., Yuan, J., Wang, Y., Si, H.B., Shan, X.M.: Exploring space–time structure of human mobility in urban space. Phys. Stat. Mech. Appl. **390**, 929–942 (2011)
25. Kung, K.S., Greco, K., Sobolevsky, S., Ratti, C.: Exploring universal patterns in human home- work commuting from mobile phone data. PLoS ONE **9**, e96180 (2014)
26. Calabrese, F., Diao, M., Di Lorenzo, G., Ferreira, J., Ratti, C.: Understanding individual mobility patterns from urban sensing data: a mobile phone trace example. Transp. Res. Part C **26**, 301–313 (2013). https://doi.org/10.1016/j.trc.2012.09.009
27. Liu, X., Gong, L., Gong, Y., Liu, Y.: Revealing travel patterns and city structure with taxi trip data. J. Transp. Geogr. **43**, 78–90 (2015). https://doi.org/10.1016/j.jtrangeo.2015.01.016
28. Padgham, M.: Human movement is both diffusive and directed. PLoS ONE **7**, e37754 (2012)
29. Kaltenbrunner, A., Meza, R., Grivolla, J., Codina, J., Banchs, R.: Urban cycles and mobility patterns: exploring and predicting trends in a bicycle- based public transport system. Pervasive Mob. Comput. **6**, 455–466 (2010). https://doi.org/10.1016/j.pmcj.2010.07.002
30. Vogel, P., Greiser, T., Mattfeld, D.C.: Understanding bike-sharing systems using data mining: exploring activity patterns. Procedia - Soc. Behav. Sci. **20**, 514–523 (2011)
31. Andrienko, N., Andrienko, G.: Exploratory Analysis of Spatial and Temporal Data: A Systematic Approach. Springer, Heidelberg (2006). https://doi.org/10.1007/3-540-31190-4
32. Shalizi, C.R.: Methods and techniques of complex systems science: an overview. In: Thomas, D., Yasha, K. (eds.) Complex Systems Science in Biomedicine, pp. 33–114. Springer, New York (2006). https://doi.org/10.1007/978-0-387-33532-2_2
33. Haghani, A., Lee, S.Y., Byun, J.H.: A system dynamics approach to land use/transportation system performance modeling part I: methodology. J. Adv. Transp. **37**, 1–41 (2003)
34. Batty, M.: The New Science of Cities. MIT Press, Cambridge (2013)
35. Forrester, J.W.: Urban Dynamics. MIT Press, Cambridge (1969)

An Ecology of Conflicts

Using Network Analytics to Explore the Data of Building Design

Daniel Cardoso Llach[(✉)] and Javier Argota Sánchez-Vaquerizo

Computational Design Laboratory, School of Architecture,
Carnegie Mellon University, Pittsburgh, PA, USA
dcardoso@cmu.edu, reivajar@gmail.com

Abstract. The scale and socio-technical complexity of contemporary architectural production poses challenges to researchers and practitioners interested in their description and analysis. This paper discusses the novel use of network analysis techniques to study a dataset comprising thousands of design conflicts reported during design coordination of a large project by a group of architects using BIM software. We discuss in detail three approaches to the use of network analysis techniques on these data, showing their potential to offer topological insights about the phenomenon of contemporary architectural design and construction, which complement other forms of architectural analysis.

Keywords: Architecture · Network analysis · Design ecology · BIM · Data visualization

1 Introduction

Network science techniques allow for the relational analysis, management, and representation of data [3]. These have been used in multiple fields including, for example, medicine and pharmacology studies [4], security and defense [5], humanities research [6, 7], and organizational management [8] among others. In the design fields, network analysis techniques have been applied, for example, to spatial analysis for architectural [9], and urban [10, 11] studies, and—more recently—to the analysis of the dynamics of product adoption [12]. Novel in our approach is the use of network analysis techniques on trace data about design conflicts reported during the collaborative process of building design and construction coordination. The data was collected semi-automatically using a custom software tool installed in the coordination logs of a group of architects using BIM software during several months [1]. Each tuple in the dataset includes information about a design conflict—a problem arising in the process of coordinating different design and construction trades, such as architecture, mechanical systems, structure, concrete, etc. The dataset includes information about each conflict's location, the organizations involved, an index number, among others.

Design conflicts are central to the processes of design and construction enabled by Building Information Modeling (BIM). A design conflict, such as a clash between a structural column and a ventilation duct, typically arises from the clash between two

© Springer Nature Singapore Pte Ltd. 2019
J.-H. Lee (Ed.): CAAD Futures 2019, CCIS 1028, pp. 198–212, 2019.
https://doi.org/10.1007/978-981-13-8410-3_15

different models provided by different organizations such as, for example, the architecture and the mechanical engineering contractors. In the project documented here, the design conflicts are identified in the BIM model, documented through screenshots (see Fig. 1), and registered in a spreadsheet sometimes called "issue log." These live documents and the conflicts they describe are central to the everyday coordination of this project—a large hospital complex in the Middle East. For detailed descriptions about this project, its coordination, and the collection of these data—as well as some earlier data visualizations—see [1, 2].

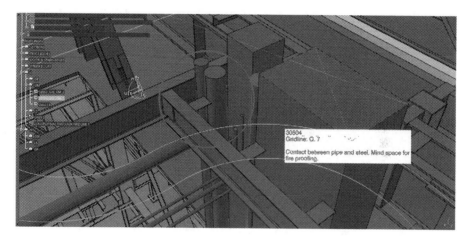

Fig. 1. A screenshot of a design conflict caused by a clash between the steel and the MEP model. The annotations indicate the conflict's location and description.

In this paper we focus on how network analyses of design conflict data can make visible relationships between entities across dissimilar categories including concepts, spaces, materials, people, and organizations, offering what Drieger has termed 'topological insights' [14] on the evolution of a design process. The analyses presented demonstrate that the combination of static and dynamic networks, and text analysis, can enrich our understanding of contemporary architectural production. By documenting concrete approaches to applying network science techniques to study design conflict data, this paper offers architecture and design researchers conceptual and analytical tools to approach the increasingly complex socio-technical practices of building design.

The first analysis aggregates the conflicts into a basic static network (Fig. 2). Focusing on high-level features of each conflict (its location and the organizations involved) this analysis offers a spatial and organizational portrait of the design process through a directed-force graph. The second analysis explores the temporal dimension of the dataset, creating a dynamic network able to capture shifting trends in the data, such as the changing importance of locations and organizations over time. The third analysis uses text mining techniques on coordinators' descriptions of each conflict, revealing how concepts (e.g. 'beam,' 'steel,' or 'clash') cluster along different spatial, organizational or temporal dimensions. Finally, we present a low-level semantic analysis based on Cube Analysis [15], which offers valuable insight into workflow and managerial aspects of this specific design ecology.

The following sections offer details and illustrations of three network analyses performed, and a discussion of their potentials and limitations.

2   Methods

2.1   Static Network Analysis: Tracing Actors and Features

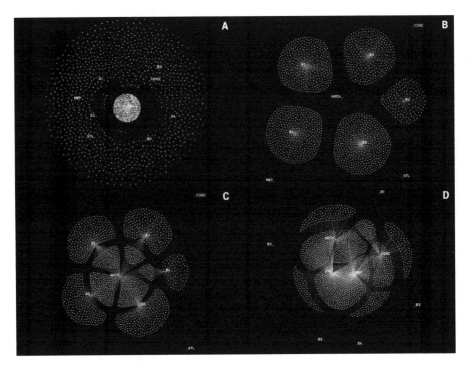

Fig. 2. Different clustering outputs depending on the activated network links: conflicts x trade with only ARCH trade links (A), conflict x location with independent clusters for each building (B), conflict x trade x location with only ARCH related trade links (C), and conflict x trade network showing different clusters depending on the related trades (D).

The first analysis is realized by constructing a simple static network based on high-level features in the design conflict data. Basic static networks are the simplest representations in network science. A common example of static networks is a network based on friendships ties in a class. The network is defined by the links between pairs of individuals. However, the network's analytical potential is realized in its representation of overlapping and coincident connections (incidents) across the whole group. There are two approaches to static network analysis. In the first one, networks comprise nodes belonging to the same category. Their connections are built implicitly from incidents of their variables. In the second approach (our choice for this analysis), networks comprise nodes belonging to different categories [16, 17]. For example, between nodes representing the instances and those representing the variables' values. In our dataset, design conflicts are the high-level features configuring the nodes, which are organized in relating to values such as location and organization. These values are key to the management of the architectural project. The result of this analysis is a "meta-network" [19] composed by two distinct networks: one relating conflicts and their locations, which provides information about the spatial dimension of design coordination, and another relating conflicts and the organizations involved in their resolution, which provides information about managerial aspects of the design process.

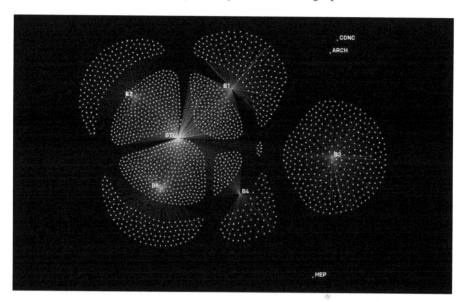

Fig. 3. Clustering of conflicts based on Steel related issues (STL) grouped by trade and location networks. 'B' labels indicate a specific zone and the number indicates the floor.

For example, the visualization of the resulting static network, a force-directed graph [18], creates clusters of design conflicts in relation to the variables analyzed. Force-directed graphs minimize intersections while clustering related nodes. This rendering can outline automatically clusters of data with similar features. For example, Fig. 2B renders conflicts in each part of the building in a single image. Figure 2C, by contrast, renders the relative importance of ARCH (Architecture) at each building area—thus spatializing coordination trends. Similarly, Fig. 3 offers a focused picture of the relative importance of conflicts in a specific zone of the project.

Displaying all the possible links between conflicts, locations, and trades can offer a high-level insight about coordination, but the resulting analysis can be confusing. For example, by combining 50 interconnected clusters we produced a network displaying the relative importance of different types of conflicts during the process of design coordination. However, while a high-level picture of the state of coordination is useful, conflict features are lost, and important aspects of hierarchy and centrality are glossed over—we therefore omit it. Instead, using only high-level features makes possible a clearer and more actionable analysis.

2.2   Dynamic Network Analysis: Tracing Change

Our second analysis uses dynamic networks to explore how the design process evolves over time. Dynamic network analysis adds to conventional network metrics the capacity to observe the evolution of the network's density over time—defined as the ratio of existing links over the maximum possible number. This is a good indicator of the relative importance of each network within the whole "meta-network." Further, the link count over time is an indicator of a network's overall activity. Taking design conflicts' timestamps indicating the moment when the conflict was reported by a BIM coordinator, this analysis makes visible the evolving relationships between types of conflict, locations, and trades, over their lifetime [22].

Table 1. Dynamic metrics for trades related networks

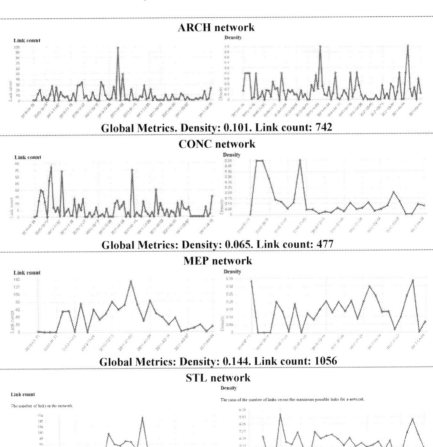

Table 2. Dynamic metrics for location-based network.

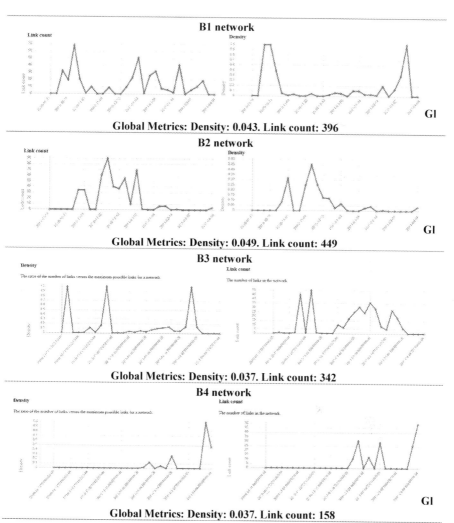

Global Metrics: Density: 0.043. Link count: 396

Global Metrics: Density: 0.049. Link count: 449

Global Metrics: Density: 0.037. Link count: 342

Global Metrics: Density: 0.037. Link count: 158

A resolution of weekly increments eases distortions caused by unusual reporting frequency on specific days. A comparison between the density of the network and its total number of links offers a perspective on the relative weight of each location and each trade at each time frame. For example, in the ARCH (Architecture) network (see Table 1) we can see ARCH related design conflicts peaking in the middle of the observation period. The coincidence of peaks across the network indicates a managerial focus on this type of design conflict. The STL (Steel) network, in contrast, exhibits a different trend. The peak of conflict activity does not align with the peak density of steel issues in the overall network—which occupies the beginning and end of the observed period. Finally, the total link counts and density indicate that MEP (Mechanical, Engineering, and Plumbing) conflicts were the most active, and offered the most challenges to the design coordination team—a result consistent with direct ethnographic observation of this design process [13].

Comparing density and link count in trade networks (Table 1) and location networks (Table 2) offers a glimpse of their distinctive dynamic signatures. Trade networks (networks organized by the trade organization in charge of conflicts) show a higher variability in their size and density values, while location networks (networks organized by the location of conflicts) are more homogenous. The temporal patterns also differ. Salient in the trade network is the mismatch between the peaks highlighting higher-incidence of issues across the whole set. This hints at specific managerial challenges during coordination. However, when checking the temporal trends of the location of the issues, there are alignments between both temporal targets. These delineate the hierarchy and division of the work within the project—and a managerial focus on coordination progress by building, and not by work trades or packages. This outlines a specific managerial trait of this project.

2.3   Text Analysis: Tracing Concepts

The third and last analysis explores the potential of text analysis techniques to explore design coordination data. We discuss three approaches to text mining, each facilitating a different type of analysis: stems-count, text mapping, and cube analysis.

Stems-Count
Stems-count is a basic text-mining strategy that identifies the most frequent stems—roots of words—throughout the design conflict descriptions. The use of stems instead of tokens allows us to identify terms without the noise of word derivation. Using Python Notebook we tokenize each description and rid it of "stopwords" such as prepositions, and articles, obtaining 374 different roots with a typical power law distribution of natural language [20]. For legibility purposes, only the 24 stems with a frequency over 50 were selected:

```
listOfKeywords = ['beam', 'ceil', 'clash', 'column', 'concret',
'corner', 'discrep', 'door', 'duct', 'edg', 'fireproof', 'fur',
'issu', 'level', 'mep', 'miss', 'model', 'partit', 'pipe',
'slab', 'stair', 'steel', 'support', 'wall']
```

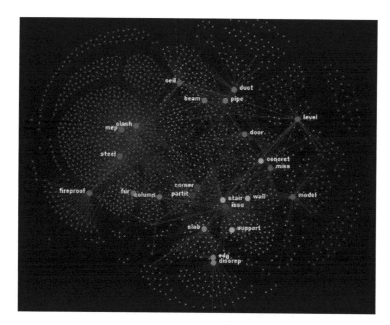

Fig. 4. Static network conflict (small nodes) x Stem (large nodes). Links colored by Louvain grouping for improving visualization. Louvain value: 0.4916405.

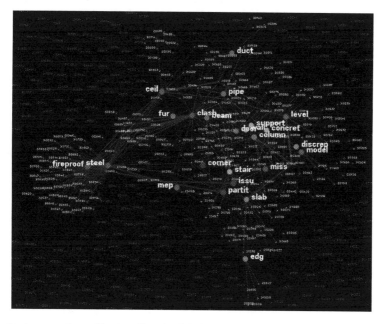

Fig. 5. Static network conflict (small nodes labelled with the ID) x Stem (large nodes). Links colored by Louvain grouping [19]. Louvain value: 0.4916405. Showing only links with an Issue_length (Issue string length) over 49 as simplification method for the network.

Following the process described in the previous section, we created a static network connecting two different classes of nodes: conflicts and stems. The resulting network was too complex to offer useful insights (Fig. 4), so we simplified it by focusing our analysis on the subset of 224 design conflicts with the longest descriptions (Fig. 5). This introduced a bias which may be avoided in future analyses by focusing instead on conflicts of a single trade, building zone, or timeframe. The resulting network shows a central core of highly correlated and common issues and conflicts comprising stems such as 'steel', 'mep', 'clash', 'fireproof', and their close periphery 'corner', 'partit', 'ceil', and 'issu.'

Stem-count analysis offers visual insight into the concept-scape of this design process, mapping the relative importance of certain problems (such as clashes between steel and mechanical systems) in the process of designing this specific building. An important limitation of this analysis is the fact that the data can vary significantly from coordinator to coordinator, and from issue to issue. This reflects their different habits of record-keeping and areas of professional specialization [1]. A second limitation to this analysis is that it does not account for the relevance of each term in the network from a communicative point of view. This is a subject we explore in our next analysis.

Text Mapping

In addition to occurrence and frequency, text mapping techniques can help make visible relations across concepts and their meanings. Based on cognitive and communicative models [21], they examine a text and produce semantic networks based on these relations.

To transform the tabular original data into the text-only data, we used a Python Notebook. We then used ORA-Netmapper to map the text into two static networks: one based on the cross-classification of concepts depending on their context, meaning, and ontological category, and a semantic network based on the relationship between concepts. For the first, we mapped each relevant term to one of the following categories: "agent," "belief," "location," "organization," "resource," "task," or "unknown" (see Fig. 6), often used in text-mapping analyses, following the MetaOntology algorithm already implemented on ORA-Netmapper [15]. Ignoring the most common classification ("unknown", in grey), the two categories more populated are "resource" (in turquoise) and "task" (in blue). It is important to note that this pre-defined set of categories is a limiting factor in our study, and may explain the over-classification of data as "unknown." For the highly idiosyncratic data studied in this paper such generic settings don't seem to fit. Getting rid of the "unknown" category, however, unveils a nuanced landscape of interrelated meanings across nodes classified as "Resource" and "Task" (see Fig. 7). Unsurprisingly, labels for trade names ("arch", "conc", "mep", and "stl") were highly ranked. This analysis reveals topics that would be overlooked by a frequency and occurrences analysis. For example, seldom mentioned terms such as "land-water-use" and "tools_and_appliance" seem relevant because of their position in the semantic network. Their position suggests that addressing the design issues underlying those terms would have significant impact on the overall design coordination of the project.

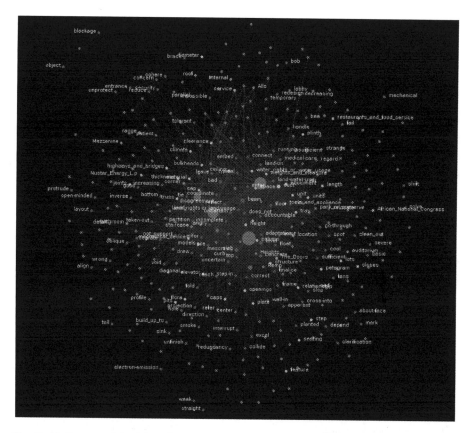

Fig. 6. Static network based on the terms cross-classification from the descriptions on the field Issue. Each color denotes a term category: red = agent, purple = belief, orange = location, green = organization, turquoise = resource, task = blue, grey = unknown. (Color figure online)

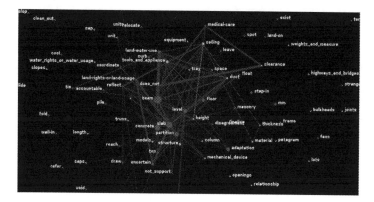

Fig. 7. Static network based on the cross-classification of terms from the field issue, only displaying nodes and links labelled as "Resource" (in blue) and "Task" (in green). Link with values over 50. (Color figure online)

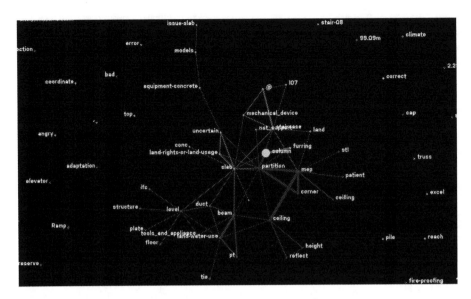

Fig. 8. Regenerated semantic static network with Louvain clustering (Louvain value 0.4557173), removing trade labels.

A second semantic network shows connectivity across concepts. It is a representation focused on knowledge, while cross-classification focuses on the role of each term. Rather than representing the whole network, we again isolate the core using Louvain clustering. Trades labels again occupy key positions, so we remove them in order to focus our analysis on less obvious connections (Fig. 8). This results in concepts such 'column', 'mep', and 'level' occupying a central position in the network. The remaining terms are key concepts identified only in this analysis. Those concepts are 'false', 'ramp', 'ifc', 'uncertain', and 'park_or_preserve'. As they only appear in this analysis, it can be assumed that there are underlying factors fostered by the metrics which drive semantic relationships.

Cube Analysis

Lastly, we conducted a cube analysis of the dataset. Cube analysis is a technique that seeks to describe the communicative power of different concepts in a static semantic network. It analyzes the words in a dataset from three perspectives: consensus (frequency), betweenness (a measure of how frequent a particular node (or stakeholder) is a broker of connections among all the other nodes in the network), and total degree (the number of direct connections that a node has in a network [15]). Depending on the combination of those three vectors, concepts can be classified as ordinary words, factoids, buzzwords, emblems, allusions, stereotypes, placeholders, and symbols [15]. The presence of a word in either of these categories suggests it plays a distinct role in the conceptual scaffolding of the design process.

Table 3. The cube analysis identified different typical measurements as "buzzwords."

Rank	Concept	Consensus	Degree centrality	Betweenness centrality
1	4350 mm	0.0002276	0.00001442	0.005
2	cross-into	0.0002276	0.00001442	0.003
3	1675 mm	0.0002276	0.00002164	0.003
4	2350 mm	0.0002276	0.00001683	0.002
5	1750 mm	0.0002276	0.00001683	0.002
6	dgmsst18	0.0002276	0.00001442	0.002
7	470 mm	0.0002276	0.00001923	0.002
8	oblique	0.0002276	0.00002164	0.002

Somewhat perplexingly, the concepts classified as buzzwords by our analysis were measurements (see Table 3). In network analysis, buzzwords are concepts with a low degree and a low consensus, but a high betweenness. Often these important topics because they appear in many lines of thought, despite not being repeated frequently, and not being necessarily connected with many other concepts. Out of context, measurements are not meaningful concepts, and yet their relevance as buzzwords indicates that they are important elements in the spatial language of the building. In this case, these measurements referred to typical proportion and distances related to the structure, installations, distances between floors, etc. Their presence as buzzwords in our dataset of design conflicts indicates that discrepancies between these measurements in plans and on the real construction was a common source of conflict.

Emblems are concepts with high consensus and betweenness values. This means that they appear frequently, and in many lines of thought—although they may not be connected directly to them apparently in the text (low total degree). The only emblem in our analysis is 'concrete-mep' (Table 4). This indicates the prominence of this coupling of trades in the concept-scape of the project. Even when trade tags are not considered as a source field for our analysis, conflicts between the concrete structure and mechanical systems are foregrounded by the analysis. Ethnographic descriptions of the project confirm this relative importance in the project [1].

Table 4. The "concrete-mep" concept was classified as an "emblem" by the cube analysis.

Rank	Concept	Consensus	Degree centrality	Betweenness centrality
1	Concrete-mep	0.001	0.00002164	0.006

Table 5. Stereotypes from the cube analysis on the static semantic network.

Rank	Concept	Consensus	Degree centrality	Betweenness centrality
1	ceiling	0.006	0.00025	0.00003925
2	±50 mm	0.005	0.0006587	0
3	−stair	0.001	0.000101	4.049E−06
4	detail	0.001	0.000101	0
5	stair-23	0.001	0.00007212	0
6	gridline	0.0009105	0.000101	0.00001763
7	clashes	0.0009105	0.00006731	0
8	parallel	0.0009105	0.0000625	0

Stereotypes (Table 5) are concepts with a high degree, high consensus, and low betweenness. It means concepts which are both frequent and highly connected, but not central in the network. Our analysis identifies as stereotypes some commonly used concepts such as "clashes" and "ceiling" (sic). Stereotypes don't play a key role in the concept-scape. They can be seen as common but unimportant issues. Finally, the misspelling of 'ceiling' is an issue which would be addressed later by data cleaning.

On the other hand, symbols (Table 6) are the concepts with the highest values in the three parameters. They offer an initial metric for detecting important concepts in the dataset. The cubic analysis yields some coincidences with past metrics, e.g. "column," "mep," "ceiling," and "level." Others, such as "false," "ifc," "Ramp," and "uncertain" were already identified using simply the betweenness centrality. There are, however, two new concepts: "beam" and "slab." Those are key elements which have an important presence in the recorded issues but were missed previously.

Our analysis did not find factoids, allusions, or placeholders in our dataset of design conflicts. Factoids are defined by a high frequency and low levels of betweenness and total degree. Differently, allusions have a high score of total degree but low levels of frequency and betweenness. Finally, placeholders combine a high value of betweenness and total degree with a low frequency. Their absence may be explained by the unconventional style of conflict descriptions, which is utilitarian, often rushed, and thus highly economical in its vocabulary.

Table 6. Symbols in the cube analysis of communicative power on the static semantic network.

Rank	Concept	Consensus	Degree centrality	Betweenness centrality
1	column	0.035	0.002	0.253
2	mep	0.123	0.004	0.108
3	False	0.002	0.0001611	0.109
4	slab	0.045	0.003	0.035
5	ifc	0.008	0.0007933	0.072
6	RAMP	0.002	0.0001563	0.073
7	uncertain	0.022	0.001	0.051
8	ceiling	0.036	0.002	0.03
9	level	0.026	0.002	0.038
10	beam	0.034	0.002	0.029

3   Conclusion

A premise of this paper has been that the socio-technical complexity of today's design and construction industries pose challenges to researchers and practitioners interested in their description and analysis. By documenting the novel use of network analysis techniques on a dataset of design conflicts produced during the design coordination of a large architectural project, we show that computational methods of data collection and analysis offer additional tools to address these challenges, enriching our understanding of contemporary modes of architectural design and construction. Particularly, as this paper has shown, they allow us to collect and navigate larger datasets of digital traces of the design process, and to obtain high-level topological insights about them. As documented above, a combination of static and dynamic networks, and text analysis, can help uncover patterns of conflict in the design process by relating conflicts, concepts, organizations, and spaces. They may also be useful to explore comparatively how different teams—or cultures of architectural production—coordinate their efforts.

As a study of design coordination, the focus of this project is strictly interpretive and analytical—in fact, the analyses were conducted after the project was finished. However, these methods could also play a role during the design and construction of the building. Real-time topological insights about the coordination process could help design coordination teams identify and solve design problems—and problem "patterns." This remains to be tested.

While BIM coordination processes offer relatively large and tractable sources of data about building design, it is very important to remember that these do not account for the full complexity of the project, which includes a much richer ecosystem of material practices and social interactions. Similarly, the data itself should not be understood as an inherently truthful nor neutral account of the coordination process, but rather as a collection of situated artifacts—each contingent upon the specific habits of record keeping and professional inclinations of the people and organizations defining them and collecting. Therefore, as proposed in [1], computational methods of data analysis work best in combination with other methods of qualitative observation and reflection. Accordingly, the methods presented in this paper do not aim at replacing or automating design research, but rather at expanding the repertoire of tools available to those interested in developing rich, performative accounts of the socio-technical processes of architectural design.

Acknowledgements. The authors wish to thank Dr. Kathleen M. Carley and the CASOS Group at CMU for their valuable guidance in employing network science techniques.

References

1. Cardoso Llach, D.: Tracing design ecologies: collecting and visualizing ephemeral data as a method in design and technology studies. In: Vertesi, J., Ribes, D. (eds.) DigitalSTS Handbook. Princeton University Press (2019)
2. Cardoso Llach, D.: Builders of the Vision: Software and the Imagination of Design. Routledge, London, New York (2015)

3. Brandes, U., et al.: What is network science? Netw. Sci. **1**, 1–15 (2013)
4. Hopkins, A.L.: Network pharmacology. Nat. Biotechnol. **25**, 1110–1111 (2007)
5. Arquilla, J., Ronfeldt, D.: Networks and Netwars: The Future of Terror, Crime, and Militancy. RAND, Santa Monica (2001)
6. Weingart, S.: Topic modeling and network analysis. The Scottbot irregular, 15 November 2011. http://www.scottbot.net/HIAL/?p=221
7. McCallum, A., Corrada-Emmanuel, A., Wang, X.: Topic and role discovery in social networks. In: Proceedings of the 19th International Joint Conference on Artificial Intelligence, IJCAI 2005, pp. 786–791. Morgan Kaufmann Publishers Inc., San Francisco, CA, USA (2005). http://dl.acm.org/citation.cfm?id=1642293.1642419
8. Wu, L., et al.: Mining face-to-face interaction networks using sociometric badges: predicting productivity in an IT configuration task. In: Proceedings of the International Conference on Information Systems (2008)
9. Porta, S., Crucitti, P., Latora, V.: The network analysis of urban streets: a primal approach. Environ. Plann. B: Plann. Des. **33**, 705–725 (2006)
10. Alexander, C.: A city is not a tree. Archit. Forum **122**, 58–62 (1965)
11. He, Y., Luo, J.: Novelty, conventionality, and value of invention. In: Gero, J.S. (ed.) Design Computing and Cognition '16, pp. 23–38. Springer, Cham (2017). https://doi.org/10.1007/978-3-319-44989-0_2
12. Sarkar, S., Gero, J.S.: The topology of social influence and the dynamics of design product adoption. In: Gero, J.S. (ed.) Design Computing and Cognition '16, pp. 653–665. Springer, Cham (2017). https://doi.org/10.1007/978-3-319-44989-0_35
13. Ammon, S., Hinterwaldner, I. (eds.): Architecture and the Structured Image in Imagery in the Age of Modelling: Operative Artifacts in the Design Process in Architecture and Engineering. Springer, Heidelberg (2017)
14. Drieger, P.: Semantic network analysis as a method for visual text analytics. Procedia Soc. Behav. Sci. **79**, 4–17 (2013)
15. Carley, K., et al.: ORA User's Guide 2013. ISR, SCS, Carnegie Mellon University, Pittsburgh (2013)
16. Borgatti, S.P., Everett, M.G.: Network analysis of 2-mode data. Soc. Netw. **19**, 243–269 (1997)
17. Latapy, M., Magnien, C., Del Vecchio, N.: Basic notions for the analysis of large two-mode networks. Soc. Netw. **30**(1), 31–48 (2008)
18. Eades, P.: A heuristic for graph drawing. Congr. Numer. **42**, 149–160 (1984)
19. Carley, K.: Smart agents and organizations of the future. Handb. New Media **12**, 206–220 (2002)
20. Fagan, S., Gençay, R.: An introduction to textual econometrics. In: Handbook of Empirical Economics and Finance, pp. 133–153. CRC Press (2010)
21. Johnson-Laird, P.: Mental Models. Harvard University Press, Cambridg (1983)
22. Pfitzner, R., et al.: Betweenness preference: quantifying correlations in the topological dynamics of temporal networks. Phys. Rev. Lett. **110**, 198701: 1–5 (2013)

High-Rise Building Group Morphology Generation Approach Based on Wind Environmental Performance

Yuqiong Lin, Yanan Song, Jiawei Yao, and Philip F. Yuan[(✉)]

College of Architecture and Urban Planning, Tongji University, Shanghai, China
{1630237,jiawei.yao,philipyuan007}@tongji.edu.cn,
862724182@qq.com

Abstract. In the urbanization process, high-rise is favored and popularized, while results to the high-density urban space which aggravated the deterioration of urban wind environment. Using quantifiable environmental factors to control the building, is promoting a more meaningful group formation of the sustainable high-rise buildings. Thus, taking wind performance into account in high-rise design infancy is essential. According to the achievement of CAADRIA2018 "SELF-FORM-FINDING WIND TUNNEL TO ENVIRONMENTAL-PERFOR-MANCE URBAN AND BUILDING DESIGN" workshop, a preliminary set related to the environmental performance urban morphology generation system and method was constructed. In this study, various of high-rise building forms that might be conducive to urban ventilation were selected, such as "hollow-out", "twisting", "façade retracting" and "lift-up", to design the Dynamic Model System with multi-dimensional motion.

Keywords: High-rise · Group morphology · Wind tunnel · Dynamic models · Environmental performance

1 Introduction

With the advance of the "Performative Urbanism" Design paradigm, it has become a design trend to bridge the urban morphology to the social aspects through the parametric design tools [1]. Applying environmental performance as driven parameters in the design generation and optimization process help the architecture decisions become more environmentally responsible and reality-based, rather than subjective and empirical as usual.

In the urbanization process, high-rise is favored and popularized because of its intensive and comprehensive nature, but at the same time it results to the high-density urban space which aggravated the deterioration of urban ventilation, heat island effect, air pollution and so on. The bulky volume of the high-rise and the formation of the numerous clusters, impacts malignantly on the outdoor wind environment through the overall effect of the wind funnel effect in the urban space, which Leads to wind retention and local eddies as well as local strong winds such as high-rise winds and corner winds, strongly affect pedestrian comfort and safety [2]. Meanwhile, the wind

© Springer Nature Singapore Pte Ltd. 2019
J.-H. Lee (Ed.): CAAD Futures 2019, CCIS 1028, pp. 213–227, 2019.
https://doi.org/10.1007/978-981-13-8410-3_16

direction and wind speed greatly affect the location and strength of urban heat island phenomenon [3]. Therefore, it's worthwhile to study the high-rise buildings' group formation design based on wind environmental performance, through the adjustment of the morphology and layout of the building group, thus to reduce the deterioration of outdoor wind-heat environment.

With the proposed of "Arcology" in the 1960s, wind is more usually to be regarded as an important ecological factor to drive the layout and shape of buildings through digital design approach [4]. It's a trend to adjust the pedestrian wind environment and urban bioclimatic conditions from the urban planning level [5, 6]. The building morphology generation approach based on environmental performance, using quantifiable environmental factors to control the building, is promoting a more meaningful emerge of the architectural form. Therefore, through the adjustment of the morphology and layout of the building group, the building group's morphology can interact with the trajectory of the surrounding airflow to a certain extent, and give positive feedback to the wind environment. The "City in Wind Tunnel" dynamic model device (Fig. 1) aims to explore how the morphology of high-rise buildings in high-density cities can be optimized through wind tunnel experiments, to weaken the negative impact of high-rise buildings on the post-construction environment.

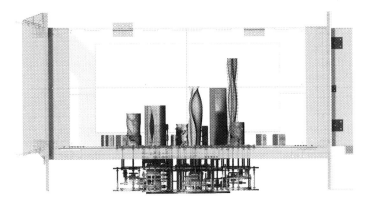

Fig. 1. The "City in Wind Tunnel" dynamic model device in CAADRIA2018 "SELF-FORM-FINDING WIND TUNNEL TO ENVIRONMENTAL-PERFORMANCE URBAN AND BUILD-ING DESIGN" workshop

During the previous research, a design method for the physical performance of the building morphology generation using the physical wind tunnel under the intervention of the dynamic model has been proposed [7]. The platform constructed by the method improves the feedback loop of environmental information and experimental morphology, which, at the same time, compensates for the transmission crack of wind tunnel simulation data in building generation design. Meanwhile, the integration of dynamic model abandons the functional definition of traditional static model simulation analysis that really changed the "post-evaluation" mode of environmental performance. In this condition, "performance evaluation" and "design optimization" are tightly coupled.

However, the dynamic simulation of this "self-forming" by mechanical devices based solely on a single motion change pattern can lead to limitations in the choice of building. Therefore, in this study, the author carried out the optimization design of three different motion modes of "rotation", "shifting" and "lifting" and the corresponding control programs to achieve a more complex and diverse architectural dynamic model. Take CAADRIA2018 Workshop Group 7 A "SELF-FORM-FINDING" WIND TUNNEL TO ENVIRONMENTAL-PERFORMANCE URBAN AND BUILDING DESIGN as an example, we selects twisting, setback, concave-convex façade, penetration through the volume and elevating ground floor as the morphology design strategies of high-rise buildings, which are conducive to urban ventilation. Based on the custom design of physical wind tunnels, a set of system and method for environmental performance based high-rise group morphology self-generation are preliminarily constructed, with a city-scale initial design study carried out.

2   Design Strategy

2.1   The Relationship Between Buildings' Morphology and Surrounding Wind Environment

High-rise buildings have a strong interference with the natural flow of the surrounding wind due to their large volume. The original wind direction is forced to change when it collides with the building: part of the wind flows downwards, forming a lower wind with a faster speed, which in turn creates a vortex area in front of the building, which affects the wind field of the pedestrian height; A part of the wind can flow over the upper edge of the building to the rear of the building, resulting in negative pressure on the leeward and crosswind surfaces of the building due to the thinness of the flow, forming a wind shadow area. The two wind directions affect the local wind field around the high-rise building and form a high-rise wind. According to the flow direction of the wind, the high-rise wind is divided into a split wind and a return wind. This two actions cause the airflow to be chaotic and accelerate the wind speed to be too fast, which strongly interferes the outdoor wind environment [8].

High-rise buildings directly determine the urban spatial morphology because of their height and volume. Under the same boundary wind speed, the urban spatial morphology determines the urban ventilation to a large extent [9]. High-density urban space is prone to wind retention and local vortex, which decline the urban ventilation and self-purification capacity; local strong winds such as high-rise wind and corner wind will affect pedestrian comfort and safety; the distribution and arrangement of buildings will change the airflow direction significantly [8].

2.2   Common Forms of Contemporary High-Rise Buildings

Due to its unique humanistic attributes and scientific rationality, contemporary high-rise buildings produce a unique value system of "technical aesthetics" and "art aesthetics" that satisfy the theory of dissipative structure [10]. Based on this aesthetic background, architects tend to select two forms of expression: "structural expression-ism" and "form sculptureism" when designing high-rise buildings: the "structural expressionism" is to free the formal beauty of structure itself from a large number of cumbersome decorations for an intuitive artistic expression. This method can clearly and precisely express the structural logic of the building, and can also make the structure and space uniform expression. The "form sculptureism" is based on the sculpture method to shape the form of the building - through the addition and sub-traction process, the three-dimensional space abstraction, volume sense, virtual and real relationship and detail design of the building form [11].

2.3   Case with Wind Environment Performance

In the context of the digital design paradigm, the cognition and quantitative generation of high-rise buildings based on wind environment performance has become an important method for building a livable city. The unique spatial form of the high-rise and high-density urban areas determines the urban area where the ventilation mode is various from other forms. Among them, split and return winds are formed due to the blockage of high-rise buildings, which changes the direction of airflow and increases the wind speed. At present, the influence of high-rise wind field on buildings is mainly concentrated on the windward, wind shadow areas and corner areas [8].

Through the research, the author found that the height of the building, the layout of the plane, the shape of the facade, the way of opening the window, the size of the opening and the angle between the building and the wind direction of the incoming wind may all affect the wind environment around the building. At present, the common spatial methods for the wind environment optimization are: mass transfer; morpho-logical change; elevating ground floor; wind-proof facilities and green vegetation [12]. The wind speed fluctuation in the corner area of the building will decrease as the number of geometric edges of the building plane increases, while the torsion and scaling along the height will guide the flow of the wind. For example, the Shanghai Tower (Fig. 2) was designed with a spiral-up façade that directs the strong airflow from the corners of the building, enables it attached to the facade, spiraling up to reduce wind loads. Besides, the indentation of the windward side of the building can weaken the impact of the sinking wind on pedestrians [13]. For example, the "Abeno Harukas" building (Fig. 2) in Japan uses setback to weaken the influence of high-rise buildings on the upper wind environment as well as alleviate the vortex airflow of the windward side and downwind energy; In addition, setting "ventilation holes" penetrating through the building can weaken the impacts of strong wind in front of the building [14], reduce the scope of the wind shadow area, promote the outdoor ventilation, and optimize pedestrian comfort, such as the Pearl River Building (Fig. 2) which is designed by SOM. Thus, the research summarizes several commonly used physical strategies for optimizing the wind environment performance of high-rise buildings, including twisting, setback, concave-convex façade, penetration through the volume and ele-vating ground floor.

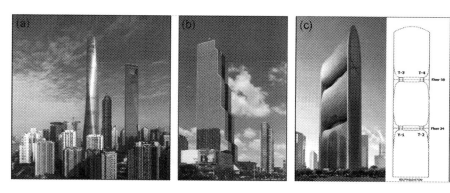

Fig. 2. Shanghai Tower (a), "Abeno Harukas" building (b), Pearl River building (c)

Since the existence of high-rise buildings has an inevitable objective impact on the surrounding wind environment, the adjustment of the building morphology and overall layout can interact with the trajectory of the surrounding airflow to a certain extent, and has positive feedback on its wind environment. Therefore, the preliminary design using the wind environment performance as a morphogenetic guide factor can effectively reduce the negative impact of high-rise buildings on the post-construction environment. This kind of environmental performance architectural design is a scientific, rational, and bottom-up design method in the digital age.

3 Dynamic Model Mechanical System Design

This paper takes the results of CAADRIA2018 Workshop Group 7 A "SELF-FORM-FINDING" WIND TUNNEL TO ENVIRONMENTAL-PERFORMANCE URBAN AND BUILDING DESIGN as an example to carry out the relevant optimization design of the physical wind tunnel and dynamic model linkage platform. The principle of the dynamic model, which composed of mechanical model device and Arduino electronic control platform, was adopted in this study for the city's formation, The dynamic model system in the method uses Arduino, an open source platform to connect virtual information and material entities, and the corresponding motion control programs were designed for different dynamic model motion patterns. The program directly controls the parameters of different servos, that are the active parts to drive the follower through the meshing of the gears. The followers' shape can be designed to convert the moving direction and speed of the mechanical models into the expected morphology changing mode, so that the orientation of each building model, the size of setback and the concave-convex facade, as well as the height of elevating the ground floor are enabled for continuous variation and quantitative control. Among them, each set of mechanical devices adopts standardized design, so that its position on the bottom board of the wind tunnel test section can be changed flexibly according to various design schemes. With matching different building model, which can be seen as the shells of the mechanical devices, to realize the sustainable use of physical tools.

3.1   Mechanical Transmission Principle

The mechanical transmission of the main building model provides feasibility for the diverse generation of the building morphology. The core mechanical transmission of this experiment is based on the Arduino electronic control system operating the servo system. The device controls series of different morphologies by the electronic signal generated by the wind pressure or wind speed sensor. As Fig. 3 shows, the steering gear (also known as servo motor, SERVO) is a position servo drive with an electromechanical structure of a closed-loop control system consisting of small DC motors, variable speed gear sets, adjustable potentiometers, control boards and other components [15]. The workflow is as follows: (1) The controller of the steering gear drives the motor to rotate by receiving the signal source; (2) The gear set receives the motor signal, and processes it to rotate the corresponding angle; (3) The potentiometer follows the gear set Synchronous rotation, measure the angle of rotation; (4) The board receives the potentiometer signal to determine whether the servo is rotated and maintained at the target angle. The experiment completes the morphological change of the main body model by driving the gears or other parts through the steering gear [16].

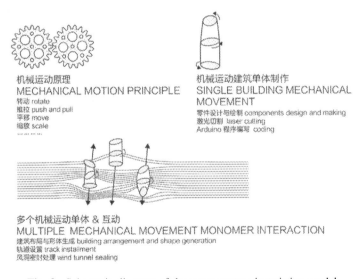

机械运动原理
MECHANICAL MOTION PRINCIPLE
转动 rotate
推拉 push and pull
平移 move
缩放 scale

机械运动建筑单体制作
SINGLE BUILDING MECHANICAL MOVEMENT
零件设计与绘制 components design and making
激光切割 laser cutting
Arduino 程序编写 coding

多个机械运动单体 & 互动
MULTIPLE MECHANICAL MOVEMENT MONOMER INTERACTION
建筑布局与形体生成 building arrangement and shape generation
轨道设置 track installment
风洞密封处理 wind tunnel sealing

Fig. 3. Schematic diagram of the servo system in twisting model

3.2   Combination of Various Mechanical Transmission Mechanisms

Based on the three transmission mechanisms, which are rotation, shifting and lifting, the "City in Wind Tunnel" dynamic model device selects the high-rise building forms that are favorable for urban ventilation, such as twisting, setback, concave-convex façade, and penetration (Fig. 4), to carry out the mechanical system design of the dynamic model, with the corresponding control programming. The programming code controls the signal parameters of the servos, utilizing the gears as the active part to mesh the experimental model to perform the driven motion to generate the expected form. The direction and speed of motion of the follower are controlled by Arduino, a electronic platform, so that the orientation of each building model, the size of twisting, setback, the concave-convex facade and penetration through the volume, and the height of the elevating ground floor are realized to achieve continuous change and quantitative control. Among them, each set of mechanical devices adopts standardized design, which can flexibly to be changed its position on the bottom board of the wind tunnel test section according to different design schemes, and match different building forms (i.e., the main part of the building model) to realize the sustainable use of physical tools. The number of servos increases the diversity of motion throughout the system, resulting in richer morphologies.

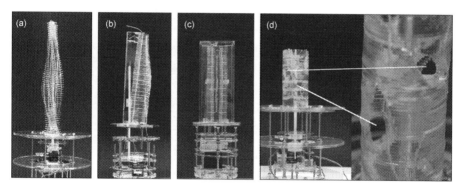

Fig. 4. Dynamic model of twisting (a), concave-convex façade (b), shifting penetration (c), rotary penetration (d)

Twisting Model

The twisting model (Fig. 5) consisted of a stack of several 4 mm thick laser-cut acrylic boards. Several active rotating boards are settled on the upper, middle and lower sides of the model according to different schemes. Besides, the remaining acrylic boards are placed between the active boards as the passive rotating boards. For instance, there're four active rotating boards of the main building model in Fig. 6 (left), which are controlled by four different servos, and the servos rotates the gears to drive the four rotating shafts that are nested together to rotate. The four rotating shafts are all made of hollow ABS tubes, so that to respectively transmit the rotation of the corresponding servo to the corresponding active rotating board. Inside the building model, a set of rotating shafts and two elastic threads are inserted. After the first and last ends of the threads are fixed, the active boards can drive the passive boards to rotate, maintaining the continuity of the entire model's motion. The elastic thread has a moderate elastic force, so that it can avoid the affect by the rotation of the servos while pulling the passive rotating boards for rotation [17].

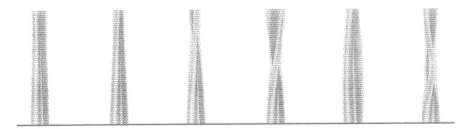

Fig. 5. Dynamic change of the twisting model

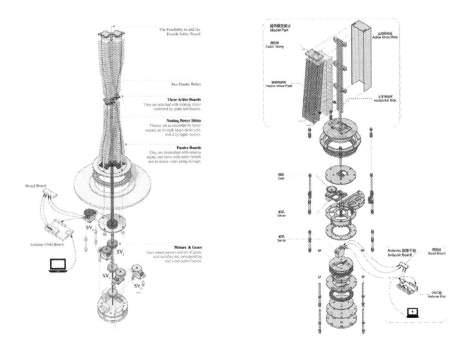

Fig. 6. Construction diagram of the twisting (left) and concave-convex (right) model

Concave-Convex Model

The concave-convex model consists of motion parts and a static cuboid enclosure. The passive part of the motion parts is formed by a stack of 4 mm thick laser-cut acrylic boards, while the active part is composed of a horizontal sliding rod arranged in the middle of the building model, and an active shifting board placed in the upper middle and lower parts. As Fig. 6 (right) shows, the active shifting boards are controlled by first servo synchronously, which drives the rod to move through the rotation of the gear, and then transmits the corresponding moving signal to the corresponding passive moving boards. The second servo, as to produce another kind of motion, that is, rotation, to realize the changing of the orientation of the building. The interior of the building model runs through two elastic threads, the principle is the same as above. The experimental model simulates the unevenness of the facade of the building by moving the board forward and backward in the horizontal direction.

Penetration Model

The experiment of penetration through the building volume includes shifting penetration and rotary penetration. The shirting penetration building model (Fig. 7) consists of the inner driven part and the static enclosure parts on both sides. As Fig. 8 (right) shows, the dynamic part is a stack of 4 mm thick laser-cut acrylic boards, which is symmetrically distributed along the central axis of the long-side of the building model. In the middle of the dynamic part and the static part, a horizontal sliding rod is disposed

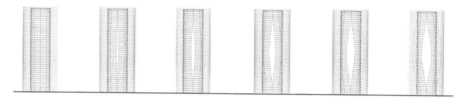

Fig. 7. Dynamic change of the shifting penetration model

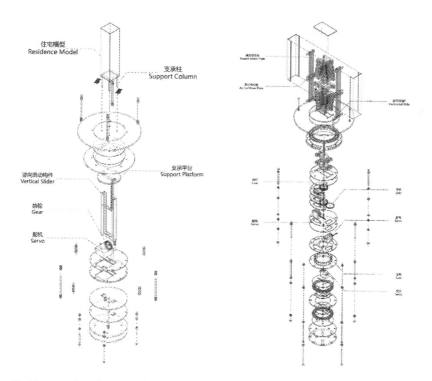

Fig. 8. Construction diagram of the elevating the ground floor (left) and shifting-penetration (right) model

on each of the left and right sides, and each of the two rod members has an active motion board in the middle thereof, which are respectively controlled by different servos. The two servos drive the left and right horizontal sliding rods to mirror the horizontal sliding by the rotation of the gears. The sliding member further transmits the motion trend to the active moving board and drives the passive moving board to perform mirrored follower motion along the long-side central axis. There are two elastic threads running through the inside and outside of the building model. The principle is the same as above.

It shows the section diagram of rotary penetration in Fig. 9, which's principle is similar to that of twisting, which's motion is based on the rotating motion mechanism. However, the model is a stack of 4 mm thick laser-cut acrylic which are punched inside in advance to simulate the internal holes of the building in a variety of internal spatial forms. The model is provided with four active rotating boards from top to bottom, and the remaining boards are regularly stacked between as passive rotating boards. The four active rotating boards of the main building model part are controlled by four different servos. The servo rotates the gears to drive the four rotating shafts that are nested together to rotate. The rest of the principle is the same as the above-mentioned "twisting" model. This experiment forms a different internal penetration space form by rotating the boards.

Basic Morphology Design

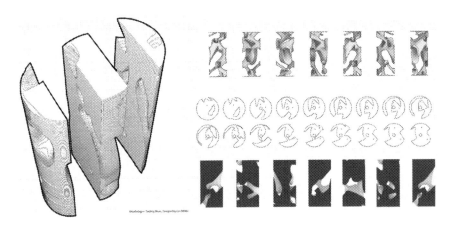

Fig. 9. Section diagram of the rotary-penetration model

4   Generation Workflow

(See Fig. 10).

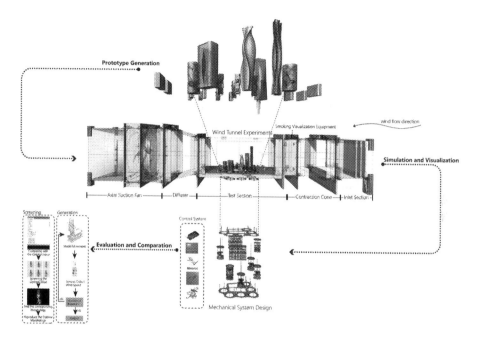

Fig. 10. Generation system based on wind tunnel experiment

4.1   Urban Wind Environment Assessment Method

The prerequisite for achieving a good urban wind environment is to be able to make scientific, reasonable and practical evaluations of the wind environment in urban design. As an analysis and generation tool [18], the algorithm can evaluate the environmental data obtained by the experiment and convert it into an environmental performance score that meets the designer's requirements. Because high-rise buildings are more likely to form strong undershoot airflow than multi-storey buildings, the surrounding ground wind speed is four times that of low-rise buildings, pedestrian comfort is greatly affected [13], while high-rise and high-density urban center area is a densely populated area, more attention should be paid to the wind environment at the pedestrian level. Therefore, in this experiment, the wind speed is measured at a pedestrian height of 1.5 m as the basic data of the wind environment evaluation.

Since the influence of the building on the surrounding environment differs from various specific site, the layout of the sensors' measuring position on the baseboard of the wind tunnel is depend on the design requirement, according to the criticality of social attributes such as the functional elements and crowd objects at various points around the building. Since the air flow at the pedestrian level is complex and variable, it cannot be judged only from the wind speed value. At present, the common evaluation methods of wind environment data, such as wind speed probability evaluation, thermal comfort evaluation, wind speed ratio, wind speed dispersion, comfortable wind speed ratio, etc., can be used as a standard for constraining the building morphology generation. In this study, in the evaluation of the wind environment comfort of pedestrians, it is necessary to eliminate the building form that causes excessive wind speed dispersion. Secondly, the form with low comfortable wind speed ratio is also need to be avoided. Then, determine the range of the comfortable wind speed based on the summer average temperature value in the site environment, and obtain the different wind speed probability values of the same measuring position through a certain time measurement, so as to comprehensively evaluate the wind environment performance of the building form. Thus, three valid criteria in the wind environment evaluation—the deviation value V_{de} of the comfort temperature, the discrete value V_{di} of the wind speed of the measuring point, and the probability of the uncomfortable wind speed value P_{uc} are selected to evaluate the effective data generated in the experiment. The weight of different measuring point of the overall environmental performance score in the scheme x and the weight of the different environmental evaluation indicators:

$$E(x) = aV_{de} + bV_{di} + cP_{uc} \tag{1}$$

If the difference in criticality of each measuring point isn't obvious, the weight of the environmental data evaluation can be set to: $a = 70\%$, $b = 15\%$, $c = 15\%$, while for the homogeneity of the surrounding airflow, the evaluation weights are: $a = 60\%$, $b = 30\%$, $c = 10\%$ [20].

4.2 Optimization of High-Rise Building Group Layout

The urban space porosity is reduced when high-rise buildings form a cluster layout, which worsen the street natural wind environment permeability and make the urban pollutants more difficult to be eliminated in time, resulting in more serious environmental pollution. Therefore, in this study, the initial step is to control the spatial position of each high-rise building model and optimize the overall layout combination [5].

The orientation and layout of high-rise buildings should be staggered as much as possible, and sufficient space should be reserved between the buildings to prevent the formation of narrow-tube effects. The front and rear high-rise buildings should be staggered to reduce the wind blockage of the front-row buildings and on the main wind channel. Properly setting up squares and connect open areas of the block is to ensure that the prevailing wind of the main air duct can penetrate all corners of the area, reduce the scope of the wind and shadow area, and optimize urban ventilation [19]; the building combination should adopt a gradual height distribution, which is beneficial to reduce The sudden change of wind speed; under the premise of ensuring that sunshine meets the standard, the building is oriented to reverse the appropriate angle, which is conducive to saving land and obtaining a better wind environment [20]. Therefore, in the experiment, we use the building permeability (P-building permeability) and the site coverage ratio (λp-site coverage ratio) as reference factors to make a simple evaluation and optimization of the overall layout of the experiment [21].

4.3   Optimization of High-Rise Building Morphology

After optimizing the layout of the main model, this section focuses on the calculation logic of the servo factor in the iterative algorithm. By quantitatively translating a series of spatial servo data of the building model in time dimension into a mathematical language that can be scored and compared, and then weighting calculation, screening and comparison by pre-set wind environment assessment criteria, the best value is obtained and the building form is reappeared. The servo calculation logic is specifically described below in combination with model motion of twisting, concave-convex, penetration and elevation.

The principle of the twisting model is that the servos drive the building plane to rotate and generate the twisting morphology. Its deformation angle can be quantitatively controlled by four servos through controlling their degree of rotation, that is, in combination to be the degree of distortion. The rotation angle of the active board is proportional to the servo's angle. The servo angles are $D_{sv_1}, D_{sv_2}, D_{sv_3}, \cdots, D_{sv_n}$ and the degree of deformation can be quantitatively expressed by the formula:

$$N = \left(\frac{D_{sv_1}}{D_{sv_2}} + \frac{D_{sv_2}}{D_{sv_3}} + \cdots + \frac{D_{sv_n}}{D_{sv_1}} \right) / n \tag{2}$$

The concave-convex model is changed by the servo driving the active board for forward and backward telescopic movement. The form variable can be quantified as the displacement distance of the active moving board controlled by the three servos, that is, the indentation rate. The moving distance of the three active moving boards is proportional to the rotation angle of the corresponding steering gear. The degree of deformation can be expressed by the formula:

$$T = \left(\frac{|D_{sv_1} - D_{sv_2}|}{D_{sv_2}} + \frac{|D_{sv_2} - D_{sv_3}|}{D_{sv_3}} + \cdots + \frac{|D_{sv_n} - D_{sv_1}|}{D_{sv_1}} \right) / n \tag{3}$$

The calculation principle of the penetration model is more complicated, and the author summarizes it into continuity. The principle of shifting penetration is similar to that of concave-convex facade. The volume change of the form can be visually expressed as the displacement distance of the active moving board, which can be quantified by:

$$K = (D_{sv_1} + D_{sv_2} + \cdots + D_{sv_n}) / n \tag{4}$$

In the rotary penetration, the penetration portion only undergoes shape adjustment during the deformation process, and its volume doesn't change. Therefore, the principle of rotary penetration is that the servo drives the hollow space of the building to undergo torsional deformation. The calculation of "emptiness" can be equivalent to the previous calculation of "torsion". The quantitative formula is:

$$R = \left(\frac{D_{sv_1}}{D_{sv_2}} + \frac{D_{sv_2}}{D_{sv_3}} + \cdots + \frac{D_{sv_n}}{D_{sv_1}} \right) / n \tag{5}$$

Fig. 11. Simulation diagram of the wind tunnel experiment

5 Summary

The design of the "City in Wind Tunnel" experimental device developed the multi-dimensional motion mechanism, which enables the physical building models to generate active and dynamic feedback changes to its environment (Fig. 11). The interactive programming technique combined with environmental performance and digital building profile algorithm brings a new definition of non-deterministic patterns and convertible properties to the dynamic model. With the help of the new parametric design platform, designers can instantaneously obtain a large number of different physical data in the same environment background, satisfying the requirements of machine learning for massive sample data such as genetic algorithm or neural network algorithm, and bridged the building geometry generation parameters and urban wind environment parameters.

Acknowledgements. This research is funded by the National Natural Science Foundation of China (Grant No. 51578378), the Special Funds for State Key R&D Program during the 13th Five-year Plan Period of China (Grant No. 2016YFC0702104), the Sino- German Scientific Research Program (Grant No. GZ1162) and Science and Technology Commission of Shanghai Municipality (Grant No. 16dz1206502, Grant No. 16dz2250500, Grant No. 17dz1203405).

References

1. Yuan, W., Xu, W.: Research on algorithmic shape based on environmental performance analysis. In: 2013 National Architectural Institute Digital Architecture Teaching Seminar and International Symposium on Digital Architectural Design, Tianjin, China (2013)
2. Yang, X.: High-rise building shape design strategy under the influence of wind environment. Tianjin University (2014)
3. Oke, T.R.: City size and the urban heat Island. Atmos. Environ. (1967) **7**(8), 769–779 (1973)
4. Lan, M.: Create a harmonious environment together of ecological architecture design method. Procedia Environ. Sci. **10**, 1774–1780 (2011)
5. Ng, E., et al.: Improving the wind environment in high-density cities by understanding urban morphology and surface roughness: a study in Hong Kong. Landsc. Urban Plann. **101**(1), 59–74 (2011)
6. Kormaníková, L., et al.: Parametric wind design. Front. Archit. Res. **7**(3), 383–394 (2018)
7. Lin, Y., Zheng, J., Yao, J., Yuan, P.F.: Research on physical wind tunnel and dynamic model based building morphology generation method. In: CAADRIA 2018, Fukuda, W.H. T., Janssen, P., Crolla, K., Alhadidi, S. (eds.), pp. 165–174. Beijing (2018)
8. Xie, Z., Yang, J.: Optimization design strategy for high-rise building forms to improve outdoor wind environment. J. Archit. (2), 76–81 (2013)
9. Zhu, Y.: Research on the evaluation method of stroke environment in urban planning and design. Southeast University (2014)
10. Yang, Y.: Research on the aesthetic value of high-rise buildings. Chongqing University (2006)
11. Wang, R.: Conceptual design of high-rise building plastic art and structure. Chongqing University (2007)
12. Ye, Z., Chen, Y.: The spatial pattern design of urban plots oriented by wind environment: taking the plot of the school of architecture and urban planning of Tongji University as an example. In: the International Conference on Urban Development and Planning (2010)
13. Xie, Z., Yang, N.: Optimization design strategy for high-rise building shape to improve outdoor wind environment. Acta J. (2), 76–81 (2013)
14. Guo, F., Li, P.: Building morphing strategy based on wind environment. Hous. Ind. (7) (2016)
15. Hu, X., et al.: Research on semi-physical simulation system of steering gear based on virtual instrument. J. Measur. Control Technol. **30**(01), 75–78 (2011)
16. Cai, R.: Arduino based steering gear control system design. J. Comput. Knowl. Technol. **8**(15), 3719–3721 (2012)
17. Lin, Y., et al.: Research on the architectural properties of environmental performance based on wind tunnel visualization (2) (2018)
18. Maxwell, I., Pigram, D.: Algorithmic typology: towards an operational model. In: Scripting the Futures, pp. 107–112. Tongji University Press, Shanghai (2012)
19. Wang, H.: Research on the shape control of high-rise buildings in Shenzhen Qianhai No. 3 unit based on wind environment. Harbin Institute of Technology (2013)
20. Yao, X., Leng, H., Sun, Q.: Research on wind environment optimization strategy in high-rise residential areas. Ind. Constr. (s1), 9–11 (2013)
21. Yuan, C., Ng, E., Norford, L.K.: Improving air quality in high-density cities by understanding the relationship between air pollutant dispersion and urban morphologies. Build. Environ. **71**, 245–258 (2014)

Rethinking Space and Spatial Behavior

Encoding Design Process
Using Interactive Data Visualization

Naghmi Shireen$^{(\boxtimes)}$, Halil Erhan$^{(\boxtimes)}$, and Robert Woodbury$^{(\boxtimes)}$

Simon Fraser University, Surrey, Canada
{nshireen,herhan,rw}@sfu.ca

Abstract. The existing research on design space exploration favors the exploration of multiple parallel designs, however the act of exploring a design space is still to be integrated in the design of new digital media. We conducted an experiment to understand how designers navigate through large numbers of design alternatives generated from parametric models. We analyzed the data with a purpose-built visualization tool. We observed that participants changed the task environment and took design actions, frequently combining these into action combinations. Five tasks emerged from our analysis: Criteria Building, Criteria Testing, Criteria Applying, Reflection and (Re)Setting. From our analysis, we suggest several features for future systems for interacting with design alternatives.

Keywords: Design space exploration · Design alternatives ·
Coding protocol and analysis · Creativity support tools ·
Interfaces for design galleries

1 Introduction

Generative tools and increased computational processing power have enabled designers to rapidly create thousands of design alternatives to explore the previously seldom-implemented, but much discussed design space [1, 3, 17, 24, 25]. Representing this design space, even partially, remains a research challenge across disciplines [7, 8, 10, 11, 13, 14, 23, 27]. A common approach centres around viewing, managing, and editing multiple designs through gallery-like interfaces, which seems promising. However, there is a need to identify fundamental actions, interactions and interfaces that can seamlessly support working with large numbers of design alternatives. Current interfaces are usually built on assumptions of how designers must work, rather than understanding what designers actually do. We address the latter by observing designers working in a simulated environment supporting exploration of computationally generated design solutions and propose tool features based on our results.

Our argument for exploring new tools features by observing designers in a simulated environment is based on Human Problem-Solving theory [18]. It suggests that the structure of a task environment is the major determining factor of the structure of a problem space in which a cognitive agent performs a task. This predicts that changing the task environment may radically change observed designer behaviour. Indeed, the very notion of an alternative may change as the available design operators are different.

© Springer Nature Singapore Pte Ltd. 2019
J.-H. Lee (Ed.): CAAD Futures 2019, CCIS 1028, pp. 231–246, 2019.
https://doi.org/10.1007/978-981-13-8410-3_17

For example, expert designers generate four to five design alternatives on average when using sketching [1, 3], whereas when using generative systems, this number can grow to hundreds if not thousands. Sketching and generative systems present two different task environments with different problem space structures, hence lead to different sets of moves. We cannot expect a designer to explore 1000 solutions using sketching only, nor expect a designer using generative systems to interact with only a few designs. Hence, using existing design media for understanding design moves when working with a generative system can result in misleading conclusions.

Our research premise is that, if designers can access and work directly with a large number of designs in a design task environment with new representations and tools as part of the design workflow, we should expect new action patterns, task sequences and strategies to emerge and thus change design processes. What are the new actions, action patterns and task sequences in this new task environment that would enable working with multiple designs? Our research program aims to answer this (and similar) questions; this paper looks at a partial design process at an action-level granularity. It addresses the basic actions performed interacting with large design spaces. How and when these actions appear with respect to the design process? In what sequence they are performed? Is there an overlapping pattern of design tasks? Answering these questions will help us identify a set of potential user interactions and operations on gallery-like design exploratory tools.

In the following sections, we first address the existing literature, followed by our larger research goals and the more specific goals for this paper. Since we have previous publications [16] documenting the details of the experimental setup, we only provide an overview here and proceed to reporting design media, action and task coding and analysis.

1.1   Background

The literature on simultaneously working with a large number of alternatives has emerged quite recently. It finds that multiple alternative designs allow for more accurate comparative evaluation [21] and suggests 'selecting the right design,' before 'getting the design right'. Working with multiple designs helps designers to explore more design space faster and efficiently [5]. Smith et al. [19] suggest exploratory interfaces to support switching between ideas, viewing, labeling, grouping and classifying multiple ideas, and providing an explicit means to capture the design situation, and, finally, to support fluid composition and decomposition of ideas.

Exploration techniques include *Set Evolution* by Xu et al. [26], *Shape Evolution* by Chouchoulas and Day [4], *d.tour* by Ritchie et al. [15]. A few present parallel viewing & editing techniques that include *Parallel Paths* [20], *Design Galleries* [13], *Linked Editing* [22], *Subjunctive Interfaces* [11], *Juxtapose* [8], GEM-NI [27] Design Gallery [23], and CAMBRIA [10].

Terry et al.'s [20] *Parallel Paths* argues that there is a potential alternative, before, during or after a command is evoked. Drucker et al. [6] presents an interface that helps comparing and managing multiple presentation slides. Toomim et al. [22] present *Linked Editing* technique to support parallel editing of duplicated code. Hartmann et al.'s [8] *Juxtapose* is built on top of this technique with interactive parameter tuning for runtime provision and exploration. Lunzer and Hornbaek [11] propose and evaluate parameter-based exploration interfaces called *Subjunctive Interfaces*. *Design Gallery* by Marks et al. [13] presents a computer-assisted parameter setting mechanism with passive display of results.

1.2 Research Objectives

The systems discussed present valuable techniques to develop and edit multiple alternatives, but there is little evidence of what may happen when working with multiple designs. Our research is an attempt towards understanding the process of managing multiple designs based on a low-fidelity prototype of a task environment. Our study has two general research objectives:

1. *To explore how a design process is manifested in a task environment that enables working with a large number of computationally generated alternatives.*
2. *To identify the characteristics of this task environment—including tools, representations, and logical and spatial structure of an environment—that can support managing a large number of alternatives.*

These two objectives are tightly coupled. In our larger research, we intend to relate them and report the spatial patterns of design media use with the design process observed. In this paper, we report our findings related to this design process. The analysis of the data concerning strategies in relation to actions and space use is out of scope here. More specifically, this paper reports a set of common design actions executed by the participants performing the same design task, under the same design situation, and using the same design instruments. We identified these actions through iterative qualitative coding as we relied less on previous research and more on what our data presented. The set of actions is a starting point to our larger research objective, namely developing better support for working with alternatives in design environments with generative and computational tools. We also investigated and report here, how the identified actions relate to each other and to the study design task at large. We further speculate how these actions can be translated or manifested into system functions for gallery style design interfaces.

2 Research Design

We conducted a lab experiment where a sample of designers (selected by referral sampling) were given a set of 1000 design alternatives printed on index cards. We made the following assumptions. (1) Workspaces with secondary cognitive artifacts (e.g., pencil and paper) can be considered part of a 'prototype' information system [2] and considered a basic work environment representing an interface. (2) Designers moves back and forth between design phases opportunistically, e.g., conceptualizing may overlap with prototyping. Our scope is a part of the conceptual design phase only, as it is likely to involve exploring alternatives; (3) Generative methods can be integrated into the conceptual design workflow such that sketching-a-solution is now complemented by filtering and selecting of plausible solutions out of a large set. With these assumptions, we developed a design task for which 1000 alternatives were computationally generated, filtered based on their diversity, and presented back to the designers (participants) for exploration and reflection. Filtering was designed to ensure that the generated 1000 designs are visually different from each other (Fig. 1) [7].

As a design scenario, we developed an open-ended task to promote exploration using incomplete requirements rather than well-defined goals to avoid mere selection [16]. We asked participants to consider themselves as the chief architect in a team tasked with devising a large set of computer-generated conceptual models for a multi-storey residential building. Participants were unaware of the exact number of designs in the set. They were asked to review the designs and set goals for the next phase.

Fig. 1. A small sample of the dissimilar design alternatives

2.1   Coding the Design Process

Nine participants and one pilot participant took part in the study. We video recorded each session using four cameras. The placement and the coverage details of each camera is shown in the Fig. 2, Right. Participants were encouraged to voice their thinking. Once completed, the audio-video data collected was converted into a unified video stream. The video was analyzed and coded at three levels determined after the pilot study and literature review: change-events, design-actions and design-tasks.

Change-Events. As one of the larger research goals involved understanding the spatial structures adapted by the participants when managing multiple designs; hence, close attention was given to all those events/instances that resulted into a *change* in the workspace environment. We called these instances a *change-event* (Fig. 3). They were marked every time a physical action or a sequence of actions changed the overall spatial structure of a worksurface.

Coding spatial change-events helped us identify patterns adapted by participants to off-load their memory using spatial conjectures, such as zoning, orientation, positioning, visual marking, etc. [16]. Two researchers coded these spatial events separately to validate the coding schema. Their inter-rater reliability was calculated at three rounds of fresh video encoding (5–10 min of video used per round), until a desired value of Cronbach's alpha (20 events; $\alpha = .80$) was achieved. Later one of the researchers coded all the video data and divided the entire design process for participants into chunks of observable change-events. A spatial snapshot of each event was logged from each four cameras with a time stamp.

Fig. 2. (Left) Experimental material; (Right) experimental setup

1. The participant brings a stack of cards from the side table to his front.
2. He divides the selection pile into five smaller piles.
3. He spreads out designs to see as many designs as possible side by side

Fig. 3. A change-event demonstration

Design Actions. In our coding the smallest unit of analysis was an *action*. It is defined as an observable move by a participant without any interpretation or association with the design intent. The process of identifying these actions was iterative and ran multiple times until we reached an exhaustive list. Once the definitions of these actions were finalized, two researchers coded the video-audio data simultaneously for correctness and reliability (Cronbach's alpha for 40 actions = 0.82). See Table 1.

Please note that there might be instances where multiple simultaneous actions were observed, but for simplicity and clarity one of those actions at a time was recorded. For example, a participant who was *comparing* multiple designs may also be *focusing* on one design at the same time. To accommodate these overlapping action sequences, actions were coded within a period of a change-event. This means, researchers looked at actions within a time-period of a change-event and listed them as one set of actions performed between two consecutive change-events. The final coded sheet can be seen in Fig. 4, Left.

Design Tasks. A design task is defined as a group of actions performed to achieve a certain design goal explicitly stated by a participant. In total, five design tasks emerged (Table 2): *Criteria Building, Criteria Testing, Criteria Applying, Reflection and (Re) Setting*.

Consistent with the design literature, participants followed a cyclic design process (Fig. 4, Right) that began by clarifying and defining the initial design criteria based on their preliminary immediate study of a randomly selected set of alternatives. This initial criterion could be based on experience, understanding, knowledge or designer insight; it could be subjective/objective, internal/external. As the understanding of the overall design task developed, the criteria matured.

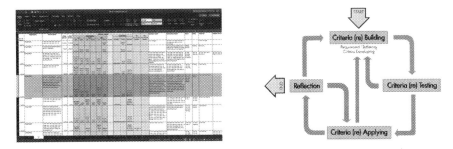

Fig. 4. (Left) The coded excel sheet. (Right) A cycle of design tasks

Once the preliminary criteria were identified, participants tested the criteria over few designs before they continued using them in the next cycles. In each cycle, the search became faster and participants very often reflected on their design decisions. They orally confirmed their decisions, spent time looking at a collection, asked questions for clarity, looked for inspiration, and did (re)setting (clearing up the table for the next filtering cycle for instance).

Table 1. Defining design actions

Action	Definition
Drawing	A participant draws a card (design alternative) from a pile
Selecting	(S)he selects a design card based on a criterion for further exploration
Eliminating	(S)he is discarding a design card based on a criterion
Stacking	(S)he is placing cards one over the other (overlay)
Spreading	(S)he lays out the design cards side-by-side
Sorting	(S)he lays out the cards based on some sequence or rank in mind
Splitting	(S)he splits a pile into two or more stack of piles
Flickering	(S)he flickers through multiple cards in hand very quickly
Scanning	A participant gives a quick look on multiple design cards simultaneously
Focusing	(S)he is focusing on one design card for more than 3 s
Comparing	Participant is comparing back and forth between two or more design cards in hand or on table
Reading	(S)he is reading from the requirement sheet
Noting	(S)he is writing on the sticky notes, or on the white board or anything else
Marking	(S)he places a written/color-coded tag on a design or a set of designs
Revisiting	(S)he revisits one of the previous designs or a previous design decision

Interactive Timeline Visualization. Due to the limitation of spreadsheets, that is, their inability to transform and synchronize snapshots along with the codes, we developed our own interactive timeline visualization system. It displays action and task durations, along with the snapshots from the cameras (Fig. 5). It enables selecting a spatial snapshot via brushing the respective actions and tasks and vice versa. The spatial snapshots can be enlarged to have a closer look of the spatial arrangements. This interactive visualization became our primary analytic tool. Two researchers carefully analyzed these timeline visualizations for each participant initially one by one and then in combinations on a large display system (3 × 2 HD monitors). The analysis sessions ran over two weeks, for around four to five hours each day.

Table 2. Defining design tasks

Design task	Definition
Criteria (re) Building	Whenever a participant is observed to have found a criterion to sort the design cards. This also includes the instances when the participant changes a criterion with a different one, rearranges criteria, eliminates a criterion, or redefines its meanings Examples: "I should look for designs with more green spaces from now on". "I am going to start looking for building designs facing North" (building criteria) "Let's combine earthquake proof designs and stilt building designs, since they both seems to have things in common" (redefining criteria) "Well I am thinking that I should rather start with looking at if I understand the building structure at all?" (rearranging criteria sequence)
Criteria Testing	When a participant introduces a criterion, the first round of selection made under that criterion is considered as for testing of that criterion. Once tested, next is the applying and reapplying of the criterion multiple times, without any hesitation Note: This task should not be confused with Criteria Applying. In many instances, participants tested a criterion and later would reject it, noting that it did not work
Criteria (re) Applying	When the participant is found to be considering the qualities of a design against one of his chosen criteria Example: "Too bulky….", "Doesn't look interesting….", "Has less green space…" etc.
Reflection	When participant takes a step back, talks about (explains) what he has done so far, what is his next move. At this point, he may continue what he has been doing so far, or he may simply reject his previous moves and restarts the whole process with a new perspective
(Re)Setting	When the participant (re)sets the physical work environment for next round of filtering or to make space for his/her next actions

Descriptive Statistics. We ran a descriptive analysis by compiling the raw codes into five main variables. (1) *Participant ID*. Each participant was given an ID, e.g., p01. (2) *Action Combinations*. Actions were coded in a time period spanning a change-event. We first analyzed the actions individually and then in pairs; therefore, we could focus on action-pair frequencies for understanding the correlation between them and the design tasks. (3) *Actions.* action-level data was visualized to see if there was any significance in its occurrences. (4) *Time period.* The time taken for each action and action-pair was normalized, i.e. time period of a change-event divided by total number of actions or action-pairs in that change-event. This gave us a uniform comparable data on actions. (5) *Tasks.* Tasks are a group of goal-oriented design actions identifying designer intent and reinforced by verbal confirmation.

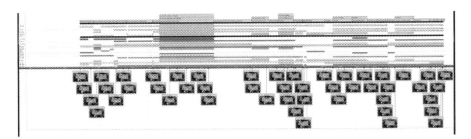

Fig. 5. Customized interactive data visualization showing design actions, design tasks and space-use data on a single timeline

3 Findings and Results

3.1 Change-Events

Table 3 compares the total time spent by each participant and the total number of change-events recorded during that time. It is clear that the number of change-events are independent of total time spent by a participant. Please note that the data in the table is purely for confirmation, i.e., it may have no research significance as is. A qualitative analysis of the change-events in the overall design process may yield insight, but is out of scope for this paper.

Table 3. Total time spent by each participant and the number of change-events coded

Participant ID	p01	p02	p03	p04	p05	p06	p07	p08	p09
Number of change-events	49	29	25	24	9	11	8	7	13
Total time spent (s)	6322	7081	2921	3077	5652	1622	4718	1494	3448

3.2 Actions

In total we identified 15 recurring actions. These actions were recorded once within a period of a change-event, even though they might have appeared multiple times. Every time an action appeared, it was counted individually and in combination with its co-occurring actions to estimate the number of actions and combinations performed. For example, in Fig. 4, there are six co-occurring actions in the highlighted change-event, for which actions and action combinations appear in Table 4.

Table 4. Calculating action combinations

Change-Event #	4
Event Begin Time	00:24:51
Event End Time	00:26:00
Actions (within this event)	*Drawing, Comparing, Sorting, Eliminating, Spreading, Selecting*
Number of actions (n)	6
Action combinations (during this event)	*Drawing Comparing, Drawing Sorting, Drawing Eliminating, Drawing Spreading, Drawing Selecting, Comparing Sorting, Comparing Eliminating, Comparing Spreading, Comparing Selecting, Sorting Eliminating, Sorting Spreading, Sorting Selecting, Eliminating Spreading, Eliminating Selecting, Spreading Selecting*
Number of action combinations of arity $k = 2$ Possible combinations $\binom{n}{k} = \frac{n!}{(n-k)!k!}$	15

The action-combinations were calculated per change-event separately and then added together for each participant. Table 5 shows the total actions and action-combinations counts.

Count of Actions. Combining all participants' data and looking at the frequency of individual actions revealed the most frequent actions as; *Stacking, Selecting, Eliminating, Focusing, Comparing and Drawing* (Table 6). As expected, participants managed the exploration of huge design space by making collections, based on common design attributes. While making collections, they *Stacked* designs belonging to one group either *completely* or *partially*. In contrast to *Stacking*, participants also arranged designs by *spreading* them over a surface in form of a layout. They *Focused* on designs individually and collectively to identify their features and *Compared* designs with each other to justify their *Selection* or *Elimination* patterns.

Table 5. Number of design actions and action combinations for each participant

	p01	p02	p03	p04	p05	p06	p07	p08	p09
Action combinations	382	206	272	70	29	123	149	35	294
Action count	199	105	115	64	25	57	50	25	80

Table 6. The above average actions and their frequencies

Actions	Stacking	Selecting	Eliminating	Focusing	Comparing	Drawing
Frequencies	90	83	79	76	70	69

Time Spent on Actions. We observed participants spending more time *Focusing* and *Comparing* designs than any other action, maybe because one analyzes properties of a design to make a decision. *Focusing, Comparing, Eliminating, Stacking, Drawing* and *Selecting* all had more than the average number of action occurrences.

Actions Per Design Task. Plotting actions versus design tasks revealed that a few actions were performed more often in a certain design situation. Criteria Building involved understanding the design space and devising strategy to group similar designs, hence frequent actions included *Scanning, Focusing, Eliminating* and *Spreading*. For Criteria Testing to validate a criterion's effectiveness, participants' most frequent actions were *Eliminating, Selecting, Focusing* and *Stacking*. The number of actions during Criteria Applying was highest as participants made quick decisions. This task included *Selecting, Stacking, Focusing, Drawing and Eliminating* as frequent actions.

During Reflection, participants revisited previously seen designs and planned next moves. The frequent actions during this task were *Revisiting and Comparing*. In between design tasks of *Criteria Building, Testing, Applying* and *Reflection*, participants managed their workspace. We called it *Setting/Resetting*. During this task, participants were mostly *Sorting, Spreading* and *Stacking* design alternatives.

3.3   Action Combinations

In total we observed 15 design actions. Consequently, there were 105 mutually exclusive action-combinations (pairs) and if we added the basic 15 actions that might appear individually, there exist 120 possible action-combinations.

Count of Action-Combinations. We arranged the combined participants' data radially to observe frequently used combination (Fig. 6, Left). The top ten action-combinations included one of these five actions: *Stacking, Selecting, Eliminating, Focusing* and *Drawing* (Fig. 6, Right), which is consistent with our action-count data in Sect. 3.2. The least frequent action-combinations contained *Marking, Noting, Flickering* and *Splitting* actions.

Time-Spent on Action-Combinations. In contrast to the frequent action-combinations, we found different results for percentage of time spent on each combination. For example, *Marking* and *Noting* were the least used action combinations but were used for ∼9% of the normalized time spent by all participants in combination with *Comparing*.

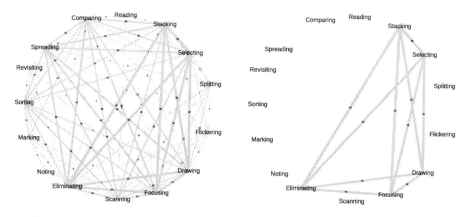

Fig. 6. (Left) All action combinations, (Right) The most frequent action combinations

In detailed analysis, we discovered two outliers (Fig. 7). We found that these top two action combinations were because of the unexpectedly large time spent by one of the nine participants. Further investigation of the videos revealed the first case was when p04 went through 20–25 designs (initially) selected from a randomized pile of alternatives and quickly made a judgement on those and started sketching his own version of a design. (S)he spent 80% of time on comparing those designs and sketching variations (Fig. 7, Left). The second outlier appeared when p05 spent almost an hour comparing 10 designs selected from a randomly picked ∼40 designs and made notes on the white board about their differences and commonalities (Fig. 7, Right).

Removing these data points presented a more reliable time-use graph. It showed that *Focusing-Drawing, Eliminating-Stacking, Selecting-Stacking* were among the highly weighed action-combinations in terms of time spent. It made sense now as these combinations were also the frequently used combinations. *Revisiting* stood out; participants did not use it very often but did spend 3.6% of combined normalized time on it.

Fig. 7. (Left) *p04* sketching design alternatives, (Right) *p05* noting differences and commonalities between design alternatives.

Action-Combinations Count Per Design Task. Plotting action combinations versus design tasks revealed similar results as action counts within design tasks (see Sect. 3.2).

3.4   Design Tasks

We normalized action counts and time, to compare data across participants and to evaluate actions and time independent of participant's design process and thinking. In terms of design tasks, we observed participants spent more time developing design criteria than they spent testing. They spent ~20% time Criteria Building, 13% Testing, 49% Criteria Applying, 11% Reflecting and 7% rearranging the workspace. Similarly, participants performed 15% of total actions during Criteria Building, 14% Testing, 52% Criteria Applying, 10% Reflecting and 9% Re-setting.

These suggest two findings: (1) although Criteria Applying was the longest phase overall, Criteria Building stood second longest. This is consistent with the design literature where experts spend more time structuring and restructuring design problem than detailing it; (2) there was a significant amount of time invested (7%) and actions executed (9%) to arrange and layout the design work surface. This led us to a result: the workspace plays an active role in exploring design space.

4   Summary

We present the data coding process along with descriptive statistics on an action-level protocol analysis from the lab experiment with nine participants working in a simulated task environment with 1000 design variations. Results show that frequent and long-drawn-out design actions executed by the participants include *Stacking, Selecting, Eliminating, Focusing, Comparing* and *Drawing*. Among these frequent actions, participants spent most time *Focusing* and *Comparing* designs. All actions were performed in multiple cycles of five repeated design tasks: Criteria Building, Criteria Testing, Criteria Applying, Reflection and (Re)setting. In each task, the frequency and time spent on design actions varied. Overall, participants spent half of their time (49%) and performed half of their actions (52%), filtering design variations into collections during the Criteria Applying task. In this task, participants performed multiple quick episodes of five frequent actions performed rapidly (as fast as sub-second): *Draw-Focus-Select-Eliminate-Stack*. Criteria Building was the second dominant task in terms of both action count and time. During this task, participants identified design patterns by *Scanning-Comparing-Focusing* on samples of designs spread side-by-side over a work surface. These patterns later became filters to form an initial set of design criteria. For Criteria Testing, which is the first round of filtering, participants *Focused-Selected-Eliminated-Stacked* but did not *Draw*. They spent more time testing a criterion compared to the applying the same criterion. During Reflection, participants revisited their decisions by comparing designs to validate their choices. Participants spent a significant amount of time (7% overall) arranging, setting and laying out their worksurface, i.e., (Re)setting. They are largely observed *Sorting, Spreading* and *Stacking* designs during this task. Mostly this task was used to clean up the worksurface for the next Criteria Applying cycle; many times, it also overlapped with the Reflection design task.

5 Discussion and Future Work

The findings from the study provided valuable insights for the design of new task environments enabling designers to work with large numbers and collections of design alternatives. We suggest that tools in such environments may focus on the following.

Visually-Accessible Collections. Stacking—the frequently performed action—implied a collection along with visual marking and tagging. Even though the physicality of the experimental material did not allow much, participants still used several spatial tactics to inform visibility of collections. They plotted cognitive cues [9] within their stacked designs. For instance, several participants placed design cards upside down (Fig. 8, Right) to visually mark them as 'seen and rejected', eliminating the need to remember and to minimize the visual clutter on the worksurface. Another interesting mechanism was to stack designs partially; affording a visual access to a design collection. p06 simplified the visual perception by partially over-laying designs based on their visual weights and content (Fig. 8, Left). (S)he made visual groups of designs, such as, minimum to no-red group, too much red, too little green, too much gray etc. (S)he used partial overlapping to highlight visual content without having a need to remember. Consequent to her visual process of rejection, her final selection was designs with balanced distribution of red, green and gray. We envision new task environments to enable interactions with the visual accessibility of a design collection, perhaps through reduced resolution visualizations of representative designs with semantic zoom to reveal collection details.

Collections and Sub-collections. All participants began with two primary collections, which later branched out into multiple sub-collections. They selected designs for further viewing, or they rejected designs based on certain attributes. Most of the participants, did not care about the designs ending in the rejection pile, however, some of them made collections within the rejection group as well. p03 made two groups initially of do's and don'ts to group designs for selection and rejection. However, at later stages, (S)he re-grouped designs into sub-groups of two extremes of the same criteria, one as the best implementation of a criterion and other as the worst (Fig. 9).

Fig. 8. (Left) P06 clustering designs using visual properties of designs; (Right) A participant creating physical constraints by placing designs upside-down (Color figure online)

Fig. 9. P03 grouping designs using two extremes of a design attribute/criterion.

Design Tasks. *Criteria Building.* All participants began by clarifying and defining the initial design criteria based on preliminary immediate study of a randomly selected set (~ 23) of alternatives. They moved back and forth between sub-tasks interacting-with-criteria and interacting-with-designs. Interacting-with-criteria included:

- Creating a new criterion, explicitly. This could be physical or non-physical.
- Removing a criterion that is no longer needed.
- Merging two criteria into a single criterion based on a similarity.
- Branching a criterion into multiple categories.

Interacting-with-designs included *Scanning-Comparing-Focusing* on samples of designs that were spread side-by-side over a worksurface. We envision new task environments with multiple design spaces to enable both types of interactions. They should support sampling of designs per designer's need; should allow several display arrangements on a sample, such as grid, circular, random, etc.; should support one-to-one, one-to-many and many-to-one comparing operations. These comparisons can be visual and/or structural (comparing parametric values). They should also allow group-actions on a sample set, such as creating visually-accessible/constrained collections of selected designs, rejecting all designs at once and shuffling designs.

Criteria Testing and Applying. The new task environments supporting multiple designs should allow many small and quick episodes of *Draw-Focus-Select-Eliminate-Stack*. This means they should enable a variation of sprinting or visual-brain-dumping techniques, popular in the graphic design domain [12], where designers can time themselves, such as one-minute-a-design. This task may also support rapid serial viewing of designs for high-speed off-loading of internal computation that heavily rely on visual memory and contrast. The operations should support arrangement of crowded collections in focus of the analysis zone [16] with design viewing space.

Reflection and (Re)Setting. New task environments should allow revisiting design decisions, may be a flexible and editable timeline. They should allow display settings; such as saving an arrangement, applying saved display, clearing the worksurface, etc.

Future Work. The system features proposed are motivated by the results of the study. We contend that they can be important to the success of a task environment supporting large numbers of alternatives. However, their effectiveness should be verified on prototypes of system interfaces and by conducting separate evaluations.

References

1. Akin, O.: Variants in design cognition. In: Design Knowing and Learning: Cognition in Design Education, pp. 1–17 (2001)
2. Blackwell, A.F., Green, T.R.G.: Notational systems - the cognitive dimensions of notations framework. In: Carroll, J.M. (ed.) HCI Models, Theories and Frameworks: Toward a multidisciplinary science, pp. 103–134. Morgan Kaufmann, San Francisco (2003)
3. Cross, N.: Design cognition: results from protocol and other empirical studies of design activity. In: Eastman, C., McCracken, M., Newstetter, M. (eds.) Design Knowing and Learning: Cognition in Design Education, pp. 79–103. Elsevier Science (2001)
4. Chouchoulas, O., Day, A.: Design exploration using a shape grammar with a genetic algorithm. Open House Int. **32**(2), 25–35 (2007)
5. Dow, S., Glassco, A., Kass, J., Schwarz, M., Schwartz, D., Klemmer, S.: Parallel prototyping leads to better design results, more divergence, and increased self-efficacy. ACM Trans. Comput.-Hum. Interact. **17**(4), Article no. 18 (2010)
6. Drucker, S.M., Petschnigg, G., Agrawala, M.: Comparing and managing multiple versions of slide presentations. In: Proceedings of the 19th Annual ACM Symposium on User Interface Software and Technology (UIST 2006), pp. 47–56. ACM, New York (2006)
7. Erhan, H., Wang, I., Shireen, N.: Harnessing design space: a similarity-based exploration method for generative design. Int. J. Archit. Comput. **13**(2), 217–236 (2015)
8. Hartmann, B., Yu, L., Allison, A., Yang, Y., Klemmer. S.R.: Design as exploration: creating interface alternatives through parallel authoring and runtime tuning. In: Proceedings on UIST 2008, pp. 91–100. ACM, New York (2008)
9. Kirsh, D.: The intelligent use of space. Artif. Intell. **73**(1–2), 31–68 (1995)
10. Kolarić, S., Woodbury, R., Erhan, H.: CAMBRIA: a tool for managing multiple design alternatives. In: Proceedings of the 2014 Companion Publication on Designing Interactive Systems (DIS Companion 2014), pp. 81–84. ACM, New York (2014). https://doi.org/10.1145/2598784.2602788
11. Lunzer, A., Hornbæk, K.: Subjunctive interfaces: extending applications to support parallel setup, viewing and control of alternative scenarios. ACM Trans. Comput.-Hum. Interact. **14**(4), 1–44 (2008)
12. Lupton, E.: Graphic Design Thinking Beyond Brainstorming. Princeton Press, Princeton (2011)
13. Marks, J., et al.: Design galleries: a general approach to setting parameters for computer graphics and animation. In: Proceedings of the 24th Annual Conference on Computer Graphics and Interactive Techniques (SIGGRAPH 1997), pp. 389–400. ACM Press/Addison-Wesley Publishing Co., New York (1997)
14. Matejka, J., Glueck, M., Bradner, E., Hashemi, A., Grossman, T., Fitzmaurice, G.: Dream lens. In: Proceedings of the 2018 CHI Conference on Human Factors in Computing Systems - CHI 2018, April 2018, pp. 1–12 (2018). https://doi.org/10.1145/3173574.3173943
15. Ritchie, D., Kejriwal, A., Klemmer, S.: d. tour: style-based exploration of design example galleries. In: Proceedings of the 24th Annual ACM Symposium on User Interface Software and Technology, pp. 165–174 (2011)
16. Shireen, N., Erhan, H., Woodbury, R., Wang, I.: Making sense of design space. In: Çağdaş, G., Özkar, M., Gül, L.F., Gürer, E. (eds.) CAADFutures 2017. CCIS, vol. 724, pp. 191–211. Springer, Singapore (2017). https://doi.org/10.1007/978-981-10-5197-5_11
17. Shneiderman, B.: Creating creativity: user interfaces for supporting innovation. ACM Trans. Comput.-Hum. Interact. (TOCHI) **7**(1), 114–138 (2000)

18. Simon, H.A., Newell, A.: Human problem solving: the state of the theory in 1970. Am. Psychol. **26**(2), 145–159 (1971)
19. Smith, B., Xu, A., Bailey, B.: Improving interaction models for generating and managing alternative ideas during early design work. In: Proceedings of Graphics Interface 2010 (GI 2010), pp. 121–128. Canadian Information Processing Society, Toronto, Canada (2010)
20. Terry, M., Mynatt, E.D., Nakakoji, K., Yamamoto, Y.: Variation in element and action: supporting simultaneous development of alternative solutions. In: Proceedings of the SIGCHI Conference on Human Factors in Computing Systems (CHI 2004), pp. 711–718. ACM, New York (2004)
21. Tohidi, M., Buxton, W., Baecker, R., Sellen, A.: Getting the right design and the design right. In: Grinter, R., Rodden, T., Aoki, P., Cutrell, E., Jeffries, R., Olson, G. (eds.) Proceedings of the SIGCHI Conference on Human Factors in Computing Systems (CHI 2006), pp. 1243–1252. ACM, New York (2006)
22. Toomim, M., Begel, A., Graham, S.L.: Managing duplicated code with linked editing. In: Proceedings of the 2004 IEEE Symposium on Visual Languages - Human Centric Computing (VLHCC 2004), pp. 173–180. IEEE Computer Society, Washington, DC, USA (2004)
23. Woodbury, R., Mohiuddin, A., Cichy, M., Mueller, V.: Interactive design galleries: a general approach to interacting with design alternatives. Des. Stud. **52**, 40–72 (2017)
24. Woodbury, R.F.: Elements of Parametric Design. Routledge, London (2010)
25. Woodbury, R.F., Burrow, A.L.: Whither design space? AIEDAM **20**(2), 63–82 (2006)
26. Xu, K., Zhang, H., Cohen-Or, D., Chen, B.: Fit and diverse: set evolution for inspiring 3D shape galleries. ACM Trans. Graph. **31**(4), 1–10 (2012)
27. Zaman, L., et al.: GEM-NI: a system for creating and managing alternatives in generative design. In: Proceedings of the 33rd Annual ACM Conference on Human Factors in Computing Systems, Seoul, Republic of Korea, pp. 1201–1210. ACM, New York (2015). https://doi.org/10.1145/2702123.2702398

Examining Potential Socio-economic Factors that Affect Machine Learning Research in the AEC Industry

Nariddh Khean[1(✉)] ⓘ, Alessandra Fabbri[1(✉)] ⓘ, David Gerber[2,3(✉)],
and Matthias H. Haeusler[1,4(✉)] ⓘ

[1] Computational Design, University of New South Wales, Sydney, NSW 2052,
Australia
{n.khean,a.fabbri,m.haeusler}@unsw.edu.au
[2] Ove Arup and Partners, London, UK
david.gerber@arup.com
[3] Viterbi School of Engineering and School of Architecture, University of Southern
California, Los Angeles, CA 90007, USA
dgerber@usc.edu
[4] CAFA Visual Innovation Institute, Beijing, China

Abstract. Machine learning (ML) has increasingly dominated discussions about the shape of mankind's future, permeating almost all facets of our digital, and even physical, world. Yet, contrary to the relentless march of almost all other industries, the architecture, engineering and construction (AEC) industry have lagged behind in the uptake of ML for its own challenges. Through a systematic review of ML projects from a leading global engineering firm, this paper investigates social, political, economic, and cultural (SPEC) factors that have helped or hindered ML's uptake. Further, the paper discusses how ML is perceived at various points in the economic hierarchy, how effective forms of communication is vital in a highly-specialized workforce, and how ML's unexpected effectiveness have forced policy makers to reassess data governance and privacy; all the while considering what this means for the adoption of ML in the AEC industry. This investigation, its methodology, background research, systematic review, and its conclusion are presented.

Keywords: Machine learning · Artificial intelligence ·
Research and development ·
Architecture, engineering and construction industry · Social factors ·
Political factors · Economic factors · Culutral factors

1 Introduction

The field of artificial intelligence (AI) has accelerated over the last decade. According to the *Artificial Intelligence Index*'s 2017 report, the heightened volume of activity – demonstrated by upsurges in published academic papers, course

J.-H. Lee (Ed.): CAAD Futures 2019, CCIS 1028, pp. 247–263, 2019.
https://doi.org/10.1007/978-981-13-8410-3_18

enrolments, job postings, start-ups, venture capitalist funding, and public perception – is indicative of society's willingness to invest in AI [1]. Recent breakthroughs in this field of research have predominantly been fueled by the successes of a subset of AI, known as machine learning [2]. Machine Learning (ML) has been so transformative, that it has come to permeate almost all facets of our digital, and even physical, world.

In 2012, journalist and author Charles Duhigg recounts the events surrounding Andrew Pole, a statistician working for *Target*. Pole was tasked to develop an algorithm to automatically determine *'which of Target's customers were pregnant'* [3]. In response, Pole and his team leveraged Target's data on the buying patterns of their customers. Their solution was so effective that, through targeted advertising, they uncovered a case of teen pregnancy before the teen's family were even aware themselves. As ethically controversial as this example may be, it is illustrative of the value that companies place on data. Fast forward half a decade, sprinkle in a handful of new ML algorithms, and the petabytes of data that has been collected gives rise to powerful new ways through which companies can influence consumers. From determining optimal store layouts and what gets end-of-aisle fame, to clustering collectively purchased items to make consumers spend more. From creating individualized promotions and coupons, to monitoring customer movements and predicting potential theft [4] machine learning is astonishingly pervasive, and it is accelerating.

Companies are undergoing a digital transformation. Our highly-interconnected economy has conditioned consumers to expect an infinite amount of choice, accessible remotely, and purchasable within minutes. How efficiently a company can develop algorithms to sift through the magnitudes of choice and select the few most suited to the individual consumer is one of the modern hallmarks for success. Pedro Domingos posits that *'as companies grow [...] after a point, there just aren't enough programmers and consultants to do all that's needed, and the company inevitably turns to machine learning'* [5]. In conjunction, Thomas H. Davenport argues that in the era of big data, where *'it would simply be impossible for humans to deal with all of this data without an automated process, organizations that can recognize and react quickly and intelligently have the upper hand'* [6]. Companies embrace ML because they are racing to create the best algorithms, where failure to do so means losing that advantage. *'They embrace it because they have no choice'* [5].

The imminent inevitability of ML adoption provides an opportunity to understand how this transition will affect business. As with all transitions, comes transition costs. Variations in the geopolitical landscape, economic environments, and even cultural differences have resounding implications on the rate and success of technological integration. Understanding the factors that influence this critical moment is an opportunity to mitigate barriers and enhance potential. As such, this research examines the social, political, economic, and cultural (SPEC) factors that affect how ML is being adopted by the architecture, engineering, and construction (AEC) industry.

2   Research Questions

In accordance to the purpose of this research – examining SPEC factors that influence the integration of ML in the AEC industry, and therefore understanding the cultural and organizational context of our profession – a series of questions were developed to direct the study and inform the objectives:

- To what extent has the AEC industry invested in ML research and development?
- What insights can be gathered from analyzing previous instances of ML research in the AEC industry?
- What are the potential SPEC factors that have affected the integration of ML in the AEC industry?

3   Objectives

As the AEC industry increasingly invests in ML research and development, social, political, economic, and cultural factors can both facilitate and hinder its success. If identical research projects were conducted in different locations, their outcomes would be heavily influenced by the disposition of their respective SPEC climates. Thus, one can argue for internal (within the organization) and external (the geospatial location of the organization) factors and the overarching objective of this research is to identify and analyze these instances. Consequently, the research has investigated ML research projects within the AEC industry to understand and derive SPEC factors involved.

To do so, this research intends to:

- Co-develop with a global AEC firm to systematically analyze their previous and current investments in ML (internal factors),
- Identify potential SPEC factors that might have affected ML research and development projects (external factors), and
- Examine how the respective research projects may have been influenced by the identified SPEC factors (externals effect on internal factors).

4   Methodology

The present research was carried out in partnership with Arup Engineering due to their global presence and extensive involvement across the AEC industry. Still, the objective of this research is to identify SPEC factors that aren't only specific to Arup Engineering as such but aims to be applicable across the whole industry. Arguing that Arup Engineering, with over 16,000 employees in more than 30 countries, in conjunction with Arup's well-established approach to encouraging and investing in employee ideas, Arup is an apt candidate for this study.

A systematic review – outlined in *Towards Evidence-Based Research* as requiring *'inclusion criteria, search methods, selection procedures, quality assessment, data extraction, and data analysis'* [7] – was conducted to assure valid and accurate results. Focusing specifically on the *Invest in Arup* (IiA) database, this research started with a quantitative, inductive methodology, seeking to identify patterns and interpolate potential SPEC factors from Arup's research and development in ML. Beyond IiA, there are a number of ML initiatives at Arup that impacts ML culture, with many containing a significant research component. These works are worthwhile to acknowledge, however, as they are not documented within the IiA database, they fall outside the purview of this study.

The IiA database contains over 19,000 investment proposals. A preliminary extraction of those using ML revealed over 170 proposals at varying stages of development. However, further observations showed some to be misleading, incomplete and/or duplicates. Thus, a set of criteria was developed and employed to assure valid inclusion for this study, resulting in 105 proposals. The IiA proposals deemed relevant were spatially and temporally mapped to identify any emerging patterns that can be potentially attributed to SPEC factors.

To examine the validity of these factors, this research isolated a subset of proposals that was investigated further. Shifting into a qualitative, deductive methodology, project managers of the isolated subset were asked to partake in an interview series to discuss how the SPEC disposition of their office, country, and region affected their research. The intention of the interviews was threefold: to validate the factors gathered from the data analytics, to identify other factors undetected from the data, and to examine the impact of these factors to the integration of ML in the AEC industry.

5   Data Analytics

Using a systematic review methodology, the research concentrated its curatorial research process on the intersection of the key contributing fields. A preliminary search through the roughly 8,000 research and development projects in the *Invest in Arup* database revealed over 170 research proposals with an ostensible connection to ML. The connections could have been established as IiA proposals contain information about the project's aims, methods, and intellectual context. Due to the latter, false positives, namely proposals which mentioned ML peripherally, were a common occurrence. Incomplete, dormant, or duplicated proposals also emerged. To narrow the focus of our search and retain the integrity of our project scope, invalid IiA studies, specifically data points which were likely to skew the research analytics, were excluded. For this purpose, a set of criteria was developed to determine the suitability of a proposal. The systematic review revealed that only 105 proposals of the initial 170 directly incorporated ML, thus relevant for the second phase of the research. Two Python libraries (i.e. NumPy and Pandas) were utilized for scientific computing and high-performance data structures respectively. The data underwent a process of mapping, both spatially (i.e. at an office, country, and regional scale) and temporally (i.e. on a yearly basis).

Noteworthy in this context is the correlation between the employee count of an office and the number of IiA proposals originating from that office. Arup's

UKIMEA (UK, India, Middle East and Africa) region, for instance, has roughly three times more employees than other regions, resulting in a proportional increase in IiA proposals. Thus, comparing the number of proposals without taking in consideration other factors (such as an office's or a region's population size) will eventuate in a heavy bias (see Fig. 1).

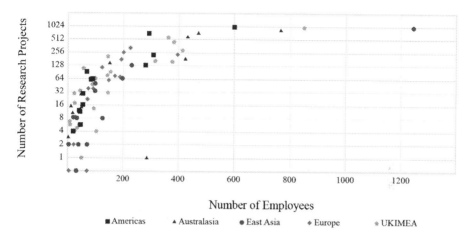

Fig. 1. The number of IiA proposals from Arup offices compared against the office population size and region. (Note: The London office, with an employee count of roughly 3000 and over 5000 IiA proposals, was intentionally omitted for greater clarity on the plot).

In light of this, descriptive and diagnostic data analysis was undertaken with the goal of identifying the potential SPEC factors that could affect ML adoption in the AEC industry. Results from the analyses led to formulating several observations.

First, when the allocated funding for approved ML proposals were averaged across the five regions, it was found that those in the East Asia region were provided with over 50% more funding than other regions (see Fig. 2).

A subsequent question emerged: Was the reason for this disparity an internal anomaly specific to Arup, or is there a larger force at play (a culture of techno-optimism or even government-level financial incentives)?

Second, the approval rate of all IiA proposals appeared to be proportional to those that were R&Ds, while showing a 15% increase when compared to those using ML (see Fig. 3).

In aggregate, ML proposals are more likely to be approved. But it goes further than that. From the analyses of approval rates at a regional level, the largest difference between the R&D proposals and the ML ones could be found in the East Asia and Australasia region. The Australasia region has an approval rate of 100%, which indicates that Australasia has yet to decline any ML proposals. From this second set of observations, a new consideration emerged: Does this

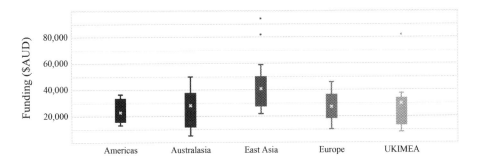

Fig. 2. The funding for machine learning IiA proposals per region.

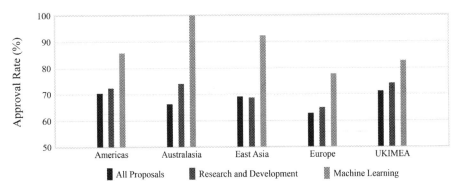

Fig. 3. The average approval rates for all IiA proposals, only R&D proposals, and only ML proposals per region.

imply a forward-thinking investment strategy or a blind pursuit of what author of *Artificial Unintelligence* calls, *'technochauvinism'* [8]? These two hypotheses were the catalyst for the investigations in the following section, where a series of interviews with Arup staff involved in these projects were conducted to identify and examine factors the data could not reveal.

6   SPEC Factors

Thirteen Arup employees, who had been directly involved with the identified ML R&D projects out of the IiA database, were contacted to speak about the insights gathered from the data analytics. The interviewees were based in nine offices across four regions and possessed varying levels of technical ML expertise.

A general structure was developed to direct the interview, while project and context specific questions were also pursued. By way of explanation, if the interviewee was based within the European Union (EU) and their proposal stated concerns about data collection or privacy, they were asked to comment on the implications of the EU General Data Protection Regulation (GDPR) implemented in 2018. Alternatively, interviewees based in Singapore or China were asked if they experienced any influence from their respective government's AI strategies.

In analyzing and examining the results of the thirteen interviews, eight potential SPEC factors were identified and structured into three overarching categories: perceptions of ML; the communication of knowledge and education; and data governance and privacy. These are listed and outlined in the following sections.

6.1   Perceptions

Doer Resistance. Within the AEC industry, those that implement ML are also those that have shown the most resistance to its adoption. Architects and engineers have been taught how to approach existing problems, emboldening and validating their use of current methods, and in turn, building a resistance to new ones. This leads to the industry's resistance technological adoption, on par with that of the agriculture and transportation industries [9–11]. Due to the considerable distance between the fields of computer science and architectural engineering, and the tendency towards Occam's razor – a philosophical principle stating that the simplest solution is probably better – the doers cause the most immediate form of resistance to ML adoption in the AEC.

An interview with an Arup employee working in digital transformation revealed a substantial willingness at the managerial level to invest in new technologies. The interviewed stated that despite the evident long-term profitability of ML, the doers still show a fundamental resistance to its adoption. Architectural engineers have a toolbelt of programs and software that match up to a list of problems they face in their work. This rigidity facilitates a psychological attachment toward that toolbelt of proven successes. The interviewee further states that the doers more open to ML still embark on their own standards of testing to validate the accuracy of the new ML methods. This is inherently detrimental for ML adoption, as ML processes favor speed and efficiency over accuracy. During an interview with a key proponent for ML processes in the AEC, they stated that a new approach to problems requires *'180-degree thinking'*, and that *'for digital transformation to occur, it takes a certain amount of unlearning before learning'*. This is echoed in a 2017 McKinsey report, that argues the following: to leverage full digital opportunity requires a *'shift [of] cultures and ways of working rather than just systems and tools'* [11].

Further, the field of computer science, wherein ML sits, is of considerable distance from that of architecture. As such, architects are not trained, nor expected, to have the required skills to implement ML. Combined with its steep learning curve, using ML becomes a daunting task. In parallel with Occam's razor, Domingos argues that *'simple theories are preferable because they incur in a lower cognitive cost (for us) and a lower computational cost (for our algorithms)'* [5]. The doers are resistant to ML due to an attachment to current methods and their proven successes, in combination with the sheerness of ML's learning curve. Thus, significant consideration for more effective ML adoption in the AEC should be placed towards how ML can be integrated rather than what ML can do.

Misconceptions and Funding. Despite management's willingness to invest in ML, how technology is perceived greatly affects its implementation. As with any technology that dominates the public eye, over-hype and misconceptions run rampart. Leadership positions rarely contain *'digital natives'* and misconceptions can lead to an *'uncertain[ty] about what exactly AI can do for them'* [2]. Any resistance to the allocation of funding compounds resistance to the application of ML. Further, even when funding is reduced, expectations remain that lead to inevitably underwhelming results and, as a consequence, a disincentivization of future implementations.

When ML misconceptions underpin business decisions and goals, expectations and results are pushed further apart. A 2017 McKinsey report highlights a lack of *'digital natives'* in leadership positions [11] which is a major contributor to this problem. Any misconceptions at the managerial level exasperates resistances felt by those conducting ML's implementation.

Arup's R&D application process asks applicants to request a specific amount of funding. This could be altered if deemed necessary after receiving Arup's approval. Of the 64 ML-related projects that have been funded, 37 received more or on par with the funding they requested. This leaves 27 projects that have had their funding reduced, with an average reduction of 46% compared against the requested funding (see Fig. 4).

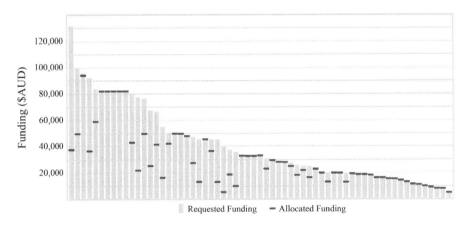

Fig. 4. The difference between requested and allocated funding for the 64 ML projects that received funding.

During the interview series, five interviewees made statements relating to how the scope of their projects were severely limited due to the reduction of funding. One interviewee asserted that the reduction led *'to a simplification of the process'*, while a second one stated that the reduction turned *'an initially global project into a local one'*. Regardless of whether expectations are bred from misconceptions over ambitious scoping, or a lack of research – the disparity between managerial expectations with what the project team can deliver may lead to unmet goals and has the potential to disincentivize future ML research.

Governmental Strategies and Incentives. The impact of ML extends well beyond firms, and as governments catch onto its potential value, several nations have developed and implemented AI/ML strategies to capture this potential. Minute differences in these policies – such as their focus, goals, and the speed at which they were released – may have resounding implications for the implementation of ML in the AEC. Further, as these strategies are developed for a national scale, multinational companies may undergo disproportionate levels of incentives, and ML investment may proceed at different rates. Conversely, these strategies may have little influence on the AEC industry, as they target "digital" firms. However, the cultural significance they instill encourages its investment, as it is demonstrated by the following the data.

The varying perceptions and values governments place on ML is visible through an examination of their AI strategies. With foci ranging from scientific research to ethics and inclusion, certain countries vocalize their ambition to lead the world in AI, while others favor future-proofing their economy. These vast differences have the potential to affect multinational companies, by influencing company goals set by different regions, countries, and offices. Despite all 13 interviewees claiming that there was no direct effect any AI strategy had on their ML-related projects, a correlation between the more aggressive policies with greater funding was evident. China, Singapore, and Japan were part of the earliest countries to have released national AI strategies. The eagerness shown from the East Asia region is similarly echoed as the first two explore ML at Arup, where, in 2012, a team from the Shenzhen office explored how ML can be used to intelligently control the actuation of windows.

Despite how the UKIMEA region has since developed the largest quantity of annual ML IiA proposals – potentially a by-product of the region's comparative population size (see Fig. 5) – the East Asia region commits the largest average financial investment of all the regions by a significant margin (see Fig. 2). Further, comparing the 24 funded ML-related projects in 2017 against the 28 in 2018, the East Asia region was the only region to have an increased average of allocated funding, with an increase of 14.45%. Finally, the approval rate for the East Asia region is second only the Australasian region. It is evident that the East Asia region has a heightened willingness to invest in ML, however, it is ultimately unknowable if the AI strategies directly influenced their successes.

6.2   Communication

Digital-Focused Communities. Firms in the AEC are not traditionally considered "digital" firms, thus digital standards and practices are not yet a priority.

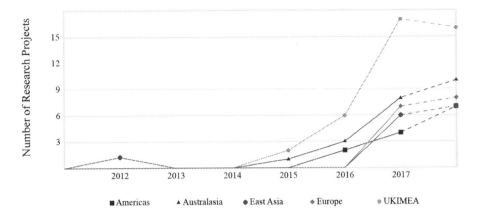

Fig. 5. The number of ML proposals per region per year. (Note: The data for 2018 is only partially complete as the analysis was conducted before the end of 2018).

Key minds in the field of computer science and ML have continuously introduced new approaches in the form of different programming languages, frameworks, and algorithms, each one of with their own nuances and intricacies. As favor and popularity varies over time, learners will be introduced to ML with different preferences and opinions. Furthermore, lacking a central location where an internal community of ML-enthusiasts in AEC firms can communicate and share knowledge and code can lead to overlapping work, incomprehensible code, and incompatible communication.

As ML is still within its infancy in the AEC, Arup has conducted a greater amount of ML research and development compared to incorporating ML in client-facing work. As such, Arup has yet to apply company-wide digital standards and practices (though they are currently in development). One aspect of ML that is vital to standardize is the preference of ML frameworks. TensorFlow, a low-level Python ML framework developed by Google, has garnered the most popularity in the ML community – popularity measured by job posting requirements, usage surveys, GitHub activity, and publication mentions [12]. However, the Arup interviews revealed that very few ML developers were using TensorFlow in favor for less popular frameworks such as CNTK and MXNet. The disparity between Arup's ML developers and the greater ML community has the potential to cause friction in its adoption. The more popular a framework, the more likely it will be maintained and the greater number of resources, both factors that can ease ML adoption. Arguably, the granularity of TensorFlow is not necessary for the applications within the AEC, and that a higher-level framework such as Keras or Caffe would suffice, however Arup developers have yet to reach a consensus. Furthermore, during an interview with an Arup developer, there was mention of a neural network architecture, called "ShuffleNet" [13], being a standard across Arup. However, the other interviewees have not even heard of this architecture. Small differences and inconsistencies, due to a lack of an internal

ML community, is a barrier for effective communication, leading to incompatible code and reduced comprehension.

Dissemination is a big focus for Arup research, however, as stated in an interview, *'just because a model was disseminated, doesn't necessarily mean it's being used'*. At Arup, company-wide dissemination can occur through several channels; namely skills networks. However, Arup lacks a single central repository for trained ML models to be shared and reused. For instance, a ML research project based in the Dublin office used local traffic data to train a ML model for the prediction of traffic congestion after accidents. The model itself would be useless in other locations, however, disseminating the code itself in a central, easily-accessible repository would allow others to modify the training data to train their own local model. What is required is not simply bottom-up innovation, but also a systematized top-down initiative and structure. Without this, what can be expected is, at best, overlapping work and wasted time, and at worst the stagnation of ML integration in the AEC.

Expertise. The AEC is an incredibly multidisciplinary industry, requiring a lot of different domain experts to collaborate on projects that can span several years, and even decades. With expert knowledge becoming more and more specialized, effective communication between fields has become vital. However, due to ML's steep learning curve, and the differences between the architectural engineering and computer science fields, communication when integrating ML in the AEC can become tenuous. Furthermore, with the development of ML-based tools, intended to be used by non-experts, developers not only need to train a robust ML model, but also present it in an easily-accessible, user-friendly interface, for greater ML uptake.

Effective ML models often require problem domain knowledge. More robust ML models can be developed with data validation, data normalization, feature engineering, and edge cases addressed by the domain expert. However, in the age of splintered expertise, rarely is the ML engineer and the domain expert the same person. Thus, effective communication between the parties is key. *'High-proximity, high-bandwidth communication can happen relatively easily in a small start-up firm with only a few employees. It is of course more difficult in a large firm'* [6]. The impact of communication is evident through the examination of two PhD students conducting ML research with Arup. One student, a mathematician, received a comparatively low "objectives/deliverables" rating than that of the other student, a software developer, with their research reported as *'slow progressing'*. When questioned about the cause of the disparity, the candidates' supervisors stated that the field of mathematics is a further step removed from the built environment than that of software development. This added an unforeseen strain to effective communication. Moving forward, *'roles that companies need to fill are the "translators" and data scientists ("quants")'* [2]. *'However, the specific percentage of projects that fail is questionable, there is no doubt that lack of communication in small and big data projects causes big problems'* [6].

The translation of a digital tool or service into one accessible by a non-expert audience is an important process seemingly lacking in the AEC industry. An interviewee recounted a completed research project that yielded a robust and accurate ML model, however, after its dissemination, it was found that the tool itself was not being used. The interviewee attributed this failure to the lack of an interface; they did not make a front end, and so *'it wasn't used in the office'*. On two ends of the spectrum, Arup has the ML experts to train good models, and the engineers who will use the tool, however there is a lack of software developers to bridge the gap between the tool and the users. This ultimately harms the integration of ML in the AEC industry.

Education. ML's climb in popularity has garnered a plethora of formal education, i.e. university courses [1], in addition to informal resources, such as online tutorials and blog posts. Because ML has flourished only recently, a considerable amount of ML developers were not formally taught ML and have gained their ML knowledge from autodidacticism. However, the culture of self-education may lead to incongruencies in ML knowledge as the informal resources of knowledge can be opinionated, outdated, or even invalidated. And with the plethora of resources available, this leads to a fragmentation of knowledge and a difference of opinions with standards and practices.

Some perceive ML as a magic solution, whereby premade algorithms and pretrained models can simply be taken and applied to any problem. With this mentality, understanding the corresponding programming language is all that's required to produce results. However, to effectively train a robust ML model to a high degree of accuracy, a considerable understanding of regularization techniques, hyperparameter tuning, data engineering, and normalization are required. An out-of-the-box solution is inherently limited when shoehorned into more complex problems. An example of this can be seen in an early Arup project exploring ML, where the model achieved a maximum accuracy of 60%. The disseminated research documentation revealed that a standard ML architecture was used without any hyperparameter tuning. This was the main reason for below average results. Inconsistent and incomplete ML education acts as a barrier for ML integration, however, Arup has taken steps to standardize and formalize ML developers' education. On multiple occasions, Arup has partnered with universities to allow Arup employees in ML-focused workshops and courses, in addition to the dissemination of validated educational resources and the development of its own curriculum.

A McKinsey report revealed in an investigation into digital transformation that *'many companies are attempting to make use of the large volume of unstructured data at the disposal, but do not have the data science and data engineering capabilities to generate game-changing insights'* [11]. While Arup is reasonably supported by internal engineers with data science expertise, two interviewees mentioned a lack of ML expertise within specific subdomains of ML, forcing the team to seek experts in other offices.

6.3 Data

Data Governance. The accumulation of data is accelerating. *'Of the 3.5 trillion photos that have been snapped since the first image of a busy Parisian street in 1838, fully 10 percent were taken in the last year'* [14]. With new methods of data analytics and algorithms that can convert vast quantities of data into valuable insights, the governance of data is a question that will become increasingly discussed. Due to the requirement for data in the field of ML, data governance has the potential to greatly determine the shape of ML integration in the AEC.

An often-overlooked step in the process of ML research is the collection of data. And investigation reveals that a lot of time and money is wasted in this process. Following a developed risk classification schema, of Arup's 76 ML projects that had stated potential risks, and second only to the availability of their team, the most prevalent risk identified was the collection of data. When projects were proposed, more teams stated that they were concerned about the collection of data, than about the quality and quantity (see Fig. 6).

Fig. 6. The prevalence of risks indicated by 76 ML proposals in accordance to the developed classification of risks. (Note: 29 proposals indicated no risks).

As the documented risks are completed during the application process, these risks are speculative. Unfortunately, concerns about data collection were founded. When interviewees were asked about the issues of data collection, four voiced concerns about its governance, one stating that *'there is an ongoing issue on who owns the data'*. The sheer quantity of data needed to adequately train a ML model required another team to source their data from multiple third parties, thus requiring *'a lot of time cleaning the data'*. Davenport poignantly states that *'since big data is often external to the organization, governance of it is often a tricky issue. Data ownership is much less clear, and responsibilities for ongoing data management haven't been defined either in most cases. We're going to be wrestling with big data governance for quite a while'* [6].

Data governance is a web of boundaries that become increasingly difficult to draw as parties undergo constant data revaluation. *'As the economy has changed so, too, must our metrics. More and more what we care about in the second machine age are ideas, not things – mind not matter; bits, not atoms'* [14]. And in a world where data is virtually infinite, and ML algorithms are vying for beyond-human level performance, the question of how data is valued is brought to a head. *'The basic tenet is that the world – and the data that describes it – are in a constant state of change and flux, and those organizations that can recognize and react quickly and intelligently have the upper hand'* [6]. Because of this instability, Arup has faced instances of third parties denying them data. An interviewee described a project focused on geotechnical analysis that received only a fraction of the initial training data from a third party. Another interviewee recounted a project that required a vast amount of tree species data, yet the universities they were working with no longer wanted to share their data. Those in possession of data are starting to reassess what it's worth, which acts as resistance for successful implementation of ML in the AEC.

Data Privacy. The rapid rise of data accumulation, in combination with a plethora of new algorithms, have made way for powerful predictive models. A common statistics aphorism states that *'all models are wrong, but some are useful'*, with some so useful, that their uncanny accuracy has sparked concerns about data and privacy. *'New resources – whether a better spyglass or print or a new method – extend not only what is known but, crucially, the range of what can be known'* [15]. Instances like the case of Andrew Pole and *Target'*s pregnancy predictor, mentioned in the introduction, revealed the benefits of data for companies, but also has amassed a public outcry concerning the power companies wield. Outcries have ignited responses from policy makers to enact restrictions. Any limitation to the accessibility of data is ultimately detrimental for ML, as ML models are only as effective as the data, creating barriers for the use of ML in the AEC.

Despite some governments advocating for more open data, others are limiting and disincentivizing it for fear of data privacy infringement. The governments of Germany, Denmark, India, Japan, and Taiwan have released AI strategy plans that dedicates a portion to *'policies aimed at promoting data access, as well as their circulation and sharing'*, an excerpt taken from France's *For a Meaningful Artificial Intelligence: Towards a French and European Strategy* [16]. However, strict regulations and heavy fines have been enforced on the misuse of personal data, a severe deterrent for ML research. Most notable is the European Union's General Data Protection Regulation (GDPR), with companies set to receive fines of up to four percent of global revenue or twenty-million euros. An interview with an Amsterdam-based employee revealed an ongoing research project that has been stalled due to concerns about the GDPR. The interviewee stated that the external partner for the research project *'is being more difficult,'* as they *'don't want data to leave the Netherlands'*. Data's importance for ML combined with new regulations acts as a barrier for the successful implementation of ML.

7   Conclusion

The purpose of this research was to identify and examine potential SPEC factors that influence the adoption of ML in the AEC industry by:

- Co-developing with a global AEC firm (Arup) to systematically analyze their previous and current investments in ML,
- Identifying potential SPEC factors that might have affected ML research and development projects, and
- Examining how the respective research projects may have been influenced by the identified SPEC factors.

To reiterate, the following conclusions have been shaped by conversations with a subset of those from one AEC firm. Further research – analysis of ML innovation outside of formal research databases, conversations with more project managers and technical experts, and investigations in more than one firm – is require to capture a more holistic insight into the state of ML adoption across the entirety of the AEC industry. Upon reflection of the objectives set at the beginning of the paper, one can conclude that out of the eight SPEC factors that were identified and structured into three overarching categories – perceptions of ML, the communication of knowledge and education, and data governance and privacy – there are two SPEC factors that cause the greatest effect on ML adoption, but conversely can be controlled.

As discussed in the subchapter *Doer Resistance*, the hesitancy from those applying ML poses an immediate problem. This is compounded when the desire to validate the accuracy of an inherently inaccurate model yields a misleading underperformance. An interviewee, described as a *'key progenitor and proponent for the shift in ML-based research'*, asserts that the underlying cause can be attributed to a rigidity in the current *'approach'* or *'mindset'*. They call for doers to undergo a *'complete 180-degree turn in thinking'*, and places incredible importance on the process of *'unlearning, before learning'*. Moving toward a greater degree of computer-aided work, cognitive flexibility and agile thinking are skills that are increasingly valued. The more willing those are to adopt machine intelligence into their workflows, the greater their potential output.

From the perspective of AEC firms, the facilitation of ML adoption starts with the development of a supportive digital ecosystem. The subchapter *Digital-Focused Communities*, the second pertinent SPEC factor, emphasizes this. Pragmatic standards and practices, central and accessible repositories, and a common platform for open and informal communication fosters a culture of ML-driven innovation. *'At the speed at which innovation and disruption are taking place, [the] world of data requires new forms of collaboration'* [17].

Returning to Pedro Domingos and his views on the ML-driven future, *'when someone talks about exponential growth, ask yourself: How soon will it turn into an "S" curve?'* [5]. Many theorists claim that we currently sit at the inflection point of the exponential rise of ML, and that a plateau is on the horizon. During this transition period, it is of vital importance that companies take advantage of the current upwards gradient and mitigate any hindrances (Fig. 7).

'The future belongs to those who understand at a very deep level how to combine their unique expertise with what algorithms do best' [5].

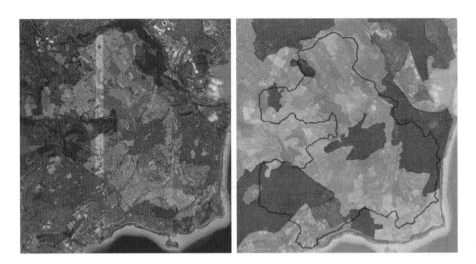

Fig. 7. High-resolution satellite imagery segmentation (left) with the existing equivalent (right). An example of Arup's ML adoption on AEC problems, taken from one of Arup's 2017 Global Research Challenges: *'Unlocking the Potential of Natural Flood Management with Machine Learning'*.

Acknowledgements. A huge thank you to the thirteen Arup interviewees who put aside time to share their knowledge and experience. Despite only a few being directly quoted, each conversation helped shaped the main ideas that drove this research. Thank you to Giulio Antonutto, Steven Downing, Veronika Heidegger, Jorke Odolphi, and Alvise Simondetti for sharing their experience with technological integration at Arup. Further, a big thank you to those in Arup University – Bree Trevena, Alex Sinickas, Esther Wheeler, and Kim Sherwin – without whom this research would not have been possible. Finally, thank you to both Arup Engineering and the University of New South Wales for their continual support.

References

1. Artificial Intelligence Index: 2017 Annual Report. Artificial Intelligence Index. http://cdn.aiindex.org/2017-report.pdf. Accessed 12 Dec 2018
2. Bughin, J., et al.: Artificial Intelligence: The Next Digital Frontier? McKinsey Global Institute, New York City (2017)

3. Duhigg, C.: The Power of Habit: Why We Do What We Do in Life and Business. Random House, Great Britain (2012)
4. De Jesus, A.: Artificial Intelligence in Groceries and Produce. Emerj. https://emerj.com/ai-sector-overviews/artificial-intelligence-in-groceries-and-produce-current-applications/. Accessed 14 Dec 2018
5. Domingos, P.: The Master Algorithm: How the Quest for the Ultimate Learning Machine Will Remake Our World. Basic Books, New York City (2015)
6. Davenport, T.H.: Big Data at Work: Dispelling the Myths. Uncovering the Opportunities. Harvard Business School Publishing Corporation, Boston (2014)
7. Lund, H., et al.: Towards evidence based research. Br. Med. J. **355**, i5440–i5445 (2016). https://www.bmj.com/content/bmj/355/bmj.i5440.full.pdf
8. Broussard, M.: Artificial Unintelligence: How Computers Misunderstand the World. The MIT Press, Cambridge (2018)
9. Manyika, J., et al.: Digital America: A Tale of the Haves and Have-Mores. McKinsey Global Institute, New York City (2015)
10. Bughin, J., et al.: Digital Europe: Pushing the Frontier. Capturing the Benefits. McKinsey Global Institute, New York City (2016)
11. Blackburn, S., Freeland, M., Grätner, D.: Digital Australia: Seizing the Opportunity from the Fourth Industrial Revolution. McKinsey Global Institute, New York City (2017)
12. Hale, J.: Deep Learning Framework Power Scores 2018. Towards Data Science. https://towardsdatascience.com/deep-learning-framework-power-scores-2018-23607ddf297a. Accessed 14 Dec 2018
13. Zhang, X., Zhou, X., Lin, M., Jian, S.: ShuffleNet: an extremely efficient convolutional neural network for mobile devices. In: Proceedings of the IEEE Conference on Computer Vision and Pattern Recognition, pp. 6848–6856 (2018)
14. Brynjolfsson, E., McAfee, A.: The Second Machine Age: Work, Progress, and Prosperity in a Time of Brilliant Technology. W. W. Norton & Company Ltd., New York City (2014)
15. Siskin, C.: System: The Shaping of Modern Knowledge. The MIT Press, Cambridge (2016)
16. Villani, C.: For A Meaningful Artificial Intelligence: Towards a French and European Strategy. AI For Humanity. https://www.aiforhumanity.fr/pdfs/MissionVillani_Report_ENG-VF.pdf. Accessed 19 Dec 2018
17. Schwab, K.: The Fourth Industrial Revolution. Crown Publishing Group, New York City (2016)

Investigating the Social Impacts of High-Density Neighbourhoods Through Spatial Analysis

Sahar Soltani[1]([✉]), Ning Gu[1] [ID], Jorge Ochoa Paniagua[1] [ID],
Alpana Sivam[1] [ID], and Tim McGinley[2]

[1] University of South Australia, Adelaide, SA 5000, Australia
sahar.soltani@mymail.unisa.edu.au
[2] Technical University of Denmark, Lyngby, Denmark

Abstract. Studies argue that higher density areas incur social problems such as lack of safety [1], while other studies provide evidence for the positive impact of high-density urban areas, for instance opportunities for social interactions and equal form of accessibility [2]. This paper argues that design factors can mediate the impacts of density on social aspects. Therefore, this study explores the extent to which design factors can be correlated to the social outcomes of different density areas. To do this, data from an empirical study conducted in the UK, which identified the relationship between density and social sustainability through cases of fifteen neighbourhoods, have been utilised. This paper has conducted further analysis based on these cases using a mixed method with spatial analysis tools. Outcomes show that some of the social results in the UK study such as safety are correlated with spatial factors like normalised angular choice. Moreover, the regression model created from the spatial indices can be used to predict the overall social sustainability index reported by the UK study.

Keywords: Urban density · Social sustainability · Spatial analysis · Space syntax · Urban Network Analysis

1 Introduction

As the world's urban population continues to grow, the shift towards more compact cities seems inevitable in most countries. Many scholars believe making cities more compact is a sustainable strategy which supports the environmental and economic growth of cities while having benefits for the population as well. The social benefits of intensifying the urban areas, however, remain controversial. Some studies argue that higher density areas incur social problems such as lack of sense of safety [1], while other studies provide evidence for the positive impact of high-density urban areas, for example more opportunities for social interactions and equal form of accessibility that promotes walking and cycling [2]. Although a large body of the literature contends that increasing density can improve social sustainability, we argue that increasing density does not always lead to the same impact unless we optimize design factors as well. The dilemma between a compact city and its social impact triggers the necessity to explore

© Springer Nature Singapore Pte Ltd. 2019
J.-H. Lee (Ed.): CAAD Futures 2019, CCIS 1028, pp. 264–278, 2019.
https://doi.org/10.1007/978-981-13-8410-3_19

the design role in improving the life quality of the residents while considering this mainstream urban strategy. Therefore, this study, with the focus on computational approaches, attempts to explore how the spatial design factors interact with the change of density. Moreover, the extent to which these design factors can be correlated to the social sustainability outcomes will be investigated. To do this, the paper uses the centrality graph theory and spatial network analysis [3] to study the street and building networks of fifteen suburbs characterised by various density ranges. The qualitative results on the relationship between density and social sustainability have been utilized as stated by the CityForm UK study [1], enabling further computational exploration of the cases possible for this paper. To quantify the network structure of the urban form, mathematical measurements are applied. Most of the methods employ the graph theory to model the urban structure into a more abstract graph consisting of nodes and edges which streamlines its measurement and interpretation. Using centrality, graph theory can identify the most important nodes in a network [3]. One of the primary methods in this approach is space syntax [4, 5]. Allowing for the statistical description of human behaviors such as movement and navigation, space syntax is based on a representation of the space which is inherently social [5]. Another method which is based on the graph theory is the Urban Network Analysis toolbox (UNA), developed in the City Lab at Harvard University; it addresses the buildings and their functions as the third element in the graph along with the street network [6]. This paper explores the correlation between some social sustainability aspects which are investigated in the UK study, namely social interaction, safety and the overall index of social sustainability with spatial indices, i.e. gravity, normalized angular choice and intelligibility. The outcomes confirm that when employing a suitable method, some social outcomes of densifying an area can be correlated and measured with the spatial indices. To measure these social impacts, the study needs to identify the key indicators of social sustainability which can be defined within the realm of the built environment. This can be a challenging task since there is rarely a widely accepted and commonly used category and measurements for this concept exclusively investigating the role of the built environment's design. Moreover, the existing studies generally do not provide a unified category, and some of the results are contradictory or inconsistent.

2 Social Impacts of High-Density Neighborhoods

A growing body of research shows that the concept of "compact city" has the potential to play an influential role in human well-being, quality of life and livability through the provisioning of a state of social sustainability [7–9]. Earlier studies approach this topic via a wide spectrum of definitions and perceptions of social sustainability. For instance, research on the social impacts of 25 medium-sized UK cities confirms the positive role of high-density housing on social equity [10]. Similarly, Yang [11] found that neighborhood satisfaction in high density areas in Portland (US) is higher than the same-attributed neighborhoods in Charlotte (US) which suggests consideration of spatial scale and context in studying the relationship between density and quality of life. Conversely, in Raman's [9] study on six neighborhoods in the UK, the greater emphasis on layout and design of the neighborhoods, shows that the relationship between density and social sustainability is nonlinear. Instead, the spatial configuration of neighborhoods wields a stronger impact on experiential outcomes rather than density.

In one of the most comprehensive studies named "CityForm", three neighborhoods with different density ranges (high, medium and low) in five UK cities were selected to examine the assertion that denser forms support better transportation, economic viability and social merits. Through questionnaires and interviews, they conducted a research asking residents to describe and rate their living environment based on social sustainability measurements in the dimensions they had defined. The results of this study show that although denser areas facilitate environmental and social equity by providing better access to services and facilities, this process adversely affects the sustainability of a community by reducing perceived safety, social interaction and group participation. This in turn leads to a lack of community stability and sense of place [8, 12]. The same outcomes were extracted in a study on other cases in some small towns outside Helsinki, Finland, whereas the results of the research on the urban core areas were contradictory [13]. Kytta et al. [7] found that the correlation between density and social sustainability is rather complex and context dependent. Similar to previous studies, they demonstrate that high-density areas support better accessibility in both urban and suburban neighborhoods. Nevertheless, contrary to urban areas, better accessibility does not support perceived environmental quality by the residents in suburban areas, which induces poor well-being conditions as well. They believe that this contradiction is a result of misinterpreting the outcomes without considering the specific context or scenario in each case. They found that perceived environmental quality reaches its peak at a relatively high level of density (100 housing unit/ha), and then starts declining as the density increases. Although densifying the cities' inner areas can help to provide better social sustainability, the layout and configuration of density play a more important role than density alone. The same population density can be manifested in a quite different dwelling and built form configuration, layout, and design which can lead to different types of accessibility and physical proximity [14]. However, a limited number of studies attempt to define density based on the design of the physical elements.

3   Indicators of Social Sustainability in the Built Environment

Social sustainability in relation to the design of the built environment comprises various aspects, which can be directly affected by the urban form. In this regard, one major influential factor is accessibility. This is a mediated factor linking social sustainability to the built environment and addresses a major concern in social sustainability – equity. Accessibility is defined by the design layout and spatial configuration of the built environment and impacts on people's experience of living in the environment.

In a nutshell, social sustainability indicators in the built environment include:

- **Accessibility:** which refers to equal and convenient access to the key facilities and services and public transportation. This is how the design of the built environment can contribute to better experiential outcomes of the community and potentially lead to more sustainability.
- **Community sustainability or experiential outcomes:** this dimension refers to the provision of social interaction, social participation, safety and security, sense of place, and community stability which collectively can sustain a livable neighborhood [15].

These indicators have been selected exclusively for the built environment, however, as stated in the previous section, the results of the empirical studies are not always consistent in the densified areas in terms of social impacts. Thus, we argue that optimizing some of the design factors can mediate the impact of density. We assume that the spatial design factor can be correlated to the social impacts of density as the spatial analysis also explains social phenomena through the physical configuration.

4   Mixed Method Using Spatial Analysis

Spatial analysis enables the "morphological description" of a physical entity, for example a building or an urban setting to be directed in a systematic way, and to be associated with the social aspects of the built form. This paper utilizes a mixed method[1] using spatial analysis to analyze the role of design in the trade-off between social sustainability and density. Space syntax serves to explore the socio-spatial aspects of the built form, and the Urban Network Analysis toolbox (UNA) is employed to investigate the spatial accessibility of the cases. The two tools are used in a complementary way to overcome their limitations and measure the intended study goals more comprehensively [16]. To quantify the network structure of the urban form, mathematical approaches are required. Most methods employ the graph theory to model the urban structure into a more abstract graph which streamlines its measurement and interpretation. Graph theory represents the urban network with two key elements: nodes and edges [17]. In the space syntax analyses, the graph represents configurational relationships where spatial elements are nodes connected to each other through lines which denote the relationships. Spatial relations in space syntax analysis are based on the approach that is taken for measuring the distance between the spatial elements of a network. To measure the distances in a network of disaggregated lines, space syntax defines three distances according to the relationships between adjacent segments: firstly, Metric distance or "shortest length" measures the Euclidean distance between the two spatial elements; secondly, Topological distance, referred as "fewest turns", is the number of turns (change of directions) to get to a destination; and thirdly, Angular distance which denotes the angular changes that have to be taken in the travel between

---

[1] The detailed justification, mapping and critical description of the method is presented in another paper which is published as part of the CAADRIA 2019 conference proceedings.

two points in a graph [18]. According to the angular distance definitions, Space syntax measures various spatial relations including depth, integration, choice and connectivity. Depth index is measured by the shortest distance between the spatial elements whether metric, angular or topological, based on how it is abstracted in human navigation. This is related to the definition of the connectivity parameter which denotes the number of immediate neighbors of each node. Integration value can calculate the closeness and accessibility of a point in a graph with reference to the other surrounding spaces. Integration is similar to closeness in centrality measurements except that integration calculates the angular distance while closeness takes metric distance into account. This value can predict the number of people presenting in a given area [19]. Choice in the space syntax analysis is mathematically similar to Betweenness centrality which refers to the probability of falling on any shortest path that links any pair of segments for a street segment. Interpretative models of space syntax can be developed using the parameters above whether intuitively or mathematically, which enables the statistical explanations of human behavior.

Addressing the shortcomings of space syntax, UNA includes the buildings' fabric and their function in a weighted graph. Thus, along with nodes and edges in the traditional network analysis, they include buildings as the third element. Unlike space syntax, they follow the conventional assignment of the edges to the streets, which the commuter needs to pass, and nodes to the intersections, where two or more edges meet, and the added element represents the origins and destinations of the traffic. Each building is connected to the closest street from its internode via the shortest perpendicular line. It is argued that in a spatial network, two lines with different building type - for example, one with high rise buildings and the other with detached houses - should not be treated in the same way and receive the same weight in the analysis [20]. Furthermore, missing buildings and activities, and assigning similar weights for all of them regardless of their function, location and distance from a node, overlooks some essential information about land use and density distribution [6]. UNA indices can be utilized for a wide range of analyses, for example from spatial accessibility to trip estimation derived from a particular building to other destinations. Some of the main indices which can be conducted to explore the impacts of density on the accessibility of various services in an area; reach, and gravity. These are explored in more detail below.

Considering each building as a node in the graph, reach measures the number of destinations and opportunities around each node within the radius R which determines the mode of transportation (walking, biking or driving). Each node can be weighted according to the study's desired features, e.g. floors, jobs or residences which can be interpreted as areal density measures [20]. In this case, reach calculates the weights instead of the number of destinations.

$$Reach^r[i] = \sum_{j \in V(G) - \{i\}; d[i,j] \leq r} W[j] \qquad (1)$$

Where [i, j] is the shortest path distance between nodes i and j in G, and W[j] is the weight of a destination node j.

In contrast to the reach index which only informs us about the accumulated weight or number of destinations, the gravity index provides additional information about the attractiveness of the destinations and associated travel costs based on the distance between two or more nodes in the graph. It is inversely related to the shortest path between building i and other buildings in G. The exponent β determines the distance effect.

$$Gravity^r[i] = \sum_{j \in V(G)-\{i\}:d[i,j] \le r} \frac{W[j]}{e^{\beta.d[i,j]}} \tag{2}$$

5 Analysis

Considering the built form as two networks of streets and buildings, space syntax can be used to analyze the street network. The street layout provides a long-lasting framework that embodies various social behaviors such as movement, interaction and activity. As per density, since this paper uses the data from another research study which already provided data around density and social outcomes, the focus will be on the opportunities that density of the cases has provided through spatial accessibility. Studying the building network, UNA will measure the spatial accessibility according to the contextual condition of the cases particularly addressing building density and attraction distribution.

5.1 Summary of the CityForm-UK Project

The data have been extracted from the CityForm-UK project [21] which was funded by the Engineering and Physical Sciences Research Council conducted in five British cities. Its aim was to explore the extent to which the urban form can contribute to sustainability. As one of the imperative objectives, they attempted to test the claim that a compact city can improve aspects of social sustainability. Following this study, the authors conducted another empirical analysis by choosing three different neighbourhoods of approximately c.2000 households in each to represent a specific range of density. In the case selection process, they targeted those areas that represent the most varied social, economic and urban form. The fifteen cases explored in the UK studies are categorised into three groups, i.e. inner, middle and outer areas. Each of these groups represents a different range of density from low to high. In this paper, we also followed their categories.

5.2 Spatial Analysis

Angular segment analysis was chosen for the space syntax investigation as Hillier et al. [18] have shown that angular analysis (which is based on the angular distance) is more representative of the actual pattern of people's movement given how they perceive the environment. That is, people tend to consider topological and geometric attributes while choosing the shortest path, rather than calculating the metric distance. Accordingly, as the cases are of different sizes, they have been normalized to be comparable using the following formula [22]:

Normalized angular choice

$$NACH = logCH + 1/logTD + 3 \qquad (3)$$

Where CH is choice and TD is total depth.

Normalized angular integration

$$NAIN = NC^{1.2}/TD \qquad (4)$$

Where NC refers to the number of nodes and TD is total depth.

Since the CityForm-UK study was conducted almost 10 years ago, the maps were compared with the historical database available from Google Earth Pro to do the adjustments to the network maps. Despite the new developments which have mainly occurred at the building level, the street network of most cases has remained the same. However, there are a few cases whose street network has also been changed. Such alterations have been applied to the cases' maps manually to be as close as possible to the actual network as it looked back in 2006. This was possible with Google Earth providing 3D virtual tours (Fig. 1) and various street views in any direction. The maps were double-checked to control if all the road lines in the map actually meet, and to unlink those lines that do not exhibit continuous traffic flow, for instance, where an overpass bridge cuts the link between two segments. Such circumstances have been inspected and modified in the AutoCAD files.

Fig. 1. 3D views from Google Earth in 2006 (in the left) and 2018 (on the right)

We chose to use the road-centreline for our space syntax analysis instead of the conventional axial maps created by the UCL DepthMap software to run the angular segment analysis. There is strong theoretical and cognitive evidence that the angular segment analysis, driven from the road-centrelines, are more representative of the actual patterns of people movement [23]. The same maps were used for the UNA analysis which is done on Rhino 3D. The radius used for both sets of analysis were 600 meters close to walking distances. For analyzing vehicle movement and accessibility higher radius are needed which is not discussed in this paper.

6 Results and Discussion

6.1 Spatial Accessibility

As reported in the UK study, the low-density outer areas revealed a better rate of social sustainability. Apart from the socio-demographic characteristics of each neighbourhood, the outer areas have a relatively high proportion of green spaces. Bearing this information in mind, it is expected that the outer areas are provided with better spatial accessibility on a global level and local level where the residents can reach various destinations easily. It is also confirmed in the UK study that the socially sustainable areas provide an equal level of environmental and social accessibility. We examine this expectation with the UNA toolbox using gravity index. As the buildings are assigned to be the nodes in the analysis, the results examine the accessibility to the buildings in the global scale (r = n). The gravity index, first introduced by Hansen [29], can be assumed as a spatial accessibility indicator for pedestrians. For instance, in one study conducted on several grid layouts from cities throughout world including Adelaide, Manhattan, and London, Sevtsuk et al. [24] show how this index can help explore the role of block size in pedestrian accessibility. They demonstrate that the gravity values are greater in the larger blocks which relates to more pedestrian accessibility [24]. Table 1 shows that the outer areas have a better gravity value and thus better accessibility is provided. This is compatible with the UK study result where the more accessible areas provide better social sustainability, however, it is not consistent with what we expect from denser areas. As density arises, the layout also starts getting compacted and thus the various attraction points are getting closer which implies a better range of accessibility. In this case, however, the lower density area presents a better range of attraction. It could also be due to the layout form which might have a more influential role in improving accessibility than density itself.

Table 1. Descriptive data of gravity index in the three ranges of density

Gravity	Minimum	Maximum	Mean
Inner	1.02	142.38	22.9315
Middle	1.03	66.50	15.6497
Outer	1.07	170.52	44.0369

Figure 2 depicts the accessibility maps of three cases within their three selected areas that represent different density levels. The warmer colors refer to the better accessible areas, while the cooler colors show less accessible areas.

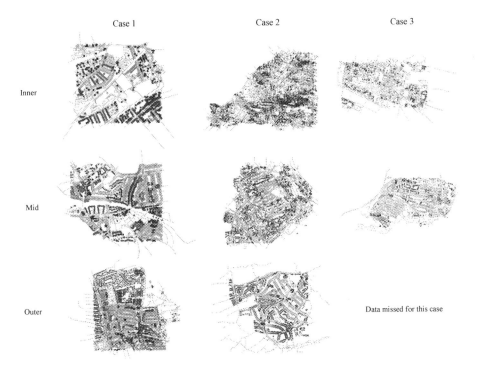

Fig. 2. Gravity index shows spatial accessibility in different areas of selected cases

6.2   Visual Accessibility: Intelligibility

Apart from the physical accessibility and the reachness of the cases, visual accessibility has also been identified as an influential factor in the relationship between density and social sustainability. Raman [9] demonstrates that the visibility from and to the main facilities and public spaces in a neighborhood are closely linked to social activities. When the activities and opportunities are visible to people, they tend to participate and use such places more resulting in a higher rate of social activities in relatively higher density areas. Thus, the UK cases have been studied in terms of visual accessibility or as defined in space syntax terms, intelligibility. The intelligibility of a space is a Pearson correlation between the connectivity and integration values of that given area [22]. The middle areas show a higher score of intelligibility while the inner and outer areas, respectively, show the lower scores (Table 2). This has also been confirmed in the UK study where the middle areas are reported to be the safest compared to the inner and outer areas. Furthermore, for the other two categories (inner and outer), it seems that the values vary according to the layout form. Whether in the outer or inner area, the intelligibility values are higher where the cases benefit from a grid layout.

Table 2. Intelligibility index which is measured by the Pearson Correlation coefficient between connectivity and integration

Category		NAIN	
		Pearson Correlation	Sig. (2-tailed)
Inner	Connectivity	.261**	.000
Mid	Connectivity	.302**	.000
Outer	Connectivity	.143**	.000

**. Correlation is significant at the 0.01 level (2-tailed).

6.3 Safety and Security

Feeling safe is repeatedly associated with the level of social sustainability and is known as an important identifier of a liveable area. In the UK study, the level of safety and crime rate have been studied as one aspect of social sustainability. They report that the suburbs are or feel safer especially where the layout is a less elemental network (cul-de-sac or grid). Inner areas have the smallest score of being "safe" while the middle areas show a higher score and outer areas the highest.

In the literature, depth is generally declared to have a nuanced association with the rate of crime. Some studies show that the crime rate on the more integrated and thus shallower areas is higher, where there are more people living and are victims of a burglary. Yet other studies also provide evidence for safer environments located in the shallower spaces, so therefore much care should be taken when interpreting the results. As Hillier et al. [5] suggest, the formula of safety does depend on the probability of encountering strangers in a given area. People may not expect to interact with strangers in some deep areas, especially in the residential areas close to their territory, and find it not safe in some spatial configurations like estate housing, while the same encounter with strangers is normal in other configurations, for instance street-based systems [4] (p. 46). Depth index has a lower value in the inner areas and on the contrary, it shows a higher value in the suburban area. This could be due to having a well-connected (as shown in connectivity value as well) and compact network the inner areas that depth rated a lower score. We proceed with the analysis to further explore the potential correlation between the reported safety rate and spatial design metrics. Figure 3 shows a scatterplot investigating the pattern of safety as the spatial metrics arise. We conduct the Kendall's Tau correlation to run the analysis. The data that we are dealing with in this dataset are non-parametric as they reject the assumption of normal distribution, and the sample size is relatively small. Therefore the Kendall's Tau is a suitable correlational test [25]. The Kendall's Tau correlation analysis on the same value shows;

- There is a significant relationship between connectivity and safety, $r = 0.41$, p (2-tailed) < 0.05.
- Choice is significantly correlated with safety, $r = -0.63$, $p < 0.05$.

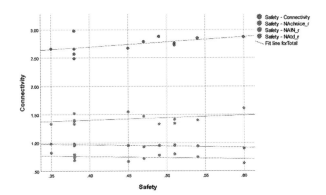

Fig. 3. Simple scatterplot with fit line of NAchoice_r of connectivity, of NAIN_r, of NATD_r by safety

6.4   Overall Social Sustainability Index

The rest of the analysis will focus on the NACH role in improving the social sustainability results and investigate if there could be any pattern explained by this metric in the angular segment analysis (ASA). We have constructed the basic regression models to dig deeper into the potential relationship that design metrics can shape the results on the social sustainability aspects (Table 3). According to the initial findings yielded from this set of analyses, not all the design metrics have a significant meaningful correlation with the various aspects of social sustainability. However, the interesting pattern that is visible in the regression models is the significant role of the NACH in all the models of social sustainability including the overall index. normalized integration in the axial map (normalized with D-value) is effectively used to predict the movement pattern in the design stage so the choice value in the previous analysis of space syntax, axial maps, was not normalized as the integration proved to be enough [26].

However, in the ASA where the distance is based on the directional turn similar to the actual movement behavior, normalized choice turned out to be as powerful as the integration value in the post-prediction of movement, and plays an integral role in the angular segment analysis [18]. Hillier et al. [26] suggest that the normalized integration and normalized angular choice (NACH) can yield a deeper understanding of the spatial morphology. The higher total value of choice means the layout is becoming more segregated. The mean NACH can also measure the level of deviation from a straight line or a regular grid. The maximum value of the normalized Choice is an indicator of the degree of the structure of a city, while the mean NACH can represent the degree of grid-like properties, bearing in mind that these two values do not necessarily have any correlation with each other.

Table 3. Regression model summary, ANOVA test results, and Coefficients

Model Summary				
Model	R	R Square	Adjusted R Square	Std. Error of the Estimate
1	.811[a]	.658	.463	1.63864

a. Predictors: (Constant), Connectivity, NAIN_r, NAchoice_r, NAtd_r

ANOVA[a]						
Model		Sum of Squares	df	Mean Square	F	Sig.
1	Regression	36.181	4	9.045	3.369	.077[b]
	Residual	18.796	7	2.685		
	Total	54.977	11			

a. Dependent Variable: Overall_Social_Sustainability

b. Predictors: (Constant), Connectivity, NAIN_r, NAchoice_r, NAtd_r

Coefficients[a]						
Model		Unstandardized Coefficients		Standardized Coefficients	t	Sig.
		B	Std. Error	Beta		
1	(Constant)	-224.533	93.639		-2.398	.048
	NAchoice_r	176.688	60.788	1.746	2.907	.023
	NAIN_r	-14.761	26.379	-.374	-.560	.593
	NAtd_r	25.718	17.129	1.089	1.501	.177
	Connectivity	13.741	7.756	.866	1.772	.120

a. Dependent Variable: Overall_Social_Sustainability

7 Conclusion

Studies on the social impacts of urban density are sometimes contradictory and inconsistent. We propose that one reason could be due to the lack of studies on the role of design and the specific physical patterns that density can create. This paper aimed to investigate this claim that the design factors can also contribute to the provision of better social sustainability while increasing density. This is especially important when considering the compact city as an inevitable scenario of what future cities will look like and the expected wide range of environmental and economic benefits. Empirical studies of the social impacts of such changes are valuable, however, there is a lack of research and practice on the computational models and tangible guidelines for the future designs or development of existing areas. While computing the social impacts is a difficult task, there is still much potential for minimizing the likely social problems incurred by the design and spatial agreement of the built form. Thus, using a mixed-method spatial analysis approach, this paper attempted to explore how the spatial design factors can be correlated to the social sustainability outcomes provided by previous studies in the literature. Considering the built form as two networks of streets and buildings, space syntax was used to analyse the street network. The street layout provides a long-lasting framework that embodies various social behaviours such as movement, interaction and activity. The building network, to target density and the opportunities it provides, was investigated through the UNA analysis.

According to the results of the spatial analysis, some of the social sustainability dimansions (introduced in Sect. 3) can be correlated to spatial design factors. Spatial accessibility was explored through UNA analysis using gravity index which matched the UK study recognizing better rate of accessibility in the low-density outer areas reported by the residents. Visual accessibility or Intelligibility was examined with Pearson correlation between connectivity and NAIN yielded from space syntax analysis which showed higher values in the medium-density middle areas. This also was in line with UK study results where they report greater safety for the middle areas. Safety was further explored with NAchoice and connectivity using Kendall's Tau correlation which suggested a significant level of correlation. Finally, various spatial design factors were employed as dependent variables to predict the overall social sustainability rate using multiple regression analysis. While not all the variables showed a significant level of prediction, the main index in the angular segment analysis, normalized choice, received a significant p-value in the regression model. The findings confirm that using a suitable method, some social outcomes of densifying an area can be correlated and measured with the spatial indices.

The study faced several limitations which motivate future analyses of this topic in more detail and with more precision. The measurements of density in this paper do not reveal everything about the design and physical attributes of the cases. Provided that more data are available about density and physical features, the research can benefit from novel methods which attempt to relate the density measurements to the morphology as well. Berghauser-pont et al. [27] believe that to describe the compactness of an area only referring to the Floor Space Index (FSI), reflecting the building intensity, does not adequately capture either its physical density or its spatial features. They have developed a system, Spacemate, which consists of three additional variables, i.e., compactness (GSI), pressure on non-built space (OSR) and height (L) which create a more efficient index in combination to show the distribution of density. According to all these variables, Spacemate provides a comparative platform illustrating the range of intensity and compactness and network density of various cases [27].

Nevertheless, adding density into the spatial analysis measurements, merely focusing on the planar properties of the street network does not seem adequate enough. Thus, mixing Spacemate matrix with the UNA analysis can be useful focusing on the density analysis to the benefits that density can create and to explore the distribution of movement flow among the various beneficiaries that density generates. Another limitation of the study is the availability of data through open online sources such as OSM where sometimes the missing data means that UNA analysis cannot be completed in Rhino 3D. UNA itself is also only a recently developed tool and not currently widely supported by empirical studies. One challenge is that OSM maps require simplification and modification and this needs to be manually done for space syntax analysis in order to be as accurate/similar as possible to the traditional axial maps [28].

This paper is a part of an ongoing research focusing on the impacts of urban density on social sustainability and served as the first step towards the overall aim, by first revealing the correlations with space syntax and UNA measures; and in the next stage, they will be mapping onto explicit design metrics or design. In future studies and looking at new cases, density can be defined with a close relationship to the design and morphology of such scenarios. This will generate a better understanding of the design role. Such explorations will enable planners and designers to identify the most influential design factors and optimize their designs to minimize the potential social problems that can be incurred by the spatial arrangement of the built form.

Acknowledgements. This research is supported by an Australian Government Research Training Program (RTP) Scholarship.

References

1. Bramley, G., et al.: What is 'social sustainable', and how do our existing urban forms perform in nurturing it? In: Proceedings of Planning Research Conference, pp. 1–40 (2006)
2. Newman, P.: Density, the sustainability multiplier: some myths and truths with application to Perth, Australia. Sustainability **6**(9), 6467–6487 (2014)
3. Newman, M.E.J.: Networks: An Introduction. Oxford University Press, Oxford/New York (2010)
4. Hillier, B.: Space is the Machine: A Configurational Theory of Architecture (1996)
5. Hillier, B., Hanson, J.: The Social Logic of Space. Cambridge University Press, Cambridge (1984)
6. Sevtsuk, A., Mekonnen, M.: Urban network analysis toolbox. Int. J. Geomatics Spat. Anal. **22**(2), 287–305 (2012)
7. Kyttä, M., et al.: Urban happiness: context-sensitive study of the social sustainability of urban settings. Environ. Planning B: Planning Des. **43**(1), 34–57 (2016)
8. Dempsey, N., Brown, C., Bramley, G.: The key to sustainable urban development in UK cities? The influence of density on social sustainability. Prog. Plann. **77**(3), 89–141 (2012)
9. Raman, S.: Designing a liveable compact city: physical forms of city and social life in urban neighbourhoods. Built Environ. **36**(1), 63–80 (2010)
10. Burton, E.: Housing for an urban renaissance: implications for social equity. Hous. Stud. **18**(4), 537–562 (2003)
11. Yang, Y.: A tale of two cities: physical form and neighborhood satisfaction in metropolitan Portland and Charlotte. J. Am. Planning Assoc. **74**(3), 307–323 (2008)
12. Bramley, G., et al.: Social sustainability and urban form: evidence from five British cities. Environ. Planning A **41**(9), 2125–2142 (2009)
13. Kyttä, M., Broberg, A.: The multiple pathways between environment and health. In: Wellbeing: A Complete Reference Guide 2014. Wiley (2014)
14. Berghauser Pont, M.Y., et al.: Space, Density and Urban Form, in Urbanism, TUDelft (2009)
15. Soltani, S., et al.: Social sustainability in the built environment: a critical conceptual framework. In: Unmaking Waste 2018, Adelaide (2018)
16. Soltani, S., et al.: A computational approach to measuring density through mixed methods. In: The 24th Annual Conference of the Association for Computer-Aided Architectural Design Research in Asia (CAADRIA 2019), Wellington, New Zealand (2019)

17. Blanchard, P., Volchenkov, D.: Mathematical Analysis of Urban Spatial Networks. Understanding Complex Systems (2009)

18. Hillier, B., Iida, S.: Network and psychological effects in urban movement. In: Cohn, Anthony G., Mark, David M. (eds.) COSIT 2005. LNCS, vol. 3693, pp. 475–490. Springer, Heidelberg (2005). https://doi.org/10.1007/11556114_30

19. Penn, A., et al.: Configurational modelling of urban movement networks. Environ. Planning B: Planning Des. **25**(1), 59–84 (1998)

20. Sevtsuk, A.: Analysis and planning of urban networks. In: Alhajj, R., Rokne, J. (eds.) Encyclopedia of Social Network Analysis and Mining, pp. 25–37. Springer, New York (2014). https://doi.org/10.1007/978-1-4614-6170-8

21. Bramley, G., et al.: Social sustainability and urban form: evidence from five british cities. Environ. Planning A: Econ. Space **41**(9), 2125–2142 (2009)

22. Al-sayed, K.: Space Syntax Methodology. Bartlett School of Architecture, UCL, London (2018)

23. Turner, A.: From axial to road-centre lines: a new representation for space syntax and a new model of route choice for transport network analysis. Environ. Planning B: Planning Des. **34**(3), 539–555 (2007)

24. Sevtsuk, A., Kalvo, R., Ekmekci, O.: Pedestrian accessibility in grid layouts: the role of block, plot and street dimensions. Urban Morphol. **20**(2), 89–106 (2016)

25. Field, A.: Discovering Statistics using SPSS. SAGE Publications, Thousand Oaks (2009)

26. Hillier, B., Yang, T., Turner, A.: Normalising least angle choice in Depthmap and how it opens new perspectives on the global and local analysis of city space, vol. 3, pp. 155–193 (2012)

27. Berghauser Pont, M., Haupt, P.A.: The spacemate: density and the typomorphology of the urban fabric, pp. 11–26 (2007)

28. Kolovou, I., et al.: Road centre line simplification principles for angular segment analysis. In: Proceedings of the 11th Space Syntax Symposium, Instituto Superior Técnico, Lisbon, Portugal (2017)

29. Hansen, W.G.: How accessibility shapes land use. J. Am. Inst. Plann. **25**(2), 73–76 (1959). https://doi.org/10.1080/01944365908978307

Joint Parametric Modeling of Buildings and Crowds for Human-Centric Simulation and Analysis

Muhammad Usman[1(✉)], Davide Schaumann[2(✉)], Brandon Haworth[1],
Mubbasir Kapadia[2], and Petros Faloutsos[1,3]

[1] York University, Toronto, Canada
{usman,brandon,pfal}@eecs.yorku.ca
[2] Rutgers University, New Brunswick, USA
{ds1540,mk1353}@cs.rutgers.edu
[3] UHN–TRI, Toronto, Canada

Abstract. Simulating groups of virtual humans (crowd simulation) affords the analysis and data-driven design of interactions between buildings and their occupants. For this to be useful in practice however, crowd simulators must be well coupled with modeling tools in a way that allows users to iteratively use simulation feedback to adjust their designs. This is a non-trivial research and engineering task as designers often use parametric exploration tools early in their design pipelines. To address this issue, we propose a platform that provides a joint parametric representation of (a) a building and the bounds of its permissible alterations, (b) a crowd that populates the environment, and (c) the activities that the crowd engages in. Based on this input, users can systematically run simulations and analyze the results in the form of data-maps, spatialized representations of human-centric analyses. The platform combines Dynamo with SteerSuite, two established tools for parametric design and crowd simulations, to create a familiar node-based workflow. We systematically evaluate the approach by tuning spatial, social, and behavioral parameters to generate human-centric analyses for the design of a generic exhibition space.

Keywords: Human-centric analytics · Crowd simulation ·
Parametric modeling · Building occupancy · Multi-agent systems

1 Introduction

Architectural design involves the systematic exploration of design options to identify solutions for a given social, physical, and environmental context [16,31]. This is an iterative process that involves the progressive refinement of design solutions to achieve a target performance [27]. Computer-Aided Design (CAD) and Building Information Modeling (BIM) tools have been developed in the last decades to assist architects in such a process. These tools help architects

© Springer Nature Singapore Pte Ltd. 2019
J.-H. Lee (Ed.): CAAD Futures 2019, CCIS 1028, pp. 279–294, 2019.
https://doi.org/10.1007/978-981-13-8410-3_20

evaluate design solutions mostly in terms of energy performance, cost, lighting, and structure. However, predicting the impact that a building produces on its occupants is often left to intuition. Poor assessments at the design stage can lead to under-performing buildings and diminished user satisfaction or productivity.

Simulation methods have been developed to represent human behavior in day-to-day and emergency scenarios [17,28]. Some of these approaches have been used to evaluate how a building design affects the behavior of the building occupants [14,15]. However, with few exceptions [35], these simulation frameworks are often decoupled from digital building modeling tools used by architects (e.g. CAD or BIM tools), hampering the designer's abilities to seamlessly simulate, analyze, and incorporate human-centric dynamics in practice.

In this work, we introduce a joint parametric representation of buildings and crowds for modeling design options, simulating human behavior, producing human-centric analyses, and incorporating the results. In conventional approaches designers modify a building model to generate a unique design solution. *Parametric modeling* explicitly encodes the relationship between building components. In this way, a designer can explore the large space of possibilities by simply modifying component parameters [36]. Our framework directly embeds, within a parametric design framework, not only traditional building modeling features, but also the modeling of crowds and the activities they engage in. Designers can leverage the node-based visual data-flow of parametric design tools to model the relationships and constraints between building design elements, crowd properties and activities in order to perform iterative human-centric analyses aimed at informing decision-making in architectural design. The proposed platform couples Dynamo – a BIM-based parametric modeling tool embedded into Revit – with SteerSuite – an established crowd simulator [33]. With newly modeled Dynamo nodes and pre-existing SteerSuite capabilities, our platform provides an integrated framework for simulation-based human-centric analyses in the domain of architectural design.

The first step of the framework involves generating a parameterized representation of (a) a *building*, which includes bounds of permissible alterations and additional data to support human behavior simulation (e.g. building semantics, spawning regions, movement targets); (b) the *crowd* that populates the buildings (e.g. number, types, distributions); and (c) the *activities* people are engaged in (e.g. day-to-day or emergency evacuation activities). The designer can then simulate a broad range of parametric behaviours and activities and then quantitatively analyze the results. The framework provides several human-centric analyses such as crowd measures, e.g. evacuation times, or spatiotemporal data-maps, e.g. aggregated density, speed, and movement maps [24].

We illustrate the capabilities of the proposed approach using a case study where we systematically tune spatial, social, and behavioral parameters to simulate and analyze dynamic situations in the design space of a gallery. We argue that the proposed approach holds promise to augment the iterative design process with human-related factors.

2   Crowd Simulation in Architectural Design

Several approaches have been proposed to address the gulf between static representation of buildings and the impact of design choices on the intended building occupants and the activities they engage in.

Static Human Behavior Analyses. Static analyses of building layouts, such as Space-Syntax, calculate spatial features such as visibility, connectivity, accessibility, and organization of a space using an abstract representation of a building geometry and topology [2,12,34]. Other approaches extend building models with information pertaining to occupant activities [20] and spatial cognition abilities [5,13]. These approaches, however, do not consider dynamic features of human behavior such as occupant movement and activities.

Dynamic Human Behavior Simulations. In contrast, dynamic analyses of human behavior provide a time-based representation of a building in-use by their prospective occupants. Beyond a building model, these methods explicitly model individual occupants or crowd entities who will populate the space (specifying occupant types, density, desired velocity, and grouping), and the activities they will engage in (e.g. moving to a target location, gathering with other agents, etc.). The problem is commonly addressed by coupling BIM with a video game engine to generate dynamic visualizations of a building in use from a first-person perspective [37]. This approach, however, requires the manual operation of a human-controlled avatar, limiting a designer's ability to analyze how a building affects the behavior of multiple people at the same time. Multi-agent systems (MAS), instead, use autonomous virtual agents to simulate the mutual interactions between people and their surrounding environment [17]. Particle-based approaches model crowd behaviors while accounting for local-level interactions between homogeneous entities by simplifying crowd agents to particle dynamics [26]. A common approach is to derive movement updates from physically modelled social forces [11,19]. Hybrid frameworks combine rules, prediction, and planning methods to avoid future collisions in a crowd [33]. Event-driven approaches coordinate the behavior of large groups of agents to perform collaborative behaviors [18,29]. Data-driven methods adopt learning techniques to capture realistic crowd behaviors [22,23].

Human Behavior Simulation in Architectural Design. MAS techniques have been applied to represent pedestrian movements [38] in emergency evacuation activities [8,25] and day-to-day behavior in different workplaces, such as offices [9], universities [30], and hospitals [28]. Preliminary studies have shown that human behavior analyses can support the iterative refinement of design solutions in terms of day-to-day and emergency behaviors [14,15]. Human behavior simulation methods, however, are often decoupled from a building modeling environment, possibly hampering their use to evaluate design solutions iteratively. To address this issue, static and human behavior analyses have been incorporated in a BIM framework where designers can generate a design and then run static and dynamic analyses to evaluate their design [35]. However, in this approach, the designer needs to manually specify building, crowd, and activity parameters in a disconnected fashion, since they are not integrated in a shared environment where the relationships and constraints between different parameters can be explicitly modeled.

Our Approach. In this work, we provide a shared modeling environment where designers can jointly model buildings, occupants, activities and the connections among them. Specifically, we leverage the workflow proposed by node-based parametric design, where buildings are modeled not as monolithic objects but as relationships between building components. In this way, a designer can manually specify the constraints between buildings, occupants, and activities as well as the bounds for admissible conditions (e.g. the maximum number of agents that can be spawned in a specific space region). Additionally, the designer can run dynamic analysis of human behavior activities and manually tune visualization and analysis parameters to gather insights that may inform successive design iterations or behavior simulations.

3 Parametric Modeling of Buildings and Crowds for Human Behavior Simulation and Analysis

3.1 Overview

We propose a platform that couples parametric design of buildings and crowds to support analyses of human spatial behavior in not-yet-built environments. Specifically, a user can model a parametric building design, crowds and their activities in a combined framework, where relationships between components can be explicitly modeled. After designing a parametric simulation configuration, the user can simulate crowd behavior over time and observe dynamic crowd-based analytics in the form of aggregate data-maps, spatialized representations of human-centric objectives over time [24]. Based on the simulation results, a user can iteratively fine-tune building, crowd, and activity parameters to simulate additional activities and gather insights that can inform decision-making in architectural design. Figure 1 shows an overview of the framework.

3.2 Main Components

The platform couples Dynamo, an established tool for parametric modeling, with SteerSuite, an established crowd simulator.

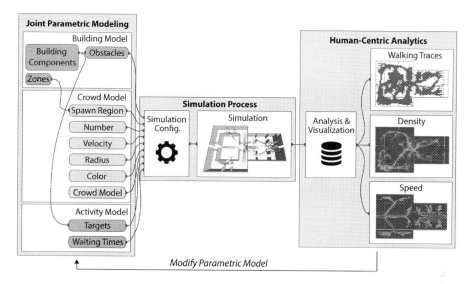

Fig. 1. Framework for parametric modeling and analysis of crowd behaviors in built environments.

Dynamo. An Autodesk Revit ® plugin that enables visual programming of building components and the relations between them [1]. Each visual component is represented as a node in a workflow. Each node encodes a script that can create a geometry in Revit, read-write data from a file, perform some operations on BIM data, or communicate data with another program. Multiple nodes can be connected so that the output of a node can be used as input for a different node. Different from other parametric modeling approaches, such as Grasshopper, Dynamo is coupled directly with Revit. BIM models – beyond geometric data – store meta-data that can be used to perform static and dynamic human-centric analyses [35].

SteerSuite. An open framework for developing and evaluating steering algorithms, simulating crowd behavior using established simulation approaches, and sharing the results with other researchers [32]. Several industry standard simulation approaches are currently incorporated in Steersuite including: (a) *Social Forces* – a method to compute attraction and repulsion forces among agents and with obstacles [10], (b) *RVO* – a widely used approach that uses reciprocal velocity obstacles for collision avoidance [3], (c) *PPR* – a rule-based approach which combines reactions, predictions, and planning [33], and (d) *FootSteps* – a biomechanical approach that simulates agent foot steps to support realistic movement and interactions [4]. In this work, SteerSuite is used for dynamic crowd simulations with parameterized crowd and space inputs. Custom Python nodes facilitate the integration of SteerSuite and Dynamo.

3.3   Joint Parametric Modeling of Buildings and Crowds

In a joint parametric modeling environment, the components required to simulate human behavior in a building are the *building's* layout, the *crowd* that populates the building, and the *activities* that the virtual people engage in, as well as the relationships among these different components. These relationships and parameters are outlined in the following subsections.

Building Modeling. A building layout is composed of architectural components (e.g. walls, doors, floors, and equipment) as well as *zones* – discrete portions of space that host different kinds of activities [7]. Both types of entities, which can be modeled using traditional CAD and BIM approaches, are defined as sets of adjustable parameters and can be used as input to define additional crowd parameters. For instance, the building components can be used as obstacles that the agents must avoid. Zones can be used to define regions where agents are spawned at the beginning of the simulation, or are associated with behaviours. Figure 2 shows a parametric building model of an art gallery designed and visualized in Dynamo with different possible layouts generated by tuning building parameters.

Crowd Modeling. A crowd is composed of a user-defined number of agents that move in a space. Additional parameters include the speed at which agents will move, one or more target goals, a color with which an agent is rendered, the radius of the disk which represents geometrically a virtual agent in the simulation, and a steering model. A user can select between the available steering models, such as social forces, RVO, and PPR, as described in Sect. 3.2. The joint parametric modeling proposed in this work enables using space parameters as input for crowd parameters. For instance, zone models can be used as spawning regions were agents are created at the beginning of the simulation, or may be associated with agent behaviours. Figure 3 shows a parametric crowd model in Dynamo.

Activity Modeling. A crowd can be engaged in different activities, such as a day-to-day use of space or an emergency evacuation. Such activities can be modeled by specifying agent movement targets, or behaviours, and the duration of their performance at each destination. A straightforward example may be specifying as movement target at emergency exists, thus modelling a simplified evacuation scenario. More complex scenarios can be modelled by identifying series of movement targets in a space (e.g. the location of the art works), or behaviours (like behaviour trees, and/or zone dependent behaviours) where agents move in space from one location to another. The proposed joint parametric representation enables using input from the building model to define input for the activity model. For example, the location of the art works specified in the building model can be used to define movement targets in the activity model. Figure 4 shows the activity model visualized in Dynamo.

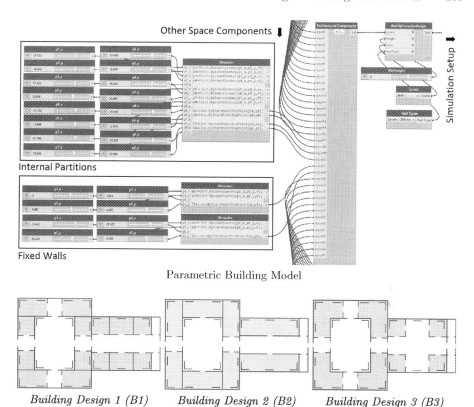

Parametric Building Model

Building Design 1 (B1)   *Building Design 2 (B2)*   *Building Design 3 (B3)*

Fig. 2. *Top*: parametric building modeling of an art galley visualized in Dynamo. The model is composed of a set of fixed and movable partitions, which parameters can be tuned to generate different building layouts. *Bottom*: three variants of the art gallery created by tuning the parameters of the internal partitioning walls. Grey regions indicate the spawn regions of the crowd; red lines indicate the fixed walls; dark gray lines indicate the partitioning walls; blue lines represent the art works (i.e. potential targets for the crowd). (Color figure online)

3.4   Crowd Simulation

The building, crowd, and activity models are used as input for a simulation phase, which computes the movement and behavior of the crowd over time. The Dynamo node workflow is designed to aggregate the different input data and generate a scenario, effectively defining the simulation to execute in SteerSuite.

A user can visualize the simulation in real-time, live update simulations in the background as parameters change without visualizing the 3D graphics. As a simulation is completed, the data, the set of spatio-temporal trajectories, are communicated back to Dynamo for the analysis phase. This process closes the loop of data-driven design without breaking the workflow of the designer. Figure 5

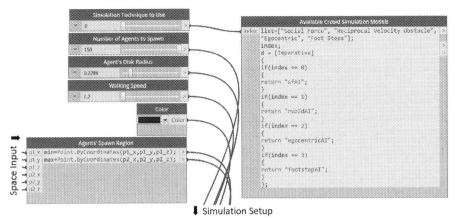

Parametric Crowd Model

Fig. 3. A parametric crowd model that allows a user to tune different crowd parameters. Input data for the spawning regions originates from the parametric building model.

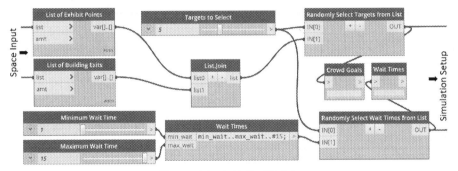

Parametric Activity Model

Fig. 4. The crowd activity model visualized in Dynamo. The parameters can be tuned to generate different activities, such as evacuation or day-to-day scenarios in an art gallery.

shows the simulation nodes visualized in Dynamo as well as a snapshot from a running simulation.

3.5 Crowd Behavior Analysis

The simulation output can be analyzed with respect to different analysis methods including (but not limited to) density, trajectory, and speed data maps. *Density*: defined as the number of agents per square meter. We calculate the average density per square meter for the building space over the course of a simulation. *Trajectory*: the path that an agent in motion follows over the course of the simulation. *Speed*: defined as the distance traveled over time. We calcu-

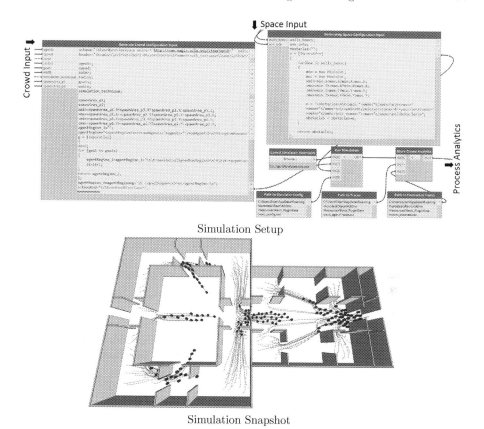

Simulation Setup

Simulation Snapshot

Fig. 5. *Top*: crowd simulation setup visualized in Dynamo. *Bottom*: screenshot of a simulation for an evacuation activity run through SteerSuite. The blue circles represent the occupants. The red lines represent occupants' movement traces. (Color figure online)

late the average speed over all agents for each sample point during the course of simulation. Figure 6 shows the crowd behavior analyses, parameterized and visualized in Dynamo, as well as the output of the analyses, visualized in Revit. Architects and designers can use these results to systematically examine the interaction between a building and its occupants.

4   Case Study

In this section we preset a few demonstrative examples to illustrate the potential of the proposed platform and how it may be used.

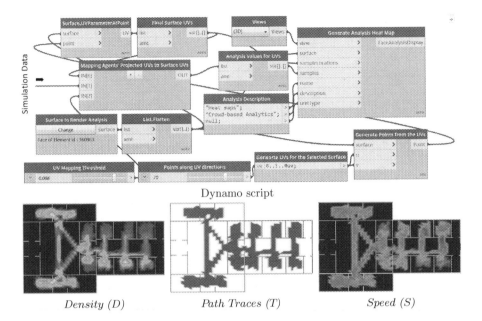

Dynamo script

Density (D)   Path Traces (T)   Speed (S)

Fig. 6. Top: modeling of crowd behavior analysis visualized in Dynamo. Bottom: examples of human-centric analysis for an exhibition activity. Left–Right: Density (red regions are the most congested areas compared to blue ones), Trajectory (red regions are the areas traveled by virtual agents during the course of simulation) and Speed (red regions are the areas where agents traveled with high speeds compared to blue ones) heat maps are shown. (Color figure online)

4.1   Simulation Setup

Building Parameters. Three variations of a floorpan are created by tuning the parameters of the adjustable partitions of an art gallery (Fig. 2: Bottom). In the remainder of this section, these variants are named *B1*, *B2* and *B3*.

Crowd Parameters. A total of 150 autonomous agents are randomly distributed and initialized in 14 different spawn regions for building (B1), 8 different regions for building (B2) and 8 different regions for building (B3), as shown in Fig. 2 (Bottom). We parameterize the crowd movement into two categories in terms of walking speed. *Adults (C1):* represents the adult walking. A speed of 1.2 m/s is considered an average walking speed of an adult with normative gait and without to use of mobility aids [6,21]. *Mix-Adults (C2):* represents mix-adult (heterogeneous) walking. Depending on the age, height, weight and health conditions, a human can walk with a wide speed range. In this study, *C2* adults walk in a range of 1.1 – 1.8 m/s. In the remainder of this paper, crowd heterogeneity levels will be referred as *C1*, and *C2*, respectively.

Activity Parameters. We consider two different simulation activities. *Day-to-day (A1):* represents a day-to-day situation where people come to an art gallery and walk from one exhibit point to another until they have seen all the exhibits or those aligned with their interest. Agents spend a random time between $5-20$ s with each exhibit before moving to the next. *Evacuation (A2):* represents an emergency situation (e.g. fire egress) where all the occupants vacate the building through their nearest exits.

Human-Centric Analyses. In this study we consider three types of analyses, namely density, walking traces, and average speed, as previously described in Sect. 3.5.

4.2   Results

Figure 7 shows data maps of density, trajectory, and average speed analyses, for all three building spaces with both day-to-day and evacuation activities.

In building $(B1)$ and for adult crowds $(C1)$, in the density map (D) for exhibition activity $(A1)$, the red regions in the corridors and hallways are more congested as they are common passages to connect different exhibit points. However, during the evacuation activity $(A2)$, this congestion is mostly found near the building exits due to bottlenecks near egress points. For the trajectory map (T) during a day-to-day activity $(A1)$, we see complex trajectories because the crowd moved from one exhibit point to the other in order to explore the exhibition, whereas in the evacuation activity $(A2)$, we see symmetric trajectories as the agents tried to vacate the building from their nearest exits. For the average speed map (S) during exhibition activity $(A1)$, the higher walking speed is recorded in the corridors and hallways, whereas in evacuation activity $(A2)$, the highest speed is recorded near the building exits.

In building $(B2)$ and for adult crowds $(C1)$, in the density map (D) for exhibition activity $(A1)$, the regions in the middle corridor are comparatively more crowded especially at the very center of the hallway, whereas during the evacuation activity $(A2)$, the congestion is found near the egress points as well as around the regions connecting the middle hallway and the exhibit areas. For the trajectory map (T) during exhibition activity $(A1)$, we see comparatively more complex trajectories and for evacuation activity $(A2)$, the symmetric trajectories are found as the agents vacated the building from their nearest exits. However, for both activities, the trajectories show that virtual crowds traveled more areas compared to areas traveled in building $(B1)$. For the average speed map (S) during exhibition activity $(A1)$, the higher walking speed is recorded not just in the corridors but also at the exhibit areas, whereas in evacuation activity $(A2)$, high walking speed is only recorded near the egress points.

In building $(B3)$ and for adult crowds $(C1)$, in the density map (D) for exhibition activity $(A1)$, the areas at exhibit points as well as the middle corridor exhibit increased density levels, whereas during the evacuation activity $(A2)$, the congestion is only found near the egress points. For the trajectory map (T)

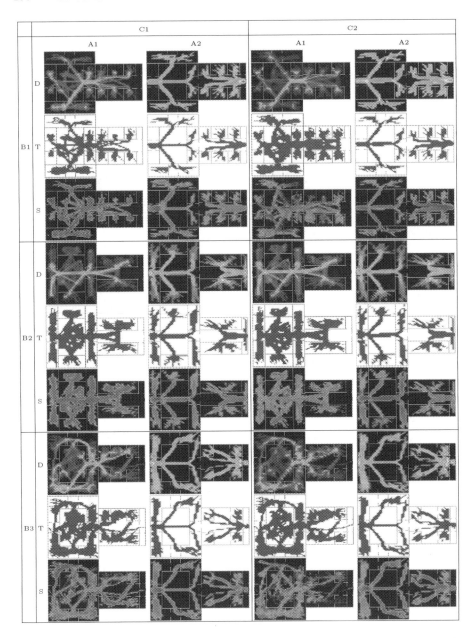

Fig. 7. Selected results for different iterations of human-centric analyses. Specifically, we considered three building layouts (B1, B2, B3), two crowd configurations – "Adults" (C1), and "Mix-Adults" (C2), two activities – "Day-to-day" (A1), and "Evacuation" (A2), and three analyses – "Density" (D), "Path Traces" (T) and "Speed" (S).

during exhibition activity $(A1)$, we see complex trajectory structures at the middle corridor as well as at the exhibit points with multi-route trajectories, and for evacuation activity $(A2)$, the symmetric trajectories are found as agents moved to the nearest building exit. For the average speed map (S) during exhibition activity $(A1)$, since there are multiple routes to the exhibition rooms, high walking speed is recorded around the exhibit areas as the agents moved in from one side of the room and exit from the other side. However, in evacuation activity $(A2)$, high walking speed is only recorded in the middle hallway near the building exits.

The speed analysis also reveals interesting patterns. In the case of evacuation $(A2)$ the mix-adult crowd $(C2)$ shows more variation and asymmetry in speed than $(C1)$. Interestingly, the more uniform crowd $(C1)$ seems to exhibit more speed variation and slower regions in everyday exhibit browsing $(A2)$.

The above analyses are simply for proof for concept. In a realistic setting a user would use multiple levels of analysis to identify and analyse further areas of interest or use patterns. For example, a trajectory analysis could identify the most visited areas, where a subsequent speed analysis could identify the specific use patterns in those areas.

Implementation Details. All case study experiments are run on a Lenovo laptop with the following specifications: Intel(R) Core i7-6700HQ CPU @ 2.60 GHz (8 CPUs), 16 GB of RAM (DDR4), Nvidia GeForce GTX 1060 (Graphics Card) and Microsoft Windows 10 Home (OS).

5   Conclusions and Discussion

In this work, we presented a joint parametric design workflow where users can specify a parameterized representation of (a) an environment (with bounds of permissible alterations of an environment), (b) the agents that populate the environments, and (c) the activities agents are engaged in. Such representation can be used to run human behavior simulations and fine-tune the aforementioned parameters based on visual feedback of human-centric analyses (e.g. density, trajectory, and average speed maps). The proposed platform couples Dynamo – an established tool for parametric modeling, with SteerSuite – an established crowd simulator to support analyses of human spatial behavior in not-yet-built environments.

A case study is conducted to analyze the effectiveness of the proposed framework. Three variants of an exhibition space are created by parameterizing the partitioning walls of an art gallery. Two diverse crowd behaviors are selected in terms of walking speed namely "Adults", and "Mix-Adults". Finally, two sets of crowd activities are performed namely "Day-to-day" – a normal day-to-day scenario and "Evacuation" – an emergency evacuation scenario. The framework allows users to systematically run simulations with the defined input parameters and analyze the results in the form of data-maps – spatialized representations of human-centric analyses to gather insights that can inform the design process.

While in this study we analyzed a selected number of building, crowd, and activity configurations, our platform can simulate infinite variations of these parameters in a systematic fashion.

Future work will involve: (a) extending the activity and crowd models to account for additional parameters; (b) incorporating additional human-centric analyses, such as crowd flow, evacuation times, and exit usage; (c) representing the simulation results by means of a dashboard that supports the storing and exploration of the different design solutions; (d) embedding into the platform an optimization process that systematically tunes selected building, crowd and activity parameters to improve a building design and operation; and (e) conducting a user study to determine how the platform can be used by architects to simulate and evaluate design options.

Acknowledgement. This research has been partially funded by grants from the NSERC Discovery and Create programs, ISSUM and in part by NSF IIS-1703883, NSF S&AS-1723869 and the Murray Fellowship.

References

1. Dynamo: Open source graphical programming for design. https://dynamobim.org/
2. Bafna, S.: Space syntax: a brief introduction to its logic and analytical techniques. Environ. Behav. **35**(1), 17–29 (2003)
3. van den Berg, J., Guy, S.J., Lin, M., Manocha, D.: Reciprocal n-body collision avoidance. In: Pradalier, C., Siegwart, R., Hirzinger, G. (eds.) Robotics Research. Springer Tracts in Advanced Robotics, vol. 70, pp. 3–19. Springer, Heidelberg (2011). https://doi.org/10.1007/978-3-642-19457-3_1
4. Berseth, G., Kapadia, M., Faloutsos, P.: Robust space-time footsteps for agent-based steering. Comput. Animation Virtual Worlds (2015). https://www.semanticscholar.org/paper/Robust-Space-Time-Footsteps-for-Agent-Based-Berseth/21d3e445853bf9852b6f10d56f473aef7b18f98c
5. Bhatt, M., Schultz, C., Huang, M.: The shape of empty space: human-centred cognitive foundations in computing for spatial design. In: IEEE Symposium on Visual Languages and Human-Centric Computing, pp. 33–40 (2012)
6. Bohannon, R.W.: Comfortable and maximum walking speed of adults aged 20–79 years: reference values and determinants. Age Ageing **26**(1), 15–9 (1997)
7. Brodeschi, M., Pilosof, N.P., Kalay, Y.E.: The definition of semantic of spaces in virtual built environments oriented to BIM implementation. In: Proceedings of Computer Aided Architectural Design Futures, pp. 331–346 (2015)
8. Chu, M.L., Parigi, P., Law, K., Latombe, J.C.: Modeling social behaviors in an evacuation simulator. Comput. Animation Virtual Worlds **25**(3–4), 373–382 (2014)
9. Goldstein, R., Tessier, A., Khan, A.: Schedule-calibrated occupant behavior simulation. In: Proceedings of the 2010 Spring Simulation Multiconference, p. 180. Society for Computer Simulation International (2010)
10. Helbing, D., Farkas, I., Vicsek, T.: Simulating dynamical features of escape panic. Nature **407**(6803), 487–490 (2000)
11. Helbing, D., Molnar, P.: Social force model for pedestrian dynamics. Phys. Rev. E **51**(5), 4282 (1995)

12. Hillier, B., Hanson, J.: The Social Logic of Space. Cambridge University Press, Cambridge (1989)
13. Hölscher, C., Büchner, S.J., Meilinger, T., Strube, G.: Adaptivity of wayfinding strategies in a multi-building ensemble: the effects of spatial structure, task requirements, and metric information. J. Environ. Psychol. **29**(2), 208–219 (2009)
14. Hong, S.W., Lee, Y.G.: The effects of human behavior simulation on architecture major students' fire egress planning. J. Asian Archit. Build. Eng. **17**(1), 125–132 (2018)
15. Hong, S.W., Schaumann, D., Kalay, Y.E.: Human behavior simulation in architectural design projects: an observational study in an academic course. Comput. Environ. Urban Syst. **60**, 1–11 (2016)
16. Kalay, Y.E.: Architecture's New Media: Principles, Theories, and Methods of Computer-Aided Design. MIT Press, Cambridge (2004)
17. Kapadia, M., Pelechano, N., Allbeck, J., Badler, N.: Virtual crowds: steps toward behavioral realism. Synth. Lect. Vis. Comput. Comput. Graph. Animat. Comput. Photogr. Imaging **7**(2), 1–270 (2015)
18. Kapadia, M., Shoulson, A., Steimer, C., Oberholzer, S., Sumner, R.W., Gross, M.: An event-centric approach to authoring stories in crowds. In: Proceedings of the 9th International Conference on Motion in Games, pp. 15–24. ACM (2016)
19. Karamouzas, I., Heil, P., van Beek, P., Overmars, M.H.: A predictive collision avoidance model for pedestrian simulation. In: Egges, A., Geraerts, R., Overmars, M. (eds.) MIG 2009. LNCS, vol. 5884, pp. 41–52. Springer, Heidelberg (2009). https://doi.org/10.1007/978-3-642-10347-6_4
20. Kim, T.W., Fischer, M.: Automated generation of user activity-space pairs in space-use analysis. J. Constr. Eng. Manag. **140**(5), 04014007 (2014)
21. LaPlante, J.N., Kaeser, T.P.: The continuing evolution of pedestrian walking speed assumptions. ITE J. Inst. Transp. Eng. **74**(9), 32 (2004)
22. Lee, K.H., Choi, M.G., Hong, Q., Lee, J.: Group behavior from video: a data-driven approach to crowd simulation. In: Proceedings of the 2007 ACM SIGGRAPH/Eurographics Symposium on Computer Animation, pp. 109–118. Eurographics Association (2007)
23. Lerner, A., Chrysanthou, Y., Lischinski, D.: Crowds by example. In: Computer Graphics Forum, vol. 26, pp. 655–664. Wiley Online Library (2007)
24. Morad, M., Zinger, E., Schaumann, D., Pilosof, N.P., Kalay, Y.: A dashboard model to support spatio-temporal analysis of simulated human behavior in future built environments. In: Symposium on Simulation for Architecture and Urban Design, June 2018
25. Pan, X., Han, C.S., Dauber, K., Law, K.H.: A multi-agent based framework for the simulation of human and social behaviors during emergency evacuations. AI Soc. **22**(2), 113–132 (2007)
26. Reynolds, C.W.: Flocks, herds and schools: a distributed behavioral model. In: ACM SIGGRAPH Computer Graphics, vol. 21, no. 4, pp. 25–34 (1987)
27. Rittel, H.: Some principles for the design of an educational system for design. J. Architectural Educ. **26**(1–2), 16–27 (1971)
28. Schaumann, D., Breslav, S., Goldstein, R., Khan, A., Kalay, Y.E.: Simulating use scenarios in hospitals using multi-agent narratives. J. Build. Perform. Simul. **10**(5–6), 636–652 (2017)
29. Schaumann, D., Date, K., Kalay, Y.E.: An event modeling language (EML) to simulate use patterns in built environments. In: Proceedings of the Symposium on Simulation for Architecture and Urban Design, Toronto, pp. 189–196 (2017)

30. Shen, W., Shen, Q., Sun, Q.: Building information modeling-based user activity simulation and evaluation method for improving designer-user communications. Autom. Constr. **21**, 148–160 (2012)
31. Simon, H.A.: The Sciences of the Artificial. MIT Press, Cambridge (1969)
32. Singh, S., Kapadia, M., Faloutsos, P., Reinman, G.: An open framework for developing, evaluating, and sharing steering algorithms. In: Egges, A., Geraerts, R., Overmars, M. (eds.) MIG 2009. LNCS, vol. 5884, pp. 158–169. Springer, Heidelberg (2009). https://doi.org/10.1007/978-3-642-10347-6_15
33. Singh, S., Kapadia, M., Hewlett, B., Reinman, G., Faloutsos, P.: A modular framework for adaptive agent-based steering. In: Symposium on Interactive 3D Graphics and Games, pp. 141–150. ACM (2011)
34. Turner, A., Doxa, M., O'Sullivan, D., Penn, A.: From isovists to visibility graphs: a methodology for the analysis of architectural space. Environ. Planning B: Planning Des. **28**(1), 103–121 (2001)
35. Usman, M., Schaumann, D., Haworth, B., Berseth, G., Kapadia, M., Faloutsos, P.: Interactive spatial analytics for human-aware building design. In: Proceedings of the 11th Annual International Conference on Motion, Interaction, and Games, p. 13. ACM (2018)
36. Woodbury, R.: Elements of Parametric Design. Taylor & Francis Group, Abingdon (2010)
37. Yan, W., Culp, C., Graf, R.: Integrating BIM and gaming for real-time interactive architectural visualization. Automa. Constr. **20**(4), 446–458 (2011)
38. Yan, W., Kalay, Y.E.: Simulating the behavior of users in built environments. J. Archit. Plann. Res. **21**(4), 371–384 (2004)

The Social Life of Small Urban Spaces 2.0

Three Experiments in Computational Urban Studies

Javier Argota Sánchez-Vaquerizo[(⊠)] ⓘD
and Daniel Cardoso Llach[(⊠)] ⓘD

Computational Design Laboratory, School of Architecture,
Carnegie Mellon University, Pittsburgh, PA, USA
reivajar@gmail.com, dcardoso@cmu.edu

Abstract. This paper introduces a novel framework for urban analysis that leverages computational techniques, along with established urban research methods, to study how people use urban public space. Through three case studies in different urban locations in Europe and the US, it demonstrates how recent machine learning and computer vision techniques may assist us in producing unprecedently detailed portraits of the relative influence of urban and environmental variables on people's use of public space. The paper further discusses the potential of this framework to enable empirically-enriched forms of urban and social analysis with applications in urban planning, design, research, and policy.

Keywords: Data analytics · Urban design · Machine learning ·
Artificial intelligence · Big data · Space syntax

1 Introduction

William Whyte's well known study of "The Social Life of Small Urban Spaces" sought to understand what factors contributed to making a city's public space vibrant and engaging. He—and his team—used film, qualitative observation, and clever counting and mapping techniques to document people's use of public spaces in cities across the United States [9]. They observed how people moved around and used urban artifacts such as benches, waste baskets, building steps, sculptures, retail, and movable chairs. They were interested in determining what public space features made people comfortable, or made strangers engage with each other. While other strands of quantitative urban analysis exist [10–12], the visual and methodological repertoires employed by Whyte—and his ambition for an empirically-grounded practice of urban research—remain influential in urban studies, planning, and policy [13, 14].

This paper demonstrates how recent advances in computer vision and machine learning open the possibility for revisiting and extending Whyte's distinctive approach. It describes a novel framework for urban analysis that leverages computer vision, machine learning, and urban design techniques to study how people move around in and interact with environmental features in public urban spaces. Discussing three case

© Springer Nature Singapore Pte Ltd. 2019
J.-H. Lee (Ed.): CAAD Futures 2019, CCIS 1028, pp. 295–310, 2019.
https://doi.org/10.1007/978-981-13-8410-3_21

studies, it demonstrates the framework's potential to enhance traditional spatial analysis tools, and to reveal the relative impact of urban features such as building form, vehicular traffic, and residential and retail functions on people's use of public space. The case studies span different urban conditions: a public square in a European old city at plaza del Callao in Madrid, Spain; a central lawn of a North American campus at Carnegie Mellon University in Pittsburgh, PA, and a public square in North America in Pittsburgh Downtown's Market Square.

The paper reports on the methods employed, and on the findings of each analysis. It concludes with a discussion of the potential of this framework to enable new, data enriched, forms of urban analysis with applications in urban planning, design, research, and policy. The aim of this framework is to leverage the data gathering, processing and analysis capacities of modern computation in order to create an enriched and nuanced portrait of the connection between urban spaces and the human experience. As the following sections show, the analysis of these data yields an unprecedently detailed portrait of the relative influence of urban and environmental variables on people's utilization of public space.

2   Methods

2.1   General Approach

Our portrait of each built environment is supported on three categories of data classified according to two parameters: time range –how frequently the data changes– and nature –how the data is generated– (Fig. 1): First, we account for spatial features including conventional urban design and planning parameters such as distances to Points of Interests (POIs) and sunlight, as well as "synthetic" parameters [7] derived from Space Syntax metrics such as compactness and occlusivity [4]. Second, we account for the visual complexity of the built environment using visual entropy [6], a measure of the perceptual and cognitive conditions of human experience in urban space [3, 6]. It's worth noting that this parameter evokes early 20th century Gestalt and constructivist postulates on spatial perception [1, 5, 8]. Finally, we account for geolocated levels of detection of activity in the space, which we classify by type (e.g. pedestrians, cars, trucks, buses, bikes, motorbikes, and police cars). These are derived computationally from anonymized video data captured on site using computer vision techniques.

These different data are aggregated into a spatial grid (Fig. 5), each cell indexing the corresponding parameters as an array of vectors with the same dimension. Thus codified, the collected data can be analyzed for correlations between the different variables in space. This data architecture, developed in Python data processing pipeline enriches conventional computational representations of the city, typically alien to this type of information and level of detail.

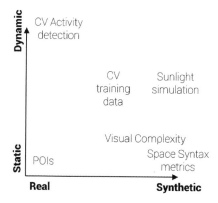

Fig. 1. Types of data according to their nature and time range.

We stacked data (Fig. 4) corresponding to 24 h periods and analyze their correlations longitudinally during the day (Figs. 3, 5 and 6). Broadly speaking, the relations between the different variables presented can be inferred using regression analysis. This allows for testing bivariate correlations between the more than 30 variables considered. Bivariate analysis—one of the simplest statistical methods for checking the empirical relationship between two variables [2]—is computed with three different mathematical methods with similar outcomes: Pearson's correlation coefficient [15], Spearman's rank correlation coefficient [16], and Kendall's tau coefficient [17] (Fig. 5). Additionally, in the campus case, we segmented the data corresponding to different zones based on patterns of pedestrian utilization. Video of each site was captured using cameras located at a distance to keep the data anonymous.

An important technical challenge was to accurately map the data collected from the video into a digital geometric model of the site. We achieved this by using different machine learning methods, including deep learning to detect and identify correlations in the features in the images from different sources, and other statistical techniques. The resulting model innovatively matches temporal signatures of the detected occupations with a digital representation of the site to offer a detailed portrait of people's behavior in that urban space over a period of time.

The first two case studies illustrate the framework's initial implementation in Madrid and Carnegie Mellon University. They both include a bivariate analysis of the parameter-space of each site which measures correlations between spatial features and patterns of spatial use. The third—and more advanced—case study illustrates a multi-camera activity detection strategy, which is introduced in order to account for a more complex urban space. In this case a bivariate analysis is developed using historical weather data. New detectable objects are added to the system (i.e. urban furniture). Finally, a controlled experiment changing the location of furniture is introduced for a sensitivity test and to interrogate the framework's capacity to yield actionable planning and design insights.

2.2   First Case Study: Plaza del Callao (Madrid, Spain)

Plaza del Callao is a public open space in central Madrid located at the intersection of Gran Vía, calle Preciados, calle del Carmen, calle del Postigo de San Martín, calle de Jacometrezo, and calle de Miguel Moya. Despite being located in the city's old town, its design is relatively recent—it aligns with the opening of the new Gran Via at the beginning of the 20th century. It's important to note that Plaza del Callao is located in one of the denser and more compact areas of the city. It is not a space for staying, but mostly a crossroad between very active areas of the city center. Narrow and lively streets connect to Callao, and the flow of people is channeled and compressed through these pathways while spreading out across a square which has no remarkable landmarks or resting areas: it is simply paved square (Fig. 2).

Fig. 2. View of plaza del Callao, Madrid (Spain)

Table 1. Data specifications for location 1.

Data description	Source	Features
Space Syntax metrics	3D model	Area, Distance Weighted Area, Perimeter, Compactness, Circularity, Convex deficiency, Occlusivity, Min radial, Max radial, Mean radial, Standard Deviation, Variance, Skewness, Dispersion, Elongation, Drift Magnitude, Drift Angle
Sunlight simulation	3D model	Continuous numeric value

(*continued*)

Table 1. (*continued*)

Data description	Source	Features
POIs	3D model	10 locations (metro entrance, Eastern access from Gran Vía, Starbucks, access from calle del Carmen, access from calle Preciados, access from calle del Postigo de San Martín, Western access from calle Preciados, Callao Theatre, Western Access from Gran Vía and calle Jacometrezo, tree)
Activities detections	CV system	Latitute, longitude, time, class (pedestrian, car, police car, bike, bus, truck, motorbike)
Visual complexity	Google Street View	Continuous numeric value

The data (Table 1) for this case study comes from three sources: (a) a 3D model of the built environment elaborated in Rhinoceros from information available at Google Maps and from NASA digital elevation models; (b) spherical panoramas from Google Street View; and the (c) anonymous video data recorded with a camera specially located in the square for this project. The 3D model is used for simulating the sunlight conditions and for the space syntax analyses of the physical environment. The period of observation lasted 12 days, from 12 pm on April 1st, 2018 through 1:10 pm on April 12th, 2018. An average of 1.2 million detections were collected per day. The data analyzed in this paper corresponds to a subset of this dataset including 24 h of data from April 2nd, 2018.

Aside from considering the patterns of pedestrian occupation detected using the cameras, we considered space syntax metrics characterizing users' perception of the directionality and centrality in the space provides insights into the underlying factors affecting pedestrian movements.

Results: A Geography of Pedestrian Use

Our analysis shows low correlation between areas with greater amount of sunlight and the areas most used by pedestrians (see correlations on Fig. 5). Unsurprisingly, the Subway entrance is a key attractor of pedestrian traffic. Other points of interest around the square seemed to have comparatively little impact on pedestrian behavior. Interestingly, the central areas of the square are the most important for pedestrian use as indicated by the centrality measures (area, mean radial, and drift magnitude) generated by space syntax techniques. Finally, the Easternmost areas of the plaza are more frequently used during the evening, while morning activity tends to concentrate on different spots around the West part of the square (Fig. 3). This may correlate with the character of the commercial uses in that part of the square.

Fig. 3. Spatial segmentation based on temporal patterns of use. Each color is a different cluster of cells where the temporal patterns of pedestrians' detection is similar. (Color figure online)

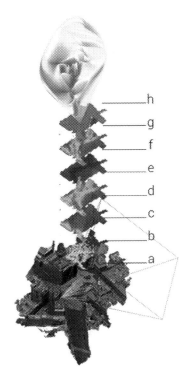

Fig. 4. Multidimensional aggregation of data on analysis discreet cells in one of the studied locations (plaza del Callao). Only some databases are shown, from top to bottom: (a) 3D environment Virtual Entropy, (b) aggregation of pedestrian detections (c) Space Syntax (SS) area, (d) SS perimeter, (e) SS skewness, (f) SS elongation, (g) SS max radial, (h) Space Syntax (SS) max radial, (h) Visual complexity Z graph.

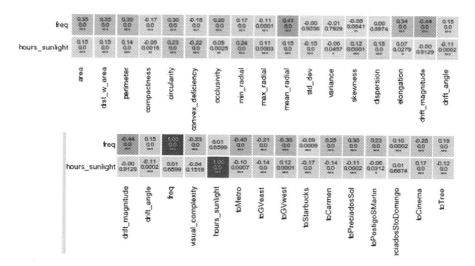

Fig. 5. Detail of correlation matrix for plaza del Callao, Madrid. Values and significance for *freq* (detections of pedestrians in the space) and *hours_sunlight* (number of sunlight hours).

2.3 Second Case Study: Carnegie Mellon Campus Lawn (Pittsburgh, PA)

The second case study focuses on a completely different urban environment: the "Cut," one of the meadows located in the historical core of the campus of Carnegie Mellon University in Pittsburgh, Pennsylvania, US (Fig. 6). This is the biggest open public space of the campus, located between the College of Fine Arts, and the tennis courts by the Margaret Morrison Carnegie Hall in the East and the School of Drama, Doherty Hall, and Baker Hall in the West. It is a key area for the functioning and communication of the campus as it is the main crossroads connecting some of the main facilities of the campus with a clear pedestrian character. It highlights the walkable character of the environment, as well as a place for gathering and leisure whose best-known landmark is the Fence.

The three sources for data are detailed in Table 2. The timeframe for this location is shorter and covers 13 h of data, from 8 am to 9 pm on April 30th, 2018. The shorter period explored in this location allows us to focus on the quicker patterns of use in a university campus—where night activity is almost nonexistent comparatively with the center of a large European city.

Fig. 6. Perspective of location analyzed on central lawn of Carnegie Mellon University campus in Pittsburgh, PA (USA)

Table 2. Data specifications for location 2.

Data description	Source	Features
Space Syntax metrics	3D model	Area, Distance Weighted Area, Perimeter, Compactness, Circularity, Convex deficiency, Occlusivity, Min radial, Max radial, Mean radial, Stadard Deviation, Variance, Skewnes, Dispersion, Elongation, Drift Magnitude, Drift Angle
Sunlight simulation	3D model	Continuous numeric value
POIs	3D model	5 locations (flag, Doherty Hall entrance, inflatable Sled, fence, path to Hunt Library)
Activities detections	CV system (wide angle lenses)	Latitute, longitude, time, class (pedestrian, car, police car, bike, bus, truck, motorbike)
Visual complexity	Google Street View	Continuous numeric value

Results: A Map of the Campus' Everyday—With Few Surprises

Our analysis shows that pedestrian behavior is strongly conditioned by the design of paved paths. We found that space syntax metrics relating to the perception of urban space have little effect on the behavior of people (Fig. 7). Finally, we found higher levels of activity during the morning closer to education buildings entrances. Afternoon activity moves towards the central part of the lawn (Fig. 8).

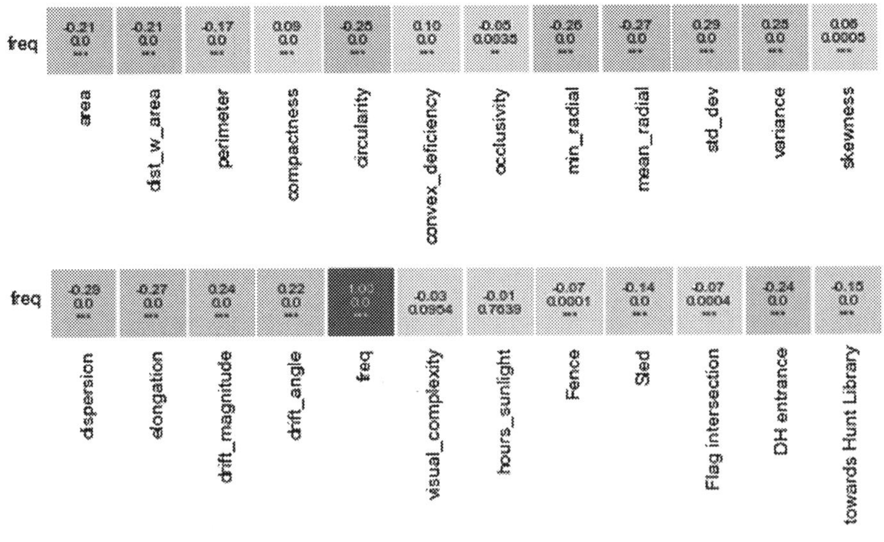

Fig. 7. Detail of correlation Matrix for Carnegie Mellon University campus (the whole matrix is equivalent to the one shown on Fig. 3). Only freq-related values (detection of pedestrian) are shown: correlation coefficients and significances with other parameters are shown.

The trends seem to match the expected behavior of this setting, which is highly conditioned by students' highly-regimented class schedule. As it has been already pointed out, the spatial design of the common areas at Carnegie Mellon University campus is defined by a clear separation between the communication pathways with a concrete pavement, and the greenery of grassed areas in between. It conditions the patterns of utilization of the space, and this trait is picked up by our analysis. An important benefit of this case study was to test the framework for capturing special structure information from the behavior (it means, pedestrians' detections) without implicitly introducing this information in the system. Accordingly, we are able to automatically detect the underlying segregation of the space in paved paths and grass just by inferring it from the data (Fig. 9)—a feature that plays an important role in our third and last case study.

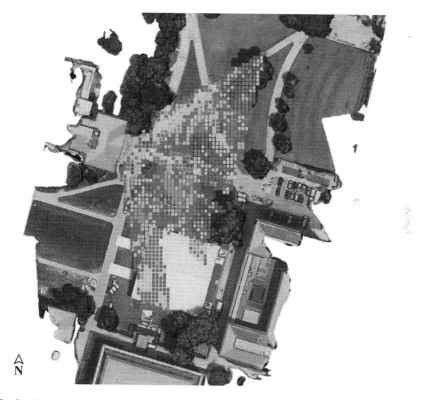

Fig. 8. Spatial segmentation of the central lawn at Carnegie Mellon University campus based on common temporal pattern of utilization. Paths and paved areas are identified.

2.4   Third Case Study: Market Square (Pittsburgh, PA)

Our third and last case study is located in the main urban public space of downtown Pittsburgh: Market Square. This is one of the few spots of the city with a pure built-up

Fig. 9. Cameras use for Market Square data collection. Pittsburgh, PA (USA).

and very urban setting, surrounded by dense commercial activity. The closest example to a traditional "European" urban square embedded in a dense city fabric. As many downtown areas in North America's rust-belt cities, it has a complicated history of economic and environmental degradation. However, during the last several years, it has been central to important urban renovation efforts. In this context, the city of Pittsburgh has been collaborating with the Pittsburgh Downtown Partnership (PDP) for more than 20 years with the goal of improving this area. Currently, this organization is the main stakeholder in activating and taking care of downtown. As part of this collaboration Market Square was renovated in 2006, and since then PDP has sought to establish this iconic space as a vibrant activity hub.

Data was collected over a period of 5 weeks, from August 24th to September 28th, 2018, using four cameras placed in different locations around the square (Fig. 9). The multiple cameras were an innovation of this case study and were key for providing a good coverage of the space—over 97% of the square's surface. Another improvement relative to the other two case studies is that the system is able to detect a larger repertoire of classes. Public urban elements such as umbrellas, tents, seats, and tables, for example, are added as objects of interest that might enrich our portrait of the activities taking place on the square. During the 5-week period 3,200 h of video were captured, and over 250 million of detections were processed. A final feature of this analysis is the observation of specific changes to the urban furniture, which enabled us to study the impact of these changes on the activity on the square and its spatial distribution.

In addition to the bivariate analysis, a quantitative and qualitative comparative analysis of the data is performed checking the alignment between weather conditions and levels of utilization of the square (Table 3).

Table 3. Data specifications for location 3.

Data description	Source	Features
Weather information	Historical data	Hourly historical record on temperature and rain
Activities detections	CV system (4 cameras)	Latitude, longitude, time, class (pedestrians, trolleys, seats, tables, sun umbrellas, tents, cars, pickups, vans, trucks, bikes, motorcycles)

Results: A Detailed Picture of Pedestrian Activity

Our analysis of Market Square, which was longer and more technically complex, yielded interesting insights concerning three different aspects of this urban space. First, it allowed us to study the impact of weather over relatively long periods of time (Fig. 10). Second, it allowed us to study the spatial distribution of activities in relation to specific changes on the square's urban furniture layout. Finally, it allowed us to examine how special events impact the amount of people visiting the square, and their behavior.

Concerning weather, while our analysis shows how short and episodic periods of rain have little effect on the medium- and long-term activities on the square, it also shows how rain has an immediate effect on pedestrian activity (Fig. 10). On the other hand, persistent and longer periods of rainy conditions have a very different effect on activity levels detected on the square. In average, they cause a drop of 60% of the activity on the square. Interestingly, however, there is a "compensation effect" the following day, which can show an activity increase ranging between 20% and 30%. This trend can have important implications on activities planning and design changes on the square. It allows to predict important shifts on activity level on the square depending on weather conditions.

Regarding the spatial distribution of activity, the levels of correlation between pedestrians' presence and furniture is moderately high. In general terms, the central part of the square is used around 8 times more than the edges and trees quadrants. Additionally, these patterns seem to be closely connected to the distribution of elements around the square: urban furniture and tents for markets (Fig. 11).

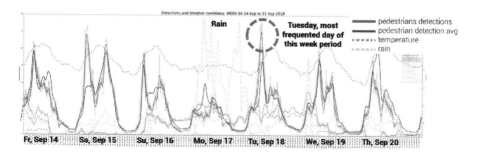

Fig. 10. Pedestrian detections and weather information for Market Square, Pittsburgh PA.

In order to study the effect of urban furniture distribution on pedestrian activity, we changed the location of the chairs and tables. Instead of concentrating all these elements in the central part of the square, we placed them under the trees, closer to the edges of the square. This produced a significant shift in pedestrian activity by redistributing the occupancy between the edges of the square and the center. It means that the difference between central and peripheral use of the square was 4 times higher with this new setting for the urban furniture, rather than 8 times higher as recorded in the previous setting (Fig. 12), while the absolute activity level of the square was similar.

We were also able to observe how the events and venues programmed in the space (i.e. markets, concerts, games and shows for kids, yoga sessions, etc.) have an important effect on pedestrian use. The measurable increase of activity in the space during the last week of August—when daily events are programmed for the summer season—is around 20%. Later on, from a more qualitative point of view, the succession of events generates some degree of synergy which causes a rise in the number of people in the square. This suggests that event frequency (i.e. events programmed over several days) has an important "snow-ball" impact on the square's activity trends (Fig. 13).

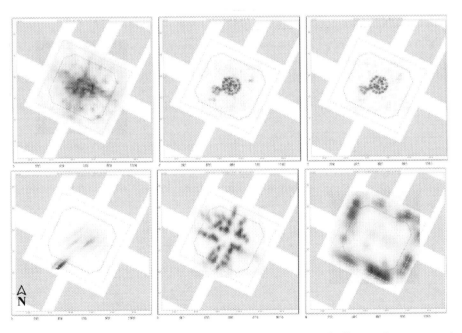

Fig. 11. Spatial distribution of pedestrians, seats, tables, sun umbrellas, market tents, and vehicles on Market Square. Initial setting. Thursday September 6th.

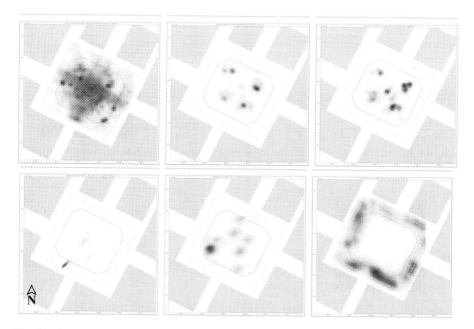

Fig. 12. Spatial distribution of pedestrians, seats, tables, sun umbrellas, market tents, and vehicles on Market Square. After modification of urban furniture. Wednesday September 28th.

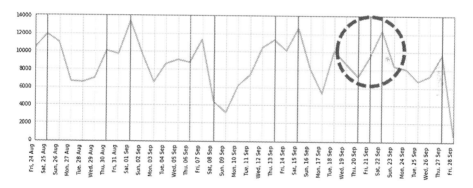

Fig. 13. Total count of people per day during the whole data collection period. Red lines indicate events programmed in the space. (Color figure online)

3 Conclusion

3.1 Contributions

We have introduced a novel framework for urban analysis that leverages computational techniques, along with established urban research methods, to study how people use urban public space. Through three case studies in different urban locations, we have shown how machine learning and computer vision techniques may assist us in producing unprecedently detailed portraits of the relative influence of urban and environmental variables on people's use of public space. As shown above, this framework has the potential to enrich our empirical accounts of urban activity, and has multiple applications in urban planning, design, research, and policy. We thus build on a tradition of quantitative urbanism, updating it to reflect recent developments in computer vision and machine learning. More specifically, we show specific applications of machine learning—from the simplest linear regressions to the use of deep learning techniques—to urban data. We think there is great potential in these methods to make visible trends and patterns hidden in historical data, thus helping ground architectural and urban hypothesis.

An additional contribution of this research is the data themselves. The datasets including the anonymous data for the three case studies can be downloaded from [19]. We invite other urban researchers to study these urban conditions, ask different questions, and perhaps enrich—or challenge—our own interpretations.

3.2   Limitations

Our approach has important limitations. First, it is key to acknowledge that urban life comprises a much richer repertoire of situations and experiences that inevitably escape any computational framework [20]. There is an indescribably finer granularity to urban life, situations, timing, uses, and experiences which exceed the technical formalizations of our framework. For this reason, we think of our framework not as a replacement but rather as a complement to other types of analysis and reflection, including ethnographic engagements across media, and other forms of qualitative research. In the future, we expect to work on these "thicker" urban descriptions combining computational as well as qualitative, ethnographic, and visual data and interpretations.

Second, despite the academic nature of this project, a latent risk in any framework leveraging algorithmic techniques of observation and analysis is that it is misused as a tool of surveillance and/or policing. To minimize this risk, we took measures to prevent the system from capturing data that would enable the identification of individuals. The cameras, for example, were placed at a certain distance from the activity, making identification difficult if not impossible. In addition, the computational techniques employed deliberately focus on patterns of movement and activity, and not on individual behavior. Finally, the data collected is abstract and the source data is disposed immediately after the analyses.

Finally, aside from the non-digital factors considered above, the data currently considered in the framework has important gaps and limitations. There is missing data, as well as limitations on the collected data. There is, for example, an implicit bias in using 2-D analytical tools [18] to the study of a complex 3-D environment. There is room in our field for developing better spatial analysis techniques offering insight into the perception of the space. Our approach to measuring these factors, while somewhat innovative, is the most uncertain.

3.3   Future Work

The methods and evidence described above open questions as well as avenues for future work. On a technical level, improving the computer vision algorithm for extracting features from video frames would yield immediate analytical benefits. Further, adding new detectable features, and active tracking of objects, would enrich the analysis as well as overcome visual occlusions. Similarly, reducing the depth of the network architecture for improving performance, and developing a more precise evaluation method for testing accuracy, would increase the reliability of the results.

Expanding the project to other urban conditions, while refining our repertoire of questions, will offer additional insight, and start to configure a comparative approach to computational urban studies. To achieve this, the technical instruments, frameworks, and processes employed need to be streamlined.

Finally, as indicated above, we are interested in further developing this framework and in combining it with other forms of analysis and media. Our larger goal is to be able to produce "thicker" accounts of urban life, which can serve as reference for urban designers, scholars, and researchers, and which reflect glimpses of the incommensurable spatial and sensorial complexity of urban experience.

Acknowledgements. This research has been possible thanks to the Fulbright Foundation that supported my stay in the United States at the MS in Computational Design at CMU; to R. Delso, I. Romero and A. Gómez as partners for developing the whole computer vision algorithm; and to Metro 21 Institute for Smart Cities at CMU, Heinz Endowments, Pittsburgh Downtown Partnership and Pittsburgh Supercomputing Center for supporting the Market Square implementation in Pittsburgh.

References

1. Arnheim, R.: Art and Visual Perception. University of California Press, Berkeley (1954)
2. Babbie, E.R.: The Practice of Social Research. Wadsworth Cengage, Belmont (2010)
3. Derix, C.: The Space of People in Computation. Archit. Des. **84**, 14–23 (2014)
4. Hillier, B., Leaman, A., Stansall, P., Bedford, M.: Space syntax. Environ. Plan. B **3**, 147–185 (1976)
5. Janofske, E.: Architektur-Räume: Idee und Gestalt bei Hans Scharoun (1984)
6. Li, X., Hijazi, I., Koenig, R., et al.: Assessing essential qualities of urban space with emotional and visual data based on gis technique. ISPRS Int. J. Geo-Inf. **5**, 218 (2016). https://doi.org/10.3390/ijgi5110218
7. Parker, S.P. (ed.): McGraw-Hill Dictionary of Scientific and Technical Terms. McGraw-Hill, New York City (2003)
8. Piaget, J., Inhelder, B.: La représentation de l'espace chez l'enfant. [Representation of space by the child.]. Presses Universitaires de France, 75006 Paris, France (1948)
9. Whyte, W.H.: The Social Life of Small Urban Spaces. Municipal Art Society of New York, USA (1979)
10. Jacobs, J.: The Death and Life of Great American Cities. Vintage Books – Random House, New York (1961)
11. McMahon Catherine in Dutta, A., Tuerk, S., Kubo, M., et al.: A Second Modernism: MIT, Architecture, and the "Techno-Cultural" Moment. MIT Press, Cambridge (2013)

12. Bettencourt, L.M.A.: The Kind of Problem a City is. Santa Fe Institute, Santa Fe NM, USA (2013)
13. Adler, J.: Life in the City is Essentially One Giant Math Problem. Smithsonian mag. (http://www.smithsonianmag.com/innovation/life-in-the-city-is-essentially-one-giant-math-problem-37759041/) (2013)
14. Sisson, P.: Your City is Watching You. Curbed (2018)
15. Pearson, K.: Note on regression and inheritance in the case of two parents. Proc. Roy. Soc. Lond. **58**, 240–242 (1895)
16. Spearman, C.: The proof and measurement of association between two thing. Am. J. Psychol. **15**, 72 (1904). https://doi.org/10.2307/1412159
17. Kendall, M.G.: A new measure of rank correlation. Biometrika **30**, 81 (1938). https://doi.org/10.2307/2332226
18. Ratti, C.: Space syntax: some inconsistences. Environ. Plan. B: Plan. Des. **31**, 487–499 (2004). https://doi.org/10.1069/b3019
19. Argota Sánchez-Vaquerizo, J.: CMU Codelab: Github repository for understanding public space use in market square. In: Github (2018). https://github.com/c0deLab/UDE_MarketSq
20. Mattern, S.: A city is not a computer. Places J. (2017). https://doi.org/10.22269/170207

Visualization of Occupant Behavior in an Open Academic Space Through Image Analysis

Mathew Schwartz[(✉)]

New Jersey Institute of Technology, Newark, NJ 07003, USA
cadop@umich.edu

Abstract. Between agent simulation and circulation diagrams within design pedagogy, the prediction of occupant movement in space is integral to the informed design process. At the same time, trends in higher education have led to more open-ended spaces that are then studied for the unexpected ways in which students collaborate. These studies, by the unpredictable nature, must be done post-occupancy. In this paper, occupant behavior is visualized from an image dataset over a 9 day period in an open student environment. The methods for extracting behavior through this large dataset are presented. The results are then reflected on in regard to the role of circulation diagrams for interior design and spatial planning.

Keywords: Occupant behavior · Circulation · Computation · Post-occupancy evaluation · Interior design

1 Introduction

The use of circulation diagrams can be seen in many stages of design: from planning of space and program [7] to monitoring occupant behavior for egress [6]. The simulation of circulation and occupants in the built environment can provide lifesaving design decisions and changes [1]. A key element in interior design and architecture pedagogy is the drawing of circulation diagrams to describe how occupants will behave in their space. One way of simulating occupant behavior and circulation is with the use of agent based modeling which has ranged from simple localized agent decisions [13] to more complex definitions [10].

While circulation diagrams are an often used visual tool for a designer to demonstrate perceived paths from a building occupant, the visuals generated are more accurately described as design intent than in occupant behavior. Pedagogically, these visual and diagrammatic tools are used to show a student how their design decisions in a spatial context impact human behavior. While occupancy tracking in a residential space has shown the random space utilization that is difficult to predict [4], in a class Studio, students are taught to use the plan to describe entry, path, and goal [7].

© Springer Nature Singapore Pte Ltd. 2019
J.-H. Lee (Ed.): CAAD Futures 2019, CCIS 1028, pp. 311–324, 2019.
https://doi.org/10.1007/978-981-13-8410-3_22

The reality of human behavior in interior spaces is far more complex than what is generalized by these traditional circulation diagrams, in particular due to social and cultural variables [15]. Educational environments in particular demonstrate the unpredictable aspect of occupant behavior. While methods for generating circulation diagrams have been developed with an element of social awareness [8], the mixture of social networks and coincidental connections with adaptable furniture and layouts frequently in open collaborative spaces [2] make models based on general social or visual cues inaccurate. Likewise, the importance of furniture layout and the direct impact on occupants interactions has been studied for decades [11]. The combination of a collaborative and flexible open academic space and the importance of furniture and seating arrangements on occupant interactions provides an important area of observation to better understand how these various configurations can change collaborative work. Due to the infinite combinations of layouts in real-world environments, a system for long term data recording and processing behavior into a consolidated format is important for human interpretation for future modifications of the space, as well as input data for simulation.

To better understand occupant behavior for both refinement of agent based systems and furthering the understanding of how occupants use particular spaces, numerous researchers have conducted studies to track occupants. Although RGB cameras are well established technology, recent research towards extrapolating occupant data has been focused on developing new systems. In [14], multiple depth cameras were used to line a hallway, however this is an expensive proposition with available technology. [4] implemented a similar technique for interior residential monitoring. Combining basic video techniques and human intervention [5] was able to map consumer behavior in a grocery store. In a less intrusive method, [3] uses passive infrared sensors to generate a grid of occupant locations, although this method drastically reduces accuracy. Through combining an RGB camera with recent image processing techniques, a lower cost and informative system that still provides high resolution data for visualizing occupant behavior is demonstrated in this paper.

In this paper, a study of occupant circulation and activity in an open space of a university campus center is presented as a case study for a visualization method and platform for recording occupants. Through a camera installed in the ceiling, a large dataset of occupant behavior was recorded and analyzed. A method for generating what is referred to as motion maps of the space is detailed in the methodology. Understanding the utilization of the space, and the interaction the university community has within it, can provide further insights into both circulation diagram generation and agent based modeling for educational environments. The results show multiple data aggregation and consolidation techniques that can be used with the motion map system.

1.1   Methodology

The experiment was installed in the campus center of the university. The IRB granted an exemption for the recordings on the basis of a public space. Notices around the area of recording were posted, notifying that a study was being conducted to record activity. This area of the campus center was chosen for its open ended definition not connected to any particular college or department. Multiple chairs and tables are available, with some ottomans that are movable (although university notices ask not to move furniture).

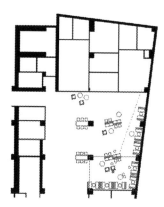

Fig. 1. The floorplan of the campus center space. The red box highlights the view of the camera with the circle as the camera location. The dashed line shows the path of the wiring system into a secured space for data collection. (Color figure online)

In Fig. 1, the floorplan of the surrounding area is shown. Offices and resources such as the Dean of Students are located in this space. The red circle shows the location of the ceiling mounted camera with the red rectangle outlining the camera view. To maintain security of the data without integrating into the networked security camera system a hardwired and local setup was created, with storage of the drives wired into an office space (represented by the dashed line in the figure).

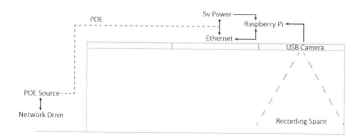

Fig. 2. Experiment setup. The camera module is powered by the Pi3 over USB. A power over ethernet (POE) cable is used to connect the storage device to the Pi3. The same cable splits to a power supply for the Pi3.

A RGB USB camera module (IMX179 image sensor) with a resolution of 3264 × 2448 pixels was used for the recordings. However, due to the high number of image files the stored data 640 × 480 pixels. The camera was installed flush within a ceiling tile and had a 145° field of view. Using this USB camera module, a type of network camera system was created at a low cost with more control. The sensor data is easily retrieved with standard libraries such as opencv, the module itself does not contain any casings so it is easily adaptable to different locations, and the on-board processing for exposure and color can be directly controlled rather through proprietary software. The challenge with this is the length limit for USB cables. While there are methods to extend the length of a USB cable there must be a power supply available at the source end (in this case, where the camera is). A power over ethernet (POE) cable was used to connect the hard drive and power the RPi3 (Fig. 2).

A balance between recording a large amount of data and the difficulty with processing it is a challenge. To track an occupant moving in the scene while reducing the images needed, a rate of 3 frames per second were stored. The recording started on Monday Sept. 24th at 16:00 and continued until Wednesday October 3rd at 03:00 (2018), producing 204 h groups of data. Over this time period, with each 640 × 480 pixel image is 901 kb in size and 2,142,381 images recorded and stored, 1.8 TB of space was used.

Fig. 3. A frame from the ceiling mounted camera recording in the campus center open space.

To understand the way the target space is used by students, two fundamental metrics were created: a method for quantifying and displaying motion within an image, and a way to track an occupant for circulation. Both metrics rely on the fixed camera position and relatively static environment, with the exception of a few moveable pieces of furniture. A sample frame from the study is shown in Fig. 3.

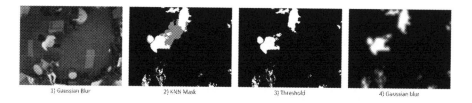

1) Gaussian Blur   2) KNN Mask   3) Threshold   4) Gaussian blur

Fig. 4. Process for generating a motion map frame.

Data processing was done using the Python programming language and OpenCV library. With the fixed camera position, a difference between two image frames (i.e., background subtraction) can be considered a moving occupant. The OpenCV KNN background subtractor method [17] provided the most accurate representation for this study. Additional filtering was applied on the images for each intended use. In Fig. 4, the four step process to generating a given frames motion values is shown.

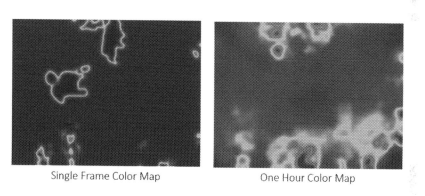

Single Frame Color Map   One Hour Color Map

Fig. 5. Color mapping of (left) a single frame of data and (right) the averaged motion data across one hour (approx. 10000 frames).

As the goal for the motion map is to represent active areas in the space, background subtraction that includes image noise must be removed. The first step is in applying a Gaussian blur to the image. Next the KNN mask is applied, which separates the calculate difference as well as putting the assumed shadow into a grey value. A threshold is applied to remove the shadow, and finally a Gaussian blur is applied to reduce the impact of hard edges and small remaining noise. For each hour of the study the motion map is summed from every frame. The final values for each hour are then mapped to a color scale. The color mapping for the final processed image of Fig. 4 can be seen in Fig. 5. The average value for each pixel across the hour containing the sample frame is shown on the right.

The processing of images for identifying moving objects is largely similar, with a few extra steps, as shown in Fig. 6. At first, a bilateral filter is applied

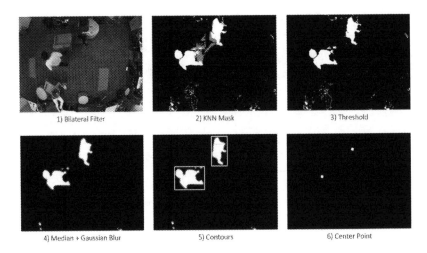

1) Bilateral Filter   2) KNN Mask   3) Threshold

4) Median + Gaussian Blur   5) Contours   6) Center Point

Fig. 6. Process for detecting moving occupants in the frame.

to reduce noise and maintain defining lines. The KNN mask is applied and again the calculated shadow is removed. The goal in this process is to determine the location of a moving person (in relation to the camera). As such, small motions that provide incremental information to the motion map create noise when defining regions of interest. A median and Gaussian blur are applied to the frame, which largely eliminates smaller motion. The OpenCV method for detecting contours [16] is applied. As the contours are indiscriminate of size, a minimum area of 1400 pixels is used as the threshold to store a contour. The center point of the contour is stored and used in another process for tracking.

While plotting the found points over time would provide a general visualization of location history over time, understanding circulation paths would be limited as the association of one point over time would not exist. To track paths taken within the space, initial thresholds are set for the identification of a point to an ID over each frame of data within a day. As an occupant may sit for extended periods of time with little movement, and the process for determining the location of an occupant relies on motion, it is possible multiple frames would pass before a point is associated with that occupant. A threshold of 3000 frames (approximately 16 min) is set as the time limit before an ID is discontinued. On initialization for the day no IDs exist, and the first point found is then associated to a new ID. After the first frame, a point in a frame could either be associated to an existing ID, or a new ID.

To determine if a point should be associated to an existing ID, the distance between the point and the last known point of all IDs that are within the time threshold is checked. For this study, a threshold of 50 pixels between points was applied. However, as an occupant walks across the image frame, the speed of movement impacts the distance between frames. To better estimate the association of the current point to the ID, the vector between the last known point of an ID and its previous one is calculated, and applied with a weight to predict where the ID may be. This predicted point is used for the distance threshold. In many instances, the relation between known IDs and current points is complex, and can be broken into the following cases in each frame.

1. multiple points fall within the threshold of a single ID
2. multiple IDs are within the threshold of a single point
3. multiple IDs are within the threshold of multiple points, with overlapping values.

In these more complex cases the Kuhn-Munkres algorithm [9,12] for assignment problems is used. The matrix used for the algorithm input is constructed as rows of known IDs and columns as points existing in the current frame. The cost factor for an ID to a point is calculated by multiplying weighted values for time and distance.

$$d = d_p^{1/3}$$
$$t = (t_c - t_l)^{1/8} \tag{1}$$
$$C = d \times t$$

Where tc is the current frame, tl is the last frame the ID was associated in, and dp is the distance from the predicted value. The resulting assignments are stored and each ID with a new assignment is updated for its last known frame and position.

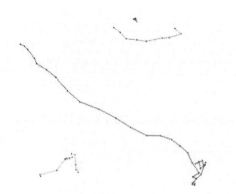

Fig. 7. Tracked path and assignment of IDs over 45 frames of data. Each color represents a unique ID, and each black circle is a motion point defined in the frame. (Color figure online)

An example of the result can be seen in Fig. 7. Four IDs are identified in the span of 45 frames. One ID has very little motion to the point of noise at the top of the image, and one ID is largely static at the bottom of the image.

The frame in which the center points found and shown in Fig. 6 is contained within the path in Fig. 7. The purple path shows an occupant leaving the space, while the orange path shows an occupant walking around an ottoman. The paths associated to the individual IDs are stored, along with each frame and point pair and are used to visualize the results.

2   Results

By aggregating the motion and tracking data detailed in the Methodology section, various map visualization can be generated to understand the space utilization. As the recording of data stopped at 3am, the last day is disregarded for aggregated day based analysis.

2.1   Tracking

For tracking occupants to better understand circulation, the speed of an occupant determines the intensity of the value. Important to note, as an occupant moves out of the scene, their velocity approaches 0 and therefore the extreme edges cannot be considered. When visualizing the aggregated data across the entire study (Fig. 8), a clear relationship of the space emerges. Specifically, the center of the image contains the majority of fast moving subjects. However, as the entrance and exit are on the left side and upper two corners, the assumed paths that are often shown in circulation diagrams do not appear.

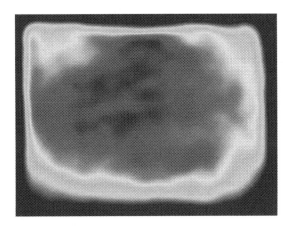

Fig. 8. Velocity visualization for occupant paths across the entire studies dataset.

As the open space was used by a variety of groups, the circulation of the space became nearly indiscriminate of entrance and exit, with occupants moving back and forth between tables. To further inspect the space utilization a list of maps for each day are shown in Fig. 9.

As can be seen, each day in the study has a slightly different mapping. When considering the 3rd of the study (Wednesday), a unique pattern to the velocity

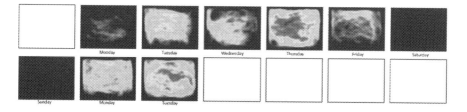

Fig. 9. Intensity map showing velocity of occupant paths.

Fig. 10. Frame of data from the 3rd day of recording. The chairs and table were organized for a group lunch and not moved back, preventing circulation in that area. The image is blurred for protecting occupant identities.

becomes apparent. Upon inspection of images taken in the study (Fig. 10), occupants moved furniture to eat in a group setting, blocking an area used in other days for circulation.

The final velocity based map is broken into hourly data across the study (i.e., the aggregate of all 09:00–10:00 in one image, etc.) for Fig. 11. While each image is normalized within the set, some faint details of occupants circulating can be seen at 06:00 and increasing from 07:00.

2.2   Motion Map

A key insight to the space utilization is provided by the generation of motion maps. Unlike a metric mapping the location of occupants over time, the motion map specifically shows physical activity that occurs. Therefore, a student sitting at a table alone and reading a book generates a lower scoring motion map than two people playing a board game. Similarly, an exam period where multiple students are studying would have a different motion map than a conference group doing a meet and greet. Likewise, a person sleeping in a chair or on a couch provides little impact on a motion map, while logging occupant location

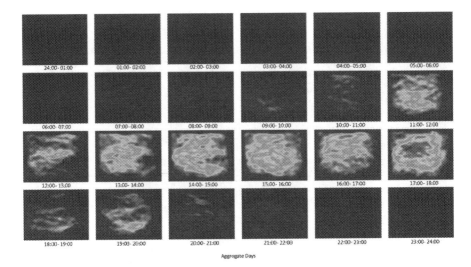

Fig. 11. Velocity paths aggregated by hours across the study.

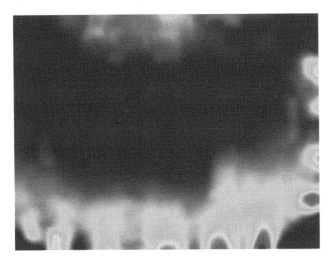

Fig. 12. The motion map generated from all data recorded during the study.

or utilization times of a chair would be greatly impacted. The fundamental difference in this metric belongs to the encouragement of collaborative spaces common in modern educational environments.

In Fig. 12, the motion map of the space over the multi day recording period is shown. When compared to the view of the environment shown in Fig. 3, it becomes apparent the bottom corner generates the highest rate of activity. Notably, this map of motion shows a near inverse of the previous maps of velocity, while they rely on different calculations. The motion map does not consider the speed of motion, only the existence of it. When compared to the velocity visualization it becomes apparent that the middle space is largely left empty and mostly used for circulation.

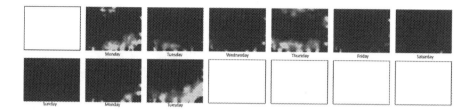

Fig. 13. Motion maps generated for each day of the study. Data was aggregated for each hour of the day. The maps were normalized across the study.

When aggregating data into days, logical trends can be seen. For example, there is a drastic reduction in activity on Saturday and Sunday (Fig. 13). Also of note is the difference in space utilization between the same day of different weeks (i.e., the Monday and Tuesday pairs). In comparison to Fig. 9, both have low activity on the weekend, with some circulation being shown and a small amount of space utilization in the lower seating area.

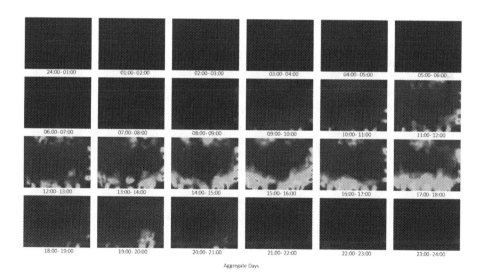

Fig. 14. Motion maps for each hour recorded in the study. Multiple days are represented within each image and normalized across the entire dataset.

By aggregating data hourly, each hour is comprised of 9 samples (one for each day of the study). The amount of activity and space utilization within a day can be easily seen. Through Fig. 14 it is clear the space has the least occupant motion from 21:00 to 09:00. Likewise, the peak of activity in the space occurs between 13:00 and 18:00. Furthermore, the small seating area in the top middle of the recording space is used in relation to the other seating areas. Further examination between the tracking paths and the hourly data could provide insights as the reason.

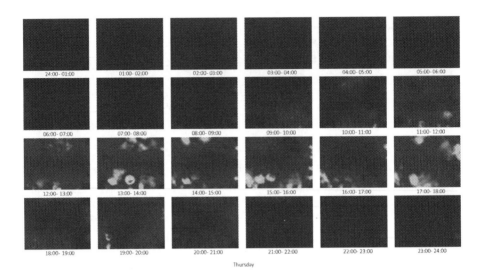

Fig. 15. An hourly motion map representation for a Thursday recorded in the study. The values are normalized for the day.

By examining the hourly data of a specific day, a higher bias to the data is visible, with more occupant specific behaviors appearing. From 09:00 to 12:00, Fig. 15 shows three clusters appearing over time. As the data is aggregated within this specific day (Thursday) and within the corresponding hour group, areas of motion activity that exist between frames are likely continuous. Importantly, the isolated regions that develop over the day suggest groupings of occupants that are socially connected. Similarly, the distance between each cluster can suggest some level of avoidance by each group. Further analysis of the dataset could help in understanding the dynamic between separate groups.

3   Discussion

The work presented here demonstrates a few initial insights as to the space utilization of an open and ill-defined collaborative educational environment. While others have used depth cameras to record and be able to extract similar information the cost of the devices are significantly more expensive. Furthermore, isolated case studies of a single occupant [4] or controlled hallway [14] have made the recording of occupant movement more straightforward. In this paper, the real-world case study demonstrated the significant challenges to monitoring flexible environments used for a variety of purposes. For example, the ability to move furniture makes it difficult to simply apply a background separation from an ideal state. However, through the techniques of motion mapping and abstraction from the activities over a significant timespan, post occupancy evaluation and understanding of the space utilization can be gained.

The motion mapping, through its simplicity, is shown to be a robust tool. The tracking of individual occupants has remained a challenge. While detection of a moving occupant has been demonstrated, the assignment of unique IDs is limited to travel within a specific course of travel as the occupant themselves are not recognized. Further work in the labeling of individual users through face or image recognition would allow further metrics and insights to be gained. This aspect is vital for the understanding of social arrangements in the space to identify when the open environment is being used for collaboration, as this is highly suggestive in the way occupants move within the space. Additionally, the logical insights seen, such as a reduction in motion depending on time of day, could be more accurately understood as an occupant number causing the reduction or the time of day reducing actual motion. Finally, additional sensors, such as microphones, could be used to correlate against the motion map and provide insight into the relationship between noise and activity in the space.

Acknowledgements. I thank Richard O'Brien from the Digital Learning and Technology Support department in NJIT for assisting in the setup of the networked hard drive for storing recorded data. Additionally, the support of the Facilities department and Murray Center for Women in Technology was instrumental in allowing and assisting with the camera installation. Finally, Florencia Pozo, who worked on early versions of the literature review.

The study was reviewed by the NJIT IRB: Number F373-18.

References

1. Exodus Software. https://fseg.gre.ac.uk/exodus/
2. Barritt, M., et al.: Observations from an open, connected, and evolving learning environment the improvisational, risk-taking, and risky culture of openness, evolution, and connection most define design Lab 1 and its ability to support effective, authentic learning and engage (2013). www.scup.org/phe. https://search.proquest.com/openview/7669d0f141710ad071745c2580a25ff3/1?cbl=47536&pq-origsite=gscholar
3. Berry, J., Park, K.: A passive system for quantifying indoor space utilization (2017). http://papers.cumincad.org/cgi-bin/works/Show?acadia17_138
4. Dziedzic, J., Yan, D., Novakovic, V.: Occupant migration monitoring in residential buildings with the use of a depth registration camera. Procedia Eng. **205**, 1193–1200 (2017). https://doi.org/10.1016/J.PROENG.2017.10.352. https://www.sciencedirect.com/science/article/pii/S1877705817350270
5. Gil, J., Tobari, E., Lemlij, M., Rose, A., Penn, A.R.: The differentiating behaviour of shoppers: clustering of individual movement traces in a supermarket. Royal Institute of Technology (KTH) (2009)

6. Groner, N.E.: A decision model for recommending which building occupants should move where during fire emergencies. Fire Saf. J. **80**, 20–29 (2016). https://doi.org/10.1016/J.FIRESAF.2015.11.002. https://www.sciencedirect.com/science/article/pii/S0379711215300412

7. Hing, A.: Understanding the plan: a studio experience. J. Inter. Des. **31**(3), 10–20 (2006). https://doi.org/10.1111/j.1939-1668.2006.tb00528.x. http://doi.wiley.com/10.1111/j.1939-1668.2006.tb00528.x

8. Kontovourkis, O.: Design of circulation diagrams in macro-scale level based on human movement behavior modeling. Autom. Constr. **22**, 12–23 (2012). https://doi.org/10.1016/J.AUTCON.2011.10.002. https://www.sciencedirect.com/science/article/pii/S0926580511001944

9. Kuhn, H.W.: The Hungarian method for the assignment problem. Naval Res. Logist. Q. **2**(1–2), 83–97 (1955). https://doi.org/10.1002/nav.3800020109. http://doi.wiley.com/10.1002/nav.3800020109

10. Langevin, J., Wen, J., Gurian, P.L.: Simulating the human-building interaction: development and validation of an agent-based model of office occupant behaviors. Build. Environ. **88**, 27–45 (2015). https://doi.org/10.1016/J.BUILDENV.2014.11.037. https://www.sciencedirect.com/science/article/pii/S0360132314004090

11. Mehrabian, A., Diamond, S.G.: Seating arrangement and conversation. Sociometry **34**(2), 281 (1971). https://doi.org/10.2307/2786417. https://www.jstor.org/stable/2786417?origin=crossref

12. Munkres, J.: Algorithms for the assignment and transportation problems. J. Soc. Ind. Appl. Math. **5**(1), 32–38 (1957). https://doi.org/10.1137/0105003. http://epubs.siam.org/doi/10.1137/0105003

13. Narahara, T.: The Space Re-Actor : walking a synthetic man through architectural space (2007). https://dspace.mit.edu/handle/1721.1/39255

14. Seer, S., Brändle, N., Ratti, C.: Kinects and human kinetics: a new approach for studying pedestrian behavior. Transp. Res. Part C: Emerg. Technol. **48**, 212–228 (2014). https://doi.org/10.1016/J.TRC.2014.08.012. https://www.sciencedirect.com/science/article/pii/S0968090X14002289

15. Spankie, R.: Drawing Out the Interior. AVA/Academia (2009). https://westminsterresearch.westminster.ac.uk/item/90zqv/drawing-out-the-interior

16. Suzuki, S., Be, K.: Topological structural analysis of digitized binary images by border following. Comput. Vis. Graph. Image Process. **30**(1), 32–46 (1985). https://doi.org/10.1016/0734-189X(85)90016-7. https://www.sciencedirect.com/science/article/pii/0734189X85900167

17. Zivkovic, Z., van der Heijden, F.: Efficient adaptive density estimation per image pixel for the task of background subtraction. Pattern Recogn. Lett. **27**(7), 773–780 (2006). https://doi.org/10.1016/J.PATREC.2005.11.005. https://www.sciencedirect.com/science/article/pii/S0167865505003521

Fabrication and Materialization

Pneumatic Origami Joints

A 3D Printed Flexible Joint

Heng Lu[1], Daekwon Park[2(✉)], Chen Liu[1], Guohua Ji[1(✉)],
and Ziyu Tong[1(✉)]

[1] Nanjing University, Nanjing, China
childswim@gmail.com, lc-nju@outlook.com,
{jgh, tzy}@nju.edu.cn
[2] Syracuse University, Syracuse, USA
dpark103@syr.edu

Abstract. This paper describes the design and fabrication process of an adaptive joint using foldable 3D printed structures encased in heat-sealed synthetic polymer films (e.g. airtight plastic casing). The proposed joint can be pneumatically actuated using the airtight casing, and the shape of the deformation can be controlled using origami-inspired 3D printed structures. A zigzag-gap microstructure is designed for the connection portion of the origami structure inside the joint, in order that the rigid 3D printed material (PLA) acquires properties of mollusk material, such as flexibility and softness. Finally, the paper presents some applications adopting pneumatic origami joints which can interact with people or adapting indoor environment, and compares the advantages of this pneumatic technology with mechanical technology.

Keywords: 3D printing · Adaptive joint · Pneumatic architecture · Origami structure

1 Introduction

The concept of pneumatic architecture appeared in the 1960s with the interests in creating large-scale air-supported structures [1]. This system enabled the construction of lightweight buildings with extremely large-span and temporary buildings that can be inflated or deflated in a relatively short amount of time. For instance, the Beijing Olympic Games Water Cube's envelop consists of ETFE air pillow membrane (Fig. 1 (a)), with a total area of 100,000 square meters. The entire building has a light transmission of 94% and is resistant to UV and noise [2].

More recently, pneumatic architecture is designed to be interactive or responsive with its physical environment. In this case, pneumatic components are designed to change with physical factors such as sunlight, temperature, humidity and airflow to achieve a relatively stable interior environment [3]. Furthermore, with the rapidly evolving technologies in the industry, human interaction with the built environment is becoming more accessible and achievable [4]. Components that change according to human behavior can create a sense of communication and interaction, adapting and

© Springer Nature Singapore Pte Ltd. 2019
J.-H. Lee (Ed.): CAAD Futures 2019, CCIS 1028, pp. 327–340, 2019.
https://doi.org/10.1007/978-981-13-8410-3_23

responding to human behavior. In this context, the pneumatic architectures including adaptive building skins and breathing facades are focusing on human interactions with its built environment [5–7].

Origami is a handcrafted art with centuries of history that folds flat paper into three-dimensional object and creates some structural stability. The origami structure is inspired by this art and is widely used in engineering, machinery, aviation, architecture and other fields. In the architecture sector, origami structures can provide stability over large spans. The Yokohama International Passenger Terminal designed by Japan's Foreign Office Architects is a famous case (Fig. 1(b)). Its inner roof is made up of folded diamond-shaped units, and the shape of the entire roof can be folded from a single piece of paper [8]. This origami structure is often used as a structural form to withstand more loads and remain stable. There is another application, for example, the Festival Hall of the Tiroler Festspiele (Fig. 1(c)), designed by Delugan Meissl Associated Architects, using origami inspired geometry in the exterior shape and interior spaces, making the building more versatile and dynamic. In these cases, origami inspired geometry is used primary as a means for generating and rationalizing complex architectural form.

(a)　　　　　　　　　　(b)　　　　　　　　　　(c)

a. ETFE air pillow membrance of Water Cube *(from: www.cscec.com.cn)*
b. Yokohama International Passenger Terminal origami structure *(from: www.archdaily.com)*
c. Festival Hall of the Tiroler Festspiele *(from: www.archdaily.com)*

Fig. 1. Pneumatic architecture and origami-inspired architectures

Origami structures also enable space and structure to expand or contract. In 1961, the Spanish architect Pinero E.P. successfully applied the concept of folding structure to the design of movable theaters [9] (Fig. 2(a)). In the aerospace field, the Miura origami structure invented by Miura Koryo from University of Tokyo provided a novel solution to the solar cell expansion problem [10] (Fig. 2(b)). In these cases, origami structures are effective in achieving flexibility and adaptability for architecture and mechanical applications.

Li from Harvard University had conducted explorations of the pneumatic origami muscles and their movements in the field of machinery [11] (Fig. 2(c)). Based on their research, we adopted origami structures as joints for adaptable and flexible architectures. These joints are fabricated by additive manufacturing technology (3D printing), which enables mass customization of intricate components. The final pavilion and shading system use the origami joints as connections of common materials, and the movements of structures are actuated by air suction to achieve flexibility and adaptation as pneumatic architectures.

In this context, the following will describe the design, fabrication, kinematics and applications of an origami inspired joint system.

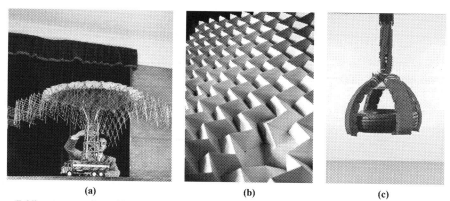

(a)   **(b)**   **(c)**

a. Folding structure of movable theatre *(from: www.arquitecturaviva.com)*
b. Miura Folding Origami *(from: mappingignorance.org)*
c. Pneumatic Origami Muscles *(from: phys.org)*

Fig. 2. Origami structure studies in other areas

2 Pneumatic Origami Joint

Pneumatic Origami Joint can generate three types of motions: stretch, bending and compound movement. To achieve the targeted motion, the geometry of the 3D printed joints is designed to deform in specific ways during inflation and deflation of the airtight casing (Fig. 3).

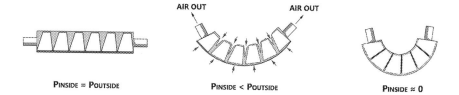

AIR OUT   AIR OUT

$P_{INSIDE} = P_{OUTSIDE}$ $P_{INSIDE} < P_{OUTSIDE}$ $P_{INSIDE} \approx 0$

P_{INSIDE}: **Air pressure inside the airbag**
$P_{OUTSIDE}$: **Standard atmospheric pressure**

Fig. 3. Airtight casing encapsulating principle

2.1   Stretching Motion Joint

In stretching motion, we fold the cardboard strip back and forth into a wavy shape. After the air in the bag is pulled out, the cardboard will be folded along the creases and drag the end of the airbag. Conversely, when the bag is inflated, the cardboard will stretch. The length of the stretch in this type of motion is affected by the distance of the adjacent creases. However, the recovery performance of this joint is poor, and it is difficult to recover by itself when there is no force at the end (Fig. 4).

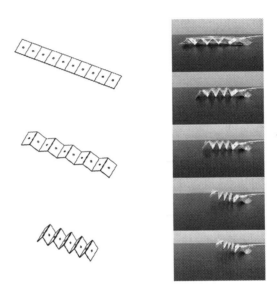

Fig. 4. Stretching motion joint

2.2   Bending Motion Joint

The bending motion joint is based on the stretching motion. When the origami structure in the stretching motion is folded to some extent, fixing bottom of the structure. The origami structure inside is similar to a truss structure. In this case, each of the origami units can be regarded as triangular prisms and when they are squeezed, the volume can be compressed only by reducing the angle between adjacent triangular prisms. A bending motion is achieved in this way (Fig. 5). The bending shape is related to the angle of the triangles in cross section.

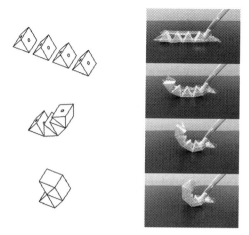

Fig. 5. Bending motion joint

In the following research, we experiment different triangular prism units and test their performance at variable angles. Similarly, the bent body can ensure a good bending effect when air out, but the recovery performance is also poor.

2.3   Compound Motion Joint

The compound motion joint is based on the bending motion. It can be viewed as a superposition of bending in two dimensions. The shape of the unit transforms from triangular prism to quadrangular prism and the intersection part transforms from an edge to a point. These allow the joint to not only have a contracted space in the vertical direction but also bend in the horizontal direction. The two motions superimposed produce the rotating motion.

In this combination, there is a problem that when a sufficient number of units are reached, the joint will rotate back to the starting position and meet the first unit. Therefore, in order to achieve a general rotation such as a space spiral, it is also necessary to adjust the combination. When the sum of the angles in vertical direction between the unit blocks is greater than 180°, the next unit block needs to be flipped back and forth in horizontal direction. In this way, the joint could continue to rotate forward (Fig. 6).

Two variables could control the shape of the compound motion joint. The angles between the units in the vertical direction determine the height of the space spiral and the angles in the horizontal direction determine the diameter of the spiral. Both of them are positively related.

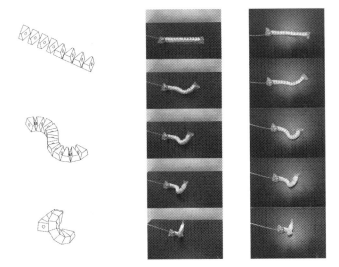

Fig. 6. Compound motion joint

2.4   Bending Curvature Simulation

Bending motion joint has many variants, and complex bending curvatures can be simulated by combinations of different triangular prisms. The characteristics of the bending motion joints are determined by the angle between the two adjacent units of the origami structure and the length of each unit. By changing the angle between the units, you can change the amplitude of the bending. When the angle is smaller, the amplitude of the bending is smaller. Conversely, the angle of the rotation will be larger (Fig. 7).

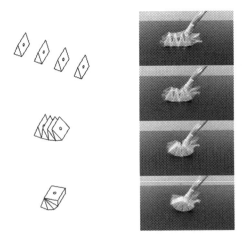

Fig. 7. Smaller angles bending motion joint variant

The length of each unit affects the curvature of the joint. A long unit block can be seen as a number of short unit blocks that are closely attached together at zero degree. Thus, the curvature of the entire joint will be smaller at the longer units and larger at the shorter ones (Fig. 8).

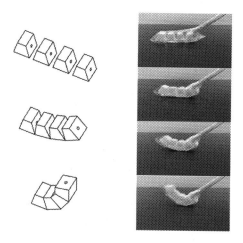

Fig. 8. Longer units bending motion joint variant

According to the above two characteristics, by changing the angles inside the bending joint and the length of the units, it is possible to simulate bending motion of different curvatures (Fig. 9).

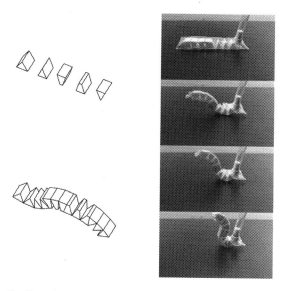

Fig. 9. Complex combination of the bending motion joint variant

3   Fabrication

3.1   Additive Manufacture Technology

The joints are fabricated by Addictive Manufacture technology. There are several reasons for using 3D printing techniques: First, 3D printing manufacturing is more customizable. Different joints will be located in different parts of the building, and their movement, bending amplitude and intensity can be completely different. 3D printing technology can adapt to this feature very well. Secondly, the rigid 3D printed components can increase the strength of the joints. Because each joint is in a stressed position and needs to move the entire structure, the material needs to have a certain strength and durability. At the same time, the pneumatic joints need to withstand the atmospheric pressure under vacuum condition, which also increase the requirement of the strength. Finally, the production process is simplified and the efficiency is raised by using this technology. 3D printing is generally processed directly by using only one material, and if a joint is made by ordinary materials, various materials combinations are required to achieve complex movements. If the different material connections are not designed properly, the joint's usability will be reduced.

However, the use of additive manufacture technology to fabricate joints still requires solving some technical problems. The most critical one is how to make a rigid material like PLA or ABS, be bent to some extent like a mollusk material in the integrated printing process. The project achieves this target by designing the microstructure of the joint to make the rigid material have the characteristics of a flexible material.

3.2   Microstructure

The design was inspired by a manufacturing method that transforms wood into a flexible material. The wood board or the wood strip in the origin state is difficult to complete a flexible bending at a large angle, and it can be regarded as a rigid material. Serge Lunin and Christian Kuhn from the Zurich University of the Arts created a flexible wood that can be bent widely by designing the microstructure of the wood [12]. They achieved this flexibility by cutting zigzag incisions on a wooden board (Fig. 10). This flexibility occurs in the opposite direction of the incisions, and in the direction of the incisions, the stability of the wood as a rigid material itself is maintained. This flexible wood has been used in wall and ceiling of the building.

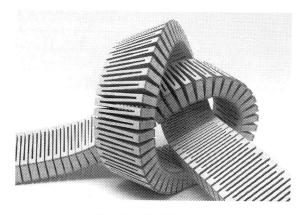

Fig. 10. Flexible wood

By changing the microstructure of this flexible wood, softness and bending direction of the wood can be adjusted. The deeper and larger the incisions of the zigzag are, the higher the softness of the wood can be achieved. If the incisions are sparse, the inherent hardness of the wood becomes more pronounced. At the same time, the zigzag incisions can be processed simultaneously in both the lateral and longitudinal directions of the wood board, so that the entire panel can be bent in three-dimension.

This fabrication methodology helps us investigate the optimum geometric configuration of the 3D printed structures to enhance the mechanical and kinematic performance of each joint. The main body of the origami structure requires a rigid material as support, and all connections require flexibility to achieve bending motion. If two materials are used separately, the origami structure will lose its integrity, resulting in a decrease in structural stiffness. In response to this, at the junction of the two adjacent units, the microstructure is designed as the zigzag gaps like the flexible wood.

However, unlike flexible wood, this structure is designed in the beginning and fabricated directly by 3D printing, rather than cutting incision in an integrated block. The 3D printing zigzag structures acquire higher strength and toughness than the method of cutting or milling, and also save materials and processing time. On the other hand, according to different requirements, the gap density and size of this structure can also be flexibly adjusted. For joints with small angles between units, the density of the gaps can be sparser and the depth can be shallower. On the contrary, joints with larger angles require tighter gaps. This design has different connection microstructures for different joints requirements to ensure good mechanical properties (Fig. 11).

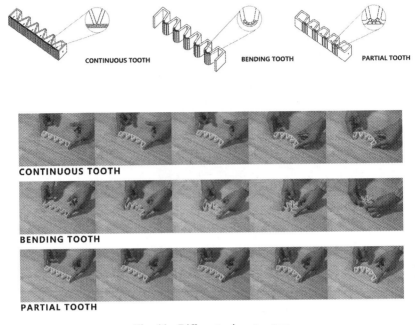

Fig. 11. Different microstructure

3.3   Airbag

A variety of choices for the material of the sealed bag have been tested. The materials of common plastic sealing bags people use in daily life are mainly polyethylene, polypropylene, polyester and nylon. The requirements of the airbag are strong enough to sustain barometric pressure and cannot have deformation when being stretched. Thermoplastic PE material (polyethylene) is selected as the airbag material according to the requirements.

The airtightness of the cavity is a key requirement for pneumatic systems. Due to the size limitations of our heat seals, we adjust the joints within the allowable range of dimensions. A joint airbag fabrication requires the preparation of the corresponding area of sealing film according to the size of the origami structure, and then double sealing to ensure good air tightness.

4   Application

4.1   Pavilion

Pneumatic joints can provide flexibility and adaptability to structures without relying on complex mechanical components. It is possible to configure the three types of joints to create adaptive structures with a wide range of movements. Furthermore, the capability to dynamically control the actuation (e.g., response time) provides opportunities for interactive and responsive building applications.

To test the Pneumatic Origami Joints in real-world conditions and scale, the joints are applied to a pavilion design (Fig. 12). The pavilion consists of six sets of PVC tube frames, with white elastic fabric as a covering. The joint between the pipes uses the bending motion joints, and the cloth is pulled by stretching motion joints to form a space (Fig. 13). As the bending motion joints are actuated, the PVC frames deform in various configurations. The space under the elastic fabric changes in response to the frame configurations (Fig. 14). The actuation of the stretching motion joints can further refine the shape of the elastic fabric.

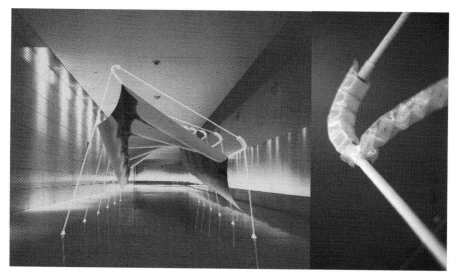

Fig. 12. Interactive pneumatic joints pavilion with its partial frame

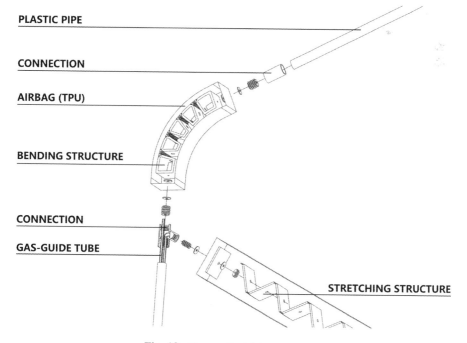

PLASTIC PIPE

CONNECTION

AIRBAG (TPU)

BENDING STRUCTURE

CONNECTION

GAS-GUIDE TUBE

STRETCHING STRUCTURE

Fig. 13. Pneumatic joint axonometry

Fig. 14. Movement simulation

4.2   Building Shading System

At present, shutter shading is the main method to adjust indoor light environment. This method requires manual pulling of the rope to produce a fixed angle of the blade to obtain different amounts of light. Although this method is simple, it cannot cope with large-scale glass curtain walls. At the same time, such a system cannot automatically adjust the light environment according to the complex needs of the indoor environment. Another way is to automatically adjust the blinds through a complex mechanical system. However, the conventional gear transmission structure has the problems such as a large self-weight, high price, high maintenance cost, and noise during operation.

The pneumatic shading system is light-weight, easily installable, and low-maintenance. The stretching motion joint is built in behind the louvers, and the opening or closing of the louvers can be realized by air pressure. Meanwhile, the pneumatic system uses the solenoid valves to control the airflow in the gas-guide tubes, combined with the sensor to detect the indoor light and heat environment. In this way, the independent and controllable adjustment of each group of louvers can be realized (Fig. 15).

Fig. 15. Pneumatic shading system

5 Discussion

With the gradual development of new technologies, flexible materials have become more and more popular, because of their excellent performance. Combined with pneumatic technology, it can achieve most of the functions of traditional mechanical systems. Moreover, compared with mechanical system, the flexible material occupies less space and light-weight. Moreover, the price of pneumatic system is comparatively low, and the maintenance is relatively easy. Another significant advantage is that it can carry greater loads at the same quality as the mechanical structure. Finally, the pneumatic joints have higher mechanical efficiency than the mechanical transmission system, and the energy loss is small during the movement. In the field of human-computer interaction, lightweight materials and flexible systems are also increasingly used because it reduces the damage that users may experience when colliding with other components.

The origami pneumatic joint research still has areas for improvements. First, the strength of the joints needs to be increased to make it able to withstand heavier loads. At present, origami pneumatic joints can only be used for the connection of temporary architecture with lightweight materials. Its strength can be enhanced by using hydraulic driving, which provides stronger power, and a tighter and stronger material as an airbag cover. This requires more experiments to explore. Second, the connection between joints and common materials requires optimization. The existing connection method is only applicable to lightweight materials such as plastic tubes. Finally, the design of the gas-guide tubes path is also critical. Excessive paths can make the entire structure complex and redundant, while too few air tubes can make the pneumatic structure less powerful. Reasonable design of its path deserves further study.

6 Conclusion and Future Work

This paper introduces the design and fabrication process of an origami pneumatic joint for flexible architecture applications. The movement of the joint is generated by the change of the air pressure and the configurations of the internal origami structure. Through the microstructure design of the connection point in the origami structure, the rigid material (PLA) gains flexibility, making it possible for 3D printing technology to produce the pneumatic joint.

By implementing pneumatic joints only to the nodes of architecture and using common materials like tubes and membranes for the rest of the structure, adaptive or interactive architecture becomes affordable and easier to construct. The pneumatic actuation method is safe, convenient and controllable, avoiding using large-scale mechanical devices as well.

The two design cases discussed in the previous section is the application of pneumatic flexible joints in building. Although the field is still in its infancy with material research and system design needs to be developed, it is apparent that pneumatic flexible joints can replace many of the traditional kinetic joints in the future.

As future works we plan to investigate optimization of the system in order to enhance the strength and durability of the joint. Furthermore, scale-up study is needed to meet extensive usage requirement.

Acknowledgements. The research was conducted as a workshop project of the NJU IPTP program, under the supervision of Prof. Daekwon Park from MATR (Material Archi-Tectonic Research) Lab & Studio in Syracuse University, Huayin Zhong, research assistant of NJU, Guohua Ji, dean of NJU and Ziyu Tong, director of Digital Fabrication and Construction Lab in NJU. This research was also supported by National Natural Science Foundation of China (51578277).

References

1. Herzog, T.: Pneumatic structures. A hand book of inflatable architecture. J. Soc. Archit. Hist. **37**(3), 222–223 (1976)
2. Zheng, F., Zhang, X.: Water cube. National aquatics centre. Archit. J. **6**, 36–47 (2008)
3. Velikov, K., Thün, G., O'Malley, M.: PneuSystems: cellular pneumatic envelope assemblies. In: ACADIA 2014: Design Agency, Proceedings of the 34th Annual Conference of the Association for Computer Aided Design in Architecture, pp. 435–444 (2014)
4. Daniel, F., Ryan, G., Kathy, V.: Pneuma-technics: methods for soft adaptive environments. In: ACADIA 2105: Computational Ecologies: Design in the Anthropocene, pp. 274–283 (2015)
5. Mendelez, F., Gannon, M., Jacobson-Weaver, Z., Toulkeridou, V.: Adaptive pneumatic frameworks. In: ACADIA 2014: Design Agency, pp. 427–434 (2014)
6. Park, D., Martin, B.: Designing biologically-inspired smart building systems: processes and guidelines. Int. J. Archit. Comput. **4**, 437–463 (2013)
7. Hinz, K., Alvarenga, J., Aizenberg, J., Bechthold, M., Kim, P., Park, D.: Pneumatically adaptive light modulation system (PALMS) for buildings. Mater. Des. **152**, 156–167 (2018)
8. Foreign Office Architects: Yokohama International Port Terminal, AA Files, no. 29, pp. 14–21 (1995)
9. Pinero, E.P.: Expandable space structures. Progress. Archit. **43**(6), 154–155 (1962)
10. Miura, K.: Method of packaging and deployment of large membranes in space. Institute of Space and Astronautical Science Report (1985)
11. Li, S., Vogt, D.M., Rus, D.: Fluid-driven origami-inspired artificial muscles. Proc. Natl. Acad. Sci. U.S.A. **114**(50), 13132–13137 (2017)
12. Serge, L., Christian, K.: Two-dimensional component (2009)

Robot-Aided Fabrication of Light-Weight Structures with Sheet Metal Expansion

Elif Erdine(✉), Giulio Gianni, Angel Fernando Lara Moreira,
Alvaro Lopez Rodriguez, Yutao Song, and Alican Sungur

Architectural Association (AA) School of Architecture, London, UK
{elif.erdine, giulio.giannil, lara-moreira,
Lopez-Rodriguez, alican.sungur}@aaschool.ac.uk,
yutaosong@yahoo.com

Abstract. This paper presents a novel approach for the creation of metal light-weight self-supporting structures through the employment of metal kerfing and robotic sheet panel expansion. Research objectives focus on the synthesis of material behavior on a local scale and the structural performance on a global scale via advanced computational and robotic methods. There are inherent structural properties to expanded metal sheets which can be employed to achieve an integrated building system without the need for a secondary supporting structure. A computational workflow that integrates Finite Element Analysis, geometrical optimization, and robotic toolpath planning has been developed. This workflow is informed by the parameters of material experimentation on sheet metal kerfing and robotic sheet metal expansion on the local panel scale. The proposed methodology is applied on a range of panels with a custom-built robotic fabrication setup for the design, fabrication, and assembly of a one-to-one scale working prototype.

Keywords: Robotic fabrication · Robotic sheet metal expansion · Light-weight structure · Metal kerfing · Metal expansion

1 Introduction

The research presented in this paper aims to outline an innovative strategy for the creation of metal lightweight self-supporting structures through the employment of metal kerfing and robotic sheet metal expansion. Research objectives focus on the synthesis of material behavior on a local scale and structural performance on a global scale via advanced computational and robotic methods.

Traditional sheet forming techniques employ incremental deformations to a sheet until it is formed into its final shape, and the forming tool can be attached to a CNC machine or a robotic arm. Robotic metal sheet forming opens new opportunities in the design and fabrication of component-based aggregations that can be facilitated for cladding purposes or spatial enclosures. The versatility, multi-axis freedom, precision, and adaptable programmability of a generic robotic arm introduces new approaches and techniques to the metal sheet forming process [1]. By the careful correlation of form-finding techniques and various analysis methods, structural, environmental, and other

© Springer Nature Singapore Pte Ltd. 2019
J.-H. Lee (Ed.): CAAD Futures 2019, CCIS 1028, pp. 341–355, 2019.
https://doi.org/10.1007/978-981-13-8410-3_24

critical performative properties can be articulated via robotic metal sheet forming. The investigation of performance facilitates the consideration of pattern that moves away from sole ornamentation towards processes that trigger pattern formation in natural systems [2].

The research presented focuses on the geometrical, structural and material properties within the agency of robotic sheet metal expansion. Expanded metal surfaces have gained widespread use in architecture, and they are typically adopted as facades, cladding panels, rainscreen systems, and in ventilation units. Double-skin load-bearing structures, typically referred to as "stressed skins", have widespread use in the automotive and aerospace industries where monocoque chassis and airplane wings make structural use of the exterior skin as well as the internal network of ribs to create structural elements with high flexural stiffness and low weight per unit area. A typical stressed-skin section works like a conventional I-beam, where the top and bottom skins bear tensile and compressive forces, and the expanded cones transfer shear forces, enabling the two skins to work in a composite manner [3] (Fig. 1).

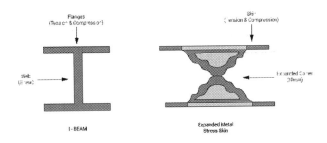

Fig. 1. Conventional I-beam versus stressed skin.

There are several precedent research studies and explorations that have undertook different aspects of the outlined research area. One such research focuses on the failure mechanism of expanded metal tubes under axial crushing [4], investigating the structural behavior of expanded sheet tubes without elaborating on architectural applications. Other research investigations have concentrated on the design, manufacturing and construction concept for self-supporting lightweight freeform structures that integrates load-bearing, functional properties and façade design into one unit, using a double-skin structure (RWTH Aachen University) [5], as well as the development of a modelling approach for the design and fabrication of an incrementally formed, stressed skin metal structure (Stressed Skins, CITA, The Royal Danish Academy of Fine Arts) [6]. In both cases the stressed skin is produced by bolting together panels which have been formed using Incremental Sheet Metal Forming techniques.

The research described in this paper aims to propose a holistic approach that facilitates the structural performance of expanded metal sheets for the design, robotic fabrication, and construction of light-weight and self-supporting structures (Fig. 2). There are inherent structural properties to expanded metal sheets which can be employed to achieve an integrated building system capable of modulating and responding to various environmental conditions without the need for a secondary supporting structure.

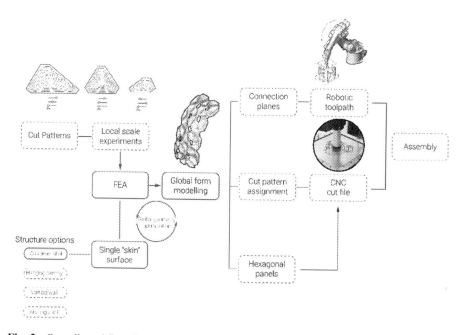

Fig. 2. Overall workflow for the design and fabrication of sheet metal panels with kerfing and robotic expansion.

The one-to-one scale prototype presented in this paper is a case study to test the proposed methodology through the design and construction of a freeform structure with the employment of metal kerfing and robotic sheet metal expansion. The structure lies in a bounding box of 1,300 mm width, 1,665 mm length, and 2,290 mm height. The location of the case study is the outdoor area of Architectural Association (AA) School of Architecture, London. The research is conducted as part of an international workshop, AA Summer DLAB.

2   Preliminary Experimentation and System Development

2.1   Expanded Sheet Metal as Stressed Skin

The many advantages of linearly expanding single metal sheets are hindered by a series of factors, namely the complex connections the raised edges a mesh presents, a limited load carrying capacity when it comes to covering large spans, and their inadequacy for surfaces with complex curvatures. A novel configuration of strands arranged concentrically and yielding expanded "cone" shapes with the potential to be configured as a double-layer structure will be investigated in the following sections (Fig. 3).

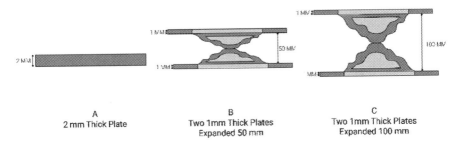

A
2 mm Thick Plate

B
Two 1mm Thick Plates
Expanded 50 mm

C
Two 1mm Thick Plates
Expanded 100 mm

Fig. 3. Left: Flat plate; Middle: Expanded linear mesh; Right: Expanded cone panel.

When considering the structural performance of this proposed system, assuming a perfectly composite behavior between the structure skins, and comparing a 2 mm. thick sheet of steel with two 1 mm. thick sheets expanded apart 100 mm from each other, the bending stiffness of the latter has increased by three orders of magnitude, while the weight/meter has remained constant (Table 1). It is hence possible to achieve a stiffer structure with the same amount of structural material.

Table 1. Structural properties of expanded metal shell cross-sections.

		A	B	C
W	kg/m^2	15.7	15.7	15.7
A	mm^2/m	2	2	2
D	mm	2	50	100
$I = \sum (A_i * d_i^2)$	mm^4	667	1.25×10^6	5.00×10^6
I/W	mm^6/kg	42.5	7.96×10^4	3.18×10^5

Where: W = weight per surface area; A = cross-sectional area; D = overall structural depth; I = second moment of area; I/W = specific stiffness.

2.2 Physical Experimentation on Local Scale

For preliminary experiments on the sensitivity of the chosen material system, 1.2 mm. Zinc panels have been employed. These preliminary tests focus on understanding the main variables dictating the expansion, deformation and overall structural behavior of kerfed metal sheets. Panels are placed on a rigid frame and expanded downwards using a simple wooden tool. The tested panels have various sizes and shapes, with a typical dimension of 200–300 mm. in width, and are expanded to about 150–300 mm. depth. Some of the results of these experiments are illustrated in Fig. 4.

Fig. 4. Various panel geometries and sizes for local experiments.

A qualitative assessment on the tested samples has highlighted the most influential parameters dictating the expansion of a panel. These parameters are: (i) Relation of width and length of strands; (ii) Panel shape (panel perimeter geometry, number of sides, and overall size); (iii) Shape of un-kerfed panel center; (iv) the transition between these two parameters affecting the geometry of the circumferential kerfs. These variables are summarized in Table 2 and Fig. 5 below. The effect of these variables and their interaction is further explained in the following sections.

Table 2. System variables in tested panels.

System variable	Variable range
Strand width [A]	10 to 20 mm
Strand length [B]	50 to 200 mm
Number of sides [N]	Triangle to circle
Panel aspect ratio [S]	1 to 6
Maximum size [w]	600 mm
Circumferential cuts geometry	Offset or tweened
Maximum expansion depth [D]	100 mm to 400 mm

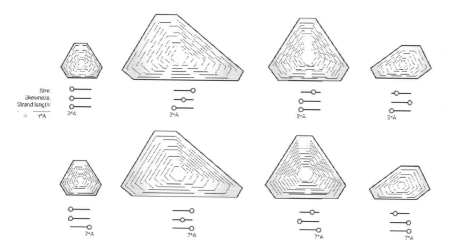

Fig. 5. Sample of tested panels with extreme-case variables.

Cut Length and Width. The expansion process relies on the formation of staggered load paths in the kerfed sheets, causing the slender strands of metal to bend beyond their elastic limit and yield to achieve their at-rest position once the panel is unloaded. Bending of these strands is a function of the plate geometry, its thickness, strand width, the amount of load each strand receives (a function of the cutting pattern, further discussed in Sect. 3.4), and the length of the kerf which determines the span of the centrally-loaded strand. After a series of tests, the team determined that the most suitable strand width was 12 mm. This parameter could be varied depending on the structural or environmental performance required by each panel, further discussed in Sect. 5.

Panel Shape. It has been observed that circular panels with the same offset center geometry perform better for expansion, as the forces are evenly distributed across the mesh from the center of the sheet. As shown on Fig. 6, a very even expanding profile can be observed on the circular panel as opposed to the rectangular one. The rectangular panel failed to expand evenly along all its edges since excessive expansion occurred along the corners.

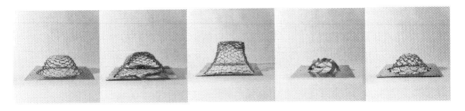

Fig. 6. Rectangular panels exhibit deformation as opposed to circular panels.

However, the aim to achieve a double layer shell consisting of circular panel geometry introduces excessive constraints to the edge to edge connections between any two given panels. Due to the inherent impact of this edge to edge panel joinery on the overall structural performance, it has been concluded to proceed with an N-gon panel geometry. The adopted panelization strategy is further outlined in Sect. 4 and is aimed at achieving panels with internal angle dimensions greater than 120° to achieve polygons which are as regularly-shaped as possible.

Panel Center. The nature of the metal expansion process requires a relatively small part of the panel's central section to remain un-kerfed. Advantages of this solution are two-fold: It allows the robotically controlled pushing tool to have a section that remains planar during this process, and the property of planarity is necessary to keep bearing stresses low and evenly distributed while the robotic arm applies the downwards force required to expand the metal panels. Furthermore, this flat central section is provided with a hole for a M6 bolt used to connect two facing panels in the final structure's double-layer shell.

The location of the hole on the panel and its relationship to the center section is one of the most challenging aspects of the design of every panel. In fact, the location of the hole is dictated by the position of the opposing panel on the other skin, which is governed by the overall curvature of the structure's surface. Simultaneously, the hole location has a significant impact on the allowable number of concentric kerfs that can physically fit on a panel.

As previously discussed, kerfs need to be staggered along concentric curves for the metal sheet to be expanded. These curves must form closed loops to ensure a sufficient number of load paths is evenly distributed around the panel. In fact, sections that do not have closed kerfed loops will not expand at all. Therefore, the outcome is that the maximum number of allowable concentric kerf paths is dictated by the smallest distance between the panel's central section and its edge as demonstrated in Fig. 7.

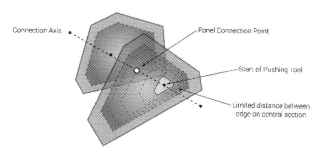

Fig. 7. Panel to panel connection area and the organization of the kerfing pattern in between panel boundary and center.

Transition Between Panel Outline and Center. Experimentation on various panel geometries and panel central section has been simultaneously coupled with the testing of the geometry of the concentric kerfing paths in relation to the panel's perimeter and the central section. Different methods of transitioning between a polygonal panel boundary to a circular central profile (initially adopted with the aim of having one single pushing tool for all the panels) have included 'tweening' these two curves. Tween Curve is a frequently used Rhinoceros 3D command for interpolating a series of curves between two open or closed input curves. This method helps to achieve a smooth transition between the panel boundary and central area, but limits the control of the strand width and has eventually been discarded in favor of a repeated offset inwards of the panel perimeter. This means that every central section and its associated pushing tool is of a unique geometry; nevertheless, it gives the designers more control over the various parameters affecting the panel's expansion process (Fig. 8).

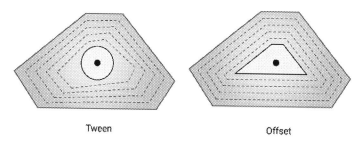

Tween   Offset

Fig. 8. Tweening versus offsetting of kerfing pattern.

3   Robotic Fabrication

Metal forming is a well-known and documented traditional manufacturing technique, and it comprises the application of a force to a target object in order to strengthen, stretch or shape its original geometry [7]. The research introduces kerfing as the initial step to facilitate the expansion process and its output geometry. Kerfing aids with the removal of material in order to obtain a light-weight structure while reducing manufacturing time, in comparison to other forming processes such as Single Point Incremental Forming (SPIF).

Sheet metal Zinc, with a thickness of 1.2 mm., has been selected for its malleability and lightness as the material for the prototyping process. Kerfing has been completed with a CNC router, and subsequently the metal sheets have been formed by a unidirectional pressure applied by a 6-axis robotic arm, allowing for a streamlined and flexible process for the fabrication of each expanded metal panel.

The robotic fabrication process has been developed using a KR30-3 KUKA robot, and the toolpaths have been generated by Robots, an add-on for Grasshopper, in order to deliver a series of unique panels with various stretching depths and angles. An algorithm has been developed to determine the starting and ending angles from the flat surface to the summit and generate a series of planes. These planes interpolate the normal plane angle from the entry plane progressively into the final position at the summit through a gradual rotation from 0° to the final rotation at the summit. The toolpath for each panel has been unique due to the angle of the summit and the depth of the panel (Fig. 9).

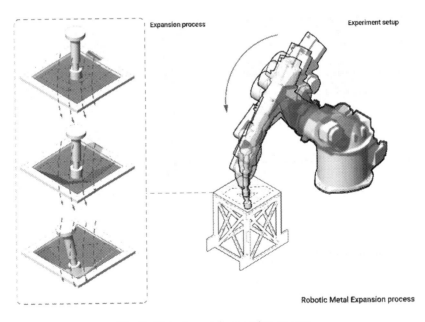

Fig. 9. Robotic metal expansion process.

The toolpath accommodates the transformation of said plane by incorporating a series of resting targets at different stages in order to gain better control of the deformation, thereby allowing the material to reach plastic deformation and avoid any possible overstress areas in the panel. This strategy also accommodates for the reduction of spring-back in the final stage of deformation, as it incorporates a 1 to 3 s stop at every stage of the toolpath. Furthermore, iterative physical experimentation conducted in the early stages has demonstrated that lengthening the toolpath by an additional 15% from the summit plane aids with the reduction of spring-back, hence this parameter has also been added to the toolpath setup.

During the fabrication setup for robotic sheet metal expansion, a series of frames and pushing tools have been created to deliver a series of unique panels with various stretching depths and summit angles. Initial testing has revealed two key challenges that had to be resolved in order to achieve high accuracy; namely metal sheet displacement during the forming process, and maintaining the uniformity of the applied force to the sheet. Throughout the design development stages, students proposed and tested various solutions to resolve these challenges. These solutions include the creation of different wooden templates in between the metal sheets and the rigid frame in order to create a homogeneous distribution of applied force during the forming process, as well as the fabrication of custom-made pushing tools for each unique panel geometry to aid in the forming process.

The resulting robotic fabrication setup comprises a rigid frame with dimensions of 500 mm. by 500 mm., and a wooden forming tool, attached to the KUKA robot as an end effector, with a replaceable acrylic head that can be adjusted to match the geometry of the summit surface for each individual panel (Fig. 10). It has been concluded that the employment of a wooden template was not effective in stabilizing the counter-forces generated in the metal sheet during the forming process. Instead, a locking system has

Fig. 10. Robotic fabrication setup.

been devised by adding a hole to the center of each panel and a pin to the end of the forming tool. The hole in the center of each panel is also advantageous for the assembly process, as described in Sect. 2.2. The uniformity of the stresses occurring in the metal panel has been increased by coating the tool head with a high-density neoprene rubber sheet. With a constant pushing force adapted according to the length and speed for the deformation process, the toolpath was executed with precision, and was able to achieve the expansion depths and angles of each individual panel.

4   Computational Methodology for the Global Scale

During the initial stage of the workshop, students were divided into 6 groups to investigate and explore ways of devising metal lightweight self-supporting structures through the employment of metal kerfing and robotic sheet metal expansion. Key design constraints included the location of the structure, AA's outdoor area that is open to public access, fabrication time, structural stability, and an efficient assembly process. The design phase was concluded by the collective decision on one design option based on structural performance, fabrication time, and proposed assembly sequence. The selected design option, illustrated in Fig. 11, is a semi-vault structure that receives additional support from the existing columns on the terrace, and it is formed of hexagonal panels.

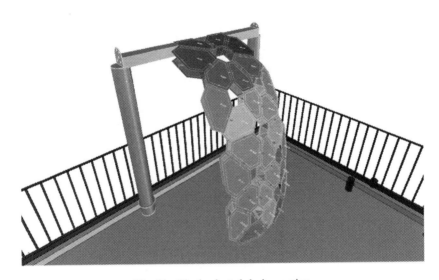

Fig. 11. Final selected design option.

Once a primary structural form for the surface had been selected, the double layer shell was modelled with varying offset to follow the principle stress in the shell. An initial finite-element (FE) analysis has been carried out with the Grasshopper add-on Karamba in order to identify the areas where highest bending moments and deflections occur on a single layer shell. This initial analysis informs an iterative design process where the global height to span ratio and local double-curvature of the arch are increased to enhance its stiffness. Bending moment results from the Karamba analysis are then translated to a value map on the surface which informs the offset distance between the two surface skins and in turn also the panel size.

"Mesh machine" is a component embedded in the Grasshopper add-on Kangaroo, and it allows the user to re-mesh a given geometry iteratively with varying controls on mesh size, density and aspect ratio. This tool has been utilized to equalize the interior angles of each triangle mesh face in order to reduce potential issues during the expansion process that would result from narrow angles of skewed panel geometries.

The triangular mesh resulting from this process has been used as the basis for further geometrical modelling such as generation of the hexagonal panels planes, panel centers and connection points between the two double layer shell's surfaces. This geometry has been stored to be used for generating the robotic tool path at a later stage. For example, the panel's hinge connections, which are fabricated from scored plates riveted to the panel edges, are derived from a custom-built script using the perimeter of the panel's plane (Fig. 12).

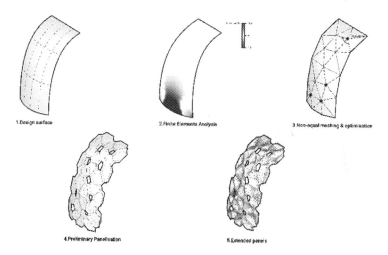

Fig. 12. Computational workflow demonstrating the transition from a single shell to a double-layered shell with the distribution of panels.

Furthermore, the fact that all the hexagonal panels are irregularly distributed across the doubly-curved surface means that: (i) No evident failure line will occur as multiple load paths are provided (ii) Once a panel has two edges connected this can be free-standing and self-supported, meaning that simple hinge detail connection can be used across all the panels as previously explored in the "Ramboll 2015 Trada Pavilion" [8] (Fig. 13).

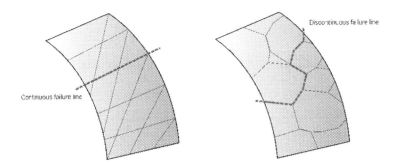

Fig. 13. Staggered panel subdivision aiding with multiple load paths.

Finally, the assembly sequence and panel connection detailing are also generated within the custom-built script, further aiding in the fabrication and assembly processes. The hexagonal panels constituting the global assembly are organized into groups for ease of assembly in the regional scale. The panels within each group are connected to each other with rivets, and subsequently each group of panels are connected to each other with M6 screws and nuts (Figs. 14 and 15).

Fig. 14. Final one-to-one scale prototype.

Fig. 15. Final one-to-one scale prototype.

5 Discussion

The main ambition of the research has been to devise a methodology for the creation of metal lightweight self-supporting structures with advanced computational and robotic methods. A computational workflow that integrates Finite Element Analysis, geometrical optimization, and robotic toolpath planning has been developed. This workflow is informed by the parameters of material experimentation on sheet metal kerfing and robotic sheet metal expansion.

The research demonstrates that the incorporation of robotic sheet metal expansion as a driver during the early stages of design can facilitate the development of lightweight structures that can withstand different loading conditions. A further advantage of employing expanded sheet metal, in comparison to perforated metal, is that a very small fraction of material is removed from the sheet during kerfing, leading to greater structural performance, material efficiency, and reduced waste during the fabrication process.

While one of the research ambitions was to create a self-standing structure within the research domain, the final prototype is defined as a semi-vault structure that receives additional support from the existing columns on the terrace. This result was a design decision based on the time constraints for fabrication and assembly stages. Nevertheless, the proposed methodology can be utilised for the design and fabrication of a free-form self-standing structure. This objective entails further research to address several key areas in relation to material experimentation on the local panel scale.

Firstly, the associations between panel geometry, kerfing pattern, required panel depth, and summit angle need to be studied further through an iterative material experimentation process in order to obtain a dataset which maps the relationships between such parameters numerically. In this way, the amount of panel expansion for a specific panel strength and kerfing pattern can be prescribed. This approach necessitates quantifying the structural behavior of local panels for a specific set of kerfing patterns through the application of various loading conditions. This study will initially be conducted for regular panel forms, and will further be developed for irregular/skewed panel forms. Through the understanding of material behavior for regular and irregular panel forms and kerfing patterns, a more informed and holistic approach can be developed to achieve complex doubly-curved global geometries. Furthermore, the robotic fabrication process will particularly benefit from the incorporation of a simultaneous feedback setup in order to record the amount of spring-back during the expansion process and modify the toolpath in real-time. This feedback system can also be employed to record the visual data of panel deformation and the distribution of material stresses in relation to the application of forces with varying pressures and angles.

Kerfing and expanding the steel sheet implies that the in-plane shear is transferred between each shell face follows a limited amount of load paths (i.e. the un-cut strands) down the kerfed pattern, through the connecting bolt, and into the panel below. Due to the sharp cuts it is expected that local stress concentrations will occur around the cuts or strand corners. Local failure of the expanded cones under such loads has not been tested and it is proposed that this forms part of the future research on the system. Physical or finite-element testing should also take into account the local strain hardening of the strand corners once the metal is expanded as this will increase the overall stiffness of the cone.

One of the key aims of this research is to illustrate the architectural possibilities of using sheet metal in a nonconventional way by creating strong associations between computational design methodologies and robotic fabrication processes. Through the adoption of material and fabrication parameters as design drivers from the conceptual design phase onwards, the high level of complexity inherent in design processes can be discovered to serve multiple aspects of performance.

Acknowledgements. The work presented is part of the research undertaken at Architectural Association (AA) Summer DLAB 2018. We would like to thank the faculty and students for their great efforts.

Head of AA Visiting School: Christopher Pierce

Head of AA Summer DLAB: Elif Erdine

Faculty: Elif Erdine, Giulio Gianni, Angel Lara Moreira, Alvaro Lopez Rodriguez, Yutao Song, Alican Sungur.

Students: Laura de la Torre, Montei di Matteo, Bryan Edward, Angelina Garipova, Vanda Hajizadeh, Jill Hartley Yokota, Ahmed Hassan, Hsin-Ying Huang, Harun Ishak, Maciej Kanarkowski, Kseniia Kondratovich, Roberto Marin, Sahil Mohan, Elena Nuñez Segura, Rajiv Parekh, In Pun, Francesca Savanco, Hugh Taylor, Ziqing Xu, Fan Yang, Masashi Yaushira.

References

1. Kalo, A., Newsum, M.J.: An investigation of robotic incremental sheet metal forming as a method for prototyping parametric architectural skins. In: McGee, W., de Ponce Leon, M. (eds.) Robotic Fabrication in Architecture, Art and Design 2014, pp. 33–49. Springer, Cham (2014). https://doi.org/10.1007/978-3-319-04663-1_3
2. Hensel, M., Menges, A.: Patterns in performance-orientated design: an approach towards pattern recognition, generation and instrumentalisation. Archit. Des. **79**(6), 88–93 (2009)
3. Gerber, C., Crews, K.: Timber stressed-skin panels: design guidelines for australian practice. Aust. J. Struct. Eng. **9**(3), 207–216 (2009). https://doi.org/10.1080/13287982.2009.11465023
4. Graciano, C., Martinez, G., Gutierrez, A.: Failure mechanism of expanded metal tubes under axial crushing. Thin Walled Struct. **51**, 20–24 (2012)
5. Bailly, D., et al.: Maufacturing of Innovative self-supporting sheet metal structures representing freeform surfaces. Procedia CIRP **18**, 51–56 (2014)
6. Nicholas, P., Stasiuk, D., Nørgaard, E., Hutchinson, C., Thomsen, M.R.: A multiscale adaptive mesh refinement approach to architectured steel specification in the design of a frameless stressed skin structure. In: Thomsen, M.R., Tamke, M., Gengnagel, C., Faircloth, B., Scheurer, F. (eds.) Modelling Behaviour: Design Modelling Symposium 2015, pp. 17–34. Springer, Cham (2015). https://doi.org/10.1007/978-3-319-24208-8_2
7. Emmens, W.C., Sebastiani, G., Van den Boogaard, A.H.: The technology of incremental sheet forming—a brief review of the history. J. Mater. Process. Technol. **210**(8), 981–997 (2010)
8. Harding, J., Lewis, H.: The TRADA pavilion: a timber plate funicular shell. In: Obrębski, J. B., Tarczewski, R. (eds.) Proceedings of the International Association for Shell and Spatial Structures (IASS) Symposium 2013 (2013)

Soft Additive Fabrication Processes: Material Indeterminacy in 3D Printing

Rachel Dickey[(✉)]

University of North Carolina Charlotte, Charlotte, USA
rachelldickey@gmail.com

Abstract. This description of Soft Additive Fabrication Processes, documents ways in which chance and randomness might be treated as values rather than problems. The production of a series of robotically controlled extruder experiments explore integrating material volition with the rigid order of machine control. Specifically this paper outlines the development of tooling procedures that harness emergent conditions in the automation of qualitative material effects. A key question for the research asks, how might architects imagine a design and construction scenario, which is no longer confined to prescriptive material dimensions, but is instead driven by digitally calibrated stochastic material processes? What opportunities might arise from developing an automated system, which does not rely on direct translation, but instead operates and predicts outcomes within a range of potential results?

Keywords: Additive manufacturing · Robotics · 3D printing · Indeterminacy · Material volition

1 Introduction

As robots and intelligent machines find their way onto construction sites, this research proposes ways they might contribute not only through highly measured and controlled processes, but also through a soft systemic approach to explore material indeterminacy. While technological advancements in fabrication today enable an increasingly direct relationship between design and translation and a future of machine processes driven by interests in precision and efficiency, methods and theories of the past have found validity in the celebrated flaws of construction and the handiwork of the craftsman. Negotiating between the rigid order of machine control and material volition, these Soft Additive Fabrication Processes interrogate the strictly measured paradigms in fabrication by exploring the dichotomies of the determinate and the indeterminate, the repeatable and the unrepeatable, and the intended and the accidental. It does so integrating the creative process in the development of tooling procedures that harness emergent material conditions requiring an optimistic stance on chance and randomness in the automation of qualitative material effects.

This research develops automated tooling processes that produces multiple material variations by harnessing material fluidity and malleability. Specifically it does this by means of the robotically controlled extrusion of Acrylonitrile Butadiene Styrene (ABS), which creates subtle material variations from repeating identical machine

© Springer Nature Singapore Pte Ltd. 2019
J.-H. Lee (Ed.): CAAD Futures 2019, CCIS 1028, pp. 356–371, 2019.
https://doi.org/10.1007/978-981-13-8410-3_25

processes. These processes move beyond direction translation and instead provide an instrumental framework for the material to perform in a way that produces a range of results. This method takes an opportunistic approach to design research as a means for advancing tooling processes based on material effects. The evaluation criteria and research questions include: what are the ways design research can promote a greater understanding of materiality relative to fabrication processes? How can we rediscover materiality through experimentation and computation? What opportunities might arise from developing an automated system, which does not rely on direct translation, but instead operates and predicts outcomes within a range of potential results? How can we develop a consistent tooling process, which produces a range of material variations from conditions of material and machine indeterminacy?

1.1 Soft Systems and Fabrication

Architecture's relationship with indeterminate systems or unmeasured conditions has a varying history, ranging from the visionary projects of the 1960's to the contemporary appropriation of computation as a domain for integrating feedback with the work of Phillip Beesley and Minimaforms. Implementing emergence, flexibility, or indefinite-ness into a measured process relates to Sanford Kwinter's ideas of soft systems, which he defines when he writes:

> "The system, one might say, is driven by its very 'softness,' its capacity to move, to differentiate internally, to absorb, transform, and exchange information with its surrounding [...] A system is 'soft' when it is flexible, adaptable, and evolving, when it is complex and maintained by a dense network of active information or feedback loops, or put in a more general way, when a system is able to sustain a certain quotient of sensitive, quasi-random flow." [1]

In other words, a system is soft when it is driven by dynamics, responsive to change, and able to accommodate chance and indeterminacy. In the 1960's, soft systems were under investigation in many disciplines, including philosophy and the sciences, and represented a common thread of speculation. Architecture in the sixties included visionary projects of Cedric Price's Fun Palace and Yona Friedman's Ville Spatiale, which offered an occupational agenda for soft system approaches that would allow for contingency and change based on the needs of the occupants. Soft systemic approaches are also currently common in other disciplines, such as computer science. These methodologies, known as soft computing, often involve the development of approximate solution and are often applied for the development of intelligent systems, which *"aim to exploit tolerance for imprecision, uncertainty and partial truth"* [2]. Negro-ponte's book, Soft Architecture Machines, was perhaps the first formal introduction of soft computing in architecture and proposed ideas of softened collaboration with machines in design [4].

Looking into the pre-computing origins of soft systems relative to acts of fabri-cation and construction are most apparent in John Ruskin's 19th century descriptions of the Gothic, especially through the characteristic he classifies as "savageness". Ruskin explains that savageness resulted from the idiosyncrasies, mistakes, and imperfections in the construction of gothic cathedrals. Such rough details were made by craftsmen, often due to harsh climates and conditions in which they built. Ruskin saw these rough details as aesthetic attributes because they told a story of the workers and were markers of the act of construction [5]. An additional characteristic of savageness was that the design of the cathedrals often emerged during the process of building, due to the length of construction and number of architects involved. The decisions for placement of elements overtime would alter the overall design and inform the subsequent procedures, suggesting a feedback or *"quasi-random flow."* Lars Spuybroek connects the relationship of emergence to the ideas of contemporary fabrication processes. In discussing Spuybroek's work, Swiatkowski clarifies the notion of emergence in the context of contemporary fabrication processes. His description similarly relates to the notion of soft systems in that the methods of construction *"allow for variety and profoundly accept change and mistakes"* [6], thus savageness involved flexibility in acts of construction and a feedback that allowed the process of design and fabrication to build on previous acts over time.

1.2   Neo-Savageness in Digital Fabrication

Just as the craftsman of the gothic worked and negotiated around a process of orders and logic, today machines too might allow for accidents and flexibility during acts of fabrication [6]. In the design methodology described here, fabrication processes were developed to harness material volition and explore opportunities for emergence in digital fabrication. Embracing the Ruskinian notion of savageness, this work steers away from the tendency of technology to generate uniform results and embraces the idea that qualitative attributes arise from imperfections, even material irregularities made by machines.

The difference between the Ruskinian notion of savageness, which described labor and craft and this proposal for neo-savageness made by the machine, is that computational control is consistent over time. Thus, the subsequent prototypes allow for an alternative savageness based on a material logic that is intuitive and directly relates its means of manipulation. In other words, in this study the rules of material change, such as viscosity and malleability, are instrumental in testing and informing design. Also, creating processes that produce material volition enables indeterminate or unknown conditions to result by providing a framework for the material to have inherent behavior, almost personifying the material as having a will or desire. Just as the materiality of architecture embraces firmness when *"clay is fired into brick, wood is dried and compressed, and sand is melted and annealed into its solid form"* [7], this design methodology explores moments of translation from soft to hard.

The loose process of leaving room for accident that builds up to a more directed and tight approach is a similar to Spuybroek's description of the Gothic when he writes:

> *"That is Gothic ontology: there is plenty of accident, yes, but accident leading to substance, and there are huge amounts of flexibility, but flexibility leading to rigidity. Things do not miraculously meet in a single moment either through magical emergence or magical intervention; rather, they settle step by step, in a process that takes on more direction the more it progresses, trading the initial vagueness for increased determination."* [8]

The methods by which gothic craftsman worked involved not a one to one translation, but a step by step emergence, scanning the previous step as a way of evaluating and determining the subsequent steps. This process of emergence influenced design at various scales, from the scale of the cathedral to the placement of individual stones. The framework for the subsequent fabrication studies also leaves room for the unintended, but builds up sequentially into a process, which becomes more ordered and rigid.

This study provides designers with a scenario where they could start with material execution strategies and develop a range of possibilities from there. Also, the material which builds up in excess and informs the location of the next moves is reminiscent of Ruskin ideas of the grotesque:

> *"The overabundance of matter visible in the Gothic cathedral does not mean that the construction sinks into chaos. There is active rigidity in place. Various levels of organization emerge during the subsequent steps of construction. The forces eventually solidify into a given structure. Nevertheless, the procedure characterizing Gothic architecture always involves risks. It frequently leads to grotesque results. Some cathedrals are 'over the top' [...] For Ruskin, this grotesque aspect is nevertheless fundamental. It shows the true freedom of the Gothic."* [6]

1.3 Material Volition

This uses an alternative form of measurement in the act of fabrication based on emergence and abundance. It does not rely on traditional ideas of tolerance, which only work within a small deviation of the intended dimensions, but instead expands the notion of tolerance to allow room for a broader material behavior and effect. Such tolerances involve risks sometimes resulting in collapse and excess material use; however, they permit for a true freedom of the material.

While uncertainty and imprecision are often avoided in manufacturing and construction, these procedures explore the possibilities of emergence in fabrication and look to unmeasured moments of material consequences to inform potential forms of construction. This research draws on the traditions of digital fabrication centered on material techniques [9], but differs by celebrating material irregularities and manufactured imperfections. It negotiates between the measured and unmeasured, perceiving the moments of indeterminacy not as a hindrance, but as an opportunity.

1.4 Background

Other additive-based systems which capture similar moments of material volition and in 3d printing include: Roxy Paine's automated sculpture makers (1996–2001) and Anish Kapoor's 3d printed concrete (2012). The 3D printing research of Virginia San Fratello and Ron Rael similarly uses gravity and adjustments in typical stacking of layers to generative various patterns in their "Clay Bodies" project [10]. Other work also steers away from traditional horizontal layering during deposition by exploring alternatives to horizontal banding by inserting voids without losing the structural rigidity during additive production process. This work includes Isabella Molloy and Tim Miller's industrial design scale printed objects, Gramazio and Kohler's mesh structures and Jose Luis García del Castillo 3D printed lattice structures [11–13]. Similar research, which looks at material behavior relative to speed and complexity in toolpath includes the "Spatial Print" project by Bechthold [14]. However, this paper and research presented differs by exploring moments of material indeterminacy, which deviate from the prescribed toolpath to generate irregularities. It does not focus on direct translation, but instead celebrates variations caused by material and machine volition.

2 Methodology

The goal for the research is to develop a consistent automated tooling process that produces multiple material variations by harnessing material fluidity and malleability. The strategy creates subtle material variations from repeating identical machine processes. These processes move beyond direction translation and instead provide an instrumental framework for the material to perform in a way that produces a range of results. This method takes an opportunistic approach to design research as a means for advancing tooling processes based on material effects and demonstrates alternatives to the traditional ideas of measurement in fabrication.

The method for the research involves a two-part process of first, material testing and second, an automated fabrication strategy. Working with the parameters of the plastic extruder, different panel types are created in order to further push the capabilities and understanding of irregularities. Once the automation tests are run, the research team catalogs the range of material effects to accompany the tooling development. The strategy used to keep track of the different methods of manipulation was to catalog of a series of material deviations through three different tests. The first set of experiments explore material interpolation, where the tools moves in rectilinear toolpaths, but the material bends and curves. The second set of experiments involve glitches inserted into the machine code would cause the tool to hesitate causing a buildup of material. A third set of experiments, deviate from their tool path by exploring the pull of gravity on the material during deposition.

2.1 Research Setup and Material Testing

The research setup includes a Kuka KR-60 robot, Kuka-prc plug-in for Grasshopper for machine code development, an electrically heated base plate, and a BAK Micro Extruder (made by Hapco). The material tests began by experimenting with various filaments. These tests included factors such as filament temperature, filament adhesive and layering qualities, horizontal and vertical movement, speed of extrusion, and the angle of deposit. The temperature tests involved by increasing the temperature by ten-degree increments and documenting the malleability and molten consistency. Too high of temperatures caused burning, discoloration, or accelerated cooling. A certain degree of workability and material fluidity was necessary beyond the typical desire for the filament to hold a tubular form after the extrusion process.

2.2   High Density Polyethylene (HDPE) vs. Acrylonitrile Butadiene Styrene (ABS)

Based on temperature tests for the High Density Polyethylene (HDPE) the highest extrusion temperature to permit maximum malleability without burning or loud fumes is 330°. The maximum temperature for the Acrylonitrile Butadiene Styrene (ABS) is 280°. These temperatures permit the most thick and viscous moments and create a range of discrepancies from the toolpath. By analyzing the differences between the two filaments the team deemed the ABS best suitable for exploration of variations produced by material fluidity paired with the speed of the robotic arm, while still maintaining typical printing attributes of layering and adhesion.

2.3   Variables and Constants

The constant variables set from the material tests include: room temperature, extruder temperature, extruder spooling speed, base plate temperature, and distance between deposited layers. The constant variable of layering of the extruded filament is kept at 1.5 mm. If the distance between the layers is too small the next layer of extruded filament will be pressed into the layer below. If the spacing between the layers of filament is too large, the inconsistency and stability decreases.

The extruder spooling speed affects the consistency of the plastic through the control of the amount of material that comes out, as well as the amount of exposure to the heated air. The spooling settings work best between the range of one to six, one being the slowest and six being the fastest. The slower the speed setting, the more melting occurs, due to longer exposure to hot air.

The size of each experiment was kept within a five-inch cubic boundary to keep the toolpath run time between ten and thirty minutes. Testing the various speeds involved increasing the intervals of velocity by five percent each time (which is what is permitted through manual overrides to the machine code). The final outputs for changes in velocity are made through the Kuka PRC velocity input. This variable change impacts either the Point to Point movement or the Linear movement speed. The linear speed ranged from 0.01 m/s to 0.10 m/s. A faster speed allowed for a smother appearance in the extrusion with less time for gravity to pull the material. The strategy used to keep track of the different methods of manipulation was to catalog a series of panels that show material deviations through three different tests classified as material interpolation, gravity pull intervals, and material buildup glitches.

3   Results

3.1   Material Interpolation

The first set of experiments explore material interpolation. Interpolation is a term used here to describe the material negotiation between the robotically controlled toolpath and the actual material behavior, which deviates from the path. The material behaves similarly, to a non-uniform rationale b-spline (nurb) which geometrically follows the same knot count formula as a polyline with equal number of control points; however, instead of a geometric interpolation there is a material deviation. Using rectilinear toolpaths the material interpolates the tool's movement, and cuts or smooths at the corners (Figs. 1, 2, 3 and 4). This set of experiments demonstrates the opportunities for integrating stochastic material engagement with automated tooling by capturing effects made from dynamic processes.

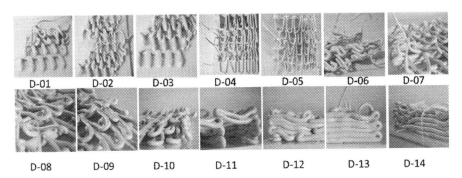

Fig. 1. Taxonomy of interpolation studies showing deviated material conditions from rectilinear tool path.

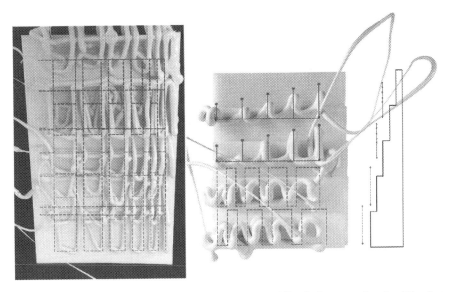

Fig. 2. Diagram illustrating material interpolation. The red line indicates tool path while photo below initiates the material deviation. (Color figure online)

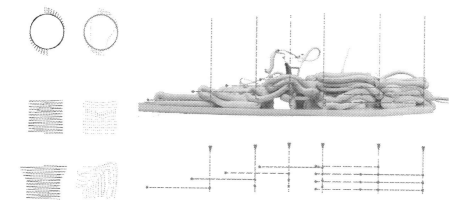

Fig. 3. Diagrams of material interpolation. Tool paths (in black) and actual filament (in red). (Color figure online)

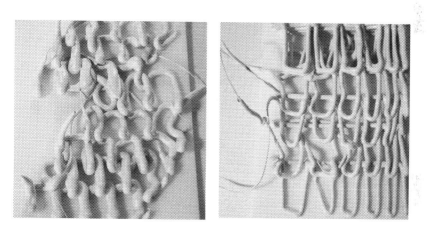

Fig. 4. Detail images of material interpolation.

3.2 Material Buildup Glitches

Glitches inserted into the machine code would cause the tool to hesitate causing a buildup of material. These glitches cause robot hesitations and changes in velocity. Since the filament builds up the subsequent layers are impacted causing a ripple effect (Fig. 5). These glitches could be caused by an overload of points in the grasshopper script's tool path or the speed of the tool movement. The glitches occur in groups of points relating to similar x and y locations, but the locations of the individual groups did not relate to one another. The slower the speed of the tool movement, the amount of filament deposited increases (Figs. 6 and 7).

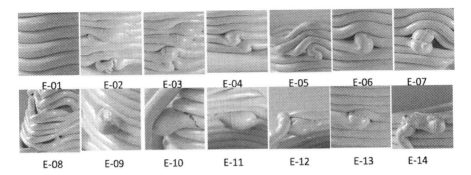

Fig. 5. Taxonomy of material buildup glitches

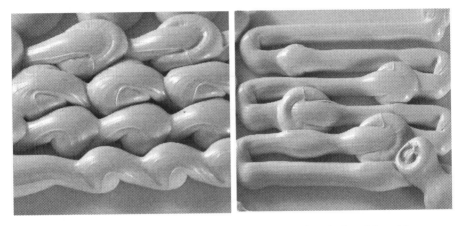

Fig. 6. Images of repetitive glitches inducing changes in velocity of deposition.

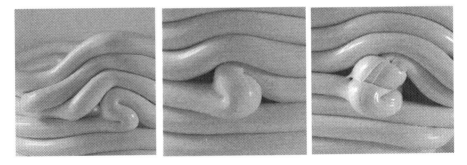

Fig. 7. Detail images of material buildup glitches.

3.3   Gravity Pull Intervals

A third set of experiments, which deviate from their tool path by using gravity to pull the material downward by stepping outside of the layering process. These tests track how the material behaves when deposited at various distances from the preceding layer. By controlling the space between each outward stepping motion, the filament can either be spread out or it can start to overlap. The filament will only fall as far as the movement of the tool allows before changing directions and pulling the filament along with it. If the speed of the tool along the toolpath is consistent with the rate at which the filament is being extruded, there remains a constant pull and tension resulting in a straight line. When the tool moves slower than the rate at which the filament is being extruded, inconsistencies arise and the filament begins deviating from the toolpath. This deviation is when the filament becomes uncontrolled and begins to create indeterminate moves. It begins to follow the path of least resistance, layering and piling onto itself creating more subsequent moves (Fig. 8). When the outward-stepping layers overlap, it allows the filament more time to dry before finding its resting place. When there is no support the tool makes an outward movement, the filament pulls downward as far as the extrusion extends.

Fig. 8. Taxonomy of gravity pull interval tests.

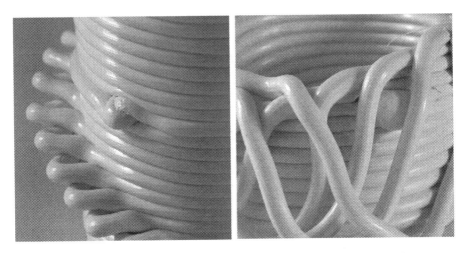

Fig. 9. Detail images of gravity pull intervals with material build up glitches.

Fig. 10. Detail image of gravity pull interval.

The instability of the material after being extruded is caused by the high temperature at which it remains for more than a minute. While it is still in this softened state it will deform and react to its environment by deflecting, sticking, curving, etc. until it has found a resting position in which it can cool. The time it requires to cool and harden is also a factor of the positioning and directionality of the tool. Directly adjacent to the filament extruder tip is the hot air supply that constantly exerts air flow onto the extruded ABS, while the air temperature can be raised or lowered it cannot be completely turned off. This air flow directly impacts the movement and consistency of the filament. The hotter the air, the longer the cooling time of the deposited filament. When there is an increased cooling period, there is also an increased level of instability and a decreased level of consistency in placement and behavior. This slow rate of cooling does not allow for filament to cool and remain suspended mid-air or to build upon itself mid-air. The filament pulls downward until it reaches the next point of contact (Figs. 9, 10 and 11).

Fig. 11. Detail image of gravity pull interval with glitch.

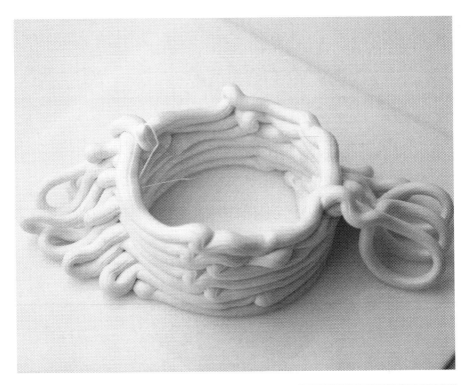

 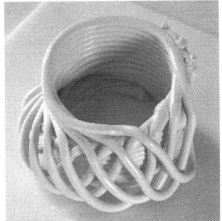

Fig. 11. (*continued*)

4 Reflection

While these additive processes are only an initial study of how construction methods might integrate ideas of material indeterminacy, it provides designers with a scenario where they could rethink existing methodologies—perhaps no longer working from intent to execution, but starting with material execution strategies and speculating on the range of possibilities from there. This area of pure research seeks to inform and encourage larger scale applied research, which could be adapted to architectural design and construction. For instance, with the scaling up of the material such fast curing concrete and large scale 3d printing, the question arises regarding how feedback could allow the system to scan and recalibrate in order to provide sufficient structure or delineate and differentiate space. With this type of development, lies the potential for integrating machine-learning processes as an additional method for appropriating soft computing techniques within the system.

Further development of this research would entail a feedback process by integrating sensors or laser scanners, which would allow the system to respond to material discrepancies in real time, as appose to predicting them and setting the toolpaths based on those predictions. This feedback would allow for subtle changes in the toolpath to help optimize and celebrate the material irregularities and subsequently allow the automation procedures to build upon themselves, creating a quasi-intelligent fabrication system. A set of secondary questions arise for the development of the research: How will the development of digital fabrication devices built for stochastic material processes respond to change? How might the system scan or recalibrate in order to provide sufficient structure or delineate and differentiate space? How might we imagine a design and construction scenario, which is no longer confined to prescriptive material dimensions, but is instead driven by a digitally calibrated stochastic material processes?

Other potential applications from integrating feedback and intelligence would be in the development of site-specific applications. The Markus Kayser's Solar Sinter project (2011) provides an example of how fabrication systems might draw on the availability of resources relative to geography. Kayer's project deploys a portable 3D printer on dessert sites to convert sand into annealed glass using lens directed heat from the sun. The printer is able to adapt and respond to the sun by tracking its position and harnessing its rays. Adding the idea of indeterminacy into such a site-specific intervention could allow for rich possibilities and additional design potential.

5   Conclusion

With developments in large scale 3D printing at University Southern California, the appropriation of robots on construction sites at the University of Stuttgart, and the integration of drone technology in construction at ETH Zurich (Eidgenössische Technische Hochschule Zürich), technological advancements are impacting the way buildings are both designed and built. Integration of feedback loops with 3D scanning and sensors are allowing for additional developments in decision-making machines; fabrication robots will one day be capable of learning from data in real time and make decisions about the next moves. Spuybroek recalls artificial intelligence scientist Marvin Minsky theorizing of a system that might sort through unprocessed materials and have the capacity to build like a bird assembles a nest entirely intuitively with flexibility in the system:

"Nobody's ever tried to make a machine that could build a bird's nest. Instead they're all out there in factories assembling motors. People say, 'Oh yes, the bird gets straws and it sticks them in the nest and glues them in.' But a motor is designed to be put together. The debris lying around on the floor of a forest isn't described to made into nests." [8]

One could say the same about our industrial robots. "They are all out there in factories assembling motors" and we have been appropriating them to do the same within in architecture schools making and assembling parts "designed to be put together".

Antoine Picon, in his assessment of robots in architecture, points out, "Robotic fabrication may confront us for the first time directly with the need to cooperate with our technological auxiliaries rather than simply use them" [15]. Looking beyond material and tooling methods, Picon draws upon Negroponte's ideas and opportunistically calls for the emancipation of robots, no longer acting as a workforce, but as a contributors to the discourse of design. Similarly, Greg Lynn calls for alternative ways of thinking about robots, suggesting the ability to go beyond "robotic fabrication of primitive huts" [16]. Perhaps instead of an obsession with efficiency, predictability, and precision, we should start the quest for opportunistic alternatives for robotics in design, by finding ways to integrate responses to change, uncertainty, and imprecision. This research outlined here focuses on indeterminacy centered on material and machine agency in architecture. Promoting such agency requires less rigidity in authorship, which promotes softness not only in terms of materials and movements, but also in allowing machines to have an agency that exists beyond the designer's facilitation. Such a softening of authorship requires room for indeterminacy and a willingness to collaborate with computer-controlled methods.

This research proposes ways which robots and intelligent machines might contribute not only through the highly measured and controlled processes, but looks toward integrating a soften approach exploring opportunities for embracing material indeterminacy through soft systems. Embracing the Ruskinian notion of savageness, it steers away from the tendency of technology to generate uniform results and embraces the idea that originality arises from imperfections, even material irregularities made by machines. In a future of buildings constructed in collaboration with intelligent robots, what Ruskinian markers or savage details will result? Will the buildings tell of extreme precision and control or will they deviate and embrace material indeterminacies? Might robots scan and process material data and behavior better than ourselves to help celebrate and execute their design potential? It is within this immense range of potential applications that these Soft Additive Processes provide a way for framing and pursing optimistic alternatives for appropriating technology in design by taking an opportunistic approach to indeterminacy in additive manufacturing.

Acknowledgements. This work was supported, in part, by funds provided by the University of North Carolina at Charlotte. The work was produced in collaboration with Meritt Foreman.

References

1. Kwinter, S.: Soft systems. In: Culture Lab 1, edited B. Boigon, p. 211. Princeton Architectural Press, New York (1993)
2. Applied Soft Computing, in The Official Journal of the World Federation on Soft Computing (2016)
3. Rutkowski, L.: Artificial Intelligence and Soft Computing – ICAISC 2008. 9th International Conference Zakopane, Poland, June 22–26, 2008 Proceedings. Springer, Berlin (2008). https://doi.org/10.1007/978-3-540-69731-2
4. Negroponte, N.: Soft Architecture Machines, p. 54. MIT Press, Cambridge (1975)
5. Spuybroek, L.: The Sympathy of Things: Ruskin and the Ecology of Design, 2nd edn. Bloomsbury Publishing Plc: Bloomsbury Academic (2016)
6. Swiatkowski, P.: How to think constructivism? Ruskin, spuybroek and deleuze on gothic architecture. Footprint **14**(1), 44–45 (2014)
7. Beaumont, J.R.: Architectures of firmness and softness, from interactive architecture lab. The Bartlett School of Architecture, 5 November 2015. Accessed 13 Feb 2017
8. Spuybroek, L.: The Sympathy of Things, pp. 45, 67. Bloomsbury Publishing Plc: Bloomsbury Academic (2011)
9. Kolarevic, B., Kevin, K.: Manufacturing Material Effects: Rethinking Design and Making in Architecture, pp. 5–24. Routledge, New York (2008)
10. Rael, R., San Fratello, V.: Clay bodies: crafting the future with 3D printing. Archit. Des. **87**(6), 92–97 (2017)
11. Isabella, M., Miller, T.: Digital dexterity: freeform 3D printing through direct toolpath manipulation for wellington crafted artifacts. In: Recalibration: on Imprecision and Infidelity. Proceedings Catalog of the 38th Annual Conference of the Association for Computer Aided Design in Architecture (ACADIA) edited by Phillip Anzalone, Marcella Del Signore, Andrew John Wit, Mexico City, pp. 266–275 (2018)
12. Helm, V., et al.: Iridescence print: robotically printed lightweight mesh structures. 3D Print. Addit. Manuf. **2**(3), 117–122 (2015)
13. Im, H.C., AlOthman, S., del Castillo, J.L.G.: Responsive spatial print: clay 3D printing of spatial lattices using real-time model recalibration using spatial lattices similar to space frame. In: Recalibration: on imprecision and infidelity. Proceedings Catalog of the 38th Annual Conference of the Association for Computer Aided Design in Architecture (ACADIA) edited by Phillip Anzalone, Marcella Del Signore, Andrew John Wit, Mexico City, pp. 286–293 (2018)
14. AlOthman, S., Im, H.C., Jung, F., Bechthold, M.: Spatial print trajectory: controlling material behavior with print speed, feed rate, and complex print path. In: Willmann, J., Block, P., Hutter, M., Byrne, K., Schork, T. (eds.) ROBARCH 2018, pp. 167–180. Springer, Cham (2019). https://doi.org/10.1007/978-3-319-92294-2_13
15. Picon, A.: Robots and architecture: experiments, fiction, epistemology. Archit. Des. **84**(3), 58–59 (2014)
16. Lynn, G.: Giant Robots. RoboLog. Winter 2016, p. 14. Cambridge. (2015)

The Effect of Hygroscopic Design Parameters on the Programmability of Laminated Wood Composites for Adaptive Façades

Sherif Abdelmohsen[1,2(✉)] ⓘ, Passaint Massoud[1,3],
Rana El-Dabaa[2,4] ⓘ, Aly Ibrahim[1], and Tasbeh Mokbel[1]

[1] Department of Architecture, American University in Cairo, Cairo, Egypt
{sherifmorad,drpassaint,aly_magdy,
tasbeh_mokbel23}@aucegypt.edu
[2] Department of Architecture, Ain Shams University, Cairo, Egypt
[3] Department of Architecture, French University in Egypt, Cairo, Egypt
[4] Department of Architectural Engineering and Environmental Design,
Arab Academy for Science, Technology and Maritime Transport, Cairo, Egypt
rana.bahaa@aast.edu

Abstract. Typical adaptive façades respond to external conditions to enhance indoor spaces based on complex mechanical actuators and programmable functions. Hygroscopic embedded properties of wood, as low-cost low-tech programmable material, have been utilized to induce passive motion mechanisms. Wood as anisotropic material allows for different passive programmable motion configurations that relies on several hygroscopic design parameters. This paper explores the effect of these parameters on programmability of laminated wood composites through physical experiments in controlled humidity environment. The paper studies variety of laminated configurations involving different grain orientations, and their effect on maximum angle of deflection and its durability. Angle of deflection is measured using image analysis software that is used for continuous tracking of deflection in relation to time. Durability is studied as the number of complete programmable cycles that wood could withstand before reaching point of failure. Results revealed that samples with highest deflection angle have least programmability durability.

Keywords: Wood · Hygroscopic design · Lamination · Deflection · Durability · Adaptive façades

1 Introduction

Wood is an anisotropic material whose mechanical properties vary according to the orientation of its fibers. Studying the hygroscopic properties of wood allows for the control and programming of its response behavior to the fluctuation of humidity levels. Several studies have been conducted to explore and capture the hygroscopic behavior of wood for adaptive building facades. Little has been done however to address the effect of hygroscopic design parameters on the durability of programmable wood.

© Springer Nature Singapore Pte Ltd. 2019
J.-H. Lee (Ed.): CAAD Futures 2019, CCIS 1028, pp. 372–383, 2019.
https://doi.org/10.1007/978-981-13-8410-3_26

Previous relevant studies tend to fall into one of three categories; physical experiments to control and program the response of wood [1], fabricating architectural prototypes and full scale models [2], and numerical simulations for wood response [3]. In the architectural realm, this type of motion has been explored as a low-tech low-cost motion mechanism to enhance the behavior of adaptive and responsive structures. The programmability of wood has been extensively studied and tested at the Institute for Computational Design (ICD) at the University of Stuttgart [4] and the Self-Assembly Lab (SAL) at MIT [5].

Different hygroscopic design parameters affect the response behavior of wood such as the type of wood, wood thickness, moisture content, sample dimensional ratio, grain orientation, and lamination. Lamination involves a specifically fabricated wooden composite with two layers of wood, where one acts as the active layer that initiates the motion, while the other acts as the passive layer that restrains motion. When varying the level of humidity, the difference in the response behavior of each layer causes one layer to expand more than the other, thus causing the overall motion. This motion mechanism has been studied as a novel way for responsive and adaptive architectural facades. Hygroscopic motion is a motion mechanism that requires no additional energy or any complex mechanical system, but rather relies on the latent properties of wood that expands and shrinks according to the embedded moisture content.

This passive motion mechanism of wood is introduced in the adaptive architecture realm to program responsive facades. Their actuation is through variation in humidity levels. Also programming the wood initial state can be programmed though moisture content in the laminated sample, thus controlling it to turn from flat to curved state or vice versa. Two adaptive structures used this property showing the difference in wood response when increasing humidity. The HygroScope pavilion opens when humidity increase, while Hygroskin pavilion closes when humidity increase [6].

As a natural material, the inherent characteristics of response behavior and durability are keys to its sustainable use in adaptive façade prototypes. To address the durability dimension – and consequently the "programmability" – of laminated wood composites, this paper focuses on physically investigating the lamination of a variety of configurations involving different hygroscopic parameters and their effect on the programmability of wood over time. The paper is divided into two parts: (1) the physical experimentation of laminated wood samples with different hygroscopic design parameter configurations, and (2) tracking and analyzing the response behavior of wood using image analysis software.

2 Methodology and Procedures

This research is part of an ongoing research that utilizes hygroscopic properties of wood as a low-cost low-tech approach for passive adaptive façades, as shown in Fig. 1. Several hygroscopic design parameters were previously studied and analyzed to physically and numerically program specific motions such as wood response to humidity [7], to use different methods of tracking hygroscopic response using tangible interfaces [8], and to analyze its motion via computational methods [9].

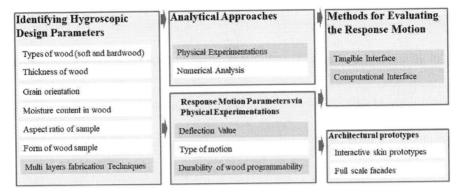

Fig. 1. Scope of paper within larger research framework

This paper focuses on studying the programmability of wood through recording the value of the angle of deflection of wood upon response to humidity and studying the durability of that value, represented in the number of cycles before wood loses its programmability. Two sequential methods are used to study the deflection value and durability with respect to the effect of number of complete response cycles on deflection value. The complete response cycle is represented in this context by the behavior of wood from one humidity level to another then its reversible motion till it reaches its initial point. In terms of tools and interfaces, a physical experimental setting, including a sealed humidity chamber and humidity sensor, was used as a tangible interface, while the Kinovea image analysis software was used as a computational interface, as shown in Fig. 2. A video camera on a tripod with a fixed distance of 60 cm from the samples was used as a link between these two interfaces.

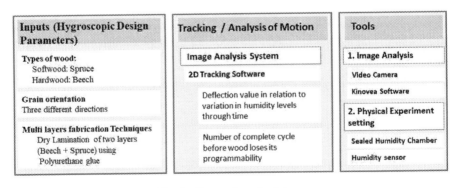

Fig. 2. Research methodology

2.1 Experiment Setup

Beech (hardwood) and spruce (softwood) with tangential cuts were used as a base for the laminated composite in this experiment. The dimensions of the laminated wooden sample used were 40 mm × 120 mm × 1.22 mm. The parameters of the laminated sample are shown in Table 1.

Table 1. Parameters of laminated wooden sample

Beech (American)	
Wood type	Hardwood
Thickness	0.60 mm
Shrinkage value	11.9% tangential
Spruce (Sitka)	
Wood type	Softwood
Thickness	0.60 mm
Shrinkage value	4.3% radial
Adhesive layer	
Polyurethane glue	Water-resistant glue

Wood samples were fixed to clamps inside a controlled humidity chamber. A video camera was fixed on a tripod with a fixed distance from the samples. Three samples of the same configuration were aligned inside the chamber (for consistency of applied conditions), as shown in Fig. 3. A digital humidity sensor was used for accurate tracking of the level of humidity inside the chamber. The wood samples were exposed to an increase in humidity level till 90% for 5 min duration, and then humidity level decreased till it reached 50%.

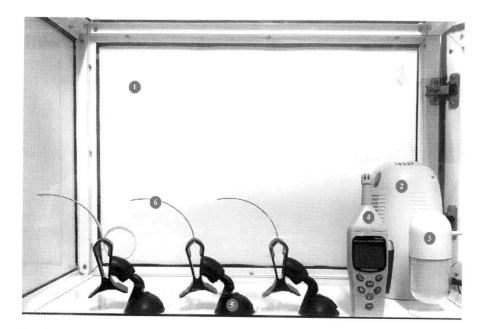

Fig. 3. Experiment setup (1. Controlled humidity chamber, 2. Dehumidifier, 3. Humidifier, 4. Humidity and temperature sensor, 5. Clamps, 6. Tested laminated samples)

2.2   Lamination Experiments

Experiments were conducted on nine different configurations of laminated samples in a humidity-controlled environment. Several configurations were used for the lamination of different grain orientations and wood types with tangential cuts as shown in Fig. 4.

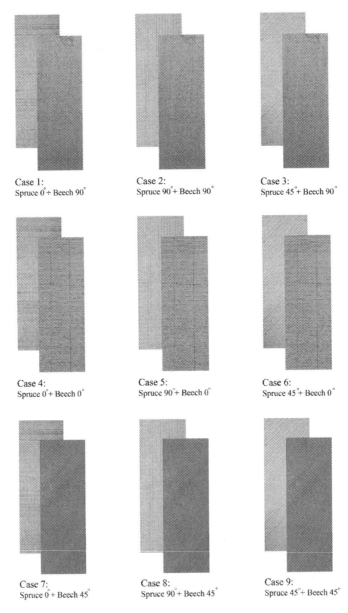

Case 1:
Spruce 0° + Beech 90°

Case 2:
Spruce 90° + Beech 90°

Case 3:
Spruce 45° + Beech 90°

Case 4:
Spruce 0° + Beech 0°

Case 5:
Spruce 90° + Beech 0°

Case 6:
Spruce 45° + Beech 0°

Case 7:
Spruce 0° + Beech 45°

Case 8:
Spruce 90° + Beech 45°

Case 9:
Spruce 45° + Beech 45°

Fig. 4. Configurations of the tested laminated cases

Three grain orientations were tested: 0° (grain parallel to short axis of wood sample), 90° (grain parallel to long axis of wood sample) and 45°. Each experiment was repeated on three samples, and the average of deflection value and durability was taken for the validity of results. The analysis and comparison of the response behavior of these configurations was done by comparing the maximum deflection angle with respect to the time consumed. This was done using the Kinovea image analysis software to trace the effect of the different hygroscopic design parameters in the laminated wooden composite configurations.

2.3 Durability of Wood Programmability

The second phase of analysis involved exploring the durability of the programmed laminated wood composites. This was done by tracking the difference in wood response through several cycles and its deflection angle over time. Motion tracking software was used to compare the difference in wood response to each time [8]. This phase demonstrated the difference in deflection angle each time wood reacted to a change in humidity level. For time limitations, the durability of wood was tested in three cycles, where the change in response behavior was tracked and analyzed.

3 Image Analysis

The laminated wood samples were marked to facilitate tracking, such that three markers were located in the center and on the two ends of the samples. Three aspects were measured: response time, angle of deflection in single curved samples, and twisting and deflection in double curved samples. The deflection angle was measured between the location of the initial and final state points, while the twist angle was measured between location of the first and second points, as shown in Fig. 5.

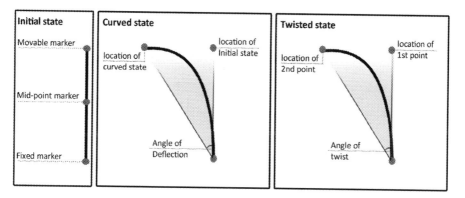

Fig. 5. Method of measurement of the deflection and twist angles

The Kinovea image analysis software was used to track the motion of wood, as shown in Fig. 6. Recorded videos were used as an input for the software, in addition to calibrating its dimensions, and locating fixed and movable markers to be tracked.

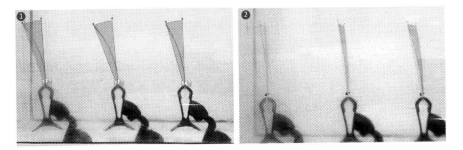

Fig. 6. Kinovea tracking (1. Angle of curvature, 2. Twist angle)

4   Results and Discussion

Nine different laminated cases were tested to study the effect of different grain orientations on the wood behavior response, represented in the deflection angle value. This was tested, as a limited durability test, on three continuous wood expansion cycles in relative humidity ranging from 50% to 90%, and shrinkage cycles in relative humidity ranging from 90% to 50%. Each case was repeated three times on three samples for the validity of the results, where an average of the readings was taken.

4.1   Deflection Angle

Two types of curvature occurred with respect to wood response to humidity: single curvature and double curvature. Double curvature is due to the 45° grain orientation. Cases 1, 2, 4 and 5 featured single curvature, while cases 3, 6, 7, 8 and 9 featured double curvature. Samples with double curved response were analyzed with respect to two angles; a vertical angle for measuring deflection, and another angle to measure twisting. Results were divided into three groups according to the properties of the active layer (beech with grain orientation 90°, 0°, and 45°) as shown in Tables 2, 3, and 4 respectively.

It was shown that high twisting values were related to samples with beech at 45° grain orientation, such as in cases 7, 8 and 9. The highest twisting angle was demonstrated in case 8 (Spruce 90° + Beech 45°).

Table 2. Tracking deflection and twisting angles with respect to response time for cases with beech as active layer at 90° grain orientation

		Case 1: Spruce 0° + Beech 90°			Case 2: Spruce 90° + Beech 90°			Case 3: Spruce 45° + Beech 90°		
		Cycle 1	Cycle 2	Cycle 3	Cycle 1	Cycle 2	Cycle 3	Cycle 1	Cycle 2	Cycle 3
Time (minutes)	RH (50%:90%)	5:23	5:31	5:33	5:39	4:35	5:32	2:40	4:29	5:27
	RH (90%:50%)	10:05	10:12	10:50	9:08	9:23	9:44	8:00	10:56	7:20
Deflection Angle (°)	Sample 1	3	2	2	0	1	1	2	1	2
	Sample 2	2	2	1	1	2	0	2	2	2
	Sample 3	2	3	4	1	1	0	2	3	3
	Average	2.33	2.33	2.33	0.67	1.33	0.33	2	2	2.33
Twist Angle (°)	Sample 1	/	/	/	/	/	/	1	1	0
	Sample 2	/	/	/	/	/	/	1	1	1
	Sample 3	/	/	/	/	/	/	1	1	1
	Average							1	1	0.67

Table 3. Tracking deflection and twisting angles with respect to response time for cases with beech as active layer at 0° grain orientation

		Case 4: Spruce 0° + Beech 0°			Case 5: Spruce 90° + Beech 0°			Case 6: Spruce 45° + Beech 0°		
		Cycle 1	Cycle 2	Cycle 3	Cycle 1	Cycle 2	Cycle 3	Cycle 1	Cycle 2	Cycle 3
Time (minutes)	RH (50%:90%)	5:41	4:08	4:13	7:07	6:38	7:06	6:27	4:55	6:47
	RH (90%:50%)	11:21	10:40	10:02	10:41	11:20	10:56	11:15	10:56	10:48
Deflection Angle (°)	Sample 1	16	16	20	7	7	8	13	15	17
	Sample 2	17	18	19	6	6	7	12	15	17
	Sample 3	16	16	17	5	6	5	12	13	14
	Average	16.33	16.67	18.67	6	6.33	6.67	12.33	14.33	16
Twist Angle (°)	Sample 1	/	/	/	/	/	/	1	0	0
	Sample 2	/	/	/	/	/	/	1	1	1
	Sample 3	/	/	/	/	/	/	1	1	1
	Average							1	0.67	0.67

Table 4. Tracking deflection and twisting angles with respect to response time for cases with beech as active layer at 45° grain orientation

		Case 7: Spruce 0° + Beech 45°			Case 8: Spruce 90° + Beech 45°			Case 9: Spruce 45° + Beech 45°		
		Cycle 1	Cycle 2	Cycle 3	Cycle 1	Cycle 2	Cycle 3	Cycle 1	Cycle 2	Cycle 3
Time (minutes)	RH (50%:90%)	5:32	6:11	6:12	6:55	7:12	7:19	6:36	6:58	7:48
	RH (90%:50%)	11:17	11:20	11:02	11:06	11:18	11:15	10:40	10:45	12:03
Deflection Angle (°)	Sample 1	2	2	1	5	6	5	8	9	12
	Sample 2	2	3	1	5	6	6	5	7	9
	Sample 3	1	2	2	7	9	10	5	6	8
	Average	1.67	2.33	1.33	5.67	7	7	6	7.33	9.67
Twist Angle (°)	Sample 1	4	5	4	4	4	4	4	6	6
	Sample 2	4	4	5	3	4	4	2	3	4
	Sample 3	3	4	3	5	6	6	2	3	3
	Average	3.67	4.33	4	4	4.67	4.67	2.67	4	4.33

A comparison between the deflection angles for all the nine laminated cases is shown in Fig. 7. Results show that the highest deflection angles occur where beech grain orientation is at 0°, as in case 4, 5 and 6. In those laminated samples with beech and spruce, beech is the active layer that initiates and controls the movement. The least deflection angles however are shown in samples with beech at 90° grain orientation, as in cases 1, 2 and 3. Cases 7, 8 and 9, with beech at 45° grain orientation, demonstrate an intermediate deflection angle.

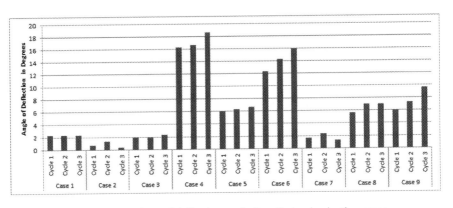

Fig. 7. Comparison of deflection angle for all nine lamination cases

In the twisting cases, it was demonstrated that the fastest response with the highest twisting angle was represented in those cases with the active layer at 45° grain orientation and the passive layer at 90° grain orientation. Cases however with the active layer at 45° grain orientations and the passive layer at 0° grain orientation were demonstrated to exhibit the least twisting angles, as shown in Fig. 8.

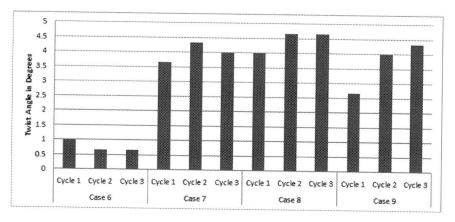

Fig. 8. Comparison of twisting for cases with 45° grain orientation

4.2   Durability of Wood Programmability Analysis

As shown in Fig. 7, the difference in the response value between each cycle within the same case represents the change in wood programmability after each cycle. From the previous experiments, it was demonstrated that the variation in programmable durability is affected by the lamination properties of each layer. Laminated samples with beech at 90° grain orientation showed the least variation values between cycles, thus having the most stable programmable durability. Laminated samples with beech at 0° grain orientation tended to have the least programmable durability that decreased from the first cycle till the third cycle. For laminated samples with beech at 45° grain orientation showed varying results from high programmable durability as in case 7 to medium programmable durability as in case 9.

4.3   Response Time

A comparison of the response time for all nine laminated cases is shown in Fig. 9. The response time shows two segments; the time needed for expansion to reach the highest angle of deflection, and the shrinkage time of the sample to return to its initial state. It was shown that the time needed for sample expansion is half the time needed for the sample to shrink and return to its initial state.

Although veneer with grain orientation at 0° is known to be fastest in response with a high deflection angle, it was shown in this experiment that the response is quite different in laminated composites. From the previous experiments, it was shown that the behavior of wooden laminated samples differs from that of single layer wood samples.

It was also demonstrated that beech as a hardwood was the main driver for motion in the samples, where it acted as an active layer that has the ability to change the laminated sample behavior according to its configuration. Spruce as a softwood on the other hand acted as a passive layer that restricts sample behavior.

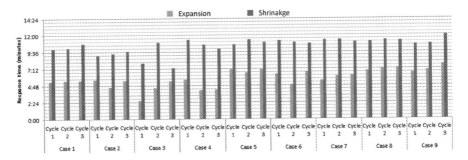

Fig. 9. Comparison of response time for all nine lamination cases

5 Conclusion

The study introduced a framework to develop, control and program the response behavior of wood to difference in humidity levels. A matrix was introduced to show the effect of hygroscopic design parameters on the response of laminated wooden composites through the angle of deflection, twisting and response time of expansion and shrinkage of laminated samples. This provides a benchmark for controlling the deflection of wood through fabricating laminated wooden composites with specific hygroscopic design parameters such as grain orientation, wood cut and type, thus enriching the hygroscopic design control of adaptive facades.

Acknowledgment. The authors are grateful to the Bartlett Fund for Science and Engineering Research Collaboration in supporting the 'Soft Adaptive Building Skins for Energy-Efficient Architecture' research project.

References

1. Wood, D.M., Correa, D., Krieg, O.D., Menges, A.: Material computation—4D timber construction: towards building-scale hygroscopic actuated, self-constructing timber surfaces. Int. J. Architect. Comput. **14**, 49–62 (2016)
2. Krieg, O.D., et al.: HygroSkin – Meteorosensitive pavilion. In: Fabricate 2014, pp. 61–67. Zurich (2014)
3. Rüggeberg, M., Burgert, I.: Bio-inspired wooden actuators for large scale applications. PLoS ONE **10**, e0120718 (2015)
4. Dierichs, K., Menges, A.: Towards an aggregate architecture: designed granular systems as programmable matter in architecture. Granular Matter **18**, 25 (2016)

5. Correa, D., et al.: 3D-printed wood: programming hygroscopic material transformations. 3D Printing Addit. Manuf. **2**, 106–116 (2015)
6. Reichert, S., Menges, A., Correa, D.: Meteorosensitive architecture: biomimetic building skins based on materially embedded and hygroscopically enabled responsiveness. Comput. Aided Des. **60**, 50–69 (2015)
7. Abdelmohsen, S., Adriaenssens, S., El-Dabaa, R., Gabriele, S., Olivieri, L., Teresi, L.: A multi-physics approach for modeling hygroscopic behavior in wood low-tech architectural adaptive systems. Comput. Aided Des. **106**, 43–53 (2019)
8. Abdelmohsen, S., Massoud, P., El-Dabaa, R., Ibrahim, A., Mokbel, T.: A computational method for tracking the hygroscopic motion of wood to develop adaptive architectural skins. In: eCAADe 2018: 6th Annual Conference on Education and Research in Computer Aided Architectural Design in Europe, Poland, vol. 2, pp. 1–9 (2018)
9. El-Dabaa, R., Abdelmohsen, S.: A Methodology for Evaluating the Hygroscopic Behavior of Wood in Adaptive Building Skins using Motion Grammar, vol. 362, pp. 1–8 (2018)

Tooling Cardboard for Smart Reuse: A Digital and Analog Workflow for Upcycling Waste Corrugated Cardboard as a Building Material

Julio Diarte[1,2]([⊠]) [iD], Elena Vazquez[1] [iD], and Marcus Shaffer[1]

[1] Stuckeman School of Architecture and Landscape Architecture,
The Pennsylvania State University, University Park, PA 16802, USA
{jcd40,emvl0,mus39}@psu.edu
[2] Facultad de Arquitectura, Diseño y Artes, Universidad Nacional de Asuncion,
Campus Universitario, San Lorenzo, Paraguay
julio.diarte@cidi.fada.una.py

Abstract. This paper is a description of a hybridized digital and analog workflow for reusing waste corrugated cardboard as a building material. The work explores a combination of digital design and analog fabrication tools to create a workflow that would help designers/builders to negotiate with the material variability of waste cardboard. The workflow discussed here was implemented for designing and fabricating a prototypical modular floor panel using different sheets of waste cardboard combined with repurposed wood. The implementation shows that combining digital and analog tools can create a novel approach to material reuse, and facilitate a design/fabrication culture of *smart* reuse that supports informal building and making at recycling collection centers in developing countries for housing alternatives.

Keywords: Smart reuse · Waste cardboard architecture ·
Digital analog workflow · Parametric design

1 Introduction

The work detailed in this paper is part of a research agenda that is currently exploring technological methods and tools (from low-tech to digital) for upcycling waste cardboard that is taken directly from the urban waste stream in developing countries, and its reuse/transformation as a resource for architecture. The central thesis presented in this paper is that parametric and other digital design tools can help designers-builders negotiating with the material variability of waste cardboard. This first section of the paper provides an overview of precedents of cardboard architecture including a discussion of the challenges and opportunities of using cardboard as a building material. A brief review of digital design tools used for negotiating variable material is thereafter presented, describing the strategies adopted for this study. Next, in the methods section, the authors describe the workflow proposed for fabricating prototypical modular floor panels reusing sheets of waste cardboard. Finally, the authors analyze and discuss the outcome in the results and conclusion sections.

© Springer Nature Singapore Pte Ltd. 2019
J.-H. Lee (Ed.): CAAD Futures 2019, CCIS 1028, pp. 384–398, 2019.
https://doi.org/10.1007/978-981-13-8410-3_27

1.1   Precedents of Cardboard Architecture in Research and Practice

A systematic review of the literature of cardboard as a construction material in research and practice reveals that the interest in the use of cardboard started in the mid-twentieth century. Nevertheless, it was not until the 1990s that cardboard architecture became noteworthy – especially in the work of Shigeru Ban. Figure 1 illustrates the number of related research publications and buildings that used cardboard products during the last seventy-five years. A possible explanation for this increment might be the emergence of Shigeru Ban's paper buildings in the 1990s and the establishment of research groups in relevant academic centers and universities in the 2000s – particularly Delft University of Technology and ETH Zurich. These research groups; strategically associated either with Shigeru Ban Architects, the paper industry, or engineering consulting companies, developed comprehensive studies on cardboard applications for architecture and structural engineering [1–7].

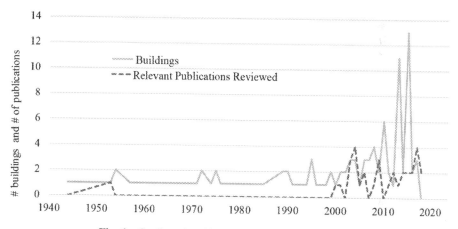

Fig. 1. Cardboard architecture in research and practice

According to the review, architects and engineers were and still are motivated by the eco-friendliness, relative strength, low-weight, and low-cost of the material. 56% of the reviewed publications mentioned cardboard as a sustainable product, and 32% included the reusability and recyclability of the material as an advantage for construction. Other aspects of cardboard products that stand out include the worldwide availability of the material, one that could facilitate a potential mass production system, its fabrication technologies, and its relatively sound acoustic and thermal insulation capacities.

Currently, there is a wide range of applications of cardboard products in building construction. The most common application of cardboard products – specifically paperboard, paper tubes, corrugated cardboard, honeycomb boards, and L and U-shape profiles – is in the fabrication of composite walls panels for walls (for both load and non-load bearing), floors, and roof. This application is found in short-span structures in small residential and commercial buildings. The second most common application, particularly for paper tubes, is for constructing arches, barrel vaults, domes, shells, and formwork for columns. This application is found in short and long-span structures. The most common type of buildings on which these applications are found are mostly temporary pavilions for exhibitions (26%), public buildings (26%), emergency shelters (21%), and housing and multifunctional buildings (15%) among others.

Overall, there has been extensive formal research into the use of cardboard products as a building material. However, the focus has typically been on brand-new and engineered cardboard produced by the paper factories, and geographically located in developed countries (50% in Europe, 21% in North America, and 17% in Japan) where the recovery rate of waste cardboard is very high – above 90% in North America, West Europe, and Japan [8]. On the other hand, waste cardboard has a different story in developing countries where it is commonly underutilized; the recovery rate is very low – barely above 60% in Latin American countries [8], there has been very little formal research about used cardboards potential reuse for designing and producing waste cardboard architecture.

The research described in this paper focuses on how a combination of digital and analog tools could facilitate reinserting waste cardboard collected from the urban waste stream in developing countries into a "smart" reuse process for housing alternatives. The work includes a case study developed in an academic setting that is intended to be tested in Asuncion, Paraguay, where the formal recovery system of recyclable materials including waste cardboard is deficient or non-existent [9], and there is a population that needs housing and cannot afford building using conventional materials.

1.2   Reusing Waste Cardboard – Opportunities and Challenges

Waste corrugated cardboard occupies a large volume of the residential and commercial municipal solid waste produced globally – particularly in urban areas – and it is also one of the least valuable products among all collected recyclables [10]. This situation, in addition to associated material advantages mentioned previously, presents an opportunity for the potential use of waste cardboard as a building material for the construction of affordable housing systems in places (cities) where cardboard is a common waste and the material is insufficiently recovered or recycled.

In some developing countries, for example, waste cardboard is commonly recovered by an informal network of self-employed collectors or "cardboard pickers" who eventually use this material for building temporary shelters. Although the material is highly available and almost free, the vulnerability of cardboard against the elements, and the lack of technologies and knowledge for processing and improving the material on-site, prevents pickers from using it for constructing long-term use buildings.

Upcycling waste cardboard, however, presents several challenges, ranging from advancing collection methods, improving the mechanical properties of the material – cardboard, for example, loses resistance to puncture and long-term loads – and improving its resistance to humidity and fire, to negotiating with the variability of the material for designing building parts (waste cardboard, as opposed to brand-new cardboard, is heterogeneous in size and thickness). In this paper, we present a design and fabrication workflow for upscaling waste cardboard as a building material, using digital tools to negotiate with the variability of the material. The goal is to fabricate building parts using sheets of waste cardboard that are taken directly from "the street". Additional aspects considered for this work were the structural limitations of the material and the potential constraints of the target context – urban areas in developing countries with little or no access to digital fabrication tools.

1.3 Incorporating Digital Design Tools

Digital design tools can be used for negotiating the variability of non-standardized or irregular materials in frameworks where the final design is conditioned by the existing material. One strategy is to incorporate material feedback in design and automated fabrication processes. An example of this approach is presented by Amtsberg et al. [11] were the authors developed a digital setup to adapt non-standard parts to a predefined geometry using 3D scanning and nesting tools. Other more theoretical studies explored flexible and adaptable systems to incorporate indeterminacy in materials and machine processes as an advantage for design [12].

Another group of studies developed parametric tools for dealing with the variability of reclaimed materials. Here the literature includes: parametric scripts that accommodate shifting dimensional variables in reclaimed materials for reusing lumber from an old barn to configure new building components such as building skins [13]; insertion of digital information into material system for reusing waste sheet manufacturing products into a flat-pack building system [14]; parametric scripts for designing foldable trusses made from sheet steel using two-dimensional CNC fabrication tools for minimizing waste [15]; and negotiating inherent irregular geometries with unconventional technologies – industrial robotic arms—for designing and fabricating large capacity structures made of forked tree limbs [16].

Together, these studies indicate that combining variable materials and digital design and fabrication tools requires a workflow that can adjust to the indeterminacies of non-standardized materials without compromising their efficiency, stability, and aesthetics. The main strategies adopted in the described studies, such as parametric tools for minimizing waste and design algorithms for accommodating the variability of reclaimed materials, serve as precedents for this study.

1.4 Proposing a Hybridized Digital/Analog Workflow

Our study proposes a digitally-aided workflow for both designing and fabricating cardboard architectures using waste cardboard. The digital tools developed with this workflow aid the materialization of the cardboard elements using analog means. In other words, while the design part of the workflow relies on parametric design tools, the fabrication process is very much manually made, using (common) low-tech tools. With this combined use of digital and analog strategies, we argue for the need to develop decentralized and accessible fabrication tools that are to be physically associated with recycling environments, where the access to automated machinery might be limited.

In this context, we propose a hybridized digital/analog workflow to support the design and fabrication processes of building components made with waste cardboard in combination with other standard building materials – primarily repurposed plywood or particle board. Our workflow was designed to be applied in a recycling environment in a developing country. The novelty of this approach relies both on the use of waste material (waste cardboard collected from the urban waste stream as opposed to brand new cardboard provided on demand by paper manufacturing companies) and the methodology – incorporating digital design and fabrication tools into the workflow combined with low-tech methods and tools.

2 Methods

As explained in the introduction, the proposed workflow relies both on digital and analog strategies. In the workflow, we use parametric tools for helping design with non-standard building materials and for providing materialization instructions for fabricating cardboard architectures. Previous studies have also used parametric tools for aiding materialization processes. For instance, Çapunaman et al. [17] developed computer algorithms in Grasshopper for Rhino to generate patterns for (hand) making three-dimensional objects previously modelled using CAD software. Another study used parametric design tools for creating templates to help materialize a parametric wall using low-tech masonry techniques [18]. These studies demonstrated how computer algorithms and parametric tools can help translate design from digital environments to fabricated elements, by providing materialization instructions and guides rather than fabrication technologies.

As a proof of concept, a case study was developed (in an academic) setting where we repurposed sheets of waste cardboard collected from a university waste stream, in combination with common, repurposed wood and conventional hardware for producing a prototype of a modular floor panel. The floor panel consists of a "sandwich structure" comprised of two particle boards sheets with a core made of structural ribs that are fabricated with folded sheets of repurposed waste cardboard. What follows is a description of the workflow, detailing the tools developed in each step.

The workflow, illustrated in Fig. 2, includes (1) **material collection**; (2) the **documentation** and inventory of the collected sheets of waste cardboard; (3) **digital design tools** for designing the panel with structural ribs of waste cardboard, adapting available material to the designed component, and for providing materialization instructions; (4) **fabrication** of the structural ribs of waste cardboard using digital and analog tools to produce the floor panels; and (5) manual **assembly** of the floor panels. Through the implementation of a workflow for producing simple building components made of waste cardboard, this paper provides a reflective account of digital and analog techniques for reusing and upcycling common waste into building elements.

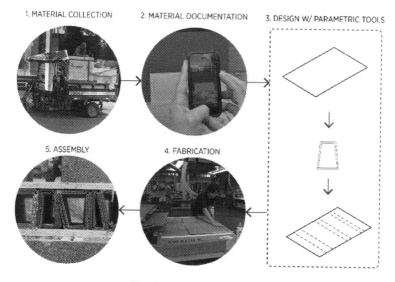

Fig. 2. Proposed workflow

2.1 Material Collection

The first step, ***material collection***, involves recovering and sorting sheets of waste cardboard that are not contaminated with food or medical waste, wet, and torn. This process is intended to be developed in association with waste collection systems available in the local context. For instance, in Asuncion, Paraguay – where we are planning to apply this workflow – the municipal collection system does not segregate neither residential nor commercial waste sending everything to landfills. Consequently, the recovery system of common recyclable materials, including waste cardboard, is dependent upon the work of self-employed collectors who harvest recyclables from the streets (Fig. 3). According to Medina, an specialist on informal recycling in the region, these unofficial collection systems "have been essential for the paper industry in Latin America" contributing to increasing the recovery rate of waste cardboard in, for example, Mexico and Brazil (see p. 21 in [19]).

Fig. 3. Self-employed collectors in Asuncion, Paraguay

In Paraguay, however, recycled cardboard only contributes 30% of material to the local production of new cardboard products and, according to a representative of the largest paper factory in the country, there are no expectations that this amount will grow in the near future [20]. Consequently, waste cardboard has the lowest value among local recyclable materials and collectors receive only between 5–10 cents (US Dollars) for each kilogram of recovered waste cardboard. We can compare this to at least double the amount for white, color or mixed paper, and ten times more for aluminum [21]. In an effort to imbue both collecting waste cardboard, and the material itself with more value, we are proposing that this workflow could support upscaling waste cardboard as a recyclable with a combination of digital and analog tools.

2.2   Material Documentation

The second step, *material documentation*, is shown in Fig. 4 and it consists of recording the dimensions of the recovered sheets of waste cardboard. The documentation is made by assigning an identification number to each sheet (variable a) and recording its length (variable b), width (variable c), and thickness (variable d). The scanning process of these variables is made by the user, employing a smartphone with a common tape measure application. In this research, we used a mobile app called *EasyMeasure* – as smartphones are widely available in the deployment context and this application is very inexpensive.

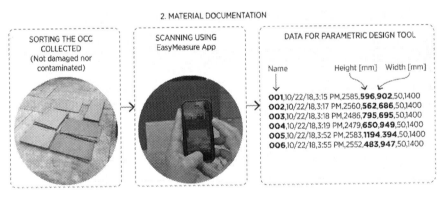

Fig. 4. Material documentation process using the *EasyMeasure* mobile app

The user simply places the sheet on a board and records the first three variables using the camera of the phone. The thickness is taken manually using a regular tape measure or similar measuring device. The material information recorded using the application is then exported to a text file, and this data is imported into a parametric script (detailed in the next section). The script selects the data needed from the text file and excludes all other information provided by the application that is not required. This documentation procedure automates the creation of a database that in turn facilitates the next step of the process when the designer needs to choose the appropriate sheet(s) of waste cardboard for the building component needed.

2.3   Designing with Digital Tools

The material documentation provides all the information needed for the next step in the framework, where we use *digital design tools* to produce a prototypical modular floor panel using a parametric tool, and for providing materialization instructions for the next step. The parametric design tool is a script developed in the Grasshopper plugin for Rhinoceros. The script facilitates the design of building elements with cardboard pieces of different shapes and thickness, where the final design emerges in the interplay between the constraints set by the user and the shape of the material that is available. The script allows the user to define limits to the solution space of the waste cardboard elements to assess different configurations with the aim of maximizing material reuse. The digital design tool also automates the generation of materialization instructions; cutting and scoring paths for geometries that are necessary for the fabrication process, according to the configuration of the building element.

Figure 5 illustrates the logic of the parametric design tool. The inputs for the script are the dimension of the sheets of cardboard obtained in the documentation process, and a group of design variables established by the user. The variables defined by the user (user input) are the thickness of the cardboard sheet, the minimum and maximum values for the dimensions of the cross-section of the waste cardboard rib, the profile type, and the number of cardboard walls each profile has. The cross-section of the profile can be either quadrangular, rectangular, trapezoidal, or triangular. The length of the waste cardboard ribs is also defined by the user, as per the desired width of the panel and the available material.

Based on the variables and input described above, the algorithm creates a series of possible profiles and automatically selects the appropriate profile for each cardboard piece available, so as to maximize material reuse. The algorithm outputs a preview of the panel by placing the selected profiles side by side until completing the desired length of the panel. The algorithm also produces scoring and cutting paths on each one of the sheets of cardboard and places tag names to identify the sheets facilitating the work during fabrication. The script also shows the amount of waste for each design iteration.

The user can then read (on each sheet) the amount of waste in millimeters and if it is deemed as an excessive amount of waste, the user can adjust the user input variables and redesign the profiles. This step can be repeated as many times as needed. Simply put, the user designs with the digital tool, adjusting the parameters and assessing how much material is wasted, in an iterative design process.

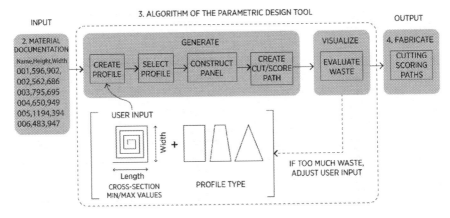

Fig. 5. Logic of the parametric design tool

Figure 6 depicts how the script creates a preview of the panel showing the flat (unfolded) waste cardboard ribs with the scoring paths and the waste generated by the design. The output of the parametric script are the materialization instructions, in the form of cutting and folding path geometries that can either be printed out as templates in paper, or simply be the geometries used to laser-cut the pieces. The workflow continues with the fabrication of the waste cardboard ribs and assembling the panel.

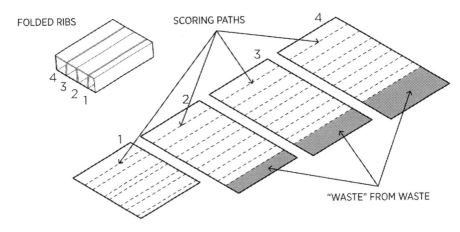

Fig. 6. Visualization

2.4   Fabrication of Building Parts

The third step, the *fabrication* process, combines digital information obtained from the previous step and analog fabrication methods associated with cardboard construction, such as scoring, cutting, and/or folding, aiding the user in producing the building components needed. At this point, the cutting and scoring paths obtained with the digital design tool need to be translated onto the cardboard pieces. Different methods can be used at this point: translating the scoring and cutting paths using printed templates, or directly laser/drag knife cutting the cardboard pieces. Figure 7 illustrates how the translation can be done with the help of printed paper templates generated by the script. Using a cutting surface, the paper template is positioned accordingly by the user as a guideline for cutting and scoring.

Fig. 7. Fabrication process

2.5 Assembly of Building Parts

The last step, the *assembly* of the panel, is realized manually using hand and power tools. The plywood/particle board is placed on top of a flat surface and the waste cardboard ribs are joined to it using a water-based adhesive. Then, the second particle board is placed on top and the panel is clamped until the adhesive is completely cured. Depending on the humidity level, the panel can be ready in between 60 to 120 min. The waste cardboard ribs can be randomly placed by the user, as the profiles are designed to have the same angle. In future studies, we intend to optimize the placement of the profiles in the panel, arranging the different profile sizes to improve the mechanical performance of the cardboard elements.

3 Results

As a proof of concept, we implemented the workflow in an academic setting for designing and fabricating a floor panel. The panel (Fig. 8) was designed to be 2400 mm long, 450 mm wide, and 150 mm high, resulting in a sandwich structure of two particle board sheets with a core fabricated from thirty-five folded sheets of six different dimensions of repurposed waste cardboard. The finished panel is intended to be moved/placed by two people. The panel is supported by two joists running on the longest side of the panel. The folded sheets act as structural ribs and they are oriented in parallel to the width of the panel and perpendicular to the joists. The particle board sheets and waste cardboard ribs are joined using a standard and inexpensive water-based adhesive.

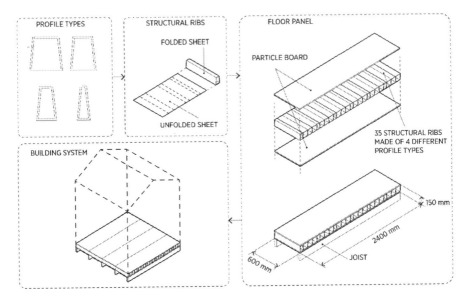

Fig. 8. Prototype of floor panel

The material collection process consisted on recovering sheets of waste cardboard from the university waste stream. We collected around forty sheets of waste cardboard, of six different dimensions, in a couple of hours in a common week day and, as mentioned above, we use thirty-five sheets for building one single floor panel. Although the reusing rate for this experiment was very high (almost 90%), we did not quantify the numbers of sheets found that did not qualify because they were contaminated, wet, torn, or were not large enough to be use as structural ribs.

The material documentation was effortlessly made by one person using the *EasyMeasure* app. We had fifty-two waste cardboard pieces of six different dimensions; the creation of the database helped in organizing and processing this information. The margin of error of the app – roughly 2.5 cm – is considered acceptable since it does not significantly affect the final dimensions of the panel profile. The app creates a database as a *.csv* file that is imported into the parametric script. Rather than manually entering the information into the parametric model, the proposed method facilitates and speeds up the recycling process by automating the creation of a database. The documentation process could also be done manually. However, the availability of smartphone applications for measuring surfaces or perimeters and its accessibility make this a viable alternative for automating the process.

The parametric tool was successfully used to design the panel as to maximize material reuse. Overall, the reusing rate of the each one of the thirty-five sheets was above 90%. The designed panel has four different dimensions of trapezoidal rib profile types, ranging from very thin ones used for the small pieces of waste cardboard, to thick profiles for the larger pieces. All the profiles have at least two cardboard walls as minimum thickness. To improve mechanical properties, this wall thickness could be increased to three or more. In this case, the cardboard pieces were not long enough to do so. One interesting aspect we discovered is that, while the parametric tool automates the creation of the profiles, the visualization of the panels, and the cutting-scoring paths, the user still is very much in control of the design process. The user defines the solution space and conditions the outcome of the system, optimizing the design so as to use as much material as possible.

In the illustrated workflow, we fabricated the panel using printed paper templates to translate the cutting and scoring paths, a utility knife and a cutting edge. Although this process can easily be made using a large laser cutter machine or a sample maker machine with a drag knife (commonly used in the packaging industry), we decided to keep the process as simple as possible considering that the access to such technology will not be easy in a context of scarce resources. Therefore, the tools used for cutting and scoring were very conventional and common. An alternative digital way for translating the scoring/cutting paths on the sheet of waste cardboard could be using virtual superimposition methods to replace templates or standard set up and measurement systems as seen in [22].

Finally, to have an idea of the structural performance of the panel, we performed an empirical load resistance test (Fig. 9) placing concrete blocks on top of the panel, taking into consideration the standard uniform live load used for residential floor designs, which is around 195 kilograms per square meter. After loading, we measured the deformation and the relative humidity levels over the course of several days. Although the waste cardboard used for building the panel did not have any protection against humidity, the panel did not show substantial deformations; however, further tests are needed to have a complete characterization of the panel's mechanical properties.

Fig. 9. Empirical load resistance test

4 Conclusions

This paper presented a workflow for upcycling waste cardboard using digital and analog tools. We propose a method for reusing waste cardboard – rather than 'new' cardboard—as a building material. The novelty of this approach relies on using digital design tools to "inform" and upscale a waste material for fabricating building elements; waste material that otherwise would be used only for producing new cardboard, or filling landfills.

Generally speaking, in the presented case study, the use of waste material with its heterogeneous nature is not evident in the resulting aesthetics of the constructed building part. Although this is not required, highlighting the heterogeneity of the material could enhance the overall aesthetics of the architecture. A variation to this approach would be to use algorithms to design a more heterogeneous building element where the formal configuration indicates the existence of materials of different sizes and thicknesses. Further studies for different application will explore this alternative. The described approaches are schematized in Fig. 10.

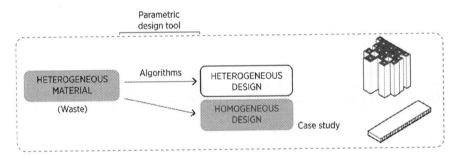

Fig. 10. Proposed approach for upscaling waste material

The reuse rate of sheets of waste cardboard for this experiment was very high (90%). However, the percentage of waste cardboard that did not meet the conditions required for the experiment was not measured. Further analysis in this aspect is, therefore, an essential next step in confirming the real impact of the project in the recovery rate of waste cardboard.

The material documentation method, using the mobile app, allows for the rapid creation of a database that is imported into a parametric model. Although the margin of error of the measurement app is around 2.5 cm, this is still acceptable considering that the edges of the sheet of waste cardboard need to be trimmed. Additionally, the proliferation of smartphones, and the low-cost and user-friendliness of the app allows almost everyone to use the tool.

The design phase of the workflow makes the process faster and more precise, giving inherent "smartness" and new value to the collected waste cardboard pieces. The algorithms of the parametric tool help transform a waste material that has variable shape and form into a relatively conventional construction component, in this case, a floor panel. The design tool also helps translating the cutting/scoring/folding paths from the digital to physical by offering printable templates that can be used without the need of a computer. Although the parametric tool works satisfactorily, the only parameter that it provides the user with for evaluating the different design iterations is how much material is wasted. Further work is required to incorporate other evaluation parameters into the parametric tool, such as an indication of the designs' mechanical performance.

The fabrication phase can be adapted to the available resources of the target context: urban areas in developing countries. The fabrication can be done either by translating the digital information into the physical realm with the use of templates – this would be the simplest way – or by using laser/drag knife-cutting machines to cut and score the cardboard pieces in situations where these tools are available. Parts of the workflow are automated, such as the creation of the database and the generation of cutting and scoring paths. Nevertheless, the automation does not mean relinquishing control over the design outcome of the cardboard architecture. Rather, the digital tools are conceived as to make the design and fabrication process faster and more efficient.

On the other hand, since cardboard is essentially a packaging material, more work could be done to determine the compatibility of the proposed tools with existing structural packaging design and fabrication tools. The existing standardized methods for fabricating packaging components and its associated tools could help inform more efficient design-fabrication workflows for repurposing waste cardboard.

Finally, the application of the workflow proposes that the combination of digital tools – increasingly ubiquitous around the world and more affordable as they proliferate – and analog tools to create a novel approach to material reuse, producing architectural and structural elements while simultaneously accommodating for waste cardboard's inherit material indeterminacies. We argue that methods that can record, and accommodate for, indeterminacies in (found, collected) waste materials will facilitate a culture of *smart* reuse that supports informal building and making at collection/recycling centers.

References

1. Eekhout, M., Verheijen, F., Visser, R.: Cardboard in Architecture. IOS Press, Amsterdam (2008)
2. Latka, J.F.: Paper in Architecture: Research by Design, Engineering, and Prototyping. Delft University of Technology (2017)
3. Salado, G.D.C.: Painel de vedação vertical de tubos de papelão: Estudo, proposta e análise de desempenho. Universidade de Sao Paulo (2011)
4. Ayan, Ö.: Cardboard in Architectural Technology and Structural Engineering. ETH Zurich (2009)
5. Pohl, A.: Strengthened corrugated paper honeycomb for application in structural elements. ETH Zurich (2009)
6. Sekulic, B.: Structural cardboard: feasibility study of cardboard as a long-term structural material in architecture. Polytechnic University of Catalonia (2013)
7. Ban, S.: Shigeru Ban. Material, Structure, and Space, 1st edn. Toto Publishing Ltd., Tokyo (2017)

8. Zhao, H.: Global OCC Market Outlook, p. 26 (2016)
9. IADB: Solid Waste Management in Latin America and the Caribbean (2015)
10. Hoornweg, D., Bhada-Tata, P.: What a waste: a global review of solid waste management (2012)
11. Amtsberg, F., Raspall, F., Trummer, A.: Digital-material feedback in architectural design. In: CAADRIA, 20th International Conference of the Association for Computer-Aided Architectural Design Research in Asia (2015)
12. Dickey, R.: Soft systems: rethinking indeterminacy in architecture as opportunity driven research. In: CAADRIA, 22nd International Conference of the Association for Computer-Aided Architectural Design Research in Asia, Hong Kong, pp. 811–821 (2017)
13. Hemsath, T.L., Mccracken, B.: Decon recon: parametric CADCAM deconstruction research. In: ACADIA 2010, pp. 291–293 (2010)
14. Wilkins, G., Zilka, L., Cherrey, J.: Scripted materials. In: ACADIA, 31st Annual Conference of the Association for Computer Aided Design in Architecture, Alberta, pp. 204–211 (2011)
15. Beorkrem, C., Corte, D.: Zero-Waste, Flat-Packed, Tri-Chord Truss: continued investigations of structural expression in parametric design. In: ACADIA, 32nd Annual Conference of the Association for Computer Aided Design in Architecture, San Francisco, pp. 199–208 (2012)
16. Vercruysse, E., Self, M.: Infinite variations, radical strategies. In: Fabricate 2017, pp. 30–35. UCL Press (2017)
17. Çapunaman, Ö.B., Bingöl, C.K., Gürsoy, B.: Computing stitches and crocheting geometry. In: Çağdaş, G., Özkar, M., Gül, L.F., Gürer, E. (eds.) CAADFutures 2017. CCIS, vol. 724, pp. 289–305. Springer, Singapore (2017). https://doi.org/10.1007/978-981-10-5197-5_16
18. Vazquez, E., Diarte, J., Gürsoy, B.: Bridging parametric design and craftsmanship: materializing the digital parametric brick wall with low-tech masonry construction techniques. In: CAADRIA, 23rd International Conference of the Association for Computer-Aided Architectural Design Research in Asia CAADRIA 2018, Hong Kong (2018)
19. Various: Revista: Harvard Review of Latin America - Garbage, 1st edn. David Rockefeller Center for Latin America Studies Harvard University, Cambridge (2015)
20. Diarte, J.: Personal Interview with Jose Mas from Cartones Yaguarete SA (2019)
21. Diarte, J.: Personal Interview with Jorge Abate from PROCICLA (2019)
22. Quinn, G.C., Galeazzi, A., Schneider, F., Gengnagel, C.: StructVR virtual reality structures. In: Mueller, C., Adriaenssens, S. (eds.) Proceedings of the IASS Symposium 2018, Boston (2018)

Weeping Brick

The Modular Living Wall System Using 3D Printed Porous Ceramic Materials

Jiyoon Bae[✉] [ID] and Daekwon Park[✉]

School of Architecture, Syracuse University, Syracuse, NY 13244, USA
{jbae05,dpark103}@syr.edu

Abstract. The goal of this research is to design and fabricate a modular living wall brick system that purifies and cools air for various indoor environments. The research utilizes ceramic 3d printing techniques for fabrication; and living plants in conjunction with evaporative cooling techniques for indoor air quality control. The brick is made of soil which become porous after firing or drying. Water from the reservoirs slowly weep through the porous brick, creating a layer of water on the surface of the brick. The air movement around the saturated brick creates evaporative cooling and the hydro-seeded plants absorb water from the surface. The shape and texture of the Weeping Brick maximizes the cooling effect via large surface area. As an aggregated wall system, the water circulates from unit to unit by gravity through interconnected reservoirs embedded within each unit. The plants and moss transform the Weeping Brick into a living wall system, purifying and conditioning the indoor air.

Keywords: Living wall system · Modular brick · Ceramic 3D printing · Evaporative cooling

1 Introduction

This research describes the design and fabrication process of the Weeping Brick, which is a modular living wall system that can house vegetation for both aesthetical and functional purposes. Inspired by traditional irrigation methods and evaporative cooling techniques, Weeping Brick can serve as passive air conditioning system for various indoor environments.

Olla, a traditional unglazed pottery used for irrigation is an excellent reference for utilizing weeping as a mechanism for slowly distributing water to the outer surface in a controlled way. Furthermore, Muscatese, a traditional evaporative cooling window system, serves as an inspiration for utilizing evaporative cooling for indoor environments.

1.1 Traditional Ceramic Technology

Traditional ceramic products such as pottery or mud brick is among the first material technology invented by humanity. The production techniques such as hand-building,

© Springer Nature Singapore Pte Ltd. 2019
J.-H. Lee (Ed.): CAAD Futures 2019, CCIS 1028, pp. 399–409, 2019.
https://doi.org/10.1007/978-981-13-8410-3_28

wheel-throwing, and casting has been developed and refined throughout the history and continues to be utilized to this day (see Fig. 1). Olla and Muscatese, which will be discussed in the following, utilizes these conventional ceramic production methods. However, in order to utilize the weeping mechanism, the ceramic is not glazed before firing to maintain its porous characteristic.

Fig. 1. Conventional ceramic production including hand-building, wheel-throwing, and slip-casting method in sequence. (Source: Shepherds Grove Studio)

Olla is an unglazed clay pot traditionally used for irrigating as well as cooking in the tradition of Northern Africa and is still practiced as an irrigation system in certain countries such as Brazil and India (see Fig. 2A). Once the unglazed clay pots are buried in the ground, the contained water slowly leaks out through the porous enclosure saturating the soil adjacent to the Olla. The plant roots absorb moisture from the wet soil around the Ollas [1]. Since the water weeps out from the pots in a consistent and extremely low rate, the water conservation is significant compared to other irrigation methods. Furthermore, the water distribution relies on weeping which is a passive process that does not require any external power sours of mechanisms (e.g. water pump or spray).

The Muscatese evaporative cooling window system has been used in Oman since the ancient era (see Fig. 2B). A porous-surfaced pottery is placed outside of Mashrabiya, a lattice screen window made of wood, controls the air temperature using the evaporative cooling effect. As the breeze from the outside enters the indoor space through the Mashrabiya screen, the air is cooled by the evaporative cooling that occurs at the moist surface of the water-saturated pot [2]. Similar to the Olla irrigation system, there is a water usage is optimized and the water distribution is passive.

In the current research, these traditional irrigation and cooling systems provide a basic understanding of the porosity of clay materials that can play significant role in water distribution and evaporative cooling.

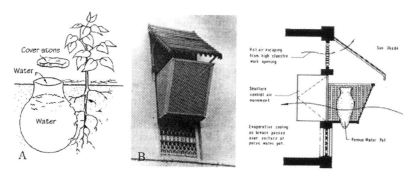

Fig. 2. A; Ollas irrigation B; Muscatese evaporative cooling (Source: A; Vukasin et al., B; Cabin et al.)

1.2   Contemporary 3D Printing Technology

With the wide spread interest in 3d printing ranging from artists to scientists, techniques to print objects beyond plastic (e.g. metal, glass, ceramic) has been in great demand. In this context, ceramic 3d printing technology has also been a focus for many researchers and developers. Currently, ceramic 3d printing can be achieved using all three platforms including fused deposition modeling (FDM), stereolithography, and selective laser sintering (Table 1). Depending on the platform, ceramic is used in the form of powder or in the plastic state (i.e. ceramic powder suspended in water or liquid plastic).

Ceramic 3d printing technology allows artists, designers, and architects to fabricate complex geometry with ease, and allow mass customization [3]. This research utilizes the FDM platform due to the simplicity of the system and the capacity to scale-up more effectively compared to other 3d printing platforms. Clay in a plastic state (clay powder mixed with water and ethyl alcohol) is used during the printing process and compressed air is used to force the clay mix through the nozzle. The viscosity of the clay mix, air pressure, print speed, and nozzle diameter needs to be optimized based on the complexity and size of the brick.

Table 1. Types of contemporary ceramic printing technology (Source: Snikhovska, K)

	FDM	Stereolithography	SLS
Mechanism			
Product	DIY Printer Delta Wasp Lutum	Formlab	Tethon3d VTech

There are a plethora of research and design utilizing ceramic 3d printing techniques. Cool Bricks (see Fig. 3A) designed by Emerging Objects utilizes evaporative cooling via micro-structured ceramic bricks [4]. The lattice structure enabled by the 3d printing process significantly increases the surface area of the bricks which enhances the rate of evaporative cooling.

Also, Ceramic Morphologies (see Fig. 3B) designed by Material Process + Systems Group, Harvard GSD investigates novel ceramic 3d printing processes for building applications. Their research pavilion not only showcases the geometric possibilities of ceramic 3d printing but also implements thermal design strategies [5]. These two precedents highlight the potential of ceramic 3D printing as an enabling technology for creating expressive ceramic components which functions beyond aesthetics.

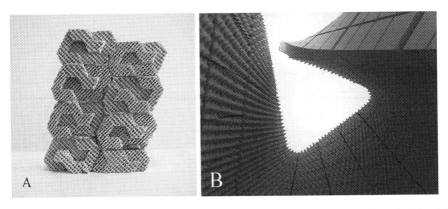

Fig. 3. A; Cool brick and B; Ceramic morphologies (Sources: A; Emerging objects, B; Material process + systems group)

1.3   Porosity and Absorption Rates of Ceramics

At the beginning of research, choosing the proper types of clay was significant to get a porous surface after fabricating, which is dependent on the mineral components and size of the particle. Therefore, the investigation into characteristics of several types of clays was required to find the appropriate material. Clay which is used for pottery or brick can be broadly divided into Porcelain, Stoneware, and Earthenware [6]. Each classified clay has its own traits such as color, porosity, absorption rates, texture and strength (Table 2).

Table 2. Broad classification of clay type and characteristics (Source: Kiln Art)

Earthenware clay	Porcelain clay	Stoneware clay
Color range from white to brick red	Color range from white to brown	Color range from gray to dark brown
Various texture	Various texture	Various texture
Porous surface	Non-porous	Slightly porous
Relatively fragile	Relatively less fragile	Relatively strong

This paper studies the three types of clay, porcelain, earthenware red, and red terracotta clay, to identify the correlation between porosity and water absorption rate. These clays have different levels of water absorption rates depending on their porosity. Also, each clay has appropriate firing temperature to get stable outcomes [7]. Table 3 below shows proper firing temperature and the characteristics of fired potteries made from each clay type. Earthenware has highest absorption rate but, porcelain barely absorbs water [8]. Accordingly, among the attributes of each clay type, porosity and water absorption rate plays a significant role in evaporation.

Table 3. Proper firing temperature and absorption rate of clay pots (Source: Zamek, J)

	Earthenware clay	Porcelain clay	Stoneware clay
Firing temperature	Cone06 (1,828 °F)	Cone09 (2,300 °F)	Cone06 (1,828 °F) Cone09 (2,300 °F)
Porosity	Porous	Non-porous	Slightly porous
Absorption	12–14%	0.5–2%	1.5–3%

2   Design and Fabrication Process

2.1   Design Parameters

The primary components of the Weeping Brick include water reservoirs, evaporative surface, structural elements and water vessels. The undulating top surface of the brick functions as a reservoir to capture water as well as provide a large surface area for evaporative cooling (see Fig. 4).

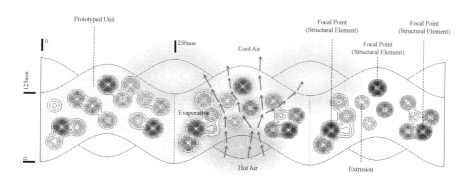

Fig. 4. Basic elements and evaporation mechanism

The structural elements consist of three vertical hollow tubes located to distribute the load evenly. These elements also serve as water vessels that circulate water (excess water after the reservoirs are full) from one unit to another. This design allows the aggregated wall to have interconnected system of water vessels that can passively distribute water using gravity and overflow (see Fig. 5).

Weeping Brick also utilizes hydro-seeding method to transform the ceramic wall into a living wall system that is attractive to the eye and contribute to air purification. Hydro-seeding is normally used for sowing seeds on irregular surface of ground efficiently by spraying a viscus mix of seeds, nutrients, water, and organic glue [9]. The textured surface of the brick facilitates hydro-seeded plants to stably root at the surface.

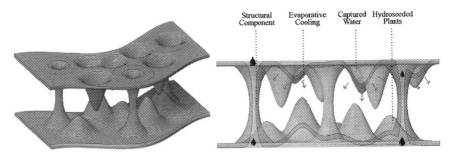

Fig. 5. Prototyped Weeping Brick unit and section which shows the basic components of unit and how water can circulate internally.

Weeping Brick is a modular system that can be flexibly configured and stacked. As an assembled system, the curvatures in the front and back of each individual unit create a wall that undulates in multiple directions (see Fig. 6). Once the units are joined horizontally and stacked vertically, air can flow between the top and bottom plate of each unit creating evaporative cooling effects through the extended undulating surfaces.

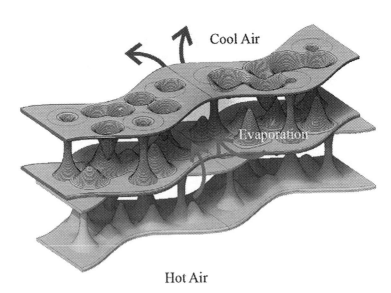

Fig. 6. Prototyped modular brick system and basic concept of evaporative cooling.

Weeping Brick living wall system can be applied to the exterior as well as the interior wall and enhance the aesthetical and environmental aspects of the space (see Fig. 7). The large porous surface saturated with water passively controls the indoor temperature by the evaporative cooling effect and the hydro-seeded plants contribute to air purification.

Fig. 7. Application of weeping brick to living wall brick system

2.2   Fabrication Process

After finishing the design process, the physical experiment, which uses Delta Wasp 2040 with a clay extruder, is conducted to fabricate actual brick units. In the beginning the fabrication process, two types of clays are prepared to compare the cooling performance. This depends on the porosity and absorption rate of each material. Each type of clay is mixed with the appropriate portion of water and ethyl alcohol to get proper softness and adhesiveness.

These prepared clays are loaded into the clay chamber that is connected to a compressor and printer. A compressor is required to squeeze the material from the clay chamber to the extruder. By using Delta Wasp 2040 3D printer and LDM (liquid deposit modeling) extruder, the prototyped unit of Weeping Brick is printed using each material, porcelain and earthenware red clay for the purpose of evaluating the materials' evaporation performances (see Fig. 8).

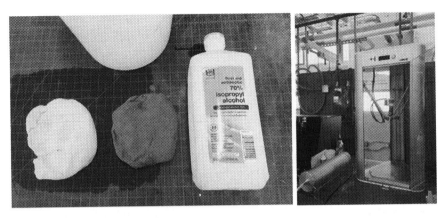

Fig. 8. 3D printing clay materials and 3D printer (Color figure online)

Once the printer is set up, the manual setting in the slice tool plays a significant role in the quality of outcomes. This research uses Slic3r as the main slicing tool. Since the outcomes can vary significantly depending on the setting in slicing tool, manual settings were utilized to find the proper parameters (see Fig. 9). During this phase, multiple samples with different variables (e.g. printing speed, infill density, and material extrusion width) were fabricated and tested.

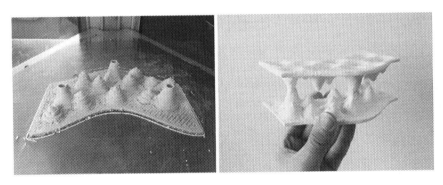

Fig. 9. Outcomes of ceramic 3D printing

The final phase in fabrication process is to plant the vegetation on the surface of the brick. Hydro-seeding method, which is a mix of seeds, nutrients, and organic glue, is utilized so that the vegetation adheres to the textured surface (see Fig. 10). The water from the reservoir weeps throughout the body of the brick providing moisture to the vegetation as well as the evaporative cooling surfaces (see Fig. 11).

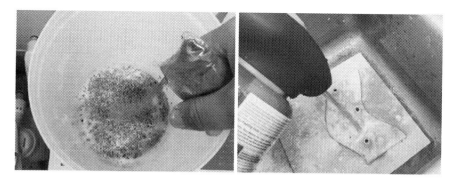

Fig. 10. Hydro-seeding

Fig. 11. Weeping brick

3   Discussion

The purpose of this research is to produce a modular brick living wall system which performs evaporative cooling and air purification. At the beginning of the research, this paper looked at the inspirational ceramic precedents in the tradition, the Olla irrigation and Muscatese window. These cases utilize the porosity of unglazed ceramics for consistent water distribution and evaporative cooling which optimized for certain environmental conditions [1, 2]. This research converts the traditional ideas of ceramic technology into contemporary interpretation by using parametric modeling, ceramic 3d printing, and hydro-seeding.

The brick can be assembled as a modular living wall system which allows nature to enter the indoor space as well as contribute to better control the indoor air quality for the habitants. Water channels and structural components embedded within each individual unit interconnect when the modules are put together for distributing the load and water throughout the assembly. Since water is distributed down the walls via gravity and overflow, the occupant can replenish the entire wall by supplying water to the top row of the assembly. After the water from the top reservoirs are full, the overflow of water trickles down to the next row via the hollow vessels embedded within the vertical structural components.

There were some challenges and limitations in the fabrication process as well as the proposed system itself. Due to the large number of variables that affect the outcome of the samples such as clay viscosity, air pressure, and print settings (speed, extrusion dimension) it is challenging to get consistent outcomes. The hydro-seeding process works in principle but similar to the delicate 3d printing setup, it is necessary to optimize the mix (seed, nutrients, water, glue) and surface texture to ensure that the batch will adhere to the brick surface properly.

Furthermore, although it is apparent that the porosity of the clay type dictates water content of the brick, it is not apparent how air flow, indoor air temperature, and vegetation covering will affect the evaporative cooling effect of the system. Therefore, further experiments are necessary for optimizing the porosity and absorption rate of the brick for both evaporative cooling and water distribution to the vegetation.

Finally, the scope of this research included prototyping of several modules for refining the 3d printing process and hydro-seeding process. During the next phase of research, it is necessary to fabricate a full-scale partition wall or a pavilion to further investigate the connection methods (e.g. mortar, gravity, or mechanical connector), and test the performance of Weeping Brick as an assembled system (e.g. structural integrity, water network, evaporative cooling performance, and aesthetics).

4   Conclusion and Future Work

This paper describes the design and fabrication process of Weeping brick, a modular living wall system made of 3d printed ceramic. This research explores the potentials of ceramic 3d printing as an enabling technology for creating both aesthetical and functional components for building applications.

Future investigations will focus on (1) further refining the 3d printing and hydro-seeding process for fabricating consistent and reliable modules; and (2) conduct physical experiments using different types of clay and firing process to optimize evaporative cooling; and (3) fabricate a building-scale prototype (e.g. partition wall or pavilion) for testing the overall system performance in terms of structure, water distribution, evaporative cooling, and aesthetics.

Acknowledgements. This research is the selected as 2018 Creative Work Grant, annual graduate school research grant program of Syracuse University School of Architecture.

References

1. Bainbrideg, D.: Super-Efficient Irrigation with Buried Clay Pots. Rio Redondo Press, San Diego (2012)
2. Rosa Schiano-Phan, R.: The development of passive downdraught evaporative cooling system using porous ceramic evaporators and their application in residential buildings. In: PLEA Conference 2004, Eindhoven, The Netherlands, pp. 19–22 (2004)
3. Suon, P.: Dynamic Ceramic, M. Arch thesis Studio 2016, Department of Architecture, University of California Berkley (2016)
4. Emerging Objects: Cool Brick, Berkley, CA (2015)
5. Seibold, Z., Hinz, K., Garcia del Castillo, J.L., Alonso, N.M., Mhatre, S., Bechthold, M.: Ceramic morphologies: precision and control in paste-based additive manufacturing. In: Proceedings of the 38th Annual Conference of the Association for Computer Aided Design in Architecture, pp. 350–357 (2018)
6. Kiln Art: Type of Clay Bodies. https://kilnarts.org/education/ceramic-pottery/the-basics-of-clay/types-of-clay/
7. Raimondo, D., Dondi, M., Gardini, D., Guarini, G., Francesca, M.: Predicting the initial rate of water absorption in clay bricks. Constr. Build. Mater. **23**, 2623–2630 (2009)
8. Zamek, J.: Clay Body Shrinkage & Absorption. Ceramic Industry (2013)
9. Oliver Brown Ltd.: History of Hydroseeding. https://oliverbrownltd.co.uk/hydroseeding/the-history-of-hydroseeding/

Shape Studies

A National Pattern Generation Method Based on Cultural Design Genetic Derivation

Lisha Ma$^{(\boxtimes)}$ ⑩, Yu Wu, Xiaofang Yuan$^{(\boxtimes)}$, and Wuzhen Zhu

School of Art and Design, Wuhan University of Technology, Wuhan, China
18612037018@163.com, Wuyu1981@gmail.com,
1126613@qq.com, 1476095124@qq.com

Abstract. It is a great challenge to digitally generate emotionally satisfying patterns with national style characteristics to meet diversified consumer demands for national patterns. As the core of national culture's gestation, growth and development, cultural genes can realize cultural inheritance and maintain national identity. From the view of design, the basic feature elements of cultural genes are extracted by original national pattern deconstruction and semantically summarized to form specific cultural design genes suitable for the rapid design of national pattern. Further, the topology principle and Computer-Aided design is introduced to simultaneously generate pattern shapes using Self-Crossing and Cross-Crossing transformation by shape grammar. Then, the pattern elements are arranged according to the initial ethnic pattern composition rules to generate new series of ethnic patterns. Finally, Chinese Tibetan pattern is patterned as an example to demonstrate that this research can creates patterns faster and in line with the user's intent.

Keywords: National pattern · Cultural design gene · Pattern deconstruction · Shape grammar · Computer-Aided design

1 Introduction

With "shape" and "semantic" features, the national pattern is a continuation and for-malized expression of minority culture, mirroring the cultural characteristics and his-torical changes of ethnic minorities [1]. As products of the times, national patterns should have national characteristics, conform to the "shape" aesthetics of modern society, and also satisfy consumers' intention. Nowadays, the demand for national patterns is growing rapidly, while the design of national patterns is time-consuming and laborious, which generates obvious contradictions between design and fast-paced consumer market [2]. Drawing the pattern based on the designer's own experience and knowledge is complicated and inefficient. Although computer-aided design can help draw pattern outlines to reduce workload, the derivative design and reuse of patterns still need to be completed by designers, with a lack of cultural depth [3].

In the perceptual consumption era, it is of vital importance to extract core con-notation of national culture and apply it to pattern to shorten national pattern design cycle and accelerate its success in market [4]. In this paper, we attempt to decompose the original ethnic patterns from the perspective of cultural semantics, and extract the

© Springer Nature Singapore Pte Ltd. 2019
J.-H. Lee (Ed.): CAAD Futures 2019, CCIS 1028, pp. 413–428, 2019.
https://doi.org/10.1007/978-981-13-8410-3_29

design features of the cultural genes that match the user's intentions as the cultural design genes. Further, we transform the process of generating new national patterns into the derivation design of cultural design genes by shape grammar. In addition, we take the Chinese Tibetan pattern as an example to carry out the derivative design research of ethnic patterns, which verifies the effectiveness of this method.

2   Cultural Design Gene Theory

2.1   Cultural Gene

Culture is the crystallization of human collective wisdom. It has different cultural features in different periods, different regions and different races. The development of culture is similar to the process of biological evolution, with characteristics such as inheritance and diversity. Cultural genes are the iconic cultural characteristics of culture that have not been buried for thousands of years. Different from biological genetics, it depends on human, social, and physical factors. Its form can be expressed as: decorative ornament, architectural style and custom. Regarding the theoretical study of cultural genes, Schipper [5] first proposed the concept of cultural gene pool and advocated the establishment of cultural gene pools. Zhao [6] constructed a cultural gene pedigree by deconstructing the intangible cultural genes and material cultural genes in regional culture. Starting with cultural genes Bao [7] explored the development background of Eastern and Western cultures, and compared the thinking and science of East and West. Therefore, cultural genes have realized cultural inheritance and maintained the sense of national identity, which is the core of the birth, growth and development of national culture.

2.2   Cultural Design Gene

Cultural design genes are a manifestation or a basic characteristic element that can be applied to design expression, and it is a core cultural feature extracted from cultural genes [8]. Professor Yair [9, 10] of Sheffield Hallam University in the United Kingdom studied how to extract the cultural characteristics of patterns such as shapes, contours and textures from traditional tin handicrafts from the perspective of applied culture and genetics. Lin [11] in Taiwan University of the Arts studied the cultural characteristics of Taiwan's aborigines, extracted cultural design genes from their living utensils, and applies them to modern design. Wang [12] in Shaanxi University of Science and Technology in China studied the composition of the triangle pattern of ancient Chinese Ban-Po painted pottery. Through the design, the traditional pattern was standardized and unified, and the inheritance of Ban-Po painted pottery culture was realized. Cultural design genes are the basic feature extraction and semantic induction of cultural genes from the perspective of design. Its purpose is to extract cultural connotation features and apply them to design activities. This paper will deeply interpret the cultural design genes from four dimensions: Semantic dimension, User dimension, Composition dimension and Environmental dimension (Fig. 1) [13].

- **Semantic dimension:** Cultural design genes have dominant semantic and implicit semantic. Dominant semantic refers to the ontological characteristics of cultural design genes, and the implicit semantics reflect the cultural connotation and spiritual symbol of cultural design genes.
- **Composition dimension:** Studying the Semantic Dimensions of Cultural Design Genes and the Compositional Rules of Cognitive Combinations.
- **Environmental Dimensions:** Cultural Design Gene Source Environment and Cultural Design Gene Reuse Environment.
- **User dimension:** the cultural background of designers and users and the user's thinking mode.

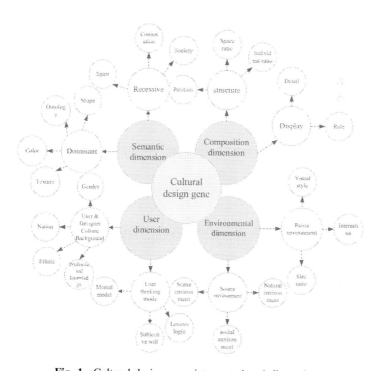

Fig. 1. Cultural design gene interpretation 4 dimensions

3 Pattern Deconstruction Description

3.1 Hierarchical Expression Model

The national pattern itself is highly standardized, and usually arranged by a series of hierarchical elements in a certain proportion, rule, size, and direction. In order to improve the efficiency of national pattern derivation and make its innovative design process intelligent, this paper introduces the conceptual relationship of "national pattern", "pattern primitive", "pattern primitive" and "cultural design gene" (Fig. 2) [14].

The national pattern can be deconstructed into various levels of concept, and the national pattern design can be finally classified into a derivative design based on the cultural design gene.

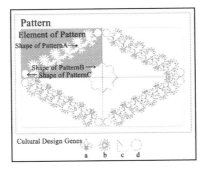

Fig. 2. Example of a hierarchical expression model of a pattern

Definition 1. A pattern with unique ethnic art style, decorative, and well-structured pattern passed down from a nation's dynasties is called national pattern.

Definition 2. The smallest independent information unit in a national pattern that needs to be transformed according to the composition rules is called a pattern element. The national pattern may be composed of one or more pattern elements, and the pattern element may generate a new national pattern according to the composition rules of the initial national pattern.

Definition 3. The so-called pattern shape refers to the shape formed by the cultural design gene derivative design. Different pattern shapes are arranged according to different coding rules to jointly form pattern elements. The pattern elements can be composed of one or more pattern shapes.

Definition 4. Cultural design genes are the smallest structural units that can be used in design, and have a cultural heritage. It has the characteristics of stability, inheritance, culture and indivisibility. One or more cultural design genes can be derivatized to form a pattern shape.

3.2   Pattern Deconstruction Principle

Chinese traditional aesthetics pays attention to the "neutral beauty". Traditional patterns often contain multiple elements. Therefore, it is necessary to decompose the original patterns, simplify the constituent elements, remove the extra decorative parts of the pattern main body pattern, and preserve the main meaning related to the pattern meaning. For the deconstruction and reuse of national patterns, Wang [15] deconstructed the Han costume culture from four aspects: color, form, ornamentation and recessive design factor, and carried out factor extraction and reuse research. Zhao [16] decomposed the Xinjiang national carpet pattern into three types of corners, the main body and the frame, and realized the innovative pattern by adjusting the content and structure of the pattern. Cui [17] integrated the shape grammar into the Zhuang embroidery design system, and divided the Zhuang embroidery pattern into three categories: single stem, double stem and quadruple stem, and decomposed the shape grammar into two stages: the rough stage and the precise stage. Prats [18] proposed four shape description methods: contour, decomposition, structure, and design. He claimed that specific deconstruction can be used to identify shapes and analyzed their properties. One of the key methods for deconstructing national patterns is to make bold choices for the national patterns containing more cultural elements, to understand the cultural connotations, then to take the essence of them, to maintain the semantic and visual language of the symbols. The key to In-Depth deconstruction of ethnic patterns using "pattern" - "pattern elements" - "pattern shapes" - "cultural design genes" hierarchy concept is the establishment of cultural design genes. (Fig. 3, show examples), the end point of deconstruction is the cultural design gene, which is the smallest structural unit with cultural symbolic meaning. Its morphological structure is relatively stable and cannot be further decomposed. This method effectively helps designers avoid subjective amplification in complex national pattern deconstruction and affects the objectivity of cultural design gene extraction work.

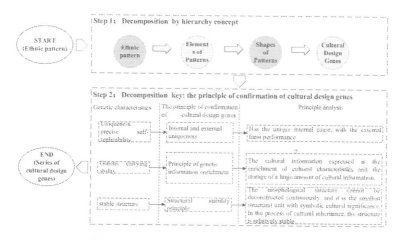

Fig. 3. National pattern deconstruction guide

3.3   Cultural Design Gene Extraction Principle

After deconstructing ethnic patterns at a hierarchical level, how to effectively extract the deconstructed cultural design genes as the initial cultural design genes derived from the new national pattern design is the focus of national pattern design research. Gou [19] studied the culture of Ban-Po pottery, and adopted the gene extraction method based on genetic theory of Ban-Po pottery culture. Liu [20] used quantitative methods to extract four cultural design factors: window, cave, color and implication, constructed the extraction model of Jiangnan garden culture factor, and scientifically extracted the design elements with recognition. As a visual symbol carrier for transmitting national information and transforming into a visual image, the cultural design gene is used to describe the pattern of the national pattern on the one hand, and to bind the national pattern with the corresponding cultural semantics on the other hand, so the culture extraction of design genes should have the following principles:

(1) Comply with the user's semantic intent. Based on the user's intention, the cultural design genes containing the user's desired cultural semantics are extracted from the deconstructed cultural design genes by the national pattern, so that the information can be expressed more quickly and clearly.

(2) Meet the user's usage intention. The extracted cultural design genes should conform to the use environment of the new ethnic pattern and conform to the user's aesthetic.

3.4 Deconstructive Description of Tibetan Patterns

The Tibetan pattern has a long history and a wide variety of forms. It embodies the profound essence of the Tibetan people and is the perfect combination of art, culture, aesthetics and religion. According to the performance theme, Tibetan patterns can be divided into geometric patterns, animal print patterns, plant pattern patterns, natural sky patterns and Buddhist patterns. Patterns with different symbolic meanings also have corresponding usage scopes. As an aesthetic symbolic language, Tibetan patterns are created to convey specific concepts and emotions, and have symbolic and emotional characteristics. This research takes the Tibetan pattern wisdom sword as an example to carry out the pattern deconstruction description, deconstructs it hierarchically to the cultural design gene with symbolic semantics, and describes it from semantic dimension and context dimension (Fig. 4, show examples). In essence, Tibetan art is a kind of religious art. The image itself is meaningless while the metaphor behind the image is

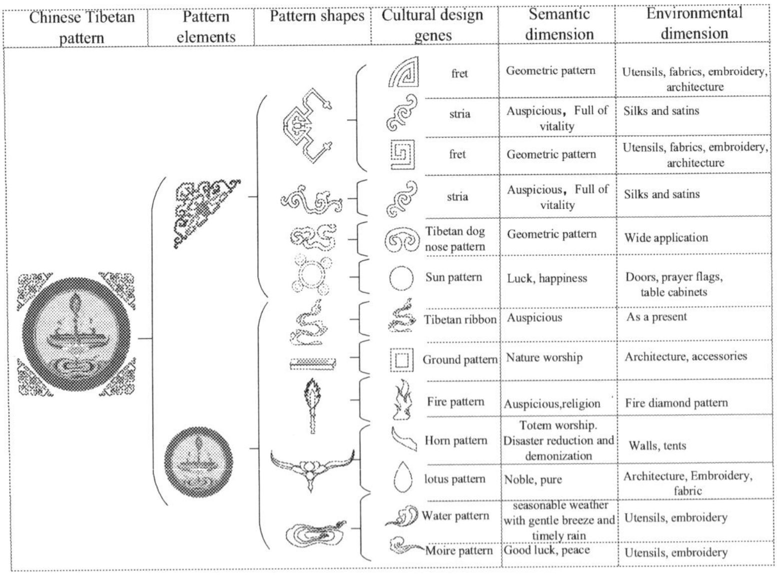

Chinese Tibetan pattern	Pattern elements	Pattern shapes	Cultural design genes	Semantic dimension	Environmental dimension
			fret	Geometric pattern	Utensils, fabrics, embroidery, architecture
			stria	Auspicious, Full of vitality	Silks and satins
			fret	Geometric pattern	Utensils, fabrics, embroidery, architecture
			stria	Auspicious, Full of vitality	Silks and satins
			Tibetan dog nose pattern	Geometric pattern	Wide application
			Sun pattern	Luck, happiness	Doors, prayer flags, table cabinets
			Tibetan ribbon	Auspicious	As a present
			Ground pattern	Nature worship	Architecture, accessories
			Fire pattern	Auspicious, religion	Fire diamond pattern
			Horn pattern	Totem worship. Disaster reduction and demonization	Walls, tents
			lotus pattern	Noble, pure	Architecture, Embroidery, fabric
			Water pattern	seasonable weather with gentle breeze and timely rain	Utensils, embroidery
			Moire pattern	Good luck, peace	Utensils, embroidery

Fig. 4. Deconstructive description of Tibetan patterns

the real intention, such as the symbolic meaning of lotus in Buddhist art. "The Lotus Flower" is a metaphor for lotus, symbolizing the elegance of teaching, and the Bodhisattva image also holds lotus, symbolizing the noble and pure Dharma. "Wisdom Sword" represents Tubo Zanpu Chisong Dezan, who is regarded as the incarnation of Manjushri with the ignorant. Symbolic carriers generally contain deep meanings, which are both normative and customary.

4 Cultural Design Gene Derivation Based on Shape Grammar

In the era of intelligent design, national pattern design will face two problems: 1. How to use the cultural design genes to quickly generate ethnic patterns in accordance with consumer intentions, to meet the diverse needs of consumers for national patterns. 2. How to maintain the continuity and consistency of the digital design of national patterns. In the design research process, it can be found that the same rules and morphological elements can produce a plurality of patterns with similar style images, which is an effective way to solve the above problems. As a derivative design method, shape grammar plays an important role in national pattern design analysis, deconstruction, reuse, and style inheritance.

4.1 Shape Grammar

The shape grammar was first proposed by George Stiny and James Gips, which was originally used in the field of architecture and sculpture, and later extended to the fields of pattern design and industrial design [21]. According to Stiny's definition of the shape grammar, the shape grammar can be represented by a quad $SG = (S, R, L, I)$. Here $S = \{s_1, s_2, s_3, \ldots, s_n\}$ that represents a finite set of shapes. $R = \{r_1, r_2, r_3, \ldots, r_q\}$, which is a finite set of shape inference rules containing the following specific inference rules: $r_1 \leftarrow Replacement$, $r_2 \leftarrow$ Additions and deletions, $r_3 \leftarrow Scaling$, $r_4 \leftarrow$ Duplicate, $r_5 \leftarrow Rotating$, $r_6 \leftarrow Shear$, $r_7 \leftarrow$ Coordinate change. The inference rule r is expressed as: $a \rightarrow b$, where a is the shape inference starting shape and b is the ending shape, $a \subset S \cup L$, $b \subset S \cup L$. $L = \{l_1, l_2, l_3, \ldots, l_m\}$, which is a finite set of markers with shape style features, s.t. $S \cap L \neq \emptyset$. $I = \{i_1, i_2, i_3, \cdots, i_q\}$, which is a finite set of initial shapes, s.t. $I \subset S \cup L$.

Shape grammar is a rule-based morphological derivative design method. The graphics of architecture, machinery and other industries are mostly composed of modular parametric graphics. The grammar rules are simple and easy to construct, but for art pattern design, the pattern is complicated and difficult. Therefore, there are few studies using shape grammars for design. Cui [22] believed that shape grammar has good potential in the design and application of art and culture. Based on the shape decomposition method, in the application of Zhuang embroidery, the Two-Level shape grammar with coarse level and refined level has been developed to improve the efficiency of the national pattern generation system. Based on the shape grammar, Zhang studied the rules of drawing and modeling elements in Tibetan Thangka art, trying to explore the aesthetic standards of Tibetan culture and provide significant guidance for current design [23]. Cui [17] investigated Yunnan national embroidery, and analyzed the characteristics of national embroidery through decomposing the curve embroidery patterns in different colors using shape grammar, and realized the automatic generation of new patterns. Sayed [24] used a parametric shape grammar to design Islamic geometric patterns.

4.2   Tibetan Culture Design Gene Derivation Design

The design process of national pattern can be regarded as the process of derivation of cultural design genes. Designers can create pattern shapes by manipulating the "dominant" and "recessive" patterns of cultural design genes. "dominant" refers to the design features that cultural design genes can be visualized, while "recessive" refers to the images, emotions, and spirits reflected by the design motifs. In the shape grammar, the dominant feature of the cultural design gene can be regarded as the initial shape, a new series of pattern shapes generated after limited rule processing. In the research, the Tibetan design is taken as an example to extract the cultural design genes of Tibetan patterns through the user's semantic intentions and using intentions. Suppose the user needs to design a picture that reflects the vitality, purity and beauty of nature. The cultural design genes extracted through screening include: the "stria" and "lotus petals" culture design gene. Then:

$$SG = (S, R, L, I)$$
$S = \{s_1, s_2, s_3, \cdots, s_n\}$, represents the pattern shapes.
$$R = \begin{cases} r_1 \leftarrow replacement;\ r_2 \leftarrow add, delete;\ r_3 \leftarrow scaling \\ r_4 \leftarrow duplication;\ r_5 \leftarrow rotation;\ r_6 \leftarrow superposition \\ r_7 \leftarrow coordinate, changes \end{cases}$$

$$L = \left\{ \begin{array}{c} \boxed{\ \blacklozenge\ } \end{array} \right\},$$

Where "⌐ ¬" represents the smallest rectangular boundary of the cultural design gene shape; "_____" indicates the length and width of the cultural design gene. The intersection of the two dashed lines uses the red dot "●" to indicate the center point of the gene shape, representing the relationship between the shape rule operation of the cultural design gene and the space.

$$I = \left\{ \bigcirc, \mathrm{\textit{⊱}} \right\}$$

When we consider shape grammar as a design method, we can combine a limited initial shape set with the rules in the rule base to generate an infinite shape terminal instance to show the style continuation of the design. On this basis, this paper introduces biological theory and uses two main derivation rules (Self-Crossing and Cross-Crossing transformation) to generate Multi-Patterned shapes. The advantage of this is to ensure that the cultural design gene is the smallest unit of pattern design, and the national pattern design can be regarded as the derivative design of the cultural design gene.

Therefore, in the shape grammar of this paper, the first level is Self-Crossing transformation, which is the design thinking process of the cultural design gene unit and its own multiple execution of inference rules (replication, rotation, superposition, etc.) derived from specific cultural design genes that can eventually form more pattern shapes. The Self-Crossing process of the lotus flower culture design gene is shown in Fig. 5. Multiple transformations can be performed to form a variety of pattern shapes as shown in Fig. 6. The self-crossing transformation process of the stria culture design gene and the resulting are shown in Figs. 7 and 8. The Self-Crossing transformations are applicable to design processes that have only one cultural design gene or are applied to Cross-Crossing transformations.

Fig. 5. Self-Crossing of "lotus petals" cultural design genes

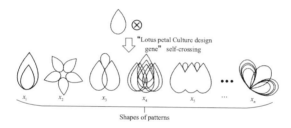

Fig. 6. "Lotus petals" pattern shapes

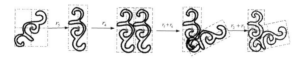

Fig. 7. Self-Crossing of "stria" cultural design genes (Color figure online)

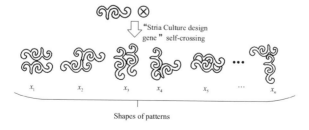

Fig. 8. "Stria" pattern shapes

In the second level, Cross-Crossing transformation, refers to a design thinking process where inference rules (replication, rotation, superposition) are performed multiple times by two or more cultural design gene monomers. The Cross-Crossing transformation process of the "lotus petals" culture design gene and the "stria" culture design gene is shown in Fig. 9; The Cross-Crossing transformation process of the "lotus petals" culture design gene Self-Crossing and the "stria" culture design gene is shown in Fig. 11; The Cross-Crossing transformation process of the "lotus petals" culture design gene and the "stria" culture design gene Self-Crossing is shown in Fig. 13; The Cross-Crossing transformation process of the "lotus petals" culture design gene Self-Crossing and the "stria" culture design gene Self-Crossing is shown in Fig. 15; Each of the Cross-Crossing transformation is formed as shown in Figs. 10, 12, 14, and 16 after a plurality of executions. Each of the cultural design genes may be a monomer, or a complex cultural design gene formed by Self-Crossing transformation or Cross-Crossing transformation of a cultural design gene monomer. The Self-Crossing transformation has higher priority than the Cross-Crossing transformation. If there are more than two cultural design genes, the Cross-Crossing transformation execution order is from left to right; The complex cultural design genes after the Cross-Crossing of the first two culture design genes can be regarded as new cultural design genes, and then Cross-Crossing with the next cultural design gene, until a variety of pattern shapes are derived.

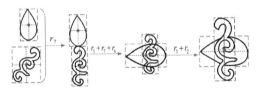

Fig. 9. "Lotus petals and stria" culture design gene Cross-Crossing (Color figure online)

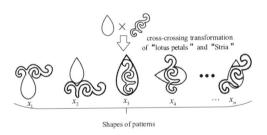

Fig. 10. Pattern shapes of "lotus petals and stria" Cross-Crossing

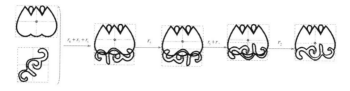

Fig. 11. "Lotus petals Self-Crossing and stria" culture design gene Cross-Crossing (Color figure online)

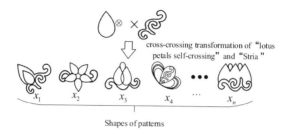

Fig. 12. Pattern shapes of "lotus petals Self-Crossing and stria" Cross-Crossing

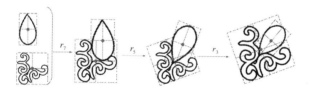

Fig. 13. "Lotus petals and stria Self-Crossing" culture design gene Cross-Crossing (Color figure online)

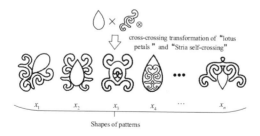

Fig. 14. Pattern shapes of "lotus petals and stria Self-Crossing" Cross-Crossing

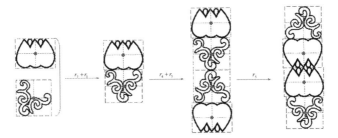

Fig. 15. "Lotus petals Self-Crossing and stria Self-Crossing" culture design gene Cross-Crossing (Color figure online)

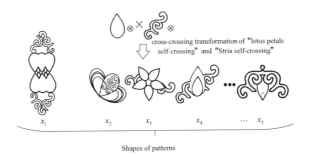

Shapes of patterns

Fig. 16. Pattern shapes of "lotus petals Self-Crossing and stria Self-Crossing" Cross-Crossing

5   National Pattern Generation

The pattern shapes reorganization can generate new pattern elements, and the design process can be combined with processing computer aided design software. The pattern shape position is marked by adopting the rectangular boundary of the shape in the above and the red center dot. The initial Tibetan pattern shape are analyzed, and the initial pattern elements can be considered to consist of two concentric rings and an intermediate portion. The coding rule is formulated according to the position, and the extension idea of "one object, multiple signs, and multiple values" is introduced. Each pattern element position can be placed with a pattern shape class containing different cultural design genes, and each type of pattern element can be a plurality of pattern shape feature values exhibited, the process of which is shown in Fig. 17. The resulting pattern elements pool is shown in Fig. 18.

Fig. 17. Processing Computer-Aided design pattern element process (Color figure online)

Fig. 18. Pattern elements pool

Taking the Tibetan pattern of China as an example, the pattern composition rules of the initial national pattern are analyzed, and the basic categories and arrangement methods of the pattern elements are sought. The pattern elements can be reconstructed into new series according to the pattern of the original national pattern. The ethnic pattern, (Fig. 3, show examples), achieves the design reuse of the "initial ethnic pattern - cultural design gene - derived national pattern" (Fig. 19, show examples),

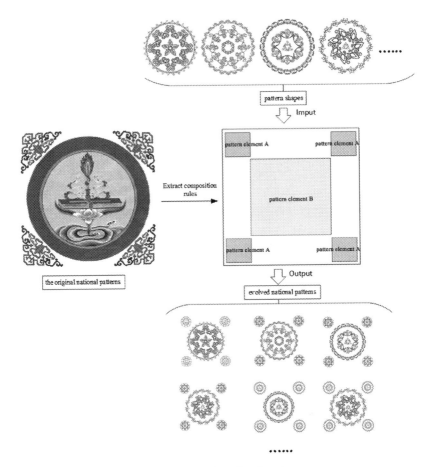

Fig. 19. A new series of national patterns

6   Conclusion and Future Research

In this research, we obtained a Chinese Tibetan pattern as an example to expound national pattern generation method based on cultural design genetic derivation. Under the premise of deep understanding of cultural genes and cultural design genes, concepts, elements of patterns and shapes of patterns and cultural design genes were defined by pattern decomposition to build the conceptual pattern hierarchy. Furthermore, we established the principles of pattern deconstruction and cultural design gene extraction. Based on shape grammar a design method for gene design of Tibetan culture design was proposed which contained two main derivation rules (Self-Crossing and Cross-Crossing transformation). We used Processing computer-Aided design software to assist the redesign of the pattern shapes. The transformation rules of the pattern shapes discharge position are performed by Shape border and red center point, and the topology principle is introduced to generate a plurality of pattern elements. Following the original pattern element composition rules, the pattern elements can form a new series of national patterns, thus realized the design reuse of "the original national patterns – cultural design genes – evolved national patterns". Taking the Chinese Tibetan pattern as an example, we demonstrated how to obtain the design requirements and how to derivatively design the cultural design genes "lotus petals" and "stria". This paper shed light on how to generate a series of national patterns in line with consumer emotional images, which also demonstrated the national vitality of cultural design genes. Unlike other pattern generation methods, here, a method of generating national patterns was raised based on cultural design genetic derivation as follow: from the perspective of design intent, integrated with the concept of genetics in biology, the problem of ethnic pattern generation can be solved by the derivative design of cultural design genes under computerized parameter constraints, with a large improvement on the pattern design efficiency.

This research can be further studied in several ways. First, to study the genes of national culture design more deeply, the deconstruction method that can be applied to more complex ethnic patterns such as Thangka. Second, the Self-Crossing and Cross-Crossing transformation in the current shape grammar will produce countless kinds of solutions, study optimization algorithms, and converge on thinking. In the current research stage, the computer only plays a role in assisting the designer's design. In the future research, the intelligent design of the national pattern design generation system will be designed and developed for users to directly use, realize the individualization of the design and enhance the user's participation.

Acknowledgements. Thanks to University for its technical support for this research, and also for the references provided by scholars. You are welcome to discuss this research.

References

1. Zhao, H.Y., Yang, Y.F., Xu, G.M.: Design method for Xinjiang folk art pattern. Comput. Syst. Appl. **20**(7), 94–99 (2011). http://kns.cnki.net
2. Zhao, H.Y., Peng, H., Zhang, X.L.: A generation method of carpet pattern based on evolutionary computation. J. Graph. **36**(1), 41–46 (2015). http://kns.cnki.net
3. Yang, Y.P., Chen, D.K., Yu, S.H.: Extraction and reuse of pattern configuration based on ontology and shape grammar. J. Zhejiang Univ. (Eng. Sci.) **52**(3), 461–472 (2018). http://kns.cnki.net
4. Lu, X., Leng, T.X., Zhang, H.X.: The application of parametric shape grammar in exploring the design of traditional decorative patterns—take islamic pattern generation as a case study. Archit. Cult. **155**(2), 135–136 (2017). http://kns.cnki.net
5. Schipper, K.: Chinese Cultural Gene Bank, Peking, chap. 1 (2002)
6. Zhao, H.L., Wang, J., Yuan, Z.J.: Study on the genealogy map construction and inheritance path of cultural genes-a case study of ancient Shu culture genes. Mod. Urban Res. **5**, 90–91 (2014). http://kns.cnki.net
7. Bao, J.Q., Lu, C.R., Huang, N.N.: Interpreting the scientific traditions and ways of thinking of the East and the West from the perspective of cultural genes. Future Dev. **1**, 59–63 (2010). http://kns.cnki.net
8. Wen, C.G., Gou, B.C., Wu, L.J.: Extraction and application research of culture design gene based on eye movement analysis, vol. 11, pp. 217–224 (2018). http://en.cnki.com.cn

9. Yair, K., Press, M., Tomes, A.: Crafting competitive advantage: crafts knowledge as a strategic resource. Des. Stud. **22**(4), 377–394 (2001). https://doi.org/10.1016/s0142-694x(00)00043-0

10. Yair, K., Tomes, A., Press, M.: Design through marking: crafts knowledge as facilitator to collaborative product development. Des. Stud. **20**(6), 495–515 (1999). https://doi.org/10.1016/s0142-694x(98)00040-4

11. Lin, R.T.: Transforming Taiwan aboriginal cultural features into modern product design: a case study of a cross-cultural product design model. Int. J. Des. **1**(2), 47–55 (2007). https://doi.org/10.1007/s00170-006-0583-6

12. Wang, W.W., Wei, T.: Redesign and application of the triangle pattern of banpo painted pottery. Packag. Eng. **8**, 42–46 (2018). http://kns.cnki.net

13. Zhu, S.S., Luo, S.J.: Reconstruction of cultural relic elements based on design semiotics in product design. J. Zhejiang Univ. (Eng. Sci.) **11**, 2065–2072 (2013). http://kns.cnki.net

14. Zhang, X.W., Wang, J., Chen, G.D.: Pattern configuration extraction and reuse based on ontology and shape grammar. J. Zhejiang Univ. (Eng. Sci.) **3**, 461–472 (2018). http://kns.cnki.net

15. Wang, W.W., Kou, R., Yang, X.Y.: Research on extraction and application of clothing culture factors in han dynasty. Mach. Des. Manuf. Eng. **1**, 79–83 (2015). http://kns.cnki.net

16. Zhao, H.Y., Peng, H., Zhang, X.L.: Evolutionary calculation based carpet pattern generation method. J. Graph. **1**, 41–46 (2015). http://kns.cnki.net

17. Cui, J., Tang, M.X.: Integrating shape grammars into a generative system for Zhuang ethnic embroidery design exploration. Comput. Aided Des. **45**, 591–604 (2013). https://doi.org/10.1016/j.cad.2012.08.002

18. Prats, M., Earl, C., Garner, S., Jowers, I.: Shape exploration of designs in a style: toward generation of product designs. AI EDAM-Artif. Intell. Eng. Des. Manuf. **20**(3), 201–215 (2006). https://doi.org/10.1017/S0890060406060173

19. Gou, B.C., Yu, H., Li, Z.F.: Study on gene extraction, design and application of ban-po painted pottery culture. J. Northwest. Polytech. Univ. (Soc. Sci.) **4**, 66–69 (2011). http://kns.cnki.net

20. Liu, L.P., Li, Y.: Study on the extraction and design application of Jiangnan garden culture factors. Packag. Eng. **24**, 57–62 (2016). http://kns.cnki.net

21. Manuela, R.M., Belmonte, M.V., Boned, J.: Layered shape grammars. Comput. Aided Des. **56**, 104–119 (2014). https://doi.org/10.1016/j.cad.2014.06.012

22. Cui, J., Tang, M.X.: Chinese pattern design using generative shape grammar. In: The GA 2010, Milan, Italy (2010). http://dx.doi.org/

23. Zhang, W.L., Lin, S.N.: Research on Tibet Tangka based on shape grammar. Comput.-Aided Ind. Des. Conceptual Des. **1**, 373–376 (2008). https://doi.org/10.1109/caidcd.2008.4730591

24. Sayed, Z., Ugail, H., Palmer, I.: Parameterized shape grammar for generating n-fold Islamic geometric motifs. In: 2016 International Conference on Cyberworlds, Chongqing, China (2016). https://doi.org/10.1109/cw.2015.54

Bauhaus Internationalism to College Town Modernism

Exploring Bauhaus Culture in Hajjar's Hybrid Architecture

Mahyar Hadighi$^{(\boxtimes)}$ and Jose Duarte

Penn State University, University Park, USA
{mzh221,Jxp400}@psu.edu

Abstract. The purpose of this study is to analyze William Hajjar's single-family houses in State College, PA, and compare them with the European modernist work of Walter Gropius and Marcel Breuer in the United States. This analysis is performed using shape grammars as a computational design methodology. Hajjar was a member of the architecture faculty at the Pennsylvania State University, a practitioner in State College, and an influential figure in the history of architecture in the area. Shape grammars are used specifically to verify and describe the influences of Bauhaus/European modernism on Hajjar's domestic architecture. The focus is on establishing Hajjar's single-family architectural language and comparing it to the architectural language of Gropius (Gropius-Breuer partnership) as the founder of the Bauhaus architecture and a prominent practitioner in introducing European modernism to American architecture students in the mid-twentieth century like Hajjar.

Keywords: Shape grammar · Modern architecture · Bauhaus modernism · William Hajjar · Walter Gropius

1 Introduction

In documenting examples of mid-century modern architecture in State College, PA, home of Penn State's University Park campus, the authors discovered that many of the single-family houses in the area mix formal and functional features typical of European modern architecture with those of traditional American architecture. Further, many of these houses were designed by William Hajjar, a faculty member at Penn State, or his followers in the mid-twentieth-century period. Hajjar was a researcher—mainly in the area of passive energy and energy efficiency—and a successful practitioner who designed and built thirty-two single-family houses in the vicinity of the University Park campus. His work in the area may be unique to a certain kind or practitioner in a certain place and time—i.e., to architecture faculty producing single-family houses in American college towns in the mid-twentieth century.

Many such faculty members who practiced modern architecture—or a hybrid modern-traditional architecture—in college towns throughout the US during this period had studied at American schools at a time when they were moving away from a

© Springer Nature Singapore Pte Ltd. 2019
J.-H. Lee (Ed.): CAAD Futures 2019, CCIS 1028, pp. 429–443, 2019.
https://doi.org/10.1007/978-981-13-8410-3_30

longstanding focus on the Beaux-Arts toward a new focus on European modernism instead. Of these schools, which included the Illinois Institute of Technology (IIT), the Massachusetts Institute of Technology (MIT), and Harvard's Graduate School of Design (GSD), with the latter leading the way in championing the new European style, becoming the nation's most prominent school training students in modernist architecture. With the appointment of Walter Gropius, founder of the Bauhaus School, as director of Harvard's Department of Architecture, the process of introducing American students to European modernism had officially begun.

Except for Harvard and the Armour Institute of Chicago, the latter of which was led by Mies van der Rohe from 1938 to 1959 and later became IIT, most U.S. architecture programs remained under the Beaux-Arts system of education (or alternatives) until after World War II. The fact that the GSD and the Armour Institute were the two pioneer schools in training students according to modernism demonstrates the importance of Gropius (and Breuer) and van der Rohe to architectural design in the United States and likewise the importance of the Bauhaus to the country's architectural pedagogy.

While many other schools continued to focus on the Beaux-Arts, some individual architecture professors and even entire architecture programs followed Gropius and Mies by teaching students according to the principles of modern architecture. Among the professors was Lawrence Anderson at MIT, and with the appointment of William Wurster as Dean of architecture in 1945, MIT became the third major program to promote modernism [1]. As Alofsin notes, Anderson, '*a longtime bastian of the French approach*,' was '*instrumental in bringing in modernist thinking*' [2]. Anderson was hired by MIT in 1933 and served as head of the department from 1947 to 1965 and as Dean of the school from 1956 until his retirement in 1972. He was one of a few instructors at MIT in the 1930s who pushed the school's teaching philosophy toward modernism. In addition, he introduced a new system to review the students' work by bringing outside critics to MIT. Gropius and Breuer were among those frequently invited to MIT for this purpose, such that MIT students (including Hajjar) were introduced to Gropius's philosophy of modern architecture [3].

Anderson was especially interested in Scandinavian modernism. With Wurster, he paid a visit to the great modern Finish architect and designer, Alvar Aalto in the late 1930s and secured Aalto's appointment as a Research Professor in Architecture in 1940 [4]. Anderson worked hard to bring a modern outlook to the MIT program, and in 1939 (with his colleague, Herbert Beckwith) he designed one of the first modernist buildings on an American campus, i.e., MIT's Alumni Swimming Pool [2]. Most probably, Anderson, as Hajjar's advisor, was responsible for pushing him toward European modernism/Bauhaus internationalism introduced to American architectural students by Gropius and Breuer.

To verify and describe the influences of Bauhaus internationalism on the work of Hajjar in State College, PA, this study offers an investigation of the faculty-practitioner's hybrid architecture by comparing and contrasting it with Gropius's architecture, with a focus on single-family houses produced by the Gropius-Breuer partnership in the United States. Via computational design methodology, this comparison will provide information to serve as a basis for determining the nature of

Hajjar's single-family architectural language including by verifying and describing the influence of Gropius-Breuer's architectural language.

2 Methodology

This paper is part of a larger study undertaken with the purpose of verifying and describing the hybrid expression of European modern and American traditional architecture in Hajjar's work in State College, PA. The larger study is based around five central steps: (1) tracing Hajjar's life and practice to identify likely influences on his work; (2) developing a shape grammar for the houses Hajjar designed in the State College area; (3) identifying or developing grammars for those influences; (4) comparing Hajjar's grammar to the grammars of these influences in order to determine the nature of these and the likely impact of each on Hajjar's work; and (5) identifying aspects of the social and technological context that may explain these influences—i.e., trends in regard to lifestyle and availability of materials and technologies. Whereas a previous paper [5] described Hajjar's single-family architecture by developing a grammar of his work, the focus of the current paper is on studying the influence of Bauhaus internationalism, as expressed in the work of the Bauhaus founders, on Hajjar's architectural language. This influence is demonstrated through a comparison of the grammar developed for Hajjar's single-family architecture [5] with the grammar developed for the Gropius-Breuer partnership in the United States. Future papers will focus on further methodological steps related to the notion of hybridity.

2.1 Shape Grammar

Defined as a set of rules of transformation applied recursively to an initial form in order to generate new forms, shape grammar formalism was introduced by Stiny and Gips in 1972 and further developed by Stiny [7] and Knight [8]. In other words, a shape grammar is a rule-based system for analyzing, describing, and generating visual or spatial designs. Shape grammars began as a concept, with early applications focused on fine arts [9], decorative arts [10, 11], architecture [12, 13] and eventually on design [14, 15], including urban design [16, 17]. Given that the work of the present study's focal architect shows some evidence of shapes and transformation rules shared with the work of other architects in a distinctly different style, the shape grammar methodology is appropriate for testing the hypothesis.

An important question regarding comparing shape grammars pertains to how detailed they need to be. This question can be answered in the process of developing grammars by finding where hybridity exists, whether in the functional organization (layout), building systems, and/or decoration. The next step would be to determine the extent to which the rules of the respective grammars are similar or different. By comparing the shape rules of Hajjar's grammar to those of the Gropius-Breuer grammar, we may be able to determine rules that have been adapted, deleted, changed, and created (added), which may, in turn, explain similarities and differences between the two architectural languages.

2.2 Related Work

The current study, and the larger research project, follow in the footsteps of research studies published by several authors. In 1983, taking the transformation of Frank Lloyd Wright's Prairies houses into Usonian houses as one of her focal cases, Knight showed how stylistic evolution in art and design can be explained by the evolution of the underlying grammars. In 2005, Çolakoğlu used this idea to propose a methodology to design contemporary houses based on vernacular Turkish Hayat houses. Using the idea of grammatical transformation, Chase and Ahmad [19] described hybridity in design. Then, in 2011, Eloy and Duarte proposed the concept of transformation grammar to adapt existing house types to the needs of contemporary life. In the same year, Kruger et al. [21] advocated the use of transformation grammar to study Alberti's influence on classical Portuguese architecture, and more recently Benrós [22] used transformations in design to study the phenomenon of hybridity in architectural languages. Against this background, the present paper is principally concerned with using shape grammars to describe the influence of Bauhaus internationalism—brought to the US by Gropius and Breuer—on Hajjar's single-family architecture.

3 A. William Hajjar

Abraham William Hajjar (1917–2000), the youngest of a large immigrant Lebanese family, was born on February 11, 1917, in Lawrence, MA. In 1936, he left the family's grocery store business to study architecture at the Carnegie Institute of Technology (now Carnegie Mellon). He received his professional Bachelor of Architecture degree in 1940. A year later, he received a master's degree from MIT. After teaching for a few years at the State College of Washington, he joined the Department of Architecture at the Pennsylvania State University in State College in 1946 [23]. He then focused on securing tenure for a number of years. However, from 1952 when he built his first design in the area to 1963 when he moved to Philadelphia on a leave of absence from Penn State to work with Vince King, a friend from MIT and a successful Philadelphian architect, Hajjar designed and built thirty-two single-family houses in the Penn State area (Fig. 1).

In the late 1930s, when Hajjar was at Carnegie, the school, like most of the architecture programs in the country, was dominated by the Beaux-Arts. However, he came into contact with some of the young faculty members teaching freshman and sophomore studios who favored a modernist design philosophy. In addition, and perhaps, critically, Walter Gropius, founder of the Bauhaus School and a pioneering master of modern architecture, delivered a lecture at Carnegie in 1938, when Hajjar was a sophomore. This was probably, the first interaction between Hajjar and Gropius.

As explained in a previous paper [5], while at MIT, Hajjar became well-versed in modernism under the supervision of Lawrence Anderson. Anderson would have been an important influence given that he both designed the first modernist building on an American campus (MIT Alumni Pool-1939) and endeavored to bring a modern outlook to MIT's program in the late 1930s. It is likely that Hajjar was influenced by modernist ideas propagated by the German émigrés: that is, he was at MIT when Gropius and Breuer were at Harvard and would have been included in the collaborations orchestrated by Anderson between the two schools referenced earlier [3]. Also, while Hajjar was at MIT, the architecture program collaborated with Harvard on a summer semester design project whereby a class from each institute, probably a small number of students, rented a house in the cape where they lived and worked on a project together. These collaborations between MIT and Harvard introduced not only Hajjar, but also his schoolmates, to Gropius's philosophy of architecture. Other well-known architects who were students at MIT under Anderson's supervision at the time include Gordon Bunshaft, George Nakashima, I.M. Pei, Bill Hartmann, Clarence Y. Yokomoto, and Vince Kling. During a leave of absence from Penn State in the mid-1960s, Hajjar worked as a senior designer at a large practice that Kling eventually established in Philadelphia.

3.1 Hajjar's Architecture

In 1946, when Hajjar first moved to State College with his family to teach at Penn State, he bought a traditional two-story Georgian revival house close to campus (Fig. 1). The house had a traditional four-square plan with an organization similar to Hajjar's own future designs, although that latter is rendered in a more modern way. To be different, and to make it easier for his family to recognize the house from other similar houses of the area, as he mentioned to his son, he painted the street face of the house white, a move that shows his philosophy of improving traditional American architecture by mixing it with modern ideas/elements. His first design in the area, a house for his own family, was built in 1951–1952. Hajjar's first family house represents his main idea of volumetric design and interior planning: the house consists of a simple shoebox, i.e., the main house, with a garage connected to it by a breezeway. At that time, most of the single-family houses in the area were in the Georgian revival, Colonial revival, Tudor, and Cape Cod styles, although ranch and split-level houses were also starting to appear. Hajjar designed and built thirty-two single-family houses in the area, many of which were very similar to his first family house in State College. As explained in a previous paper [5], many of his houses blend into the traditional houses in the neighborhood in terms of exterior building materials, volumes, and roof shapes. However, Hajjar's houses have an internal organizational structure that is both modern for the time and unique to his work.

In the plans, the entryway to Hajjar's houses on the main floor is through the breezeway and generally in the middle open space, which could include a hall and a family/sitting room on the private floor. Hajjar's typical plan can be read as a modern layout with an open space in the center, rooms organized on both sides, and the service spaces, including the bathroom, staircase, and hallway, in the middle. However, it can also be read as a very traditional plan as used in the Georgian period and the Georgian Revival, i.e., a developed hall-parlor organization, or as a developed foursquare design, similar to the plan of the first house Hajjar bought in the area.

main entrance

Fig. 1. Hajjar's first house in the area and its schematic layout.

As explained in a previous paper [5], the houses Hajjar designed for the area can be grouped according to five subtypes based on the volumetric relationship and spatial organization: (1) tri-partite organization, where a breezeway connects the garage to the inhabitable space, the lower floor hosts the living areas, and the upper floor the sleeping area; (2) split-level organization, where the sleeping area is a half floor above the living area; (3) butterfly, where a cross-shape or U-shape organization prevails; (4) compact organization, where a square-shaped plan reflects Hajjar's idea of a core area; and (5) linear organization, where two square-shaped plans forms a rectangular/linear plan.

A comparison between Hajjar's plans with both traditional houses in the area and modern houses designed by pioneers of modern architecture, such as Gropius and Breuer, reveals their likely influence on his architectural production. This architectural observation will be scientifically tested by comparing Hajjar's grammar with that of the Gropius-Breuer partnership.

3.2 Hajjar's Grammar

A detailed account of the development of the grammar for Hajjar's work is available in a previous paper by the authors [5]. In general, the grammar of Hajjar's single-family houses was developed based on the five subtypes described in the previous section. The grammar encompasses four phases or groups of rules:

(1) Rules that capture the way in which Hajjar situated his houses on the lot (Rules 1–2);
(2) Rules that describe the formal relationships between mass volumes (Rules 3–5);
(3) Rules that describe the way in which the interior space is divided into smaller rooms or spaces (Rules 6–29); and
(4) Rules that generate details such as the placement of closets and wall thickness (Rules 36–39).

The grammar can both produce all the houses designed by Hajjar in the area and generate new designs based on Hajjar's architectural language (Fig. 2).

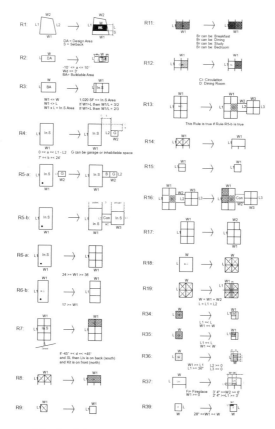

Fig. 2. Selected rules of Hajjar's grammar.

4 Walter Gropius and the Bauhaus Culture

Finding solutions to the problems experienced by the working classes after World War I in Germany was fundamental to the Bauhaus school of design, a group of architects and artists led by Walter Gropius that formally came into existence in 1919, in Weimar, Germany. Their core concept was to reimagine the material world in order to express unity among all the arts. Gropius described this concept of unifying arts and design in the Proclamation of the Bauhaus (1919), in which the Bauhaus was described as a craft organization combining architecture, sculpture, and painting into a unified creative expression [24]. However, because of the rise of political dictatorship in Europe and its detrimental effects on German culture, Gropius resigned from the Bauhaus in 1928, followed by Breuer, Moholy-Nagy, Bayer, and Schawinsky. When Hitler closed the Bauhaus in 1933, most its members left Germany to take teaching positions abroad. By the time World War II broke out, most were teaching at major schools in the United States, where they were to influence an entire generation of American artists and architects. Therefore, the first point that comes to mind in regard to European influence on American architectural culture in the modern era is the direct legacy of the Bauhaus—not its continuation, but its postscript.

Among the members of the Bauhaus who played an important role in American architecture as faculty members were Walter Gropius, Ludwig Mies van der Rohe, and Marcel Breuer. Their contributions were supported by the efforts of three other Bauhaus teachers: Herbert Bayer (graphic designer), and especially Josef Albers and Laszlo Moholy Nagy [25]. Other leaders of modern architecture who had been part of the Bauhaus also immigrated to the United States and also contributed to the modern movement in the country. However, as William Jordy argues, in no sense did their influence on American architecture match that of Gropius, Mies, or Breuer [25].

Having determined that the U.S. offered a receptive environment for their work and views, the German immigrants arrived in the country in the late 1930s. As noted earlier, Harvard's GSD was the first school in the nation to officially train students in modernist architecture with the appointment of Gropius as the Director of the Department of Architecture in 1937. Soon, Marcel Breuer joined Gropius in the U.S., not only to teach with him at Harvard but also to form a brief architectural partnership. It is worth adding here that the teaching of Gropius and Breuer at Harvard and van der Rohe at IIT marked '*the beginning of systematic training in modern principles in American architectural education*' (see p. 486 in [26]).

In Germany, Gropius had focused on large-scale buildings, such as apartment buildings and institutional projects. The only residential house that he designed in Germany was "Master's House," a group of combined single-family houses for the Bauhaus masters, commissioned by the City of Dessau in 1925–1926. He started designing single-family architecture when he immigrated to the United States. He (with Breuer) designed his first house, Gropius House, for his own family in Lincoln, MA, in 1937 with the construction ending in 1938 (Fig. 3). Modest in scale in comparison to other houses in the area, Gropius House was revolutionary in terms of its impact. The house incorporates traditional elements of New England architecture, such as wood, brick, and local stones, combined with modern materials, such as glass block, acoustical plaster, and chrome banisters. A National Historic Landmark, Gropius House is the posterchild for localized Bauhausian architecture in the New England area and in the United States more generally.

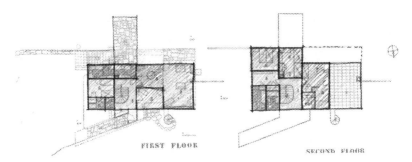

FIRST FLOOR   SECOND FLOOR

Fig. 3. Spatial relationship in Gropius House. Color representation: green represents the living room, light red represents bedrooms, blue represents service space, and orange represents transitional space/corridors. (Color figure online)

Many of the features of Gropius House can be seen in Hajjar's designs in State College. For example, many of Hajjar's houses combine minimal, simple, and modest modern design with local materials; have large panes of glass to obtain a picturesque view of the landscape; and include a screened porch as an American architectural element. Also, Hajjar's use of a rectangular pattern/grid and the dividing elements of his interior plans are to some extent similar to the interior plan of Gropius House. Further, these similarities become more pronounced following the period Breuer spent studying binuclear organization for American houses: In 1943, Breuer was studying his idea of using a two-part organization for residential houses. The Geller House in Lawrence, NY is one of the first houses that employs Breuer's idea of a binuclear house, with two wings/parts for day-time activities and night-time activities separated by an entry hall. Most of the houses designed by Breuer/Gropius from this point onwards, including Robinson House (1946), Alworth House (1954–1955), and Hooper House (1956–1959), have a similar organization. Many of the houses that Hajjar designed in the 1950s also have a two-part organization in the same style.

4.1   Gropius-Breuer Grammar

The grammar for the work of Gropius and Breuer in the United States was developed with the same strategy as that used for the grammar of Hajjar's work. Generally, to compare grammars with each other, they should be developed in the same way at the same level of detail. When this is the case, it is easiest to compare the grammars by determining which rules are adapted, deleted, changed, or added (created).

Figures 4, 5, 6 and 7 show selected rules of the grammar developed for Gropius and Breuer's work in the United States. The grammar can produce both early houses that the architects designed in style that closely resembles the Bauhaus and the binuclear plans. Figure 8 shows a step-by-step derivation of Gropius and Breuer's Robinson House, which was used to infer the grammar. In addition to all the houses designed by Gropius and Breuer in the United States, the grammar can generate additional plans in the architectural language of the Gropius-Breuer partnership.

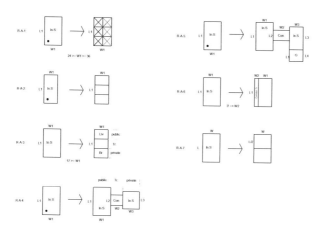

Fig. 4. Selected rules of Gropius-Breuer's grammar: define relationship between volumes

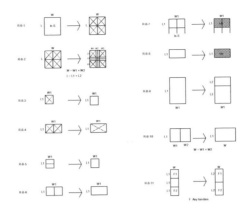

Fig. 5. Selected rules of Gropius-Breuer's grammar: divide interior space into smaller space

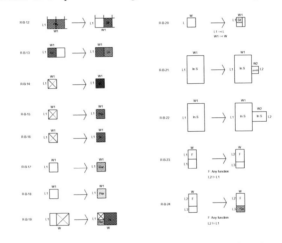

Fig. 6. Selected rules of Gropius-Breuer's grammar: assigning functions to interior space

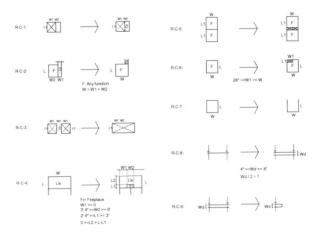

Fig. 7. Selected rules of Gropius-Breuer's grammar: interior detailing

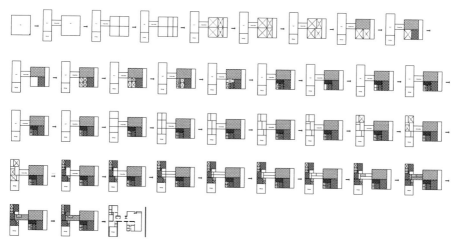

Fig. 8. Derivation of the Robinson House designed by Gropius-Breuer in 1946

5   Grammar Comparison

As noted earlier, using shape grammars, the authors focused on comparing Hajjar's architecture in State College with single-family houses designed by the Gropius-Breuer partnership in the United States. In order to do this, the rules of the two grammars should be compared and contrasted. There are two ways to test similarities between the rules of the two grammars: (1) compare step by step the derivation of a house designed by the Gropius-Breuer partnership and the derivation of a house by Hajjar, and (2) produce a Gropius-Breuer house through the grammar of Hajjar's work and compare it with the original design.

Figure 9 shows a comparison of a step-by-step derivation of the James Ford House designed by the Gropius-Breuer partnership in 1939 and the Higdon Residence designed by Hajjar in 1955. Higdon House is one of the few houses designed by Hajjar with a linear organization and a division between daytime and nighttime activities such that each is assigned to its own floor. It is also possible to produce the James Ford House using the Hajjar grammar. Although the part that projects out to expand the dining area is unique to the Gropius-Breuer design. The same strategy is demonstrated in Fig. 11, which shows a comparison between Alworth House designed by the Gropius-Breuer partnership and built in 1954 and the Eakin Residence designed by Hajjar and built in 1955 (Fig. 10). It is important to note that with this comparison, the authors do not suggest that Hajjar's Eakin House is directly influenced by Gropius-Breuer's Alworth House. Instead, Hajjar's architectural language in general was influenced in some ways by European modernism through the work of Gropius and Breuer. The grammar comparison reveals similarities in interior planning, spatial organization, separation of day-time and night-time activities, and geometry and volumetric organization between the respective architectural languages of Hajjar and Gropius-Breuer.

It is worth noting that many of Hajjar's design decisions may reflect an influence that is cultural and/or contextual in nature rather than a formal influence from modernism or traditional architecture. For example, placing the living room at the back of the house facing the backyard and having the kitchen face the street were common organizational features of mid-twentieth-century houses in the United States. Other decisions would have been based on the availability of materials or building technology, i.e., the width/length of the open living room was dictated by the structural system.

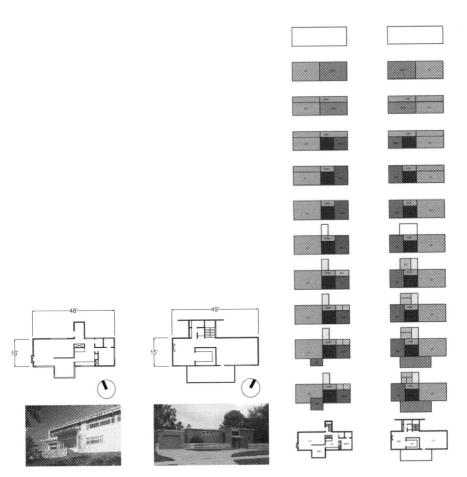

Fig. 9. Comparison of a step-by-step derivation of the James Ford House designed by Gropius-Breuer (left) and the Higdon Residence designed by Hajjar (right).

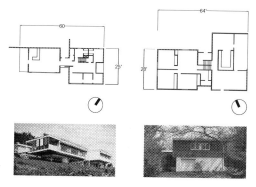

Fig. 10. Alworth House designed by Breuer-Gropius in 1954 (left) and the Eakin Residence designed by Hajjar in 1955 (right).

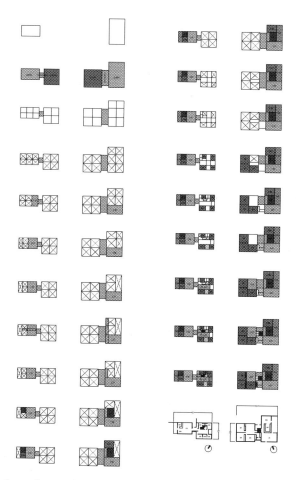

Fig. 11. Comparison of a step-by-step derivation of the Alworth House designed by Gropius-Breuer (left) and the Eakin Residence designed by Hajjar (right), organized in two columns.

6 Discussion

As noted earlier, this paper is part of a larger study undertaken with the purpose of analyzing Hajjar's hybrid single-family architecture by developing a grammar of his work and comparing and contrasting its shape rules with those of works of modernist and traditional American architecture. The purpose of the present paper, however, is to test the effectiveness of shape grammar as a computational design methodology in comparing architectural languages and analyzing hybridity in architectural design. Comparing the grammar of Hajjar's work with the grammar of the Gropius-Breuer partnership's work in the United States demonstrates that shape grammar as a computational design methodology can be an effective way for architectural historians to verify and describe such influences and, therefore, for identifying hybridity in architectural design.

In relation to Hajjar's architecture in the State College area, this study highlights his contributions to the stability and popularity of modern architecture in the United States and his roles as a teacher and practitioner who followed in the steps of Gropius and Breuer in localizing/Americanizing Bauhaus culture in the United States.

Acknowledgments. This research is partially supported by the Stuckeman School of Architecture and Landscape Architecture at Penn State, the Stuckeman Center for Design Computing, and the Hamer Center for Community Design.

References

1. Ockman, J. (ed.): Architecture School. Three Centuries of Educating Architects in North America. The MIT Press, Cambridge (2012)
2. Alofsin, A.: American modernism's challenge to the beaux-arts. In: Ockman, J. (ed.) Architecture Schools, Three Centuries of Educating Architects in North America, p. 115 (2012)
3. Oral history interview with Lawrence Anderson. Smithsonian Archives of American Art, 30 January–30 March 1992
4. President's Report, Massachusetts Institute of Technology, October 1940
5. Hadighi, M., Duarte, J.: Adapting modern architecture to a local context: a grammar for Hajjar's hybrid domestic architecture. In: 36th eCAADe Conference, Lodz, Poland, pp. 515–524 (2018)
6. Stiny, G., Gips, J.: Shape grammars and the generative specification of painting and sculpture. Inf. Process. **7**, 1460–1465 (1972)
7. Stiny, G.: Introduction to shape and shape grammars. Environ. Plann. B **7**, 343–351 (1980)
8. Knight, T.: Transformations of languages of designs: part 3. Environ. Plan. **10**, 155–177 (1983)
9. Knight, T.: Transformations of De Stijl art: the paintings of Georges Vantongerloo and Fritz Glarner. Environ. Plan. **16**, 51–98 (1989)
10. Knight, T.: The generation of Hepplewhite-Style chair-back designs. Environ. Plan. **7**, 227–238 (1980)
11. Stiny, G.: Ice-ray: a note on the generation of Chinese lattice design. Environ. Plann. B **4**, 89–98 (1977)
12. Stiny, G., Mitchell, W.J.: The Palladian grammar. Environ. Plann. B **5**, 5–18 (1978)

13. Koning, H., Elizenberg, J.: The language of the Prairie: Frank Lloyd Wright's Prairie houses. Environ. Plann. B **8**, 295–323 (1981)

14. Agarwal, M., Cagan, J.: A blend of different taste: the language of coffeemakers. Environ. Plann. B: Urban Analytics City Sci. **25**, 205–226 (1998)

15. Costa, E., Duarte, J.: Mass customization of ceramic tableware through digital technology. In: Bartolo, H., Bartolo, P. (eds.) Green Design, Materials and Manufacturing Processes, pp. 467–471. CRC Press, Lisboa (2013)

16. Beirao, J., Duarte, J., Stouffs, R.: Creating specific grammars with generic grammars: towards flexible urban design. Nexus Netw. J. **13**, 73–111 (2011)

17. Mendes, G., Beirao, J., Duarte, J.: Implementing a generative urban design model: grammar-based design patterns for urban design. In: 28th eCAADe Conference, Switzerland, pp. 265–274 (2010)

18. Çolakoğlu, B.: Design by grammar: an interpretation and generation of vernacular Hayat houses in contemporary context. Environ. Plan. **32**, 141–149 (2005)

19. Chase, S., Ahmad, S.: Grammar transformations: using composite grammars to understand hybridity in design with an example from Medieval Islamic courtyard buildings. CAAD Futures, pp. 89–98 (2005)

20. Eloy, S., Duarte, J.: Transformation grammar for housing rehabilitation. Nexus Netw. J. **13**, 49–71 (2011)

21. Kruger, M., Duarte, J., Coutinho, F.: Decoding de re aedificatoria: using grammars to trace Alberti's influence on Portuguese classical architecture. Nexus Netw. J. **13**, 171–182 (2011)

22. Benrós, D.: A generic housing grammar for the generation of different housing languages: a generic housing shape grammar for Palladian villas, Prairie and Malagueira Houses, Ph.D. dissertation, London's Global University Bartlett School of Graduate Studies (2018)

23. Hadighi, M., Poerschke, U., Pisciotta, H., Goad, L., Goldberg, D., Ling, M.: The "Air-Wall": a mid-twentieth-century double-skin façade by William Hajjar, the Façade Tectonics World Congress, Los Angeles, CA, pp. 473–482 (2016)

24. Winton, A.G.: The Bauhaus, 1919–1933, in Heilbrunn timeline of art history, Metropolitan Museum of Art, New York (2000)

25. Jordy, W.H.: The aftermath of the Bauhaus in America: Gropius, Mies, and Breuer, Perspectives in American History, Volume II, Charles Warren Center for Studies in American History, Harvard University (1968)

Defining Rules for Kinematic Shapes
with Variable Spatial Relations

Laura Harrison, Iestyn Jowers[(⊠)], and Chris Earl

The Open University, Milton Keynes, UK
{laura.harrison,iestyn.jowers,c.f.earl}@open.ac.uk

Abstract. Designing mechanisms can be a challenging problem, because the underlying kinematics involved are typically not intuitively incorporated into common techniques for design representation. Kinematic shapes and kinematic grammars build on the shape grammar and making grammar formalisms to enable a visually intuitive approach to model and explore mechanisms. With reference to the lower kinematic pairs this paper introduces kinematic shapes. These are connected shapes with parts which have variable spatial relations that account for the relative motion of the parts. The paper considers how such shapes can be defined, the role of elements shared by connected parts, and the motions that result. It also considers how kinematic shape rules can be employed to generate and explore the motion of mechanisms.

Keywords: Shape grammars · Kinematic design · Making grammars · Boundaries

1   Introduction

In shape grammars, abstract shapes model the pictorial representations used during design activities [1]. The shape grammar formalism is well suited to visual explorations of these representations, and the computational mechanism of shape rules has been applied to describe and support creative design processes [2]. This is because the shapes used in shape grammars are visually dynamic, supporting reinterpretation and recognition of emergent forms. In recent years, shape grammars have been extended to *making grammars* [3], where the aim is to formalise physical manipulations of material and objects, and to represent processes of making that take place in arts, crafts, and manufacturing. Consideration of *things* made from *stuff*, introduces new constraints to ensure that shapes mimic the behaviour of physical objects in physical space, for example to take account of collisions [4]. This paper is concerned with a subclass of physical objects, mechanisms with moving parts [5], and explores the constraints that arise when shapes are used to represent and explore mechanisms, in *kinematic grammars*.

A variety of well-proven methods exist for designing mechanisms, e.g. [6], but the underlying kinematics involved are typically not intuitively incorporated into common techniques for design representation. In some instances, linked static representations (such as series of images) may communicate the combined effects of the possible motions of parts within a design. Alternatively, physical or virtual models can be used

© Springer Nature Singapore Pte Ltd. 2019
J.-H. Lee (Ed.): CAAD Futures 2019, CCIS 1028, pp. 444–458, 2019.
https://doi.org/10.1007/978-981-13-8410-3_31

to test motion – either through simulation or material interaction. But in general, exploration depends on a designer's ability to apply understanding of potential motions between parts to independently predict and model (mentally or otherwise) the combined effects within a designed object.

Building on shape grammars, kinematic grammars aim to provide a formalism which will enable a visually intuitive approach to model and explore mechanisms [5]. In abstract terms, the motion of mechanisms can be modelled according to connected objects that move relative to each other. Consequently, kinematic grammars incorporate shapes with explicit but connected parts that have variable spatial relations between them. In this paper, kinematic grammars are introduced with reference to a specific class of mechanisms, the *lower kinematic pairs*. The paper proceeds in the next section by introducing the lower kinematic pairs; Sect. 3 considers the concept of *kinematic shapes* as models of physical mechanisms; Sect. 4 explores how mechanisms can be explored using kinematic grammars; and, Sect. 5 discusses kinematic grammars with reference to lower kinematic pairs.

2 Mechanisms in Motion

At its most basic, the design of a mechanism can be described according to combinations of the relative motions of connected parts [8]. The pairs of parts that give rise to motions are often referred to as kinematic pairs, and are subject to certain spatial conditions. Firstly, one of the parts needs to be fixed with respect to the local spatial neighbourhood. Which of the two parts is fixed is of no consequence because the motion is relative, and temporally the part only needs to be fixed for the duration of the motion. Secondly, the geometry of the two parts needs to restrict the relative motion in some way. The result of this is that the fixed part determines an envelope of motion for the moving part. In order to ensure motion, the shared geometry of the connected parts must have the same curvature. This means that the shared geometry of parts must either be a point, or it must have constant curvature, i.e. it is either rectilinear, circular, or a helical combination.

Kinematic pairs are classified in various ways: according to types of connection, i.e. surface, line or point; according to the type of relative motion, e.g. sliding or rolling; or according to the type of constraint applied to the pair, e.g. mechanical or due to gravity. Here, the focus is on a particular classification of kinematic pairs, referred to as lower pairs. These are identified according to a surface connection, and are differentiated from higher pairs, where connection is a point or a line, e.g. the connection between a cam and its follower. In total, there are six lower pairs, as illustrated in Fig. 1. The lower pairs enumerate spatial restrictions on motion, resulting in pairs of parts with relative motions of varying degrees of freedom (DoF):

– *Prismatic pair* (slider), e.g. Fig. 1i: the axes of the two parts are aligned, allowing translation along the axes and no rotation. This results in one DoF
– *Revolute pair* (hinged joint), e.g. Fig. 1ii: the axes of the two parts are aligned, allowing rotation about the axes and no translation. This results in one DoF

- *Screw pair*, e.g. Fig. 1iii: the axes of the two parts are aligned, allowing a combination of translation and rotation relative to the axes. This results in one DoF
- *Cylindrical pair*, e.g. Fig. 1iv: the axes of the two parts are aligned, allowing independent translation and rotation relative to the axes. This results in two DoF
- *Spherical pair* (ball joint), e.g. Fig. 1v: the spherical centres of the two parts are aligned, allowing rotation about three axes and no translation. This results in three DoF
- *Planar pair*, e.g. Fig. 1vi: the surfaces of the two parts are in contact, allowing translation in two directions and rotation about one axis, perpendicular to the surfaces in contact. This results in three DoF

In the design of a mechanism, kinematic pairs can be combined in chains to create models of complicated motions [6]. These are often abstracted as graphs or hypergraphs of links and nodes which can be used to determine the potential motion of a mechanism, based on connections, but without consideration of geometry [7]. Consequently, when a design is realised as a physical model, complications can arise when geometry interacts or collides during the motion of parts.

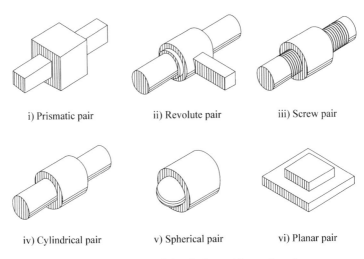

| i) Prismatic pair | ii) Revolute pair | iii) Screw pair |

| iv) Cylindrical pair | v) Spherical pair | vi) Planar pair |

Fig. 1. Examples of the six lower kinematic pairs

The spatial nature of kinematic pairs implies that mechanisms can be readily described as shapes in shape computations, and there are certain benefits in doing so. Shapes can provide a model of a mechanism that includes geometry as well as connection of parts, whilst retaining a level of abstraction that can support creative exploration. Designers are primarily concerned with modelling physically realisable designs. However, real motions are not necessarily easily described using shape computation. Conversely, more abstract notions of motion which could not be achieved in the physical world can give interesting results when modelled virtually, and therefore should not be precluded from investigation. Shape computations can be used to design and explore mechanisms in a designer-friendly way which is visually intuitive [5]. In this paper, kinematic shapes are used to model mechanisms and their motion, with reference to the lower kinematic pairs.

3   Kinematic Shapes

In a shape grammar, shape rules are used to generate designs through consideration of shapes and the spatial relation between shapes and/or parts of shapes [1]. Any two shapes (or parts of a shape) define a spatial relation. For example, all of the shapes in Fig. 2 are composed of the same three parts: a small square, a larger square, and a point located at their shared vertex. But, the shapes are all distinct from each other because of the different spatial relation between the two squares. Shape grammars often make use of such relations through applications of shape rules which produce repetition of form and arrangement and can result in visually cohesive patterns, or designs consistent with a particular style [9].

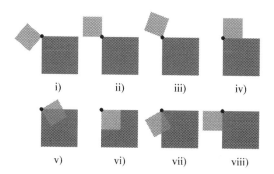

Fig. 2. Examples of spatial relations

The spatial relations used in a shape grammar are typically fixed, or for parametric shape grammars are instantiated during application of a shape rule. Spatial relations can change via application of shape rules but this does not reflect the behaviour of mechanisms, such as the lower pairs illustrated in Fig. 1, where spatial relations between parts change continuously according to their motion. Therefore, to support formal exploration of mechanisms via shape computation, it is necessary to consider the motion according to *variable spatial relations* (VSR) between parts, i.e. the continuously changing relation between parts that are in motion.

VSRs result from well-defined motions of parts, and a *kinematic shape* is a shape which includes one or more VSRs between its parts. For example, in the eight shapes in Fig. 2 the spatial relations between the small and large squares vary according to the rotation of the small square about the point. These eight shapes can be recognised as instantiations of a kinematic shape in which there is a VSR between the two squares, defined according to a rotation of the small square. This motion is not a consequence of transformations realised during application of shape rules, it is instead an implicit property of the kinematic shape. As kinematic shapes, all eight of the shapes in Fig. 2 are equal, and comparison with Fig. 1 reveals that they are a two-dimensional equivalent of a revolute pair (Fig. 1ii). This example highlights the key features of kinematic shapes; they include connected parts that are in motion.

3.1   Shapes in Motion

Shape algebras [1] provide a framework suitable for exploring motion of shapes, as summarised in Table 1. The algebras are denoted U_{ij}, where i is the dimension of the shape elements used to construct a shape, j is the dimension of the embedding space, and $i \leq j$. Motion of a shape is defined according to a reference shape which is a shape element of dimension k, where $k < j$, and the lower dimensional embedding spaces, defined by points and lines, are more restrictive with respect to motion than the higher dimensional spaces of planes and volumes.

Table 1. Shape motion in algebras U_{ij}

Algebra	Space	Motion	Reference	DoF
U_{00}	Point	-	-	-
U_{i1}	Line	Translation	Point	1
U_{i2}	Plane	Rotation	Point	1
		Translation	Point	2
		Translation	Line	1
U_{i3}	Volume	Rotation	Point	3
		Rotation	Line	1
		Translation	Point	3
		Translation	Line	1
		Translation	Plane	2

In the algebra U_{00}, the embedding space is a single point, and no motion is possible. While in algebras U_{i1}, the embedding space is a straight line, shapes are composed of points or lines, and the only possible motion is translation. This is defined relative to a point, with one degree of freedom (DoF). Algebras U_{i2} are familiar to designers who work with sketches to develop design concepts. The embedding space is a plane, shapes are composed of points, lines or planes, and motion is composed of rotations and translations. Rotation is defined relative to a point, with one DoF, and translation is defined relative to a point, with two DoFs, or relative to a line with one DoF. Algebras U_{i3} are analogous to physical space, or the 3D space within a CAD system. The embedding space is a volume, shapes are composed of volumes, planes, lines or points, and as with U_{i2} motion is composed of translations and rotations. Rotation is defined relative to a point, with three DoFs, or a line, with one DoF, while translation is defined relative to a point, with three DoFs, or a plane, with two DoFs. As an example, Fig. 3 illustrates moving shapes in the algebra U_{22}, where shapes composed of planes are arranged in a plane. Representing motion in a static image can be difficult, and Fig. 3

adopts a convention of using arrows to indicate the motion of the squares. In Fig. 3i, a square is rotated around a reference point, in Fig. 3ii, a square is translated relative to a reference point, and in Fig. 3iii a square is translated relative to a reference line.

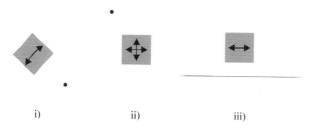

i)   ii)   iii)

Fig. 3. Moving shapes in U_{22}

Shapes with moving parts, i.e. kinematic shapes, can also be formalised in algebras U_{ij}, by considering relative motions of the parts that results in a VSR. The simplest kinematic shapes are described by a triple of shapes, $\{s, \alpha, e\}$, where s represents a static part, α represents a moving part, and e represents a reference shape, as enumerated in Table 1. The existence of multiple parts which move independently distinguishes the kinematic shape from a shape in motion, but the motion of α, the moving part, is not defined relative to s, the static part. For example, the kinematic shape in Fig. 2 is composed of two squares, and the rotation of the small square is not defined relative to the large square, it is instead defined relative to the point, which acts as the reference shape. In general, the motion of a moving part α is defined relative to e, the reference shape, which is a shape element, of dimension k, in an algebra U_{ij}, $k < j$. The VSR therefore defines the spatial relationship between α and e, and $VSR(\alpha, e)$ is a shape given by an instantiation of the motion of α relative to e. A simple kinematic shape is therefore given by $s + VSR(\alpha, e)$. For connected kinematic shapes, such as the shape illustrated in Fig. 2, the VSR can be determined by considering the connectivity of the parts s and α.

3.2 Shapes with Connected Parts

Shapes are connected when they touch, and a shape is said to be a *connected shape* when each part touches some other part [1]. For example, Fig. 4 illustrates different connected shapes in U_{22}, composed of two squares, labelled x and y. In Fig. 4a, the squares are connected because x is a subshape of y; in Fig. 4b, they are connected because they overlap; and in Fig. 4c–f they are connected because they touch, either at their edges or at their vertices.

Shape connectivity can be defined in terms of the recursive embedding relation applied to parts, boundaries of parts, boundaries of the boundaries of parts, etc. [1]. The boundary of a shape in an algebra U_{ij} is a shape in an algebra $U_{(i-1)j}$, and the operator $b^i(S)$ formalises this recursive relation between boundaries b, and shapes S, with integer $i \geq 0$ and $b^0(S) = S$. For example, a shape S in U_{33} is composed of volume shape elements and has a boundary $b(S)$ composed of planes in U_{23}. This in turn has a boundary $b^2(S)$ composed of lines in U_{13}, which in turn has boundary $b^3(S)$ composed of points in U_{13}. For all the connected shapes in Fig. 4, x and y contain parts that share a boundary, i.e. an edge, or a boundary of a boundary, i.e. a vertex.

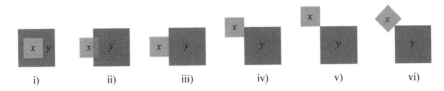

Fig. 4. Examples of connected shapes in U_{22}

Generalising this example, using the boundary operator and subshape relation $\leq$, two shapes, x and y, can be defined as connected if there are shapes z and z' such that $z \leq b^i(x)$ and $z' \leq b^j(y)$, and $b^k(z)$. $b^l(z')$ is not the empty shape, with integers $i, j, k, l \geq 0$. This definition can be applied to the connected shapes in U_{22} illustrated in Fig. 4, as follows, although there may be many possible choices of z and z' in each case:

- in Fig. 4i, x is embedded in y; z and z' are both in U_{22}, $z \leq x$ and $z' \leq y$ so that $z.z'$ is not the empty shape
- in Fig. 4ii, x and y overlap; z and z' are both in U_{22}, $z \leq x$ and $z' \leq y$ so that $z.z'$ is not the empty shape
- in Fig. 4iii, x and y share part of their boundary; z and z' are both in U_{12}, $z \leq b(x)$ and $z' \leq b(y)$ so that $z.z'$ is not the empty shape
- in Fig. 4iv, x and y share part of their boundary; z and z' are both in U_{12}, $z \leq b(x)$ and $z' \leq b(y)$ so that $z.z'$ is not the empty shape
- in Fig. 4v, x and y share a vertex; z and z' are both in U_{02}, $z \leq b^2(x)$ and $z' \leq b^2(y)$ so that $z.z'$ is not the empty shape
- in Fig. 4vi, an edge of x touches a vertex of y; z is in U_{12}, z' is in U_{01}, $z \leq b(x)$ and $z' \leq b^2(y)$ so that $b(z)$. $b^0(z')$ is not the empty shape

This definition of shape connectivity is fairly intuitive, and captures the idea that shapes are connected if their parts touch. It also applies to shapes in composite algebras, which are composed of spatial elements of different dimensions.

In shape grammars, connectivity between parts of a shape is temporary and changing, depending on the application of rules that dynamically alter the structure of a shape [1]. Similarly, in kinematic shapes, the connectivity between parts also changes, but not according to rule applications, instead according to different instantiations of the VSR, given by $VSR(\alpha, e)$. For example, in Fig. 2 as the small square rotates about the point, the connectivity of the two squares changes: in Fig. 2i–iii, the two squares are connected due to the shared vertex, but in Fig. 2iv & viii, they are connected due to a shared boundary, while in Fig. 2v & vii, they are connected due to a shared part, and in Fig. 2vi, they are connected because the small square is embedded in the large square. If they are retained, these different connections have implications with respect to the potential motion of the small square, as illustrated in Fig. 5. In these examples, connectivity of the small and large squares is explicitly identified by the shape elements drawn in black, and the arrows are used to indicate the motion of the small square according to the VSR. Figure 5i combines all the shapes from Fig. 2 into a single kinematic shape; the two squares are connected at a shared vertex and the VSR is defined by the rotation of the small square about this point. The shape is a U_{22} equivalent of a revolute pair (Fig. 1ii). In Fig. 5ii, the two squares are connected at a shared edge, and the VSR is defined by the horizontal translation of the small square parallel to the edge. The shape is a U_{22} equivalent of a planar pair (Fig. 1vi). In Fig. 5iii, the two squares overlap and are connected by a shared subshape. Consequently, they are locked in position and the small square cannot move. In these three examples, the spatial relations of the two squares are instantiations of the kinematic shape illustrated in Fig. 2, but different interpretations of the connectivity of the kinematic shape give rise to different possible motions. Ambiguity about how connectivity of shape is interpreted can be reduced by explicitly including connecting shape elements as part of the shape; for example these are drawn in black in Fig. 5.

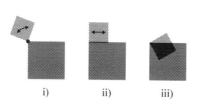

i)   ii)   iii)

Fig. 5. Motion of connected shapes

In these examples, the connecting elements also act as a reference shape, and define the motion of the small square, and this is potentially of benefit. When the connecting shape element and the reference shape are different a restriction of potential motion can result, as illustrated in Fig. 6. In Fig. 6i, rotation of the small square about the reference point, identified at its centre, is restricted due to the connectivity of the two squares, as specified by the black line on the shared boundary. The connectivity of the two squares is such that only vertical translation of the small square is possible, as illustrated in Fig. 6ii, where the connecting shape is the reference shape. Alternatively, if a rotating part is required, then this issue can be resolved by changing the geometry of the parts, as illustrated in Fig. 6iii where the small square is replaced with a circle. The boundary of a circle is invariant under rotation, and as a result the specified motion is not restricted by the connectivity of the parts. The shape in Fig. 6iii is a U_{22} equivalent of a spherical pair (Fig. 1v).

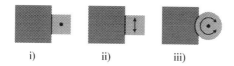

i)   ii)   iii)

Fig. 6. Exploring the consequences of shape connectivity

The explicit inclusion of connecting shapes means that kinematic shapes begin to behave more as physical objects, where motion is defined not only according to abstract concepts such as reference shapes, but also according to interactions between parts. However, this gives rise to a conflict between the expected behaviour of shapes in a shape grammar, and the expected behaviour of a mechanism. For example, in Fig. 2, as the small square rotates it overlaps the large square so that there are parts of both that occupy the same region of the embedding space. Since shape grammars are a visual formalism, when this situation arises, it is common for overlapping shapes to merge and form a single shape element. However, for physical mechanisms it not possible for parts to occupy the same region of space, and parts in motion should remain distinct. This issue can be resolved by recognising that physical mechanisms behave as things made of stuff, and should be modelled within making grammars [5].

3.3   Kinematic Shapes as Things Made of Stuff

Making grammars [3] apply the computational framework of shape grammars to physical objects, and model processes of making that take place in the arts, crafts, and manufacturing. To support this, shape algebras are extended to include spatial *stuff*, which is the composite matter of physical *things*, and making grammars incorporate actions applied to stuff as consequences of sensing its properties, e.g. by seeing or touching. Examples include knotting of strings in Incan khipu and painting with watercolours [3]. However, as discussed in the previous section, physical objects exhibit different behaviours to shapes, and these should be taken into consideration when exploring how computations for making grammars might work within shape algebras. Krstic [4] identified key factors that distinguish things and stuff used in making grammars from shapes and parts used in shape grammars. These are concerned with the equivalence of representations in different algebras, and the treatment of boundaries.

Stuff and things are by definition three-dimensional, and in shape algebras are therefore most naturally represented in algebras U_{33}, where volumes are arranged in three-dimensional space. For the purposes of illustration, it is also useful to consider two-dimensional equivalents in algebras U_{22}, where planes are arranged in two-dimensional space. In design, it is common to use boundaries as a representation for a shape, e.g. in solid modelling surface-based models are common, with U_{33} objects represented in U_{23}. However, representing material things for making in an algebra U_{ij}, where $i < j$ can give rise to conceptual inconsistencies. This is illustrated in Fig. 7 where a shape rule $a \rightarrow b$ is represented in three different algebras, which are visually similar but conceptually very different.

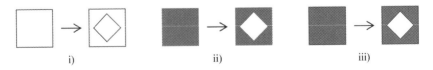

Fig. 7. Examples of shape rules in (i) U_{12}, (ii) U_{22} and (iii) $U_{22} \times U_{12}$

In the rule in Fig. 7i, the shapes a and b are both in U_{12} and this is a typical example of a rule from a shape grammar for design applications. It is an addition rule, with a square (composed of four lines) added to the square recognised by the left-hand side, and the partial order of the shapes in the rule is $a < b$. Compare this to the rule in Fig. 7ii, where the shapes a and b are both in U_{22} and the rule could be from a making grammar, e.g. to model cutting a hole in a sheet of material. It is a subtraction rule, with a planar square subtracted from the square recognised by the left-hand side, and the partial order of the shapes in the rule is $a > b$. These two rules are related by the boundary function $b(S)$, with the shapes in the rule in Fig. 7i being the boundaries of the shapes in the rule in Fig. 7ii. Because of this, and despite the visual similarity of the two rules, they perform opposite functions, one adds a square, while the other subtracts a square [4]. This example illustrates that the logic of rules for boundaries, e.g. the U_{12} rule in Fig. 7i, does not reflect the logic of making, which in this example is better modelled by the U_{22} rule in Fig. 7ii. But, rules for shapes in a U_{ii} algebra (such as U_{22}), where shapes and the embedding space are of the same dimension, are also problematic, because they are unconstrained, and can be applied to any shape in U_{ii} in infinitely many ways. Because of this, Krstic [4] suggests that in making grammars rules should include shapes and their boundaries, as illustrated in Fig. 7iii. This rule includes shapes from the composite algebra $U_{22} \times U_{12}$, and works as expected for a making grammar because the inclusion of boundaries provides context to ensure that the rule is applied correctly. Shapes in U_{ii} algebras together with their boundaries form a subalgebra of $U_{ii} \times U_{(i-1)i}$, denoted UB_i, which contains ordered pairs of shapes and their boundaries [11]. These algebras are weaker than shape algebras U_{ij}, because they lack Boolean operations of sum, product and difference, and partial order is defined component-wise, for shapes and their boundaries. But they are useful for modelling things in making grammars because they preserve the boundaries of shapes, which are useful to streamline rule application [4].

The UB_i algebras are closed under symmetric difference which can be used in the application of shape rules in a shape grammar. The symmetric difference of two shapes, x and y, is composed of the parts that are in either of the shapes, but not in their intersection   and   is   given   by $x \oplus y = (x-y) + (y-x)$,   or   equivalently $x \oplus y = (x+y) - (x \cdot y)$. For the boundaries of shapes in U_{ii} algebras symmetric difference is distributive, so that $b(x \oplus y) = b(x) \oplus b(y)$, where x and y are in U_{ii}, and for shapes in U_{ij}, it can replace sum when shapes are disjoint or difference when one shape is embedded in the other [10]. Specifically, $x \oplus y = (x+y)$ if $(x \cdot y) = 0$, and $x \oplus y = y - x$ if $x \leq y$. Using symmetric difference, a shape rule $a \rightarrow b$ can be applied to shape c under a transformation t when $a \leq c$ and $[c - t(a)] \cdot t(b) = 0$, to give $c' = [c \oplus t(a)] \oplus t(b)$ [4]. The subshape condition, $a \leq c$, ensures that the first instance of the symmetric difference results in a subtraction of $t(a)$ from c while the discrete condition, $[c - t(a)] \cdot t(b) = 0$, ensures that the second instance results in the addition of $t(b)$ to $c - t(a)$. A further condition on the boundaries of the shapes, $b(t(a)) \cdot b(c) \neq 0$, can be applied to provide registration for transformation t and restrict the applications of rules.

The discrete condition $[c - t(a)] \cdot t(b) = 0$ has the additional benefit of giving shapes the behaviour of physical objects during rule application, by avoiding collisions between parts. It ensures that the shape b on the right-hand side of the rule does not collide with the shape that remains after subtracting the shape a from the left-hand side of the rule. For kinematic shapes this mechanism for collision protection is useful, and should be applied continuously to moving parts. To achieve this, a VSR condition should also be included, so that that in a simple kinematic shape composed of a triple of shapes, $\{s, \alpha, e\}$ the static part s and the moving part α should always be discrete, i.e. $s \cdot VSR(\alpha, e) = 0$. This will ensure that the parts of a kinematic shape do not overlap as a result of its motion.

4   Kinematic Rules for Kinematic Grammars

Inclusion of kinematic shapes in shape/making grammars requires a mechanism for distinguishing between parts of shapes that are in motion and those that are static. For this purpose, one of two opposing philosophical approaches can be adopted. It can either be assumed that, by default, parts are in motion, or that they are static. In the first approach, all parts of a kinematic shape are free to move around the embedding space, except for parts which are explicitly identified as being static. In the second approach, all parts of a kinematic shape are static relative to the embedding space, except for parts which are explicitly identified as being in motion relative to specified reference shapes. In terms of physical intuition, either approach is equally valid, since it can be recognised that, in general, objects tend to be free to move, unless they are constrained in some way while, when designing mechanisms, it is common to assume that parts are static unless their motion is specified. In this paper, the second approach has been assumed, and the notation used in the examples presented identifies parts of a kinematic shape that are in motion. Symbolically, the moving parts are represented with a Greek letter, while visually they are represented using a lighter shade of grey and are labelled with an arrow to indicate the resulting motion. This notation is simplistic, and useful for the exploration presented here, but there is perhaps benefit in exploring alternative representations using colour grammars [12] or weights [13] to support greater exploration of languages of kinematic designs.

In a kinematic grammar, motion can be introduced to a static shape by applying kinematic shape rules which take the form $a \to b + VSR(\alpha, e)$. Here, a and b are static shapes in UB_i, α is a moving shape, also in UB_i. e is shape element in U_{ki} ($k < i$) and acts as both a connecting shape element for b and α, and as a reference shape for the motion of α. $VSR(\alpha, e)$ is a UB_i shape given by an instantiation of the motion of α relative to e. Figure 8 illustrates an example of a kinematic shape rule (Fig. 8i) and its application to a static shape (Fig. 8ii) to produce a kinematic shape (Fig. 8iii).

i) Shape rule:	ii) Static shape:	iii) Kinematic shape:
$a \to b + VSR(a, e)$	s	$(s - a) + VSR(a, e)$

Fig. 8. Example of a kinematic shape rule and its application to a static shape

In Fig. 8iii the motion of the kinematic shape is illustrated by the inclusion of overlapping instantiations of the moving part, all of which observe the collision protection condition $s \cdot VSR(\alpha, e) = 0$. The result is a shape that is a two-dimensional equivalent of a revolute pair (Fig. 1ii). In this example, the logic of rule application follows the shape grammar formalism, and since $a \cdot b \neq 0$ the rule proceeds by recognising and replacing the shape $a - b$ with $VSR(\alpha, e)$. Alternatively, if $a \cdot b = 0$ then the rule would proceed by replacing a with b and adding a moving part.

Kinematic shapes can also be combined into chains, to model mechanisms with more complicated motions. In a kinematic grammar this can be achieved by applying kinematic shape rules which take the form $VSR(\alpha, e) \rightarrow VSR(\beta, e) + VSR(\gamma, f)$. Here, α, β and γ are moving shapes in UB_i. e is a shape element in U_{ki} ($k < i$) and is the reference shape for the motion of α and β. f is both a connecting shape element for β and γ and is also the reference shape for the motion of β. $VSR(\alpha, e)$, $VSR(\beta, e)$ and $VSR(\gamma, f)$ are UB_i shapes given by instantiations of the motion of the moving shapes α, β and γ relative to e, e and f, respectively. Figure 9 illustrates an example of a kinematic shape rule (Fig. 9i) and its application to the kinematic shape in Fig. 8iii. In this example $\alpha \cdot \beta = 0$ and the rule proceeds by adding the second moving part, modelled by $VSR(\gamma, f)$. Alternatively, if $\beta < \alpha$, then $VSR(\alpha, e)$ is replaced with two moving parts modelled by $VSR(\beta, e)$ and $VSR(\gamma, f)$. As a result of applying the rule, the kinematic shape in Fig. 9ii has two parts in motion, both of which rotate about a connecting point. The result is a shape that is a two-dimensional equivalent of two revolute pairs (Fig. 1ii) combined in sequence. The motion of the kinematic shape is too complicated to be illustrated according to the method used in Fig. 8. Instead, in Fig. 9iii it is illustrated according to the envelopes of motion of the two moving parts. These define a sub-space of the embedding space and are represented as shaded regions. For both moving parts, the motion is restricted according to the connectivity of the parts, and according to the collision protection conditions $s \cdot VSR(\beta, e) = 0$, and $VSR(\beta, e) \cdot VSR(\gamma, f) = 0$, where s is the stationary part of the shape, and β and γ are the moving parts.

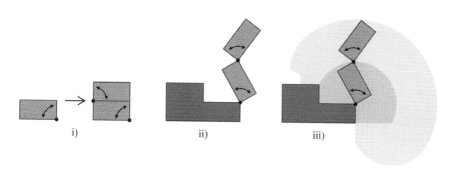

i)   ii)   iii)

Fig. 9. Example of a kinematic shape rule and its application to a kinematic shape

Application of kinematic shape rules requires a mechanism for recognising embedded parts of a shape. This is complicated by VSRs, since spatial relations between moving parts are dynamic and cannot be used to provide registration for determining where shape rules can be applied. For example, the kinematic shape rule illustrated in Fig. 10i is of the form $a + VSR(\alpha, e) \rightarrow b$ and its application requires recognition of both a static part and a moving part. Rules of this form can be used to remove moving parts from a kinematic shape, and include static shapes a and b, both in UB_i, moving shape α, also in UB_i, shape element e in U_{ki} ($k < i$) and $VSR(\alpha, e)$, a UB_i shape given by an instantiation of the motion of α relative to e. In applying the rule, recognition of a, the static shape on the left-hand side of the rule, follows the logic of rule application from shape grammars, where rule $a \rightarrow b$ applied to a shape c proceeds by first identifying a transformation t such that $t(a)$ is an embedded part of c, $t(a) \leq c$. The rule is then applied by removing the transformed instance of the shape a and replacing it with a similarly transformed instance of the shape b. In practice, identification of the transformation t is implemented by considering how distinct elements of a, such as vertices, are transformed and ensuring that all distinct elements of $t(a)$ are embedded in c [14]. For the moving shape on the left-hand side of the rule, this approach does not work, because the spatial relation between its distinct elements is changing according to the motion of α relative to e, and an alternative approach must be identified for recognising the moving parts of a shape. For this purpose, the invariants of the motion can be employed to identify the VSR between distinct elements, and the reference of motion. For example, to apply the rule in Fig. 10i to the kinematic shape in Fig. 10ii requires that the static and moving parts of the shape on the left-hand side of the rule are recognised as parts. Figure 10iii illustrates the distinct elements of the shape in Fig. 10ii that are used to support this recognition. The motion of the moving part is a rotation about the connecting point, and consequently the distance from this point is invariant. In Fig. 10iii this is illustrated by dashed lines, which are of equal length for the two instantiations of the motion. These provide enough information to determine how the shape rule can be applied, and the result is the shape in Fig. 8ii.

i)   ii)   iii)

Fig. 10. Recognising parts of a kinematic shape

5 Discussion

This paper has explored how the shape grammar formalism can be applied to the problem of designing mechanisms with moving parts. With reference to the lower kinematic pairs (Fig. 1), kinematic shapes were introduced as connected shapes composed of static parts, moving parts and shape elements used as reference for motion. In essence each kinematic shape represents an infinite number of static shapes, each of which is given by an instantiation of the moving parts. Despite this it is still possible to recognise kinematic shapes and their moving parts for the purpose of rule application in a kinematic grammar by considering the invariants of motion.

A variety of kinematic shapes were introduced as illustrations, and these were identified to be two-dimensional equivalents of the revolute pair (Fig. 5i), the spherical pair (Fig. 6iii) and the planar pair (Fig. 6ii). The other lower kinematic pairs, the prismatic pair, the screw pair and the cylindrical pair, do not have two-dimensional equivalents, because they would violate the collision condition, which ensures that parts of shapes do not occupy the same region of an embedding space. For visual shapes this is common, e.g. overlapping planes, intersecting volumes, etc., but as models of mechanisms, kinematic shapes should behave as physical things composed of spatial stuff, and collision between moving parts should be avoided. However, the prismatic pair, the screw pair and the cylindrical pair can be represented as three-dimensional shapes, in an UB_3 algebra, as illustrated in Fig. 11. For each of these kinematic shapes, the moving cuboid is connected to the static shape by a shared surface, and the motion of the cuboid is with reference to a line that is parallel to this surface. If the collision condition is adhered to, then motion is defined and constrained both by the reference line and by the geometry of the static and moving parts. As a result, in the prismatic pair only translation parallel to the line is possible, in the screw pair, only a screw rotation with dependent motions about and parallel to the line is possible, and in the cylindrical pair two independent motions are possible, rotation about the line and translation parallel to the line.

To be of use in the design of mechanisms, kinematic grammars should give some indication of the resulting behaviour of kinematic shapes, i.e. the extent of the motion of the moving parts. Representing motion in a static image can be difficult, but in this paper various approaches have been employed to give some insight, including the use of arrows, Fig. 5, inclusion of multiple instantiations of moving parts, Fig. 8iii, and inclusion of envelopes of motion of moving parts, Fig. 9iii. Envelopes of motion are perhaps the most expressive of these, and as regions of space can themselves be modelled and analysed using shape arithmetic.

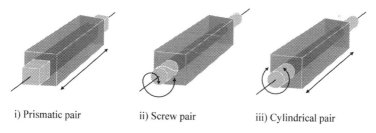

i) Prismatic pair   ii) Screw pair   iii) Cylindrical pair

Fig. 11. Modelling kinematic pairs in U_{33}

The use of the lower kinematic pairs as a reference for defining kinematic shapes has resulted in certain restrictions. Only the motions of connected shapes have been considered, and as a consequence not all the motions enumerated in Table 1 are applicable. For example, in a two-dimensional embedding space, the moving parts of a connected kinematic shape can rotate about a point or translate parallel to a line, but cannot translate according to a point. A more general consideration of kinematic shapes could take into account all of the possible motions. Also, kinematic grammars have been identified as a variation of making grammars, where shapes adhere to physical constraints, but with the inclusion of VSRs to account for moving parts. As a result, kinematic grammars do not readily support the visual emergence that typifies shape grammar applications, and much of the richness of the shape formalism has been lost. This is perhaps true for all making grammars since it is not obvious how visual emergence can work in a U_{33} algebra, when from any given view-point only part of a shape is visible, and only the boundaries (i.e. surfaces) of a part can be seen. However, there is still scope for reinterpretation of shape structure via shape rule applications, and emergence can arise in material behaviours of shapes in motion [15]. Kinematic connections between parts permit relative motions, and kinematic behaviours (or motions) emerge, as indicated in Fig. 9iii; also, when material deformations permit relative motions, elastic, plastic or even auxetic behaviours may emerge. Consequently rules acting to add multiple interacting VSRs within designs, can give rise to emergent kinematic behaviours that may be complex and surprising.

Future work will explore how kinematic shapes can be included in shape computation to formalise motions of physical materials and objects. A more general treatment could include broader categories of mechanisms than those considered here. Of particular interest is whether a visual approach can result in interesting designs, previously only found through application of analytical techniques.

References

1. Stiny, G.: Shape: Talking about Seeing and Doing. MIT Press, Cambridge (2006)
2. Prats, M., Lim, S., Jowers, I., Garner, S., Chase, S.: Transforming shape in design: observations from studies of sketching. Des. Stud. 30(5), 503–520 (2009)
3. Knight, T., Stiny, G.: Making grammars: from computing with shapes to computing with things. Des. Stud. Part A 41, 8–28 (2015)
4. Krstic, D.: Grammars for making revisited. In: Gero, J.S. (ed.) DCC 2018, pp. 479–496. Springer, Cham (2019). https://doi.org/10.1007/978-3-030-05363-5_26
5. Harrison, L., Earl, C., Eckert, C.: Exploratory making: shape, structure and motion. Des. Stud. Part A 41, 51–78 (2015)
6. Tsai, L.-W.: Mechanism Design: Enumeration of Kinematic Structures According to Function. CRC Press, Boca Raton (2000)
7. Berge, C.: Graphs and Hypergraphs. North Holland, Amsterdam (1973)
8. Reuleaux, F.: The Kinematics of Machinery. Outlines of a Theory of Machines (trans. and edited by A. B. W. Kennedy). Macmillan and Co., London (1876)
9. Prats, M., Earl, C., Garner, S., Jowers, I.: Shape exploration of designs in a style: Toward generation of product designs. Artif. Intell. Eng. Des. Anal. Manuf. 20(3), 201–215 (2006)
10. Earl, C.F.: Shape Boundaries. Environ. Plan. 24(5), 669–687 (1997)
11. Krstic, D.: Algebras and Grammars for Shapes and their Boundaries. Environ. Plan. 28(1), 151–162 (2001)
12. Knight, T.W.: Color grammars: designing with lines and colors. Environ. Plan. 16(4), 417–449 (1989)
13. Stiny, G.: Weights. Environ. Plann. B: Plann. Des. 19(4), 413–430 (1992)
14. Krishnamurti, R.: The arithmetic of shapes. Environ. Plann. B: Plann. Des. 7(4), 463–484 (1980)
15. Gürsoy, B., Özkar, M.: Visualizing making: shapes, materials, and actions. Des. Stud. Part A 41, 29–50 (2015)

Shape Clustering Using K-Medoids in Architectural Form Finding

Shermeen Yousif$^{(\boxtimes)}$ ⓘ and Wei Yan ⓘ

Texas A&M University, College Station, TX 77843, USA
{shermeen, wyan}@tamu.edu

Abstract. As the number of design candidates in generative systems is often high, there is a need for an articulation mechanism that assists designers in exploring the generated design set. This research aims to condense the solution set yet enhance heterogeneity in generative design systems. Specifically, this work accomplishes the following: (1) introduces a new design articulation approach, a Shape Clustering using K-Medoids (SC-KM) method that is capable of grouping a dataset of shapes with similitude in one cluster and retrieving a representative for each cluster, and (2) incorporate the developed clustering method in architectural form finding. The articulated (condensed) set of shapes can be presented to designers to assist in their decision making. The research methods include formulating an algorithmic set with the implementation of K-Medoids and other algorithms. The results, visualized and discussed in the paper, show accurate clustering in comparison with the expected reference clustering sets.

Keywords: Generative design systems · Clustering · Form finding · K-Medoids

1 Introduction

Generative design systems are now routinely used in the architectural design process with the integration of computational tools, such as parametric modeling [1] and numerical simulations [2], into the design process [3]. In parametric design, designers can generate a large set of design alternatives based on explicit rules and parameters, allowing for evaluation of those design alternatives in terms of design quality [4]. A significant drawback in generative protocols is that they may generate an excessive number of solutions for a designer to manage [5], and thus can be overwhelming in terms of decision-making and interaction with the systems. An example of a large set of solutions is the Pareto front illustrated in (Fig. 1) that shows hundreds of data points as Pareto optimal solutions which satisfy three objectives: cost, weight, and performance [6]. Pareto optimality is a sample model of methods that are often integrated into generative systems, a search mechanism to find a family of promising non-dominated solutions known as the Pareto front that simultaneously satisfy multiple predefined objectives [7].

Collectively, there is a need to organize the design solutions resulting from generative systems to be presented to designers so they can examine the generated

© Springer Nature Singapore Pte Ltd. 2019
J.-H. Lee (Ed.): CAAD Futures 2019, CCIS 1028, pp. 459–473, 2019.
https://doi.org/10.1007/978-981-13-8410-3_32

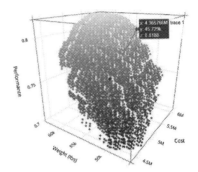

Fig. 1. The test-data solution set of Pareto optimization with three objective functions; each point is an optimal solution (image courtesy of Kalvelagen [6]).

solutions in a feasible way, as an organized set. A related problem is that design alternatives that emerge in the generation process can be similar and redundant, with extended computation time. This redundancy distracts designers from examining the diverse design candidates. For managing the excessiveness and redundancy problems, the solution set should be condensed to a highly diverse set, and similar designs need to be eliminated [8, 9]. Clustering is one of the reliable methods for managing a collection of data, it is a process of partitioning or separating a set of data objects into multiple subsets or clusters in a way that objects within a cluster have high similarity, yet are very dissimilar to objects in other subsets [10]. However, the integration of clustering methods into generative design systems remains limited.

In response to the identified problems, this research is targeted to improve generative design systems in terms of organizing the generated design forms/shapes, since forms/shapes are one of the essential considerations of architects and designers. Therefore, corresponding methods that tackle handling the emerged designs are needed. Clustering algorithms that have been applied in other disciplines can be implemented to achieve this goal. Thus, in this study, development of an algorithmic set that is capable of clustering design shapes in groups of similar characteristics and finding the representative design shape for each group, based on their geometric differences, has been pursued.

This work is directed to (1) achieve a successful articulation of design shapes in terms of geometric correspondences through developing a new shape clustering method, and (2) build a system that incorporates the developed clustering method in the form finding process. The condensed yet diverse set of shapes can be presented to designers to assist in their evaluation of designs and in decision making in generative systems. In this paper, we introduce a new robust Shape Clustering using K-Medoids (SC-KM) method that is applicable to a wide range of design problems and shape-related studies. To explain the developed clustering method, there is a need to introduce key concepts and algorithms, detailed in Sect. 2. In Sect. 3, the methods used in this study are described, and the results of the experiment are visualized and discussed in Sect. 4. Finally, conclusions are drawn and future work is summarized in Sect. 5.

2 Background

Research on articulating design solutions produced in computational generative schemes in architecture has been only recently addressed [5, 8]. In organizing big data, two methods are typically pursued: classification and clustering [5]. Clustering is an important research area in handling big data; it refers to the process of creating groups of objects that are similar in some way [11]. Clustering is labeled as an unsupervised learning method, as it deals with finding a structure or organizing a collection of unlabeled data [11, 12]. Unlike classification, which deals with predefined classes, clustering does not tackle classified data, which makes it advantageous in finding interesting hidden patterns with no predefined knowledge [11].

There is limited use of clustering methods in generative design systems in architectural design. One of the few related studies is the work of Rodrigues et al. that compares multiple descriptors of 2D shapes and utilizes the Ward linkage clustering method for architectural floor plans [5, 13]. Ward's linkage is a hierarchal clustering technique that starts with considering all available data points as clusters and proceeds with merging two clusters that satisfy an objective function, such as a variance criterion, reducing the overall within-cluster variance [5]. The method was used to cluster a synthetic dataset of 72-floor plans, applying and comparing four shape representations: (1) point distance, (2) turning function, (3) grid-based model, and (4) tangent distance [5]. Analyzing the results, Rodrigues et al. assert that the best clustering performance is achieved by the non-fixed aspect ratio scenario of the grid-based shape representation, and points out the need to further study of clustering algorithms in computational design [5]. Also relevant to this work is the study of Brown and Mueller [8] on exploring and reviewing different diversity metrics used in generative design protocols. Seeking design diversity amongst the possible design alternatives is important to avoid obtaining, or simulating repeated and similar candidates, and to enhance generative mechanisms guaranteeing that the resulting designs are diverse enough to be interesting to designers [8].

Shape representation and shape comparison are significant for performing clustering. Shape representation is concerned with finding effective and perceptually important shape features based on either shape boundary or/and interior features [14]. An area related to shape comparison is pattern recognition; the work of Cha and Gero has laid foundations for a shape pattern recognition system based on structural shape representation [15]. de las Heras, et al. have used an approach to retrieve designs with similar properties from a data set [16], and Dutta et al. applied a graph-based method to recognize symbols in floor plans such as furniture and fenestration [17]. Another approach to identify shape difference is CAD-based geometric comparison. A survey of some commercial tools used for geometric comparison was carried out by Brière-Côté, Rivest, and Maranzana [18]. As part of the preparatory studies for this work, testing the industrial tool "Kubotek3D Compare", one of the available modeling software, was conducted. This software accepts CAD-based models, performs a pair-comparison of 3D CAD models to find discrepancies between the two models, and it highlights the discrepant elements. The tool is often used for mechanical products, however, when tested with two Revit models of a single-family house design, the tool successfully found the different elements. One of its drawbacks is that it does not provide a shape difference score between the compared models, which is needed for our clustering method.

Given this initial literature background, the lack of articulation methods in form finding remains an unsolved problem. Therefore, this study was targeted to introduce a new SC-KM method that improves form finding and can be integrated into generative design systems and used for other applications. To achieve the research objectives, the system's tasks/processes were determined to be the following: (1) a parametric modeling functionality, to allow for parametric modifications leading to a rapid generation of multiple design shapes, and (2) a clustering process in which the generated designs are clustered according to their content-based geometric differences. The complete process of the SC-KM consists of sub-tasks to (1) describe shapes and find and compute the geometric dissimilitude, and (2) perform clustering. For shape description, a grid-based descriptor was followed, and to find geometric differences, a cross-reference shape analysis amongst all the compared solutions was conducted. This shape comparison method consists of a set of algorithms, incorporating the Hungarian algorithm in shape comparison. The K-Medoids algorithm, a distance-based cluster analysis, was implemented to cluster the shapes into groups of similarities and find the representative of each group. To describe the clustering method developed in this work, there is a need to introduce some relevant concepts and technical areas of generative systems, the Hungarian algorithm, and the K-Medoids clustering algorithm, described in the following sub-sections.

2.1 Parametric Generative Systems

Parametric design is a model of generative systems; it represents design process as a constrained collection of design schemes in which two interaction levels are needed: the definition of the parameters and constraints of the scheme, and the search within the system for meaningful schemes [4]. Generative systems support the exploration of multiple design alternatives and parametric-based analysis, with automatic updates of the design scheme when the parameters change. The change in parameters can be done through running a generative tool or simply through manual manipulation to allow for the parameters to change and to capture and evaluate the resulting design options at every iteration of change. The importance of this study is to improve the capabilities of generative systems in articulating the large set of design solutions in terms of geometric shapes and to support successful evaluation of those designs.

2.2 The Hungarian Algorithm

Developed by Kuhn and later revised by Munkers, the Hungarian algorithm is a combinatorial optimization algorithm, often used to solve assignment problems, applicable to many fields [19]. It can be explained using the following example: when given a matrix of workers and the cost of each worker to perform a certain job, the Hungarian algorithm can find the best possible assignment of workers to jobs so that the total cost is minimized [19]. In this paper, the Hungarian algorithm is used to match the geometric components (cells in grid-based shapes) between each pair of shapes, in

order to find the smallest overall Euclidean cell distance between the pair, for calculating the shape difference score of the compared pair.

2.3 K-Medoids Clustering

There are certain clustering algorithms developed and investigated in research, of
which K-Means and K-Medoids are considered significant [11]. K-Means is a simple
distance-based clustering algorithm that can solve well-known clustering problems
through partitioning the data set into a number of clusters (k) [11]. K-Means clustering
proceeds by calculating k initial cluster centers (means) and iteratively refining them as
follows: (1) each datum is assigned to its closest cluster, (2) each cluster center is
updated to be the mean of its constituent data, and (3) the algorithm then converges
when there is no further update in assignment of data to clusters [20].

In K-Medoids clustering, the algorithm considers a Medoid, which is the most
centrally located object (datum) in the cluster, as an alternative to the mean in K-
Means. Since the means can be easily impacted by extreme values, the K-Means
algorithm becomes sensitive to outliers and can significantly distort the partitioning
[11]. K-Medoids clustering is more robust to outliers [21]. It is based on a partitioning
method that minimizes the sum of dissimilarities between each object and its corresponding reference or Medoid [11]. Importantly, the K-Medoids algorithm is faster and
saves computation time when compared to the K-Means, for cases of normal and
uniform distributions [11]. As such, the rationale for using K-Medoids in this research
can be explained as follows: (1) the K-Medoids algorithm uses data points' dissimilarities for clustering and it minimizes the sum of general pairwise dissimilarities; the
possible choice of the dissimilarity function is very rich, however, in our application we
used the Euclidean distances, (2) the Medoids are representatives for clusters, and thus
in our work they are actual design solutions, and (3) the K-Medoids algorithm doesn't
need data points (or a quantified shape definition, which is difficult to define), rather,
their shape differences. Finding a shape difference score is targeted in this work.

The SC-KM method presented in this paper is built upon the authors' previous
experiments on shape clustering using the K-Means algorithm [22, 23]. This paper
showcases a new and complete framework of the algorithmic set that performs shape
clustering with the novel inclusion and implementation of the Hungarian algorithm, the
K-Medoids and other related algorithms, applied to a set of shapes generated from a
generative system. The work includes the fully working prototype of the proposed
generative system with the developed clustering method integrated, and with testing
and validation procedures, as described in detail in the following sections.

3   Methods

The research methods used in this study can be identified as multi-methods, comprised
of literature study, experimenting, prototyping, testing, and validation of findings.
A prototype was developed as an integrated framework of a generative system that
includes articulation of design candidates' shapes through clustering. Figure 2 illustrates the overview of the prototype, and the multiple processes and tools developed

and implemented within the framework. The prototype includes three primary tasks (processes). First, in the parametric form definition, a mass model of a selected test-case is initiated parametrically to allow for a possibly heterogeneous set of design options to be generated, leading to synthesize a dataset of shapes. Another task, form generation, can be either performed using methods for building environmental evaluation and optimization of the generated design or simply using a manual change in parameters, generating a set of design alternatives. The emphasis in this prototype was on the clustering method; therefore, optimization was not pursued. Third, in clustering, a shape clustering algorithmic set has been formulated, with the implementation of other algorithms such as the Hungarian algorithm, and the K-Medoids.

To communicate the system prototype, the selected platform had to be compatible with the determined tasks of parametric modeling and clustering algorithms and has to accept external input, store and display data, in addition to its capability of representing architectural geometric models. Therefore, the modeling and visual programming environment (Rhino/Grasshopper) was selected as the interface platform; however, other platforms, such as Revit/Dynamo, can be used alternatively. Importantly, the programming tool (GH_CPython) that allows for incorporation of numerical and scientific Python libraries to develop and perform the clustering and related algorithms was used for the SC-KM. The developed system is a framework of algorithms and nodes inside the Grasshopper platform that can be adapted to other test-cases and design problems. To apply the prototype, demonstrate its framework, explore its functionalities, and to test and evaluate those functionalities, a test-case was developed, described in detail in the following subsections.

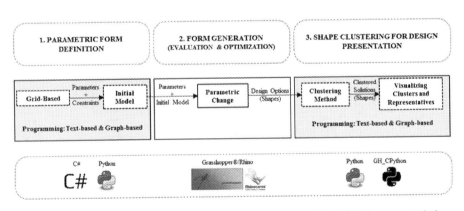

Fig. 2. Workflow and tools of the developed overall prototype in which the presented shape clustering is a major component.

3.1 Synthetic Set of Shapes

The set of shapes in this experimental test-case was synthesized using a generative algorithmic layout, a grid-based setup. This algorithmic layout was formulated combining the use of available nodes in Grasshopper for parametric modeling and specifically written algorithms using C# and Python programs to define the layout parameters and constraints. The layout was initiated on a grid, with a cell allocated in the center of the grid, and nine more cells added accumulatively. Adding each cell, the model was constrained based on three main constraints: adjacency, non-overlap (no-collision), and boundary-detection [22]. A sample of the resulting shapes of this layout is represented in (Fig. 3). The reason for using this grid-based layout was due to its capability to allow for a diverse/similar set of shapes and its appropriateness to test the clustering algorithm as will be explained next. The grid-based pattern can also approximate more complex forms characterized by curvatures or angles, using a high-resolution grid. In addition, the application of the clustering algorithmic definition to this grid-based descriptor will be feasible as the clustering will consider shape difference based on the center points of the grid cells.

3.2   Developing the Shape Clustering Method

For formulating the clustering algorithms, applying and testing the clustering method, a sample of shapes was needed. In this case, the grid-based layout was changed manually and purposefully to generate three perceptually identified clusters. This was done to produce twenty shapes comprised of three groups; each group contains shapes with only one cell-location changed within the group, as illustrated in (Fig. 3). In this set, one group of seven vertically linear shapes, another of seven horizontally linear shapes, and the third group of six zig-zag (meandering) shapes were created. The shapes were intentionally shuffled and randomized for verification purposes.

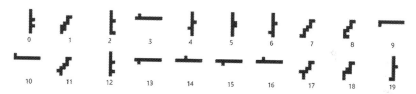

Fig. 3. A sample of shapes used to apply and test the clustering method.

The clustering method was developed using two main algorithms: the pair-wise shape difference with the Hungarian algorithm, and the K-Medoids algorithm, as explained in the following sub-sections.

The Pair-wise Shape Difference and the Hungarian Algorithm

In formulating this algorithm, the objective was to compare all the sample shapes in an agglomerative pair-wise method, pair by pair. In each pair comparison, the pair is overlapped, moving, for example, each cell of shape 0 over all the ten cells of shape 1, leading to hundred cases of overlap, of which 4 cases are shown in (Fig. 4). In shape comparison analysis, there is often a need to align the compared shapes, using transformation operations such as scale, translation, rotation, or mirror to best find their similarities and differences [24]. We utilized the alignment approach for overlapping the shapes to compare them, and ignored the need for transformations such as scale, rotation, and mirror in this experiment.

In each overlap case, the non-overlapping cells between the two shapes are subjected to a Euclidean distance measure, considering their center-points. The reason for the 100 cases of translation (overlap) is to check all possible shape overlap cases and to find the smallest sum of Euclidean distances between cells in the pair. This exhaustive search for best overlap leads to a problem of assignment. The optimum assignment is to determine what non-overlapping cells of shape 0 that would be best assigned to the non-overlapping cells of shape 1 for a minimum sum of distances, for which we will utilize the Hungarian algorithm to resolve.

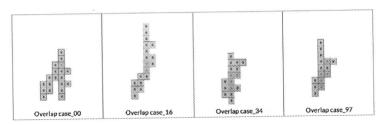

| Overlap case_00 | Overlap case_16 | Overlap case_34 | Overlap case_97 |

Fig. 4. Four selected of the hundred overlap cases of the compared pair (shape 0 in grey, shape 1 in blue, and the overlapping cells are in red). (Color figure online)

The shape comparison algorithmic node is represented in (Fig. 5) and is composed primarily of two functions: (1) a shape difference calculation for a pair of shapes, and (2) get the shape difference score matrix.

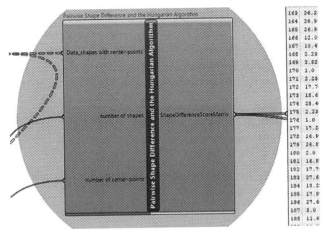

Fig. 5. The GH_CPython-based Grasshopper node of the pair-wise shape difference algorithm, with its input and output.

Function 1: Shape Difference Calculation for a Pair of Shapes
As an input to this function, the main important input variable is a data tree (a list of lists) that represents the list of shapes, each with its ten cells' center-points. In this function, a "Shape Difference Score" is defined as a pair-wise shape comparison result, which is, across all overlapping cases, the smallest sum of distances for the best matching non-overlapping cells. In every overlap case, to achieve the best matching of the non-overlapping cells, the Hungarian algorithm was implemented to compute the optimum assignment of matching cells between each pair of shapes so that the sum of Euclidian distances between the non-overlapping cells of the pair is minimized. As an example, in Overlap Case 97 in (Fig. 6), the optimum assignment of the non-overlapping cells (1–5) of shape 0, to the non-overlapping cells (a–e) of shape 1, which has been shaded in (Table 1), was needed.

Fig. 6. Overlap case 97 of the pair-wise comparison of two overlapping sample shapes (Shape 0 in grey and Shape 1 in blue), with five cells overlapping (in red). (Color figure online)

Table 1. Matrix for distance calculations for center-points' coordinates (a–e), and (1–5). Border-outlined boxes are for a random assignment and shaded boxes for the optimum assignment.

		a	b	c	d	e
		(5, 5)	(4, 4)	(2, 2)	(2, 1)	(2, 0)
1	(3, 6)	2.24	2.24	4.12	5.10	6.08
2	(3, 5)	2.00	1.41	3.16	4.12	5.10
3	(3, 4)	2.24	1.00	2.24	3.16	4.12
4	(3, 7)	2.83	3.16	5.10	6.08	7.07
5	(3, 8)	3.61	4.12	6.08	7.07	8.06

In Overlap case 97, depicted in (Fig. 6), an assignment makes a one-to-one match between the non-overlapping cells of shape 0 and shape 1. Thus, the number of all possible assignments is 5! (factorial of 5), from which we need to find the best assignment. For instance, to understand the need of the best assignment, we have the following two possible assignments: one is random, which results in the sum of Euclidean distances between the 5 pairs of cells (center points) to be 21.91, while the optimum assignment selected by the Hungarian algorithm is 19.13, the minimum sum of distances possible. (Note that the 19.13 may or may not be the overall minimum for all 100 overlapping cases.)

$$\text{sum of distances (random assignment)} = (a, 3) + (b, 2) + (c, 1) + (d, 4) + (e, 5)$$
$$= 21.91 \tag{1}$$

$$\text{sum of distances (optimum assignment)} = (a, 5) + (b, 4) + (c, 1) + (d, 2) + (e, 3)$$
$$= 19.13 \tag{2}$$

After finding the minimum sum of distances in each overlap case, 100 shape difference values are retrieved of which the minimum value is selected to represent the actual difference between the pair. The algorithm for calculating the "Shape Difference Score" of the two shapes can be expressed as follows:

```
Shape Difference Score = min ((min sum of distances of overlap case 1),
                              (min sum of distances of overlap case 2),
                              ......
                             )
```

As a result, across all the 100 overlap cases of the pair, the minimum sum of distances is 9.30 for Overlap cases: 34, 41, 52, and 95 (identical overlaps). It is important to note that a repetition of overlap was expected (but they could be eliminated to make the algorithm more efficient).

Function 2: Get the Shape Difference Score Matrix

For all the paired shapes, the algorithm constructs a "Shape Difference Score Matrix": a cross-reference matrix of values that represents the Shape Difference between each two compared shapes of the twenty sample shapes illustrated in (Table 2). In (Fig. 5), the "Shape Difference Score Matrix" (as a list of lists in Grasshopper) is illustrated as an output of the (pair-wise shape difference and the Hungarian algorithm) node.

Table 2. A triangle of the symmetric "Shape Difference Score Matrix" of Shapes 0–19 in the explained sample.

	0	1	2	3	4	5	6	7	8	9	10	11	12	13	14	15	16	17	18	19
0		9.30	2.00	27.14	2.00	1.00	2.24	10.71	8.89	27.91	27.91	11.12	1.00	27.14	25.55	26.37	26.37	11.54	9.48	2.83
1			10.67	20.38	7.89	9.06	8.71	2.24	1.00	20.72	21.38	2.00	9.89	19.94	18.38	19.16	19.38	2.24	1.41	9.71
2				28.39	2.83	3.00	2.24	11.54	9.89	29.17	29.16	12.08	1.00	28.39	26.87	27.62	27.62	12.72	11.48	2.00
3					27.10	26.51	27.74	20.52	21.21	2.24	1.00	19.88	27.74	2.00	2.00	2.24	1.00	19.16	18.97	28.40
4						2.24	1.00	8.89	7.06	27.88	27.87	9.30	2.24	27.10	25.55	26.32	26.32	9.89	9.30	2.00
5							2.83	10.47	8.65	27.28	27.28	10.89	2.00	26.51	24.91	25.73	25.73	11.30	8.48	3.61
6								9.30	7.89	28.51	28.51	9.89	2.00	27.74	26.21	26.96	26.96	10.67	10.12	1.00
7									2.00	19.80	21.33	1.00	11.12	19.16	18.52	18.52	19.52	2.00	3.61	9.89
8										21.33	22.21	2.24	9.30	20.56	19.21	19.80	20.21	2.83	2.24	8.89
9											2.00	19.16	28.51	1.00	3.61	2.00	2.83	18.52	19.35	29.15
10												20.56	28.51	1.00	2.24	3.00	2.83	19.80	19.97	29.16
11													11.54	18.38	17.88	17.75	18.88	1.00	3.16	10.71
12														27.74	26.20	26.96	26.96	12.08	10.48	2.24
13															2.83	1.00	2.24	17.75	18.61	28.40
14																2.24	1.00	17.29	16.97	26.87
15																	2.00	16.97	17.79	27.65
16																		18.29	17.97	27.65
17																			3.00	11.64
18																				11.12
19																				

Implementing the K-Medoids Algorithm

The next task was to implement the K-Medoids algorithm, with additional modifications, to apply it to the sample shapes, using their "Shape Difference Score Matrix". A typical K-Medoids algorithm performs the Partitioning Around Medoids (PAM) method [11] as follows:

- **Input:**
    ```
    K: The number of clusters
    D: The matrix of data containing n objects
    (shapes)
    ```
- **Method:**
    ```
    Random initiation of cluster medoids: first, the
    algorithm arbitrarily selects medoids in D as the
    initial representative objects. Next, the algorithm
    assigns each remaining object to the cluster with
    its nearest medoid.

    Repeat, update of cluster medoids:
    While the total cost (sum of distances of points to
    their medoid) of the assignment decreases:
        For each medoid m, for each non-medoid data
        point o:
            1. Swap m and o, assign each data point to
               the closest medoid, recompute the cost
            2. If the total cost increased, undo the swap
    ```

- **Output:** A set of k clusters that minimizes the total cost.

The specific K-Medoids implementation here is based on a NumPy/SciPy function. Our algorithm called the function inside the GH_CPython coding tool that enables the importation of NumPy/SciPy. The reason for selecting this implementation of K-Medoids is due to its validated method and robustness to applications, designed particularly to consider distance matrices and cluster them based on user-defined difference values [25].

According to the algorithm's author [25], the distance matrix-based K-medoids clustering method solely relies on distances between data points (or shapes), therefore, the distance matrix becomes the most important component of the algorithm. The "Shape Difference Score Matrix" was already retrieved from the shape difference algorithm described in the previous section. The input data of the K-Medoids becomes the following: the number of shapes, the "Shape Difference Score Matrix" (as a list of lists), the number of clusters, and the number of iterations of the K-Medoids as illustrated in (Fig. 7).

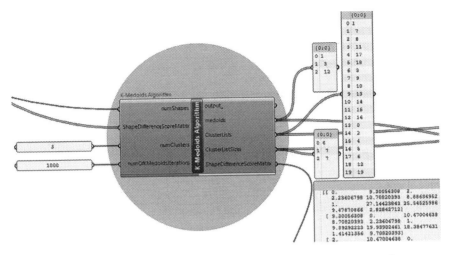

Fig. 7. The Grasshopper node of the K-Medoids algorithm with its input and output.

The outputs of the K-Medoids are primarily the list of clusters of shapes and the medoids. The outputs have been articulated as lists of clusters (each cluster with their shape IDs), the medoids' indices (IDs), and the cluster size (number of shapes in each cluster) as depicted in (Fig. 7).

4   Experimental Outcome and Discussion

Applying the described clustering algorithmic set to the above-illustrated sample of twenty shapes, the results showed correct clustering of shapes with the given numbers of clusters (3) and identified the medoid of each cluster (Fig. 8). Further, more scenarios were tested and the results were perceived accurate too (Fig. 9). To analyze the outcome of this clustering method, it is important to note that the sample cases used were intentionally created in advance to have three clusters each by manually typifying shapes from the grid-based layout to create three groups of perceptually similar shapes. Therefore, the samples were already clustered as reference clusters. For instance, in (Fig. 8), the selected sample of shapes includes a group of seven horizontally linear shapes (in cyan color) with only one cell changing in location, making the change of shape minimal. The method resulted in accurately identified clusters. Despite that in the bottom of (Fig. 9) the shapes become more complex to differentiate, the clusters were correctly identified by the clustering method.

For verification purposes, before clustering each test case, the shapes were shuffled randomly in location to make sure the algorithmic set worked regardless of the order of shapes in terms of locations. In addition to the presented samples, more tests were conducted, applying the algorithmic set to multiple scenarios, and the algorithm identified the clusters as expected.

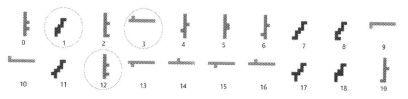

Fig. 8. Three groups of shapes are automatically clustered, represented in three colors, with the Medoids circled. (Color figure online)

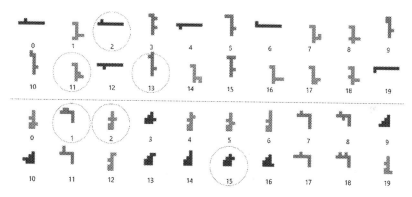

Fig. 9. Two additional test cases (top and bottom, respectively) with correct clustering results: the same colored shapes indicate that they are in the same cluster, with the Medoids circled in each group. (Color figure online)

As a measure to determine the accuracy of the clusterings, the results were compared to the reference clustering; the algorithmic set is expected to cluster the similarly typified shapes in one cluster, given the same number of clusters determined in the reference clustering such as 3 in the illustrated samples. Also, perceptual coherence was considered a measure for clustering accuracy; a cluster is considered coherent if it presents a dominant shape that appears at a high number of times in the cluster [5]. In the results of our method, a full number of the dominant shape was attained in each cluster with no outliers. For all the tested samples, the results showed a successful outcome of the clustering method to determine dominant shapes in a cluster, and correct clusters compared to the intended reference clusters.

5   Conclusions and Future Work

A method of Shape Clustering using K-Medoids (SC-KM) with a grid-based shape representation has been developed and tested in this study. The algorithm performs as expected, however, a complete evaluation and performance comparisons with other algorithms are being carried out. To apply the method to other shape analysis problems, one task is needed beforehand, which is to use a bin-packing algorithm to convert boundary-based shapes into grid-based ones. Also, the number of packed cells in each shape needs to be matched for all the analyzed shapes for the accuracy of shape comparison. The grid-based shape representation is highly dependent on resolution (the number of cells in the shape layout); thus, a bin-packing with a given number of cells will be the next algorithmic component added to this method. The integration of the bin-packing algorithm is ongoing, which will lead to producing a full package of algorithms to be used as a plugin of Rhino/Grasshopper for designers' applications. It is expected that the higher number of cells packed into the analyzed shapes, the better the results would be, but the more computation needed.

It is important to note that current or conventional use of parametric design may not necessarily give different design forms, rather, the same geometric form can be parameterized according to fenestration ratio or building materials' properties. However, we argue that we now have the capability to explore different geometry and shapes in parametric methods, so we will encounter more variable design shapes, in which the developed algorithm could be applied. Overall, this clustering mechanism has applications in generative design systems to organize the resulting data in a conceivable manner to support designers' exploration and evaluation. The articulation process can be done at any time in the generative run, to filter the shapes with high dissimulate in the process. For instance, in early iterations, this organization of shapes will help eliminate the shapes with similar geometric characteristics and select the representative shapes of these many similar ones. This way, the set becomes diverse and smaller in population for designers to examine, which leads to a reduction in computational burden for the following processes of performance simulation or optimization. Another use of the method is to help designers focus on their shapes of interest, the typological shape they want to further evolve. Future work also includes extending the application of the method to different test-cases with a wide range of shapes. In addition, the method will be compared and contrasted to the results of other shape clustering methods. Further investigation also includes applications on shape grammar research. Other applications include computer vision and machine learning.

References

1. Woodbury, R.: Elements of parametric design (2010)
2. Malkawi, A.M.: Performance simulation: research and tools. In: Performative Architecture: Beyond Instrumentality, pp. 85–96. Spon Press, New York (2005)
3. Wortmann, T., Nannicini, G.: Introduction to architectural design optimization. In: Karakitsiou, A., Migdalas, A., Rassia, S.T., Pardalos, P.M. (eds.) City Networks. SOIA, vol. 128, pp. 259–278. Springer, Cham (2017). https://doi.org/10.1007/978-3-319-65338-9_14
4. Aish, R., Woodbury, R.: Multi-level interaction in parametric design. In: Butz, A., Fisher, B., Krüger, A., Olivier, P. (eds.) SG 2005. LNCS, vol. 3638, pp. 151–162. Springer, Heidelberg (2005). https://doi.org/10.1007/11536482_13
5. Rodrigues, E., Sousa-Rodrigues, D., de Sampayo, M.T., Gaspar, A.R., Gomes, Á., Antunes, C.H.: Clustering of architectural floor plans: a comparison of shape representations. Autom. Constr. **80**, 48–65 (2017)
6. Kalvelagen, E.: Visualization of large multi-criteria result sets with plot.ly. http://amsterdamoptimization.com/viz/plota1.html

7. Radford, A.D., Gero, J.S.: Design by Optimization in Architecture, Building, and Construction. Wiley, Hoboken (1987)
8. Brown, N.C., Mueller, C.T.: Quantifying diversity in parametric design: a comparison of possible metrics. AI EDAM **33**, 1–14 (2018)
9. Yousif, S., Clayton, M., Yan, W.: Towards integrating aesthetic variables in architectural design optimization. Presented at the 106th ACSA Annual Meeting, the Ethical Imperative, the Association of Collegiate Schools of Architecture (ACSA) (2018)
10. Han, J., Pei, J., Kamber, M.: Data Mining: Concepts and Techniques. Elsevier, New York (2011)
11. Velmurugan, T., Santhanam, T.: Computational complexity between K-means and K-medoids clustering algorithms for normal and uniform distributions of data points. J. Comput. Sci. **6**, 363 (2010)
12. Jain, A.K., Murty, M.N., Flynn, P.J.: Data clustering: a review. ACM Comput. Surv. (CSUR) **31**, 264–323 (1999)
13. Ward Jr., J.H.: Hierarchical grouping to optimize an objective function. J. Am. Stat. Assoc. **58**, 236–244 (1963)
14. Zhang, D., Lu, G.: Review of shape representation and description techniques. Pattern Recogn. **37**, 1–19 (2004)
15. Cha, M.Y., Gero, J.S.: Shape pattern recognition using a computable pattern representation. In: Gero, J.S., Sudweeks, F. (eds.) Artificial Intelligence in Design 1998, pp. 169–187. Springer, Dordrecht (1998). https://doi.org/10.1007/978-94-011-5121-4_9
16. de las Heras, L.-P., Fernández, D., Fornés, A., Valveny, E., Sánchez, G., Lladós, J.: Runlength histogram image signature for perceptual retrieval of architectural floor plans. In: Lamiroy, B., Ogier, J.-M. (eds.) GREC 2013. LNCS, vol. 8746, pp. 135–146. Springer, Heidelberg (2014). https://doi.org/10.1007/978-3-662-44854-0_11
17. Dutta, A., Lladós, J., Bunke, H., Pal, U.: A product graph based method for dual subgraph matching applied to symbol spotting. In: Lamiroy, B., Ogier, J.-M. (eds.) GREC 2013. LNCS, vol. 8746, pp. 11–24. Springer, Heidelberg (2014). https://doi.org/10.1007/978-3-662-44854-0_2
18. Brière-Côté, A., Rivest, L., Maranzana, R.: Comparing 3D CAD models: uses, methods, tools and perspectives. Comput.-Aided Des. Appl. **9**, 771–794 (2012)
19. Mills-Tettey, G.A., Stentz, A., Dias, M.B.: The Dynamic Hungarian Algorithm for the Assignment Problem with Changing Costs. Robotics Institute, Pittsburgh (2007)
20. Wagstaff, K., Cardie, C., Rogers, S., Schrödl, S.: Constrained k-means clustering with background knowledge. Presented at the ICML (2001)
21. Jin, X., Han, J.: K-Medoids clustering. In: Sammut, C., Webb, G.I. (eds.) Encyclopedia of Machine Learning and Data Mining, pp. 1–3. Springer, Boston (2016). https://doi.org/10.1007/978-1-4899-7502-7
22. Yousif, S., Yan, W.: Clustering forms for enhancing architectural design optimization. Presented at the Learning, Adapting and Prototyping, the 23rd Conference of the Association for Computer-Aided Architectural Design Research in Asia (CAADRIA) (2018)
23. Yousif, S., Yan, W., Culp, C.: Incorporating form diversity into architectural design optimization. Presented at the ACADIA 2017: DISCIPLINES & DISRUPTION [Proceedings of the 37th Annual Conference of the Association for Computer Aided Design in Architecture (ACADIA) (2017)
24. Funkhouser, T., Kazhdan, M., Min, P., Shilane, P.: Shape-based retrieval and analysis of 3D models. Commun. ACM **48**, 58–64 (2005). https://doi.org/10.1145/1064830.1064859
25. Bauckhage, C.: Numpy/Scipy Recipes for Data Science: k-Medoids Clustering, February 2015. researchgate.net

Shape Rule Types and Spatial Search

Rudi Stouffs[(✉)]

National University of Singapore, Singapore, Singapore
stouffs@nus.edu.sg

Abstract. Searching for spatial objects in CAD tools is mostly based on the ability to compare properties of different objects. Instead, the matching mechanism(s) underlying a shape grammar interpreter offers a much wider potential for search, including the emergence of shapes that were unanticipated at the point of specification. This paper provides an overview of different rule types that can be discerned in the context of shape grammars, and explores the impact these have on the ability for search. It specifically considers two alternative matching algorithms, either determining a transformation matrix or an association of graphical elements, the latter complemented with constraining predicates, applying over different data types, e.g., shapes, shapes augmented with attributes, and descriptions, to provide for a wide range of spatial search variations.

Keywords: Spatial search · Shape rules · Description rules · Rule types

1 Introduction

A rule-based design generation scheme can be considered to consist of a set of generative rules that can be applied to a set of initial objects in order to generate a variety of solutions or design objects. The set of rules, together with the initial object(s) and the vocabulary of elements from which the rules are composed, is termed a grammar and the objects resulting from a generative application of such a grammar constitute the derived language. Specifically, a shape grammar is a formal rewriting system for producing languages of shapes [1].

However, the paradigm of design as search [2, 3]—within which rule-based design generation fits particularly well—is more fundamental to design than its generational form alone might imply. Any mutation of an object into another one, or parts thereof, whether as the result of a transformation or operation, constitutes an action of search. A rule can be deemed to constitute a particular compound operation or mutation, that is, a composition of a number of operations and/or transformations that is recognized as a new operation and can be applied as such. Similarly, a grammar may be viewed as just a collection of rules or operations that yields a certain set (or language) of design objects given an initial object (or set thereof). As such, the creation of a grammar is only a tool that allows a structuring of a set of operations that has proved its applicability to the creation of a certain set of objects, rather than a framework for generation.

A rewriting rule can generally be expressed in the form $lhs \rightarrow rhs$, with the left-hand-side (lhs) of the rule specifying the part to be recognized in the current design and the right-hand-side (rhs) of the rule specifying the part to replace the recognized part

J.-H. Lee (Ed.): CAAD Futures 2019, CCIS 1028, pp. 474–488, 2019.
https://doi.org/10.1007/978-981-13-8410-3_33

with. Thus a rewriting rule specifies two actions, an action of search or recognition specified by the left-hand-side and an action of mutation specified by the right-hand-side with respect to the left-hand-side. Recognizing the left-hand-side of the rule in the current design involves determining a transformation under which the left-hand-side becomes part of the design, that is, denoting the current design d and the transformation f, determining f such that $f(lhs) \leq d$. Once f is found, the mutation involves replacing the left-hand-side with the right-hand-side under the same transformation, that is, the resulting design is the result of $d - f(lhs) + f(rhs)$. An additive rule is a rule that only adds elements to the current design, that is, $lhs \leq rhs$. Similarly, a subtractive rule only removes elements from the current design, that is, $lhs \geq rhs$.

Transformations may be of different kinds [4]. A shape grammar commonly considers transformations of similarity, allowing for translation, rotation, reflection and uniform scaling. However, a more narrow or broad definition of transformations can be considered as well. For example, Stiny and Mitchell's Palladian grammar [5] can be considered to allow for only isometric (or Euclidean) transformations, including translation, rotation and reflection, but no scaling, as the rules potentially operate on a simple grid of rectangular shapes of equal size. In practice, as exemplified by the underlying grid for the Villa Malcontenta [5], the size of grid cell may vary implying the inclusion of non-uniform scaling or, instead, the specification of parametric shape rules. Theoretically, in a parametric shape rule, the left-hand-side and right-hand-side of the shape rule can have parameters specified and constraints over these parameters [6]. However, no implementation of a general parametric shape grammar interpreter exists that allows for the explication of parameters, unless for description rules. So-called parametric shape grammar interpreters instead allow for the recognition of associations between spatial elements that serve to constrain rule matching. For this reason, we prefer the term *associative* (or parametric-associative) shape rules. Applied to shapes of line segments, associations that are recognized may include intersecting lines, parallel or perpendicular lines, or segments of equal length. Depending on the associations recognized, a rectangle may be a set of four line segments, either with twice two parallel segments that are perpendicular with respect to one another, or with twice two segments of equal length and with diagonals of equal length as well.

It is obvious that the types of allowable rules greatly impact the expressiveness and applicability of a grammar system. In this paper, we present an overview of different types of rules (not entirely exhaustive) that can be discerned in the context of shape grammars. Subsequently, we narrow our focus to the left-hand-side of the shape rule and the related action of search or shape recognition, in the context of different types of rules. That is, we focus our attention on search not as a paradigm of design but as a technique of recognizing shapes within a design. Specifically, we explore to what extent the shape recognition mechanism underlying a shape grammar interpreter can support graphical search within a Computer Aided Design (CAD) environment. Currently, searching and finding spatial elements and objects in CAD software tools, if available, is mostly based on the ability to compare properties of different objects, for example, object type, area, etc. The shape recognition or matching mechanism(s) underlying a shape grammar interpreter offers a much wider potential for search, including the emergence of shapes that were unanticipated at the point of specification.

2   Types of Rules

We base our exploration on an overview of different types of rules, as these support different approaches to search. Shape grammar rules can be distinguished, among others, by data type, e.g., shape and description rules, by the relationship between the rule's left-hand-side and right-hand-side, e.g., addition and subtraction rules, and by matching algorithm, parametric-associative and non-parametric rules. In the context of search, where the emphasis lies on the left-hand-side of the shape rule, the first and last categorization are the most interesting, as the right-hand-side of the rule doesn't affect the search process. We limit our exploration to these two categorizations.

2.1   By Data Type

Most examples of shape grammars rely on labeled shapes, a combination of line segments and labeled points (in two dimensions) [1]. Krishnamurti [7, 8] extends the underlying maximal element representation to plane segments and Stouffs [9, 10] to volume segments and higher-dimensional hyperplane segments. Jowers [11, 12] considers the application of shape grammars to curves, such as quadratic Bezier curves.

Next to labels, other non-geometric attributes have been considered for shapes. Stiny [13] proposes numeric weights as attributes to denote line thicknesses or surface tones. Knight [14, 15] considers an extension to the shape grammar formalism that allows for a variety of qualitative aspects of design, such as color, to be integrated in the rules of a shape grammar. Though not specific to colors, the resulting grammar is called a *color grammar* and notions of transparency, opacity and ranking are introduced to regulate the behavior of interacting quality-defined areas or volumes. Stiny [16] also proposes to augment a shape grammar with a description function in order to enable the construction of verbal descriptions of designs. Although most authors do not consider descriptions as attributes to shapes, Beirão [17] specifically considers descriptions as attributes to spatial objects. Other kinds of attributes, or even variations in the specification of a kind of attribute, can also be considered. For example, colors can be specified in different ways, as a three-dimensional RGB or HSV (Hue, Saturation, Value) space, or in an enumerative way as Knight [14, 15] considers.

Sortal grammars [18, 19] are a class of shape grammar formalisms that enable a single *sortal* grammar interpreter to support all of the above shape grammars, and any variations thereof. Adopting an algebraic abstraction enabling the algebraic derivation of combinations of basic shape algebras with attribute algebras, this abstraction at the same time serves as a procedural abstraction, giving insights into the modular implementation of a general shape grammar interpreter for different grammar forms [20]. Representationally, *sortal* grammars utilize *sortal* structures as representational structures, where these structures are defined as formal compositions of other, primitive, *sortal* structures, termed *sorts* [21]. *Sortal* grammars benefit from the fact that every component *sort* specifies a partial order relationship on its individuals and forms, defining both the matching operation and the arithmetic operations for rule application. The SortalGI *sortal* grammar interpreter [22], developed as a library and API in the Python programming language, implements this approach and supports most data types and their combinations identified above. Specifically, SortalGI operates on points, lines and planes, line segments and (rectilinear) plane segments, circles and ellipses, circular and elliptical arcs, quadratic Bezier curves, labels, weights, colors, enumerated values, dates, and descriptions, and any combination thereof, within both 2D and 3D.

2.2 By Matching Mechanism

As stated above, applying a rule *lhs* → *rhs* onto a design *d* requires determining a transformation *f* such that *f(lhs)* is a part of *d*, *f(lhs)* ≤ *d*. The mechanism that supports this shape recognition process is called the *matching mechanism*. It generally relies on the identification of distinguishing elements within the rule's left-hand-side and the design under investigation, and mapping distinguishing elements of the same kind between both shapes in order to determine the corresponding transformation. Distinguishing elements are commonly points that form part of the shape or points of intersection among infinite lines that carry line segments forming part of the shape [23, 24].

As noted above, transformations may be of different kinds [4] and the kind of transformation necessarily impacts the matching mechanism. In three dimensions, three distinguishable points from the rule's left-hand-side and three mapped counterparts from the design under investigation uniquely determine up to two possible similarity transformations (under reflection). Evaluating each possible transformation can take two steps: a first step focused on the selected distinguishable points and a second step involving the entire left-hand-side shape. The first step looks at invariants under similarity transformations, e.g., angles and length ratios, that can be compared between the two sets of distinguishable points. The second step applies the respective transformation to the entire left-hand-side in order to check its embedding in the design under investigation. Note that it is assumed that the embedding relationship for shape grammars supports emergence. For example, when matching for a square of line segments, any square of line segments from the given shape will do, even if these line segments extend beyond the corner points of the square. The same applies when matching for a rectangle, however, only rectangles with the same ratio between length and width will be matched.

If the allowable transformations are reduced from similarity to, e.g., isometric transformations, the number of invariants will increase, thus constraining the matching process and, potentially, reducing the number of possible matches [4]. However, in the case of isometric transformations, or whenever rotations are allowed, three distinguishable points remain necessary in three dimensions and, therefore, the same matching mechanism, with the additional constraints, may be adopted. Relaxing the allowable transformations is, in principle, also possible, although a so-called parametric matching process may become more appropriate. Woodbury [25] presents the mechanisms of a shape schema grammar, a grammar specifying parametric shape rules that operate on parametric shapes. The matching mechanism is one of constraint satisfaction. However, the algorithm is intractable, no shape grammar interpreter yet exists, and there is no indication as of yet of how designers would use shape schema grammars or rules.

All other (proposed) implementations of a parametric shape grammar rely on a graph-based representation to underlie the matching process [26–29]. Although the exact graph representation may differ from one implementation to another, commonly, intersection points between line segments, or between the infinite lines carrying these segments, are considered as distinguishable points. As such, graph-based implementations can be used to find polygons of a specified number of sides, while additional constraints can be specified on (the coordinates of) the vertices, in a similar way to the shape schema grammar. In that sense, graph-based implementations are much more general than Stiny's [6] parametric shape grammar implies. Where Stiny adds parameters to loosen the matching constraints, graph-based implementations can ignore geometric coordinates altogether and, instead, require constraints to be added where invariants should apply. However, rather than requiring such constraints to be explicated, graph-based implementations generally consider implicit constraints that can be automatically recognized from associations between spatial elements. For example, Grasl and Economou's *GRAPE* shape grammar interpreter considers equal length as an associative relationship among line segments [26]. As such, an equilateral triangle will only match onto equilateral triangles and an isosceles triangle onto isosceles triangles. Any other triangle will match any triangle, irrespective of its shape. The lengths of diagonals are also considered to apply under this associative relationship. Therefore, any regular polygon only matches onto a regular polygon with the same number of sides.

Instead, the SortalGI *sortal* grammar interpreter considers associative relationships of parallelism and perpendicularity among lines and planes, instead of length. As such, an equilateral or isosceles triangle of line segments will match any triangle of line segments, as there are no parallel or perpendicular lines involved. Only a right-angled triangle will limit any matches to right-angled triangles. Similarly, a rectangle of line segments will only match rectangles of line segments, although, a square of line segments will also match all rectangles of line segments, as equal lengths are not recognized. To allow for further fine-tuning of the matching process, SortalGI allows for additional constraints to be specified in the form of predicates [30, 31]. We elaborate on the roles of associative relationships and predicates below.

3   Shape Recognition and Search

In the sequel, we narrow our focus to the left-hand-side of the shape rule and the related action of search or shape recognition, while reflecting on the different rule types identified above. Specifically, we investigate to what extent the shape recognition mechanism underlying a shape grammar interpreter can support graphical search within a CAD environment. If available, searching for spatial objects in CAD software tools is mostly based on the ability to compare properties of different objects, for example, object type, area, etc. Instead, the shape recognition or matching mechanism(s) underlying a shape grammar interpreter offers a much wider potential for search, including the emergence of shapes that were unanticipated at the point of specification.

We adopt the SortalGI shape grammar interpreter [22] as the reference point for our exploration of spatial search. As a modular implementation of a generalized shape grammar interpreter for different grammar forms, it supports both parametric-associative and non-parametric shape grammars, including points, line and plane segments, circular and elliptical arcs, quadratic Bezier curves, labels, weights, colors, enumerated values, and (parametric) descriptions, in 2D and 3D. Emergence is naturally supported. As such, it supports both different types of rules by data type and by matching mechanism, at least to some extent.

The SortalGI shape grammar interpreter exists in the form of a library and API in the Python programming language, as well as a Rhino/Grasshopper plug-in. As such, the SortalGI library can be accessed and employed in at least three different ways: within a Python development environment, within the Rhino 3D modeling environment and within the Grasshopper algorithmic modelling environment. Note that the API and plug-in necessarily limit the extent of geometric and non-geometric element types that are supported, due to the need to graphically visualize the data within the Rhino 3D modeling environment. Nevertheless, we adopt the plug-in as a reference for this study for reasons of simplicity and reproducibility. The SortalGI Grasshopper plug-in encapsulates the SortalGI library and supports the specification and application of shape rules, both non-parametric and parametric-associative, including points, line segments, plane segments, circles, ellipses, (circular) arcs and quadratic Bezier curves, descriptions and attribute descriptions (or labels), and the generation of single or multiple rule application results. It also includes a node that, given a shape rule and a shape under investigation, returns a list of all possible matches, without rule application. As such, it can be used for spatial search, depending on the left-hand-side of the rule and irrespective of the right-hand-side of the rule.

3.1 Emergence

The SortalGI plug-in offers two different components to create a rule object. The Rule component constructs a non-parametric rule object from a rule name and brief explanation of the rule, a left-hand-side shape object and a right-hand-side shape object. While the right-hand-side of a rule may be left empty, the left-hand-side must have a minimum set of geometry and/or descriptions present. The pRule component takes the same inputs as the Rule component but returns a parametric-associative rule object.

The SortalGI library, underlying the plug-in, only supports transformations of similarity for non-parametric rules, allowing for translation, rotation, reflection and uniform scaling. As such, a rule's left-hand-side specifying a simple square composed of four line segments will match any square of four line segments, irrespective of size, orientation and position. In addition, any of these four line segments may be part of longer line segments that extend beyond the corner points of the square, or they may (originally) be drawn as multiple smaller pieces of line segments that extend one another or even overlap (Fig. 1). Internally, the matching mechanism will automatically reduce any line segments that overlap or extend one another into the corresponding maximal line segment and match maximal line segments, in the left-hand-side of the rule, onto (parts of) maximal line segments, in the shape under investigation. This mechanism specifically supports emergence, the square emerges from any number of line segments that together cover the four sides of the square and, possibly, more. The same applies to any other shape of line segments.

Fig. 1. A single line (left) may constitute one or more line segments that touch or overlap (right). The matching mechanism automatically reduces any such line segments to the single maximal line segment (left).

To constrain the matching process, the rule application node additionally accepts a subshape as input. While rule application always applies to the entire shape specified, the matching mechanism compares the left-hand-side of the rule only to the subshape, if specified, thereby ignoring any spatial elements that do not belong to the subshape.

3.2   Shape Descriptions

While the non-parametric matching mechanism only supports similarity transformations, it is not impossible to require only a subset of transformations, such as Euclidean transformations (omitting scaling). However, the process will not be as straightforward. In principle it is possible to use shape descriptions to constrain rule application. Shape descriptions are verbal descriptions accompanying a shape; these can be structured or unstructured [32, 33]. When included in the left-hand-side of the shape rule, they may include parameters that are matched onto part of the respective descriptions of the shape under investigation, as well as conditional expressions that constrain these matches. Such conditional expressions can include explicit references to shapes and shape rules. Such a reference must minimally specify the spatial data kind and its numeric property but, in the case of multiple elements of the same spatial data kind, must additionally specify a filter to distinguish the specific spatial element.

In the SortalGI plug-in, the spatial data kinds can be identified as 'point3D', 'lineSeg3D', 'planeSeg3D', 'circle3D', 'ellipse3D', 'arc3D', 'bezier3D', respectively, for points, line segments, plane segments, circles, ellipses, circular arcs and (quadratic) Bezier curves. Note that these names are specific to non-parametric rules and are slightly different within parametric-associative rules. Attribute labels as a data kind are identified as 'labelD' (or a variant thereof). As such, the length of a line segment with label "l1" can be retrieved using the partial description 'lineSeg3D.length:labelD.-value = "l1"'. The colon should be read as 'where', as in the length of a lineSeg3D where the value of labelD equals l_1. However, this will only work if at least one of the line segments of the square has been labelled uniquely with respect to the other line segments of the square. Unfortunately, any rule to do so would necessarily match the same square four times, as each of the four line segments may receive the label. Therefore, a better approach may be to add an extra spatial data kind to the rule, such as a plane segment covering the square, that can be used to constrain the allowable matches (Fig. 2). Given that the plane segment retains the full symmetry of the square, a rule that adds such plane segment to a square will only match each square once. The plug-in includes a component 'Apply All Together' that applies a rule in parallel according to every match found. As each square specifies a single plane segment, no additional label is necessary to uniquely identify the plane segment. Given a description specifying the exact area of the square to be matched, a description rule 'prescribed_area? = planeSeg3D.area → prescribed_area' will constrain the rule matching appropriately. Here, *prescribed_area* is a parameter matching whatever (numeric) value is specified in the description accompanying the shape under investigation, and will constrain rule matching to squares that have the exact area, thus omitting scaling as an allowable transformation. Note that the rule necessarily also specifies a right-hand-side. In this case, the rule leaves the description unchanged.

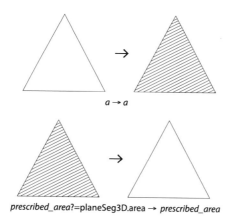

Fig. 2. A preparatory rule to add a plane segment to the triangle (top), and the search rule constraining matching to triangles with a given area (bottom). Each rule combines a shape rule and a description rule, although the description rule of the preparatory rule may be omitted.

In general, description rules with conditional expressions referencing shape rules can assist in constraining rule matching, but may require a preparatory rule that is performed first and matches a larger set of shapes, and adds additional information to the shape in the form of spatial elements or attribute labels, or both, before a second rule including an appropriate description rule can be applied to retrieve only the desired matches.

3.3 Parametric-Associative Rules: Searching Triangles

The parametric-associative matching mechanism supports a much wider set of transformations, although the matching transformation is not specified numerically, e.g., in the form of a transformation matrix. Instead, the transformation associates specific spatial elements in the given shape with respective spatial elements in the left-hand-side of the rule. For example, revisiting Stiny's [6] grammar for Chinese ice-ray lattice designs, one rule splits (almost) any triangle into a triangle and a quadrilateral by placing a single line segment between two of the original triangle's edges. As stated before, any triangle that does not include a right angle will match any other triangle, including right-angled triangles. At a minimum, searching for arbitrary triangles within a given shape only requires the specification of a non-right-angled triangle as the left-hand-side of a rule (ignoring the right-hand-side of the same rule). However, Stiny's grammar is not intended to apply to any triangle, but only to triangles of a certain minimum size that have not been the subject of a rule application—have not been split —before. Addressing the latter condition first, one solution is to label the edges of each polygon and include the labels as parametric descriptions using the same parameter in the left-hand-side of the rule. However, this procedure works fine within the context of a grammar application/derivation, but is rather useless as a search mechanism. Instead, SortalGI supports Liew's [30] *void* predicate, prescribing the area to be devoid of any spatial elements. The specific area is necessarily a polygonal area specified by its vertices, i.e., a list of position vectors. While these position vectors are defined in absolute coordinates in order to achieve a compact description, it is of utmost importance that the vertices coincide with points, line segments or intersection points between line segments, or between the infinite lines carrying these segments. Such associations will be automatically recognized by the matching algorithm and applied in the matching process, instead of the actual coordinates. As a necessary consequence, note that only the inside of the area must be devoid of spatial elements, the vertices themselves and the edges of the polygon may coincide with, overlap or partially bound a spatial element in the given shape.

To address the other condition, we can apply the plane segment trick previously described to compute the area of the triangle and constrain this area to be larger than a specified value. However, adding a plane segment will violate the void clause and open the possibility to match a larger triangle composed of smaller triangles. One solution to this problem is to assign each plane segment a unique label, such that the individual plane segments remain distinguishable, rather than possibly combining into a maximal plane segment. The parametric description assigned to the corresponding plane segment in the left-hand-side of the rule will match only a single label, limiting the matching to an individual plane segment. It should be noted that while this is a perfectly valid solution it is not a very efficient one. The matching mechanism will initially focus on matching the triangle, before checking the presence of the plane segment and its label. This means that all possible triangles will be exhaustively found and tested. While this is no different from the void rule (without the plane segment), the trick with the plane segment necessarily requires the void rule to be applied previously, adding the plane segment with a unique label within the right-hand-side of the rule. Improving efficiency could be achieved by labelling the edges of the triangle, in addition to or instead of the plane segment. The edge labels will already play a role in the matching of the triangle, before the plane segment is matched. Of course, this comes at the cost of even more additional information added to the shape. Another solution to the problem may be to use a variant of the void predicate as provided by SortalGI. The void predicate additionally allows one to specify a type of spatial element that should be absent from the area, while spatial elements of other types are ignored. In the case of searching for a triangle as defined by three line segments, specifying a void predicate to apply only to 'lineSegP3D' (the parametric-associative equivalent of 'lineSeg3D') spatial elements, would be able to complement the plane segment in the left-hand-side of the rule and the corresponding matching process. Note that this doesn't address the efficiency problem but it does avoid cluttering the shape with numerous labels (Fig. 3).

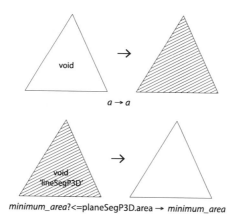

$a \rightarrow a$

$minimum\_area? <= planeSegP3D.area \rightarrow minimum\_area$

Fig. 3. A preparatory rule (top) and search rule (bottom) to identify an empty triangle with a specified minimum area. Each rule combines a shape rule and a description rule, although the description rule of the preparatory rule may be omitted.

So far, we have focused on searching for arbitrary triangles, but we might also be interested in more specific kinds of triangles. Searching for right-angled triangles is straightforward. If the left-hand-side of a rule constitutes a right-angled triangle than the rule will match only right-angled triangles. The matching mechanism automatically recognizes parallel and perpendicular associations between spatial elements (of the same kind). However, if the left-hand-side of a rule constitutes an equilateral triangle then the rule will still match an arbitrary triangle, as equal length associations are not automatically recognized. For this purpose, we can make use of a description that collects the lengths of the respective line segments and compares them. Unfortunately, this requires a preparatory rule to collect the lengths of the respective line segments, before the search rule can compare the different lengths.

SortalGI allows spatial elements within the left-hand-side of a parametric-associative rule to be tagged. Tags may be considered similar to labels, to some extent, but tags only exist within the matching process of the rule. The ability to tag a spatial element is mainly intended to support predicate specifications. As predicate specifications form a separate input, the tag serves to identify the spatial element the predicate is referencing. As such, tagging is only available in parametric-associative rules. However, tags as references can also be used in description rules that accompany parametric-associative shape rules. Thus, the description rule can identify different line segments by their tag, without these tags to be assigned as labels in another preparatory rule application. Instead, assigning tags as actual labels would not only require an additional preparatory rule but also have the labels persist unless another rule is used to remove the labels once again.

Assuming the line segments of the triangle are tagged as #l1, #l2 and #l3 (tags are recognized by the '#' symbol), the description rule to collect the lengths of the line segments may take the form 'a → (#l1.length, #l2.length, #l3.length)' where 'a' is a parameter that will be assigned any and all content of the description, to be subsequently ignored and replaced by a tuple of three length values. Next, the description rule to compare the lengths of the line segments can take the form '(l1, l2? = l1, l3? = l1) → nil'. Here, the tuple '(l1, l2, l3)' matches the tuple available in the description and the conditional expressions assigned to 'l2' and 'l3' ensure all lengths are the same. *Nil* is a keyword to indicate an empty value, however any other value might be assigned to the description as well.

As there may be any number of triangles in the shape under investigation, any number of descriptions may be created as a result of the parallel application of the preparatory rule. To link each description with the respective triangle, a labelled plane segment is created. However, rather than labelling the triangle and adding this label into the description, instead, we assign the description itself as attribute to the plane segment. The same applies to the description rule (at least the left-hand-side of the rule) comparing the lengths (Fig. 4).

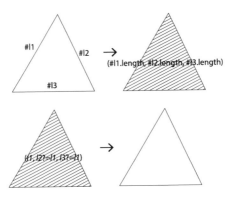

Fig. 4. A preparatory rule (top) and search rule (bottom) to identify an equilateral triangle. The preparatory rule adds a plane segment and adds the edge lengths as an attribute description to the plane segment. The search rule checks whether the edge lengths have equal values.

The search rule (Fig. 4 bottom) could be easily adapted to search for isosceles triangles by removing one of the conditional expressions. Instead of line lengths, it is also possible to identify equilateral and isosceles triangles by computing and comparing angles between respective line segments. The right-hand-side of a description rule may include an expression specifying an angle function that calculates the (counterclockwise) angle between two direction vectors (from the first to the second vector), e.g., 'a → (angle(#l1.direction, #l2.direction), angle(#l2.direction, #l3.direction), angle(#l3.direction, #l1.direction))'. However, it should be noted that the direction of a line segment is not always univocal. In principle, the direction vector reflects on the direction the line was drawn in, from one end to another. However, if the maximal line segment is the result of multiple overlapping or touching line segments, then the direction may be overwritten by the maximalization process, which specifies that the tail of the line segment has the lowest x-value, or if both x-values are equal then the lowest y-value, etc.

3.4   Parametric-Associative Rules: Searching Quadrilaterals

To further clarify the search and matching process, let us consider quadrilaterals instead of triangles. If the left-hand-side of a rule specifies a convex quadrilateral without any parallel or perpendicular line segments, then this rule will match any convex quadrilateral, irrespective of whether the matching quadrilateral has parallel or perpendicular segments. If, instead we want to search for concave quadrilaterals, we must specify a concave quadrilateral as the left-hand-side of the search rule. The matching process identifies all points of intersection among infinite lines that carry line segments forming part of the shape as well as their ordering along the infinite lines. In the case of a convex quadrilateral, all intersection points either define the vertices of the quadrilateral or lie outside of the quadrilateral (Fig. 5). In the case of a concave quadrilateral, the two intersection points each lie on a line segment in between its two vertices (not coinciding with any vertex).

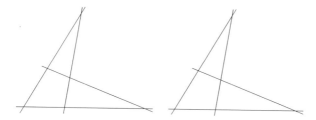

Fig. 5. A convex (left) and concave (right) quadrilateral. Each infinite (edge) line specifies (at most) three intersection points with the other infinite (edge) lines, two of which are vertices of the quadrilateral. In the case of the concave quadrilateral, the third intersection point lies between the two vertices for two of the edges. In the case of the convex quadrilateral, this never happens.

As indicated before, if the left-hand-side of the search rule specifies a rectangle, the rule will match any rectangle. However, the same applies as well for a square, that is, if the left-hand-side of the search rule specifies a square, the rule will still match any rectangle, because associations of equal lengths are not automatically recognized. Instead a description (and a preparatory rule) can be used to constrain matching rectangles to squares. The same applies to the relationship between a parallelogram and a rhombus. Where a rectangle is uniquely defined by its perpendicular corners (the parallel edges are an automatic consequence), a parallelogram is uniquely defined by its parallel edges. Thus, if the left-hand-side of the search rule specifies a parallelogram, the rule will match any parallelogram. Similar to a square with respect to a rectangle, a rhombus can be conceived as a parallelogram where all four sides have the same length. Thus, if the left-hand-side of the search rule specifies a rhombus, the rule will still match any parallelogram, because associations of equal lengths are not automatically recognized, and a description (and a preparatory rule) can be used instead to constrain matching parallelograms to rhombi. Note that an arbitrary convex quadrilateral with the additional constraint of equal length sides will also match rhombi only, however, the matching process will be less efficient as associations of parallelism and perpendicularity will be considered at an earlier stage, whereas constraints of equal length expressed through a description rule will necessarily need to be checked after the respective quadrilateral has been identified. Similarly, if the left-hand-side of the search

Table 1. Overview of the relationship between the left-hand-side of the search rule and matching shapes for various quadrilaterals. Restricting the matching to a smaller set of shapes necessarily requires the use of descriptions and a preparatory rule.

Left-hand-side of the search rule	Matching shapes	Left-hand-side of the search rule	Matching shapes
A convex quadrilateral without parallel or perpendicular edges	Any convex quadrilateral	A rectangle or square	Any rectangle or square
Any parallelogram or rhombus	Any parallelogram or rhombus	A non-right-angled trapezoid	Any trapezoid
A right-angled trapezoid	Any right-angled trapezoid	A concave quadrilateral without perpendicular edges	Any concave quadrilateral
A concave quadrilateral with a 90 degrees exterior angle	Any concave quadrilateral with a 90 degrees exterior angle	A concave quadrilateral with a 90 degrees interior angle	Any concave quadrilateral with a 90 degrees interior angle

rule specifies a non-right-angled trapezoid, the rule will match any trapezoid; a right-angled trapezoid will match only right-angled trapezoids. In order to search for isosceles trapezoids, an additional description rule will be required. The same applies if we would like to distinguish trapezoids with an obtuse angle from trapezoids with only acute angles. Any other quadrilateral figures that rely on equal lengths (such as a kite) or particular types of angles require a similar approach (Table 1).

4 Conclusion

The combination of two alternative matching algorithms, either determining a transformation matrix or an association of graphical elements, the latter complemented with constraining predicates, applying over different data types, e.g., shapes, shapes augmented with attributes and descriptions (the latter allowing for parametric description rules) provides for a wide range of spatial search variations, beyond what CAD software tools mostly offer today. Obviously, the elaboration above far from exhausts the possibilities of search based on the shape recognition or matching mechanism(s) underlying a shape grammar interpreter, in general, and SortalGI, in particular.

Acknowledgments. I would like to thank Bui Do Phuong Tung for his development work on the SortalGI library, Bianchi Dy for her development work on the SortalGI plug-in for Grasshopper, and Dan Hou for her inputs regarding predicates.

References

1. Stiny, G.: Introduction to shape and shape grammars. Environ. Plann. B: Plann. Des. **7**, 343–351 (1980)
2. Akin, Ö.: A formalism for problem restructuring and resolution in design. Environ. Plann. B: Plann. Des. **13**, 223–232 (1986)
3. Woodbury, R.F.: Searching for designs: paradigm and practice. Build. Environ. **26**, 61–73 (1991)
4. Wortmann, T., Stouffs, R.: Algorithmic complexity of shape grammar implementation. Artif. Intell. Eng. Des. Anal. Manuf. **32**, 138–146 (2018)
5. Stiny, G., Mitchell, W.J.: The Palladian grammar. Environ. Plann. B: Plann. Des. **5**, 5–18 (1978)
6. Stiny, G.: Ice-ray: a note on Chinese lattice designs. Environ. Plann. B: Plann. Des. **4**, 89–98 (1977)
7. Krishnamurti, R.: The maximal representation of a shape. Environ. Plann. B: Plann. Des. **19**, 267–288 (1992)
8. Krishnamurti, R.: The arithmetic of maximal planes. Environ. Plann. B: Plann. Des. **19**, 431–464 (1992)
9. Krishnamurti, R., Stouffs, R.: The boundary of a shape and its classification. J. Des. Res. **4**, 75–101 (2004)
10. Stouffs, R., Krishnamurti, R.: Algorithms for classifying and constructing the boundary of a shape. J. Des. Res. **5**, 54–95 (2006)
11. Jowers, I., Earl, C.: The construction of curved shapes. Environ. Plann. B: Plann. Des. **37**, 42–58 (2010)

12. Jowers, I., Earl, C.: Implementation of curved shape grammars. Environ. Plann. B: Plann. Des. **38**, 616–635 (2011)
13. Stiny, G.: Weights. Environ. Plann. B: Plann. Des. **19**, 413–430 (1992)
14. Knight, T.W.: Color grammars: designing with lines and colors. Environ. Plann. B: Plann. Des. **16**, 417–449 (1989)
15. Knight, T.W.: Color grammars: the representation of form and color in design. Leonardo **26**, 117–124 (1993)
16. Stiny, G.: A note on the description of designs. Environ. Plann. B: Plann. Des. **8**, 257–267 (1981)
17. Beirão, J.N.: CItyMaker: designing grammars for urban design. Ph.D. thesis, Delft University of Technology, Delft, The Netherlands (2012)
18. Stouffs, R., Krishnamurti, R.: Sortal grammars as a framework for exploring grammar formalisms. In: Burry, M., Datta, S., Dawson, A., Rollo, J. (eds.) Mathematics and Design 2001, pp. 261–269. Deakin University, Geelong (2001)
19. Stouffs, R.: On shape grammars, color grammars and sortal grammars. In: Achten, H., Pavlicek, J., Hulin, J., Matejovska, D. (eds.) Digital Physicality, vol. 1, pp. 479–487. eCAADe, Brussels (2012)
20. Stouffs, R.: Implementation issues of parallel shape grammars. Artif. Intell. Eng. Des. Anal. Manuf. **32**, 162–176 (2018)
21. Stouffs, R.: Constructing design representations using a sortal approach. Adv. Eng. Inform. **22**, 71–89 (2008)
22. Dy, B., Stouffs, R.: Combining geometries and descriptions: a shape grammar plug-in for Grasshopper. In: Kepczynska-Walczak, A., Bialkowski, S. (eds.) Computing for a Better Tomorrow, vol. 2, pp. 509–518. eCAADe, Brussels (2018)
23. Krishnamurti, R., Earl, C.F.: Shape recognition in three dimensions. Environ. Plann. B: Plann. Des. **19**, 585–603 (1992)
24. Krishnamurti, R., Stouffs, R.: Spatial grammars: motivation, comparison and new results. In: Flemming, U., Van Wyk, S. (eds.) CAAD Futures '93, pp. 57–74. North-Holland, Amsterdam (1993)
25. Woodbury, R.: An introduction to shape schema grammars. Environ. Plann. B: Plann. Des. **43**, 152–183 (2016)
26. Grasl, T., Economou, A.: From topologies to shapes: parametric shape grammars implemented by graphs. Environ. Plann. B: Plann. Des. **40**, 905–922 (2013)
27. Wortmann, T.: Representing shapes as graphs. Master's thesis, MIT, Cambridge (2013)
28. Yue, K., Krishnamurti, R.: Tractable shape grammars. Environ. Plann. B: Plann. Des. **40**, 576–594 (2013)
29. Strobbe, T., Pauwels, P., Verstraeten, R., De Meyer, R., Van Campenhout, J.: Toward a visual approach in the exploration of shape grammars. Artif. Intell. Eng. Des. Anal. Manuf. **29**, 503–521 (2015)
30. Liew, H.: SGML: a meta-language for shape grammar. Ph.D. thesis, MIT, Cambridge, MA (2004)
31. Stouffs, R., Hou, D.: The complexity of formulating design(ing) grammars. In: Fioravanti, A., et al. (eds.) Shock! Sharing of Computable Knowledge, vol. 2, pp. 443–452. eCAADe, Brussels (2017)
32. Stouffs, R.: Description grammars: a general notation. Environ. Plann. B: Urban Anal. City Sci. **45**, 106–123 (2018)
33. Stouffs, R.: Description grammars: precedents revisited. Environ. Plann. B: Urban Anal. City Sci. **45**, 124–144 (2018)

Towards Urban Densification

Using Shape Grammar to Develop Components for Retrofitting Street Design

Marcela Noronha Pinto de Oliveira e Sousa$^{(\boxtimes)}$ (ID)
and Gabriela Celani (ID)

The University of Campinas, Campinas 13083-970, Brazil
m024502@dac.unicamp.br, celani@unicamp.br

Abstract. Cities will have to become denser to accommodate expanding urban populations, creating a challenge for urban mobility. Existing urban infrastructure must be retrofitted to promote the use of collective and active modes of transportation. This article presents a prescriptive grammar, for retrofitting urban street design in the context of densification, based on patterns extracted from current guides and manuals. This prescriptive grammar is a crossover between concepts of shape grammar and pattern language, joining generative capabilities of geometric shape grammars with descriptive and prescriptive approaches commonly referred to as design patterns. An example is presented to illustrate its application.

Keywords: Shape grammar · Parametric urbanism · Travel behavior

1 Introduction

Urban design that prioritizes the use of private cars is a contributing factor for urban sprawl. The expected growth of urban population and the limitations imposed on urban growth by the need for land for food and energy production, as well as other environmental services, demonstrate that urban containment is a necessary strategy for the future of cities [1, 2]. Nonetheless, the concentration of origins and destinations produced by this approach is a challenge for urban mobility [3]. Thus, existing urban infrastructure must be adapted to expand the use of collective and active modes of transportation, i.e. walking and cycling, and allow for a greater number of displacements in the same amount of space.

This need to retrofit urban streets to promote walkability and transit use has been addressed by several guides and manuals over the past decade such as recent traffic engineering handbooks [4–6], geometric design policies [7, 8], guides and toolkits grounded on philosophies such as New Urbanism, Transport Oriented Design and Smart Growth [9–14]. The design rules conveyed by these guides are presented in the form of texts, sometimes accompanied by figures and tables, relating each mode of transportation to street dimensions and the advantages of each design approach. Many rules are recurrent across guides and, even though, most of them were developed in the United States, their rules are not context specific, and are recurrent across different

© Springer Nature Singapore Pte Ltd. 2019
J.-H. Lee (Ed.): CAAD Futures 2019, CCIS 1028, pp. 489–503, 2019.
https://doi.org/10.1007/978-981-13-8410-3_34

countries [11]. However, analyzing all these recommendations and combining them in a project is a highly complex task with numerous possible- and potentially conflicting-responses.

In order to improve the application of these rules in the design process this research proposes the use of Pattern Language [15] as a method to extract and combine recurrent design prescriptions for retrofitting urban streets, from the above mentioned guides and manuals. In his seminal book [15], Alexander presents patterns as prescriptions, with parameters and schematic drawings to aid their application. Alexander's method of hierarchically organizing recurrent design strategies to improve the quality of the built environment has been previously applied to structure design knowledge. These patterns, encoded in the form of shape grammar rules [16] can be applied to generate new design solutions, which belong to the language of designs described by the patterns [17–19].

A shape grammar [16] is essentially formed by initial shapes, rules written in the a - > b (If/Then) form, and labels to constrain and guide rule application. Rules are applied to the initial shapes, and each shape a is erased and substituted by shape b. The set of possible solutions that can be derived from initial shapes and rules form a language of designs. Transformations such as scaling, translation, rotation and mirroring can be used to match the left side of the rule to a given shape in order to enable the application of the rule. Rules can be applied if any part of a shape, including its labels, corresponds to a. Labels guide how rules can be applied and ensure that the shape grammar generates only valid designs.

The shape grammar formalism has been widely used to encode design knowledge related to specific styles or authors of urban design [20], houses [21], furniture [22] and objects [23]. A more recent use of the formalism is the development of generic shape grammars, which encode design knowledge related to certain design domains such as housing or urban design [19, 24]. A generic grammar should be able to derive a language of all designs belonging to its domain, through the selection of specific grammars contained within it. Thus, to develop a generic grammar for housing design, different styles and types of houses should be analyzed as a corpus to extract rules that are common to all houses. The rules will vary in their degree of specificity, and some rules are applied only to designs from a specific style. Within a generic grammar, infinite specific grammars can exist, including those for hybrid designs.

In cases like urban design or housing rehabilitation the concept of transformation grammar is relevant, because it proposes the use of shape grammar rules to adapt existing design products to a different, desired state. Eloy and Duarte [25] propose a transformation grammar to adapt existing housing stock of a specific type to the needs of modern dwellers. The authors observed the design strategies used by expert designers to adapt the existing plans to their briefs and encoded the moves into a transformation grammar that could potentially be used to rehabilitate any plan of that type.

This paper describes the development and structure of a prescriptive shape grammar based on patterns for retrofitting urban streets in the context of densification. A prescriptive grammar is understood here as a combination of different concepts from the shape grammar formalism, such as generic [19] and transformation grammars [25], combined with prescriptive patterns for urban street design, extracted from recent guides and manuals for urban street retrofitting. The proposed grammar is a generic set of rules for street retrofitting. For every different street description, a specific grammar is applicable, resulting in a single final design for that street. Nonetheless, the number of specific grammars that can be selected is potentially infinite, because they relate to the countless possible compositions of urban streets.

The patterns used to develop the shape grammar herein presented were chosen based on their recurrence in guides and manuals for urban street retrofitting, and because they focus on adapting street geometry to improve pedestrian safety and to promote active modes, of transportation in urban environments. The grammar is sequential and deterministic, i.e. for each street description a specific grammar is applied, resulting in one solution for that street. It comprises 14 sets of rules, derived from 10 patterns for urban street retrofitting. The following section describes the methods and research precedents used for developing the prescriptive grammar. A derivation of an area in downtown State College, PA, is used to exemplify the application of the shape grammar for urban street design.

2   Methods

Guides and manuals for urban street design were reviewed to find recurrent strategies for adapting street geometry to promote active modes of transportation. This resulted in 10 patterns which have the common goal of increasing how much space in the right-of-way is intended for pedestrian use, to increase safety and accessibility. The patterns were divided in categories named after the concepts commonly addressed in these guides [15]. Parameters and prescriptions from the guides were combined to develop a cohesive set of shape grammar rules. Geometric rules from several guides were compared to evaluate their common traits and differences. The differences between the prescriptions from different guides were translated as ranges for the parameters of the shape grammar rules. Once the generic rule was established for each separate pattern, rules for choosing each pattern, based on the existing street context, were defined in order to develop a lattice of relationships between patterns that could be later used to orient rule choice.

Initially, two categories were developed: (1) create more space for active and mass modes of transportation, and (2) physical measures for traffic calming. The first has the broader scope of reorganizing how space is assigned to the different functions of street design. The patterns under this category requalify space that is originally assigned for traffic, and that is being underutilized, to be used by active modes of transportation. The second category comprises street design measures to improve pedestrian safety at the scale of the sidewalk by physically inducing lower traffic speeds and increasing pedestrian visibility and accessibility. These patterns were then used to develop the street components for retrofitting (SCRtFit).

The prescriptive grammar is formed by two parallel grammars, named SCRtFit and Street Cross-Section; a description and an embedded pattern. SCRtFit is the transformation grammar, which is applied to the plan view of an existing geometry. It is a parametric shape grammar defined in the U_{22} algebra of shapes, meaning that two-dimensional shapes are manipulated on a plane. Rule application is constrained by labels in the algebra V_{22}, because labels have both length and direction, and are manipulated on a plane. To differentiate between street components, the grammar also uses a W_{22} algebra of weighted lines and shaded surfaces manipulated on a plane, which represent different street components. SCRtFit is applied to the top view, and runs in parallel with the Street Cross-Section grammar, which is defined in a U_{21} algebra, in which lines and planes are manipulated in one-dimension. This grammar was augmented by weighted lines manipulated in one-dimension, algebra W_{11}, to enable the representation of the concept of empty lanes which can be redistributed among other components or reassigned to a new component. The Street Cross-Section Grammar has a description of street profile components which must be matched to the description of an existing street, so that rules from SCRtFit can be applied. When a rule from SCRtFit is applied, it can alter the Street Cross-Section and the description of street profile components.

This Street Cross-Section Grammar and description of street profile components are built upon Beirão's [18] street profile components. His grammar for describing street cross-sections through their minimum components remained largely unchanged apart from the introduction of hybrid profile components and descriptions, and the empty lane component described above. For a rule from SCRtFit to be applied in a plan view, the existing shape must match the rule in top view, in cross-section and description (Fig. 1). After the rule from SCRtFit is applied, if the cross-section geometry and/or description is modified, it is updated.

The patterns have two roles within the shape grammar: initially they trigger rules from the prescriptive grammar, based on a street's Full Description, and they are also embedded into SCRtFit through labels, to guide further rule application. The Full Description for a street, which serves as a trigger for different patterns, and consequently for different sets of rules, comprises four items: a Travel Network designation; a Street Nomenclature designation; the width of the roadbed, measured from curb to curb, in meters; and a description of its components. The Full Description of existing streets uses the concepts defined by Beirão [18] for Travel Network, Street Nomenclature and street profile components (see Table 1). The Full Description is what triggers the application of rules. For each different Full Description, a specific grammar from SCRtFit is triggered.

Correspondence between concepts and components defined by Beirão [18] and those in the present work was sought in order to enable later integration of the tool with CIM-st [26], which could be used to generate the description for existing streets. Furthermore, the definitions of Street Nomenclature (SN), Travel Network (TN) and street profile components used by Beirão [18] proved to be both generic enough to be relatable to street classifications used across the guides employed in this research, and specific enough to easily convey the overall concept of each typology.

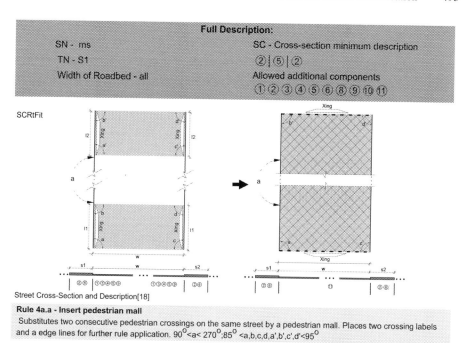

Street Cross-Section and Description[18]

Rule 4a.a - Insert pedestrian mall
Substitutes two consecutive pedestrian crossings on the same street by a pedestrian mall. Places two crossing labels and a edge lines for further rule application. $90°<a<270°;85°<a,b,c,d,a',b',c',d'<95°$

Fig. 1. Example of rule for Pattern 2 – Turn a main street into a pedestrian mall.

Table 1. Street nomenclature, travel network and street profile components [18].

Travel network	Street nomenclature	Street components
R1 - ring roads	st - street	① street parking
R2 - structural street	av- avenue	② sidewalks
S1 - distribution street	bv - boulevard	③ bicycle lanes
S2 - local distribution street	ms - main street	④ bus lanes
S3 - local access street	pr - promenade	⑤ car lanes
	gr - grove	⑥ green stripes
	la - lane	⑦ noise protection
	al - alley	⑧ tree alignments
	cs - cul-de-sac	⑨ tram lanes
	rr - ring roads	⑩ canal
		⑪ leisure walkway
		⑫ protection rails

To apply the prescriptive grammar, each street in an existing urban area, chosen for a derivation, must be assigned its Full Description as discussed above. The Initial shape for the Cross-Section grammar is then drawn using the street profile components [18]. For SCRtFit the initial shapes are GIS (Geographic Information System) shapefiles for street geometry (curb lines), street centerlines, parcels and buildings (which are used to measure the width of the right-of-way). Existing street names and street hierarchy, which is data commonly embedded in GIS street centerline shapefiles, is used to derive SN and TN. With the Full Description, Initial Cross-Section and existing geometry, the rules can be applied to arrive at a final design. The design reaches its final state when no more rules are triggered by its description and no more labels are left in the plan view. The final design comprises a final Full Description, a new Cross-Section and a new Shape, which is the plan view of the area (Fig. 2). The use of the two parallel grammars, one with the plan view and the other with a cross-section, was employed in order to allow for more detailed representations of streets. Furthermore, with a plan view and a cross-section of a street, a three-dimensional scenario can be generated as a future implementation of this research.

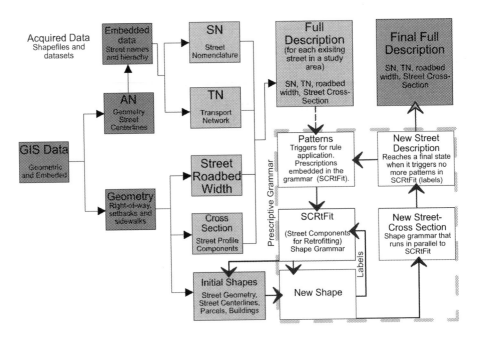

Fig. 2. Flow chart for the application of the prescriptive grammar using GIS data.

The prescriptive grammar was applied in a case study in State College, PA, in the United States. The Borough of State College provided current GIS data for this study. The files employed in the case study referred to the street centerlines [27], street polygons (curb to curb representation) [28], parcels [29], buildings [30] and zoning [31]. The street hierarchy and names of the streets contained in the GIS files [27] from State College were matched, respectively, to Travel Network and Street Nomenclature denominations using the explanations and minimum compositions provided by Beirão [18]. This correspondence between terms was done for the entire borough to have a bigger sample to test the correspondence.

3   Prescriptive Grammar for Urban Street Retrofitting

This section presents the 10 Patterns that were developed using the method discussed above. Due to space limitations only a reduced set of rules from the prescriptive grammar is demonstrated in this paper to illustrate the method. The grammar is applied sequentially, thus each rule has a number. Some patterns have several rules; thus, some rules have letters after the number to represent the sequence in which they must be applied (Fig. 3). The first category is: Create more space for active modes of transportation.

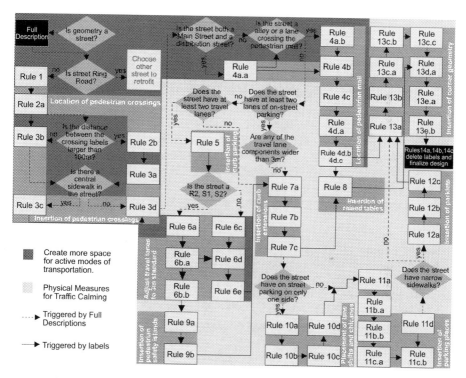

Fig. 3. Flow chart for the application of rules from the prescriptive grammar

1. Pattern 1 – All street crossings are pedestrian crossings

Wherever two streets cross, if there is a sidewalk on at least one side of the intersection, then a legal crosswalk exists, even if it is unmarked [7]. Nonetheless, marking it increases pedestrian safety [11]. Rules locate two crosswalk labels marking its size and direction everywhere the axes of two streets cross.

2. Pattern 2 – Turn a main street into a pedestrian mall

The choice to close a street for pedestrian use should be based on whether pedestrians routinely overflow onto the roadbed; if the street is located in a high-density and mixed-use area, and if it is well connected to the transit system [11, 13]. In terms of design, pedestrian streets still need to have a clear path for vehicles to provide access for individuals with reduced mobility and for controlled loading access. The pedestrian mall should be clearly distinguishable from the roadbed in contiguous streets. Considering these prescriptions for choosing streets to close for pedestrian use, one should choose those that have intense commercial use and pedestrian activity, but that will not impact negatively on urban accessibility. Thus, main streets that do not function as structural streets would be an appropriate choice. The pedestrian mall can be expanded into a pedestrian zone by closing lanes and alleys which cross it to minimize traffic intersections with the pedestrian route (Fig. 1) [11].

3. Pattern 3 – Retrofit lane width in urban settings to a 3 m Standard

Urban streets with roadbeds wider than 18 m are not conducive to active transport and encourage drivers to speed [7]. For a target speed between 40 km/h and 70 km/h, 3 m wide lanes are recommended for urban mixed-traffic lanes [7, 11, 13], and should be used as a default lane width in urban contexts [5]. After narrowing traffic lanes, leftover space can be utilized for other uses. In streets with more than three travel lanes, inserting medians can be a good option. In one and two-lane streets, if the extra space is wider than 7 m, it can be allocated to on-street parking. Between 1,5 m and 2 m bicycle lanes are an option [13]. Travel lanes on local streets can be retrofitted to 4,3 m for a two way street [32], because a yield behavior from drivers forces lower speeds, making streets safer. Left over space should be allocated to on-street parking or, if width is insufficient, to increasing the size of the sidewalks (Fig. 4).

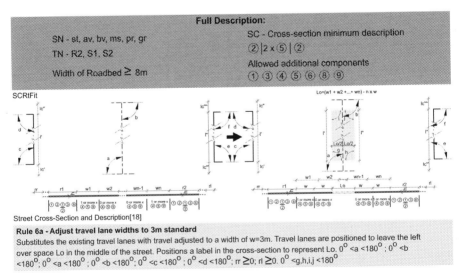

Fig. 4. Example of rule for Pattern 3 – Adjust travel lanes to a 3 m standard.

The second category is: Physical Measures for Traffic Calming. For Duany, Speck and Lydon [9], to control vehicular speed the designer should focus on changing the geometry of streets rather than just on signage. Traffic calming involves a set of design moves which generally aim at creating obstacles to speeding cars, which force them to slow down and pay closer attention to the street environment, thus making it safer for pedestrians and cyclists In commercial streets traffic calming is used to enable multiple modals to safely coexist [4, 5, 9–12].

4. Pattern 4 – Place midblock crossings wherever the distance between intersection crossings is greater than 120 m

In urban contexts, on streets with consistent pedestrian and car traffic, the distance between two consecutive pedestrian crossings should be no greater than 120 m [7]. This is important to discourage pedestrians from crossing streets in unmarked places [11]. Midblock crossings should always be marked and signalized, preferably using traffic calming measures such as curb extensions and raised tables to increase visibility [11]. Rules for this pattern insert labels for midblock crosswalks when the distance between consecutive crosswalk labels is larger than 120 m.

5. Pattern 5 – Use on-street parking as a safety barrier for pedestrians

On-street parking lanes serve several purposes such as: acting as buffer zones between traffic and pedestrians using sidewalks; slowing down traffic; supporting surrounding economic activities and improving street liveliness. It should be employed on all streets where width is enough to support it. Parallel parking is preferable in arterial streets and on main streets. It should be 2,4 m wide in commercial zones and 2,1 m in residential zones [5, 7, 13].

6. Pattern 6 – Narrow streets at crossings

Across guides a recurring design move employed to improve safety for pedestrians is to make streets narrower at crossings by. They can be achieved with curb extensions or by creating refuge islands in the middle of wide streets to decrease the distance between sidewalks and increase visibility, so that pedestrians spend minimum time on the roadbed while crossing [4, 5]. Their use presents other advantages such as relieving crowding on sidewalks by providing more space for people waiting to cross, and contribute to traffic calming [10]. The choice of geometry to narrow the street at crossings is based on the number of lanes, speed and type of street and on the location of the crosswalk, which can be either on a corner or mid-block [10–12].

Curb extensions can only be placed in parking lanes. They should be 0,3 to 0,6 m shallower than the parking lane, and at least as long as the pedestrian crossing (Fig. 5). Refuge islands are placed in the middle, or offset from the center by one lane, on streets with two or more travel lanes. They should be at least 1,5 m wide and at least as long as the crosswalk. Buffers should be placed beyond the length of the crosswalk. The tip of the buffer must be aligned with the corner of the sidewalk.

7. Pattern 7 – Use parklets to increase sidewalk space

Parking spaces can be converted to parklets to extend the sidewalk, to provide public resting areas, and to provide frontage space for restaurants and other local businesses in streets where the sidewalk is too narrow to accommodate it [5, 11]. Parklets are always placed in the parking lane. They use one or more parking spaces and must have a 1,2 m buffer zone on sides adjacent to parking. This buffer must be reinforced with the use of vertical wheel stoppers, to ensure visibility from the street. Parklets should only be considered on streets with commercial and service uses. On structural and distribution streets parklets should be considered if the sidewalk is narrower than 4,5 m. On local distribution streets, they should be considered if sidewalks are smaller than 3 m [11, 13]. If the parklets are being used as public resting areas, they should be placed adjacent to pedestrian crossings, increasing the size of curb extensions, in which case they can occupy a single parking place, because they need only one buffer zone. This strategy can be coupled with midblock crossings to increase pedestrian visibility. If they serve as a frontage area for a specific business, they should be located directly in front of it. The advantage of a parklet over a fixed sidewalk widening is that if the store moves to another building, it can also be moved, releasing a parking spot.

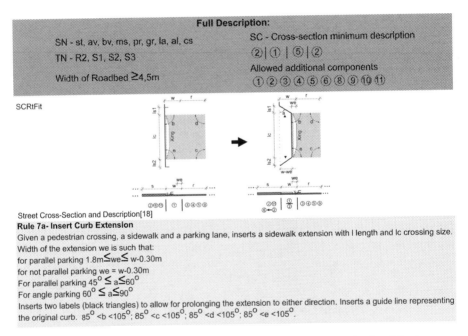

Fig. 5. Example of rule for Pattern 6 – Insert curb extension and safety islands.

8. Pattern 8 – Use lane shifts to reduce car speed

Lane Shifts, also called lateral shifts, are used to increase pedestrian space while also reducing car speed. It can be an appropriate geometry to reduce speed in streets with high volumes, where speed bumps are not recommended [5]. It can also be used to control speed in narrow streets, with one or two travel lanes and a single lane dedicated to curb parking. In one directional streets, it can be an option to reduce overall travel speed. They can be used on collectors and arterials if there is need to reduce speeding.

The length of the taper, which depends on the width of the shift and the speed limit of the street, can be calculated using the MUTCD [6] taper formula, for speeds under 70 km/h. For urban speeds of 40 km/h or lower and a shift of one lane- 3,0 to 3,6 m- a 30 m long taper is recommended.

For chicanes the same geometry can be used. Chicane geometry is different from curb extensions and lane shifts because they are designed to reduce speed more abruptly, like speed bumps and are not meant to extend pedestrian space. If designed as two subsequent lane shifts, they can be used in streets with midblock crossings, with a single parking lane to reduce speeding, while extending the sidewalk.

9. Pattern 9 – Decrease turning radii to decrease turning speed

Streets should be kept as narrow as possible at pedestrian crossing. Thus, turning radii should be limited by the space between two crossings placed on a corner. This also contributes to reducing the speed of cars turning the corner, thus increasing visibility and contributing to pedestrian safety [7, 11].

10. Pattern 10 – Raised crossings

Raised crossings or speed tables serve as speed bumps, while also increasing pedestrian accessibility and visibility. They are placed on pedestrian crossings and, when coupled with curb extensions, serve as gateways to alert drivers to speed reduction [7, 11]. These elements should be applied to local access streets where they meet structural or distribution streets. They can also be used when a pedestrian mall is crossed by structural or distribution streets. They are not compatible with streets that have tram lanes. A raised crossing is 6,6 m wide, composed of two 1,8 m ramps with a flat table in the middle as wide as the crosswalk- at least 3 m [5]. It should span the entire length of the street.

4 Derivation

The prescriptive grammar was applied in a derivation (see Fig. 6) for an area with six intersections in downtown State College. The area was chosen due to the variety of street descriptions found in a small area, including main streets. Rule 1 simplifies the geometry of the corners. Rule 2a inserts labels marking where the crossing labels must be inserted by rule 3a. These labels have both size and direction, marking where the pedestrian crossing zones will be inserted by rule 3d. The rule for midblock crossing was not used in this example, because none of the distances between consecutive crossings were larger than 120 m. These rules do not transform the cross-sections, nor the descriptions. Rule 4a.a transformed S Allen St. in a pedestrian mall. Rule 4a.b did the same to one block of Calder Way. Both these rules transformed the Cross-Section and the description for those streets. Rule 4d.c placed the labels for raised tables on Kelly Alley and Beaver Ave., where they intersect the pedestrian malls. Rule 6a adapted the size of the traffic lanes on W Beaver Ave. and S Fraser St. to a 3 m standard leaving left over space in the middle marked by a shape and a Lo lable. Rule 6b.a redistributed this labeled space between the adjacent components, one parking lane and one sidewalk for both streets. The roadbed width changed in both Full Descriptions.

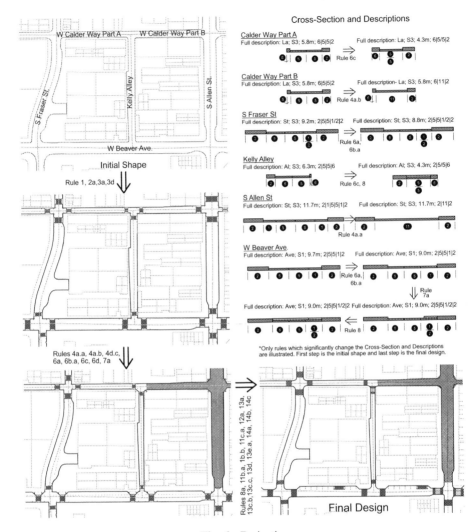

Fig. 6. Derivation

Rule 6c was applied to Calder Way-Part A and Kelly Alley, changing the width of two car lanes to a 4.3 m standard and distributing the left-over space between the adjacent components, sidewalks and green strips respectively. The width of the roadbed changed in the Full Descriptions. Rule 6d adjusted all the curbs to their new placement, and the result can be seen in the top view (third step of the derivation). Rule 7a inserted curb extensions to all the labeled crossing zones on W Beaver Ave. This altered the Cross-Section and Full Description for that street. Rule 8 inserted raised tables at the end of the pedestrian malls on W Beaver Ave. and Calder Way. They were also inserted in the Cross-Sections. Rules 11b.a, 11b.b, 11c.a inserted parking places on W Beaver Ave. Rule 12a inserted parklets on W Beaver Ave.

Rules 13a and 13c.b aligned and labeled the curb extensions on W Beaver Ave. Rule 13c.c chamfered and labeled the corner between pedestrian crossing zones on the other streets. The chamfered corners were then used in rule 13d to insert corner geometry with a curb radius defined by the placement of the pedestrian crossing. Rules 13 e.a and 13e.b extended the ramps from the raised tables to the corners and removed the labels. Rules 14a and 14b deleted leftover crossing labels, leaving the gray crossing zones to mark the pedestrian crossings. Rule 14c deleted unused guide lines from lane width retrofitting, finalizing the design.

Because of how the rules were developed, entire intersections should be selected for a derivation to generate a valid design. Otherwise, the rules for inserting the corner geometry cannot be used around the borders of the area. Thus, the minimum area for a derivation is a street between two intersections.

The result of the derivation was found to be coincident with some recently proposed changes for this area. Rule 4a.a transforms S Allen St into a Pedestrian Mall. A proposal has already been made in a Masterplan project for the town of Sate College to transform this street into a Pedestrian Mall [33], but it has never been implemented. Beaver Ave has sparse parking spaces along its length, but the proposed transformation would utilize the parking on a single side to improve safety for pedestrians. This would provide more parking and the opportunity to use some of the places for parklets to provide frontage space for small businesses on the street. Calder Way has limited traffic and is mainly used for access to parking lots.

Nonetheless, it is bordered by commercial uses, like restaurants and markets, and could be successfully integrated into a pedestrian zone. Reducing traffic lanes to the 3 m standard (or 4.3 m for local access streets) is a relevant rule for finding space for improving access to active modes in consolidated areas. S Burrowes and Beaver Ave are both wide streets within commercial zones, which can be improved by this rule, as it can be observed in the final design below. This rule could also be integrated with further rules for placing bicycle lanes.

5   Discussion

With population growth and the environmental limits imposed on urban sprawl, cities will have to become denser, and urban streets will have to be retrofitted to accommodate the use of active and public modes of transportation. This study proposes a prescriptive grammar for retrofitting urban street design in the context of densification. It reviewed several guides and manuals for urban street retrofitting from which patterns were extracted and encoded in the form of two parallel grammars and a description. It also demonstrates how data from GIS datasets can be used to generate street descriptions to trigger the application of the prescriptive grammar. An example of a derivation was presented to demonstrate its potential use. The prescriptive grammar presented in this paper does not exhaust the rules that are necessary to retrofit urban streets. It is an example of how shape grammars can be developed and used for this purpose. Rules for different scales as well as applications in larger cities are still needed and will be the object of further studies. Using the methods presented in this paper, rule sets can be developed to cover different aspects that influence walkability, cyclability and walk to transit.

The prescriptive grammar will be automatized using computational methods, in order to allow for the generation of multiple three-dimensional scenarios for urban street retrofitting, which can then be evaluated and compared on their effect on walkability, modal share, and cost-effectiveness. Future work will include using graph-based spatial analysis methods to automatically generate Transport Network classifications, using betweenness centrality. Coupled with the street descriptions and zoning, this can also be used to automatically generate Street Nomenclatures. Furthermore, existing methods to evaluate the impact of street design on travel behavior are being reviewed to develop an evaluation module. Using these methods, coupled with the generative capabilities of shape grammars, designers can generate a variety of intervention proposals, which they can compare, to choose the most adequate in terms of its impact on travel behavior. By visualizing the impacts of their projects on urban mobility, designers are expected to design more innovative solutions for a future without the prevalence of the car. This is relevant to the improvement of urban quality and to making densification viable even in cities that still do not have an efficient urban mobility system.

Acknowledgements. This study was financed by the Coordenação de Aperfeiçoamento de Pessoal de Nível Superior - Brazil (CAPES) - Finance Code 001 through PhD Scholarships in Brazil and abroad (Process 88881.187989/2018-01).

References

1. Carlow, V.M.: Limits: Space as Resource. Jovis Verlag GmbH, Berlin (2016)
2. Lehmann, S.: Sustainable urbanism: towards a framework for quality and optimal density? Futur Cities Environ. **2**, 1–13 (2016). https://doi.org/10.1186/s40984-016-0021-3
3. Ewing, R., Tian, G., Lyons, T.: Does compact development increase or reduce traffic congestion? Cities **72**, 94–101 (2018). https://doi.org/10.1016/j.cities.2017.08.010
4. Ewing, R., Brown, S.J.: U.S. Traffic Calming Manual. American Planning Association, Washington, DC (2009)
5. Pande, A., Wolshon, B.: Traffic Engineering Handbook, 7th edn. Wiley, Hoboken (2015)
6. Federal Highway Administration: Manual on uniform traffic control devices for streets and highways. United States Department of Transportation (2009)
7. Institute of Transportation Engineers: Design Walkable Urban Thoroughfares: A Context Sensitive Approach. Washington, DC (2010)
8. American Association of State Highway and Transportation Officials: A Policy on Geometric Design of Highways and Streets (2011)
9. Duany, A., Speck, J., Lydon, M.: The Smart Growth Manual. McGraw-Hill, New York (2010)
10. New York City Department of Transportation: Street Design Manual, 2nd edn. New York City Department of Transportation, New York, USA (2015)
11. Global Designing Cities Initiative: Global street design guide. Island Press (2016)
12. McCann, B.: Completing Our Streets. Island Press/Center for Resource Economics, Washington, DC (2013)
13. Speck, J.: Walkable city rules: 101 steps to making better places. Island Press (2018)

14. Farr, D.: Sustainable Nation: Urban Design Patterns for the Future. Wiley, Hoboken (2018)
15. Alexander, C.: A Pattern Language: Towns, Buildings, Construction. Oxford University Press, New York (1977)
16. Stiny, G., Gips, J.: Shape grammars and the generative specification of painting and sculpture. In: Freiman, C.V. (ed.) Information Processing 71, pp. 1460–1465. North Holland, Amsterdam (1972)
17. Vaz, C.E.V., Celani, M.G.C.: A pattern language for roberto burle marx landscape design. In: Magnani, L., Carnielli, W., Pizzi, C. (eds.) Model-Based Reasoning in Science and Technology. Studies in Computational Intelligence, vol. 314, pp. 207–219. Springer, Heidelberg (2010). https://doi.org/10.1007/978-3-642-15223-8_11
18. Beirão, J.N.: CItyMaker; Designing Grammars for Urban Design. TU Delft (2012)
19. Beirão, J., Duarte, J.P.: Generic grammars for design domains. Artif. Intell. Eng. Des. Anal. Manuf. 32, 225–239 (2018). https://doi.org/10.1017/S0890060417000452
20. Duarte, J.P., Rocha, J.M., Soares, G.D.: Unveiling the structure of the Marrakech Medina: a shape grammar and an interpreter for generating urban form. Artif. Intell. Eng. Des. Anal. Manuf. 21, 317–349 (2007). https://doi.org/10.1017/S0890060407000315
21. Koning, H., Eizenberg, J.: The language of the prairie: Frank Lloyd Wright's prairie houses. Environ. Plann. B: Plann. Des. 8, 295–323 (1981). https://doi.org/10.1068/b080295
22. Knight, T.W.: The generation of Hepplewhite-style chair-back designs. Environ. Plann. B: Plann. Des. 7, 227–238 (1980). https://doi.org/10.1068/b070227
23. Chau, H.H., Chen, X., McKay, A., de Pennington, A.: Evaluation of a 3D shape grammar implementation. In: Gero, J.S. (ed.) Design Computing and Cognition '04, pp. 357–376. Springer, Dordrecht (2004). https://doi.org/10.1007/978-1-4020-2393-4_19
24. Benros, D., Duarte, J.P., Hanna, S.: The inference of generic housing rules: a methodology to explain and recreate Palladian Villas, Prairie Houses and Malagueira Houses. In: Gero, J. S., Hanna, S. (eds.) Design Computing and Cognition '14, pp. 401–419. Springer, Cham (2015). https://doi.org/10.1007/978-3-319-14956-1_23
25. Eloy, S., Duarte, J.P.: A transformation grammar for housing rehabilitation. Nexus Netw. J. 13, 49–71 (2011). https://doi.org/10.1007/s00004-011-0052-x
26. de Klerk, R., Beirão, J.N.: CIM-St. In: Çağdaş, G., Özkar, M., Gül, L.F., Gürer, E. (eds.) CAADFutures 2017. CCIS, vol. 724, pp. 42–59. Springer, Singapore (2017). https://doi.org/10.1007/978-981-10-5197-5_3
27. State College Borough: SCB_Roads_JLW (2018)
28. State College Borough: SCB_StreetPolygons (2018)
29. State College Borough: 2018_10_01_SCB_Parcels (2018)
30. State College Borough: Buildings (2018)
31. State College Borough: 2016_SCB_Zoning (2018)
32. Burden, D., Thomas, S.: For pedestrian safety, use street design to limit vehicle speeds to no more than 20 mph. In: Farr, D. (ed.) Sustainable Nation: Urban Design Patterns for the Future, pp. 330–333. Wiley, Hoboken (2018)
33. Mahan Rykiel Associates: State College Downtown Master Plan. State College, PA (2012)

Author Index

Printed in the United States
By Bookmasters